HOTEL LAW

Amitabh Devendra

Visiting Faculty
FHRAI Hotel School, Greater Noida

OXFORD
UNIVERSITY PRESS

OXFORD
UNIVERSITY PRESS

Oxford University Press is a department of the University of Oxford.
It furthers the University's objective of excellence in research, scholarship,
and education by publishing worldwide. Oxford is a registered trade mark of
Oxford University Press in the UK and in certain other countries.

Published in India by
Oxford University Press
22 Workspace, 2nd Floor, 1/22 Asaf Ali Road, New Delhi 110 002

ISBN-13: 978-0-19-808401-3
ISBN-10: 0-19-808401-3

Typeset in New Baskerville
by Cameo Corporate Services Limited, Chennai
Printed in India by Manipal Technologies Limited, Manipal

For product information and current price, please visit www.india.oup.com

To
my parents
Devendra Kumar and Manjula Devendra
and
my grandson
Neev Devendra Rohatgi

Foreword

'Unity in diversity' symbolizes India, which is promoted by the 'Incredible India' campaign that has ushered in spectacular growth in tourism over the past decade. Economic and social changes have spurred the growth of domestic tourism, which has induced the demand for quality hotel accommodation across India. It is estimated that by the end of the decade, hotels in all the star categories would have added approximately 10,000 rooms, requiring competent managers to responsibly operate these hotels.

Hotel Law aims at educating the managers, administrators, students, and trainees on the various principles and concepts of laws governing the operations of hotels. Traditionally, some legal books have been lengthy, unmanageable, and voluminous and tend to intimidate managers and students alike from perusing them. However, in this book, the author has been able to discuss the various facets of hotel laws and their applications by dispensing with the legalese associated with such traditional legal textbooks. The book has been written in a lucid style. Each chapter is peppered with homilies and examples that enhance the presentation of the book. The book aims at setting the tone for today's managers to follow whilst operating their hotels.

The author has done justice to the cause of enhancing the comprehension of legal knowledge. With this book, managers and students alike will be able to comprehend hotel laws and apply them judiciously.

With best wishes to the author for success in his future endeavours.

Parvez Dewan
Secretary
Ministry of Tourism
Government of India

Preface

Hotels and restaurants are important components of the tourism sector. Availability of good-quality and affordable hotel rooms plays an important role in boosting the growth of tourism in the country. As on 31 December 2011, there were 2,895 classified hotels, with a capacity of 1,29,606 rooms in India. The contribution of the hotel and restaurant sector to the overall economy increased from 1.46 per cent in 2004–05 to 1.53 per cent in 2008–09, though there was a marginal decline in 2010–11. The hotel sector's compounded annual growth rate (CAGR) was 8.44 per cent from 2004–05 to 2009-10 and the growth rate in 2010–11 was 7.7 per cent. These statistics reveal that the hotel business is growing, and with a large number of star-category hotels currently under development pan India, the industry is poised to mature by 2020.

For managing hotels and restaurants successfully and efficiently in this competitive environment, one requires a dedicated team of hospitality professionals. Today's guest is educated, adventurous, conscious of money and its value, health and hygiene oriented, and definitely more demanding in his/her requirements. Decisions are mostly taken by empowered employees, enabling them to deliver quality service to guests.

It is estimated that 60–70 per cent of the decisions taken by employees can have legal implications. Knowledge of hospitality laws enables employees to operate in an ethical manner and to address issues before legal difficulties arise. Hotel laws are an integral part of the wider field of jurisprudence. Though there are some international books on this subject, few have an Indian perspective. This book is an effort to fill this void.

ABOUT THE BOOK

Hotel Law equips the reader with relevant knowledge on the diverse laws as applicable to the hotel industry. The various laws have been explained in simple, easy-to-understand, and jargon-free language. Using a practice-oriented approach, the salient features of the various acts are explained with the help of cases and examples. These will letter equip the future hotel managers to meet the challenges at their work places. The contemporary industry trends are explored and suitable illustrations provided.

The book recommends a proactive approach to managing hotels, as it is very expensive and time-consuming to fight a legal case in the courts. The legal terms have been explained with industry-related examples. Relevant figures illustrate and simplify the concepts to such an extent that the reader can easily grasp the subject. The key terms and terminologies of the discipline have been systematically defined and described in simple language.

PEDAGOGICAL FEATURES

A lot of thought and effort have gone into the making of this book to help students, researchers, faculty, and executives get a complete idea of the fundamental aspects of hotel laws. Each chapter begins with the learning objectives to help the reader conceive a broad idea about the contents. An introductory text provides the scope of the chapter. Summary and key terms given at the end of each chapter, along with review questions provide checkpoints for recapitulation of the concepts learnt. A glossary of legal terms is included at the end of the book.

The book will enable students to comprehend the content for writing assignments and making presentations. Teachers will also find it easy and interesting in the preparation of modules for classroom teaching, exercise, and evaluation, as the important concepts in each chapter are aptly supplemented with illustrations.

The key features of the book include the following:

Comprehensive and easy-to-understand text, with detailed coverage   The language of the book has been kept as simple as possible in order to enhance its reach towards professionals in the hospitality business as well students.

Blend of theory and practice   An attempt has been made to blend theory with practice by giving suitable illustrations from the hospitality business which validate contemporary trends in the hospitality industry.

Contemporary and updated information   Every attempt has been made to keep the information contemporary and relevant such as facts, figures, and industry trends for easier understanding.

Integration of the global perspective to the Indian scenario   Well-known international legal practices have been referred to whilst explaining the Indian legal scenario.

Reader-friendly features   Numerous industry-related cases and examples, figures, tables, chapter-end questions have been provided to help the reader understand the applications of the laws in the hospitality industry.

COVERAGE AND STRUCTURE

This book is divided into five parts and each part focuses upon a separate aspect of hotel law.

Part I Introduction includes two chapters.

Chapter 1, *Indian Hospitality Industry*, provides a comprehensive introduction to the Indian hospitality industry, its changing customer profile, and the role of the general manager (GM) in this new environment.

Chapter 2, *Introduction to Hospitality Laws*, briefs the reader about the evolution of law and its classification, with reference to laws governing hotel operations, food and beverage operations, employees, vendors and guest interactions, and the importance of studying them.

Part II Laws Related to Hotel Operations includes four chapters.

Chapter 3, *Doing Business in India,* dwells on the formation of various business entities in India under Indian corporate laws.

Chapter 4, *Business Contracts,* familiarizes students with different aspects of business contracts and negotiable instruments.

Chapter 5, *Hotel Licenses and Permissions,* acquaints hoteliers with the various laws and permissions that regulate hotels during project and operation stages.

Chapter 6, *Hotel Insurance,* suggests measures to protect the assets of the hotel by securing adequate insurance coverage for the property.

Part III Laws Related to Employees and Guests includes two chapters.

Chapter 7, *Labour Laws,* focusses on employee–employer relations, with emphasis on employee welfare and benefits, settlement of grievances and industrial disputes.

Chapter 8, *Hospitality Law,* discusses the legal obligations of the hotelier in providing service and meeting guest requirements round the clock. It also appraises the student of what hoteliers expect from an ideal guest.

Part IV Laws Related to Food and Beverage includes two chapters.

Chapter 9, *Food Legislation,* provides a broad discussion on the impact of the Food Preservation Act (PFA) and the Food Safety and Standards Act (FSSA) on the food business operator.

Chapter 10, *Liquor Licensing,* discusses the tenets of liquor licensing policy and the importance of maintaining the right balance between guest requirements and serving alcoholic beverages responsibly.

Part V Laws Related to Public Health and Safety includes one chapter.

Chapter 11, *Battle for a Healthy Environment,* examines the impact of environment on hotel operations and recommends steps to develop eco-friendly waste management policies and their implementation encouraging good environmental practices.

ACKNOWLEDGEMENTS

After a long stint in the hospitality industry and later teaching at the FHRAI Institute, the idea of writing a book on hotel laws germinated in my mind. It has taken approximately two years since its conception to complete the work, and it gives me great pleasure to have achieved this milestone, my contribution to the enrichment of the hotel industry.

Giving shape to the textbook required hard work, perseverance, and commitment. I deeply acknowledge the support of my wife who had taken all pains and strains in managing our household during the entire period of writing this book. I am grateful to my daughter Janubi and son-in-law Saurabh who stood steadfast behind me pushing me to meet the timeline. Cute, my pet dog was my constant companion while the book was taking shape. This book is the outcome of the support given by my well-wishers such as Alka Joshi and my students from the FHRAI Institute who at various stages gave valuable inputs. I wish to thank all my peers and colleagues in the industry for providing me the latest information and statistical data on the industry.

I thankfully acknowledge all the authors whose research papers, books, and articles have been referred to. I express my thanks to the editorial team at OUP for its coordination and support from the beginning and for the timely suggestions and encouragement, which have made this textbook more logical in its approach and presentation.

Any feedback and suggestions for further improvement of the book are welcome and can be sent to me at amitabhdevendra@gmail.com.

Amitabh Devendra

Brief Contents

Foreword   v
Preface   vii
Detailed Contents   xiii
List of Cases   xx

PART I   INTRODUCTION   1

  1. Introduction to the Indian Hospitality Industry   3
  2. Introduction to Hotel Laws   27

PART II   LAWS RELATED TO HOTEL OPERATIONS   41

  3. Doing Business in India   43
  4. Business Contracts   86
  5. Hotel Licences and Regulations   129
  6. Hotel Insurance   151

PART III   LAWS RELATED TO EMPLOYEES AND GUESTS   181

  7. Labour Laws   183
  8. Hospitality Law   239

PART IV   LAWS RELATED TO FOOD AND BEVERAGE   277

  9. Food Legislation   279
  10. Liquor Licensing   329

PART V   LAWS RELATED TO PUBLIC HEALTH AND SAFETY   359

11. Battle for a Healthy Environment   361

Glossary   393
Index   397

Detailed Contents

Foreword   *v*
Preface   *vii*
Brief Contents   *xi*
List of Cases   *xx*

PART I   INTRODUCTION   **1**

1. Introduction to the Indian Hospitality Industry   **3**

Introduction   3
Indian Hotel Industry—An Overview   4
The Colonial Era (1900–1947)   4
Laying the Foundation—Post-Independence (1947–1980)   5
Towards Economic Liberalism—First Growth Cycle (1980–2000)   6
Decade of Despair and Hope—(2000–2010)   11
Pioneering Hospitality Education   19
Changing Guest Profile   20
Challenges of the 21st Century   21
    Globalization and Diversity   22
    Safety and Security   22
    Health, Sanitation, and Hygiene   22
    Legal Issues   23
    Quality of Service and Pricing   23
    Technology Innovations   23
    Employee Retention   23

2. Introduction to Hotel Laws   **27**

Introduction   27
What is Law?   29
Role of the Legislative, Executive, and the Judiciary   31
    Legislative   32
    Executive   32
    Judiciary   32
Classification of Laws   33
Origins of Hotel Law   33
The Judicial Process   33

PART II   LAWS RELATED TO HOTEL OPERATIONS   **41**

3. Doing Business in India   **43**

Introduction   43
    Memorandum of Association   45
    Articles of Association   45
Starting a Business   48
Promotion Stage   48
Incorporation   49
Commencement of Business   49
Sole Proprietorship   49
Partnership   50
Limited Liability Partnerships   51
Private Limited Companies   53
Public Limited Companies   56
Liaison Office or Representative Office   61
Branch Office   62
Project Office   63
Joint Venture Company   64
Wholly-owned Subsidiary Company   65
Foreign Exchange Management Act, 1999 and Foreign Direct Investment   66
Regulatory Issues   73
    Taxation—Direct Taxes   73
    Taxation—Indirect Taxes   76
    Transfer Pricing   76
    Accounting Practices—Generally Accepted Accounting Principles   77
    Technology Transfer Agreements   78

4. Business Contracts   **86**

Introduction   86
Indian Contract Act, 1872   87
Essential Elements of a Contract   88
    Offer   88
    Acceptance   90
    Legal Obligations   91
    Lawful Consideration   91
    Competent Parties   92
    Free Consent   92
    Lawful Object   93
    Not Expressly Declared Void   93
    Certainty and Possibility of Performance   93
    Legal Formalities   94
Difference between Void, Voidable, and Unenforceable Contracts   95

Types of Contracts   96
   Bilateral Contract   96
   Unilateral Contract   96
   Express Contract   96
   Quasi Contract   97
   Contingent Contract   98
Discharge or Performance of Contracts   99
   By Performance (Section 37)   99
   By Tender (Section 38)   99
   By Mutual Consent or Agreement (Sections 62 and 63)   100
   By Lapse of Time   102
   By Impossibility of Performance or Operation of the Law   102
   By Breach of Contract (Section 39)   103
   By *Force Majeure* or Act of God   103
Indemnity and Guarantees   103
   Express Promise   103
   Operation of Law   104
Bailment and Pledge   107
Agency   109
   Sole Selling Agent and Subagents   110
   Commission Agents   110
   Rights and Duties of an Agent (Sections 211–221)   110
   Duties of the Principal Towards the Agent (Sections 222–225)   111
Negotiable Instruments Act, 1881   112
   Negotiable Instrument   112
   Types of Negotiable Instruments   113
   Types of Cheques   115
   Discharge of a Negotiable Instrument   117
   Steps to be Taken When a Cheque Gets Dishonoured   119
Breach of Contracts   119
   Liquidated Damages   120
   Suit for Specific Performance   120
   Arbitration   121
   Mediation   122
Hospitality Contracts   122
   Group Information Sheet   123
   Function Prospectus—Banquets   123
   Purchase Contract   123
   Franchisee Agreements   124
   Management Contracts   124
   Technical Services Agreement   125

5. Hotel Licences and Regulations   **129**
Introduction   129
Project Stage   131

Operations Stage   140
General Hotel Operating Licences   140
    Board and Lodging Licence   140
    Foreigners Regional Registration Office   140
    Shops and Establishments Act   141
    Hotel Classification   141
    NOC from Chief Fire Officer   141
    Restricted Money Changers Licence from Reserve Bank of India   141
    Export Promotion Capital Goods Scheme   141
    Lift Operating Licence from Inspector of Lifts   142
    NOC from Pollution Control Board   142
    Indian Performing Rights Society/Phonographic Performance Limited   142
    Permissions to Install Signage and Hoardings   142
    Swimming Pool and Cooling Tower Permission from the Police   142
    Website Registration   142
    Licence to Operate a Beauty Parlour and Spa   143
    Wireless Planning and Coordination Wing, Ministry of Communications   143
    Registration with Various Trade Bodies or Organizations   143
Food and Beverage Operations   143
    Health Trade Licence   143
    Eating House or Restaurant Licence   144
    Sanitary Certificate   144
    Liquor Licence   144
    Nominations under the Food Safety and Standards Act, 2006   144
    Approval of Kitchen Signage   144
    Certification of Weighing Scales and Peg Measures   144
Personnel Department   144
    Labour Department Registration   145
    Employee Provident Fund Registration   145
    Employee State Insurance Scheme   145
    Profession Tax Enrolment Certificate   145
Accounts Department   145
    Sales Tax Registration   145
    Service Tax Registration   145
    Luxury Tax Registration   146
    Value Added Tax   146
    Central Value Added Tax or Central Sales Tax   146
    Expenditure Tax   146
    Permanent Account Number   146
    Online Tax Accounting System   146
    Tax Deduction and Collection Account Number   146
    Tax Information Network   147
    Property Tax Certificate   147

6. Hotel Insurance   151
Introduction   151
What is Insurance?   155
    Salient Features of an Insurance Contract   155

Principles of Insurance Contracts 156
  Principle of Utmost Good Faith 156
  Principle of Indemnity 157
  Principle of Subrogation 158
  Principle of Insurable Interest 158
  Principle of Contribution 159
  Principle of Proximate Cause 159
Purchasing an Insurance Policy or Insurance Contract 161
  Insurance Agents 161
  Proposal Stage 162
  Cover Note 163
  Insurance Policy 163
  Renewal Notice 164
Types of Insurance Policies 164
  Life Insurance Policies 165
  Convertible Term Life Insurance 165
  General Insurance Policies 167
Insurance Coverage Commonly Availed by Hotels 171
Filing an Insurance Claim 172
Grievance Redressal Machinery 174
  Consumer Protection Act, 1986 174
  Institution of Insurance Ombudsman 175
  Grievance Cell of the Insurance Regulatory and Development Authority 175
Loss Prevention Association of India 176

PART III   LAWS RELATED TO EMPLOYEES AND GUESTS **181**

7. Labour Laws **183**

Introduction 183
Constitutional Provisions 184
  Fundamental Rights (Part III Articles 12–35) 184
  Concurrent List (Article 246 List III of the Seventh Schedule) 186
Categorization of Labour Laws 187
Categorization of Industry 188
Classification of Employees 189
  Labour Laws Defining the Relationship Between Employers, Employees,
    and Trade Unions 190
  Labour Laws That Provide for Rights of Employees at Workplace 207
  Laws Related to Equality and Empowerment of Women 224
  Employees with Special Needs 230
  Employee Safety at the Workplace 231

8. Hospitality Law **239**

Introduction 239
What is a Hotel? 240
The Sarais Act, 1867 241

Who is a Guest?   242
Law of Torts or Torts Law or Common Law   243
Duties of a Hotelier Towards Guests   245
    To Provide Accommodation against Confirmed Room Reservations 246
    To Provide Safety and Security—Exercising 'Duty of Care' 247
    Circumstances under which a Hotelier can Refuse Admission or
        Deny Accommodation to a Guest 267
    Circumstances under which a Hotelier can Evict a Guest 269
    Serving Food and Beverage Responsibly 270
    Handling Fraud Committed by Guests 271

PART IV   LAWS RELATED TO FOOD AND BEVERAGE   **277**

9. Food Legislation   **279**
Introduction   279
    The Food Adulteration Act, 1872 (UK) 280
    The Sale of Food and Drugs Act, 1875 (UK) 281
    The Margarine Act, 1887 (UK) 281
Indian Scenario   281
The Prevention of Food Adulteration Act, 1954   283
Important Legal Terms   286
    What is Food? 287
    What is an Adulterant and Adulterated Food? 288
    What is Adulteration? 290
    What is Food Poisoning? 292
    What are Food Additives? 294
    Types of Food Additives 294
    What are Food Preservatives? 296
    Defining Food Quality and Standards 296
Food Safety and Standards Act, 2006   299
    Who is a Food Business Operator? 305
    Licensing 305
    Administration of the Food Safety & Standards Act, 2006 308
    Role of Food Safety Officers 309
    Role of Food Analysts 311
    Central Food Laboratories 312
    Enforcement of the Food Safety & Standards Act, 2006 312
    Role of the Adjudicating Officer 313
Recommended Food Safety Management Plan   316
    Purchasing 316
    Receiving 319
    Stores 320
    Kitchen 320
    Kitchen Stewarding 322
    Food and Beverage Outlets 323
    Personnel 323

10. Liquor Licensing   **329**

Introduction   329
Non-alcoholic Beverages   331
Alcoholic Beverages   332
Early Initiatives to Regulate Alcohol   334
Liquor Legislation in India   335
    Prohibition   337
    Dry Days   338
    Legal Age for Drinking   338
Liquor Licensing Procedures   339
    Off Premises or Off-site Licence   339
    On Premises or On-site Licence   339
Procedure for Acquiring a Liquor Licence   340
Mandatory Compliances of a Liquor Licence   342
Service of Alcohol Beverages   344
    Factors That Affect the Rate of Absorption and BAC   346
Behavioural Traits of an Intoxicated Person   350
    Serving Drinks Responsibly   351
Sale of Cigarettes and Tobacco   353

PART V   LAWS RELATED TO PUBLIC HEALTH AND SAFETY   **359**

11. Battle for a Healthy Environment   **361**

Introduction   361
Designing a Waste Management Programme   370
Preparing a Waste Reduction Programme   371
Making a Commitment to Manage Waste   374
Implementing the Programme   375
Feedback on the Implementation   381
    EarthCheck: Green Globe Certification   382
    Leeds Building Certification: Leeds Platinum, Gold, Silver Certification   382
    International Organization for Standardization (ISO)—ISO 14001 Environmental
        Standard Certification   383
Impact of Coastal Regulation Zone on the Development of Hotels in India   386
    CRZ-I (2011 Notification)   386
    CRZ-II (1991 & 2011 Notification)   387
    CRZ-III (1991 & 2011 Notification)   387

Glossary   393
Index   397

List of Cases

Case 4.1   Gajan Moreshwar vs Moreshwar Madan   104

Case 6.1   Vasudev Mudaliar vs Caledonian Insurance Co. and Another   158

Case 6.2   Shri Kumaresh vs The National Insurance Company Ltd & Another (Supreme Court of India Civil Appeal No. 3784 of 2011)   161

Case 8.1   Connie Francis Garzilli and Joseph Garzilli, Plaintiffs vs Howard Johnson's Motor Lodges, Inc., Defendant   249

Case 8.2   Frummer vs Hilton Hotels International, Inc., 304 N.Y.S.2d 335 (1969)   250

Case 8.3   Klaus Mittelbachert vs East India Hotels Ltd. (3rd January 1997)   251

Case 8.4   Anil Virmani vs Hyatt Hotels, First Appeal No. 102 of 2004 National Consumer Disputes Redressal Commission, New Delhi   255

Case 8.5   Renate K. and Heinz K. vs Hotel "T" Liable for Theft from Safe in Hotel Room, Austrian Supreme Court (1 Ob 119/11 of July 21)   258

Case 8.6   Saunders vs Patricia Hotel   268

Case 8.7   Johnston vs Levin and Midtown Hotel Limited (1996), 25 C.H.R.R.D/82 (Ontario Board of Inquiry)   269

Case 8.8   Randhwa vs Tequila Bar and Grill Ltd. (2008), 62 C.H.R.R.D/350   269

Case 10.1   Anuj Garg and Others vs Hotel Association of India CIVIL APPEAL NO. 5657 OF 2007 [Arising out of SLP (Civil) No. 12781 of 2006] WITH CIVIL APPEAL NO. 5658 OF 2007 [Arising out of SLP (Civil) No. 16127 of 2006]   348

Part I

Introduction

Chapter 1   Introduction to the Indian
             Hospitality Industry

Chapter 2   Introduction to Hotel Laws

Introduction to the Indian Hospitality Industry

LEARNING OBJECTIVES

After going through this chapter, the reader will be familiar with the following:

- Essential characteristics of the hotel industry
- Historical perspectives of the Indian hotel industry
- Pioneers of hospitality education
- Changing guest profile
- Challenges facing the hotel general manager in the 21st century

INTRODUCTION

The hospitality industry is possibly one of the oldest forms of business. It encompasses a wide range of business activities such as travel and tourism that includes airlines, cruise ships, car rentals, railways, and bus services; management of tourism attractions, parks, and recreation facilities; lodging industry comprising hotels, motels, and resorts; and food and beverage industry comprising restaurant operations, event management, banqueting, organizing meeting, and conventions. The common denominator in all these business activities is 'service', which is based upon the 'spirit of hospitality' of welcoming guests and looking after their needs through exceptional service. It refers to the relationship between a guest and a host, and to the act of being hospitable, that is, receiving guests and visitors cordially with goodwill and friendliness.

I have collected various responses from my students as to what constitutes service:

- Pleasing guests
- Making guests happy
- Putting a smile on a person's face
- Fulfilling guests' needs unobtrusively and efficiently
- Cooking good food and serving it stylishly
- Making guests feel at home
- Welcoming guests in a friendly manner with a warm smile

Service is defined as an act of providing goods and services to guests, and offering timely assistance in a warm and friendly manner. The *Concise Oxford Dictionary eleventh edition* defines service as 'an action or process of serving' or 'an act of assistance'.

A guest cannot evaluate the quality of service in a restaurant until he has dined in it, or comment on a night's stay at a hotel without checking into a room. Quality of service in a restaurant and a one-night stay are both intangible products that are perishable in nature. In spite of their perishable nature, the services are tailor-made to the guests' requirements—for example, serving piping hot soup, cooking a lamb dish with less salt, serving scotch and soda with no ice, providing extra pillows and blankets in guests' room, shirts given for laundry returned on hangers unfolded, attending wake calls placed by the guests, delivering the choice of newspapers that guests desire, and so on.

The essential characteristics of the hospitality industry are that it is constantly striving to deliver outstanding exceptional service of intangible products that are perishable in nature throughout the year.

For the purpose of our study, we shall be restricting our discussion to the lodging industry and the food and beverage industry.

INDIAN HOTEL INDUSTRY—AN OVERVIEW

The growth story of the Indian hotel industry can be divided into four distinct phases: the colonial era, the post-Independence era, the liberalization phase, and finally the dawn of the 21st century. The first two phases spawned the five-star and five-star deluxe hotels in metro cities, whereas the liberalization phase encouraged the growth of economy and budget hotels across India.

THE COLONIAL ERA (1900–1947)

Before World War II, most hotels in India were developed in locations that were frequented by the British and the Indian aristocracy. This period saw the development of hotels being undertaken by individual British and Indian entrepreneurs, with only a few companies owning hotels in India, such as the Taj group—an Indian hotel company (owned by Jamshetji Nusserwanji Tata) and Associated Hotels of India, Faletti Family, Oberoi Group-East India Hotels (owned by Rai Bahudur M. S. Oberoi).

Karkaria (1992) lists three landmark acquisitions by Rai Bahadur Mohan Singh Oberoi—the Carlton Hotel, Shimla (today known as the Oberoi Clarkes) in 1934; the Grand, Calcutta (now Kolkata) (rechristened The Oberoi Grand) in 1938; coupled with the acquisition of Associated Hotels of India (AHI) in 1943. AHI was the only hotel chain with a north-India presence owned by the Faletti Family, consisting of the Cecil Hotels at Shimla and Muree; Dean's Hotel, Peshawar; Faletti's Hotel, Lahore; and Flashman's Hotel, Rawalpindi. These acquisitions gave the Oberoi chain a firm footing on the map of Indian hospitality. The other doyen of business—Jamsetji Nusserwanji Tata (founder of the Tata Group)—decided to build the Taj Mahal Hotel in Mumbai in 1903. This laid the foundation stone for the Taj Hotels Resorts and Palaces.

Following India's independence in 1947, the AHI properties located in Muree, Peshawar, Lahore, and Rawalpindi were treated as enemy properties by the Government of Pakistan and appropriated. These four hotels became a part of the Associated Hotels of Pakistan.

Other important hotels that were built during the British period in India are as follows:
- The Rugby, Matheran (built in 1876)
- Wildflower Hall, Shimla (built in 1911) by the Hotz family, currently an Oberoi resort
- The Savoy, Mussoorie (built in 1902), currently an ITC Fortune hotel
- The Palace Hotel, Chail (built in 1891) built by Bhupinder Singh, the Maharaja of Patalia, currently operated by Himachal Pradesh Tourism Development Corporation.
- The Imperial, New Delhi (built in 1931) was built to commemorate the Delhi Durbar of 1911 when King Emperor George V declared Delhi to be the new capital of India. The hotel was named and conferred the Lion Insignia by Lady Wellingdon.
- The Maidens Metropolitan Hotel, Delhi, (built in 1903) is now called The Oberoi Maidens Hotel.

Sharma (2011) recollects the contribution made to the hospitality industry by the Nirula and Sardari Lal families by setting up hotels in and around Connaught Place in Luyten's Delhi.
- Hotel India, New Delhi (built in 1934) owned by L. C. Nirula and family, known as the Nirula's Hotel.
- Hotel Marina, New Delhi (built in 1934) owned by Sardari Lal and Girdhari Lal, currently operated by Carlson Hospitality as Radisson Blu Hotel.
- Hotel Ambassador, New Delhi (built in 1945), currently branded as Vivanta by Taj.

During this period, the growth of hotels in British India was at its ascendency, which came to an abrupt end with the partition of the country into India and Pakistan in 1947. This ushered a period of stagnation when hotel growth and development came to a standstill.

LAYING THE FOUNDATION—POST-INDEPENDENCE (1947–1980)

Upon his return from the Non-Aligned Movement meeting held at Brioni, Yugoslavia in July 1956, Late Pandit Jawaharlal Nehru, the then Prime Minister of India, recognized that tourism could be an engine for the country's economic growth and inspired to build quality hotels in India for visiting foreign dignitaries. This led to the first-ever government-led investment in the hotel industry with the building of the Ashok Hotel in New Delhi.

The Federation of Hotels and Restaurant Association of India (FHRAI)—the apex body of the hotel industry—was created in 1955 with the amalgamation of the four zonal federations and under the guidance of the various presidents, represented the views of the industry to the government.

Their advocacy resulted in the government giving the hospitality industry another boost when it created the Ministry of Tourism and Civil Aviation in 1967, separating it from the Ministry of Transport and Shipping, thereby recognizing that tourism was not simply about transporting people from one point to another but had a much wider role to play in the nation's economy.

The India Tourism Development Corporation (ITDC) was set up in 1966 as a corporation under The Companies Act, 1956, with the merger of Janpath Hotels India and India Tourism Transport Undertaking Ltd. Today, ITDC provides a complete range of tourism services, including accommodation, catering, entertainment and shopping, hotel consultancy, duty-free shops, and an in-house travel agency.

Concurrently, Rai Bahadur M. S. Oberoi, Chairman East India Hotels Ltd., was expanding his empire by constructing New Delhi's first modern multi-storey hotel, which was franchised to US-based InterContinental Hotels. The property opened in 1965 as the Oberoi InterContinental, New Delhi. Besides the Oberoi InterContinental (now The Oberoi New Delhi), the portfolio of Oberoi Hotels consisted of six properties located at Shimla, Calcutta, Gopalpur-on-Sea, Delhi, and Darjeeling.

The Indian Hotels Company Ltd. popularly known as Taj Hotels Resorts and Palaces was next to follow the franchising trend in 1970, when it signed with the Intercontinental Hotels for its new hotel in Bombay (now Mumbai). Simultaneously, the Oberoi Hotel then under construction in Bombay (now Mumbai) entered into a franchisee agreement with the Sheraton Group. Holiday Inn—a brand owned by InterContinental Hotels—tied up with Eastern International Hotels promoted by the Khanna family to brand their 200-room hotel as Holiday Inn, Juhu, Bombay (now Mumbai).

The ITC website mentions that 'In 1975, India Tobacco Company (ITC) launched its hotel business with the acquisition of a hotel in Chennai which was rechristened ITC-Welcomgroup Chola.' Three ITC-Welcomgroup hotels were commissioned between 1975 and 1977 and were non-franchised hotels using Indian expertise. However, ultimately these hotels adopted the Sheraton brand in 1978 and employed expatriates for managing the operations of the hotel to the exacting standards of Sheraton.

All the three major hospitality chains including The Oberoi, Taj, and ITC Welcomgroup, focussed on the development of five-star and five-star deluxe categories of hotels, located in prominent metropolitan cities and a few select resorts leading to a concentration of hotels in these categories. This was the beginning of the methodical planning, designing, decorating, and furnishing of hotels in India, along with the installation of systems for operating various departments in a hotel.

TOWARDS ECONOMIC LIBERALISM—FIRST GROWTH CYCLE (1980–2000)

When India agreed to host the 1982 Asian Games, a boost was given to the country's hotel industry. The Government of India announced a National Tourism Policy and outlined the country's tourism development objectives. This policy was timed to help the country meet the huge need for hotel rooms in New Delhi, which was the venue of the Asian Games. The government granted licences for building hotels to various Indian hotel groups with a stipulation that these hotel projects should be completed within time for the Games. The groups that were sanctioned land to build hotels were Taj hotels (for Taj Palace Hotel), Asian Hotels (for Hyatt Regency, New Delhi), ITDC (for Lodhi Hotel, Samrat and Kanishka Hotel), CJ International Hotels Ltd. (for Le Meridian, New Delhi), and Surya Sofitel, New Delhi. The opening of these hotels further strengthened the hotel franchising and management contracts in the first-class/five-star segment within the metro cities. It also gave rise to the fallacy that tourism was an elitist activity that lacked mass appeal, and hotels were being built to cater to well-heeled foreign tourists.

The National Tourism Policy of 1982 was the first step towards formulating a concerted policy for the development of tourism. Tourism is one of the highest foreign-exchange contributors for the country, as illustrated in Table 1.1. The Policy laid emphasis on developing tourist circuits, a well-defined itinerary or route connecting various venues or cities regularly traversed by travellers without change of direction or returning to the starting point, for example, the Golden Triangle of Delhi–Jaipur–Agra–Delhi or the beach circuit of Mumbai–Goa–Mumbai, which would encourage foreigners to travel to India.

TABLE 1.1 Foreign Exchange Earnings from Tourism (1991–2011)

Year	FEE in ₹		FEE in US $	
	₹ Crore	**Percentage change over previous year**	**US $ Million**	**Percentage change over previous year**
1991	4318 -	nil	1861 -	nil
1992	5951	37.8	2126	14.2
1993	6611	11.1	2124	−0.1
1994	7129	7.8	2272	7.0
1995	8430	18.2	2583	13.7
1996	10046	19.2	2832	9.6
1997	10511	4.6	2889	2.0
1998	12150	15.6	2948	2.0
1999	12951	6.6	3009	2.1
2000	15626	20.6	3460	15.0
2001	15083	−3.5	3198	−7.6
2002	15064	−0.1	3103	−3.0
2003	20729	37.6	4463	43.8
2004	27944	34.8	6170	38.2
2005	33123	18.5	7493	21.4
2006	39025	17.8	8634	15.2
2007	44360	13.7	10729	24.3
2008	51294	15.6	11832	10.3
2009	53700	4.5	11136	−3.7
2010#	64889	20.8	14193	27.5
2011#	77591	19.6	16564	16.7

#Advance estimates
Source: Ministry of Tourism, Government of India, India Tourism Statistics, 2011.
Web reference
tourism.gov.in/writereaddata/CMSPagePicture/file/Primary%20Content/MR/pub-OR-
statistics/2011statisticsenglish.pdf

In line with the recommendations of the Planning Commission, the Government of India officially recognized tourism as an 'industry' in 1982. This made the industry eligible for several government incentives, which included tax incentives, subsidies, and priorities in the sanctioning of loans by banks and financial institutions, and preferences in acquiring water and electricity connections. Although these incentives were the primary reason for the boom in the development of hotel industry, there were other reasons as well, which are as follows:

- There was availability of land at reasonable prices or on lease.
- The hotel industry was perceived as a profitable industry, promising a quick return on investments.
- Hotels were viewed as best options by businessmen wishing to deploy surplus funds from their other businesses.
- Owning a hotel gave the owners recognition and greater visibility.
- Many Indian business people believed that hotels are easy to operate.

Motivated by the success stories of hotels in metro cities, individual entrepreneurs began constructing hotels and resorts in secondary cities during the late 1970s and 1980s. Many of the hotels built during this period were not well planned to facilitate operations and lacked character and standardization as they were run by individual owners as 'Mom and Pop' operations. Alarmed by the sudden proliferation of hotels in secondary locations, the Department of Tourism made it mandatory for new hotel projects having 10 or more sellable rooms or having a minimum carpet area of 120 sq. ft per room, to seek prior approval from the Hotel and Restaurant Approval and Classification Committee (HRACC). Hotel standards were formulated by the HRACC in consultation with the Department of Tourism and the concept of star categorization was developed. Under the star categorization scheme, hotels were classified and given an appropriate star rating ranging from five-star deluxe to one star, depending upon the amenities and facilities that the hotel offered. Hotels that were approved by the Committee became eligible for various fiscal relief schemes and incentives that the government announced from time to time. This 'carrot and stick' policy was aimed at controlling the mushrooming development of hotels.

However, there is a school of thought that is of the opinion that star categorization of hotels should be dispensed with; instead hotels should be categorized as luxury, up-scale, upper mid-scale, economy, and budget, reflective of the current trends being followed in hotel development.

It was only in 1987 that the government, after critical evaluation, permitted an Indian company, Choice Hotels India Private Ltd., to franchise three-star and four-star hotels in India. Choice Hotels India Private Ltd. was a joint venture between Choice Hotels International and an Indian company promoted by A. K. Dave. This was intended to help the emerging group of individual entrepreneurs whose means were just sufficient to build and run small- and medium-sized three- to four-star hotels. The franchisee route enabled these hotels the benefits of proper technical planning and international standards of comfort and hygiene with a focus on guest satisfaction.

It was also recognized that by franchising a number of hotels and resorts in tier II cities, the availability in these areas of hotel facilities that met international standards would be made known to travel agents and tourists worldwide. The dissemination of such information would help disperse tourists to new areas within India, benefitting the economies of these areas by generating more employment and support to local arts and crafts.

Tourism was made a priority sector for foreign direct investment (FDI) in 1991, making the industry eligible for automatic approvals of hotels in which up to 100 per cent of the equity was provided by a foreign partner.

Under Foreign Technology Agreements, international hotel brands could enter into management contracts and franchisee agreements with Indian hoteliers wishing to flag their properties. For foreign technology agreements, automatic approval would be granted if they met the following guidelines:

- Up to 3 per cent of the capital cost of the project paid for technical consultancy services.
- Up to 3 per cent of the net turnover payable for franchising and marketing or publicity fees.
- Up to 10 per cent of gross operating profit payable for management, including incentive fees.

A management contract draws a distinction between the ownership of the hotel and the operator while defining the business relationship between the two parties. The operator is responsible for the management of the business for an agreed fee and the owner assumes legal and financial responsibility, such as profits or the burden of any loss and any capital expenses. For example, Marriott Hotels, Accor Hotels, and InterContinental Hotel Group (IHG) enter into management contracts with the owners.

Franchisee agreement is signed between the franchisee (owner) and the franchisor (brand), where the franchisee agrees to operate the hotel as per the business model and brand standards laid down by the franchisor and in return pays a fee to the franchisor. For example, Best Western Hotels worldwide enter into franchisee agreements with owners.

A national strategy for the promotion of tourism was announced in 1996, which advocated the strengthening of human resource development, the creation of an advisory board of tourism and trade, the integrated development of tourism circuits, and the participation of the private sector in the promotion of tourism development.

Tourism was granted 'Export House Status' in 1998, making hotel owners, travel agents, tour operators, and tourist transport operators eligible for various government incentives such as the following:

- Special import licence (SIL)
- Free trading of the SIL
- Import of several types of equipment under the SIL
- Waiver of bank guarantee for imports
- Import of cars against foreign exchange earnings

Investment trends since 1996 reveal that the bulk of infrastructure investments in India is being made in the tourism sector, as compared to other industries, in order to take advantage of India's liberalized economic regime and economic developments taking place around the world.

The changed business environment led to the establishment of the Hotel Association of India (HAI) in 1996 with the objective of 'securing for the hotel industry its due place in India's economy and project its role as a contributor to employment generation and sustainable economic and social development; highlight its crucial role in the service to tourism industry as the largest net foreign exchange earner; help raise the standards of hoteliering and to build an image for this industry both within and outside the country.'

The positive investment climate encouraged new entrants to consider hospitality as a viable business proposition. The 1990s and the early part of the following decade witnessed two types of entrepreneurs coming to the fore; the first being the professional hotelier trained in hotel operations and management, while the second being the established business person seeking to diversify his or her business portfolio.

In the first category of professional hoteliers successfully launching their own hotel chains were Anil Madhok and Ajay Bakaya of Sarovar Hotels; Chender Baljee of Royal Orchid Hotels; and Patu Keswani of Lemon Tree Hotels.

Professional hoteliers like Anil Madhok and Ajay Bakaya established the Sarovar group opting for the management contract and franchisee route to establish themselves by securing an exclusive mandate from Carlson Hotels to franchise their Park Plaza brand. Chender Baljee, an IIM Ahmedabad graduate, founded the Royal Orchid Hotel chain in the early 1990s opting for the owner–operator model. Today, the chain owns hotels as well as manages properties for other hotel owners and developers. An engineering graduate from IIT Delhi and an MBA from IIM Kolkata, Patu Keswani was the chief operating officer for Taj business hotels before he decided to develop his own brand of hotels. He opted for the owner–operator model and with financial assistance from Kotak Mahindra Fund, successfully launched the Lemon Tree chain in 2002.

In the second category of successful business persons diversifying into hotels were Priya Paul of Park Hotels and S. P. Jain of Pride Hotels.

The first Park Hotel, named after Park Street in Calcutta, was opened in 1967 by Surrendra Paul. On his demise, the family's decision to give his daughter, Priya Paul, the reigns of the hotel business out of their portfolio of shipping, tea, real estate and construction, and hospitality and financial services, was a fortuitous one. Working on the owner–operator model to expand their portfolio, Park Hotels today has approximately 1400 rooms in operations. S. P. Jain, an established chartered accountant and businessman, decided to diversify into hotels by launching his first Pride Hotel property in 1988. Subsequently, with financial assistance from Kotak Real Estate Fund, the chain expanded rapidly and today they have 12 properties across India.

The last few years of the 20th century were a testing time for the hotel business with average occupancies and declining average room rates, the turn of the 21st century held promise of a better future.

DECADE OF DESPAIR AND HOPE—(2000–2010)

At the turn of the 21st century, the technology bubble that was riding the wave on the strength of the Internet and e-commerce websites registered a sharp fall in the valuations of their stock, triggering the collapse of technology stocks. Close on its heels, the tragic event of 9/11 when the World Trade Center Twin Towers in New York were attacked by terrorists jolted the tourism industry worldwide. Other significant events that impacted the Indian hospitality industry are listed in Table 1.2.

TABLE 1.2 Significant Events of the Decade

Month & Year	Event
March 2000	Internet bubble
January 2001	Gujarat earthquake
September 2001	Attack on World Trade Center twin towers
December 2001	Terrorist attack on Indian Parliament
December 2004	Indian ocean tsunami
July 2005	Mumbai deluge
October 2005	Kashmir earthquake
July 2006	Mumbai train bomb blasts
September 2008	Lehman Brothers' collapse
October 2008	Sensex losing 1100 points
November 2008	Mumbai terrorist attack
August 2009	Swine flu epidemic

Even though the decade was peppered by various disturbing events, which impacted the hospitality business, there was a silver lining too. The Indian growth story did not collapse; albeit it continued to move at a slower pace. The impact of these events on India was twofold; first, it gave impetus to enhanced security measures at airports, hotels, prominent heritage sites of tourism importance; and second, it gave the hospitality industry an opportunity to re-evaluate and reinvent itself in the changed environment.

The government announced the National Tourism Policy of 2002, which was based on the 1982 document recognizing that tourism was an engine of economic growth that would create employment. The promotion of domestic tourism marked a major shift from the 1982 policy, which had emphasized increasing foreign tourist arrivals into the country. It advocated promotion of domestic tourism and encouraging rural tourism, medical tourism, adventure tourism, and religious and cultural tourism circuits.

Rural tourism

It involves providing quality holiday experience to domestic and international travellers visiting the rural areas of India. The key rural areas identified by the government are located in remote areas such as Mokokchung (Nagaland), Lachen (Sikkim), Konaseema (Andhra Pradesh), Kumbalanghi (Kerala), and Pranpur (Madhya Pradesh), where the traveller has opportunities to experience farm stays and engage in outdoor activities like fishing, boating, and river cruise. Other sites listed for active promotion of rural tourism are the heritage sites of Karaikudi (Tamil Nadu), Hodka (Gujarat), Pragpur (Himachal Pradesh), Khultabad (Maharashtra), Pochampalli (Andhra Pradesh), Kazugumalai (Tamil Nadu), and Raghurajpur (Orissa)—famous for Pattachitra, Gotipua dance besides architectural wonders. The focus is to encourage travellers to de-stress themselves from their urban lifestyles by going back to nature by living in villages.

Medical tourism

This involves travelling abroad to receive medical treatment in another country where state-of-the-art facilities with skilled doctors and quality nursing facilities are available at an affordable cost. Traditionally, foreigners fascinated by alternative form of medicine such as *Ayurveda* and *Unani* visited India to seek treatment for ailments. However, an impetus was given to medical tourism in India with the establishment of modern world-class hospitals by companies like Fortis and Max Hospitals in metros and other cities making quality medical care available at affordable costs. Besides, medical treatment that were not covered by insurance in the parent country or medical procedures for which there were long waiting periods in the host countries gave an impetus to medical tourism.

Adventure tourism

This is recreational travel undertaken to remote or exotic destinations for the purpose of exploration or engaging in a variety of rugged activities. Adventure tourism in India, consists of water sports, aero sports, mountaineering and trekking, safaris of various natures, and so on. The top 10 adventure activities are listed in Table 1.3.

TABLE 1.3   Adventure Activities

Adventure activities	Place
Skiing	Gulmarg, J & K
Mountain biking	Ladakh, J & K
Trekking	Zanskar, J & K
Whitewater rafting	Rishikesh, Uttarakhand
Paragliding	Manali, Himachal Pradesh
Camel safaris	Jaisalmer & Bikaner, Rajasthan
Scuba diving	Andaman islands
Trekking	Lahul-Spiti valleys, Himachal Pradesh
Mountaineering	Sikkim
Forest trails	Periyar National Park, Kerala

Religious or spiritual tourism

This involves travel or pilgrimage to places of religious importance such as shrines or temples of one's faith. A study done by Delhi-based National Council for Applied Economic Research shows that of the 230 million tourist trips undertaken in India, the largest proportion is of religious tourists. Saranath, Kushinagar, Vaishali, and Nalanda are considered the key sites for Buddhist pilgrims from Japan, China, South Korea, Thailand, and Sri Lanka. The other important religious sites frequented by foreigners and Indians residing abroad are listed in Table 1.4.

TABLE 1.4   Religious Sites

Religious sites	Place
Temple of Lord Balaji	Tirupati, Andhra Pradesh
Temple of Lord Jagannath	Puri, Orissa
Golden Temple	Amritsar, Punjab
Temple of Mata Vaishno Devi	Katra, J & K
Tomb of Salim Chisti Ajmer Sharif	Ajmer, Rajasthan
Birth place of Lord Krishna	Mathura, Vrindavan, Uttar Pradesh
Temple of Saint Sai Baba	Shirdi, Maharashtra
Basilica of Bom Jesus (mortal remains of St Francis Xavier)	Panaji, Goa
Church of St Mary's Forane	Kanjoor, Kerala
The Holy Ganges	Haridwar, Uttar Pradesh

Cultural tourism

This involves travelling to experience the local traditions and lifestyles of people in various countries. Unity in diversity enshrines the variety of experiences that travellers encounter in India, which is a confluence of dialects, religions, and cultures. Some of the most frequented cultural locations are listed in Table 1.5.

TABLE 1.5   Cultural Locations

Tourist attraction	Location
Taj Mahal, Fatehpur Sikri	Agra and Uttar Pradesh
Backwaters	Kerala
Ajanta Ellora caves	Maharashtra
Virupaksha Temple	Hampi, Karnataka
Bijapur and Golconda	Karnataka
Red Fort and Chandni Chowk	Delhi
Charminar	Andhra Pradesh
Kanyakumari	Tamil Nadu
Coorg	Karnataka

The Policy also envisaged wider participative role for the private sector in developing accommodation, timeshare accommodation, restaurants, entertainment facilities, shopping complexes in identified special tourism zones, which would result in the creation of employment opportunities.

A survey of the Indian hotel market carried out by the FHRAI at the turn of the 21st century highlighted the disparity between demand and supply in hotel accommodation. There was a staggering shortfall of approximately 80,000 rooms against the projected demand and the existing inventory of 1,20,000 rooms concentrated mostly in the tier I and tier II cities and in the luxury and upper-scale business segment.

In order to bridge the wide gap in demand and supply of hotel rooms across India, the various policy initiatives taken by the government encouraged entrepreneurs to invest in hotel projects. The period 2000–2011 witnessed a plethora of hospitality projects being announced. Between April 2000 and April 2011, expansion was also fuelled to a large extent by FDI in the hospitality industry of ₹11,120.25 crore, representing 1.86 per cent of the total FDI into India.

Hotels being developed by both Indian and international chains were in the three- to five-star categories, spread over tier I and tier III cities across India. This class of new hotel entrepreneurs consisted of real-estate developers with large parcels of land that could be developed across India; and businessmen with investments in oil, automobiles, stock markets, tea, publishing, and so on, seeking to diversify their existing portfolios. They lacked expertise in running hotels and therefore opted for the franchising and management contract route. Table 1.6 illustrates some of the developers and the brands that they have contracted with giving them the following immediate benefits:

- It gives the hotel property an immediate identity and credibility through a generally recognized brand.
- It leverages the brand's marketing strengths, access its central reservation systems ensuring wider reach and a steady flow of reservations.
- The hotel owner gets the advantage of service inputs from the brand during the pre- and post-operations phases.
- The owning company can raise financing from banks and other institutions and is seemingly based on the view that branding is likely to support the performance of the property and thus strengthen the lender's security.
- Just as a brand influences travellers, a brand influences potential investors as or when the property is placed on sale. The franchisee can influence and facilitate the sale of the property.

TABLE 1.6   Hotel Developers and Their Brand Tie-ups

Developer	Hotel brand
Naman Builders, Mumbai	Sofitel
Phoenix Mills, Mumbai	Shangri-La
Wasan Motors, Navi Mumbai	Taj Gateway
Jalan Motors, Kolkata	Taj Gateway
KSL and Industries, Nagpur	Taj
Nirmal Lifestyle, Mumbai	Accor Hotels
Today Group, New Delhi & Gurgaon	Crowne Plaza
Brigade Group, Bengaluru	Mercure
D. J. Group, New Delhi	Mercure Hotel
Lavasa Corporation, Lavasa	Accor Group and Fortune Hotels
Bengal Greenfield Housing Development Company Ltd.	Country Inn and Suites

It also marked a shift in the development strategy being followed with developers recognizing that they had to cater to a maturing domestic Indian market. The hospitality industry was also cognizant of the changing guest profile and hotels were getting designed to suit their requirements by incorporating free Wi-Fi services, I-pod dockets, extending pick-up and drop services to railway stations besides airports, and so on.

This was borne out by the statistics released by the Ministry of Tourism and the Bureau of Immigration, which confirmed that there was an exponential growth in domestic tourist visits compared with foreign tourist arrivals, as illustrated in Table 1.7.

TABLE 1.7   Domestic Tourist Visits and Foreign Tourist Arrivals (1991–2011)

Year	Tourist visits		Annual growth rate	
	Domestic	**Foreign**	**Domestic**	**Foreign**
1991	66670303	3146652	nil	nil
1992	81455861	3095160	22.2%	−1.6%
1993	105811696	3541727	29.9%	14.4%
1994	127118655	4030216	20.1%	13.8%
1995	136643600	4641279	7.5%	15.2%
1996	140119672	5030342	2.5%	8.4%
1997	159877208	5500419	14.1%	9.3%
1998	168196000	5539704	5.2%	−0.7%
1999	190671034	5832015	13.4%	5.3%
2000	220106911	5893542	15.4%	1.1%
2001	236469599	5436261	7.4%	−7.8%
2002	269598028	5157518	14.0%	−5.1%
2003	309038335	6708479	14.6%	30.1%
2004	366267522	8360278	18.5%	24.6%
2005	392014270	9947524	7.0%	19.0%
2006	462321054	11738892	17.9%	18.0%
2007	526564478	13256637	13.9%	12.9%
2008	563034107	14380633	6.9%	8.5%
2009	668800482	14372300	18.8%	−0.1%
2010	747703380	17910178	11.8%	24.6%
2011	850856640	19494879	13.8%	8.85%

Source: Ministry of Tourism, Government of India, India Tourism Statistics 2011

Most of the hospitality projects that were approved during the period 2005–2010 were in the mid-sized economy three- and four-star categories as compared to five-star hotels. These three- and four-star hotel projects were a part of larger multiuse developments encompassing shopping malls with multiplex cinema halls, food courts, and so on. In certain projects, they also had a residential component. Independent research conducted by Karma Hotels and Hospitality Consultants highlights that 60 per cent of the hotel projects that were under construction were in the three- and four-star categories, adding another 25,000 rooms to the existing inventory of the mid-sized economy segment. This includes all the major domestic and foreign players operating in the Indian hotel sphere.

The development that was underway clearly highlighted the distinction that existed between hotel ownership, hotel brands, and hotel operators. It also emphasized the various routes they would take to grow their portfolios.

In the first category were the traditional players who owned the hotels and believed in running their own operations under their own brand; for example, Oberoi Hotels, Pride Hotels, Royal Orchid Hotels, and Taj Hotels.

In the second category were the new set of hotel entrepreneurs who lacked expertise in running hotels and took the conventional way of retaining the ownership of the asset while handing over the management to well-established hotel operators who flagged the property with their brand, as illustrated in Table 1.6.

International hotel operators strategically adopted the management contract and franchising route to expand their presence in India as there was a large group of developers keen to own the hotel asset without getting involved in the day-to-day operations.

In the third category were the unconventional owners who entered into a tripartite agreement with the brand that would flag the property and with a hotel operating company that was brand agnostic to run the hotel for them; for example, the Marriott Hotel, Ahmedabad is owned by the Pacifica Group of Companies and branded by Marriott Corporation as Courtyard by Marriott and the operations are run by Interstate Hotels Private Ltd.

In India under all the three categories, besides the time-honoured tradition of taking bank loans to fund the project, the entry of dedicated hospitality funds changed the way hotel projects were funded. The fund would take a position or stake in the hotel-owning company that was developing the hotel and would cash out after a predetermined mutually-agreed time period. Once the hotel commenced operations, the fund would exit after taking its share of the profits on the amount that was invested.

Other than hospitality funds, hotel operating companies that were keen to make an entry into India in strategic locations or to strengthen their position in the key markets were willing to partner with developers who enjoyed a pristine reputation and had land parcels that fitted the requirements of the brand. Typically, the investment in such cases would range from 10 to 26 per cent by way of a soft loan with a seat on the management of the board till the hotel-operating company's investment had been paid. Some of the funds that were active in the hospitality sphere were Starwood Capital, Eredine Capital, Red Fort Capital, Kotak Mahindra, Duet Hotels, Milestone Capital, and so on.

Although numerous projects were announced by the developers, the subprime financial crises that led to the downfall of Lehman Brothers and other financial institutions worldwide in 2008 had a direct impact on hotel development. Financial institutions and funds that had committed funds to various projects being promoted by real-estate companies, withdrew their commitments resulting in projects being delayed or abandoned by developers. Although four years have passed, the current political climate does not auger well for investments and many projects are still shelved for need of finances. Besides financial woes the hotel industry was further affected because of the earthquake in Sikkim in September 2011 and the north-India power grid failure in July 2012. It is to be seen if the hospitality industry will be able to fulfil its dreams of bridging the supply and demand gap.

Some of the key domestic hotel companies and their brands are listed in Table 1.8.

TABLE 1.8 Domestic Hotel Companies and Their Brands

Company	Brands
ITC Hotels	Fortune Hotels, Welcomheritage hotels
Taj Hotels and Resorts	Taj, Vivanta by Taj, Gateway Hotels,
Berggruenn Hotels	Keys
Lemon Tree Hotels	Lemon Tree, Red Fox Hotels
Pride Hotels	Pride Hotels, Pride Biznotel & Resorts
Royal Orchid Hotels Ltd.	Royal Orchid Hotels, Regenta, Spree Hotels, Peppermint Hotels
East India Hotels Ltd.	Oberoi Hotels and Resorts, Trident Hotels
Surrendra Park Hotels	Park Hotels
Roots Corporation Ltd.	Ginger Hotels
India Tourism Development Corporation (ITDC)	Ashok
Leela Hotels	Leela Kempinski, The Leela
The Lalit Hotels	The Lalit

Some of the international hotel management and franchisee companies and their brands operating in India are illustrated in Table 1.9.

TABLE 1.9 International Hotel Management and Franchisee Companies

Company	Brands
Accor	Sofitel, Pullman, Mercure Hotels, Novotel, Ibis
Best Western Hotels	Best Western, Best Western Plus, Best Western Premier
Choice Hotels International	Clarion Hotels, Quality Inns, Comfort Inn, Sleep Inns
Carlson Rezidor Hotels	Radisson Blu, Radisson, Park Plaza, Country Inn & Suites, Park Inn
Hyatt International	Park Hyatt, Andaz, Hyatt Regency, Hyatt, Grand Hyatt, Hyatt Place
Hilton Hotels	Hilton, Double Tree by Hilton, Embassy Suites, Hilton Garden Inns, Hampton, Homewood Suites
InterContinental Hotel Group	InterContinental Hotels, Crowne Plaza, Holiday Inn, Express by Holiday Inn
Kempinski Hotels	Kempinski Hotel, Kempinski Residences
Louvre Hotels Group	Golden Tulip Hotels, Tulip Inns, Royal Tulip
Marriott Corporation	The Ritz Carlton, JW Marriott, Renaissance, Courtyard by Marriott, Marriott

(Contd)

TABLE 1.9   (Contd)

Company	Brands
Oakwood	Oakwood Suites, Oakwood Residences
Starwood Hotels Corporation	'W' Hotels, St. Regis, Sheraton, Aloft, Le Méridien, Four Points by Sheraton, Westin, Luxury Collection, Elements
Shangri La Hotels	Shangri La Hotels, Traders Hotel
Wyndham Hotels	Wyndham Hotels, Wyndham Grand, Days Inn, Ramada Inn, Ramada, Howard Johnson, Travelodge, Microtel, Planet Hollywood

PIONEERING HOSPITALITY EDUCATION

The government took the lead in hospitality education under the aegis of the National Council for Hotel Management and Catering Technology (NCHMCT) by establishing four Indian Institutes of Hotel Management in 1962 in Bombay, Delhi, Calcutta, and Madras Today, NCHMCT conducts 11 full-time courses of different durations from two-year full-time MSc in Hospitality and Hotel Administration to trade-specific short courses of 1.5 years to 6- to 8-weeks duration. It has partnered with the Indira Gandhi National Open University (IGNOU) for the award of bachelor's degree in hotel management.

The training of managerial and other personnel is an important franchisee benefit. The Oberoi Hotels formally launched their management trainee programme in 1966, and the first few batches of managers trained by the Oberoi Hotels set new benchmarks of professional hotel management, which continues to influence and guide India's hotel industry today. The various training programmes conducted by the Oberoi Hotels crystallized in establishing the Oberoi Centre of Learning and Development, which is rated by the hospitality professionals as the best in India.

The growth in hotels led the Indian hotel companies to develop their own indigenous training programmes. The Taj group in collaboration with the Maulana Azad Educational Trust established the Institute of Hotel Management at Aurangabad in 1989. ITC Hotels opened the Welcomgroup Graduate School of Hotel Administration in 1994 at Manipal in association with the TMA Pai Foundation. Both institutes focussed on imparting quality education to students wishing to pursue careers in the hospitality industry. Royal Orchid Hotels Limited set up the Presidency College of Hotel Management in Bangalore (now Bengaluru) in 1994.

Besides the government and the major hotel chains setting up hotel management institutes to cater to the burgeoning demand for professional hoteliers, the FHRAI set up its own institute in Greater Noida to impart quality hospitality education in 2005.

Anticipating needs for trained manpower in the coming decade, a large number of hospitality institutes has been set up by the private sector. This mushrooming of hospitality institutes has undermined the level of education, as in most cases, the same degree course is offered but under different names as shown in Table 1.10.

TABLE 1.10 List of Degree Programmes

- BSc (Hospitality and Hotel Administration)
- BBA (Hospitality Management)
- BBA (Hotel Management)
- BSc (Hotel Management, Catering Technology & Tourism)
- BSc (Airline, Hotel & Tourism Management)
- BA (International Hospitality Management)
- BHTM (Bachelor of Hotel & Tourism Management)

This has not benefitted the hospitality industry, as today there are a large number of graduates who are in urgent need for retraining by the hospitality industry to live up to the professional standards expected from them.

CHANGING GUEST PROFILE

Changing demographics, improvement in educational standards, the technological revolution, economic growth, and social changes of the decade have influenced the profile of the new hotel guest.

- The Census of India highlighted that there was population increase in the age group of 15 to 64 years from 60.7 to 63.6 per cent in 2011, signalling the emergence of a youthful India.
- The literacy levels have registered a growth across India. The effective literacy rate in the 2001 census was 64.83, which improved to 74.04 per cent in 2011. While the effective literacy rate for males rose from 75.26 to 82.14 per cent, marking a rise of 6.9 per cent, it increased by 11.8 per cent for females from 53.67 to 65.46 per cent. Increase in the literary levels led to migration of the population from rural to urban areas.
- The latest census done in 2011 reveals that Delhi's population rose by 4.1 per cent, Mumbai's by 3.1 per cent, and Kolkata by 2 per cent compared with the 2001 census spawning large-scale urbanization.
- The revolution in communication ushered in by the Internet and the usage of mobile phone made the youth technologically savvy and well informed.
- The open sky policy for the aviation sector introduced in 1990 encouraged the urban middle class to travel exponentially at reasonable costs.
- A large workforce in the age group of 24 to 35 years encouraged spending on entertainment and lifestyle products such as fashionable designer clothes, cars, and electronic gadgets, thanks to the availability of finance from banks.

- Availability of credit cards from banks inculcated a shift in attitude from one that of savings to spending.
- High savings of the middle class owing to 'double income no kids' families increased their disposable incomes.
- With women joining the workforce in large numbers between 2001 and 2011, hotels have started to address an entirely new segment of business clientele.

The profile of the new hotel guest is that he or she is a young, educated, urban middle-class, well-informed person who is fashion conscious, has exacting dietary habits, is technology savvy, travels abroad at least once a year, and enjoys visiting hotels and restaurants.

CHALLENGES OF THE 21ST CENTURY

A hotel general manager is traditionally required to fulfil three major requirements at all times—ensure that the owners and the head office get a return on their investments, ensure that the guests are always satisfied with the quality of services given by the hotel, and finally maintain a harmonious working environment to keep the employees happy as illustrated in Fig. 1.1.

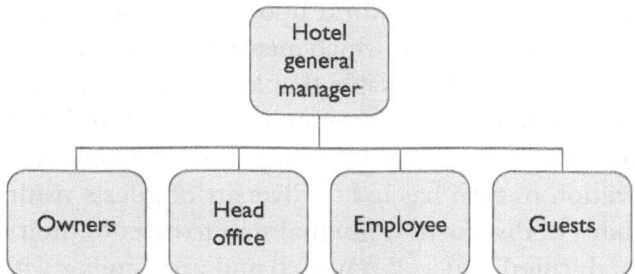

FIGURE 1.1   Roles of a Hotel General Manager

In order to do so, general managers have to lead from the front, have patience, display remarkable people management skills and an uncanny ability to delegate tasks, and maintain follow-up. They should also have a thorough understanding of the various technological systems that operate in the hotel, such as the property management system, the energy management system, and the guest reservation system to deliver guest satisfaction. They should also introduce game-changing ideas that result in empowerment of employees to deliver exceptional service.

With all the personnel skills and resources at his or her command, the general manager of the 21st century will have to address the following issues, which will put his or her business acumen to the test as illustrated in Fig. 1.2.

FIGURE 1.2 Challenges Facing the Hotel General Manager in the 21st Century

Globalization and Diversity

The term global village was coined by Marshall McLuhan in his book *The Gutenberg Galaxy* published in 1962. It is a phrase that has been touted often to describe the interdependence of people around the world upon each other and resonates with the Sanskrit phrase *Vasudeva Kutumbhkam*, which means that the whole world is a single family. Globalization has been made possible thanks to the increase in literacy, modern efficient means of transportation, the communication revolution encouraging an exchange of ideas through the Internet, and the migration of people from one country to another.

Globalization in turn has led to diversity of guests visiting hotels, which requires the availability of diverse multilingual staff to cater to their needs. These well-heeled guests are educated and well-travelled and are familiar with hotels.

Safety and Security

Post 11 September 2001 and November 2008 Mumbai terrorist attacks, hotels have had to increasingly enhance safety and security measures both for guests and employees. Terrorism is a threat, which is not likely to be contained in the near future; hence hotels will have to rely on the latest technology and staff training methods to strengthen their safety and security efforts.

Health, Sanitation, and Hygiene

Guests are increasingly getting more and more particular in their eating habits and expect their meals to be prepared in a hygienic and sanitary manner. With governments setting more and more stringent standards of sanitation and hygiene, hotels will have to maintain high standards in their properties as failure to do so may well lead to the restaurant being de-licensed by the government.

Legal Issues

It is incumbent upon hotels to seek all the permissions that are required to operate hotels from the regulatory authorities in a timely manner and to ensure that all the mandatory requirements are fulfilled. Besides licensing issues, the hotel also has to address legal claims that arise when guests are injured on account of accidents occurring in the hotel premises, as well as guests' compensation claims on account of deficiency of service.

Quality of Service and Pricing

Quality of service will always play a significant role in retaining a guest; this will involve a high level of training of employees to deliver exceptional service. Hotels will have to ensure that what they promise is actually delivered and that there is no mismatch between the level of service and the pricing. Guest expectations will have to be matched by both price and performance.

Technology Innovations

A modern hotel is an engineering marvel with plant and machinery such as an air-conditioning plant, boilers, laundry, waste management systems; a host of appliances in the kitchen, service areas, and guest rooms, electronics in telephone exchange, computer server room, business centre, and so on. The availability of these techno-logical resources makes it possible for a hotel to deliver improved service to a guest, the challenge for the hotel is to be contemporary at all times.

Employee Retention

Retaining employees will be a challenge as payroll costs will continue to escalate. Hotels will have to manage with fewer employees who are multi-skilled and proficient in handling two or more job functions. New entrants to the workforce will require intensive training to meet the exacting demands of the growing industry.

SUMMARY

This chapter traced the growth of the hotel industry in India through the pioneering efforts of Rai Bahadur Mohan Singh Oberoi, Jamsetji Nusserwanji Tata, and others from the colonial phase to the present day. The chapter highlighted the singular role played by FHRAI in changing the mindset of the government to recognize that hospitality was an engine for economic growth and poverty alleviation. The chapter also discussed how the changed business environment led to the establishment of HAI in 1996 with the objective of 'securing for the hotel industry its due place in India's economy'. The need for education in the hospitality sphere was recognized by the government as it came to the forefront to establish Institutes of Hotel Management (IHMs) that would lay the foundations for hospitality education. The chapter highlighted that the tumultuous developments of the past decade have changed the perception of hotels, which has encouraged international brands to strengthen their presence in India. Hotel development has moved from upscale luxury hotels to mid-scale economy hotels with investors tying up with local developers in order to build hotels.

The chapter also highlighted that a hotel general manager will have to manage this transition phase, which has surmountable challenges in order to be a successful hotelier in the 21st century.

KEY TERMS

Service   An act of providing goods and services to guests, offering timely assistance in a warm and friendly manner.

Characteristics of the hospitality industry   Constantly striving to deliver outstanding exceptional service of intangible products that are perishable in nature 24/7 throughout the year.

The Federation of Hotels and Restaurant Association of India (FHRAI)   The apex body of the hotel industry that was created in 1955 with the amalgamation of four zonal federations and under the guidance of various presidents representing the views of the industry to the government.

Tourist circuits   Well-defined itineraries or routes connecting various venues or cities which are regularly traversed by travellers without change of direction returning to the starting point, for example, The Golden Triangle of 'Delhi–Jaipur–Agra–Delhi' and the Beach Circuit of 'Mumbai–Goa–Mumbai'.

Hotel and Restaurant Approval and Classification Committee (HRACC)   The department of tourism has mandated that all hotel projects require to be approved by the HRACC before they can commence construction or operations.

Hotel Association of India (HAI)   Established in 1996, this association represents the entire spectrum of the hotel industry, contributing towards employment generation, sustainable economic and social development, and helping raise the standards of hoteliering in India.

Foreign technology agreements   International hotel brands could enter into management contracts and franchisee agreements with Indian hoteliers wishing to flag their properties.

Management contract   Draws a distinction between the ownership of the hotel and the operator whilst defining the business relationship between the two parties—the operator being responsible for the management of the business for an agreed fee and the owner assuming legal and financial responsibility, such as profits or the burden of a loss and any capital expenses.

Guest profile of the new hotel guest   He or she is a young educated urban middle-class well-informed person who is fashion conscious, has exacting dietary habits, is technology savvy, and travels abroad at least once a year and enjoys visiting hotels and restaurants.

Medical tourism   Involves travelling abroad to receive medical treatment in another country where state-of-the-art facilities with skilled doctors and quality nursing facilities are available at an affordable cost. It includes travel to developing countries as well.

Rural tourism   The focus is to encourage travellers to de-stress themselves from their urban lifestyles by going back to nature by living in villages.

Adventure tourism   Recreational travel undertaken to remote or exotic destinations for the purpose of exploration or engaging in a variety of rugged activities.

Religious tourism   Travel or undertake pilgrimage to places of religious importance such as shrines or temples of one's faith. Religious tourism is also called spiritual tourism.

Cultural tourism   Involves travelling to experience the local traditions and lifestyles of people in various countries.

Spirit of hospitality   Welcoming guests and looking after their needs through exceptional service. It refers to the relationship between a guest and a host, and to the act of being hospitable, that is, receiving guests and visitors cordially with goodwill and friendliness.

EXERCISES

Define the Following
1. Guest profile
2. Management contract
3. Cultural tourism
4. HRACC
5. Spirit of hospitality

6. Medical tourism
7. Tourism circuits
8. Service
9. FHRAI
10. Foreign Technology Agreements

Concept Review Questions

1. What is the difference between management contract and franchisee agreements?
2. What strategy is employed by international brands at entry level to establish their presence?
3. Write a brief note on the various types of tourism that are being promoted by the government.
4. Why is the first decade of the 21st century regarded as a decade of hope and despair?
5. Write a brief note on the growth of hospitality education in India.
6. Hospitality business was considered an elitist activity. Explain.

7. Write a brief note on the challenges faced by a hotel general manager of the 21st century.

Critical Thinking Questions

1. Review the strategies that Indian hotel chains have persued to ensure that they pose a challenge and enjoy a competitive edge over international hotel brands.
2. What made India change its tourism policy between the years 1982 and 2002?

Research Questions

1. How do general managers ensure that they stay ahead of the curve in resolving various guest-related issues?
2. Do you agree that the unconventional approach to the hospitality business is correct for the current times?

Project

1. Visit at least two or three hotels of your choice and collect data available that will help in determining and evaluating the changing guest profile.

REFERENCES

Bachi J. Karkaria, *Dare to Dream: A Life of Rai Bahadur Mohan Singh Oberoi* (Viking Press, 1992).

Mohan Sharma, 'Lodged in the Heart of New Delhi', *Hindustan Times*, 30 August 2011.

<http://oxforddictionaries.com/definition/english/service> accessed on 18 August 2012.

<http//www:theimperialindia.com> accessed on 18 August 2012.

<www.itcportal.com> accessed on 18 August 2012.

<http://www.nchmct.org/> accessed on 18 August 2012.

<http://www.ihma.ac.in> accessed on 18 August 2012.

<http://www.manipal.edu/institutions/hotelmanagement/wgshamanipal> accessed on 18 August 2012.

Planning Commission, Sixth Five Year Plan 1980–1985 <http://planningcommission.nic.in/plans/planrel/fiveyr/index9.html> accessed on 18 August 2012.

Planning Commission, Ninth Five Year Plan 1997–2002 <http://planningcommission.nic.in/plans/planrel/fiveyr/index9.html> accessed on 18 August 2012.

<http://en.wikipedia.org/wiki/Urbanisation_in_India> accessed on 18 August 2012.

<http://www.lemontreehotels.com/about-us/lemontree-hotel-management-team-humans.aspx> accessed on 18 August 2012.

Consolidated FDI Policy, Ministry of Commerce and Industry, Government of India <http://india.gov.in/allimpfrms/alldocs/16452.pdf> accessed on 18 August 2012.

Department of Industrial Policy and Promotion <http://dipp.nic.in/fdi_statistics/india_FDI_April 2011.pdf> accessed on 18 August 2012.

<http://bizfinance.about.com/od/currentevents/tp/Top_Ten_Fin_Events_Decade.htm> accessed on 18 August 2012.

<http://top10.com/top-10-events-that-shaped-the-world-2000-2010> accessed on 18 August 2012.

<http://www.bbc.co.uk/news/world-south-asia-12641776> accessed on 18 August 2012.

<http://www.theashok.com/ accessed> accessed on 18 August 2012.

<http://www.itchotels.in/> accessed on 18 August 2012.

<http://www.royalorchidhotels.com/common/about-ro.asp> accessed on 18 August 2012.

<http://www.pridehotel.com/> accessed on 18 August 2012.

<http://www.fortunehotels.in/> accessed on 18 August 2012.

<http://www.tajhotels.com/> accessed on 18 August 2012.

<http://www.accor.com/en.html> accessed on 18 August 2012.

<http://www.bestwestern.com/> accessed on 18 August 2012.

<http://www.ichotelsgroup.com/ihg/hotels/us/en/reservation> accessed on 18 August 2012.

<http://www.choicehotels.com/?refd=hotelchoice.com> accessed on 18 August 2012.

<http://www.carlsonrezidor.com/> accessed on 18 August 2012.

<http://www.hiltonworldwide.com/> accessed on 18 August 2012.

<http://www.wyndham.com/> accessed on 18 August 2012.

<http:/ http://www.shangri-la.com/> accessed on 18 August 2012.

<www.starwoodhotels.com/index.html> accessed on 18 August 2012.

<http://www.marriott.com/hotel-search.mi> accessed on 18 August 2012.

<http://www.kempinski.com/en/hotels/welcome/> accessed on 18 August 2012.

<http://www.hyatt.com/hyatt/index.jsp> accessed on 18 August 2012.

<http://www.goldentulip.com/EN/default.aspx> accessed on 18 August 2012.

<http://www.bestwestern.com/> accessed on 18 August 2012.

<http://economictimes.indiatimes.com/news/economy/indicators/census-of-india-2011-literacy-rises-by-92-per-cent-now-7404-per-cent/articleshow/7833145.cms> accessed on 18 August 2012.

<http://en.wikipedia.org/wiki/Marshall_McLuhan#The_Gutenberg_Galaxy_.281962.29> accessed on 17 August 2012.

<http://en.wikipedia.org/wiki/Vasudhaiva_Kutumbakam> accessed on 17 August 2012.

<http://www.travel-industry-dictionary.com/adventure-tourism.html> accessed on 19 August 1012.

<http://www.hotelassociationofindia.com/aboutus.html> accessed on 18 January 2013.

Introduction to Hotel Laws

LEARNING OBJECTIVES

After going through this chapter, the reader will be familiar with the following:

- Importance of studying hospitality laws
- Evolution of laws with emphasis on hotel law
- Implementation of laws by the executive and the judiciary
- Journey of a legal case through the judicial system

INTRODUCTION

For a student desirous of seeking a career in hotels, it is important to be familiar about hotel laws, which cover a wide range of legal issues ranging from hotel business contracts, front-office operations, labour laws, duties of hotels toward guests, hotel liabilities, food and beverage operations, and public health, safety and security. These laws apply to the service sector that comprises the food service, travel, and hotel industry. A hotel has a unique and diverse operating environment; it is estimated that 60 to 70 per cent of the decisions taken in this environment can have legal implications.

This chapter discusses hotel laws from a general manager's perspective, which will give an all-encompassing view of the various laws applicable to the hotel industry, in order to safeguard the interests of the hotel. Knowledge of hotel laws enables a general manager to operate his or her business in an ethical manner and to address issues before legal difficulties arise, as it is very costly to fight a legal case in the courts owing to the time-consuming judicial process.

In India, the Sarais Act, 1867, defines a general manager's role in the form of a keeper of a *sarai*: '"Keeper of a sarai" includes the owner and any person having or acting in the care or management thereof', and 'recognizes him as the person responsible for managing the affairs of the hotel'.

A simple task of choosing a name and a logo for a hotel requires that the name be registered under The Companies Act, 1956, the logo under The Patents Act, 1970, The Designs Act, 2000, and The Trademarks Act, 1999. In order to commence business, a hotel is required to register itself under the Shops and Establishments Acts of the respective states where they are located in. In case the owner desires to enter into a franchisee or management agreement with a hotel operating company, the contract has to be stamped and registered under The Indian Stamp Act, 1899 and the Registration Act, 1908. For a contract to be enforceable in a court of law it should fulfil all the conditions of a valid contract under the Indian Contract Act, 1872.

In order to commence front-office operations, the rooms division director has to ensure that the guest registration cards, arrival and departure register formats comply with the guidelines given by the police licensing authorities under The Police Act, 1861. All foreigners are required to be registered with the Foreigner's Regional Registration Office (FRRO) under The Foreigners Registration Act, 1946, and all forms to register foreigners have to be printed as per the format given by them.

If the hotel has an agreement with a hotel operating company then all printed stationery, forms, and formats, for example, purchase orders, requisition books, store-room inventory sheets, and so on, must carry the name and logo of the brand. All guest stationery such as invoices, guest bills, guest envelopes, and letterheads should carry both the logo and the name of the operating company's brand and the owning company.

Hotel accounting standards must conform to the internationally accepted Uniform System of Accounts for Hotels as well as follow the mercantile system of accounts while reporting data to the government authorities under the Income Tax Act, 1961, Service Tax Statutory Provisions Act, 1994, The Companies Act, 1956, and so on.

All food and beverage outlets have to be registered under the Food Safety and Standards Act, 2006 before commencing operations. Under the Act they are required to meet stringent licensing conditions relating to hygiene, proper storage of food articles in the kitchen just to name a few. In order to serve alcohol in the bar or through room service, they have to register under the Excise Act applicable to the respective states by paying the licence fee. The Act further requires that proper inventories of the liquor stocks be maintained at all times.

Hoteliers are required to provide a safe and secure environment to guest under the Sarais Act, 1867. Hotels take adequate precautions by putting in place adequate signage alerting guests regarding polished slippery floors, wet floors, asking to place valuables in the in-room safes or the hotel safe, and as an abundant measure of caution also take out insurance policies to protect themselves against third-party liability lawsuits.

Common crimes against hotels involve fraudulent payments by guests through credit cards, cheques, or fake currency; embezzlement by employees; theft of company property by employees; theft of services by guests and patrons, and so on.

These are just a few of the instances that require a general manager to be conversant with the laws that regulate the hotel business in order to manage hotel operations while traversing the minefield of government regulations that are administered by central, state, or municipal bodies. The later chapters will discuss the various laws that govern the relationship among the various stakeholders of a hotel—owner, operator, guest, and employee.

WHAT IS LAW?

Jean Jacques Rousseau in his treatise *The Social Contract* states that—'Man is born free, and everywhere he is in chains.'

A simple interpretation is that when man is born he is free; as he grows older he is subjected to the various norms, rules, moral strictures, religious beliefs that define his social behaviour, political preferences, personal habits, and conduct; these shackles bind him in chains from which he is freed only when he dies.

The *Oxford Dictionaries Online* define law as follows:
- The system of rules which a particular country or community recognizes as regulating the actions of its members and which it may enforce by the imposition of penalties: drunken driving leads to a fine and imprisonment.
- A rule defining correct procedure or behaviour in a sport: rules of the game.
- A statement of fact, deduced from observation, to the effect that a particular natural or scientific phenomenon always occurs if certain conditions are present: laws of gravity.
- A generalization based on a fact or event perceived to be recurrent: the change of seasons is based on the laws of nature.
- The body of divine commandments as expressed in the Bible or other religious texts: Laws of Moses.

The following statements are representative of the perception of law in the minds of the common man and they highlight the various attributes of law:
- Regulations made by the government that everyone has to follow.
- If you break the law you get punished.
- Laws are universally accepted rules passed from one generation to another; for example, speak the truth, do not steal.
- Rules that define the correct way to do a job.

Law can be defined as a universally accepted body of rules that aims at creating a social system that encourages people to interact voluntarily in an orderly civilized manner; as and when there is an infringement or a violation of these regulations, the judicial system steps in to enforce order by the imposition of penalties.

The study of law is a challenging subject as it varies from state to state, for example, the legal drinking age in India varies from 18 years in the state of Goa to 25 years in Punjab.

The basic unit of society is a family, comprising a husband, wife, and their dependent children; collectively a group of families living together constitutes a community.

In all societies families trace their lineage or *gotra* (Sanskrit for lineage in an unbroken male line from a common male ancestor). In India, the Brahmins trace their lineage to seven or eight *rishis* or sages—Gautama, Bharadvaja, Vishvamitra, Jamadagni, Vasishtha, Kashyapa, and Atri. In the Bible, Jesus and his ancestors are well documented, tracing their lineage through the male ancestor to Adam, similar to the *gotra* system practised in India.

The Ten Commandments (The Bible *Exodus* 20:1–17) given to Moses on Mount Sinai is one of the earliest references to natural law or customary law. It mentions the basic tenets of natural law for people to follow such as respect and care for your elders, do not steal, commit murder, or be envious of your neighbour's fortunes, and so on. In India, *Manu Smriti* or the Laws of Manu in the section *Dharamshastras* or 'the rules of righteous conduct', stipulates that a person is required to follow the religious customs related to marriage rituals, birth ceremonies, and burial or cremation of the dead, fulfil social obligations such as charity towards the poor, care for the elderly and the infirm, provide food and shelter for guests and travellers. It shares a commonality with *The Ten Commandments* and the *Codes of Hammurabi*, which lay down the laws that govern social interaction in business dealings, and respect and compliance of the king's or ruler's dictates.

These scriptures placed a paramount duty on the head of the family to enforce these natural laws and it is in a family environment that we learn to grapple with the basic issues of living together with parents, grandparents, brothers, sisters, spouse, friends, teachers, colleagues, and peers. The acceptance of these customary laws emerged spontaneously and were followed voluntarily, and with their extension from the family to the social sphere ensured their wider acceptance creating the glue that bound together the fabric of society. In the process of evolution natural, customary, and religious laws intermingled making it difficult to distinguish one from the other; however, by whatever name they came to be addressed these bodies of laws were universally accepted and had a common goal that of the preservation of society. Natural or customary laws are defined as unwritten norms, rules, moral strictures, religious beliefs that are followed voluntarily and universally accepted by society.

Common laws as opposed to customary laws had their origins in unwritten customs and usages that were accepted and validated by the courts and made applicable all over England. During the reign of King Henry II (1154–1189), Ranulf de Granville, a justice at the court of King Henry compiled the various decisions of the law courts, which were elaborated by Henry de Bracton, a judge in his book *On the Laws and Customs of England* in the mid-13th century.

Common law is a body of unwritten customs and usages that are validated by the courts through judgements in civil or criminal cases, thereby setting legal precedents for the courts to follow in the future when deciding cases. This process of following earlier cases is called *stare decisis*, which in Latin means 'the matter stands decided'. However, judges can choose not to base their judgement on the doctrine of *stare decisis* in any case if they are of the opinion that social changes require that the earlier precedent should not be followed in the larger interests of society; in such a situation the new legal judgement or opinion will become the precedent for future judges to follow.

English Statute Law traces its origins to the 13th century when the Kings of England made rules by proclamations. The kings issued proclamations which were written documents announcing their intention to the public to act in a certain manner or to restrain from doing an action; if it was not followed it resulted in a suitable punishment. It was during the Interregnum (1649–1660) in England that the supremacy of Parliament was firmly established over proclamations issued by the kings as the primary institutions responsible for promulgating laws. It was during this period that English became the language of the courts instead of Latin.

With the consolidation of political power—John Austin an English jurist in his book *Province of Jurisprudence Determined* (1832)—observed that law is 'a body of rules fixed and enforced by a sovereign political authority.' An outstanding example is the *Napoleonic Code* (1804) of France, which is a successful synthesis of the best from papal law, customary law, Roman law, and common law or case law.

Statute law on the other hand is a written law that is enacted by parliament which is the supreme legislative body. Unlike customary laws which are voluntarily followed, statutory laws either forbid the doing of an action or make it mandatory to do an action, and failure to follow these laws results in the imposition of penalties.

Administrative law, as the name suggests, lays down the rules and regulations that are required to be followed in order to implement the law as intended by the statute and these procedural directives derive their sanctity from it. The executive is responsible for their implementation.

The origins of laws are illustrated in Fig. 2.1.

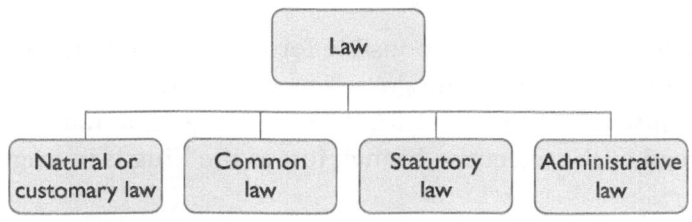

FIGURE 2.1 Origins of Law

ROLE OF THE LEGISLATIVE, EXECUTIVE, AND THE JUDICIARY

With the establishing of nation states, the principles of governance rested on the separation of power between the three arms of the government—the legislative, executive, and the judiciary as illustrated in Fig. 2.2. In India we follow this three-tier system of governance. All these three arms of the government are responsible to ensure that laws are framed and implemented judiciously.

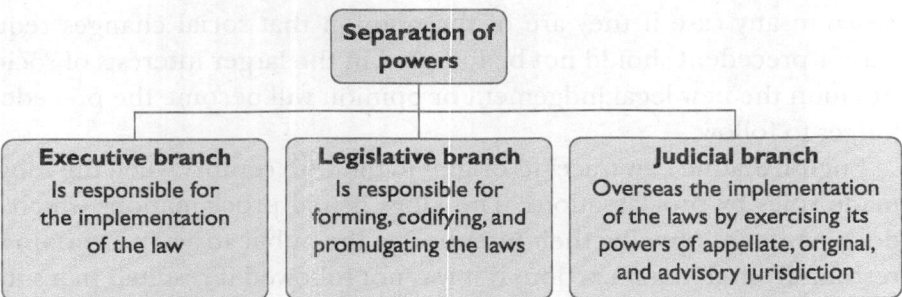

FIGURE 2.2   Separation of Powers between the Legislative, Executive, and the Judicial Branch

Legislative

In England and India, parliaments consisting of the House of Commons (Lok Sabha) and the House of Lords (Rajya Sabha) are responsible for passing statutory laws. The legislative process followed by English and the Indian parliament is similar and a bill can be introduced in either house of the Parliament, which commences the legislative process.

> **Example**   Once a bill is introduced in the House of Commons (Lok Sabha) and has been passed or approved in the House of Commons (Lok Sabha), it would be referred to the House of Lords (Rajya Sabha) and upon its acceptance by the House of Lords (Rajya Sabha) it would be sent to the King (President of India) for his assent, thereby promulgating a bill into an act of Parliament. Once the Act is notified or gazetted it becomes operational. In India, we follow the same process in enacting our laws. Legislatures recognized the evolving nature of law and addressing the changing needs of the social, economic, and political environments have been instrumental in helping societies resolve disputes and prevent conflicts.

Executive

The executive branch is responsible for the enforcement of law and order and day-to-day administration of the government; in order to achieve its goals it lays down the administrative framework for its smooth implementation. The President of India is the head of the executive branch just as the King is in England.

Judiciary

The judiciary—both in England and in India—enjoys appellate, original, and advisory jurisdiction. One of the duties of the Supreme Court is judicial review of the laws enacted by parliament and of the administrative orders issued by the executive vis-à-vis the benchmark of the constitution. Additionally, the judiciary oversees the implementation of the laws by the executive ensuring that it is carried out as per the intentions of the legislature and if the executive fails in the discharge of its functions the courts are competent to give directions to the executive, which can be in the form of judicial legislation or case law. The Supreme Court of India enjoys original jurisdiction in cases where there is conflict between the central and the state governments.

CLASSIFICATION OF LAWS

Laws are classified into either substantive or procedural and within these two broad groups all laws whether civil or criminal, public or private, corporate and commercial, and so on—addressing a wide range of activities—are categorized with further subdivisions based upon the subject and scope of their application as illustrated in Fig. 2.3.

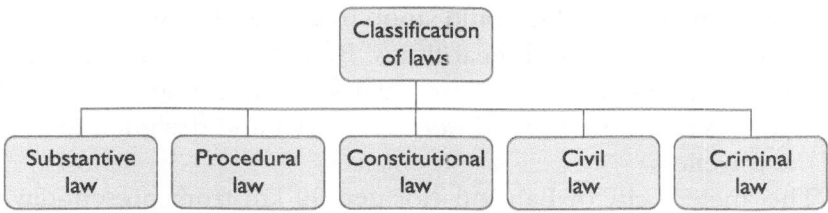

FIGURE 2.3 Classification of Laws

Substantive law It creates, defines, and regulates rights of individuals and companies, the essential substance of law, including, for example, the law of contracts, torts, wills, and property.

Procedural law or administrative law It is a body of law that governs the process prescribing the formal steps to be taken in enforcing legal rights. The implementation of civil and criminal law requires separate set of administrative procedures.

Constitutional law It defines the relationship between the three arms of the government and in a federal structure the relationship between the centre and the states, and spells out the fundamental rights and duties of citizens. All statutory laws and administrative orders cannot violate the tenants of the constitution.

Civil law It provides legal solutions to disputes involving ownership of personal property, interpretation of contracts, marriage disputes, divorce, damages for personal injury and to personal property, and so on.

Criminal law It classifies crimes under various categories such as crimes against the state, persons, and property, and crimes relating to public order, health and safety, religious affairs, marriage, decency, and morals.

ORIGINS OF HOTEL LAW

It is important to understand the meaning of the term hospitality as it is the key to a hotel's success and has its origins from the Latin word *hospes*, which literally means *hostis* or host. It involves showing respect for one's guests, providing for their needs, and treating them as equals.

In the *Taittiriya Upanishad,* chapter Shiksha Valli, verse 11, we find the earliest reference to hospitality that should be extended towards guests— *Atithi Devo Bhavah*— which in Sanskrit means that *The Guest is God.* This line is part of the verse—*Matru Devo Bhavah, Pitru Devo Bhavah, Acharya Devo Bhavah, Atithi Devo Bhavah.* The tagline of 'The Incredible India' campaign is *Athiti Devo Bhavah.* These three words enshrine the Indian values of hospitality: extending warm hospitality responsibly, respectfully, and with great humility towards guests.

However, the history of hotel laws is a sordid one. Innkeepers were regarded as persons of ill repute who would stoop to any level to steal from their guests in connivance with bandits and local thugs. Besides, the shortage of inns and hostelries made the innkeepers a law unto themselves with scant regards for the travellers. Hence laws that were framed were very strict and designed to protect the interests of the travellers.

The ancient city of Babylon (located 90 km from present-day Baghdad) had a flourishing economy with well-established trade links with neighbouring countries in the Persian Gulf and the Mediterranean. Babylon attracted numerous frequent travellers who visited the city for trade and commerce or pleasure, which required that the inns and hostelries of Babylon be regulated by the state. The Babylonian king Hammurabi passed strict laws to protect the rights of guests and travellers. These laws were documented in the *Codes of Hammurabi,* wherein an innkeeper stealing goods from a traveller, selling drinks fraudulently, not informing the authorities of a conspiracy being hatched in the tavern, and causing injury or harm to a traveller would be awarded the death penalty.

The defeat of the Spanish Armada in 1588 by the English established England as a supreme naval power. This naval success launched an age of exploration in the 16th century with merchant adventurers and explorers seeking to discover the sea route to India and further east. England during 16th to the 18th centuries was a sea-faring nation engaged in trade and commerce with Europe and Asia.

Inns in England were regulated under Common Law, which defined them as a public place directing innkeepers to offer rooms to people seeking accommodation if they were available at reasonable prices, and to provide meals if they desired. Stringent measures to ensure the safety of guests and their personal belongings by innkeepers were considered necessary as in Elizabethan England they were perceived as an unsavoury lot conniving with thieves to harm their guests. Hotels in USA and Canada were also governed by English common laws and hotel legislation reflected the legal trends that prevailed in England.

England was the first country to recognize hotelering as a business venture promulgating in The Innkeepers' Liability Act of 1863. It defined a hotel as a public place and to regulate the business made it mandatory for hotels to secure an operating licence. This Act attempted to define the duties and responsibilities of an hotelier towards his or her guests retaining the stringent measures pertaining to safety and security of guests that had been validated under common law. It gave limited powers of evicting a guest under exceptional circumstances and to refuse accommodation if required.

Sir John Lawrence, Viceroy of India from 1864 to 1868 enacted the Sarais Act in 1867 that was modelled on the Innkeepers' Liability Act of 1863. Barring the Sarais Act, there is no comprehensive legislation in India to regulate the hospitality industry defining a code of conduct or defining the limits of liability for a hotelier to follow. In some countries, there are laws defining the limits of liability towards guest, for example:

- Hotel Proprietors Act, 1956 which repealed The Innkeepers' Liability Act 1863 (UK)
- Innkeepers' Liability Act, 1902 (Australia)
- Hotel & Restaurant Act (Cap 494) 1972 (Kenya)

The Federation of Hotel & Restaurant Association of India (FHRAI) and Indian Association of Tour Operators (IATO) have put in place a self-regulatory *Agreement on Code of Practice (2005)* defining a mechanism to ensure that guests reserved by the association at various member hotels are not discriminated and are accorded equal rights in respect of reservations, no shows, turn away, and modalities of payments.

In 2010 the Ministry of Tourism adopted the *Code of Conduct for Safe and Honourable Tourism*, which was prepared in consultation with United Nations Office on Drugs and Crime; Pacific Area Travel Association, and Save the Children, India. The objective of the Code is to 'encourage tourism activities to be undertaken with respect for basic rights like dignity, safety and freedom from exploitation of both tourists and local residents i.e. people and communities that may be impacted by tourism in some way.'

Other than these self-regulatory codes that are followed voluntarily, as mentioned earlier there are a host of other statutory laws that govern the hospitality industry. These laws address legal issues ranging from hotel business contracts, front-office operations, labour laws, duty of hotels towards guests, hotel liabilities, food and beverage operations, and public health, safety and security.

THE JUDICIAL PROCESS

The three-tier Indian judicial system has a unified structure with the apex court being the Supreme Court. High court is the highest court in every state having jurisdiction over the lower courts or district courts, which are located in each administrative district. Besides, the courts there are a number of judicial tribunals or commissions that have specified areas of jurisdiction reporting to the high court. Some of the important tribunals are the Company Law Board, Monopolistic and Restrictive Trade Practices

Commission, Securities Appellate Tribunal, Consumer Protection Forum, Board for Industrial and Financial Reconstruction, Customs and Excise Control Tribunal, Income Tax Tribunal, Debt Recovery Tribunals, and so on.

We shall now review the journey of a legal case through the judicial system. In any legal proceeding there are a minimum of two parties called *litigants*.

A *plaintiff or complainant* is a person who raises allegations against the other party by suing the opposite party in a court of law demanding damages or specific performance.

A *defendant* is a person against whom allegations have been made and has been sued for damages or specific performance and is required to defend his actions. In family courts that hear cases of divorce and separation, the defendant is called the *respondent.*

A *plaint or complaint* is a document stating the allegations against the defendant and the relief being sought such as financial compensation or a suit for specific performance.

In criminal cases the plaint or complaint is normally filed by the state government and the plaintiff in the criminal court is called the *prosecutor.* The defendant is the person against whom a criminal charge has been put.

A complaint can only be filed in the court which has *original jurisdiction* over the subject matter and is competent to entertain the complaint. For example, a criminal case cannot be filed in a lower court and requires to be filed in the district and session court. Similarly, a case involving a violation of the filing of corporate income tax would have to be filed in the income tax tribunal and not at the lower court or district and session court.

Original jurisdiction implies that the court is competent to hear the case filed before it and to take the case to trial before giving its verdict.

The *trial procedure* is long drawn out and cumbersome. Figure 2.4 shows the steps that are generally followed.

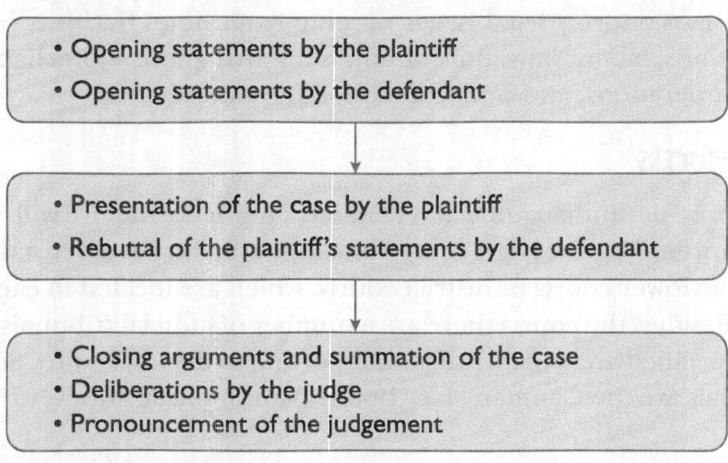

- Opening statements by the plaintiff
- Opening statements by the defendant

- Presentation of the case by the plaintiff
- Rebuttal of the plaintiff's statements by the defendant

- Closing arguments and summation of the case
- Deliberations by the judge
- Pronouncement of the judgement

FIGURE 2.4 Trial Procedure

Once the *civil complaint* or *case* has been filed in the lower court and a judgement is given in favour of the defendant, the plaintiff can appeal to the next higher court which is the district court. In case the district court gives a judgement favouring the plaintiff, the defendant can appeal in the high court. Finally, if the high court gives a judgement in favour of the plaintiff, the defendant can contest the decision by filing a case in the Supreme Court. The judgement of the Supreme Court will be binding on both the parties as there is no appeal against the decision of the Supreme Court.

Once a *criminal case* has been filed in the district and session court and a judgement is given in favour of the defendant, the prosecution can appeal to the next higher court which is the high court; if the high court gives a judgement in favour of the prosecution, the defendant can contest the decision by filing a case in the Supreme Court. The judgement of the Supreme Court will be binding on both the parties as there is no appeal against the decision of the Supreme Court.

In certain cases the plaint has to be moved in front of the appropriate tribunal; for example, Company Law Board, Monopolistic and Restrictive Trade Practices Commission, Securities Appellate Tribunal, Consumer Protection Forum, Board for Industrial and Financial Reconstruction, Customs and Excise Control Tribunal, Income Tax Tribunal; Debt Recovery Tribunals, and so on. In case the Tribunal gives a judgement against the plaintiff he or she can move the high court which enjoys *appellate jurisdiction* over judgements given by the tribunals.

Appellate jurisdiction is the privilege of the Supreme Court or high courts to hear appeals that are filed against judgements given by the lower courts or tribunals.

A *judgement* is the official decision of the court of the rights and claims of each side of the lawsuit. It is binding on both the parties to a lawsuit if it is a decision given by the Supreme Court. If the judgement has been given by a lower court, the parties have a right to appeal against the judgement on the grounds that there has been an error in the interpretation of the facts and the application of the law to the facts by the lower court. All judgements are based upon the facts and the issues raised and the decision given is based upon the reasoning given by the judge in that specific case.

In view of the legal financial costs and time consumed in pursuing a case, it is advised that general managers play a proactive role in running the operations so as to avoid unnecessary litigations.

SUMMARY

The chapter discussed the dynamic nature of law and how its origins are steeped in antiquity. It traced the evolution of natural or customary law to common law and with the rise of nation states to statutory law. All laws are classified into either of the two broad categories—substantive or procedural. The chapter highlighted the role of the executive, legislature, and the judiciary in implementing the laws. It also discussed the origins of hospitality law and the need for the general manager to familiarize himself or herself with it, and finally, the process of filing a case in the courts.

When reading any case or judgement the four main elements to identify are the facts that gave rise to the litigation; issue or the legal question that the litigants have requested the judge to resolve; the judge's decision in response to the issue; and finally the basis or reasoning that supports the judge's decision.

In view of the legal financial costs and the time spent in following a case, general managers should prudently run the operations so as to avoid unnecessary litigations.

KEY TERMS

Law A universally accepted body of rules that aims at creating a social system that encourages people to interact voluntarily in an orderly civilized manner, as and when there is an infringement or a violation of these regulations the judicial system steps in to enforce order by the imposition of penalties.

Natural or customary law Unwritten norms, rules, moral strictures, and religious beliefs that are followed voluntarily and universally accepted by society.

Common law Body of unwritten customs and usages that are validated by the courts through judgements in civil or criminal cases, thereby setting legal precedents for the courts to follow in the future when deciding cases.

Proclamations Historically, written documents announcing a king's intention to the public to act in a certain manner or to restrain from doing an action if it was not followed, which resulted in suitable punishment.

Statute law Written law that is enacted by parliament which either forbids the doing of an action or makes it mandatory to do an action, and failure to follow the law results in the imposition of penalties.

Administrative law Lays down the procedure that is required to be followed in order to implement the law as intended by the statute and derives its sanctity from it.

Substantive law Creates, defines, and regulates rights, including, for example, the law of contracts, torts, wills, and property; the essential substance of rights under law.

Procedural laws or administrative law Body of law that governs the process prescribing the formal steps to be taken in enforcing legal rights. The implementation of civil and criminal law requires separate set of administrative procedures.

Constitutional law The relationship between the three arms of the government and in a federal structure the relationship between the centre and the states. It spells out the fundamental rights and duties of citizens and ensures that all statutory and administrative laws do not violate these rights.

Civil law Provides legal solutions to disputes involving ownership of personal property, interpretation of contracts, marriage disputes, divorce, damages for personal injury and to personal property, and so on.

Criminal law Classifies crimes under various categories such as crimes against the state, persons and property, crimes relating to public order, health and safety, to religious affairs, marriage, decency and morals.

Hospitality law Covers a wide range of legal issues ranging from hotel business contracts, front-office operations, labour laws, duty of hotels towards guests, hotel liabilities, food and beverage operations, and public health, safety and security. It applies to the service sector that consists of the food service, travel, and hotel industry.

Plaintiff or the complainant Person who raises allegations against the other party by suing the opposite party in a court of law demanding damages or specific performance.

Defendant Person against whom allegations have been made and has been sued for damages or specific performance and is required to defend his or her actions. In family courts that hear cases of divorce and separation, the defendant is called the *respondent*.

Plaint or complaint Document stating the allegations against the defendant and the relief being sought such as financial compensation or a suit for specific performance.

Litigants Two parties to a lawsuit.

Original jurisdiction Implies that the court is competent to hear the case filed before it and to take the case to trial before giving its verdict.

Appellate jurisdiction Privilege of the Supreme Court or high courts to hear appeals that are filed against judgements given by the lower courts or tribunals.

Judgement Official decision of the court of the rights and claims of each side of the lawsuit. It is binding on both the parties to a lawsuit if it is a decision given by the Supreme Court.

EXERCISES

Define the Following

1. Procedural law
2. Civil law
3. Statute law
4. Original jurisdiction
5. Litigant
6. Respondent
7. Prosecution
8. Proclamations
9. Judgement
10. Constitutional law

Concept Review Questions

1. What is the difference between common law and statutory law?
2. Why is hospitality law important?
3. Write a brief note on the origins of law.

4. What is the role of the legislative, executive, and judiciary in the administration of laws?
5. Describe the process of taking a case to trial.
6. Write a brief note on the evolution of hotel laws.

Critical Thinking Question

1. Various laws apply to hotel operations; some are codified whereas others are based upon precedents. Recommend changes that may be required in order to make them more relevant to the hotel industry.

Research Question

1. Visit a court to gain first-hand knowledge of a trial procedure.

Project

1. Under what circumstances can a judge deviate from *stare decisis*?

REFERENCES

<http://oxforddictionaries.com/definition/english/law> accessed on 16 August 2012.

The Social Contract (1792) Book I, Chapter 1: Subject of the First Book <http://www.constitution.org/jjr/socon_01.htm> accessed on 14 August 2012.

<http://www.complete-bible-genealogy.com/genealogy_of_jesus.htm> accessed on 16 August 2012.

<http://www.bible-verses.net/tencommandments.php> accessed on 16 August 2012.

<http://www.hinduwebsite.com/sacredscripts/hinduism/dharma/manusmriti.asp> accessed on 16 August 2012.

<http://www.lawteacher.net/constitutional-law/essays/laws-are-rules-imposed-by-governments.php> accessed on 16 August 2012.

Bracton on the Laws and Customs of England <http://hls15.law.harvard.edu/bracton/> accessed on 16 August 2012.

<http://tarltonguides.law.utexas.edu/content.php?pid=102972&sid=1471266> accessed on 16 August 2012.

<http://www.historyguide.org/intellect/code_nap.html> accessed on 16 August 2012.

<http://legal-dictionary.thefreedictionary.com/Substantive+Law> accessed on 16 August 2012.

<http://legal-dictionary.thefreedictionary.com/Procedural+laws accessed on 15 August 2012

Taittiriya Upanishad—'Shiksha Valli' Verse 11 http://www.rayarusgrace.org/mainpage/happytoshare/religion/Taittiriya%20Upanishad%20-%20Part%20II%20A%20Dharmic%20Prescriptions.pdf accessed on 17 August 2012.

<http://en.wikipedia.org/wiki/Hospitality> accessed on 16 August 2012.

<http://en.wikipedia.org/wiki/Babylonian_law> accessed on 16 August 2012.

Robert Francis Harper, *The Code of Hammurabi, King of Babylon* (Chicago: University of Chicago Press, 1904).

<http://lawdigest.uslegal.com/travel/hotel-liability/7315/> accessed on 16 August 2012.

FHRAI & IATO, *Agreement on Code of Practice* (2005) <http://www.iato.in/pdf/FHRAI-IATO-I.pdf> accessed on 13 August 2013.

Laws Related to Hotel Operations

Chapter 3   Doing Business in India

Chapter 4   Business Contracts

Chapter 5   Hotel Licences and Regulations

Chapter 6   Hotel Insurance

Doing Business in India

LEARNING OBJECTIVES

After going through this chapter, the reader will be familiar with the following:

- Evolution of a modern company
- Business structure options available to do business in India
- Impact of Foreign Exchange Regulation Act, 1973 and Foreign Exchange Management Act, 1999 on the business environment
- Reserve Bank of India's role in attracting and regulating foreign direct investment
- Impact of taxation, accounting practices, and transfer pricing on a business
- Proposed legislative measures to improve India's business environment

INTRODUCTION

It is important to understand the business environment in India and the factors that have influenced its growth. Historically, the term 'company' is derived from the Latin word *Companis*, which means to break bread together, and originally referred to an association of persons who took their meals together. Over time, a company came to be defined as a group of people working together to accomplish a common goal.

In ancient India, the treatise *Arthashastra* by Kautilya talks about the business structures of the Mauryan Empire which predated the Roman Empire. Family-run sole proprietorships and partnerships were the most preferred business organization structures wherein people used to invest and earn profits. A partnership would be formed for a common objective, and it was understood that each partner would derive a profit proportionate to his or her share or contribution towards the business with each individual business partner retaining his individual identity.

An improvement upon the partnership model was the *Sreni* or guild model which was prevalent during Mauryan times from 322 BC to 185 BC. A *Sreni* was formed by merchants, craftsmen, and traders, and there was no limit to its membership. It was the forerunner of the modern corporation and was a separate legal entity, which had the ability to hold property separately from its owners, enter into contracts, and define its own rules for governing the behaviour of its members; it could sue and be sued in its own name.

In the western world during medieval times, the guild of merchants had the closest resemblance to a *Sreni* and modern-day companies. Guilds were associations formed by merchants and traders and those subscribed to by craftsmen in a particular town, formed to protect and promote the business interests of their members. There were guilds for craftsmen, such as weavers, masons and builders, carpenters, painters, ironworkers, leatherworkers, and so on, and then there were guilds for merchants and traders. Guilds were responsible for maintaining the quality of their products and would impose fines if members did not maintain the product standards. They also offered insurance for the goods while in transit between cities.

Over time, guilds became very powerful and exercised monopoly over the commodity, craft, and trade. In order to legitimize their monopoly, they obtained charters from the British Crown. Under the Royal Charter, each guild member conducted his or her business on his or her own account with the trading liability of each member being distinct from the guild, but they were obliged to follow the rules set by the guild. Gradually, members started to trade under the charter as joint stock companies with joint accounts and liabilities. East India Company was granted a Royal Charter in 1600 to trade with the East Indies. Other companies that were granted charters around this time were the Dutch East India Company and French East India Company.

With the passing of the Joint Stock Companies Act, 1844 by the English Parliament, a company could be incorporated by registration without obtaining a Royal Charter or sanction by a special Act of Parliament. Although the law created the office of the registrar of joint stock companies, very few companies actually went in for registration as the Joint Stock Companies Act denied to its members the facility of limited liability. Under limited liability, the loss that an owner or shareholder of a business firm may incur is limited to the amount of capital invested by him in the business and does not extend to his personal assets.

The issue of limited liability to the members of a registered company was addressed by the English Parliament when it passed the Limited Liability Act in 1855. The Act of 1844 was superseded by a comprehensive Companies Act in 1862, which laid the basic structure of the company as we know of it today. It envisaged a limited liability company, which would be limited by guarantee, after it filed two primary documents that were called The Memorandum of Association and The Articles of Associations. It prohibited any alteration in the object clause of the Memorandum of Association. The Act introduced for the first time provisions for the winding up or dissolution of a company.

Memorandum of Association

The Memorandum of Association is a document that sets out the constitution of the company and defines the relationship of the company with the outside world. It states:

- the name of the company, the type of company (such as public limited company or private company limited by shares);
- the objectives and scope of activities of the company;
- its authorized share capital; and
- names of the original shareholders of the company who were also known as its subscribers.

Articles of Association

The Articles of Association lays down the rules and regulations for the internal management of a company for achieving the objectives stated in the Memorandum of Association. These rules typically cover the issuing of shares, the different voting and dividend rights attached to different classes of share, restrictions on the transfer of shares, the rules for conducting of board meetings and shareholder meetings, and so on.

Subsequently, a series of legislative measures were passed by the English Parliament to further strengthen the scope and application of company law.

Companies (Memorandum of Association) Act, 1890 Changes in the object clause for which approval of the court was required earlier could now be made on the basis of a special resolution passed by the members in the general meeting of the shareholders.

Director's Liability Act, 1890 This Act made directors liable for the functioning of the company by introducing the concept of a director's liability.

The Companies Act, 1900 It became mandatory for companies to get their accounts compulsory audited.

The Companies Act, 1908 It permitted the formation of private limited companies.

The Companies Act, 1948 It introduced the following changes in company law:

- Shareholders were given the powers to remove directors before the expiration of their term.
- Auditors were made independent of the directors.
- Principles of accountancy were given legal sanctity and balance sheets and profit-and-loss statement had to follow a uniform pattern.
- The government-constituted company board was vested with powers to scrutinize the functioning of companies.

These changes put the organizational structure of a company on a firm footing.

Lord Justice Lindley defined a company as follows: 'By a company is meant an association of many persons who contribute money or money's worth to a common stock and employ it in some trade or business, and who share the profit and loss as the case may be arising there from. The common stock so contributed is denoted in money and is the capital of the company and the persons who contribute it, or to whom it belongs, are called as members. The proportion of capital to which each member is entitled is his share which is always transferable although the right to transfer them is more or less restricted.'

In India, the Companies Act, 1850 was modelled on the English Joint Stock Companies Act of 1844. This was repealed by The Companies Act, 1882, which remained in force till 1912. The Companies Act, 1913 was modelled on the English Companies Act, 1908. This Act was amended frequently till it was repealed by the passing of the Companies Act, 1936. After Independence, it was felt that the Companies Act, 1936 should be amended to suit the changed environment. The Indian Companies Bill was introduced in Parliament and received the President's assent in January 1956 and the Companies Act, 1956 came into force with effect from 1 April 1956. This act laid down the rules for the formation, operation, and dissolution of private limited, public limited, and unlimited companies. Besides the Companies Act, 1956, the Indian Partnership Act, 1932 and the Limited Liability Partnership Act, 2008 laid the groundwork for the formation of partnership firms and limited liability partnership (LLP) firms.

These laws laid the groundwork for the various business structure options available to do business in India, which are as follows:
- Sole proprietorship
- Partnership firm
- LLP
- Private limited company
- Public limited company

In addition to the above, the following types of business options are also available for foreign investors or foreign companies desirous of doing business in India:
- Liaison office
- Representative office
- Project office
- Branch office
- Wholly-owned subsidiary company
- Joint venture (JV) company

There has been hesitancy on the part of foreign investors to set up companies in India owing to historical reasons.

Post-Independence India had a restrictive business environment, which was aimed at protecting the nascent Indian industries from foreign competition; the emphasis was on creating a self-reliant economic base through the concept of five-year development plans. The Monopolies and Restrictive Trade Practices Act, 1969 (MRTP) and Foreign Exchange Regulation Act, 1973 (FERA) were stringent laws aimed at discouraging foreign companies from doing business in the country.

Economic liberalization started in 1985 when the government announced a series of measures described as New Economic Policy, aimed at the deregulation and liberalization of industry. These were followed by drastic changes introduced by the 1991 Industrial Policy Statement of the government. These changes gave Indian industry an opportunity to upgrade its technology and product quality and prepare for the oncoming foreign competition. This marked a shift in government's thinking from perusing a protectionist policy to one of liberalization.

Since the beginning of the 21st century, India has been pursuing liberal economic policies aimed at making Indian industry self-reliant based on technological superiority, conducive investment climate, and progressive labour reforms. In spite of these positive changes, India has a long way to go as is reflected in the *Doing Business 2013* a report by International Finance Corporation, which gives us an idea as to why this hesitancy, even though India is the world's biggest democracy and the second largest nation in terms of population.

The Report has evaluated India on 10 parameters and it has been found wanting in most of them giving the country a very poor international image. The survey has ranked India at 132 out of the total of 185 countries evaluated as illustrated in Table 3.1.

TABLE 3.1 Ease of Doing Business in India

Parameters	Ranking out of 185 nations	Average number of days to get work done
Starting a business	173	27
Dealing with construction permits	182	196
Getting electricity connection	105	67
Registering a property	94	44
Getting credit	23	–
Protecting investors	49	–
Paying taxes	152	–
Trading across borders (exports/imports)	127	16/20
Enforcing business contract	184	1420
Resolving insolvency issues	116	–
Overall ranking	132	–

Source: Mint, Times of India, (2012).

It is an undisputed fact that businesses create job opportunities leading to higher incomes, taxes, and growth. However, if the business conditions are not conducive, a country cannot move forward. Starting a business is regarded as an arduous task, securing construction or building permit can take up to 196 days; it can take as long as 1420 days to enforce business contracts. Since 2005, India has focussed on simplifying and reducing the cost of regulatory procedures related to starting a business, paying taxes, and facilitating exports and imports. The *Doing Business 2013* report indicates that starting and liquidating a business in India is rather difficult when compared to the rest of the world. For these reasons, foreign investors and businessmen find it a surmountable challenge doing business in India.

STARTING A BUSINESS

It is important to note that governments view businesses and individuals as two distinct entities and the following key considerations listed in Table 3.2 should be taken into account when finalizing a business structure. Starting a business involves setting up of the business organization that will conduct the business.

TABLE 3.2   Key Considerations in Starting a Business

Item	Aspects to be considered
Incorporating the business	Ease and cost of incorporating the company
Control	The amount of control the individual would like to exercise on the business entity
Finance	The initial investment amount or capital required and the possibility of securing institutional finance
Taxation	The tax structure applicable to the business entity and the individual
Liabilities	The liabilities of the business entity and the individual
Transfer of ownership	The ease with which the business can be exited if required

The three stages of forming a company are promotion, incorporation, and commencement of business.

PROMOTION STAGE

The business entrepreneur or promoter conceives the business idea, which could be to manufacture a product or to provide services. Once this decision is taken, the promoter would determine the quantum of capital involved and explore the sources of finance to start the company. Once these aspects have been finalized, the promoter will have to decide upon whether the company should be incorporated or a running business should be acquired. If the option of incorporating a business is exercised, then it can either be a private limited or a public limited company, or a partnership firm.

INCORPORATION

The law that will apply shall be based upon the nature of the company to be incorporated—private limited or a public limited company, which would be under the Companies Act, 1956. For a partnership firm, a partnership deed will have to be made and registered under the Indian Partnership Act, 1932 and if it is an LLP, it will require to be formed under the Limited Liability Partnership Act, 2008.

In case of a private limited or a public limited company, once the Registrar of Companies is satisfied that all the requirements have been complied with, he or she will register the company, and will issue a Certificate of Incorporation certifying the company as a private or a public limited company. Once the partnership deed has been signed, an application is moved to the Registrar of Firms for securing the Certificate of Registration. Once this is granted, the partnership stands registered as a firm. In the case of limited liability partnership, once the LLP deed has been signed, an application is moved to the Registrar of Firms for securing a Certificate of Registration. Once this is granted, the partnership stands registered as an LLP firm.

COMMENCEMENT OF BUSINESS

A private limited company can commence business upon getting incorporated while a public limited company has to secure the Commencement of Business (COB) certificate from the Registrar of Companies to commence business. A partnership firm or an LLP firm can commence business once it receives the Certificate of Registration.

Key aspects of the various business structures available in India are reviewed next to give the entrepreneurs an opportunity to decide the structure that suits best for implementing their business idea.

SOLE PROPRIETORSHIP

A sole proprietorship is the most common form of business and accounts for the largest number of business concerns in India, such as independent consultancy services, brokerages, insurance advisors, automobile repair shops, electrical equipment repair shops, grocery shops, and bakeries. It is a one-man organization where a single individual owns, manages, and controls the business.

It is easy to establish and there are no extensive legal requirements except for obtaining the necessary service tax registration, permanent account number (PAN), state value added tax (VAT), the opening of a bank account in the name of the proprietorship, and if essential, the required mandatory licence. The proprietor files income tax return in his personal name, as the PAN of the firm and proprietor are the same.

The capital normally is relatively small and is provided by the proprietor himself from his savings, and he alone enjoys the profit and loss of the business. As the proprietorship does not have a separate legal entity, the liability of the proprietor is unlimited. In case of legal claims, the personal property of the proprietor and not simply the assets used in the business can be attached to settle the claim. Upon the demise of the proprietor, the operation of the business comes to an end.

The greatest advantage that the proprietor enjoys is complete secrecy and control over the business which gives him flexibility of operations. Access to limited financial resources, unlimited liability, and incapacity to engage quality managerial talent is a distinct disadvantage. However, this type of structure is suitable for businesses that carry a moderate risk requiring limited daily-operating finances and small infusion of capital.

PARTNERSHIP

A partnership firm is defined under the Indian Partnership Act, 1932 as follows: "Partnership" is the relation between persons who have agreed to share the profits of a business carried on by all or any of them acting for all. Persons who have entered into partnership with one another are called individually "partners" and collectively "a firm", and the name under which their business is carried on is called the "firm name".

A partnership is easy to form with the various partners entering into an agreement called the 'partnership deed'. A 'partnership deed' is a stamped and registered agreement specifying in writing the rights, duties, and liabilities of the partners and is signed between two or a maximum of 20 partners in a firm. A standard 'partnership deed' contains the following details:

- Name of the firm
- Nature of the business to be carried out
- Names of the partners
- The town and the place where business will be carried on
- The amount of capital to be contributed by each partner
- Loans and advances by partners and the interest payable on them
- The amount of drawings by each partner and the rate of interest allowed thereon
- Duties and powers of each partner
- Any other terms and conditions to run the business such as allocation of responsibilities amongst themselves

In case the deed does not specify the rights and obligations, the provisions of the Indian Partnership Act, 1932 become applicable. A firm can be registered any time by moving an application with the Registrar of Firms of the area where the business is situated.

Partners of a registered firm enjoy certain rights and privileges under the Act, which are not available to unregistered partnership firms. These rights and privileges are as follows:

- Partners can file a suit in any court against the firm or its partners for the enforcement of its contractual obligations under the Act.
- Partners can file a suit to enforce its rights against third parties for failure to perform their obligations under a contract.
- Partners can claim a set off (which is the mutual adjustment of debts) in a dispute with third parties.

Even though the partnership firm may not be registered, it does not affect the rights of third parties to sue the firm and/or its partners for the realization of their dues by the attachment of the firm's and/or its partner's properties through the Court Receiver, even though the firm has been dissolved or declared insolvent.

Like a sole proprietorship, the firm and its partners are jointly and severally liable for the liabilities of the firm which is unlimited; that is, if the assets of the firm are insufficient to meet its debts, the creditors can recover their loans from the personal property of the individual partners. Furthermore, no partner can transfer his or her interest in the partnership without obtaining the consent of all the other partners. All partners have a right to participate in the management of the business, unless there is an agreement to the contrary.

The partnership firm can be easily formed, and thanks to the combined strengths of all the partners, has the capacity to infuse more capital, secure favourable credit terms, and engage a pool of managerial talent. The greatest disadvantage is that each partner is liable for the actions of the other partners with no single partner enjoying absolute control over the operations of the firm. All partners are jointly and severally liable for taxes of the firm. Finally, the firm has a limited lifespan. It must be dissolved on the retirement, lunacy, bankruptcy, or death of any partner.

Partnership firms are ideally suited for medium-sized businesses involving limited capital such as wholesale and retail trade; small service concerns like travel agents, transport agencies; or professional firms of charted accountants, doctors, lawyers.

LIMITED LIABILITY PARTNERSHIPS

A limited liability partnership business structure provides the benefits of limited liability of a company but allows its members the flexibility of organizing the internal management on the basis of a mutually-arrived agreement. This is a recent development in India and LLPs became possible with the notification of the Limited Liability Partnership Act, 2008 on 7 January 2009. The Indian Partnership Act, 1932 does not apply to LLPs which are formed under the provisions of the Limited Liability Partnership Act, 2008.

An LLP agreement is a written document between two persons with no limits as to the maximum number of partners, which determines the mutual rights and duties of the partners and their rights and duties in relation to that LLP. It can be between two individuals or even a corporate entity and an individual or two corporate entities, or between the LLP and its partners. Earlier, the Indian Partnership Act, 1932 did not permit corporate entities from entering into partnership agreements.

A standard 'limited liability partnership agreement' includes the following details:

- Name of the firm
- Nature of the business to be carried out
- Names of the partners with photographs
- The town and the place where business will be carried on
- The amount of capital to be contributed by each partner
- Loans and advances by partners and the interest payable on them
- The amount of drawings by each partner and the rate of interest allowed thereon
- Duties and powers of each partner
- Any other terms and conditions to run the business as agreed between the partners
- A minimum of two designated partners and one of them a resident of India
- The designated partners answerable for all acts of the LLP in accordance with the Limited Liability Partnership Act, 2008

An LLP is required to register itself with the Registrar of Companies and once it is registered, a Certificate of Incorporation is issued mentioning the name of the partnership suffixed by the word 'LLP'. An LLP can commence its business operations from the date of its incorporation.

An LLP is a separate legal entity which enjoys perpetual succession irrespective of change of partners and has the power to sue and be sued, hold, and dispose property, has a common seal, and can do such acts as any other corporate body.

A further distinction is drawn between the partners and the LLP, with the partners not being personally liable for the acts of the LLP; furthermore, a partner will also not be held personally liable for the acts of his or her other partners, but only for the wrongful acts committed by himself or herself. However, a partner shall be personally liable in case of any unlawful acts and fraud committed by the LLP or its partners. If at any time the number of partners of an LLP goes below two, and the LLP continues to carry on the business for more than six months, the person who is the only partner of the LLP during this time is personally liable for the obligations of the LLP incurred during this period.

Designated partners have to ensure that they fulfil all the mandatory requirements at all times in accordance with the Limited Liability Partnership Act, 2008 such as the following:

- Maintain a registered office in India to which all communications will be sent.
- Maintain proper books of accounts according to the double entry system of accounting at its registered office for the specified period of time.

- Prepare a Statement of Account and Solvency for the financial year within a period of six months from the end of each financial year.
- File annual returns duly signed by the designated partners with the Registrar within sixty days of closure of its financial year.
- Every LLP having a turnover of ₹40 lakh or a capital investment of ₹25 lakh will have to get its accounts audited.
- If the turnover exceeds ₹60 lakh, tax audit of the LLP is mandatory.
- Salary paid to the partners by the LLP is taxable in the hands of the partners.

LLPs are separate legal entities that enjoy perpetual existence and are easy to form at a minimum cost; there is no minimum capital requirement, and can be wound up or dissolved, merged, and amalgamated by fulfilling the minimum legal requirements. They enjoy the flexibility of a company with limited liability drawing a distinction between the partners and the LLPs, with the liability of the partners being limited to their agreed contributions in the LLPs. The greatest disadvantage in an LLP is that each partner is personally liable for the fraudulent actions of the other partners and the LLP.

An LLP firm is ideally suited for professionals such as charted accountants, doctors, law firms, consultants, property advisors.

PRIVATE LIMITED COMPANIES

The Companies Act, 1956 contains the necessary provisions for the formation of private limited companies. A private limited company has an independent legal existence and is a voluntary association of two and not more than 50 members with limited liability. The minimum share capital required is ₹1,00,000.

A share is a single unit of ownership in any company, and it defines the relationship between the individual holding the share (shareholder) and the company. Each share has a predetermined value, for example, a share of ₹100, called the face value of the share. Share capital is the company's capital which is divided into units based upon the face value of the share, for example, if the share capital of the company is ₹1,00,000 (one lakh) and the face value is ₹100 then there are 1000 units or shares.

Shares of a private limited company can be transferred to its members only, and it is not allowed to invite the general public to subscribe to its shares or debentures. This measure enables the directors of the company to retain control of its operations, while limiting the liability of the directors to the amount of the share capital subscribed by them.

The application for the formation of a private limited company has to be submitted to the Registrar of Companies and should contain the following information:

- Name of the company which requires to be registered followed by the word 'limited'.
- Address of the registered office where all official communications are required to be sent.

- Names of the shareholders of the company.
- Share capital of the company with the nominal share capital divided into shares of fixed amounts.
- Memorandum of Association stating the limited company's name; the situation of its registered office; its share capital; and the object for which the company has been formed must be signed by at least three shareholders.
- Articles of Association containing the internal regulations of the company, the relationship of the company to its shareholders, and the relationship between the individual shareholders.

Once the Registrar is satisfied that all the formalities of incorporation have been completed, a Certificate of Incorporation is issued, which authorizes the private limited company to commence its operations.

Upon incorporation, the directors of the company are mandatorily required to appoint the following:

- A qualified auditor who is required to certify that the balance sheet and profit-and-loss account presents a true and fair view of the company's affairs and complies with the Companies Act, 1956.
- Auditors are appointed or re-appointed at general body meetings of the shareholders.
- Maintain proper registers of the members and share ledger; a register of directors and secretaries; a register of share transfers; a register of charges; and a register of debenture holders.
- Maintain the statutory accounts comprising the profit-and-loss statement and balance sheet appended with the auditors and directors reports.
- Maintain the company seal that has to be affixed on share certificates and all other legal documents.
- Apply for permanent account number PAN, tax deduction number (TAN) from the Income Tax Department; sales tax/VAT; service tax; provident fund; Employee State Insurance Corporation (ESIC) registration, if applicable for the company.

In a private limited company, the liability of its members is limited and the company has its individual existence independent of its shareholders. The company has to fulfil less legal compliances under the Companies Act, 1956; for example, it is not required to file a prospectus, wait for a COB certificate, or file reports of the proceedings of statutory general body meetings to the registrar of companies. Its biggest drawback is that transfer of shares can only be done within the shareholders, as they cannot be sold to the public; similarly it cannot raise debt from the public by issuing debentures.

A private limited company is the best option available to small- and medium-sized business entrepreneurs engaged in manufacturing or hotels and restaurant operations that would like to maintain privacy of their business while exercising control over it.

Most of the hotel companies are private limited operating successful Indian brands, such as Lemon Tree Hotels and Red Fox Hotels and Sarovar Hotels. Even where the hotel has been flagged by any international brand, the owning company is private limited, for example, Atlantic Hotels Private Limited—Golden Tulip West Delhi, Edenpark Hotels Private Limited—The Clarion Collection, New Delhi, and Shree Naman Group—Sofitel Mumbai.

Table 3.3 gives a comparison of the salient advantages and disadvantages between private limited companies and partnerships.

TABLE 3.3   Private Limited Companies vs Partnership Firms

Private limited company	Partnership firm
The company is formed under the Companies Act, 1956.	The firm is formed under the Indian Partnership Act, 1932.
The shareholders in a company are not personally liable for the debts of the company. The creditors have recourse only to the assets of the company, and cannot recover from the directors unless they are personally liable.	Each partner in a partnership has unlimited liability and is personally liable for the debts of the partnership. This applies even when another partner commits the partnership to a debt without the knowledge of the other partner, or someone makes a successful claim against the partnership.
A company is a legal person/entity or a body corporate, able to make contracts through its directors or other staff.	A partnership, on the other hand, is made up of individuals, any one of whom may commit the partnership to any agreement. The partners have a collective responsibility for all the taxes and debts of the partnership. The partners can allocate their own division of tasks, responsibility, and liability. A partner is not an employee but the partners together may employ others.
A company exists and performs entirely within the framework contained in the Companies Act, 1956 wherein the duties are specified of the directors.	The Indian Partnership Act, 1932 applies if there is no partnership agreement. If the partnership agreement is registered, resolution of disputes between the partners and divisions of partnership assets are easy to resolve. However, less regulation gives a partnership scope for a less formal, more flexible, and more easily manageable structure.
The company records that are provided to the Registrar of Companies are open to public inspection.	A partnership is not required to disclose anything to the public.
This is a matter of practice and choice rather than of law. It is therefore easier to allocate precise roles within a company structure than in a partnership.	For a partnership, in principle, setting out a precise set of duties, obligations, and rights for each partner is possible, but in practice, partners tend to think of themselves as equals, even though some may be 'more equal than others'.
Costs of incorporation are well defined under the Companies Act, 1956.	Costs of setting up a partnership firm depend upon the fee charged by the solicitor.

PUBLIC LIMITED COMPANIES

Public limited companies are incorporated under the Companies Act, 1956. They can be privately held or government controlled, for example, Indian Hotels Company Limited (Taj Group) and East India Hotels limited (Oberoi Hotels), Bharat Hotels Ltd. (The Lalit), Pride Hotels Ltd. (Pride Hotels) or government controlled, for example, Hotel Corporation of India (Centaur Hotels) and India Tourism Development Corporation (Ashok Group).

A public limited company is a voluntary association of shareholders which should be a minimum of seven with no maximum limit having to contribute a minimum of ₹5,00,000 towards the share capital of the company with the liability of the shareholder being limited to the value of the number of shares subscribed to it by the member.

The application for the formation of a public limited company has to be submitted to the Registrar of Companies signed by at least one director and a chartered accountant or a company secretary containing the following information:

- Name of the company which requires to be registered.
- Address of the registered office where all official communications are required to be sent.
- Names of the original shareholders of the company.
- Share capital of the company with the nominal share capital divided into shares of fixed value.
- Executing power of attorney to be executed by all the directors authorizing any one of the directors to fulfil all the required formalities as required for the incorporation of the company.
- Memorandum of Association, which is the constitution of the company stating the public company's name; the situation of its registered office; its share capital; and the object for which the company has been formed. The memorandum must be signed by at least three shareholders.
- Articles of Association containing the regulations of the company for the management of its internal affairs laying down the rules and regulations for achieving the company's objectives and purpose; the different voting and dividend rights attached to different classes of share; restrictions on the transfer of shares; and the rules of board meetings and shareholder meetings.
- List of all persons who have consented to act as directors along with their individual consent letters, their individual director identification number (DIN), digital signature certificate (DSC), residential address, and nationality, date of birth and occupation, and income tax PAN.
- Declaration of compliance—certified by either an advocate of the Supreme Court or high court, company secretary or a chartered accountant, or a person named in the articles of association as a director, manager, or secretary of the company.

Once the Registrar is satisfied that all the formalities of incorporation have been completed, a Certificate of Incorporation is issued in the name of the public limited company. Once incorporated, it has its own legal identity; it can sue and be sued, becomes the owner of any property owned by the promoters, and its share capital gets authorized. The authorized share capital of a public limited company is the extent to which the company can issue shares to the public. Paid-up capital on the other hand is the extent that a company's shares have been subscribed.

However, in order to commence operations, the public limited company has to secure the COB certificate. To secure a COB certificate, the directors of the company have an option to file a Prospectus with the Securities and Exchange Board of India (SEBI) to raise capital or they can file a Statement in Lieu of Prospectus (SLP) (under Section 70 and Section 149(2)) in case the directors are contributing towards the share capital of the company without inviting the public with the Registrar of companies. In both cases, the directors are required to pay their contributions as required at the time of application and allotment of shares. Once the Registrar is satisfied, he or she issues the COB certificate.

In order to raise capital from the public, the company has to file a 'Prospectus' with SEBI after the company has received its Certificate of Incorporation. The Companies Act, 1956 defines 'prospectus as any document described or issued as a prospectus and include any notice, circular, advertisement or other documents inviting deposits from the public or inviting offer from the public for the subscription of shares. It is circulated among the public giving all the necessary information about the company so that the prospective shareholders may fully understand the objectives and the plans of the company.'

The salient features of a prospectus are as follows:
- Prospectus contains the main objectives of the company, the name and addresses of the signatories of the memorandum of association, and the number of shares held by them.
- The name, addresses, and occupation of directors and managing directors.
- The number and classes of shares and debentures issued.
- The qualification share of directors and the interest of directors for the promotion of company.
- The number, description, and the document of shares or debentures which within the two preceding years have been agreed to be issued other than cash.
- The name and addresses of the vendors of any property acquired by the company and the amount paid or to be paid.
- Particulars about the directors, secretaries, and the treasures and their remuneration.
- The amount for the minimum subscription.
- If the company is carrying on businesses, then the duration of such businesses are required.

- The estimated amount of preliminary expenses.
- Name and address of the auditors, bankers, and solicitors of the company.
- Time and place where copies of balance sheets, profits-and-loss account, and the auditor's report may be inspected.
- The auditor's report so submitted must deal with the profit and loss of the company for each year of five financial years immediately preceding the issue of prospectus.
- If any profit or reserve has been capitalized, the particulars of such capitalization will be stated in the prospectus.

The directors of the company are mandatorily required to comply with the following requirements of the Companies Act, 1956:

- A qualified auditor who is required to certify that the balance sheet and profit-and-loss account presents a true and fair view of the company's affairs and complies with the Companies Act, 1956.
- Auditors are appointed or re-appointed at general body meetings of the shareholders.
- Maintain proper registers of the members and share ledger; a register of directors and secretaries; a register of share transfers; a register of charges; and a register of debenture holders.
- Maintain the statutory accounts comprising the profit-and-loss statement and balance sheet appended with the auditors and directors reports.
- Maintain the company seal that has to be affixed on share certificates and all other legal documents.
- Apply for PAN, TAN from the Income Tax Department, sales tax/VAT, service tax, provident fund, and ESIC registration, if applicable, for the company.

A public limited company has the following advantages: It can raise capital up to the extent of its authorized share capital from the general public and its shares can be freely transferred. It can also issue debentures to the general public. The company is managed by the board of directors and the shareholders as owners are not involved in day-to-day operations. The company's operations are open to scrutiny and they are mandatorily required to comply with all the regulatory requirements of the Companies Act, 1956 and the rules and regulations imposed by SEBI.

Table 3.4 compares the salient features of a private limited company vis-à-vis a public limited company.

Besides the options discussed earlier there are other avenues of doing business in India available to foreign companies such as setting up of a liaison office/representative office, or a project office or a branch office, which can undertake activities permitted under the Foreign Exchange Management (Establishment in India of Branch Office or Other Place of Business) Regulations, 2000. These regulations are issued by the Reserve Bank of India (RBI) in keeping with the Foreign Exchange Management Act, 1999 (FEMA). Besides these options, a foreign company can also incorporate a JV or a wholly-owned subsidiary company (WOS) under the Companies Act, 1956.

TABLE 3.4 Private Limited Companies vs Public Limited Companies

Private limited company	Public limited company
Minimum number of members—two and maximum—50.	Minimum number of members—2 and maximum—unlimited.
Minimum paid-up capital of ₹1,00,000.	Minimum paid-up capital ₹5,00,000.
Public cannot be invited to subscribe to its shares or debentures.	Public can subscribe freely for shares or debentures.
A private company cannot accept public deposits at all [Section 3(1)(iii)(d) of the Companies Act, 1956]. It can accept deposits only from its members, directors, and their relatives.	A public limited company can accept public deposits if the following requirements are met: (a) Deposits can be invited only as per Rules made; (b) An advertisement giving financial position of company is published in prescribed manner; (c) The company is not in default in repayment of deposits and interest. However, there is a limit on accepting public deposits from the public which is up to 25% of its paid-up capital and free reserves. In addition, public deposits up to 10% of paid-up capital and free reserves can be accepted from shareholders of company and/or deposits guaranteed by director(s) of a company [Rule 3(2) of Companies (Acceptance of Deposits) Rules, 1975]. There are no restrictions on accepting deposits from the director of a public company.
Should contain the words 'Private Limited' at the end of its name.	Should contain the word 'Limited' at the end of its name.
SLP not required even for first issue.	SLP or prospectus is required. Prospectus is available for inspection only for 14 days after the date of publication at the ROC office under section 610 'Inspection, production and evidence of documents kept by Registrar' of the Companies Act, 1956.
Can issue any type of shares having varying and disproportionate rights in respect of voting/dividend.	Can issue only equity and preference shares.
Does not require COB certificate after incorporation.	Requires COB certificate after incorporation.
Statutory meeting and statutory reporting are not required.	Statutory meeting and statutory reporting are required.
Postal ballot is never required.	There are many resolutions for which postal ballot is required.
Further issues are not required to be rights issues to existing shareholders.	Further issues should be rights issues to existing shareholders, unless special resolution is passed.

(Contd)

TABLE 3.4 (Contd)

Private limited company	Public limited company
Annual accounts and documents can be seen by a member.	The annual returns, balance sheets, charges registered by the company, and other documents filed by it with the Registrar of Companies are available for inspection on payment of the requisite fees. Copies can also be obtained of certificate of incorporation, extract of other documents after paying the requisite fees.
Shares are transferable among the shareholders only.	Shares are freely transferable.
The quorum is two members present personally.	The quorum is five members present personally.
No restrictions apply on remunerations in a private company.	The total managerial remuneration cannot exceed 11% of the net profits, and in case of inadequate profits, a maximum of ₹87,500 can be paid.

Besides specific requirements, there are certain general requirements commonly applicable for the setting up of a branch office, liaison office/representative office, or a project office. These are as follows:

- Citizens of Pakistan, Bangladesh, Sri Lanka, Afghanistan, Iran, and China require prior permission of RBI to establish a branch, liaison office, or a project office.
- Partnership or proprietary concerns set up abroad are not allowed to establish branch, liaison, or a project office in India.
- Entities from Nepal can establish a liaison office in India.
- A branch or project office (excluding a liaison office) is permitted to purchase immovable property for its own use but not for leasing or renting it out. However, entities from Pakistan, Bangladesh, Sri Lanka, Afghanistan, Iran, Bhutan, and China are not allowed to acquire immovable property and are only allowed to lease property for a maximum period of five years.
- Branch, liaison, or project offices are allowed to open non-interest bearing current accounts in rupees and can approach any bank to open such accounts.
- A liaison or branch office can transfer its assets to subsidiaries or other liaison or branch offices with specific approval of RBI.
- Term deposits for a period of six months can be made by a branch, liaison, or project office out of temporary surplus funds. The branch, liaison, or project office has to give an undertaking that upon maturity of the term deposit, it will utilize the funds for its business in India within three months of maturity. This facility is not available to shipping or airline companies.

LIAISON OFFICE OR REPRESENTATIVE OFFICE

As per the Foreign Exchange Management Act, 1999 and Foreign Exchange Management (Establishment in India of Branch or Office or other Place of Business) Regulations, 2000,

TEXT

'a Liaison Office/Representative Office means a place of business to act as a channel of communication between the Principal place of business or Head Office by whatever name called and entities in India but which does not undertake any commercial,trading/industrial activity, directly or indirectly, and maintains itself out of inward remittances received from abroad through normal banking channel.'

Under FEMA's Notification No. 22/2000-RB dated 3 May 2000 schedule II, a liaison office can engage in the following activities:

- Represent the parent company or group companies in India
- Promote export/import from/to India
- Facilitate technical/financial collaborations between parent or group companies and companies in India
- Act as a channel for communication between the parent company or group companies and Indian companies

The company wishing to establish a liaison office/representative office in India should have a profitable financial performance for the past three years and its net worth should be more than US$50,000. It is required to submit an application in Form FNC-1 under the Foreign Exchange Management (Establishment in India of Branch Office or Other Place of Business) Regulations, 2000 to the Foreign Investment Division of RBI.

Net worth is defined as total paid-up capital and free reserves, less intangible assets as per the latest audited balance sheet certified by a certified public accountant.

The Companies (Acceptance of Deposit) Rules, 1975 define 'free reserves as the balance in the share premium account, capital and debenture redemption reserves and any other reserves shown or published in the balance-sheet of the company and created by appropriation out of the profits of the company, but does not include the balance in any reserve created:

(i) For repayment of any future liability or for depreciation in assets or for bad debts;

(ii) By the revaluation of any assets of the company.'

Approval of the application by RBI can be done under any of the following routes: the automatic route or the government route.

Automatic route   This is preferred where investments in the capital of resident companies or entities by a foreign investor do not require any prior approval from RBI or the Government of India.

Government route   This is preferred when investments in the capital of resident companies or entities by non-resident companies or entities can only be made with the prior approval of the government, for example, Foreign Investment Promotion Board (FIPB), Department of Economic Affairs (DEA), Ministry of Finance or Department of Industrial Policy & Promotion (DIPP), SEBI as the case may be.

Approval of 100 per cent FDI under the automatic route is available to a company, whose activities are already listed under the FDI regulations such as hotels; all other company's applications where 100 per cent FDI is not permitted are required to be processed through the government route. FDI is defined as 'any investment of foreign funds into a business enterprise that operates in a different country of origin from the investor'. This involves getting approvals from the Ministry of Finance and RBI.

Initial approval is granted for a period of three years and a unique identification number (UID) is issued by RBI. It is mandatory for the liaison office to obtain a PAN from the Income Tax Department. At the end of the financial year or part of the financial year ending 31 March, the office is required to file an annual activity certificate (AAC) certified by the auditors, along with the audited balance sheet confirming that only those activities permitted by RBI have been undertaken by the liaison office.

BRANCH OFFICE

The Companies Act, 1956 Section 2 sub-section (9) defines 'a "branch office" in relation to a company means any establishment described as a branch by the company; or any establishment carrying on either the same or substantially the same activity as that carried on by the head office of the company.'

Under FEMA's Notification No. 22/2000-RB dated 3 May 2000 schedule I, a branch office can engage in the following activities:

- Export/import of goods
- Render professional or consultancy services
- Carryout research work related to the business in which the parent company is engaged
- Promote technical or financial collaborations between Indian companies and parent or overseas group company
- Represent the parent company in India and act as buying or selling agent in India
- Rendering services in information technology and development of software in India

- Rendering technical support to the products supplied by parent or group companies
- Foreign airline or shipping company

In order to establish a branch office in India, the company should have a profitable financial performance for the past five years and its net worth should be more than US$1,00,000. It is required to submit an application in Form FNC-1 under the Foreign Exchange Management (Establishment in India of Branch Office or Other Place of Business) Regulations, 2000 to the Foreign Investment Division of the RBI.

Approval of the application by RBI can be done under any of the following routes: the automatic route or the government route. Approval of 100 per cent FDI under the automatic route is available to a company, whose activities are already listed under the FDI regulations, for example, hotels and all other applications of the company where 100 per cent FDI is not permitted are required to be processed through the government route. This involves getting approvals from the Ministry of Finance and RBI.

Initial approval is granted for a period of three years and a UID is issued by RBI. It is mandatory for the branch office to obtain a PAN from the Income Tax Department. At the end of the financial year or part of the financial year ending 31 March, the office is required to file an AAC certified by the auditors, along with the audited balance sheet confirming that only those activities permitted by RBI have been undertaken by the branch office.

A branch office is not allowed to engage in retail trade, manufacturing activities, or any type of processing activities. Profits earned in India can be freely repatriated after paying all applicable taxes.

PROJECT OFFICE

According to FEMA, 'Project Office means a place of business to represent the interests of the foreign company executing a project in India and Site Office means a sub-office of the Project Office established at the site of a project but excludes a Liaison Office.'

RBI has given a general permission to companies to set up a project office in India under the FEMA regulations 'provided the project is funded directly by inward remittance from abroad; or the project is funded by a bilateral or multilateral International Financing Agency, or the project has been cleared by an appropriate authority; or a company or entity in India awarding the contract has been granted Term Loan by a Public Financial Institution or a bank in India for the Project.'

The application procedure for setting up a project office is similar to setting up a branch office or liaison office with all the attendant financial and statutory requirements. On completion of the project, surpluses or excess funds can be remitted back after all taxes and statutory liabilities or any outstanding amounts have been settled and a certified copy of the final audited project accounts is submitted along with a chartered accountant's certificate to RBI.

JOINT VENTURE COMPANY

Joint venture (JV) is defined as a contractual agreement formed between two or more parties for technical or financial collaboration in order to share strengths, minimize risks, and increase competitive advantages in the marketplace so as to undertake an economic activity with each party contributing its share of the equity. Although a JV brings several benefits, it also has the potential to fail on account of incompatibility of participants, misinterpretation of roles, failure to contribute as agreed, indecisive management leading to stagnation in operations, and so on.

Joint venture means an Indian entity incorporated in accordance with the laws and regulations in India in whose capital a non-resident entity makes an investment. A JV agreement is also called a shareholders' agreement as it provides for the manner in which the shareholders of the JV company may transfer or dispose of their shares. It mentions the number of directors on the board, the quorum required for board or general meetings, policies for the day-to-day management of the company, procedure to be followed on the death or bankruptcy of a JV partner, and so on. All JVs have a non-compete fee clause that forbids each JV partner from competing with the JV. A non-compete fee is typically paid to a promoter as part of an acquisition deal to prevent it from competing with the new or sold business for a stipulated period of time.

Under the Companies Act, 1956, a JV company can be either a private limited company or a public limited company. RBI has clarified 'that a Joint Venture would be an entity in which a Foreign Institution (FI) (along with the holdings, if any, by its subsidiary) holds more than 25 per cent of equity capital pursuant to a Joint Venture agreement duly entered into between/amongst the Foreign Institution (FI) and the joint venture partner or partners for furtherance of a commercial objective. Such equity holding by the Foreign Institution (FI) would be defined under the "held to maturity" category even though equity shares have no maturity.'

Held to maturity (HTM) refers to investments in a company, until the investments reach their maturity or retirement date and therefore automatically cease to exist.

Foreign companies prefer entering the Indian market by signing JV agreements with Indian companies. This arrangement provides the Indian partner access to finance and technological inputs and gives to the foreign partner an established platform which helps him to develop and grow in the country. It is possible to start such a JV either with an existing company or to start it afresh with an Indian partner. In case it is an existing Indian company, it has to approach the FIPB and RBI giving details of the company that it wishes to associate with.

Example 1. Smart Hotel Investments Private Limited (SAMHI) is an Indian company, which has a JV partnership with GTI Capital Group and Equity International based out of Singapore. Both these companies jointly invested US$100 million in SAMHI in 2011. Funds from the foreign JV partners were routed through the automatic route which permits the inflow of 100% FDI into the hospitality sector. While getting foreign capital into the country against which SAMHI gave equity shares to the JV partners, they had to ensure that the equity shares were allotted keeping the pricing guidelines issued by RBI. SAMHI, during a short period of a year, has built up an impressive portfolio of assets, which encompasses a wide range of established international brands. It acquired a 60% ownership in Barque Hotels Pvt. Ltd by purchasing the shares of Accor in the company, thereby infusing fresh capital to develop the Formule 1 hotels in India; to develop Fairfield by Marriott branded hotels in India it has entered into a JV with Marriott International. The company is focussed on the development, acquisition, and ownership of select-service, business-class hotels across India.

Example 2. In order to tap the food and beverage potential in India, various fast food chains have entered into JV with Indian companies, for example, Jubilant FoodWorks—promoters of Domino's Pizza, Hardcastle Restaurants and Connaught Restaurants promoters of McDonald's; Devyani International promoters of Pizza Hut, Costa Coffee, and JSM Corp promoters of Hard Rock Cafe, California Pizza Kitchen, Trader Vic's.

WHOLLY-OWNED SUBSIDIARY COMPANY

Interpretation of Section 372A of the Companies Act, 1956 helps in defining a wholly-owned subsidiary company (WOS).

TEXT

'A company shall be deemed to be subsidiary of another company if:

1. *That other company controls the composition of its board of directors meaning that the holding company has the power at its discretion to appoint or remove all or a majority of the directors of the subsidiary company without consent or concurrence of any other person.*
2. *That other company holds more than half in face value of its equity share capital e.g. Company A holds 74% equity share, in company B it holds more than half in face value of its equity share capital and therefore company B is a subsidiary of company A.*
3. *Where the first mentioned company is a subsidiary company of any company which has another's subsidiary. E.g. Company B is a subsidiary of Company A and Company C is a subsidiary of Company B, therefore Company C is also a subsidiary of Company A.'*

Foreign companies are permitted to set up WOS in sectors where 100 per cent foreign direct investment (FDI) is permitted under the FDI policy. A WOS can be formed either as a private or public limited company, limited by shares or guarantee, or as an unlimited liability company under the Companies Act, 1956. In most cases, WOS are set up as private limited companies because of the ease in formation, control, and secrecy over the operations, and less statutory formalities required to be fulfilled.

Table 3.5 gives an overview of the various options available to foreign companies keen to operate in India.

TABLE 3.5 Options Available to Foreign Companies

	Wholly-owned subsidiary	Liaison office	Project office	Branch office
Characteristics	Share capital owned by parent company	Commercial activities not allowed	Temporary site office for a specific project allowed	Commercial activities allowed
Status	Shareholders	Foreign company	Foreign company	Foreign company
Tax rate	30%	Non-taxable	40%	10%
Control	Board of directors	Parent company	Parent company	Parent company
Set-up	FIPB approval or automatic route (four to six weeks)	RBI approval (four weeks)	RBI approval (four weeks)	RBI approval (four weeks)
Closure	Registrar of Companies (six to nine months)	RBI (three months)	RBI (three months)	RBI (three months)

Source: *Doing Business in India* by Shivangi and Rohit Kathuria. Free PDF E-Book June 2010 available at <http://www.cci.in/upload%5CArticle%5Cfile%5CFileTMGCQNAdoing-business-in-india.pdf> accessed on 25 January 2013.

FOREIGN EXCHANGE MANAGEMENT ACT, 1999 AND FOREIGN DIRECT INVESTMENT

At this stage, it is important for foreign investors to understand the important laws and regulations governing foreign investments in India such as the FEMA 1999, which repealed the FERA 1973 and India's FDI policy.

FERA was promulgated in 1973 with the objective of regulating foreign businesses in India, maintaining exchange rate stability, and conserving precious foreign exchange of which there was an acute shortage in the country. RBI was responsible for its effective implementation. It was a draconian law which presumed that the person was guilty unless he proved himself innocent, whereas under other laws a person is presumed innocent unless proved guilty. Foreign exchange violators were regarded as criminals and the guilty had no recourse to legal assistance.

The changing economic scenario led to the passing of FEMA in 1999. The objective of the Act was to manage foreign exchange, facilitate external trade and payments, and to encourage the orderly development of the foreign exchange market. The Act envisaged two types of transactions—capital account transactions and current account transactions—making it easier for corporates or individuals to remit or receive payments in foreign exchange.

Capital account transactions   These transactions alter the assets or liabilities, including contingent liabilities, outside India of a person who is a resident in India or assets or liabilities in India of a person residing outside India, and includes transactions referred to in Section 6(3) of FEMA.

Current account transactions   These are payments due in connection with foreign trade, other current business activities and services, and short-term banking and credit facilities in the ordinary course of business; remittances for living expenses of parents, spouse, and children residing abroad; and expenses in connection with foreign travel, education, and medical care of parents, spouse, and children, and payments due as interest on loans and net income from investments.

Key similarities and differences between FEMA and FERA are highlighted in Table 3.6.

TABLE 3.6   Comparison of FERA and FEMA

	FERA	FEMA
Similarities		
Administration	Central government and RBI.	Central government and RBI.
Jurisdiction	The Act enjoyed extra-territorial jurisdiction and was applicable to foreign exchange offences committed outside the country. In other words, it was applicable to all Indian citizens whether or not they were residents of India.	The Act enjoys extra-territorial jurisdiction and is applicable to foreign exchange offences committed outside the country by Indian citizens resident of India.
Enforcement	Directorate of Enforcement.	Directorate of Enforcement.
Differences		
Provisions	FERA was complex consisting of 81 sections.	FEMA is simple and consists of only 49 sections.
Features	Presumption of negative intention (*mens rea*) and abetment in committing an offence existed in FERA.	The presumptions of *mens rea* and abatement have been excluded in FEMA.
New terms in FEMA	Terms like capital account transaction, current account transaction, authorized person, service were not defined in FERA.	Terms like capital account transaction, current account transaction, authorized person, service have been defined under FEMA.
Definition of authorized person	Definition of 'authorized person' in FERA was a narrow one.	The definition of authorized person has been widened to include banks, money changes, offshore banking units, and so on.

(Contd)

TABLE 3.6 (Contd)

	FERA	FEMA
Meaning of 'resident' as compared to Income Tax Act, 1961	There was a big difference in the definition of 'resident' under FERA and Income Tax Act, 1961	The provision of FEMA is now consistent with the Income Tax Act. The criterion of staying in India for a period of 182 days makes a person a resident of India. Therefore, a person who qualifies to be a non-resident under the Income Tax Act, 1961 will also be considered a non-resident under FEMA. A person who is considered to be non-resident under FEMA may not necessarily be a non-resident under the Income Tax Act, 1961; for instance, a businessman going abroad and staying there for a period of 182 days or more in a financial year will become a non-resident under FEMA.
Punishment	Any offence under FERA was a criminal offence, punishable with imprisonment under the Criminal Procedure Code, 1973.	Any offence under FEMA is a civil offence punishable with a penalty. Imprisonment is prescribed only when one fails to pay the penalty.
Quantum of penalty	The monetary penalty payable was five times the amount involved.	The quantum of penalty is three times the amount involved.
Appeal	An appeal against the order of the 'Adjudicating Office' was before the Foreign Exchange Regulation Appellate Board before it went for appeal to the High Court.	An appeal against the order of the 'Adjudicating Office' is before the Special Director (Appeals). Appeal against the order of Special Director (Appeals) lies before 'Appellate Tribunal for Foreign Exchange'. An appeal from an order of the Appellate Tribunal for Foreign Exchange would lie in the High Court.
Right of assistance during legal proceedings	FERA debarred any appellant from the right to seek legal assistance.	FEMA expressly permits the appellant to take assistance of a legal practitioner or a chartered accountant.
Power of search and seize	FERA conferred wide powers on a police officer not below the rank of a Deputy Superintendent of Police to make a search.	The scope and power of search and seizure has been curtailed to a great extent.

Schedule 1 of Foreign Exchange Management (Transfer or Issue of Security by a Person Resident Outside India) Regulations, 2000 permits FDI which is an investment by a non-resident entity or person resident outside India in the capital of an Indian entity or company.

A study conducted by Associated Chamber of Commerce and Industries of India on FDI policy shows that it has gone through three distinct phases in its evolution.

Phase 1: 1969–1991   The first phase, between 1969 and 1991, called the permit or licence raj was based on tight government controls. MRTP was implemented to impose restrictions on the size of operations, pricing of products and services of foreign companies. FERA, enacted in 1973, limited the extent of foreign equity to 40 per cent; however, this limit could be raised to 74 per cent for technology or export-intensive and core-sector industries. A selective licensing regime was instituted for technology transfer, royalty payments, and applicants were subjected to export obligations.

Phase 2: 1991–2000   As part of the government's economic reforms programme, FDI underwent a process of liberalization between 1991 and 2000. In 1991, as per the 'Statement on Industrial Policy', FDI was allowed on the automatic route, up to 51 per cent, in 35 high-priority industries. Foreign technical collaboration was also placed under the automatic route, subject to specified limits. In 1996, the automatic approval route for FDI was expanded, from 35 to 111 industries under four distinct categories (Part A—up to 50 per cent, Part B—up to 51 per cent, Part C—up to 74 per cent, and Part D—up to 100 per cent). Hotels were classified under Part D, where 100 per cent FDI was permitted. Furthermore, FIPB, under the Ministry of Commerce and Industry, was constituted to consider cases under the government route.

Phase 3: 2000 till date   The third phase, 2000 to date, has been termed as the globalization phase of the Indian economy. In 2000, except for a negative list, all the remaining activities were placed under the automatic route. Negative list consists of sectors where the government expressly prohibits FDI. In a number of sectors/ activities, the sector-wise caps were introduced or enhanced. Some of the initiatives that were taken during this period were that the insurance and defence sectors were opened up with a cap of 26 per cent, the cap for telecom services was increased from 49 per cent to 74 per cent, FDI was allowed up to 51 per cent in single-brand retail. In 2010, all existing regulations on FDI were consolidated, rationalized, and compiled into a single document for easy reference by DIPP, Ministry of Commerce and Industry the latest update is effective 10 April 2012.

Currently, FDI is prohibited in the following sectors:

(i)   *Lottery business* including government/private lottery, online lotteries, and so on.
(ii)   *Gambling and betting* including casinos.
(iii)   *Chit funds.* The Chit Funds Act, 1982 defines a chit under Section 2(b) as a transaction under which a person enters into an agreement with a specified number of persons that every one of them shall subscribe a certain sum of money by way of periodical instalments over a definite period and each such

subscriber shall, in his turn, as determined by lot or by auction or by tender or in such other manner as may be specified in the chit agreement, be entitled to the prize amount.

(iv) *Nidhi company* is a company registered under the Companies Act, 1956 under Section 620-A and notified as a Nidhi company by the central government as a non-banking finance company (NBFC) doing the business of lending and borrowing with its members or shareholders. It is special class of NBFC which is outside the regulatory framework of the RBI.

(v) *Trading in transferable development rights* (TDR). TDR is a certificate issued either by the central or state government in consideration of surrender of land by the owner without monetary compensation in respect of category of land acquired for public purposes, which is transferred in part or whole. The TDR certificate entitles the certificate holder or developer to build the additional Floor Space Index mentioned in the TDR certificate on another parcel of land that is owned by the developer at another location.

(vi) *Real-estate business* or construction of farm houses.

(vii) *Manufacturing of cigars, cheroots, cigarillos, and cigarettes, of tobacco or of tobacco substitutes.*

(viii) *Activities or sectors not open to private-sector investment,* for example, atomic energy and railway transport (other than mass rapid transport systems).

The government has adopted the following methods to control the flow of FDI into the country:

- Putting a cap on the quantum of FDI that can be made in any sector, for example, 51 per cent in multi-brand retail and 100 per cent in hotels.
- It defined the route that that has to be taken by the investor in order to bring FDI into the country, for example, through the automatic route or through the government route. Hotels are permitted 100 per cent FDI through the automatic route, while in the defence sector FDI up to 26 per cent is through the government route.
- Other control measures adopted by the government are operational restrictions, licensing conditions, nationality criteria, minimum-capitalization, and lock-in period for investments.

In a note prepared by DIPP, the advantages of FDI are highlighted as follows:

- FDI helps to bridge the gap between the availability of domestic funds and the quantum of funds needed to sustain a level of growth.
- It enables the transfer of technology between the foreign company and the domestic company, thereby facilitating growth.
- It provides a platform for easy dissemination of best management practices through the tie-up between the investing foreign company and its Indian partner.

As mentioned earlier, the two routes for investing in India are through the automatic route or through the government route; however, for capital to flow into the country through either of the routes, investments can be made by foreign institutional investors (FII), foreign venture capital investor (FVCI), qualified foreign investor (QFI), non-resident Indian, and venture capital fund (VCF) in:

- Securities in the primary and secondary markets including shares, debentures, and warrants of companies unlisted, listed, or to be listed on a recognized stock exchange in India. Warrants and partly paid shares can be issued to person(s) resident outside India only after approval through the government route.
- Units of schemes floated by domestic mutual funds including Unit Trust of India, whether listed on a recognized stock exchange or not.
- Dated government securities.
- Derivatives traded on a recognized stock exchange.

FII It is an entity established or incorporated outside India, which proposes to make investments in India. In keeping with the Securities and Exchange Board of India (Foreign Institutional Investors) Regulations, 1995, an FII has to register itself after paying the requisite fee of US$10,000. Once the FII is registered along with its sub-accounts, a certificate of registration is issued valid for a period of five years, enabling it to make investments.

FVCI It is an investor incorporated and established outside India. Under the Securities and Exchange Board of India (Foreign Venture Capital Investor) Regulations, 2000, registration is mandatory to enable it to commence its operations. A requisite fees of US$20,000 has to be deposited, along with the registration application, before a certificate of registration valid for five years is issued.

QFI A QFI is a non-resident investor (other than SEBI registered FII and FVCI), which fulfils know-your-client (KYC) requirements of SEBI for the purpose of making investments.

NRI An NRI is an individual citizen of India, or is a person of Indian origin (PIO), residing outside India. A *PIO* means a citizen of any country other than Bangladesh or Pakistan, who has held an Indian passport, or either of his parents or any of his grandparents were citizens of India by virtue of the Constitution of India or the Citizenship Act, 1955 (No. 57 of 1955). A spouse of an Indian citizen or a person who has held an Indian passport is also considered a PIO.

VCF It refers to a fund established in the form of a trust, a company including a body corporate and registered under Securities and Exchange Board of India (Venture Capital Fund) Regulations, 1996. Under the regulations, a VCF should have a dedicated pool of capital, raised in the manner specified, and invested in accordance with the regulations.

It is mandated that they register with SEBI or RBI before they can make FDI investments. SEBI was established under the Securities and Exchange Board of India

Act, 1992. It was formed to regulate the capital markets by ensuring prudent and orderly development of the markets and protecting the institutional or retail investors. The Act has undergone several amendments in order to make it more attuned to the evolving financial requirements. These funds or individuals can presently only invest in approved financial instruments in order to bring FDI into the country which are describes as follows.

Derivative It is a financial contract whose value is based on or derived from a traditional security such as a stock, an asset, or a market index, designed to minimize the impact of market fluctuations by locking in the asset price to be settled at a future date, thereby serving as an instrument of risk management.

Section 45U(a) of the Reserve Bank of India Act, 1934 defines 'derivative' as an instrument, to be settled at a future date, whose value is derived from change in interest rate, foreign exchange rate, credit rating or credit index, price of securities (also called 'underlying'), or a combination of more than one of them and includes interest rate swaps, forward rate agreements, foreign currency swaps, foreign currency–rupee swaps, foreign currency options, foreign currency–rupee options, or such other instruments as may be specified by the Bank from time to time.

Warrants These can only be issued with prior approval of the central government by publicly listed companies provided the articles of association of the company expressly authorize the company to do so. The Companies Act, 1956 defines warrants as bearer instruments that entitle the holder to purchase shares of the company, which shall be delivered to the warrant holder.

Debenture It is an acknowledgment by the company that a loan has been taken at a fixed interest rate from an individual for a predetermined term period; debenture holders do not become shareholders of the company or enjoy voting rights, for example, company A has issued debentures worth ₹5,00,000 to various investors at an interest rate of 12 per cent per annum payable quarterly for a period of three years. The debenture holder will be returned the principal amount invested with interest, which is due at the end of the three-year period.

Debentures can be issued by a company at par, at a discount, or at a premium and these can be either secured or unsecured, convertible or non-convertible, redeemable or non-redeemable, registered or unregistered debentures, and can be purchased by investing in them in cash or any other consideration other than cash.

Example 1. Company A issues secured convertible debentures at par, which are non-redeemable. This means that the assets of the company have been pledged to secure the debentures that have been sold at par, that is, the face value of the debenture is equivalent to the amount paid to purchase it, and it cannot be redeemed or enchased except upon liquidation of the company but can be converted to shares upon maturity at the prevailing share price.

Example 2. Company B issues un-secured, registered non-convertible debentures at par, which are redeemable. This means that the assets of the company have not been pledged to secure the debentures, which are unsecured; however, they have been registered by entering them in the company's registers and have been sold at par, that is, the face value of the debenture is equivalent to the amount paid to purchase it. It can only be redeemed or encashed upon maturity as it is non-convertible debenture, which cannot be converted into shares of the company.

Share capital Share capital of a company is its equity. It can be either in the form of equity or preferential shares. *Equity shares* vests the shareholder with voting rights and any dividends payable are based upon the performance of the company; furthermore, they are not preference shares.

Preference shares These have two basic characteristics: they carry an affixed dividend and in the event of liquidation of the company, the capital invested in a preference share and dividend of a preference share have to be redeemed first. Preference shares can be cumulative or non-cumulative, redeemable or non-redeemable. The term cumulative implies that for this class of preference shares, in case a dividend is not paid in any year, the dividend gets accumulated and is carried forward. In the year the company makes a profit, the dividend is fully paid. Redeemable preference shares issued by the company are redeemed by it once the term is over. The Companies Act, 1956 does not authorize the issue of irredeemable preference shares as these can only be redeemed upon liquidation of the company.

REGULATORY ISSUES

Regulatory issues that affect the business environment can be classified into the following.

Taxation—Direct Taxes

Direct taxes levied by the central government are corporate tax, dividend distribution tax (DDT), minimum alternate tax (MAT), withholding tax, wealth tax, and tax on short-term capital gains (STCG) or long-term capital gains (LTCG).

Corporate tax

Corporate tax is the tax payable by a company on its income that has accrued over the previous financial year; for example, earnings of financial year 2011–2012 will be assessed to tax and will be called assessment year 2012–2013. For the purpose of taxation, companies are categorized as either domestic or foreign companies. A public or private limited company registered under the Companies Act, 1956 or whose control and management is based in India is regarded as a domestic company. A company that is not registered in India or if its management and control is exercised from a foreign country, then it is treated as a foreign company. Branch and project offices are taxed at 42.024 per cent (40 per cent plus surcharge of 2.5 per cent and education cess of 3 per cent).

Table 3.7 details the corporate tax structure for 2012–2013.

TABLE 3.7 Corporate Tax Structure for 2012–13

	Company with total income exceeding ₹10 million	Company with total income less than ₹10 million
Domestic company	32.445% (30% basic rate plus surcharge of 5% plus education cess of 3%)	30.9% (30% direct tax plus education cess of 3%)
Foreign company	42.024% (40% plus surcharge of 2.5% and education cess of 3%)	41.2% (40% plus and education cess of 3%)

Dividend distribution tax

Dividend distribution tax (DDT) is levied on domestic companies as a charge on the dividends declared, distributed, or paid by companies to their shareholders. Dividend received by the shareholder is not taxable, as dividend tax is paid by the company and not charged to the shareholders. Dividend tax is charged at the rate of 16.22 per cent and must be paid within 14 days of declaration or distribution, whichever is earlier. Deductions on account of such dividend tax are not allowed to the company.

Minimum alternate tax

Minimum Alternate Tax (MAT) was introduced in the year 1997–1998 by Section 115 JA of the Income Tax Act, 1961. It was introduced by the government as companies declaring their book profits made statutory deductions, which resulted in the taxable income being negligible. To counter this, the government made MAT payable by companies if a company's taxable income is less than a certain percentage of the booked profits, then by default, that much of the book profits will be considered a taxable income and tax has to be paid on that. MAT is payable at the rate of 18.5 per cent (plus applicable surcharge and cess). The concept of MAT credit was also introduced to give companies a benefit that could be claimed for a maximum period of 15 years.

Example If a company has a book profit of ₹20,00,000 and after applicable deductions, the taxable income is ₹2,00,000, then the MAT payable would be on the book profit of ₹20,00,000 at the rate of 18.5%, which works out to ₹3,70,000. However, the corporate income tax payable on ₹2,00,000 will be at the rate of 32.44%, which is ₹64,880. Difference between the two taxes paid, that is, ₹3,70,000 less ₹64,880, which is ₹3,05,120 would be carried forward as a MAT credit for a maximum period of 15 years.

Withholding tax

Withholding tax is a tax deducted at source from income, paid to non-residents of a country. This can be reclaimed if a double-taxation avoidance agreement exists between the country in which the income is paid and the country of residence of the recipient. Withholding tax is applicable to non-residents belonging to countries that are not party to Double Taxation Avoidance Agreements (DTAAs) with India. Rates will be competitive for DTAA partner countries.

DTAAs, as the name suggests, are agreements based on the rational that an entity or a person should not be taxed twice. Income earned by a foreigner in one country should not be taxed in the home country of the foreign national under its domestic tax laws. India currently has DTAAs with 84 countries. In all treaties, there is a standard provision that if a foreign entity has not formed a resultant Permanent Establishment in India or does not have a fixed place of business, then it shall not be taxable in India.

The current rate of withholding tax applicable to non-residents in India is shown in Table 3.8.

TABLE 3.8 Withholding Tax Rates 2012

Interest received by a non-resident from an infrastructure debt fund	5%
Dividends (domestic companies)	Nil
Royalties	20%
Technical services	10%
Any other services	40% of the income

Wealth tax

The Wealth Tax Act, 1957 stipulates that wealth tax is to be paid by every person other than a non-profit organization and the threshold limit of the net wealth is ₹30,00,000. Wealth tax is charged at the rate of 1 per cent of the amount by which the net wealth exceeds ₹30,00,000. It is being proposed that this limit be enhanced to ₹1,00,00,000.

Short-term capital gains and long-term capital gains

A capital gain is profit that is made by the sale of any capital asset such as immovable property, investments in shares, mutual funds, or jewellery.

STCG tax is levied when an asset is sold within a period of 12 months from the date of acquisition of the asset on the profit that is made upon its sale. It is taxed at the normal income tax rate.

LTCG is attracted when equity share, mutual funds, debentures are sold after 12 months and in the case of immovable property, after 36 months. The profit is subject to indexation before the tax is levied at the rate of 20 per cent with indexation, or at the rate of 10 per cent without indexation. Indexation is a process which permits the cost of the asset to be inflated, keeping in mind the cost of inflation.

Taxation—Indirect Taxes

Indirect taxes are charges levied on goods and services that are finally charged to customers. Important among these are service tax, VAT, and excise duty.

Service tax

Service tax is payable by the service provider and is levied at the rate of 12.33 per cent inclusive of education cess and surcharge. The tax is recoverable from the service receiver and has to be separately shown in the invoice. Service tax is payable by the service provider, if the turnover is more than ₹10,00,000 per annum.

Value added tax

Since April 2005, VAT has progressively replaced sales tax, which was levied on movable goods in most of the states. VAT is a multi-stage system of taxation on goods, with tax being levied on value addition at each stage of the transaction in the supply chain. It is a tax on the final consumption of goods, which is ultimately borne by the consumer. VAT comes under the state list and there are different rates of tax for different categories of goods with the tax being determined as per the category. Every state has its own tax structure for the different categories. There are five slabs for levying VAT—0 per cent, 1 per cent, 4 per cent, 12.5 per cent, and 20 per cent. Import and export of goods outside India does not attract VAT.

Excise duty

Excise duty is charged on the manufacture of goods and is payable by the manufacturer. The manufacturer is required to maintain a detailed record of stocks and accounts in respect of the duty payable. The duty varies as per the product being manufactured.

Transfer Pricing

Transfer pricing in India is a recent development. The laws relating to transfer pricing was introduced in 2001 through Sections 92A to 92F of the Income Tax Act, 1961. The purpose of the law was to ensure that dealings between two group companies or an Associated Enterprise (AE) located across borders followed Arms Length Pricing (ALP) when conducting their business transactions. ALP is the price that would be charged in a transaction had it been entered into by unrelated parties in similar conditions. The intention of the law was to ascertain that if the two companies were not related group companies but two independent companies, would the pricing be the same, or would it be different in the case of group companies engaging in a cross-border transaction. The objective was to discourage related group companies from indulging in the practice of over-invoicing or under-invoicing.

A company is an AE of another company provided the company exercises control over it. The law has taken a very wide interpretation of a company's control over an AE to include control through debt, blood relationships, and control over various components of the business activity besides holding shares or voting power, or the power to appoint the management of the enterprise. Therefore, control could be direct or indirect or even through an intermediary.

> **Example** If person A owns company A and person B owns company B and both are cousins, then both companies A and B are AEs as there is a blood relationship between persons A and B.
>
> On the other hand, if company A owns or has the power to appoint directors in company B, then company B is an AE of company A; by virtue of company A exercising control over company B's functioning.

Accounting Practices—Generally Accepted Accounting Principles

Generally Accepted Accounting Principles (GAAP) provide objective standards for judging and comparing financial data and its presentation, by laying down authoritative rules, practice, and conventions meant to provide both broad guidelines and detailed procedures for preparing financial statements and handling specific accounting situations, thereby limiting the directors' freedom in showing an unrealistic picture through creative accounting. An auditor must certify that the provisions of GAAP have been followed in reporting an organization's financial data in order for it to be accepted by investors, lenders, and tax authorities. Most of the developed countries (Canada, Japan, USA, and UK) have their own GAAP, which may differ from others in minor or major details.

In India, all businesses are required to maintain their accounts as defined by the Indian GAAP, for example, the accounting year being followed could be either a financial year or a calendar year but for taxation, all books of accounts have to follow the financial year as defined by GAAP commencing 1 April and ending 31 March. Table 3.9 gives the time frame for the filing of various reports that require to be submitted under the Companies Act, 1956 and the Income Tax Act, 1961.

TABLE 3.9 Regulatory Filing of Reports

Item	Due date
Corporate board meetings	Quarterly on a calendar-year basis
Annual general meeting (AGM)	Within 180 days of closing of the accounts
Annual returns with Registrar of Companies	Within 30 days of holding the AGM
Corporate tax returns	30 September
Tax audit report	30 September
Transfer pricing report	30 September
Tax deducted at source returns	Quarterly
Employee tax returns	31 July
Service tax returns	25 October and 25 April

Technology Transfer Agreements

Technology has been defined by the *Oxford Dictionaries Online* as 'the application of scientific knowledge for practical purposes, especially in industry'. When we talk about transfer of technology, we really mean the transfer of a body of knowledge in the fields of process, design, application, management, engineering, and manufacturing, and its application to enhance or improve the performance of the industry. A technology transfer agreement is the application of a process by which technology developed for a purpose is permitted to be used by a new user.

Ministry of Commerce and Industry, Government of India's Press Note No. 18 (1991 Series) dated 25 November 1991 has prescribed separate norms for grant of automatic approval by RBI for foreign technical collaborations with respect to hotel industry. These norms are applicable, provided the collaboration is proposed with companies running or managing hotel(s) with at least 500 rooms. The application for automatic approval of such foreign technology agreements has to be submitted in prescribed Form FC (RBI) to RBI, Exchange Control Department.

(i) Technical and consultancy services also called technical services agreements including fees for architect, design, supervision, and so on. Up to 3 per cent of the capital cost of the project (less cost of land and finance). This is a fee paid by the owners for providing services related to planning, design, and monitoring of the hotel during the project stage by the operating company.

(ii) Financing and marketing and publicity support fee: Up to 3 per cent of net turnover (net turnover is gross receipts less credit card charges, travel agents' commission, sales tax, statutory payments, and so on). This fee is payable by the owners of the hotel property to the hotel operator to meet the costs of marketing and publicity that is incurred by the hotel operator while promoting the hotel overseas and in the domestic market.

(iii) Management fees (including incentive fee): Up to 10 per cent of gross operating profit. This fee is payable by the owners to the hotel operator based upon the financial performance of the hotel.

Example InterContinental Hotels were the first international chain to enter India in 1962 as the Oberoi InterContinental Hotel through a marketing alliance with the Oberoi Group. This was followed by a marketing alliance with the Taj Group for its Delhi, Mumbai, and Agra properties. Once the rules for foreign technology agreements were announced in 1991 and the 100% FDI through the automatic route were announced by the Indian government, InterContinental Hotels were the first to sign a franchisee agreement with Eastern International Hotels Private Limited for the Holiday Inn, Juhu, Mumbai. It was in 1997 that InterContinental Hotels signed management contracts—the first one being with Grand Hotels for their chain of hotels in India. The year 2005 was another landmark in the history of InterContinental Hotels, when they opened their branch office in India at Gurgaon to service their properties in India. Another milestone was achieved when InterContinental Hotels and Duet India hotels entered into a JV to develop Express by Holiday Inn brand in India. InterContinental

Hotels is a shining example that has taken full advantage of the technology transfer agreements route and the 100% FDI through the automatic route while establishing the JV with Duet Hotels Group.

Hotels are permitted 100 per cent FDI through the automatic route. In spite of this benefit, the total FDI that the hotel and tourism sector has received during the past decade (2000–2010) is ₹15,483.19 crore or US$3372.20 million, which constitutes 1.98 per cent of the total FDI into the country. Anitha (2012) comments that 'some of the major impediments for India's poor performance in the area of FDI are: political instability, poor infrastructure, confusing tax and tariff policies, Draconian labour laws, well-entrenched corruption and governmental regulations'.

As India pursues the path of globalization, future reforms are expected to happen in the areas of taxation, accounting, and audits. A brief list of these is discussed as follows.

Direct Tax Code (DTC) 2009   It aims at reforming the cumbersome tax system replacing the Income Tax Act, 1961. Some of the recommendations that have been made regarding corporate taxation are given as follows:

Capital markets   The securities transaction tax to be abolished and the short-term gains and long-term gains should be appropriately calibrated. The distinction between listed and unlisted companies to be removed.

Dividend distribution tax DDT   Debt mutual funds will now attract a levy of 5 per cent dividend distribution tax and the dividend on non-equity mutual funds will be taxed in the hands of the investor as per his income slab.

Corporate tax and MAT   It has reduced the existing tax limit from 33 per cent to 30 per cent. MAT is a phenomenon that is applicable to capital-intensive companies that cover their book profit. MAT is increased from 18 per cent to 20 per cent under the DTC.

Resident status   NRIs and foreigners who have their source of income in foreign countries will be taxed on that income, if they have stayed in India for more than 730 days within seven years preceding the financial year in which it is taken into account.

Foreign companies   A large number of FIIs invest in India through Mauritius to avoid paying tax on capital gains in India by claiming exemptions on the basis of DTAAs. The government should ensure that the FIIs do not escape capital gains tax. The corporate bodies that have their origin abroad and hold more than 50 per cent of their assets in India are likely to pay capital gain tax based on percentage of asset holding.

Goods & services tax It aims at economically unifying the country by proposing to streamline movement of goods and services across the country with a single tax structure replacing the existing VAT, service tax, and central sales tax.

General Anti-Avoidance Rules (GAAR) These envisage the setting up of a structure that minimizes the avoidance of tax payments as opposed to tax planning, tax mitigation, and tax evasion.

Tax avoidance is to use legal means so as to avoid or reduce tax liability, which would be otherwise incurred, by taking advantage of some legal provisions in the law.

Tax planning means managing personal and/or business income in a manner so as to minimize tax liability.

Tax mitigation, on the other hand, is to take advantage of the tax incentives offered by the government by fulfilling the conditions that are required to be complied with to secure the benefit.

Tax evasion means to reduce tax liability by fraudulent or illegal means. Currently, the application of GAAR has been withheld till financial year 2015–2016.

International Financial Reporting Standards (IFRS) These have been designed to make one common language for the business community that transcends international boundaries. A road map for the convergence of the current Indian GAAP with IFRS has been unveiled and, by 2015, the process should be completed.

Companies Bill, 2011 It will replace the present Companies Act, 1956, and is likely to be passed by the Indian Parliament in 2013. Some of the concerns that the Bill proposes to address are as follows:

- It will regulate e-commerce companies that operate in the country but are not incorporated in the country.
- The Bill envisages that corporates earmark a part of their earnings for Corporate Social Responsibility activities, that is, 2 per cent of the average net profits of the last three years to be spent on fulfilling social responsibilities.
- It requires setting up of compensation committees to ensure transparency in salaries paid to senior executives; and making it mandatory for specified companies to appoint women directors.
- It requires setting standards and ensuring good corporate governance in publicly listed companies, which are being run with public monies; provision for class action suits by a specified number of shareholders or depositors; check on the loan to directors by private and public companies; individual auditors to be changed every five years and audit firms every 10 years, making it mandatory for listed and unlisted companies to obtain auditors certificate certifying the companies accounting practices.

- It envisages the setting up of a 'Dormant Company' created to deal with future projects, 'One Person Company' and 'Small Company' enabling individuals to adopt a corporate structure.
- It will permit Indian companies to merge with foreign companies subject to conditions; allows the merger of a subsidiary company with the parent company or the merger of two small companies without seeking approval from the tribunal (High Court).

In the forthcoming chapter, we will be examining the various types of contracts as defined under the Indian Contract Act, 1872, types of financial instruments under the Negotiable Instruments Act, 1881, and finally contracts that are specific to the hotel industry such as management contract, franchisee agreements, and technical services agreements.

SUMMARY

Traditional business models prevalent in India were family-run sole proprietorships, partnerships which were the most preferred wherein people used to invest and earn profits. The chapter discussed how Indian company law has followed the well-established precedents and legislative enactments emulating English company law. Doing business in India has always been a challenge, and under Indian corporate law there is a distinction between a domestic company and a foreign company. This differentiation decides the various options available to both domestic and foreign entrepreneurs though the basic modalities of starting a business remain the same—the promotion stage, incorporation of the company, and finally commencement of business. Under the FDI policy, which permits 100 per cent FDI through the automatic route for hoteliers, foreign hotel companies opt either for the JV route or the foreign technology transfer route.

The chapter highlighted that foreign companies prefer the JV route with Indian partners as it gives them access to a pool of local business knowledge that increases their chances of stabilizing their operations smoothly. Both these routes enable the foreign partner to minimize his or her risk and give them an opportunity to grow at a relatively faster pace. The chapter discussed direct and indirect taxes such as corporate tax, minimum alternative tax, securities transaction tax, value-added tax, service tax, dividend distribution tax, and so on. It explained transfer pricing and how it facilitates transparency in cross-border business transactions. Finally, the impact of the forthcoming legislation related to Direct Tax Code 2009, Companies Bill 2011, Goods & Services Tax, General Anti-Avoidance Rules, implementation of International Financial Reporting Standards and general accounting practices have also been discussed.

KEY TERMS

Company An association of many persons who contribute money or money's worth to a common stock and employ it in some trade or business, and who share the profit and loss as the case may be arising therefrom.

Partnership The relation between persons who have agreed to share the profits of a business carried on by all or any of them acting for all. Persons who have entered into partnership with one another are called individually 'partners' and collectively 'a firm', and the name under which their business is carried on is called the 'firm name'.

Memorandum of Association A document that sets out the constitution of the company and defines the relationship of the company with the outside world.

Articles of Association   Rules and regulations for the internal management of the company for achieving the objectives stated in the memorandum of association.

Authorized share capital   Of a public limited company is the extent to which the company can issue shares to the public.

Paid-up capital   The extent that a company's shares have been subscribed.

Certificate of Incorporation   Issued by the Registrar of Companies which gives a private or public limited company its own legal identity, enabling it to sue and be sued, making it the owner of any property owned by the promoters, and get its share capital authorized.

Commencement of Business Certificate   Issued by the Registrar of Companies authorizing a public limited company to commence its business operations.

Prospectus   Any document described or issued as a prospectus and includes any notice, circular, advertisement, or other documents inviting deposits from the public or inviting offer from the public for the subscription of shares.

Net worth   Total paid-up capital and free reserves, less intangible assets as per the latest audited balance sheet certified by a certified public accountant.

Permanent account number   Permanent alphanumeric identity generated by the Income Tax Department to identify individuals, corporate, firms, trusts, and others. The first five characters are letters, next four are numerals, and the last character is a letter.

Joint venture   means an Indian entity incorporated in accordance with the laws and regulations in India in whose capital a non-resident entity makes an investment.

Liaison office/representative office   A place of business to act as a channel of communication between the principal place of business or head office by whatever name called and entities in India, but which does not undertake any commercial/trading/industrial activity, directly or indirectly, and maintains itself out of inward remittances received from abroad through normal banking channel.

Branch office   Any establishment described as a branch by the company, or any establishment carrying on either the same or substantially the same activity as that carried on by the head office of the company.

Project office   A place of business to represent the interests of the foreign company executing a project in India.

Site office   A sub-office of the project office established at the site of a project but excludes a liaison office.

Capital account transactions   Those that alter the assets or liabilities, including contingent liabilities, outside India of a person who is a resident in India or assets or liabilities in India of a person residing outside India, and includes transactions referred to in Section 6(3) of FEMA.

Current account transaction   Payments due in connection with foreign trade, other current business activities and services, and short-term banking and credit facilities in the ordinary course of business; remittances for living expenses of parents, spouse, and children residing abroad; expenses in connection with foreign travel, education, and medical care of parents, spouse, and children; and payments due as interest on loans and net income from investments.

Foreign direct investment   Any investment of foreign funds into a business enterprise that operates in a different country of origin from the investor.

Nidhi company   A company registered under the Companies Act, 1956 under Section 620-A and notified as a Nidhi company by the central government as an NBFC doing the business of lending and borrowing with its members or shareholders.

Chit funds   A person entering into an agreement with a specified number of persons that everyone of them shall subscribe a certain sum of money by way of periodical instalments over a definite period and that each such subscriber shall, in his turn, as determined by lot or by auction or by tender or in such other manner as may be specified in the chit fund be entitled to the prize amount.

Automatic route   Where investments in the capital of resident companies or entities by a foreign investor does not require any prior approval from the RBI or the Government of India.

Government route   When investments in the capital of resident companies or entities by non-resident companies or entities can only be made with the prior approval of the government, for example, FIPB, DEA, DIPP, SEBI as the case may be.

Dividend distribution tax   Levied on domestic companies as a charge on the dividends declared, distributed, or paid by companies to their shareholders as dividend tax is not charged to the shareholders, the dividend received by the shareholder is not taxable.

Withholding tax   A tax deducted at source from income, paid to non-residents of a country, which may be reclaimed if a double-taxation agreement exists between the country in which the income is paid and the country of residence of the recipient.

Double taxation avoidance agreements Agreements based on the rational that an entity or person should not be taxed twice for the income earned in one country by a person resident in another country under its domestic tax laws.

Value added tax A multi-stage system of taxation on goods, with tax being levied on value addition at each stage of the transaction in the supply chain. It is a tax on the final consumption of goods, which is ultimately borne by the consumer.

Excise duty Charge on the manufacture of goods and is payable by the manufacturer.

Transfer pricing law Passed to ensure that dealings between two group companies or an AE located across borders followed ALP when conducting their business transactions.

Arms length price The price that would be charged in a transaction had it been entered into by unrelated parties in similar conditions.

Associated enterprise Of another company is one where the other company exercises control over it which could be direct or indirect or even through an intermediary.

Generally Accepted Accounting Principles Provide authoritative rules, practice, and conventions meant to provide both broad guidelines and detailed procedures for preparing financial statements and handling specific accounting situations.

Tax avoidance To use legal means so as to avoid or reduce tax liability, which would be otherwise incurred, by taking advantage of some legal provisions in the law.

Tax planning The arrangement of a person, business, or personal finances so as to minimize tax liability.

Tax mitigation To take advantage of the tax incentives offered by the government by fulfilling the conditions that are required to be complied with to secure the benefit.

Tax evasion To reduce tax liability by fraudulent or illegal means.

Foreign institutional investor An entity established or incorporated outside India, which proposes to make investments in India.

Foreign venture capital investor An investor incorporated and established outside India, which proposes to make investments in India.

Qualified foreign investor A non-resident investor (other than SEBI registered FII and FVCI), which fulfils KYC requirements of SEBI for the purpose of making investments in India.

Non-resident Indian An individual resident outside India who is a citizen of India or is a person of Indian origin.

Person of Indian origin A citizen of any country other than Bangladesh or Pakistan, who has held an Indian passport, or either of his parents or any of his grandparents was a citizen of India by virtue of the Constitution of India or the Citizenship Act, 1955 (57 of 1955); or the person is a spouse of an Indian citizen or a person who has held an Indian passport.

Venture capital fund A fund established in the form of a trust, a company including a body corporate that has a dedicated pool of capital; raised in the manner specified under the Regulations; and invested in accordance with the Regulations.

Indexation A process that permits the cost of the asset to be inflated keeping in mind the cost of inflation.

EXERCISES

Define the Following

1. Transfer pricing
2. Service tax
3. Double taxation avoidance agreements
4. Certificate of Incorporation
5. Prospectus
6. Direct tax
7. Authorized share capital
8. Person of Indian origin
9. Tax mitigation
10. Dividend distribution tax

Concept Review Questions

1. What are the salient differences between a private and a public limited company?
2. Outline the process of forming a public limited company.
3. Describe the various options available to foreign corporates to set up their operations in India.
4. Compare the salient features of FERA and FEMA.
5. What class or categories of investors are permitted to invest in India through the automatic route? Explain.

6. What is the importance of a prospectus? Give a detailed explanation.

Critical Thinking Questions

1. Examine the role of statutory organizations such as the RBI, SEBI, and Ministry of Finance in regulating FDI into the country.
2. Are joint venture companies the best option available to foreign hotel companies wishing to open hotels in India? Elucidate.

Research Questions

1. How do GAAR, IFRS, and GAAP bring about transparency in conducting business?
2. Do you agree that Indian tax laws are not investor friendly?

Project

1. Are foreign technology agreements defining the future of the hotel industry?

REFERENCES

R. Anitha, 'Foreign Direct Investment and Economic Growth in India', *International Journal of Marketing, Financial Services & Management Research* 1, no. 8 (2012) 108–125 at 122.

<http://en.wikipedia.org/wiki/Economic_history_of_India#cite_note-Jataka-5> accessed on 24 October 2012.

<http://www.ancientquest.com/embark/guilds.html> accessed on 24 October 2012.

'The Ease of Doing Business', *Mint* Page 9. <www.livemint.com/Politics/PsDkmEnSk55fd2n4blMeqJ/India-ranked-132-in-IFCs-2013-Doing Business-study.html> accessed on 24 October 2012.

The *Times of India*, 'India ranks 132nd in ease of doing biz among 185 economies: World Bank', 23 October 2013.

<http://timesofindia.indiatimes.com/business/india-business/India-ranks-132nd-in-ease-of-doing-biz-among-185-economiesWorld-Bank/articleshow/16929586.cms> accessed on 24 October 2013.

<http://www.middle-ages.org.uk/merchant-guilds-in-the-middle-ages.htm> accessed on 24 October 2012.

<http://business.gov.in/starting_business/sole_proprietorship.php> accessed on 24 October 2012.

<http://taxguru.in/finance/sole-proprietorship-in-india-meaning-advantage-disadvantage-necessity.html> accessed on 24 October 2012.

<http://business.gov.in/starting_business/org_partnership.php> accessed on 24 October 2012.

<http://wirccai.org/wirc_referencer/Income%20Tax%20&%20Wealth%20Tax/Taxation%20of%20Partnership%20Firms%20&%20LLP.htm> accessed on 24 October 2012.

<http://indiancorporatelaws.com/advantage_disadvantages_limited_liability_partnership.html> accessed on 24 October 2012.

<http://www.mca.gov.in/LLP/> accessed on 24 October 2012.

<http://business.gov.in/starting_business/org_private_ltd.php> accessed on 24 October 2012.

<http://www.cci.in/upload%5CArticle%5Cfile%5CFileTMGCQNAdoing-business-in-india.pdf> accessed on 24 October 2012.

<http://business.gov.in/starting_business/org_public_ltd.php> accessed on 24 October 2012.

<http://www.sebi.gov.in/dp/indianlof.pdf> accessed on 24 October 2012.

<http://www.mca.gov.in/Ministry/companies_act.html> accessed on 24 October 2012.

<http://www.mca.gov.in/Ministry/PS_act.html> accessed on 24 October 2012.

<www.mca.gov.in/Ministry/LLP_act.html> accessed on 24 October 2012.

<http://rbi.org.in/scripts/BS_FemaNotifications.aspx?Id=176office> accessed on 4 November 2012.

<http://legal-dictionary.thefreedictionary.com/Joint+Venture> accessed on 4 November 2012.

<www.majmudarindia.com/pdf/Joint%20ventures%20in%20India.pdf> accessed on 4 November 2012.

Companies Act, 1956, Section 2 <http://www.indiankanoon.org/doc/1455010/> accessed on 4 November 2012.

<http://business.gov.in/manage_business/joint_ventures.php> accessed on 4 November 2012.

<http://www.businessdictionary.com/definition/held-to-maturity-securities.html#ixzz2BQqkJF7k> accessed on 4 November 2012.

<http://www.rbi.org.in/scripts/NotificationUser.aspx?Id=504&Mode=0> accessed on 4 November 2012.

<http://www.mindfulmoney.co.uk/?lid=14395> accessed on 4 November 2012.

<http://www.economywatch.com/foreign-direct-investment/definition.html> accessed on 4 November 2012.

<http://www.indianresearchjournals.com/pdf/IJMFSMR/2012/August/8.pdf> accessed on 4 November 2012.

<http://www.caclubindia.com/articles/definition-type-and-issue-of-debentures-7305.asp> accessed on 4 November 2012.

<http://pib.nic.in/archieve/Ireleng/lyr2001/rsep2001/14092001/r140920012.html> accessed on 4 November 2012.

<http://www.caclubindia.com/articles/foreign-exchange-management-act-1999-fema-basic-understanding-13654.asp> accessed on 4 November 2012.

<http://indiacorplaw.blogspot.in/2008/03/derivatives-constructive-critique.html> accessed on 4 November 2012.

<http://www.nseindia.com/content/us/ismr2011ch6.pdf> accessed on 4 November 2012.

<http://www.investopedia.com/terms/d/derivative.asp#ixzz2DVu831oZ> accessed on 4 November 2012.

<http://www.vakilno1.com/nri/taxation/definitions.htm> accessed on 4 November 2012.

IFRS and GAAP difference <http://www.bdoindia.co.in/images/ifrs/Key%20differences.pdf> accessed on 14 November 2012.

<http://www.indiacompanysetup.com/india-corporate-tax-rates/difference> accessed on 14 November 2012.

<http://www.vakilsearch.com/law/tax/income-tax/minimum-alternate-tax-matdifference> accessed on 14 November 2012.

<http://law.incometaxindia.gov.in/DIT/intDtaa.aspx> accessed on 14 November 2012.

<http://oxforddictionaries.com/definition/english/technology> accessed on 14 November 2012.

<http://rbi.org.in/SCRIPTs/NotificationUser.aspx?Id=1438&Mode=0 technology transfer hotels> accessed on 14 November 2012.

<http://en.wikipedia.org/wiki/International_Financial_Reporting_Standards> accessed on 14 November 2012.

<http://www.allbankingsolutions.com/Banking-Tutor/GAAR-What-is.htm> accessed on 14 November 2012.

<http://www.allbankingsolutions.com/Banking-Tutor/Tax-evasion-avoidance-mitigation.htm> accessed on 14 November 2012.

<http://www.cci.in/upload%5CArticle%5Cfile%5CFileTMGCQNAdoing-business-in-india.pdf> accessed on 25 January 2013.

Business Contracts

4

LEARNING OBJECTIVES

After going through this chapter, the reader will be familiar with the following:

- Essentials of a valid contract and its discharge under the Indian Contract Act, 1872
- Implications of bailment and pledge, indemnity and guarantees, agency contracts
- Negotiable instruments and their importance in conducting business
- Various dispute resolution mechanisms
- Franchisee and management contracts

INTRODUCTION

Sir William Anson observed, 'As the law relating to property had its origin in the attempt to ensure that what a man has lawfully acquired he shall retain, so the law of contract is intended to ensure that what a man has been led to expect shall come to pass; and that what has been promised to him shall be performed.'

According to J. W. Salmond, a contract is an 'agreement creating and defining the obligations between two or more parties'.

Law of contracts is the foundation of business law as it postulates the principles for the formation and execution of all types of business contracts that regulate trade, business, and commerce; for example, indemnity and guarantee, bailment and pledge, and agency.

Business law is an essential part of conducting businesses worldwide as it defines the relationship between two or more individuals or business entities that come together for a common purpose to achieve their business targets for making profits in a lawful manner.

In India, the Indian Contract Act, 1872 states the essential features of a contract without which an agreement between two or more parties cannot be termed as a valid contract. Besides the Indian Contract Act, 1872 there are other acts that regulate specific types of transactions. These include Transfer of Property Act, 1882, Transfer of Property (Amendment) Supplementary Act, 1929, Negotiable Instruments Act, 1881, Companies Act, 1956, Partnership Act, 1932, Limited Liability Partnership Act, 2009, Sale of Goods Act, 1930, Indian Registration Act, 1902, Arbitration and Conciliation Act, 1996, Indian Stamp Act, 1899, Limitation Act, 1963, and Specific Relief Act, 1963.

INDIAN CONTRACT ACT, 1872

The purpose of the Indian Contract Act, 1872 is to introduce certainty to a transaction; though not exhaustive, it enunciates the principles that make an agreement into a legally enforceable contract. 'All agreements are not contracts, but all contracts are agreements.'

The Act is divided into 11 sections dealing with various aspects of contracts. Subsequently, Section 7 (Sale of Goods) was repealed when the Sale of Goods Act, 1930 was promulgated, and Section 11 dealing with partnerships has since been substituted in 1932 by the Partnership Act.

The essential differences between an agreement and a contract are stipulated in Section 2 of the Act:

TEXT

2. *Interpretation—clause   In this Act the following words and expressions are used in the following senses, unless a contrary intention appears from the context:*

(a) *When one person signifies to another his willingness to do or to abstain from doing anything, with a view to obtaining the assent of that other to such act or abstinence, he is said to make a proposal;*

(b) *When a person to whom the proposal is made, signifies his assent thereto, the proposal is said to be accepted. A proposal, when accepted, becomes a promise;*

(c) *The person making the proposal is called the 'promisor', and the person accepting the proposal is called 'promisee';*

(d) *When, at the desire of the promisor, the promisee or any other person has done or abstained from doing, or does or abstains from doing, or promises to do or to abstain from doing, something, such act or abstinence or promise is called a consideration for the promise;*

(e) *Every promise and every set of promises, forming the consideration for each other, is an agreement;*

(f) *Promises which form the consideration or part of the consideration for each other are called reciprocal promises;*

(g) *An agreement not enforceable by law is said to be void;*

(h) *An agreement enforceable by law is a contract;*

(i) *An agreement which is enforceable by law at the option of one or more of the parties thereto, but not at the option of the other or others, is a voidable contract;*

(j) *A contract which ceases to be enforceable by law becomes void when it ceases to be enforceable.*

Proposal

A *proposal* is made when a person willingly agrees to do or not to do an action with the express intention of securing the consent of the other party for his or her action or inaction. The proposal can be either oral or in writing. *Acceptance* of a proposal is secured when the person to whom the proposal is made gives his or her consent. Upon acceptance of the proposal, it becomes a promise.

A *promise* is the acceptance of the proposal.

A *promisor* is the person making the proposal.

A *promisee* is the person accepting the proposal.

Consideration for the promise is the act of doing something or not doing something by the promisee on the behest of the promisor.

An *agreement* is every set of promise or a promise for a consideration.

Contract

A *contract* is an agreement that is enforceable by law at the option of any of the parties. A *voidable contract* is an agreement that is not enforceable by the law. Any contract that is enforceable at the instance of only one party is a voidable contract.

Verbal contracts are promises entered into by hoteliers in their day-to-day interactions with guests and vendors as part of their operations and are honoured by both the parties.

> **Example 1.** Vikram requests for a table for two persons on his birthday at Blue Heaven restaurant telephonically, which is confirmed by them for 9 p.m. On arrival at the restaurant, Vikram is allotted a table for two.

> **Example 2.** Lufthansa airlines calls up Hyatt Hotel informing them that their flight has been delayed by 12 hours, and they require 40 rooms for their lay-over passengers. Room reservations of the hotel confirm the room availability at the rate of ₹4500 for a single or double room. Upon arrival of the lay-over passengers of Lufthansa's delayed flight, the front desk allots rooms to them.

> **Example 3.** The bell captain calls up the newspaper vendor indicating to him the newspaper requirement for the next day as the hotel is full. The vendor confirms that he will be able to deliver the newspapers as per the hotel's requirement.

ESSENTIAL ELEMENTS OF A CONTRACT

A contract is always between a minimum of two parties, but it can also be between two or more parties with the first party making the offer or the proposal to the second party. Once the second party accepts the proposal, it becomes a promise.

Offer

Both the offer and proposal made by the first party and the acceptance by the second party should be lawful resulting into an agreement.

An offer is an expression of willingness to contract on certain terms made with the interaction that it shall become binding as soon as it is accepted by the person to whom it is addressed.

—Gunter Treitel

For an offer to be lawful, it must fulfil four essential conditions, which can be revoked prior to its acceptance (*Smith vs Hughes* (1871) LR 6 QB 597). These are as follows:

   (i)   Delivery date
  (ii)   Price
 (iii)   Terms of payment
  (iv)   Description of the item on offer

Classification of offers

The Act draws a distinction between an invitation to an offer and various types of offers which are legally valid. These are listed in Fig. 4.1.

Invitation to offer   An offer is different from an invitation to offer. An invitation to offer is only a circulation of an offer; it is an attempt to invite offers and precedes a definite offer.

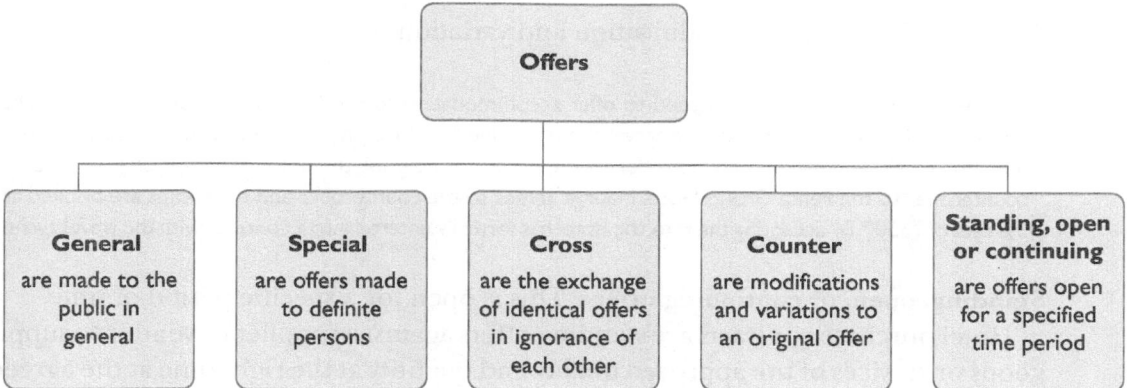

Figure 4.1   Classification of Offers

A statement made by a person who does not intend to be bound by it, but intends to further act upon it, is an invitation to offer.

> **Example**   A purchase manager invites bids for the supply of garden-fresh vegetables from interested vendors to ascertain the prevailing price of various garden-fresh vegetables. He receives five offers giving different prices for the supply of garden-fresh vegetables. Purchase evaluates all the offers made but is not bound by any of them. This constitutes an invitation to offer but does not translate into a contract until purchase decides to negotiate with any one of the parties that have quoted the rates. A final offer only emerges during the process of negotiations.

General offer   This is made to the public in general.

> **Example**   Hotel Annapurna, Kathmandu, Nepal, has advertised in the *Times of India* that it has floated special packages for Indian tourists at a special offseason price of ₹22,222 for three nights and four days inclusive of all meals, airport pick up and drop, and half-day local sightseeing inclusive of all applicable taxes. This is an offer by the hotel to the general public and in case reservation requests are received by the hotel for this package, the hotel is bound to entertain such requests and to confirm the accommodation, subject to availability of rooms.

Special offer   This is made to a specific person.

> **Example**   Hotel Shangri-La has invited Jerry Machado for a wine-tasting session to be conducted between 6 and 9 p.m. at the Aloha Bar on 26 June 2011. This is a specific offer made by the hotel and does not extend to any other person other than Jerry Machado.

Cross offer   This is an exchange of identical offer in ignorance of each other.

> **Example**   Jones sends a letter to Adam of his willingness to sell his house to him for ₹1,000,000, while Adams sends a letter offering to buy Jones house for ₹1,000,000. These offers are simultaneous

and identical and cross each other; hence, there is no binding contract as the offer and acceptance are not made in reference to each other's communication.

Counteroffer   This is a modification and variation of the original offer.

> **Example**   Hotel Maurya has agreed to offer accommodation to the Penta Group at ₹6500 per night inclusive of breakfast and taxes. The travel agent has indicated that he is willing to book rooms at the hotel for ₹5500 and makes a counteroffer to the hotel. It is now for the hotel to accept or give another counteroffer to the Penta Group. Hotel Maurya agrees to the counteroffer and the rooms are booked at the rate of ₹5500. By accepting the rate, the hotel has formally entered into a contract with the travel agent.

Standing, open, or continuing offer   This is open for a specific period of time.

Hotel purchase contracts are standing offers against a supplier or vendor to supply goods or services of the approved quality and quantity at the right time at the agreed price for a specified period.

Acceptance

The Act specifies what constitutes an acceptance and the manner in which the acceptance has to be communicated to the proposer.

TEXT

According to Section 2(b) of the Act, "When the person to whom the proposal is made signifies his assent thereto, the proposal is said to be accepted."

   (i)   For a proposal to be accepted, it must be communicated.
   (ii)   It can only be agreed to by the person to whom the offer is addressed or made.
   (iii)   Acceptance is not binding on the proposer, if it is accepted by a third party who is not the acceptor's agent.
   (iv)   If the proposer specifies a method of acceptance of the offer then it needs to be followed by the acceptor, for example, mail, fax, or unregistered post.
   (v)   Acceptance must be given within a reasonable time before the offer lapses.
   (vi)   Acceptance given by the way of conduct.
   (vii)   Mere silence or mental acceptance is no acceptance.
   (viii)   The offer has to be accepted unchanged, otherwise it becomes a counteroffer.

> **Example**   The purchase department of Hotel Shenzhen publishes the following advertisement in the *Hindustan Times*: Parties interested in supplying fresh seafood items to the hotel may submit their quotations on their company letterhead as per the itemized requirements listed in this advertisement by registered letter so as to reach on or before 10 May 2010. All quotations must be accompanied with a demand draft for ₹25,000 (rupees twenty five thousand only), which shall be refunded to parties whose quotations are not shortlisted; the amount shall be refunded within 90 days of the award of the purchase contract.
>
> From this advertisement, it is clear that vendors who fulfil all the conditions of the advertisement shall be eligible to be considered for the award of the contract subject to final negotiations.
>
> However, in case one of the parties sends its quotation by hand delivery to the purchase manager, the hotel has the right to reject the quotation, as it has not complied with the conditions of the invitation-to-bid advertisement.

Sections 5 and 6 of Chapter 1 of Indian Contract Act, 1872 define revocation of proposals and acceptance and how they are done.

A proposal may be revoked at any time before the communication of its acceptance is complete as against the proposer, but not afterwards.

An acceptance may be revoked at any time before the communication of the acceptance is complete as against the acceptor, but not afterwards.

A proposal is revoked:

(1) *By the communication of notice of revocation by the proposer to the other party;*
(2) *By the lapse of the time prescribed in such proposal for its acceptance, or, if no time is so prescribed, by the lapse of a reasonable time, without communication of the acceptance;*
(3) *By the failure of the acceptor to fulfil a condition precedent to acceptance; or*
(4) *By the death or insanity of the proposer, if the fact of the death or insanity comes to the knowledge of the acceptor before acceptance.*

Legal Obligations

Both parties must be willing to enter into a contract with each other in order to create a legal obligation, either orally or in writing, which is based on the Latin phrase *Pacta sunt Servanda* (agreements are to be kept).

Consider the example cited earlier where the purchase manager invites offers for the supply of garden-fresh vegetables from suitable vendors. The manager decides to negotiate the rates with three shortlisted vendors, which signifies the willingness of the hotel to enter into a contract with any one of them, subject to other terms and conditions of the contract. However, only two of the shortlisted vendors express their willingness to negotiate with the hotel; hence, the negotiations by the hotel will be conducted with them.

Lawful Consideration

Consideration is an essential element of a valid contract which is of value or benefit to both the parties. It is the price for which the promise of the other is bought. A contract without a lawful consideration is void. The consideration may be in the form of money, services rendered, goods exchanged, or a sacrifice which is of value to the other party. This consideration may be past, present, or future. Consideration means quid pro quo, that is, something in return.

However, under Section 25 of the Act, consideration is not required to establish a contract under the following circumstances:

(1) *It is expressed in writing and registered under the law for the time being in force for the registration of documents, and is made on account of natural love and affection between parties standing in a near relation to each other; or unless*
(2) *It is a promise to compensate, wholly or in part, a person who has already voluntarily done something for the promisor, or something which the promisor was legally compellable to do; or unless*
(3) *It is a promise made in writing and signed by the person to be charged therewith or by his agent generally or specially authorised in that behalf, to pay wholly or in part debt of which the creditor might have enforced payment but for the law for the limitation of suits. In any of these cases, such an agreement is a contract.*

Explanation I.   Nothing in this section shall affect the validity, as between the donor and donee, of any gift actually made.

Explanation 2.   An agreement to which the consent of the promisor is freely given is not void merely because the consideration is inadequate; but the inadequacy of the consideration may be taken into account by the Court in determining the question whether the consent of the promisor was freely given.

Competent Parties

The parties making the contract must be legally competent in the sense that both must not be minors, both should be of a sound mind, and not expressly disqualified from contracting. A person of sound mind is one who is able to understand the proposal and rationally evaluate it keeping his interest in mind.

Free Consent

Free consent implies that the parties must agree about the subject matter of the agreement in the same sense as it is proposed without any ambiguity at the same time, which is *consensus ad idem* meaning that there is a meeting of the minds between the two parties as to the subject matter of the agreement.

Free consent is elaborated in the Act under Sections 15–21, which stipulate that it should be obtained without coercion, undue influence, fraud, or misrepresentation, and mistake as of fact.

- *Coercion (Section 15)—threatening to commit any act forbidden by law or do an unlawful act of detaining or threatening to detain any property, with the intention of making a person enter into an agreement.*
- *Undue Influence (Section 16)—Where a person is in a position to dominate the will of another in order to secure an unfair advantage it is regarded as exercising of undue influence. A person is in a position to dominate the will of another*
  - *(a) Where he holds a real or apparent authority over the other, or where he stands in a fiduciary relation to the other; or*
  - *(b) Where he makes a contract with a person whose mental capacity is temporarily or permanently affected by reason of age, illness, or mental or bodily distress.*
  - *(c) Where a person who is in a position to dominate the will of another, enters into a contract with him, and the transaction appears, on the face of it or on the evidence adduced, to be unconscionable, the burden of proving that such contract was not induced by undue influence shall be upon the person in a position to dominate the will of the other.*
- *Fraud (Section 17)—'Fraud' means and includes any of the following acts committed by a party to a contract, or with his connivance, or by his agent, with intent to deceive another party thereto of his agent, or to induce him to enter into the contract.*
  - *(1) The suggestion as a fact, of that which is not true, by one who does not believe it to be true;*
  - *(2) The active concealment of a fact by one having knowledge or belief of the fact;*
  - *(3) A promise made without any intention of performing it;*
  - *(4) Any other act fitted to deceive;*
  - *(5) Any such act or omission as the law specially declares to be fraudulent.*

- *Misrepresentation (Section 18) means*
  (1) *The positive assertion, in a manner not warranted by the information of the person making it, of that which is not true, though he believes it to be true;*
  (2) *Any breach of duty which, without an intent to deceive, gains an advantage to the person committing it, or anyone claiming under him; by misleading another to his prejudice, or to the prejudice of anyone claiming under him;*
  (3) *Causing, however innocently, a party to an agreement, to make a mistake as to the substance of the thing which is subject of the agreement.*
- *Voidable agreements (Section 19)—When consent to an agreement is caused by coercion, fraud or misrepresentation, the agreement is a contract voidable at the option of the party whose consent was so obtained.*

  A party to contract, whose consent was caused by fraud or misrepresentation, may, if he thinks fit, insist that the contract shall be performed, and that he shall be put on the position in which he would have been if the representations made had been true.

  Exception *Even though the consent was obtained by incorrect means a contract will not be voidable if the party whose consent was so caused had the means of discovering the truth with ordinary diligence. Or if incorrect means is practised but do not influence the consent by the party it does not render the contract voidable.*
- *Mistake as of fact (Section 20)—'Where both the parties to an agreement are under a mistake as to a matter of fact essential to the agreement, the agreement is void.'*
- *Effect of mistake as to law (Section 21)—A contract is not voidable because it was caused by a mistake as to any law in force in India, but mistake as to a law not in force in India has the same effect as a mistake of fact.*

Lawful Object

The object of the agreement must be lawful. An agreement is unlawful, if it is (i) illegal, (ii) immoral, (iii) fraudulent (iv) of a nature that, if permitted, it would defeat the provisions of any law, (v) causes injury to the person or property of another, and (vi) opposed to public policy. Such agreements are void *ab initio*, that is, from the beginning.

Not Expressly Declared Void

An agreement expressly declared to be void under the Contract Act or under any other law, is not enforceable and is, thus, not a contract. The Contract Act declares the following types of agreements as expressly void:
- Agreement in restraint, to marriage (Section 26)
- Agreement in restraint of trade, profession, or business (Section 27)
- Agreement in restraint of legal proceedings (Section 28)
- Agreements having uncertain meaning (Section 29)
- Wagering agreement (Section 30)

Certainty and Possibility of Performance

The terms of a contract must not be vague or uncertain such that their meaning cannot be ascertained, or that it is impossible to carry out the contract. Such agreements are not enforceable by law.

Legal Formalities

A contract may be either oral or in writing. However, certain types of contracts are required to be in writing and may even require registration. Where law requires an agreement to be put in writing or be registered, the same must be complied with.

Compulsory registration under Section 17 of the Registration Act, 1902 is required in the following cases:

(i) Gift of immovable property

(ii) Any non-testamentary instrument that intends to create, declare, assign, limit or extinguish whether in present or in future any right title or interest of a value of ₹100 and upwards to or in an immovable property

(iii) Any leases of immovable property for any term exceeding a year or getting a yearly rent

(iv) Any non-testamentary instrument which acknowledges the receipt or payment of any consideration on account of creation, declaration assignment, limitation or extinction of any right title or interest

A testamentary document is revocable and intends to dispose of an asset upon death, for example, a will.

Section 10 of the Act clarifies what agreements are contracts. All contracts are agreements that are made by free consent of parties competent to contract, for a lawful consideration and with a lawful object, and are not hereby expressly declared to be void and are enforceable by law at the behest of either of the parties.

Example STIC Travels, New Delhi, has made a reservation request for a single room for Sanjiv at Hotel Le Méridien, New Delhi. The details of Sanjiv's room reservation are given as follows:
- Check in 15 June 2000, arrival by AI-101 from New York at 17:00 hours
- Check out 18 June 2000, departure by AI-102 from New Delhi at 01:30 hours
- Room rate ₹5500 per night inclusive of breakfast and taxes

Other instructions
- Complimentary airport pick up and drop to be provided.
- One night's deposit of ₹5500 has been paid by Visa credit card.
- Late checkout at 19:00 hours at no extra charge.
- Guest will settle the hotel bill directly.

Upon arrival at the airport, Sanjiv is received by the hotel car and taken to the hotel and allotted room no. 223. When the reservation request was communicated by STIC Travels to the hotel, the travel agency had initiated a proposal requesting for room accommodation for Sanjiv for the dates specified. The hotel by confirming the reservation request has accepted the proposal and promises to give a room to Sanjiv upon arrival. The hotel further communicates that by paying one night's room charges, the reservation will be guaranteed by the hotel and the same shall be forfeited in case the guest does not check in; the deposit is paid by STIC Travels to the hotel as a consideration to hold the room on a confirmed basis. This transaction between the hotel and STIC Travels is a contract, as it is enforceable by law by either party demanding specific performance.

Essentials of a valid contract

A valid contract is between two consenting parties who agree of their own free will to create a legal relationship by one party making the offer and the other accepting the offer for a lawful consideration either orally or in writing, where there is a reasonable certainty of the contract being fulfilled. This contractual obligation on the part of the hotel is created when the hotel confirms a guest reservation against a deposit and gets validated once the guest is received at the airport and a room is allotted to him and he signs the guest registration card.

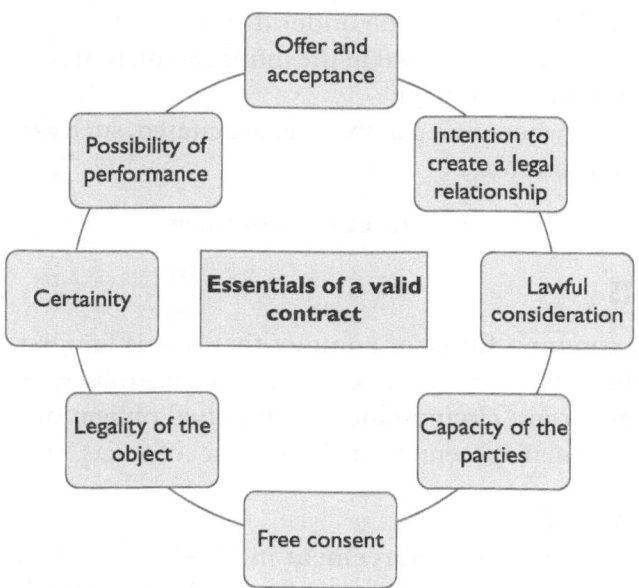

FIGURE 4.2 Essentials of a Valid Contract

Figure 4.2 illustrates the various steps that are required to be undertaken to establish a valid contract under the Indian Contract Act, 1872.

DIFFERENCE BETWEEN VOID, VOIDABLE, AND UNENFORCEABLE CONTRACTS

All void contracts are unenforceable by law. Examples of such contracts are as follows:

(i) Contracts for promoting illegal activities, such as gambling, prostitution, or other crimes

(ii) Contracts made by minors or persons of unsound mind, who do not have the legal capacity to make decisions

(iii) Contracts that were not supported by adequate consideration or where the consideration was unlawful

(iv) Contracts for the performance of impossible acts

(v) Unconscionable contracts, which are so unfair to a person that no prudent or reasonable person would enter into one

(vi) Contract that is contingent upon the occurrence of an impossible event

(vii) Agreements that are fraudulently contracted

(viii) Contracts that restrain a person's choice of marriage, trade or commerce, or legal proceedings or hearing

Voidable contracts are valid agreements where the affected party can seek the performance of the contract or rescind it on any of the following grounds:

(i) Contracts where one of the parties to the agreement is a minor

(ii) Contracts that were made under duress

(iii) Contracts involving fraud in the inducement, that is, fraud that induces a person to enter into a contract

(iv) Contracts where one party was incapacitated, such as situations involving intoxication or insanity

All void contracts are unenforceable contracts.

TYPES OF CONTRACTS

The most common forms of contract that one is familiar with are between two or more parties and contingency contracts like insurance, indemnity, and so on; however, under certain circumstances contractual obligations are created even though there is no formal agreement such as quasi contracts.

Bilateral Contract

A bilateral contract is an agreement in which both the parties make a promise to each other. For example, Rajiv decides to sell his car for ₹2,000,000 upon receipt of the payment from Sudhir.

Unilateral Contract

Unilateral contract is one where only one of the parties makes a promise to pay upon the completion of a specified action. For example, Krishna has misplaced his house keys in his office and offers a reward of ₹500 to any person who can find it for him.

Express Contract

Express contract is one that is either in writing or orally expressed between two parties promising to do or not to do an action. For example, Rajiv decides to sell his laptop to Sudhir for ₹20,000 upon receipt of the payment from Sudhir.

Quasi Contract

Quasi contracts are certain relations resembling those created by contract or implied contracts (Chapter 5 of Indian Contract Act, 1872). Situations that resemble contracts but are not formally entered into by the parties are mentioned in Sections 68 to 72 of the Indian Contract Act, 1872. In all these cases, the person receiving the benefit is bound to reimburse, compensate, or return the goods to the person who had furnished the supplies or paid the money.

Quasi contracts are those that are implied by law. These are in reality not contracts but based on the principle that one should not enrich himself at the cost of the other and, therefore, are recognized by the courts to remedy situations. For example, a doctor renders assistance to an accident victim on the site of the accident and then takes him to the nearest hospital for treatment. Upon recovery, the patient refuses to pay the doctor who helped him at the accident site. The court in all fairness directs the patient to compensate the doctor for the services rendered.

Implied contract is one in which the action of one of the parties suggests that a contract is implied even though it is not in writing. For example, Suman goes to the Skoda service station to get his car serviced; it is implied that he will pay the service station once the car servicing is completed.

TEXT

68. Claim for necessaries supplied to person incapable of contracting, or on his account

If a person, incapable of entering into a contract, or anyone whom he is legally bound to support, is supplied by another person with necessaries suited to his condition in life, the person who has furnished such supplies is entitled to be reimbursed from the property of such incapable person.

Example Singh has incurred expenses to the tune of ₹10,000 whilst looking after the parents of Gautam while he was on a tour. Gautam is required to reimburse these expenses to Singh. In case Gautam does not have the financial means, it is recoverable from the property owned by Gautam's parents.

TEXT

69. Reimbursement of person paying money due by another, in payment of which he is interested

A person, who is interested in the payment of money which another is bound by law to pay, and who therefore pays it, is entitled to be reimbursed by the other.

Example Suresh owes ₹5000 to the hotel; the hotel has inadvertently collected an excess payment of ₹10,000, which has to be reimbursed to Rajiv. Rajiv collects ₹5000 from the hotel and pays the hotel ₹5000 owed by Suresh to them on Suresh's behalf. The hotel has now squared up its accounts with both Rajiv and Suresh. Rajiv has to collect ₹5000 from Suresh, as he has discharged Suresh's debt towards the hotel.

TEXT

70. Obligation of person enjoying benefit of non-gratuitous act

Where a person lawfully does anything for another person, or delivers anything to him, not intending to do so gratuitously, and such another person enjoys the benefit thereof, the letter is bound to make compensation to the former in respect of, or to restore, the thing so done or delivered.

Example Shashi indicates to Anuj that he is keen to purchase a washing machine and is looking for the best possible rates. Anuj purchases a washing machine on a discount for Shashi and informs him of the discounted price. Shashi gets the machine installed at his residence and enjoys its benefits. He is bound to reimburse the discounted price of the washing machine to Anuj.

TEXT

71. Responsibility of finder of goods
   A person who finds goods belonging to another, and takes them into his custody, is subject to the same responsibility as a bailee.

Example The lost and found section of the housekeeping department is entrusted with the task of storing valuable and invaluable items of all guests that are surrendered to them by employees. Hurst staying in room no. 556 inadvertently leaves behind his blue shirt at the time of checking out on 5 May 2011. The same is deposited with the lost and found department. The hotel is duty bound to contact the guest and return the shirt to him irrespective of whether it has been brought to the attention of the hotel by the guest.

TEXT

72. Liability of person to whom money is paid, or thing delivered, by mistake or under coercion
   A person to whom money has been paid, or anything delivered, by mistake or under coercion, must repay or return it.

Example The concierge receives a parcel of chocolates for J. Jones staying in room no. 732. The bell boy delivers the parcel of chocolates to H. Jones staying in room no. 372. When J. Jones enquires about his parcel, the mistake is discovered by the bell desk and H. Jones is contacted to return the parcel. However, H. Jones has consumed a few of the chocolates; he is requested to return the parcel of chocolates to the bell desk. The bell desk in turn will have to replenish the chocolates that were consumed by the guest before delivering the parcel to J. Jones of room no. 732. In case the chocolates are not returned by the guest, then the bell desk will have to purchase the chocolates from the market and give to the guest.

Contingent Contract

Contingent contracts are defined under Sections 31–36 of the Indian Contract Act, 1872. A contingent contract 'is defined as contract to do or not to do something, if some event, collateral to such contract, does or does not happen'.

(i) A contingent contract can only be enforced provided an uncertain event *happens* in the future. For example, Ashu enters into an agreement with Gaurav to buy his house for ₹5,000,000, provided he agrees to get it repaired and painted. Gaurav gets the house painted and repaired. Ashu is now obliged to purchase the house from Gaurav and this contingent contract is enforceable by law.

(ii) A contingent contract can only be enforced, provided the uncertain event *does not happen*. For example, Sonam enters into an agreement with Alka that if India wins the Test match against Pakistan, she will gift a gold chain to her. India loses the match; this contingent contract is not enforceable.

(iii) A contingent contract can only be enforced provided the uncertain event happens in the future or does not happen *within a specified time frame.* For example, Ashu enters into an agreement with Gaurav to buy his house for ₹5,000,000, provided he agrees to get it repaired and painted within two months. Gaurav gets the house painted and repaired in four months. The contingent contract has expired at the end of the two-month period as the work had not been completed by Gaurav, hence the contract is void.

Agreement contingent to an impossible event is void. A agrees to pay B ₹1,000 if B will marry A's daughter C. C was dead at the time of the agreement. The agreement is void.

Contracts of insurance, indemnity, and guarantee are contingent contracts.

DISCHARGE OR PERFORMANCE OF CONTRACTS

A contract is said to be discharged or terminated under the Indian Contract Act, 1872 when the rights and obligations created by the contract are fulfilled. Contracts are discharged or terminated by any of the following actions

- (i) By performance
- (ii) By tender
- (iii) By mutual consent or agreement
- (iv) By lapse of time
- (v) By impossibility of performance
- (vi) By breach of contract
- (vii) By *force majeure* or an act of God

By Performance (Section 37)

When both parties fulfil their obligations created by the contract in the manner specified within the agreed time frame.

> **Example** Rajiv has to organize a day conference for eight people at the Taj Hotel and has requested for a meeting room to be booked for 13 April 2011. The hotel has confirmed his request. On the appointed day, Rajiv and his guests come to the conference venue and after completing their deliberations, settle the conference charges. Both the parties have fulfilled their commitments; hence the contract gets discharged by performance.

By Tender (Section 38)

Discharge by tender is an offer to perform by the promisor, which must be unconditional, given at an appropriate time and place, made under circumstances enabling the promisee to ascertain that the party by whom it is made is able and willing then and there to do the whole of what he or she is bound to do by his or her promise.

If the performance is rejected, then the promisor is discharged from any further liability.

> **Example**   Surya Travels is holding confirmed reservation for 10 standard double rooms at the Grand Hotel, New Delhi, for 2 October 2010, which is a long weekend and the hotel is fully sold out. When the group arrives at the hotel, the travel agent is informed that only deluxe rooms are available and the hotel does not have standard rooms. Surya Travels has the option of accepting the deluxe rooms or of transferring the group to another hotel where standard rooms are available. If the offer of deluxe rooms is rejected by the agent, the hotel is absolved of any further liability to provide accommodation to the group.

By Mutual Consent or Agreement (Sections 62 and 63)

Discharge of contracts by consent or agreement can be done in the following manner: novation, alteration, rescission (Section 62), or remission (Section 63). This is based upon the rule of law 'that a thing can be destroyed in the same manner that it was created' based on the Latin rule of law *eodem modo quo quid constituitur, eodem modo destruitur.*

TEXT

62. *Effect of novation, rescission, and alteration of contract*
    If the parties to a contract agree to substitute a new contract for it, or to rescind or alter it, the original contract need not be performed.

Novation is the substitution of a new contract between the same parties prior to the expiry of the existing contract. This discharges the obligation of both the partiers under the old contract and results in a new contractual relationship.

> **Example**   Manoj has made a banquet booking at the Oberoi Hotel for his sister's marriage function scheduled on 16 December 2011 and the payment terms that are agreed are as follows:
> * 30% of the consideration amount on reservation to be paid on 16 July 2011
> * 30% to be paid within 60 days from the date of reservation
> * 30% to be paid by 15 November 2011
> * 10% to be paid on the date of the function
>
> Manoj desires that the payment terms be altered after he has paid 60% of the consideration amount to the hotel.
> * 20% to be paid by 15 November 2011
> * 20% to be paid on the date of the function
>
> The hotel agrees to the revised terms of payment, thereby substituting the original contract terms with the new ones thereby discharging by novation the old contract.

Rescission is a discharge of both parties from the obligations of a contract by a new agreement made after the execution of the original contract but prior to its performance, that is, both the parties agree not to demand performance of the contract mutually, thereby discharging the original contract.

Example Manoj has made a banquet booking at the Oberoi Hotel for his sister's marriage function scheduled on 16 December 2011 and the payment terms that are agreed are as follows:

- 30% of the consideration amount on reservation to be paid on 16 July 2011
- 30% to be paid within 60 days from the date of reservation
- 30% to be paid by 15 November 2011
- 10% to be paid on the date of the function

Manoj has paid 60% of the consideration amount to the hotel, when his father expires due to a fatal accident and has to cancel the banquet booking. The hotel under these circumstances agrees to release the banquet space and refunds the amount. Both the parties have mutually agreed to the non-performance of the contract, thereby discharging the contract by rescission.

On the other hand, *waiver* is the unilateral renunciation by one party to forego its rights against the other.

Alteration of the contract happens when both the parties mutually agree to change the terms of the contract, and the original terms of the contract stand discharged. In the example cited, if Manoj had opted to postpone the wedding upon his father's demise, it would be an alteration in the contract as the contract is yet to be performed by both the parties.

Remission is the reduction or relinquishment of a payment or a penalty; or dispensing with the obligation to perform an action at the sole discretion of the promisee.

TEXT

63. *Promisee may dispense with or remit performance of promisor*
Every promisee may dispense with or remit, wholly or in part, the performance of the promisor made to him, or may extend the time for such performance, or may accept instead of it any satisfaction which he thinks fit.

Example 1. Rajiv owes ₹5,000 to Shekar. Sunder pays on behalf of Rajiv ₹3,000 to Shekar, who accepts this amount in satisfaction against his claim of ₹5,000 from Rajiv. The claim is discharged.

Example 2. Rajiv owes ₹5,000 to Suncity Hotel, Udaipur, which is payable on 30 September 2011 before 5 p.m. He pays on the required place, date, and time a sum of ₹4,000 to the hotel. The hotel accepts this amount in satisfaction against its claim of ₹5,000. The claim is discharged.

Example 3. Rajiv owes to Shekar a sum of money under a contract, the value of which has not been ascertained. Rajiv without ascertaining the amount pays to Shekar a sum of ₹2,000, which he accepts, thereby discharging Rajiv from the whole debt whatever be the amount.

Example 4. Rajiv owes ₹5,000 to Shekar. He also owes ₹15,000 to the hotel. He makes an arrangement with all his creditors including Shekar that they will accept a 20% discounted amount towards the settlement of his debts. By paying Shekar a 20% discounted sum of ₹4,000 and ₹12,000 to the hotel, Rajiv has reached a full and final settlement of his debts and both the claims are discharged.

By Lapse of Time

Under the Limitation Act, 1963, a contract must be performed within a period of three years from the date of its inception; otherwise, it stands discharged.

By Impossibility of Performance or Operation of the Law

Rule of law: *Lex non cogit ad impossibilia. Impossibilium nulla obligatio est.* The law does not compel a man to do that what is impossible and what is impossible does not create an obligation.

TEXT

56. Doctrine of frustration. An agreement to do an act impossible in itself is void. Contract to do act afterwards becoming impossible or unlawful: A contract to do an act which, after the contract is made, becomes impossible or, by reason of some event which the promisor could not prevent, unlawful, becomes void when the act becomes impossible or unlawful.

Compensation for loss through non-performance of act known to be impossible or unlawful: Where one person has promised to be something which he knew or, with reasonable diligence, might have known, and which the promisee did not know to be impossible or unlawful, such promisor must make compensation to such promise for any loss which such promisee sustains through the non-performance of the promise.

Ways in which an offer terminates by impossibility of performance or operation of law include the following:

- Termination by death or insanity of either party. If the person who makes the offer or the person who accepts the offer dies or is established as legally insane, then the offer will terminate.
- Termination by a supervening impossibility or illegality of the act agreed to be done (Section 56 of Indian Contract Act, 1872) An offer will terminate if after the offer was made, a new law prevents a party from carrying out the terms of the contract making it impossible to perform.

Example Cox & Kings, a large tour operator, has reserved a series of groups consisting of Pakistan nationals at the Lalit chain of hotels. Due to unforeseen circumstances, the Government of India enforces a ban on travel of Pakistan nationals to the country, making it impossible for Cox & Kings to operate the series of groups.

- Termination by destruction of the subject matter would terminate the offer because the subject matter of the proposed contract no longer exists.

Example About 60% of the room inventory is not available for sale due to a terrorist attack on the hotel. The hotel is compelled to cancel all room reservations as the rooms that are the subject matter of the contract have been destroyed and are not available for sale.

- Termination due to the non-occurrence of an event would result in the termination of a contingent contract.

> **Example**   Hoechst Pharmaceuticals is planning a conference for all its various divisions at New Delhi in July 2010 at the Sofitel Hotel subject to the hotel completing the hotel's refurbishment programme by December 2009. The hotel's refurbishment does not get completed by December, forcing Hoechst Pharmaceuticals to shift the conference to another venue.

By Breach of Contract (Section 39)

Effect of refusal of party to perform promise wholly
   When a party to a contract has refused to perform, or disabled himself from performing, his promise in its entirety, the promisee may put an end to the contract, unless he has signified, by words or conduct, his acquiescence in its continuance.

Consequences of a breach of contract are as follows:
- When a breach of contract happens, the aggrieved party is entitled to financial compensation to the extent that it has suffered a loss on account of the non-performance of the contract.
- If a penalty amount is specified, it becomes payable irrespective of the loss amount upon the breach of contract.
- If the contract is rescinded, then the amount spent prior to the same being rescinded is reimbursable to either party.

By *Force Majeure* or Act of God

Once a contract has been signed between two parties, natural calamities or acts of God can result in the discharging of the contract. An act of God is defined as an action that results without any human intervention.

INDEMNITY AND GUARANTEES

Indemnity and guarantee are most often confused. An indemnity is where one party agrees to pay the liabilities incurred by a party upon happening of an event, whereas a guarantee is a form of security.

124. *'Contract of indemnity' defined*
   A contract by which one party promises to save the other from loss caused to him by the contract of the promisor himself, or by the conduct of any other person, is called a 'contract of indemnity', the person who gives the indemnity is the indemnifier and the person for whose protection it is given is called indemnity holder. The loss must be caused by the promiser himself or any third party due to some human intervention.

A contract of indemnity is created by the following.

Express Promise

Express promise is a specific agreement between parties to indemnify one of the parties.

CASE 4.1

APPELLANT:　Gajan Moreshwar
　　　　　　vs
RESPONDENT: Moreshwar Madan

DATE:　(1942) Bom 302

FACTS:　G. Moreshwar took a plot in Bombay on long lease period and subsequently transferred the lease to M. Madan for a limited period. M. Madan started construction over the said plot and got his supplies from a K. D. Mohan Das. When Mohan Das asked for payment, the defendant could not pay up.

Upon request by M. Madan, G. Moreshwar executed a mortgagee deed in favour of K. D. Mohan Das the supplier after finalizing the interest rate and the date was set for the return of the principal amount with interest and G. Moreshwar put a charge over his properties. M. Madan had agreed to pay the principal amount, the interest, and to get the mortgage deed released before the set date. M. Madan did not pay anything to K. D. Mohan Das; it was G. Moreshwar who paid some interest.

When despite repeated request, M. Madan did not pay the principal amount, interest, or get the mortgage deed released, G. Moreshwar sued him for indemnity.

HELD:　The Privy Council did not accept M. Madan's stance that G. Moreshwar had suffered no loss and thus could not claim anything under Sections 124 and 125. The Council held that an indemnity holder has rights other than those mentioned in the Sections above. If the indemnity holder has incurred a liability and the liability is absolute, he can turn to the indemnifier to take care of the liability and pay it off. Thus, G. Moreshwar was entitled to be indemnified by M. Madan against all liabilities under the mortgage and deed of charge.

Example　A hotel has employed Tiptop Security Services to manage the security of the hotel night club. It has been briefed by the management that entry to the club has to be strictly regulated as it is by invitation for patrons above the age of 21 years. In case no identification or proof of age is given, the patron should be politely refused admission. These rules are also prominently displayed at the entrance of the night club.

A group of four couples invited by the hotel present themselves at the gate for admission. Three couples are admitted after they have shown their proof of identity, whilst the fourth couple is refused admission in spite of being invited, as they are not carrying any proof of identity with them. This leads to an altercation between the fourth couple and security resulting in a brawl in which the couple and a security guard are grievously injured and subsequently rushed to hospital.

Within the next few days, a case is filed against the security services by the fourth couple seeking compensation of ₹40,000 on the grounds of entry being refused in spite of an invitation. Although the case is contested by the security services, judgement is given against it. Tiptop Security Services maintains that it had acted on behalf of the hotel management, and therefore, the amount of ₹40,000 is payable by the hotel and not by the security agency. The hotel is liable to pay as it has indemnified the security agency for acts done by it in the course of the business.

Operation of Law

Under Section 145 of the Indian Contract Act, 1872, if the surety pays the creditor, the principal debtor in lieu of whom the surety was paid has to indemnify the surety.

> **Example** Ashu contracts to indemnify Bholu against the consequences of any proceedings, which Pinto may take against Bholu in respect of a particular transaction. If Pinto does institute legal proceeding against Bholu in that matter and he pays damages to Pinto, Ashu will be liable to make good all the damages Bholu had to pay in the case.
>
> Under Section 13 of the Indian Partnership Act, 1932, a firm is bound to indemnify an agent who suffers a loss by doing a lawful act of the firm and vice versa.

TEXT

(e) *The firm shall indemnify a partner in respect of payments made and liabilities incurred by him*
  (i) *In the ordinary and proper conduct of the business; and*
  (ii) *in doing such act, in an emergency, for the purpose of protecting the firm from loss, as would be done by a person of ordinary prudence, in his own case, under similar circumstances; and*
(f) *A partner shall indemnify the firm for any loss caused to it by his wilful neglect in the conduct of the business of the firm.*

Section 6, Clause 81 of the Negotiable Instruments Act, 1881 provides that any person liable to pay, and called upon by the holder thereof to pay, the amount due on a promissory note, bill of exchange, or cheque is before payment entitled to have it shown, and is on payment entitled to have it delivered up to him, or, if the instrument is lost or cannot be produced, to be indemnified against any further claim thereon against him.

TEXT

126. *'Contract of guarantee', 'surety', 'principal debtor' and 'creditor'*
  A 'contract of guarantee' is a contract to perform the promise, or discharge the liability, of a third person in case of his default. The person who gives the guarantee is called 'surety', the person in respect of whose default the guarantee is given is called 'principal debtor', and the person to whom the guarantee is given is called 'creditor'. A guarantee may be either oral or written.

127. *Consideration for guarantee*
  Anything done, or any promise made, for the benefit of the principal debtor, may be a sufficient consideration to the surety for giving the guarantee.

128. *Surety's liability*
  The liability of the surety is co-extensive with that of the principal debtor, unless it is otherwise provided by the contract.

129. *Continuing guarantee*
  A guarantee which extends to a series of transaction, is called, a 'continuing guarantee'.

130. *Revocation of continuing guarantee*
  A continuing guarantee may at any time be revoked by the surety, as to future transactions, by notice to the creditor.

131. *Revocation of continuing guarantee by surety's death*
  The death of the surety operates, in the absence of any contract to the contrary, as a revocation of a continuing guarantee, so far as regards future transactions.

A contract of guarantee is a contract to perform the promise, or discharge the liability, of a third person in case of his default. Once a surety is given, it is co-extensive with the principal debtor and the consideration can be any promise or action done by the creditor that will benefit the principal debtor. The contract of guarantee can be either oral or in writing.

When two persons give a surety for a single principal debtor in a contract, and contract amongst themselves to be liable on the default of the other, any arrangement between the two sureties between themselves has no meaning. This is because in case of a default both shall be liable jointly and severally for the default even though the arrangement is in the knowledge of the principal debtor.

> **Example** Anuj and Sanjay have given surety on behalf of Rajiv for an amount of ₹2,00,000. In case Rajiv defaults in making the payment on time to Mukesh. Anuj and Sanjay have amongst themselves arrived at an understanding that they shall be liable for the default of each other which is in the knowledge of Mukesh. However, in case Rajiv defaults, both Anuj and Sanjay have to pay the surety amount in full to Mukesh irrespective of their understanding.

Surety is the person giving the guarantee.

Creditor is the person to whom the guarantee is given by the surety in case of default by the principal debtor.

Principal debtor is the third person for whom the guarantee is given by the surety in case the creditor defaults.

Continuing guarantee is one that is given by the surety to cover multiple transactions. A continuing guarantee stands revoked upon the death of the surety; also it can be revoked any time by the surety by giving notice to the creditors. However, in both the cases, the revocation will apply to future transactions only.

A surety can be discharged of his obligations in the following manner:

- If any material change is done in the contract by the principal debtor and the creditor without the knowledge of the surety, the surety is discharged of his future obligations (Section 133).

> **Example** Rajiv contracts with Sunshine Hotels (creditor) for the supply of goods to the value of ₹100,000 within 12 months and Anuj stands surety for Rajiv (principal debtor). In case of default, Anuj (surety) will have to fulfil the contract on behalf of Rajiv. However, without the knowledge of Anuj (surety), Rajiv and Sunshine Hotels modify the contract value to ₹150,000. This modification in the contract discharges Anuj from standing surety for Rajiv.

- Any contract that results in the release of the principal debtor by the creditor discharges the surety of his obligations (Section 134).

> **Example** Rajiv contracts with Sunshine Hotels (creditor) for the supply of goods to the value of ₹100,000 within 12 months and Anuj stands surety for Rajiv (principal debtor). In case of default Anuj (surety) will have to fulfil the contract on behalf of Rajiv. Rajiv supplies goods worth ₹75,000 to the hotel. Subsequently, Sunshine Hotels (creditor) releases Rajiv (principal debtor) from his obligation to fulfil the remainder of the contract. This act on the part of the Hotel releases Anuj (surety) of his obligations.

- Any contract between the principal debtor and the creditor, where the creditor promises to give time or not to sue the principal debtor, discharges the surety of his obligations unless he agrees (Section 135).

Example Rajiv contracts with Sunshine Hotels (creditor) for the supply of goods to the value of ₹100,000 within 12 months and Anuj stands surety for Rajiv (principal debtor). In case of default Anuj (surety) will have to fulfil the contract on behalf of Rajiv. Rajiv supplies goods worth ₹75,000 to the hotel and subsequently Sunshine Hotels (creditor) gives time to Rajiv to fulfil the remainder of the contract value in excess of the contract period. Anuj (surety) stands automatically discharged of his obligations.

- If the creditor does an act that is inconsistent with the rights of a surety, or fails to do his duty to the surety as required of him, resulting in the impairment of the surety's rights against the principal debtor the surety is discharged (Section 139).

Example Rajiv contracts with Sunshine Hotels (creditor) for the supply of goods to the value of ₹100,000 within 12 months and Anuj stands surety for Rajiv (principal debtor). In case of default Anuj (surety) will have to fulfil the contract on behalf of Rajiv. Sunshine Hotels (creditor) without the knowledge of Anuj (surety) unilaterally cancels the contract with Rajiv thereby discharging the surety from his obligations.

Indemnity and surety are the most misconstrued and misunderstood aspects of contract law and the terms are synonymous in most people's minds. Table 4.1 highlights the four major differences between an indemnity and a surety.

TABLE 4.1 Differences between Indemnity and Surety

Indemnity	Surety
Between two persons: the indemnifier and the indemnified.	Between three parties: the surety, principal debtor, and the creditor.
Reimbursement of a loss.	For the security of the creditor.
Liability of the indemnifier is primary and arises when the event occurs.	Liability is secondary and arises when principal debtor defaults.
Upon discharge of his indemnity, has no legal rights against the third party.	Upon discharge of liability, steps into the shoes of the creditor and can sue the principal debtor.

BAILMENT AND PLEDGE

Bailment and pledge are by far the most common and frequent types of transactions that are entered into during the course of conducting business in a hotel. The French term *bailor* means to deliver, which implies that the possession of the property changes hands upon delivery without a change in ownership of the property.

The Indian Contract Act,1872 defines this transaction as bailment.

TEXT

Chapter 9—Section 148. 'Bailment' 'bailor' and 'bailee' defined. A 'bailment' is the delivery of goods by one person to another for some purpose, upon a contract that they shall, when the purpose is accomplished, be returned or otherwise disposed of according to the directions of the person delivering them. The person delivering the goods is called the 'bailor'. The person to whom they are delivered is called, the 'bailee'.

Bailment is the delivery of goods by one person to another for some purpose, upon a contract that they shall, when the purpose is accomplished, be returned, or otherwise disposed of according to the directions of the person delivering them.

Bailor is the person delivering the goods for safekeeping.

Bailee is the person accepting the goods for safekeeping.

Non-gratuitous bailment is when a charge for keeping the goods is levied.

Gratuitous bailment is when goods are kept without levying a charge.

Voluntary bailment is when a guest voluntarily hands over possession of his goods to the hotelier for custody.

Involuntary bailment is when the hotel comes into possession of misplaced, lost, or abandoned guest property as it has been found on the hotel premises.

It is the duty of the bailor to disclose to the bailee defects if any in the goods being handed over for safe custody and it is the duty of the bailee to exercise due care so that the goods do not get damaged whilst in his or her care. In case the bailee is required to do an act to preserve and maintain the goods, the bailor has to compensate the bailee the cost of getting the act done.

Example   Sagar has given his expensive Armani shirt to the 24 hours hotel laundry for dry cleaning. The laundry manager observes that the hemming of the shirt is frayed and two buttons are missing. The same is brought to the attention of the guest. The laundry manager offers to get the shirt repaired before dry cleaning it.

Due to an unforeseen emergency, Sagar has to check out of the hotel leaving the shirt behind in the care of the hotel. Upon his return, he is given the shirt, which has been repaired by the hotel and presented a bill of ₹500 for its repairs; this amount is payable by Sagar (bailor) to the hotel (bailee).

TEXT

Pledge   Section 172 of the Act defines 'Pledge' 'Pawnor' and 'Pawnee'

The bailment of goods as security for payment of a debt or performance of a promise is called 'pledge'. The bailor in this case is called the 'pawnor' and the bailee is called the 'pawnee'.

It is a practice followed by hotels to hold back guest belongings in case the guest does not settle his bills. This transaction is called pledging of goods by the guest as a security for payment. The hotel is entitled to recover interest along with the principal amount in case of inordinate delay in receiving the payment from the guest before returning the goods pledged.

If for any reason the guest fails to pay his dues at the appointed date and time, the hotel is entitled to dispose of the guest property to recover its dues. In the event that the sale proceeds are higher than the amount owed to the hotel, the balance shall be reimbursed to the guest and in case the proceeds partially satisfy the debt, then the guest is liable for the difference in amount.

Example Roy upon checkout owes an amount of ₹45,000 to the hotel and pledges his expensive Citizen watch and gold Parker pen as security until he discharges his debt. After waiting to receive the payment for four months, the hotel informs the guest that it shall be disposing his watch and pen to recover the outstanding dues of ₹45,000 along with interest. Both the items are sold for ₹33,000 leaving an outstanding balance amount of ₹12,000. Roy will have to pay this amount to fully discharge his debt.

  If, on the other hand, both these items had been sold for ₹60,000 then Roy's debt would have been fully discharged and the excess amount of ₹15,000 would be payable by the hotel to him.

Although there are various differences as illustrated in Table 4.2, essentially bailment is the transfer of property without transfer of ownership, whereas pledge is the transfer of ownership and property to the pawnee.

TABLE 4.2 Differences between Bailment and Pledge

Bailment	Pledge
Bailment can be non-gratuitous, gratuitous, voluntary, or involuntary.	A pledge is bailment done for a specific type of purpose, which is to secure a loan or to satisfy a debt.
The bailee does not get a right to sell the goods.	A pawnee has a right to sell the goods in case the debt is not settled.
The bailee only gets a right of lien over the goods.	A pawnee gets a right of retainer and a special interest in the goods, which is more than a lien.
The bailee can use the goods bailed.	The pawnee has no right to use the goods.
The bailee is not responsible for the loss, destruction, or deterioration if he uses the goods with reasonable care.	The pawnee is absolutely liable for the upkeep of the goods.

AGENCY

It is important for an hotelier to understand the role of an agent vis-à-vis the principal as most vendors that supply products to a hotel are agents of major companies:

- Some of the most common agency relationships are sole selling agents, subagents, commission agents, brokers, and so forth.
- When the hotel contracts with a sole selling agent, a subagent, or a commission agent, the hotel is in effect entering into a contract with the principal. The exception being that when the contract is with a subagent, it is binding on the agent and may not be binding on the principal, if the sole selling agent has not briefed the principal of the appointment.
- Inadvertently or due to oversight, in case defective material or a product whose shelf life has expired is delivered to the hotel and the sole selling agent, subagent,

or a commission agent fails to replace the product, the hotel has a right to claim against the principal to have the item replaced.

> **Example**   Qutab Hotel enters into a contract with XYZ Dairy for the supply of milk and milk products. XYZ Dairy directs Pawan, its agent, to deliver 50 litres of milk on a daily basis. For 15 days in the month of May, Pawan delivers 30 litres instead of 50 litres. The hotel cancels the purchase order by serving a notice to Pawan citing reasons of non-delivery of the required quantities by him. This cancellation of the contract is binding on XYZ Dairy.

Sole Selling Agent and Subagents

A sole selling agent is appointed by the principal, whereas a subagent is appointed by the sole selling agent, both of whom have a relationship with the principal and any lawful acts done by either of them are binding on the principal. The relationship between the agent and the principal is that of a buyer and a seller. Once the goods are purchased by the agent, he becomes the owner of the goods and upon selling it further to the hotel, the agent is entitled to his commission from the principal.

In case the appointment of the agent is revoked by the principal, then automatically the appointment of the subagent also stands cancelled.

Commission Agents

A commission agent operates on behalf of the principal and is entitled to his commission upon selling or consigning the goods that remain in the custody of the principal. The transaction is concluded when the goods are delivered.

TEXT

Section 182 of the Act defines an 'agent' and 'principal'. An 'agent' is a person employed to do any act for another or to represent another in dealings with third persons. The person for whom such act is done, or who is so represented, is called the 'principal'.

The Act further stipulates that any person who is a major and of sound mind can appoint an agent to represent him in dealings with third parties. No financial remuneration is payable to the agent to create an agency and the authority vested in the agent can be expressed, either orally or in writing or implied that is inferred by the actions of the principal towards the agent. Any lawful acts committed by the agent in the course of business are binding on the principal and in case he takes steps that any prudent person would to protect the business of the principal, the principal is bound to ratify the agent's actions.

Rights and Duties of an Agent (Sections 211–221)

- To conduct the business as per the directions of the principal
- To exercise reasonable care while conducting the business and in case a loss is suffered on account of his mistakes to make good the loss to the principal
- To maintain proper accounts of the business and pay all monies due to the principal

- In case there is an outstanding commission recoverable from the principal the agent can deduct the same before making payments to the principal or keep a lien on the goods of the principal for the recovery of his dues
- The principal has to give an imprest amount to the agent to enable him to conduct the business

Duties of the Principal Towards the Agent (Sections 222–225)

222. *Agent to be indemnified against consequences of lawful acts*
  The employer of an agent is bound to indemnify him against the consequences of all lawful acts done by such agent in exercise of the authority conferred upon him.

Example 1. Bhavesh, at Mumbai, under instructions from Ashok of Kolkata, contracts with the hotel to deliver 1000 sets of bedspreads and pillow slips. Ashok does not send the goods to Bhavesh, and the hotel sues Bhavesh for breach of contract. Bhavesh informs Ashok of the suit, and Ashok authorizes him to defend the suit. Bhavesh defends the suit, and is compelled to pay damages and costs, and incurs expenses. Ashok is liable to Bhavesh for such damages, costs, and expenses.

Example 2. Rakesh, a broker at Kolkata, by the orders of Sunil, a merchant there, contracts with the hotel for the purchase of 1000 kg of paper waste for Sunil. Afterwards he refuses to receive the paper waste, and the hotel sues Rakesh. Rakesh informs Sunil, who repudiates the contract altogether. Rakesh defends, but unsuccessfully, and has to pay damages and costs and incurs expenses. Sunil is liable to Rakesh for such damages, costs, and expenses.

223. *Agent to be indemnified against consequences of acts done in good faith*
  Where one person employs another to do an act, and the agent does the act in good faith, the employer is liable to indemnify the agent against the consequences of that act, though it may cause an injury to the rights of third persons.

Example 1. A, a decree-holder and entitled to execution of B's goods, requires the officer of the Court to seize certain goods, representing them to be the goods of B. The officer seizes the goods, and is sued by C, the true owner of the goods A is liable to indemnify the officer for the sum which he is compelled to pay to C, in consequence of obeying A's directions.

Example 2. B, at the request of A, sells goods in the possession of A, but which A had no right to dispose of B does not know this, and hands over the proceeds of the sale to A. Afterwards C, the true owner of the goods, sues B and recovers the value of the goods and costs A is liable to indemnify B for what he has been compelled to pay to C and for B's own expenses.

224. *Non-liability of employer of agent to do a criminal act*
  Where one person employs another to do an act which is criminal, the employer is not liable to the agent, either upon an express or an implied promise, to indemnify him against the consequences of that act.

Example 1. A employs B to beat C, and agrees to indemnify him against all consequences of the act. B thereupon beats C, and has to pay damages to C for so doing. A is not liable to indemnify B for those damages.

Example 2. B, the proprietor of a newspaper, publishes, at A's request, a libel upon C in the paper, and A agrees to indemnify B against the consequences of the publication, and all costs and damages of any action in respect thereof B is sued by C and has to pay damages, and also incurs expenses A is not liable to B upon the indemnity.

TEXT

225. *Compensation to agent for injury caused by principal's neglect*
   The principal must make compensation to his agent in respect of injury caused to such agent by the principal's neglect or want of skill.

Example A employs B as a bricklayer in building a house, and puts up the scaffolding himself. The scaffolding is unskilfully put up, and B is in consequence hurt. A must make compensation to B.

Effect of agency on contracts with third persons

As illustrated above, an agent is indemnified against consequences of lawful acts and acts done in good faith by the principal, and the principal has to compensate an agent for injury caused to him or her by his or her negligent act. However, the principal is not liable to condone the agent's criminal acts.

NEGOTIABLE INSTRUMENTS ACT, 1881

In the regular course of business, it is important that financial transactions are regulated to enable parties to effectively and efficiently discharge their obligations under contracts. The Negotiable Instruments Act, 1881 and the Negotiable Instruments (Amendment and Miscellaneous Provisions) Act, 2002 define negotiable instruments and the process for their discharge or encashment.

Negotiable Instrument

Negotiable instrument is a transferable signed document that promises to pay the bearer a sum of money at a future date or on demand and is transferable by way of delivery or by endorsement.

TEXT

Section 118: Presumptions as to negotiable instruments
   Until the contrary is proved, the following presumptions shall be made:

(a) *Of consideration—that every negotiable instrument was made or drawn for consideration, and that every such instrument, when it has been accepted, indorsed, negotiated or transferred, was accepted, indorsed, negotiated or transferred for consideration;*

(b) *As to date—that every negotiable instrument bearing a date was drawn on such date;*

(c) *As to time of acceptance—that every accepted bill of exchange was accepted within a reasonable time after its date and before its maturity;*

(d) *As to time of transfer—that every transfer of a negotiable instrument was made before its maturity;*

(e) *As to order of indorsements—that the indorsements appearing upon a negotiable instrument were made in the order in which they appear thereon;*

(f) *As to stamps—that a lost promissory note, bill of exchange or cheque was duly stamped;*

(g) *That holder is a holder in due course—that the holder of a negotiable instrument is a holder in due course: provided that, where the instrument has been obtained from its lawful owner, or from any person in lawful custody thereof, by means of an offence or fraud, or has been obtained from the maker or acceptor thereof by means of an offence or fraud, or for unlawful consideration, the burden of proving that the holder in due course lies upon him.*

A negotiable instrument is based on the presumptions that it has been adequately stamped, prepared on the date mentioned on it, and has been lawfully transferred to the drawee, who has accepted it before its date of maturity for the consideration amount mentioned on it the amount being payable only in money. In the event of endorsements on the instrument, it is presumed that the endorsements have been made in the order that they appear on the instrument.

Types of Negotiable Instruments

Under Section 13 of the Negotiable Instrument Act, 1881, a negotiable instrument means a 'promissory note, bill of exchange or cheque payable either to order or to bearer'.

Promissory note

4. A 'promissory note' is an instrument in writing (not being a bank-note or a currency-note) containing an unconditional undertaking signed by the maker, to pay a certain sum of money only to, or to the order of, a certain person, or to the bearer of the instrument.

Figure 4.3 is a sample of a promissory note commonly known as a pro-note, which is a written document, duly stamped under the provisions of the Indian Stamp Act, 1899. It is clear that there are two parties to a promissory note (i) the maker or drawer (Sanjiv Tayal) who has to pay (ii) the payee (Rajiv Sodhi) an amount of ₹10,000 on demand or on a certain date. A promissory note can be paid only in money and not in any other way. For example, Sanjiv Tayal cannot discharge his liability towards Rajiv Sodhi by buying him a watch costing ₹10,000.

₹10,000/-   Mumbai
12 April 2012

On demand, I promise to pay Rajiv Sondhi s/o Ramesh Sondhi R /o Nagpada, Mumbai or order a sum of ₹10,000/- (Rupees Ten Thousand Only) for value received.

To   (Signed)

Mr. Rajiv Sodhi   Sanjiv Tayal

Nagpada, Mumbai

Figure 4.3 Sample Promissory Note

Bill of exchange

5. A 'bill of exchange' is an instrument in writing containing an unconditional order, signed by the maker, directing a certain person to pay a certain sum of money only to, or to the order of, a certain person or to the bearer of the instrument.

A promise or an order to pay is not 'conditional', within the meaning of this Section and Section 4, by reason of the time for payment of the amount or any instalment thereof being expressed to be on the lapse of certain period after the occurrence of a specified event which, according to the ordinary expectation of mankind, is certain to happen, although the time of its happening may be uncertain.

The sum payable may be 'certain', within the meaning of this Section and Section 4, although it includes future indicated rate of change, or is according to the course of exchange, and although the instrument provides that, on default of payment of an instalment, the balance unpaid shall become due. The person to whom it is clear that the direction is given or that payment is to be made may be a 'certain person,' within the meaning of this Section and Section 4, although he is misnamed or designated by description only.

Figure 4.4 is a specimen 'bill of exchange' indicating that there are three parties to a bill of exchange—the drawer (Sanjiv Tayal) who authorizes the drawee (Suresh Kant) to pay a certain amount of ₹10,000 to the payee (Rajiv Sondhi) on 15 July 2012. A bill of exchange is only valid if the drawee signs the acceptance to unconditionally pay the amount and the document is duly stamped under the Indian Stamp Act, 1899. A cheque can also be regarded as a bill of exchange; however, the drawee in this case will always be a banker.

₹10,000/-   Mumbai
                                                 12 April 2012

On 15 July 2012 pay Rajiv Sondhi s/o Ramesh Sondhi R /o Nagpada,
Mumbai or to his order a sum of ₹10,000/- (Rupees Ten Thousand Only)
for value received.

To   (Signed as Accepted)   (Signed)
Rajiv Sondhi   Suresh Kant   Sanjiv Tayal

FIGURE 4.4   Specimen Bill of Exchange

Although both promissory note and bill of exchange are unconditional promises executed in writing duly stamped, yet they differ in some ways. Table 4.3 compares promissory note with bill of exchange highlighting the differences between them.

TABLE 4.3   Comparison between Promissory Note and Bill of Exchange

Promissory note	Bill of exchange
It is an unconditional promise.	It is an unconditional promise.
There are two parties—payer and payee.	There are three parties—drawer, drawee, and payee.
It is made by debtor.	It is made by creditor.
Acceptance is not required	Acceptance by the drawee is essential.
Liability of the payer is primary and absolute.	Liability of the drawer is secondary and conditional upon non-payment by the drawee.
It requires to be stamped.	It requires to be stamped.

6. A 'cheque' is a bill of exchange drawn on a specified banker and not expressed to be payable otherwise than on demand and it includes the electronic image of a truncated cheque and a cheque in the electronic form.

Explanation 1. For the purposes of this section, the expressions:

(a) 'A cheque in the electronic form' means a cheque which contains the exact mirror image of a paper cheque, and is generated, written and signed in a secure system ensuring the minimum safety standards with the use of digital signature (with or without biometrics signature) and asymmetric crypto system;

(b) 'A truncated cheque' means a cheque which is truncated during the course of a clearing cycle, either by the clearing house or by the bank whether paying or receiving payment, immediately on generation of an electronic image for transmission, substituting the further physical movement of the cheque in writing.

Explanation 2. For the purposes of this section, the expression 'clearing house' means the clearing house managed by the Reserve Bank of India or a clearing house recognised as such by the Reserve Bank of India.

Types of Cheques

The following are the various types of cheques:

Bearer cheque   This cheque can be enchased at the bank's issuing branch by any person who presents it over the counter or deposits it into an account, or is endorsed by the payee to a third party.

Post-dated cheque   Here, the date on the cheque is a later date than the date of issue. For example, if a cheque issued on 1 May 2011 is dated 10 May 2011, then the bank will issue payment for it only on 10 May 2011.

Ante-dated cheque   The date on the cheque is earlier than the date of issue, for example, a cheque issued on 10 May 2011 dated 1 May 2011.

Stale cheque or expired cheque   It is a cheque that has not been presented for payment for a period of three months from the date of its issue.

Mutilated cheque   A cheque that has been torn into pieces and if it is presented in such condition, payment shall not be made by the bank.

Crossed cheques   The Negotiable Instruments, Act 1881 makes specific provisions for the crossing of cheques under Sections 123, 124, and 130.

Cheque crossed generally   It is a cheque that bears across its face an addition of the words 'and company' or any abbreviation thereof, between two parallel transverse lines, or of two parallel transverse lines simply, either with or without the words 'not negotiable', that addition shall be deemed a crossing, and the cheque shall be deemed to be crossed generally (Section 123).

Cheque crossed specially   It is a cheque that bears across its face an addition of the name of a banker, either with or without the words 'not negotiable', that addition shall be deemed a crossing, and the cheque shall be deemed to be crossed specially, and to be crossed to that banker (Section 124).

Cheque bearing 'not negotiable' A person taking a cheque crossed generally or specially, bearing in either case the words 'not negotiable', shall not have, and shall not be capable of giving, a better title to the cheque than that which the person from whom he took it had. Thus, merely writing the words 'not negotiable' does not mean that the cheque is not transferable. It is still transferable, but the transferee cannot get title better than what transferor had (Section 130).

A valid cheque (Fig. 4.5) must have the following attributes—name of the banker, name of the party who has to receive the payment (the drawee), the amount written both in words and figures, the account number of the drawer and his signature, the individual cheque number, branch address, and finally the date of issue of the cheque.

ABCD Bank	Date: 10 March 2012
JVPD, Mumbai	
Pay__Santosh Kumar_____	or Bearer
Rupees Fifty Thousand Only	
A/C No: 12345678	₹50,000/-
	Signature
Payable at Par at all Branches of ABCD in India	
152298 987654321	345678

FIGURE 4.5 Specimen Cheque

Table 4.4 is a comparative chart listing the salient features of the most commonly used negotiable instruments in the course of business—cheques, bills of exchange, and drafts.

TABLE 4.4 Comparison between a Cheque, Bill of Exchange, and Draft

Cheque	Bill of exchange	Draft
It is drawn on a bank.	It is drawn on anyone including a bank.	It is drawn on a bank.
The amount is payable on demand.	The amount is payable on demand or within a specified period.	The amount is payable on demand.
It can be crossed to end its negotiability.	It cannot be crossed.	It can be crossed to end its negotiability.
Acceptance is not required.	Acceptance from the drawee is a must.	Acceptance is not required.
It is not required to be stamped under the Indian Stamp Act, 1899.	It is required to be stamped under the Indian Stamp Act, 1899.	It is not required to be stamped under the Indian Stamp Act, 1899.
Payment can be stopped.	Payment can be stopped.	Payment cannot be stopped.

Discharge of a Negotiable Instrument

According to Section 82 of the Negotiable Instruments Act, 1881—discharge from liability, the maker, acceptor, or endorser, respectively of a negotiable instrument, is discharged from liability thereon by the following.

By cancellation

By cancellation to a holder thereof who cancels such acceptors' or endorsers' name with intent to discharge him, and to all parties claiming under such holder.

> **Example** Sanjay gives a cheque of ₹50,000 dated 9 February 2010 to Rajiv. Rajiv cancels the cheque by crossing out Sanjay's name and signature. By this action, Rajiv has discharged Sanjay of his liability to pay him ₹50,000.

By release

By release to a holder thereof who otherwise discharges such maker, acceptor, or indorser, and to all parties deriving title under such holder after notice of such discharge. In common parlance a release letter is known as a 'no dues certificate'.

> **Example** Sanjay gives a cheque of ₹50,000 dated 9 February 2010 to Rajiv. Rajiv releases Sanjay of his liability to pay him ₹50,000 by signing a waiver letter confirming that Sanjay has no dues against him. In this case, Rajiv does not cancel Sanjay's name or signature on the cheque.

By payment

By payment to all parties thereto, if the instrument is payable to bearer, or has been indorsed in blank, and such maker, acceptor, or indorser makes payment in due course of the amount due thereon.

> **Example** Sanjay gives a cheque of ₹50,000 dated 9 February 2010 to Rajiv. Rajiv deposits the cheque with his bankers for collection. Upon receiving credit of this amount into his account, Sanjay is discharged of his liability.

By endorsement

Section 15 of the Negotiable Instruments Act 1881 defines indorsement. When the maker or the holder of a negotiable instrument signs the same, otherwise than as such maker, for the purpose of negotiation, on the back or face thereof or on a slip of paper annexed thereto, or so signs for the same purpose a stamped paper intended to be completed as a negotiable instrument, he is said to indorse the same, and is called the 'indorser'.

Types of endorsements The legal dictionary defines endorsement (or indorsement) as the act of the owner or payee signing his or her name to the back of a cheque, bill of exchange, or other negotiable instrument so as to make it payable to another or encashable by any person.

The process of endorsing a negotiable instrument is called indorsement; once this is completed the instrument has been endorsed. Partial and forged endorsements are invalid.

General indorsement   This is where the endorser signs his name only on the reverse of the cheque. This type of indorsement is also called endorsement in blank, which means that the negotiable instrument can be further indorsed by the holder of the instrument (Section 53).

> **Example**   Sanjay signs on the reverse of the cheque that he has received from Rajiv for ₹10,000 indorsing it to Aloke. Aloke in turn indorses it further to Sunder. When Sunder deposits the cheque, the amount of ₹10,000 gets credited to his account. Thereby Rajiv's liability towards Sanjay, Sanjay's liability towards Aloke, and Aloke's liability towards Sunder is settled.

Indorsement in full   This is where the endorser signs and adds the name of a person to be paid (Section 50). Section 55 permits the conversion of an indorsement in blank to an indorsement in full.

> **Example**   Sanjay signs on the reverse of the cheque that he has received from Rajiv for ₹10,000 by indorsing 'pay to Aloke' Aloke can further endorse it.

Conditional indorsement   This is the liability to be discharged upon the happening of an event.

> **Example**   Sanjay signs on the reverse of the cheque that he has received from Rajiv for ₹10,000 by indorsing 'without recourse' and gives it to Aloke. By doing this, Sanjay has absolved himself of any further liability.

Restrictive indorsement   This prohibits further negotiations and makes the amount payable to a specified person.

> **Example**   Sanjay signs on the reverse of the cheque that he has received from Rajiv for ₹10,000 by indorsing 'pay the amount to Aloke only'. Aloke cannot further endorse it and has to deposit it into his account.

By operation of law

A negotiable instrument is also discharged by operation of law under any of the following circumstances:

- By lapse of time, that is, when the claim is barred by the Limitation Act, 1963, for example, promissory note, bills of exchange have time limit of two years.
- By merger, that is, when the court passes a judgement against the endorser by merging the existing debt with the debt amount finalized by the court in its judgement.

- Under the law of insolvency, that is, when the acceptor, maker, or endorser are declared insolvent under the Provincial Insolvency Act, 1920, by an order of the Court.
- By delay in presenting the cheque within a reasonable time. If a cheque is not presented for payment within three months and there is a delay, the drawer cannot be held responsible. However, if the drawee suffers a loss due to bank failure, the drawer is discharged from his liability.

Steps to be Taken When a Cheque Gets Dishonoured

Managers accept cheques towards the settlement of dues from corporates, guests, airlines, travel agents, and so on. It is important to see that the cheques are properly made out in the name of the hotel and that there are no material alterations on it that may lead to the cheque being dishonoured by the bank. The Act specifies that the following constitute material alterations to a cheque—undated cheques, amount not matching in words and figures, and signature illegible or not matching. Besides material alterations the bank is legally bound to dishonour a cheque for the following lacunae:
- Legal order from the court attaching the account.
- Material alterations to the cheque, for example, amount not matching in words and figures, signature illegible or not matching.
- The cheque is mutilated.
- The drawer has issued a stop payment instruction.
- The bank receives notice of the drawer's death, insolvency or lunacy.
- The drawer's account has insufficient funds.
- The cheque is stale—that is, if presented for payment after lapse of three months from the date of issue.
- Notice to close the account has been served by the drawer on which the cheque is drawn.

A cheque must be issued to pay off the debt or liability. In case the cheque is dishonoured by the bank for insufficient funds in the account, Section 138 provides that a person shall be punishable with two years' imprisonment or with a fine. Once the hotel receives the dishonoured cheque from the bank with a covering memo stating insufficient funds, the hotel can serve a notice to the drawer informing him that he should make good the payment as the cheque issued by him has been dishonoured. If within 15 days no payment is received from the client, then a cause of action arises under Section 138 and the hotel can register a legal complaint on the 16th day but within 30 days.

BREACH OF CONTRACTS

A breach of contract occurs when one of the parties to a contract fails to act upon or perform on its commitment or promise as agreed in the contract. When a breach of contract occurs, the aggrieved party can claim for liquidated damages or seek performance under the Specific Relief Act, 1963, go in for arbitration under the Indian Arbitration and Conciliation Act, 1996, or go in for mediation.

Liquidated Damages

Liquidated damages are normally written into the contract, when the contract is being drawn up by the parties. In purchase contracts, it is normally mentioned that in the event a vendor or a supplier fails to deliver the produce as required by a hotel or if short delivery of the item ordered is done; the hotel has the right to purchase the product at the market price rate and debit the vendor the difference between the contract price and the market price.

Example   The hotel has a contract rate of ₹180 per kg for cottage cheese and orders 10 kg of cottage cheese. The supplier delivers 8 kg of cottage cheese, forcing the hotel to purchase from the open market the balance of 2 kg at a higher rate of ₹200 per kg. The hotel will debit the difference in price of ₹40 to the supplier as per contract.

Suit for Specific Performance

The Specific Relief Act, 1963 has provision under which the plaintiff can file a suit for specific performance in case there is a breach of contract.

The Specific Relief Act, 1963 (Section 10) stipulates that the specific performance of a contract is enforceable by the courts where:

(1) There exists no standard for ascertaining the actual damage caused by the non-performance of the act agreed to be done; or
(2) The act agreed to be done is such that compensation in money for its non-performance would not afford adequate relief.

On the other hand, specific performance of a contract that has been partially completed shall not be enforced by the courts in the following cases:

(1) *Where a party to a contract is unable to perform the whole of his part of it, but the part which must be left unperformed bears only a small proportion to the whole in value and admits of compensation in money, the court may, at the suit of either party, direct the specific performance of so much of the contract as can be performed, and award compensation in money for the deficiency.*

(2) *Where a party to a contract is unable to perform the whole of his part of it, and the part which must be left unperformed either—*
    (a) *forms a considerable part of the whole, though admitting of compensation in money; or*
    (b) *does not admit of compensation in money; he is not entitled to obtain a decree for specific performance; but the court may, at the suit of the other party, direct the party in default*

to perform specifically so much of his part of the contract as he can perform, if the other party—

(i) in a case falling under clause (a), pays or has paid the agreed consideration for the whole of the contract reduced by the consideration for the part which must be left unperformed and in a case falling under clause (b), pays or has paid the consideration for the whole of the contract without any abatement; and

(ii) in either case, relinquishes all claims to the performance of the remaining part of the contract and all right to compensation, either for the deficiency or for the loss or damage sustained by him through the default of the defendant.

(3) When a part of a contract which, taken by itself, can and ought to be specifically performed, stands on a separate and independent footing from another part of the same contract which cannot or ought not to be specifically performed, the court may direct specific performance of the former part.

Explanation   For the purposes of this section, a party to a contract shall be deemed to be unable to perform the whole of his part of it if a portion of its subject-matter existing at the date of the contract has ceased to exist at the time of its performance.

Example 1.   Centaur Hotel Juhu Beach has engaged Morani Fireworks for a fireworks display to celebrate the New Year's Eve function at the hotel. Morani Fireworks has contracted that they shall commence the fireworks display at midnight which will be for the duration of five minutes. The hotel is informed on 30 December by Morani Fireworks that they shall not be in a position to do the fireworks display for five minutes as contracted, but only for three minutes as they have not received adequate supply of fireworks from the factory. The hotel can sue for specific performance of the contract as the hotel stands committed to the New Year revellers that there will be a display for five minutes. The decision given in this case by the court will be called a 'judgement'.

Example 2.   At times, a breach of contract can occur for no fault of the hotel. For example, WC Event Management Company hosted a beauty pageant on 2 October 2009 and had booked the banquet space and rooms at QI Hotel in Udaipur. After the event, a cocktail dinner was hosted for the invitees by the hotel. It was the responsibility of the hotel to secure the necessary liquor licence to serve alcoholic beverages. As 2 October is a dry day in India when no alcoholic beverages could be served, the date of the function decided by the organizers resulted in a breach of contract on the part of the hotel.

Arbitration

Under the Indian Arbitration and Conciliation Act, 1996, arbitration is a process in which an independent, neutral arbitrator is appointed to resolve the dispute. Through a process of conciliation, the arbitrator plays a proactive role by suggesting various options or proposal for the settlement of the dispute to both the parties. The decision of the arbitrator which is binding on both is called an 'award'.

Example   Euphoria Hotels have a management contract with Keys Hotel to manage their hotel property. The owners of Euphoria Hotels construct and do the interiors of the hotel as per the guidelines and specifications given by the operator Keys Hotels. Once the hotel has been completed, the operator shows no enthusiasm to start the operations of the hotel as they have acquired the hotel plot on which they plan to construct their own property.

Euphoria Hotels initiates arbitration proceedings against it and the arbitrator gives an award that Keys Hotel should take over the property and commence operations as per the terms of management contract with Euphoria Hotels.

Mediation

Mediation is a dispute-solving process where a mediator is appointed with the consent of both the parties who is impartial, neutral, and unbiased to resolve the differences. The process is consensual and involves both the parties to the dispute presenting their viewpoints to the mediator who is knowledgeable about business matters and whose objective is to create a 'win–win' situation for both the parties. The decision of the mediator is called a 'settlement'.

Example   Orchid Hotels have a master contract with Schindler Lifts for the supply, installation, and maintenance of their lifts for all Orchid Hotels located across India. The maintenance clause in the contract reads 'Schindler maintenance service staff will attend to a complaint within eight hours of receiving the complaint from the hotel and will ensure that the lift is made operational within a reasonable period of time. In the event the lift is not made operational within 48 hours, Schindler Lifts will compensate the hotel at ₹2000 per day after the expiry of the 48-hour period.'

Orchid Hotels, Ahmedabad has made a claim against Schindler Lifts for an amount of ₹22,000 under this clause, as they had failed to repair one of the lifts of the hotel for a period of 11 days. Schindler, on the other hand, disputes the number of days that it was out of order.

In order to resolve the dispute, they appoint a mediator, who after hearing their viewpoints, gives a settlement that nine days' compensation is payable, which is agreeable to both the parties.

HOSPITALITY CONTRACTS

Special types of contracts that are peculiar to the hospitality industry are as follows:
- Group information sheet (GIS)
- Function prospectus—banquets
- Purchase contract
- Franchisee agreements
- Management contracts
- Technical services agreement (TSA)

These contracts can be classified broadly into three categories:

(i) Those that define the relationship between the hotel and the guests; for example, GIS and function prospectus—banquets

(ii) Those that define the relationship between the hotel and the vendor; for example, purchase contracts and lease deeds of hotel or shop

(iii) Those that define the relationship between the hotel owner and the operator; for example, franchise agreements, management contracts, and TSAs

Group Information Sheet

Group information sheet (GIS) is a contract between the hotel and the travel agent to provide accommodation and meals and any other services to the group during its stay at the hotel. It is governed by the Agreement on Code of Practice between FHRAI & IATO (2005) entered into between the Federation of Hotel and Restaurant Association of India (FHRAI) and Indian Association of Tour Operators (IATO).

The GIS is prepared by the front office giving details of the group movement for any given day, which is circulated internally to all the departments. A GIS has the following information—name of the group, time and date of arrival and departure, mode of transportation such as flight details or if travelling by coach, number of persons and their room requirements, single or double rooms, the group's meal plan, passenger rooming list giving the passport details in case the group members are foreigners, billing instructions such as room bill to travel agent collect extras directly from the guest, amount taken as advance and finally the name of the travel agent and the group coordinator or leader.

Function Prospectus—Banquets

A function prospectus is a signed contract between the hotel and the guests for conducting a banqueting event, listing details of the event, that is, date, time, venue, and type of function, minimum and maximum number of guests expected, rate being charged per guest, food and beverage menu (if alcohol is to be served then details of the temporary excise licence—L-20 is required in Delhi), set-up at the venue—conference, marriage, formal sit down, and so on, instructions for the decorators, mode of settlement—cash, cheque, or credit card, the amount taken as advance, and the guests' PAN card details. Any other special instructions such as wedding cake, bridal suite, bottle of champagne complimentary, and so on, are also included. This document is circulated to all the departments that are required to coordinate various tasks to ensure the success of the event.

Purchase Contract

A purchase contract specifies the goods or services that are required by the hotel from the vendor for a specific period at the agreed commercial terms indicating the quality parameters of the product or services; defining the place, time, and periodicity for the execution of the contract. The document further stipulates the grounds for termination and the dispute resolution mechanism.

Franchisee Agreements

Franchising as defined by the *Oxford Advanced Learner's Dictionary* 'is a formal permission given by a company to somebody who wants to sell its goods or services in a particular area'. In the past decade, franchising has assumed importance as a large number of developers have announced hotel projects pan India as a conscious strategic decision to diversify their business portfolios.

A standard franchisee agreement is signed between the owners and hotel franchising companies. The salient points that both the franchisee and the franchisor must adhere to are discussed subsequently.

Franchisee's (owner) responsibilities are as follows:

- Franchisee should construct the hotel as per the rules, regulations, and permissions granted to it by the local authorities. He or she should ensure that all permission to run the hotel is valid and current.
- Franchisee should take proper insurance to cover the property against fire and other hazards, employees, third-party liabilities towards guests, and so on.
- Franchisee should maintain the hotel equipment and structure, décor of the rooms, and public areas neat, clean, and welcoming at all times.
- Franchisee should make every effort to promote the hotel and increase its business through the central reservation system, trade fairs, and regional and local promotions.

Franchiser's (hotel operator) obligations are as follows:

- Franchiser should assist the owner by providing the hotels operating manuals, copy of rules and regulations for the planning and construction of back-of-the-house areas of the hotel.
- Franchiser should provide marketing support and sales promotion services through its reservation offices and marketing offices worldwide. He or she should list the hotel in the international hotel directory for worldwide circulation.
- Franchiser should carry out quality assurance inspections.
- Franchiser should establish standard accounting and reporting systems, record keeping systems as recommended by a property management system.

These points are similar to management contracts, as they spell out the duties and obligations of both the owner and the franchiser towards each other, and the terms and conditions of termination and dispute resolution.

Management Contracts

Management contracts are entered into by the owners as they lack the expertise to manage the hotels' operations themselves or are involved in multiple businesses or are hospitality funds investing in hotel projects and hence enter into an agreement with professional hotel-operating companies to manage them.

Management contract helps a new hotel property to establish an identity for itself by a tie-up with a recognized hotel brand; and gives it access to the brand's central reservation system, hotel operating systems, employee training inputs, and sales and marketing support through its international and domestic advertising campaigns, and guest recognition programmes. It makes available to the owner loans from financial institutions at preferred rates, which is based upon the brand's credibility and this in turn, influences the minds of potential investors who may be seeking to invest in sustainable hotel projects.

Management contracts are agreements that are signed between the owner of the property (hotel owner) and the operator (hotel operating company) handing over the operations of the hotel for a specific duration against the payment of the agreed management fee. The contract spells out the duties and obligations of both the owner and the operator towards each other, the terms and conditions of termination and dispute resolution.

Technical Services Agreement

A technical services agreement (TSA) is signed between the owner and the operator and forms a part of the management contract. The purpose of this agreement is to ensure that the hotel is built as per the standards and specifications of the brand and this involves the following:

- Recommending guest room specifications with interior design or decoration, furniture, fittings, and equipment (FF&E)
- Suggesting design of the projects facilities
- Recommending operating equipment and its suppliers
- Designing mechanical and electrical engineering layouts for back of the house
- Recommending property management information systems
- Attending regular development meetings with the owner and the prospective building consultants
- Training the staff
- Assisting in commissioning and handover

SUMMARY

The essential attributes of a valid contract, various types of contracts, and the subsequent modalities which ensure that the contract is performed successfully have been discussed in this chapter. Void and voidable contracts have been differentiated. Terms such as indemnity, guarantee, bailment and pledge, and surety have been clarified with examples. The relationship between an agent and the principal, and also their obligations towards each other have been discussed.

The chapter explained various types of negotiable instruments and went on to discuss the safeguards that a hotelier should take when accepting cheques from clients and the steps for handling cheques that have been dishonoured. The chapter also discussed the commonly entered contracts such as GIS and banquet function prospectus that define hotels' duties and obligations towards guests. The owner and operator relationship is defined either through a management contract or a franchisee agreement. The chapter highlighted that in case of a breach of contract remedies are available to either party to arrive at a dispute resolution through mediation, arbitration, and recourse to legal action for specific performance of the contract.

KEY TERMS

Proposal   Made when a person willingly agrees to do or not to do an action with the express intention of securing the assent of the other party for his or her action or inaction.

Acceptance of a proposal   Secured when the person to whom the proposal is made gives his or her consent. Upon acceptance of the proposal, it becomes a promise.

Promise   The acceptance of the proposal.

Promisor   The person making the proposal.

Promisee   The person accepting the proposal.

Consideration for the promise   The act of doing something or not doing something by the promisee on the behest of the promisor.

Agreement   Every set of promise or a promise for a consideration is an agreement.

Voidable contract   An agreement that is not enforceable by law or any contract that is enforceable at the instance of only one party.

Contracts   All agreements are contracts if they are made by the free consent of parties competent to contract, for a lawful consideration and with a lawful object, and are not hereby expressly declared to be void and are enforceable by law at the option of either of the parties.

Contract of guarantee   A contract to perform the promise, or discharge the liability, of a third person in case of his or her default. Once a surety is given it is co-extensive with the principal debtor and the consideration can be any promise or action done by the creditor that will benefit the principal debtor. The contract of guarantee can be either oral or in writing.

Contingent contract   Defined as a contract to do or not to do something, if some event, collateral to such contract, does or does not happen.

Surety   Person giving the guarantee.

Creditor   The person to whom the guarantee is given by the surety in case of default by the principal debtor.

Principal debtor   The third person for whom the guarantee is given by surety in case the creditor defaults.

Continuing guarantee   One that is given by the surety to cover multiple transactions. A continuing guarantee stands revoked upon the death of the surety and can be revoked anytime by the surety by giving notice to the creditors. However, in both the cases the revocation will apply to future transactions only.

Free consent   Implies that the parties must agree about the subject matter of the agreement in the same sense as it is proposed without any ambiguity at the same time, that is, a consensus ad idem.

Coercion   Threatening to commit any act forbidden by law or do an unlawful act of detaining or threatening to detain any property, with the intention of making a person enter into an agreement.

Undue influence   Where a person is in a position to dominate the will of another in order to secure an unfair advantage it is regarded as exercising of undue influence.

Voidable agreements   When consent to an agreement is caused by coercion, fraud, or misrepresentation, the agreement is a contract voidable at the option of the party whose consent was so obtained.

Novation   The substitution of a new contract between the same parties prior to the expiry of the existing contract; this discharges the obligation of both the parties under the old contract and results in a new contractual relationship.

Rescission   A discharge of both parties from the obligations of a contract by a new agreement made after the execution of the original contract but prior to its performance, that is, both the parties agree not to demand performance of the contract mutually, thereby discharging the original contract.

Waiver   Unilateral renunciation by one party to forego its rights against the other.

Remission   Every promisee may dispense with or remit, wholly or in part, the performance of the promisor made to him, or may extend the time for such performance, or may accept instead of it any satisfaction which he thinks fit.

Bailment   The delivery of goods by one person to another for some purpose, upon a contract that they shall, when the purpose is accomplished, be returned or otherwise disposed of according to the directions of the person delivering them.

Bailor   The person delivering the goods for safekeeping.

Bailee   The person accepting the goods for safekeeping.

Non-gratuitous bailment   When a charge for keeping the goods is levied.

Gratuitous bailment   When goods are kept without levying a charge.

Voluntary bailment   When a bailor voluntarily hands over possession of his or her goods to the bailee for custody.

Involuntary bailment   When the bailee comes into possession of misplaced, lost or abandoned bailor property as it has been found on the hotel premises.

Indorsement   The act of the owner or payee signing his or her name to the back of a cheque, bill of exchange, or other negotiable instrument so as to make it payable to another or encashable by any person.

Endorsement   A cheque, bill of exchange, or other negotiable instrument is indorsed so as to make it payable to another or encashable by any person.

Pledge   The bailment of goods as security for payment of a debt or performance of a promise.

Sole selling agent   Person appointed by the principal to conduct the business on his or her behalf.

Subagent   Person appointed by the sole selling agent.

Principal   Can appoint an agent to conduct the business on his or her behalf provided he is a major of sound mind.

Negotiable instrument   A transferable signed document that promises to pay the bearer a sum of money at a future date or on demand and is transferable by way of delivery or by endorsement.

Promissory note   Also called a pro-note is an instrument in writing (not being a bank-note or a currency-note) containing an unconditional undertaking signed by the maker, to pay a certain sum of money only to, or to the order of, a certain person, or to the bearer of the instrument.

Bill of exchange   An instrument in writing containing an unconditional order, signed by the maker, directing a certain person to pay a certain sum of money only to, or to the order of, a certain person or to the bearer of the instrument.

Cheque   A bill of exchange drawn on a specified bank payable on demand and includes a cheque in the electronic form or an electronic image of a truncated cheque.

Post-dated cheque   One where the date on the cheque is later than the date of issue.

Ante-dated cheque   One where the date on the cheque is earlier than the date of issue.

Crossed cheque   A cheque crossed by two transverse parallel lines across its face at the top left hand corner.

Stale cheque or expired cheque   A cheque that has not been presented for payment for a period of three months from the date of its issue.

Mutilated cheque   A cheque that has been torn into pieces and if it is presented payment shall not be made by the bank.

Breach of contract   Occurs when one of the parties to a contract fails to act upon or perform on its commitment or promise as agreed in the contract.

EXERCISES

Define the Following
1. Waiver
2. Continuing guarantee
3. Bailee
4. Surety
5. Pledge
6. Stale cheque
7. Indorsement
8. Negotiable instrument
9. Antedated cheque
10. Novation

Concept Review Questions
1. What types of contracts require stamping and registering under the Indian Registration Act, 1902?
2. What is the remedy available to a purchase manager in the event of short supply of goods by a vendor? Explain with examples.
3. What are the differences between an award, a settlement, and a judgement?
4. What are quasi-contracts? Explain by giving examples.
5. What is the purpose of a technical services agreement?

Critical Thinking Questions
1. How do hotels resolve various contractual disputes without having to approach the legal system for their redressal?
2. A banquet function prospectus is a contract between a guest and a hotel. What are the essential elements present in the function prospectus that qualifies it as a valid contract?

Research Questions
1. Are management contracts and franchisee agreements impartial and fair towards hotel owners and developers? Evaluate.
2. What aspect of the hospitality business does the contract 'Agreement on Code of Practice between FHRAI & IATO' regulate?

Project
1. Review the various remedies available to solve disputes and recommend to hoteliers the best option that can secure a speedy resolution to a contentious issue.

REFERENCES

Ashok Sharma, *Business Law* (FK Publications, New Delhi, 2010) <http://books.google.co.in/books?id=aRnqGWX BMbQC&dq=a+contract+is+an+%E2%80%9Cagreeme nt+creating+and+defining+obligations+between+the+p arties.%E2%80%9D&source=gbs_navlinks_s> accessed on 1 April 2012.

J. Beatson, *Anson's Law of Contract*, reviewed by Peter MacFarlane (28th edn, Oxford University Press, UK, 2002) <http://www.paclii.org/journals/fJSPL/vol07no2/8. shtml> accessed on 1 April 2012.

Edwin Peel and GH Treital, *Treitel on the Law of Contract*, (Sweet and Maxwell, London, UK, 2012).

Guenter Treitel, *Treitel on the Law of Contract (11th edition)* (Sweet & Maxwell, London, 2003) <http://www.law. ox.ac.uk/profile/treitelg>.

<http://www.arbitrationindia.com/pdf/mediation_india.pdf> accessed on 1 April 2012.

<http://www.clatadda.com/uploads/8/3/4/2/8342076/ legal_dictionary.pdf> accessed on 1 April 2012.

<http://www.e-lawresources.co.uk/Smith-v-Hughes-(1871). php> accessed on 1 April 2012.

<http://www.hanumant.com/index.php/academics/law-notes/10-law-of-contracts-ii-bailment-pledge-agency-etc.html> accessed on 1 April 2012.

<http://kanwarn.wordpress.com/2010/11/25/indemnity-under-indian-contract-act-1872-part-2/> accessed on 1 April 2012.

<http://www.lawyersnjurists.com/resource/articles-and-assignment/all-contracts-are-agreements-but-all-agreements-are-not-contracts-explain-the-statement/> accessed on 1 April 2012.

<http://legal-dictionary.thefreedictionary.com/ indorsement> accessed on 1 April 2012.

<http://legal-dictionary.thefreedictionary.com/ Rescission+of+contract> accessed on 1 April 2012.

<http://www.legalflip.com/Article.aspx?id=74&pageid=375> accessed on 1 April 2012.

<http://www.vakilno1.com/bareacts/negoinstruact/ chapter6/s81.htm> accessed on 1 April 2012.

<http://www.vakilno1.com/bareacts/negoinstruact/ negoinstruact.htm> accessed on 1 April 2012.

Hotel Licences and Regulations

LEARNING OBJECTIVES

After going through this chapter, the reader will be familiar with the following:

- Developmental role of the district administration in the planned growth of cities
- Concessions given to the hospitality industry during project stage
- Process of securing permissions and licences to develop hotels
- Process of managing the transition from project to operations stage

INTRODUCTION

A revolutionary step in the history of mankind was the shift from a nomadic existence to an agrarian society. Farming made it possible for people to grow their own food and to settle in communities which were located close to rivers, streams, or areas that received regular rainfall. These communities or villages supported a growing population consisting of farmers, artisans, and skilled workers such as masons, carpenters, ironmongers, traders, and merchants. To sustain themselves, people studied the various seasons that would determine the planting and harvesting of crops, as this was the mainstay of the economy. Ancient Indian cities had aqueducts to channelize water to the homes, an effective drainage system, and well-planned streets and had buffer zones segregating residential areas from commercial areas. Ancient India was an agrarian society with towns developing around a group of villages where the villagers could gather to exchange their produce. This hub-and-spoke arrangement was instrumental in villages evolving into towns that were well connected with other hubs, along well-established trade routes.

During the British rule, the existing hub-and-spoke arrangement was further developed and strengthened leading to the establishment of district headquarters, which exercised administrative control over the villages and towns in the district. The first district of Calcutta was established by the British in 1690 on land that was given by the Mughal Emperor, and the last few districts acquired after the Sikh War of 1849 were Amritsar, Rohtak, and Gurdaspur. Warren Hastings in 1772 established the office of the district collector in each district as its administrative head. The role of the district magistrate or the district collector was threefold— first, to maintain law and order, dispense justice; second, to collect taxes from the residents; and third, to oversee the development of the district.

Road and rail connectivity was established between military cantonments that were established at towns that were strategically located, pilgrimage centers that were historically important, and commercially important towns.

In popular destinations for recreation and leisure activities (such as hill stations and beach resorts), development was encouraged. Upon India's independence in 1947, the established structure of administration continued to be followed.

The establishment of city states eventually led to the growth of large urban agglomerates; it became imperative for governments to control urbanization by imposing various types of fees and levies upon the development activities being undertaken. Land is a limited resource and its use is required to be regulated. This process of regulating activities by drawing up a master plan is called zoning. This is achieved by the government by drawing up a master plan for an area, allocating parcels of lands for various purposes and activities. A master plan ensures that any development work being undertaken contributes towards the well-being of the community. Today, there is hardly any city in India that does not have a master plan for its future development.

A master plan is a blueprint that lays down the long-term development strategy and is prepared by the government that demarcates land based on the principle of separation into various parcels according to its proposed usage; for example, agricultural, residential, commercial, mixed use, institutional, and industrial, as certain activities are incompatible with each other.

The Census of India 2011 determines the classification of cities in India based upon the population of the city, available infrastructure, cost of living index, and so on. This government classification is important as it is used to determine house rent allowance and city compensatory allowance of government servants, and ready-reckoner rates that impact taxation of property. Broadly, cities are classified into Tier-I, Tier-II, Tier-III cities, and Class 'C' towns.

An urban agglomeration is defined as a continuous urban spread constituting a town and its adjoining outgrowths or two or more physically contiguous towns together with or without outgrowths of such towns. Some of the important urban agglomerations are Greater Mumbai, Delhi NCR, and Kolkata; these three cities are also classified as mega cities by the Indian census of 2011 as they have a population of more than 10 million. Hyderabad, Bangalore, and Chennai are also urban agglomeration, but not classified as mega cities. Along with Mumbai, Delhi, and Kolkata, these three cities are also commonly referred to as Tier-I cities.

We have secondary cities that may or may not be urban agglomerates with a population of a million and are known as Tier-II cities. These include Ahmedabad, Surat,

Nagpur, Pune, Jaipur, Lucknow, Kanpur, Vijayawada, Patna, Rajkot, Baroda, Bhopal, Indore, Nasik, Jabalpur, Jamshedpur, Dhanbad, Faridabad, Cochin, Madurai, Meerut, Agra, and Allahabad.

Towns with a population of more than 1,00,000 are classified as Class-I towns and also known as Tier-III cities, for example, Jamnagar, Jammu, Kurnool, Roorkee, Dehradun, Vellore, Belgaum, and so on. Finally, there are towns with a population of less than 1,00,000 also known as Class 'C' towns such as Jangipur, Asansol, Durgapur, Renukoot, Sultanpur, Khurja, Hathras, Bulandshahr, Haridwar, Sivakasi, Coonoor, and Neyveli.

Another aspect that needs to be considered is that in different states the unit of measurement of land varies. In Punjab, it is *kanal* or 605 sq. yds; *marla* or 30.25 sq. yds; in Uttar Pradesh and Rajasthan, it is *biswa* or 151.25 sq. yds and *bigha* or 3,025 sq. yds; in Uttrakhand it is *kila* or 4,840 sq. yds. When a sale deed is being executed, the land area should be mentioned in both the local unit as well in an acceptable unit such as sq. yds or sq. ft to ensure transparency in the transaction.

To encourage tourism-related activities such as amusement and entertainment centres, hotels, convention centres, and so on, city planners incorporate them in the planning stage into the city's master plan. This is done as tourism activities contribute substantially towards the government's valuable foreign exchange kitty. In view of this, hotel development is monitored by central and state laws, which regulate various aspects of the hotel and restaurant business right from purchase of the land, planning for the hotel's construction till it is commissioned. To secure the requisite licences or permissions for hotel development, at each stage the developer has interactions with various government regulatory bodies or agencies either at the central, state, or municipal level. Broadly, hotel development activities can be divided into two stages:

Project stage   Licences and permissions which are required prior to the commencement of the project and during the construction of the project.

Operations stage   Licences and permissions which are required closer to the completion and commencement of the hotel.

PROJECT STAGE

Developing a hotel is a highly capital-intensive activity with a long gestation period before the developer gets a return on his investments. Currently, there is an immense shortage of quality accommodation in India. The government estimates a current room shortage in the mid-market segment to be 1,50,000 rooms, while the industry estimates pegs the room requirement at 75,000 rooms. Today, the total number of rooms available in India is less than the rooms available in the cities of Shanghai, London, and New York.

In order to encourage hotel development, central and state governments announce various incentives from time to time. The Federation of Hotels and Restaurants

Association of India (FHRAI) has compiled a list of the concessions currently available to hoteliers. This could be in the form of a subsidy or an outright financial grant, a tax holiday for five years, land parcels on lease, a public–private partnership to develop a hotel on prime public land, and so on.

A large number of states have declared tourism as an industry. This automatically gives hotels in those states access to finance from banks at favourable interest rates for period of nine years instead of seven, including a moratorium for the first year. States that have declared tourism as an industry are: Haryana, Himachal Pradesh, Karnataka, Maharashtra, Kerala, Uttarakhand, Assam, Uttar Pradesh, West Bengal, Arunachal Pradesh, Gujarat, Assam, Pondicherry, Lakshadweep, Daman and Diu, Mizoram, Orissa, Sikkim, Manipur, Tripura, Jharkhand, and Jammu and Kashmir.

Some of the benefits that are given by the central and state governments are listed as follows:

- Subsidy up to 60 per cent against the insurance premium for the first two years.
- Subsidy on consultant fee for the preparation of the project report between 50 and 75 per cent.
- Manpower development and training subsidy up to 50 per cent or ₹3000 per trainee, whichever is higher, provided the trainee is trained in a government-recognized institute.
- Sales-tax waiver for a period of five years from the date of commencement of hotel operations or exemption from building or property tax.
- In states where tourism has been declared an industry, the hotel enjoys water at concessional charges for the first three years of operations.
- The hotel enjoys partial reimbursement of electrical expenses for the first five years of operations.
- The hotel is given a subsidy on the purchase of diesel generator (DG) sets.
- Exemption on electricity duty on the power generated by a hotel using DG sets.
- Reimbursement of transport charges on the shipment of plant and machinery from the place of manufacture to the place of installation on actual cost of transportation or waiver of octroi for a period of three years.
- Priority in the allotment of building materials cement, iron and steel, and so on.
- Allotment of land parcels at a premium or at industrial rates or long-term lease.
- Land for construction of hotels is given a 25 per cent subsidy against the acquisition costs.
- Concession in the import of equipment under the Export Promotion Capital Goods (EPCG) scheme.
- 25 per cent outright subsidy on capital investments in the hotel project including land, cost of construction, plant and machinery, equipment, and so on.
- Subsidy on the purchase of Furniture, Fixtures and Equipment (FF&E), the percentage of subsidy varies from state to state.

- Five-year tax holiday for new hotels in the two-star, three-star, and four-star categories located in all UNESCO-declared world heritage sites (excluding Mumbai and Delhi) for hotels that become operational by 31 March 2013.
- Delinking of hotels from the commercial real-estate category by the Reserve Bank of India enables hotels to secure loans from banks at lower interest rates.

In spite of the various concessions given by the government to encourage the growth of hotels across India, one of the most challenging tasks is to acquire a parcel of land that is suitable for the development of a hotel. Location, location, and location is the often repeated mantra for identifying hotel sites.

Besides location, other factors that have to be considered are the price, clarity in the ownership of the title, permitted land use, existing infrastructure in and around the site, for example, access roads, sewers and drains, streets lights, electrical and water supply, and so on. Clarity in the ownership of the title is important as any parcel of land with a defective title where the ownership is disputed will hamper the acquisition process. Curing defective titles is a cumbersome process and can completely derail a project.

Hotel, being a commercial activity, can only be developed on a plot that is earmarked for commercial activities or mixed use in the master plan. In certain states such as Delhi NCR, the government has well-defined commercial areas where plots of land are earmarked for hotel development. These hotel sites are auctioned and leased by the government to the highest bidder. Most hoteliers prefer to bid for such sites, as once the plot is registered in their company's name, development activity can be undertaken without any delay.

Most of the hotel development is currently taking place in Tier-I and Tier-II cities ranging from five-star hotels to three-star hotels. However, hotel developers are gradually moving into Tier-III cities and 'C' class towns as well. Class 'C' towns are the future for the growth of the hospitality industry. Because of affordable land rates, it is recommended that limited service hotels, for example, three-star hotels should be built in the emerging towns.

In some of the Tier-III cities and Class 'C' towns, a city master plan may not exist or the categorization of the land parcels has not been done as commercial, mixed use, and so on. In such cities, the developer will have to get the land use changed to commercial by applying to the local municipal corporation, which is a time-consuming process. Normally, when change of land use is permitted, the plot is initially made N/A (not applicable), implying that the current land use does not apply to the land and subsequently changed to commercial.

Once a land parcel has been identified, due diligence completed, legal formalities of getting the parcel of land registered in the name of the company has to be completed. Being an immovable property, registration is compulsory under the Indian Registration Act, 1908 and the documents have to be stamped as per the requirements of the Indian Stamp Act, 1899. The registration process requires the company to deposit the requisite registration fee and stamp duty which is computed using the ready reckoner.

Due diligence is the process conducted by the lawyers of the intending purchaser to ascertain the marketability of the title. This requires checking for any kind of encumbrances such as the seller having pledged the property to secure a loan, encroachments on the land, the authenticity of the seller's title to the land, and the approximate value of the land.

Ready reckoner has been defined by *Oxford Dictionaries Online* as 'a book or table listing standard numerical calculations or other kinds of information presented formulaically'. These rates are updated by the government from time to time and are used for the valuation of properties, payment of stamp duty, and registration charges.

The next step is securing building permissions or a building permit from the local municipal corporation. When applying for a building permit, hotel developers are generally required to submit the following documents to the municipal bodies:

- Proof of ownership of the land, for example, sale deed or lease deed along with location and site plans. In case the land has been leased, a copy of the no objection certificate (NOC) from the lessor authorizing the lessee to develop the plot. The NOC from the lessor also assists the hotel developer in securing a loan from the bank, provided it is a long-term lease in excess of 25 years.
- Copy of valid registration certificate from the architect, engineer, structural engineer, and plumbing engineer appointed to execute the project.
- Layout plans indicating the footprint of the building, parking facilities, and landscaping layout certified by the architect and the owner.
- Approval of height clearance from the Airport Authority of India, in case the project is located close to the airport. The maximum height normally permitted is 35 metre for hotel projects that are not located in close proximity to airports.
- Approval from the electricity department confirming that the structural drawings conform to the laid-down electrical safety standards prior to sanctioning the electrical load.
- Approval of drawings from the water department outlining the water storage tank location and capacity, location of the water metre room, and so on. Based on this information, availability of water for the proposed project is confirmed.
- NOC from the traffic department of the police authorizing vehicles carrying construction materials or construction debris to ply when there is least traffic on the roads and that construction materials or construction debris will not be stored on public roads.
- NOC from the Chief Controller of Explosives for the installation of storage tanks and transportation of liquefied petroleum gas (LPG), high speed diesel (HSD), and furnace oil.
- Permission from the electricity department under the Electricity Act, 2003 and Indian Electricity Rules, 1956 for the installation of DG sets in the hotel.

- Permission from the Chief Inspector of Boilers, if the heating surface of the boiler is more than 49 sq. metres. The drawings should indicate the location of the boiler in the building and highlight the safety measures that are being taken.
- Clearance under Urban Land Ceiling Act confirming that the plot is not under acquisition or has any restrictions placed on it. The Act has since been repealed by the government.
- Partial NOC from the Chief Fire Officer certifying that the hotel plans adhere to all the statutory fire requirements such as installation of fire risers, sprinklers, smoke detectors, fire alarms, fire control room, fire extinguishers at predetermined locations in the building, refuge floors, fire exit staircase, and so on.
- Clearance from the Pollution Control Board certifying that the hotel plans conform to its requirements; for example, installation of sewage treatment plants (STP) for the treatment of black water, DG set shall be provided with proper noise mufflers to reduce noise pollution, and provision for rainwater harvesting.
- In case a basement is being proposed, then an indemnity bond has to be submitted to the municipal corporation that no excavation shall be carried out beyond the boundary of the plot. Any damage occurring during or due to the excavation to public sewers, water pipes, drains, and adjacent structures shall have to be repaired and made good by the hotel developer.
- Affidavit confirming that no storage of construction material or debris shall be done on any public road or public property and shall be removed promptly.
- Undertaking that the construction shall not violate the building permission being granted by the corporation [Intimation of Disapproval (IOD) and Commencement Certificate (CC)]. In case of violations, the corporation is at liberty to demolish the unauthorized construction. Any demolition activity that the corporation will undertake will be at the cost of the hotel developer.
- Environment impact assessment or study (EIS) is required under the Coastal Regulation Zone regulations for projects being undertaken in coastal, eco fragile, or sensitive areas. An environment impact study attempts to provide information regarding: (i) the impact of the proposed project on the physical, social, and economic environment; (ii) the short-term versus long-term effects of the proposed project; (iii) lists any unavoidable adverse environmental effects; and finally (iv) any irreversible damage that the project will have on the environment. In brief, the purpose of an environment impact study is to evaluate the impact that a proposed development will have on the local environment of the area.
- Project approval from the Department of Tourism indicating the star category of the hotel. This enables the developer to apply for concessions under the various incentive schemes of the government especially, the Import Export Code (IEC) which is must for securing an EPCG licence or to import under an Open General Licence (OGL).

Once an IOD and a CC are granted by the municipal corporation, it is implied that the hotel will leave the necessary setbacks that are required to be left, will adhere to the height restrictions imposed on it, and will not exceed the sanctioned Floor Space Index (FSI), unless the hotel has purchased additional FSI through the Transfer of Development Rights (TDR) route.

Setback in a building is the area left between the building footprint and the boundary wall by the developer to enable the circulation of air and light in the premises. It also serves the purpose of providing circulation space for the movement of vehicles, fire tenders, and so on. These areas are usually landscaped adding to the aesthetics of the building.

FSI or Floor Area Ratio (FAR) is the ratio of construction that is permitted in relation to the street area where the plot is situated. It is also referred as buildable area and applies only to buildable plots. The method of calculating FSI or FAR is the same all over the country.

> **Example**   In Mumbai's C Ward, the area under roads is less and the area available for construction is higher: 71% buildable, 29% streets (making for a plot factor of 2.4). Once the FSI factor has been determined, it is multiplied with the plot size to determine the buildable area.
>   Plot size: 10,000 sq. ft; FSI: 2.4; total buildable area: 10,000 × 2.4 = 24,000 sq. ft

Barron's Dictionary of Real Estate Terms defines 'area' as a two-dimensional space defined by boundaries; for example, sanctioned areas, buildable area, built-up area, carpet area, and super built-up area, covered area, and sellable area. It is important to understand the difference between these terms.

Sanctioned area or buildable area is the area approved by the corporation that can be built by the developer. It is also referred to as buildable area, for example, 24,000 sq. ft in the example given above.

Built-up area is the actual area built by the developer against the sanctioned area for example, out of the sanctioned 24,000 sq. ft, in case the hotel developer builds only 15,000 sq. ft, this will be known as built-up area.

Carpet area on the other hand is the actual usable space available for occupation in the building; it excludes the thickness of the walls, shafts, common areas, and so on.

Super built-up area or sellable area is the area that includes the carpet area plus the thickness of the walls, shafts, terraces, lifts and stairs, and so on. It is normally 30 per cent more than the carpet area in residential projects and may go as high as 50 per cent; for example, if the built-up area is 24,000 sq. ft, the super built-up area at the rate of 30 per cent will be 31,200 sq. ft.

Covered area is the ground area covered immediately above the plinth level by the building but does not include the space covered by garden, rockery, well and well structures, plant nursery, water pool, swimming pool (if uncovered), platform around a tree, tank, fountain, bench, *chabutra* with open top and unenclosed on sides by walls and the like; drainage culvert, conduit, catch-pit, gully-pit, chamber, gutter and the like; and compound wall, gate, slide/swing door, canopy, and areas covered by *chajja* or similar projections and staircases which are uncovered and open at least on three sides and also open to sky.

Traditionally, the right to develop a parcel of land could not be separated from the land itself. TDR is a new concept in development. It separates the right to develop a parcel of land from the land itself. This is how the concept works: suppose there is a parcel of agricultural land which has good fertile soil, developing it would impact its utility. In such cases, the government would allow the parcel to continue to be retained as agricultural land and would transfer the development right attached to the agricultural land to an urban area. The farmer would be able to sell this TDR to any developer who develops commercial or residential properties in an urban area. After purchasing TDR, the developer can enhance the FSI that he can build on his parcel of land in the urban area. This is a win–win situation for both the developer and the farmer. The price of TDR is determined by the prevailing ready-reckoner rate of the location where it is going to be used.

The National Building Code (NBC) 2005 formulated by the Bureau of Indian Standards (BIS) is a comprehensive document providing guidelines for regulating the building construction activities across the country. The Code contains administrative regulations, development control regulations (DCRs), general building and fire safety requirements; stipulations regarding building and structural design, electrical and plumbing services, and safety standards to be followed during construction.

Depending upon the state that the hotel project is being executed, the hotel developer will have to adhere to the development norms laid down by the state.

Example Under the Maharashtra Development Control Regulation, 1991, certain areas were designated FSI-free areas such as basements, balconies, fire exit staircases, fire refugee floors, and shafts. With the passing of the Maharashtra Development Control Regulation, 2011, these areas will now be counted towards FSI. To compensate for the loss of FSI-free areas for commercial developments, Maharashtra government has agreed to sanction additional 20% as fungible FSI. Fungible FSI would be available at 60%, 80%, and 100% of the ready-reckoner rates for residential, industrial, and commercial construction, respectively. For hotels, 20% fungible FSI would be available at a premium of 80% of the ready-reckoner rate as hotel is categorized as an industry in Maharashtra. Purchasing fungible FSI increases the cost of developing hotels to go up in the state of Maharashtra, and it can be used to develop additional habitable space in commercial projects being redeveloped.

The architect, interior design consultants, heating ventilation and air-conditioning engineers, mechanical and electrical consultants, plumbing consultants, structural engineers have to complete the *construction drawings* for the hotel. *Construction drawings* consist of the *blueprint of the hotel*, which is a series of drawings showing the layout of the parts of the building. The complete set of blueprints consists of the following:

(i) *Plot and survey drawings* delineate the legal boundaries of the plot.
(ii) *Contour plans* that give a graphical representation of the land parcel.

(iii) *Floor plans* that are drawn to scale giving a bird's eye view or a horizontal perspective of the various spaces on a given floor such as rooms, corridors, lift locations, shafts, and so on.

(iv) *Elevation drawings,* as the name suggests, give a view of a building as seen from one side and is used to describe the external appearance or façade of a building.

(v) *Perspective* gives a three-dimensional view of the building.

(vi) *Cross section or simply section drawings* give a vertical perspective and highlight the relationship between different levels of a building.

(vii) *Mechanical drawings or technical drawings* enable dimensions and measurements to be taken giving details of the plumbing, sewage, electrical, TV cabling, telephone wiring, AC ducting, and hot and cold water supply system details.

Simultaneously, site development has to be undertaken prior to commencing construction. This involves demarcating the boundary of the plot, soil testing, mapping the contours of the land, levelling the land parcel, marking of the building footprint and driveways, landscaping, installation of the electrical power load, water connection, constructing temporary buildings and facilities, and so on. Upon completion of the site development, it is mandatory for the developer to give a notice to the municipal corporation advising them of his intent to commence construction. The municipal corporation grants permission to the developer by issuing an IOD and CC.

IOD is a letter approving the project, authorizing the development subject to the restrictions mentioned in the approval letter, whereas a CC permits the developer to commence construction activities on the plot of land subject to the IOD. Generally, the IOD and CC are given simultaneously by the corporation. In certain states, IOD is not required and a CC issued by the corporation is the only document required by the hotel developer to commence construction.

These permissions suffice only till the construction of the plinth level. The free dictionary.com defines: 'The plinth usually rests directly on the ground'. 'A plinth is the base or platform upon which a column, pedestal, statute, monument or structure rests'.

Once the plinth level is reached, the grid of the building, consisting of columns and beams upon which the entire load of the building will rest, is completed. Once the construction starts, it takes approximately 12–18 months for the hotel structure to be completed. An NOC from a qualified structural engineer certifying that the building's structural design meets all the safety standards, that the materials used, the workmanship, and the methodology employed for construction work are of accepted standards so as to protect the building from natural hazards such as earthquakes, hurricanes, tornadoes, landslides, and floods is submitted to the municipal corporation. During the last six to eight months of the project, the interior design team and the operations teams coordinate the final finishing of the hotel to make it operational.

The project team initiates the process for securing a partial completion certificate (PCC) from the municipal corporation. As the name suggests, a PCC issued by the municipal authorities certifies that the hotel structure has complied with all the requirements laid down in the IOD and CC, has fulfilled all the norms outlined in the NBC 2005. In order to secure a PCC, the developer has to obtain NOCs from all the agencies that have been listed earlier. Table 5.1 highlights the various certificates required to be submitted to secure a PCC.

TABLE 5.1   Certificates Required for Partial Completion Certificate

Approval Details
• Structural Engineer's Stability Certificate
• Architect's Supervision Certificate
• NOC from Airport Authority of India
• NOC from Chief Fire Officer
• NOC from Chief Engineer Electrical, Department of Electricity
• NOC from Inspector Of Lifts, Department of Electricity
• Drainage Completion Certificate (Storm water drains)
• Drainage Completion Certificate (Sewage)
• Rainwater Harvesting Completion Certificate
• Successful Installation of STP Certificate
• Boiler Inspection Certificate under The Indian Boilers Act, 1923 and the Indian Boilers (Amendment) Act, 2007
• Installation of storage tanks for LPG Gas, HSD & Furnace Oil under the Indian Explosives Act, 1884
• Clearance from the Water Department authorizing the water connection
• NOC under The Water (Prevention and Control of Pollution) Act, 1974 and the Water (Prevention and Control of Pollution) Amendment Act, 1988—to release waste water from the premises
• NOC under The Air (Prevention and Control of Pollution) Act, 1981—to operate diesel operated generators and boilers
• NOC from the Electricity and Pollution Control Board for the installation of DG sets conforming to noise pollution standards

Granting of a PCC enables the hotel developer to apply for the various operational permissions and licences.

The Ministry of Tourism has set up the Hospitality Development and Promotion Board to address these issues where a hotel developer has to visit various government agencies from time to time. The objective of the Board is to monitor and facilitate the clearances or approvals of hotel project applications with the central and state governments. It does not grant the necessary approvals. It aims at ensuring timely approvals or clearances or NOCs from multiple government agencies, thereby reducing delays in the implementation of project.

OPERATIONS STAGE

Upon completion of the building including interiors, the PCC is converted to a completion certificate by the municipal corporation. Once a completion certificate is received, an application is moved for securing an occupancy certificate (OC) from the municipal corporation. It is at this stage when all the required permissions to make the hotel operational have to be obtained from the various government authorities.

Occupancy certificate issued by the municipal corporation certifies that the building has incorporated all the safety standards and is in a habitable condition. An OC enables the residents to secure water, electricity, drainage, and sewage connection from the appropriate authorities.

Hotel operating licences broadly pertain to general hotel operations, food and beverage operations, and mandatory registrations which have to be done by the finance and personnel departments.

GENERAL HOTEL OPERATING LICENCES

General hotel operating licences are concerned with hotel classification, front-office operations, safety and security of guests, providing for guest recreation and in-room entertainment, and internal communication network of the hotel.

Board and Lodging Licence

The first and foremost licence that is required to be obtained is the Board and Lodging Licence, which is issued by the Additional Commissioner of Police, Licensing Branch. In the application, it is mandatory to disclose the names of the owners of the hotel and the name of the unit head or general manager who is responsible for the operation of the hotel. This licence enables the hotel to operate the property, permits the stamping of the visitors' register also known as the arrival and departure register maintained by the front office. It is a mandatory requirement under the licence that the hotel should collect all the relevant details of the guest at the time of registration—for Indian nationals, a photocopy of their government-issued identity card, for example, driving licence, permanent account number (PAN) card, Aadhaar card, and so on, and for foreign nationals, a photocopy of their passport.

The licence also stipulates that videography of all guests should be carried out discreetly at the time of check-in and this record should be available on site for a period of 30 days.

Foreigners Regional Registration Office

Under The Foreigners Act, 1946 and Registration of Foreigners Act, 1939, hotels are required to furnish details of all foreign nationals to the Foreigners Regional Registration Office (FRRO), Bureau of Immigration. However, Pakistani nationals are required to report within 24 hours and Afghan nationals within 14 days of arriving in the country to the FRRO office in person.

Shops and Establishments Act

Registration under the Shops and Establishment Act is mandatory for hotels and restaurants. Once registered, the owner is licenced to operate a 'commercial establishment' as defined under the Act. It is required to follow the rules and regulations relating to hours of work, payment of wages, leave, holidays, terms of service, and other conditions of employment as laid down under the Act.

Hotel Classification

Hotels are classified into five star deluxe, five star, four star, three star, two star, and one star by the Department of Tourism. A hotel must apply for classification within three months of the hotel becoming operational and the application must be submitted to the Hotel and Restaurant Approval and Classification Committee. The Committee is responsible for the classification and re-classification of hotels. The purpose of hotel classification is to ensure that hotels with comparable standards of facilities and services are graded similarly, enabling travellers to make an educated decision in choosing the kind of hotel and budget that they would like to stay in. In most states, classification is a prerequisite for availing government incentives and to secure tax advantages.

NOC from Chief Fire Officer

Each state has framed its own fire safety and prevention laws and in the state of Delhi the NOC is given by the Chief Fire Officer under the Delhi Fire Service Act, 2007 and Delhi Fire Service Rules, 2010 after inspecting the hotel premises. The advantage of the NOC is that it helps in securing preferential tariffs from the insurance company when the hotel applies for a fire insurance coverage.

Restricted Money Changers Licence from Reserve Bank of India

Restricted money changers licence is issued by the Reserve Bank of India to hotels, enabling the front-office cashiers to exchange foreign currency as well as to accept foreign exchange towards the settlement of in-house guest-stay bills. Foreign exchange received by the hotels is given to banks or full-fledged money changers who reimburse the amount spent by hotels in encashing the foreign exchange in Indian rupees.

Export Promotion Capital Goods Scheme

The EPCG scheme allows import or domestic sourcing of capital goods (including completely knocked down/semi-knocked down (CKD/SKD) at 0.30 per cent customs duty for all sectors as against the normal total of 25.852 per cent, thus providing a duty saved to the value of more than 25.55 per cent of the import value. This is subject to an export obligation (EO) equivalent to six to eight times of duty saved, to be fulfilled over a period of 6/8/12 years reckoned from the date of issuance of licence. Under this scheme, hotels import food and beverage items, FF&E items, cars for guest use, and a variety of other capital goods. To apply under this Scheme, hotels should be classified by the Department of Tourism and be members of the accredited trade bodies. This enables them to get the IE code which is a must for an EPCG licence.

> **Example**   Hotel Shenshah has imported wines worth ₹1,00,000 during the financial year 2012–2013 against their EPCG licence. If the wine was not imported under EPCG, then the customs duty payable would have been ₹25,852 at the time of delivery of the wines. However, the wines were delivered after the hotel agreed to fulfil the EO which is six times the value of the duty saved. In this case, it is ₹1,55,112 payable over the next six years from the hotel's foreign exchange earnings.

Lift Operating Licence from Inspector of Lifts

A lift is defined as a mechanically guided car, platform for transport of persons and materials between two or more levels in a vertical or substantially vertical direction. Licence to operate a lift is given by the Chief Inspector of Lifts, Office of the Electrical Inspector after verifying that the lift has been correctly balanced to carry the number of passengers or weight as indicated and that the safety features installed in the lift are functional.

NOC from Pollution Control Board

The Pollution Control Board after inspecting the installation of STPs, provision for rainwater harvesting system, and DG set shall issue an NOC.

Indian Performing Rights Society/Phonographic Performance Limited

Registration with Indian Performing Rights Society and Phonographic Performance Limited enables a hotel to play recorded music in the public areas and restaurants.

Permissions to Install Signage and Hoardings

The permission to install signage and hoardings is given by the municipal corporation for installing external hotel signage at the hotel and for hoardings for special events, for example, New Year's eve functions, food and beverage food festivals, and so on.

Swimming Pool and Cooling Tower Permission from the Police

This is given after all the safety aspects of the swimming pool and the installation of the cooling tower have been checked by the police.

Website Registration

The hotel website with all the details of the hotel requires to be registered with a website service provider. The hotel has to monitor the usage of the Internet facilities by the guests as they should not be accessing websites that display pornographic material.

Licence to Operate a Beauty Parlour and Spa

Licence has to be obtained from the municipal corporation and the health department. It has to be registered separately under the Shops and Establishment Act, even though it is located inside the hotel.

Wireless Planning and Coordination Wing, Ministry of Communications

Licence is granted by the Ministry of Communication to operate dish antennas and paging system within the building within a predefined waveband and frequency.

Registration with Various Trade Bodies or Organizations

- Federation of Indian Chambers of Commerce and Industry (FICCI)
- Punjab, Haryana, Delhi Chamber of Commerce and Industry (PHDCCI)
- Directorate General of Foreign Trade (DGFT)
- Confederation of Indian Industry (CII)
- Associated Chamber of Commerce and Industry of India (ASSOCHAM)
- FHRAI
- Hotel Association of India (HAI)
- Pacific Area Travel Association (PATA)

Membership of the above-mentioned organizations gives the hotelier an insight into the following:

- Government policies and their impact on businesses
- Awareness of the industry's best practices
- Obtaining expert advice on issues relating to foreign exchange regulations, import or export, excise and customs, industrial relations, income tax, energy conservation, and so on

FOOD AND BEVERAGE OPERATIONS

One of the key revenue-producing departments of a hotel is the Food and Beverage, which is entrusted with the task of serving healthy and nutritious food that is hygienically prepared. The primary responsibility of this department is to secure licences from the health authorities, Food Safety and Standards Authority of India, and the excise departments to operate restaurants and bars.

Health Trade Licence

The health trade licence is issued by the Director of Health Services to eating houses or restaurants. Renewable annually, it is mandatory for all food handlers to undergo periodic medical checks and get vaccinated against typhoid.

Eating House or Restaurant Licence

Eating house licence is issued by the police commissioner upon receiving the health trade licence given by the health department. With effect from 2011 with the passing of the Food Safety and Standards Act, 2006 and Standards, the restaurant licence or eating house has to be renewed with the Food Safety and Standards Authority of India (FSSAI). It is now given for a period of five years.

Sanitary Certificate

Sanitary certificate is issued by the health department giving clearance to the hotel from sanitary or hygienic point of view.

Liquor Licence

A hotel requires an on-premises or on-site liquor licence in order to serve liquor to guests in a restaurant, bar, or through room service. The hotels require L-3 Licence for room service and L-5 licence for bars located in star-category hotels.

Nominations under the Food Safety and Standards Act, 2006

FSSAI has retained the nomination Section 17(2) and rule 12-B of the Prevention of Food Adulteration Rules, 1955, which makes it mandatory for the hotel management to nominate the manager or supervisor responsible for the day-to-day operations of the restaurant. The purpose of the nomination is to hold the manager or supervisor accountable for any offences that may happen during the operations of the restaurant. The manager or supervisor of the restaurant should be a graduate from a recognized catering college.

Approval of Kitchen Signage

Under the FSSAI, all signage such as 'milk not for sale', 'vegetable oil used for cooking only', which are displayed in the kitchens are required to be displayed prominently.

Certification of Weighing Scales and Peg Measures

Certification of weighing scales and peg measures is now required to be done under the FSSAI Act with effect from 2011 as earlier calibration of weighing scales and peg measures were required to be done under the Weights and Measures Act.

PERSONNEL DEPARTMENT

The personnel department is responsible for administering welfare activities for the benefit of employees, which involves registering the hotel with the labour department, securing establishment codes from the Provident Fund and Employee State Insurance Corporation (ESIC) authorities.

Labour Department Registration

The hotel has to be registered with the labour department which approves the Model Standing Orders of the hotel. Registration requires the hotel to submit annual returns to the labour office on the manpower strength of the hotel indicating that minimum wages are being paid to the employees, date when the payment of wages will be made, list of annual holidays that will be followed by the hotel under The National and Festival Holidays Act, 1958.

Employee Provident Fund Registration

The hotel has to register itself with the provident fund commissioner's office under the Provident Fund Act, 1952 and obtain the establishment code from them. This is required of the hotel, as it has to make periodic deposits of amounts deducted from the employee salaries along with the hotel's contribution into the individual employee provident fund accounts.

Employee State Insurance Scheme

It is mandatory for the hotel under the Employee State Insurance Act, 1948 to register itself with the ESIC. This is required by the hotel as it has to make periodic deposits of amounts deducted from the employee salaries along with the hotel's contribution into the individual employee's ESIC accounts.

Profession Tax Enrolment Certificate

Under the Maharashtra State Tax on Professions, Trade, Callings and Employment Act, 1975, professional tax is payable by employees who have an annual income of more than ₹50,000 per annum. The employer is obliged to deduct this tax and deposit it on behalf of the employee.

ACCOUNTS DEPARTMENT

The accounts department is responsible for registering the hotel with the appropriate tax authorities and to ensure that the hotel fulfils all the statutory tax compliances requirements.

Sales Tax Registration

Sales tax registration from the department of sales tax is required to enable the hotel to deposit sales tax. Sales tax is levied on food and beverage and alcoholic beverages. Tax returns have to be filed monthly by the 21st day of every month.

Service Tax Registration

Service tax is the tax paid on the services being rendered by the assessee. It is levied on rooms at the rate of 5 per cent and food and beverage at the rate of 3 per cent, state value added tax (VAT) is excluded for calculating service tax.

Luxury Tax Registration

Luxury tax registration with the department of sales tax is required to enable the hotel to deposit luxury tax, which is levied on room tariff only. Tax returns have to be filed monthly by the last day of every month. There is confusion in charging luxury tax as seven states and union territories levy luxury tax on published tariff, 16 states and union territories levy luxury tax on actual invoice tariff, and the remaining 12 states and union territories do not levy luxury tax.

In case breakfast is included in the room rate, then it amounts to double taxation as VAT is charged on the breakfast and luxury tax on the total room charges, which includes breakfast upon which VAT has been charged.

Value Added Tax

VAT is a general consumption tax that is assessed on the value added to goods and services. It is an indirect tax on the consumption of the goods, paid by its original producers upon the change in goods or upon the transfer of the goods to its ultimate consumers. It is based on the value of the goods, added by the transferor. It is the tax in relation to the difference of the value added by the transferor and not just a profit.

Central Value Added Tax or Central Sales Tax

Central value added tax or central sales tax is a tax levied on the manufacture or production of movable and marketable goods in India. The tax is generally levied on an ad-valorem basis, which means that tax will be levied based upon the value of the goods which will either be expressed as a percentage of the transaction value or the maximum retail price of the goods.

Expenditure Tax

Expenditure tax is levied on rooms at the rate of 7 per cent and food and beverage at the rate of 5 per cent; state VAT is excluded for calculating tax.

Permanent Account Number

PAN registration certificate is a 10-digit alphanumeric identifier issued by the Income Tax Department. Each assessee (e.g., individual, firm, company, and so on.) is issued a unique PAN.

Online Tax Accounting System

Online tax accounting system is designed to receive information and maintain records of tax paid through banks which upload tax returns or challans through their online tax accounting system.

Tax Deduction and Collection Account Number

Tax deduction and collection account number (TAN) is a 10-digit alphanumeric number required to be obtained by all persons who are responsible for deducting or collecting tax. It is compulsory to quote TAN in all tax deducted at source/tax collected at source (TDS/TCS) returns (including e-TDS/TCS return), TDS/TCS payment challans, and TDS/TCS certificates.

Tax Information Network

Tax information network registration is required so that e-filing records of taxes can be checked by accounts.

Property Tax Certificate

Property tax certificate is required signifying that the property tax is being paid regularly on time.

As can be seen from the list of licences, permissions, and NOCs, which are required to be obtained prior to a hotel becoming operational, it is a daunting task for a hotel developer to adhere to strict timelines without incurring cost overruns.

SUMMARY

This chapter discussed how the evolution of cities into large urban agglomerates made it imperative for governments to control the haphazard growth of cities; this was achieved with the help of city master plans which segregated activities that were incompatible with each other. Additionally, governments began to grant building permits or licences to developers to encourage planned developments. The chapter discussed how in order to encourage hotel development governments both at the centre and the states have announced many incentives as hotel development is highly capital intensive with long gestation periods. In spite of these incentives there are comparatively very few hotels under development leading to a shortage of rooms in the country.

The chapter also highlighted that securing permission to develop a hotel is a cumbersome process as the hotel developer has to interact with a host of government agencies at the centre and the state levels. This leads to projects being delayed and cost overruns; the Ministry of Tourism has established the hospitality development and promotion board to streamline this. Once approvals have been obtained it takes approximately 18–24 months for the structure to be completed. The exercise to secure hotel operating licence is carried out six months prior to the commencement of operations. A hotel can commence operations after all the operational licences or permissions and mandatory registrations have been completed.

KEY TERMS

Master plan   A blueprint prepared by the government that demarcates land based on the principle of separation into various parcels according to its proposed usage, for example, agricultural, residential, commercial, mixed use, institutional, and industrial as certain activities are incompatible with each other.

Urban agglomeration   A continuous urban spread constituting of a town and its adjoining outgrowths, or two or more physically contiguous towns together with or without outgrowths of such towns.

Tier-I cities   Cities with a population of 10 million, for example, Chennai, Hyderabad, Bengaluru.

Mega cities   Those with a population of more than 10 million, for example, Greater Mumbai, Delhi NCR, Kolkata, which are also classified as Tier-I cities.

Tier-II cities   Cities with a population of 1 million, for example, Ahmedabad, Surat, Nagpur, Pune, Jaipur, Lucknow, Kanpur, Vijayawada, Patna, Rajkot, Baroda, Bhopal, Indore, Nasik, Jabalpur, Jamshedpur, Dhanbad, Faridabad, Cochin, Madurai, Meerut, Agra, and Allahabad.

Tier-III cities Cities with a population of 1,00,000 and above, for example, Jamnagar, Jammu, Kurnool, Roorkee, Dehradun, Vellore, Belgaum, and so on.

Class 'C' towns Towns with a population of less than 1,00,000, for example, Jangipur, Asansol, Durgapur, Renukoot, Sultanpur, Khurja, Hathras, Bulandshahr, Haridwar, Sivakasi, Coonor, Neyveli.

Due diligence Process conducted by the lawyers of the intending purchaser to ascertain the marketability of the title—this requires checking for any kind of encumbrances such as the seller having pledged the property to secure a loan, encroachments on the land, the authenticity of the seller's title to the land, and the approximate value of the land.

Ready reckoner Defined by the *Oxford Dictionaries Online* as 'a book or table listing standard numerical calculations or other kinds of information presented formulaically'. These rates are updated by the government from time to time and are used for the valuation of properties, payment of stamp duty, and registration charges.

Floor Space Index or Floor Area Ratio Ratio of construction that is permitted in relation to the street area where the plot is situated, which is also referred as buildable area and applies only to buildable plots.

Setbacks In a building is the area left between the building footprint and the boundary wall by the developer to enable the circulation of air and light in the premises. It also serves the purpose of providing circulation space for the movement of vehicles, fire tenders, and so on. These areas are usually landscaped adding to the aesthetics of the building.

Area Two-dimensional space defined by boundaries, for example, sanctioned areas, buildable area, built-up area, carpet area, and super built-up area, covered area, and sellable area.

Sanctioned area or buildable area Area approved by the corporation that can be built by the developer, which is also referred to as buildable area.

Built-up area Actual area built by the developer against the sanctioned area, for example, out of the sanctioned 24,000 sq. ft, in case the hotel developer builds only 15,000 sq. ft this will be known as built-up area.

Carpet area Actual usable space available for occupation in the building, which excludes the thickness of the walls, shafts, common areas, and so on.

Super built-up area or sellable area Area that includes the carpet area plus the thickness of the walls, shafts, terraces, lifts and stairs, and so on. It is normally 30 per cent more than the carpet area.

Covered area Ground area covered immediately above the plinth level by the building but does not include the spaces covered by gardens, rockeries, well and well structures, plant nurseries, water pools, swimming pools (if uncovered), platforms around trees, tanks, fountains, benches, *chabutras* with open tops and not enclosed on sides by walls and the like; drainage culverts, conduits, catch-pits, gully-pits, chambers, gutters and the like; and compound walls, gates, slides/ swing doors, canopies, and areas covered by *chajjas* or similar projections and stair-cases, which are uncovered and open at least on three sides and also open to sky.

Transfer of Development Rights Traditionally, the right to develop a parcel of land could not be separated from the land itself. TDR is a new concept in development, which separates the right to develop a parcel of land from the land itself. After purchasing TDR the developer can enhance the FSI that he can build on his parcel of land in the urban area. The price of TDR is determined by the prevailing ready-reckoner rate of the location where it will be used.

The NBC 2005 Formulated by the BIS is a comprehensive document providing guidelines for regulating the building construction activities across the country containing administrative regulations, DCRs, general building and fire safety requirements, and stipulations regarding building and structural design, electrical and plumbing services, and safety standards to be followed during construction.

Plot and survey drawings Delineate the legal boundaries of the plot.

Contour plans Graphical representations of the land parcel.

Floor plans Drawn to scale giving a bird's eye view or a horizontal perspective of the various spaces on a given floor such as rooms, corridors, lift locations, shafts, and so on.

Elevation drawings A view of a building as seen from one side and is used to describe the external appearance or façade of a building.

Perspective A three-dimensional view of the building.

Cross section or simply section drawing A vertical perspective highlighting the relationship between different levels of a building.

Mechanical drawings or technical drawings Dimensions and measurements to be taken giving details of the plumbing, sewage, electrical, TV cabling, telephone wiring, AC ducting, hot and cold water supply system details.

Intimation of disapproval A letter approving the project, authorizing the development subject to the restrictions mentioned in the approval letter.

Commencement certificate Permits the developer to commence construction activities on the plot of land subject to the IOD. Generally, the IOD and CC are given simultaneously by the corporation.

Plinth The base or platform which rests directly on the ground and upon which a column or structure rests.

Partial completion certificate Issued by the municipal authorities certifying that the hotel structure has complied with all the requirements laid down in the IOD and CC, and has fulfilled all the norms outlined in the NBC 2005.

Occupancy certificate Issued by the municipal corporation certifying that the building has incorporated all the safety standards laid down and is in a habitable condition. It enables the residents to secure water, electricity, drainage, and sewage connection from the appropriate authorities.

Zoning The process of regulating activities by drawing up a master plan for the town, city, or urban agglomerate.

EXERCISES

Define the Following

1. Intimation of disapproval
2. Area
3. Due diligence
4. Urban agglomeration
5. Plinth
6. Super built-up area
7. Mechanical drawing
8. Partial completion certificate
9. Commencement certificate
10. Mega cities

Concept Review Questions

1. Which are the licences required to open a restaurant?
2. Explain why cities prepare master plans.
3. What is the procedure to secure intimation of disapproval, completion certificate, and occupancy certificate?
4. How many general hotel operating licences are required to open a hotel?

5. What are the requirements to be fulfilled before a building permit is granted?
6. What is the importance of construction drawings?

Critical Thinking Questions

1. A blueprint is the foundation stone of a hotel development project. Do you agree?
2. If additional TDR is granted to a hotel project, how will it impact the built-up area and the overall development of the hotel?

Research Questions

1. The Hospitality Development and Promotion Board is formed to facilitate the single-window clearance of hotel projects. Give your recommendations on how this can be achieved.
2. What are the important incentives given by the government to encourage development of hotels?

Project

1. It has been observed that environment impact studies lead to project delays and cost overruns. Do you subscribe to this viewpoint?

REFERENCES

<http://history-world.org/ancient_civilization.htm> accessed on 3 December 2012.

<http://www.cambridge.edu.au/education/resource/page-proofs_8_675933.pdf> accessed on 3 December 2012.

<http://www.bis.org.in/sf/nbc.htm> accessed on 3 December 2012.

<http://www.thehindu.com/opinion/lead/article3723646.ece> accessed on 3 December 2012.

<http://oxforddictionaries.com/definition/english/ready%2Breckoner> accessed on 3 December 2012.

<http://dipp.nic.in/English/Investor/Investers_Gudlines/approval_clearances_required_for_new_projects.pdf> accessed on 3 December 2012.

<http://toolboxes.flexiblelearning.net.au/demosites/series10/10_01/content/bcgbc4010a/07_prep_documentation/02_plans/page_007.htm> accessed on 3 December 2012.

<http://en.wikipedia.org/wiki/Architectural_drawing> accessed on 3 December 2012.

<http://www.thefreedictionary.com/mechanical+drawing> accessed on 3 December 2012.

<http://encyclopedia.thefreedictionary.com/plinth 03 December 2012> accessed on 3 December 2012.

<http://businesstoday.intoday.in/story/international-hotels-investing-in-indian-hotel-biz/1/16102.html 03 December 2012> accessed on 12 December 2012.

<http://www.urbanindia.nic.in/publicinfo/byelaws/chap-1.pdf> accessed on 12 December 2012.

<http://censusindia.gov.in/2011-prov-results/paper2/data_files/India2/1.%20Data%20Highlight.pdf> accessed on 12 December 2012.

<http://www.phdcci.in/membership-overview.php> accessed on 12 December 2012.

<http://www.hotelassociationofindia.com/membership.html> accessed on 12 December 2012.

<http://www.assocham.org/> accessed on 12 December 2012.

<http://en.wikipedia.org/wiki/Classification_of_Indian_cities> accessed on 16 December 2012.

<http://www.epcg.in/> accessed on 16 December 2012.

<http://www.mcdonline.gov.in/healthdetail.php?id=37> accessed on 16 December 2012.

<http://www.aeaweb.org/aer/data/sept05_app_banerjee.pdf> accessed on 16 December 2012.

<http://www.nrai.org/ind_updates.asp?id=4> accessed on 16 December 2012.

<http://delhigovt.nic.in/dept/pubserv/liqlic.asp#4> accessed on 16 December 2012.

<https://www.tin-nsdl.com/pan/faq-pan-general.php> accessed on 16 December 2012.

<http://www.tax4india.com/vat/vat.html> accessed on 16 December 2012.

<http://www.tmf-vat.com/global-vat/india-vat-cenvat-service-tax-and-gst.html> accessed on 22 December 2012.

<http://www.wpc.dot.gov.in/faq.asp> accessed on 22 December 2012.

Hotel Insurance

LEARNING OBJECTIVES

After going through this chapter, the reader will be familiar with the following:

- Evolution of insurance and the various types of insurance policies
- Legal principles of insurance
- Process of securing hotel insurance coverage
- Insurance claim and grievance redressal machinery
- Working of the Loss Prevention Association of India

INTRODUCTION

The history of insurance is directly linked to man's desire for security and protection since the dawn of civilization. Insurance is based on the principle of distributing the risk that an individual takes in life and in any business activity by distributing the losses of one amongst the many.

A simplistic form of insurance can be attributed to the various 'kitties' that informal groups organize amongst themselves to take care of any family contingencies that may arise such as paying for children's school fees, medical bills, and so on. The underlying principle of a 'kitty' is to collect a fixed amount as contributions from its members for a predetermined period of, for example, six months or a year on a regular basis. The member who is the most in need of money makes a bid for the kitty amount, which is then given to him. The difference between the bid amount and the kitty amount is known as profit, which is allowed to accumulate over the period of the kitty. The person who is the last to bid for the kitty is entitled to the profits after deductions of any expense for managing the kitty.

The *Code of Hammurabi* from 1750 BC Babylon details the prevailing practice of insuring merchant voyages. Merchants would agree to pay a higher amount in case the goods were stolen from the ship for waiver of the loan amount that was taken by the merchant to finance the voyage. In India, insurance has a deep-rooted history, which finds mention in the writings of Manu (*Manusmrithi*), Yagnavalkya (*Dharmasastra*), and Kautilya (*Arthasastra*). The writings speak in terms of pooling of resources that could be re-distributed in times of calamities such as fire, floods, epidemics, and famine.

The Persian kings were the first to introduce the concept of insurance, with the insurance contracts being registered on the day of *Navroze* or the Persian/Parsi New Year. Different communities and those who wished to be insured would bring gifts or money as contribution to the king; gifts would be evaluated and the insurance registry would record the value of the gift in monetary terms. As and when the person who had registered his insurance with the king required financial assistance for the marriage of his children, to meet funeral expenses, or support his family, he would approach the office of the registrar, who after verifying the amount would give him an amount double the value of his contribution. The Persian kings encouraged families to provide for the security and financial needs of the infirm and the aged members giving rise to the joint-family system. In the 12th century, the Seljuk Empire introduced the concept of compensation from the royal treasury to pay off the losses suffered by traders whose goods were robbed whilst transiting Seljuk territory.

The code of Manu indicates the practice of marine insurance by Indians along with the Sri Lankans, Egyptians, and Greeks. Marine insurance is the oldest form of insurance which originated in England in the 12th century. The first known marine insurance contract was prepared in Genoa, Italy in the 14th century. The great fire of London in 1666 gave birth to the idea of insuring buildings and fire insurance was introduced to cover buildings built using bricks. The 18th and the 19th centuries witnessed the Industrial Revolution in England, which gradually spread to Europe and America. This application of science to industry powered the technology that gave an impetus to manufacturing; this resultant growth encouraged large-scale migration from villages to cities as there was a great demand for labour to man the machines. Whilst working in the factories a fair amount of workers suffered accidents, which led to the concept of accident insurance that was commonly called disability insurance.

In 1881, the German Emperor, William I, in a ground-breaking letter to the German Parliament wrote: 'those who are disabled from work by age and invalidity have a well-grounded claim to care from the state'. In 1884 sickness insurance was introduced by the state based upon mandatory contributions taken from the employees, employers, and the government. In 1889 Germany's Chancellor Otto von Bismarck introduced retirement benefits and disability benefits based upon mandatory contributions taken from the employees, employers, and the government. With the introduction of unemployment insurance in 1927, Germany had a comprehensive system of 'income security' based on social insurance principles.

During the British rule English and other foreign insurance companies operated in India. The first life insurance company—the Oriental Life Insurance Company—commenced business in 1818 in Calcutta; however, it closed down in 1834. The first general insurance company promoted by the British was the Triton Insurance Company established in 1850 in Calcutta. The British Insurance Act was passed in

1870 to encourage and regulate the insurance business, which resulted in three life insurance companies being formed with Indian promoters in Bombay, namely Bombay Mutual (1871), Oriental Insurance (1874), and Empire of India (1897). However, these companies faced stiff competition from foreign companies operating in India. The first general insurance company formed by Indian promoters was Indian Mercantile Insurance Company Limited in Bombay in 1906.

The turn of the 20th century witnessed a spate of legislative measures to regulate the business of insurance in India, as unscrupulous insurance companies had resorted to unfair trade practices. These important legislative landmarks in the history of insurance in India are illustrated in Table 6.1.

TABLE 6.1   Legislative History of Insurance in India

Year	Legislation	Objective
1912	Indian Life Assurance Companies Act	To regulate the business of life insurance
1928	Indian Insurance Companies Act	To collect statistical information on life and general insurance business in India
1938	The Insurance Act	First comprehensive act to exercise effective control over the insurance business
1950	The Insurance Amendment Act	To abolish principal agencies in the marketing of insurance
1956	The Life Insurance (Emergency Provisions) Act issued by ordinance nationalizing all the insurance companies	All life insurance companies were nationalized and merged into the newly incorporated Life Insurance Corporation of India
1957	General Insurance Council under the aegis of Insurance Association of India formed	To frame a code of conduct for insurers based upon fair and sound business practice
1968	The Insurance Amendment Act	To regulate investments and set solvency standards. Tariff Advisory Committee formed
1972	The General Insurance Business (Nationalization) Act	All general insurance companies were nationalized and amalgamated to form four companies—National Insurance Company Ltd., New India Assurance Company Ltd., Oriental Insurance Company Ltd., and United India Insurance Company Ltd. under the General Insurance Corporation of India
1999	Insurance Regulatory & Development Authority Act	An autonomous body to regulate and develop the insurance industry
2000	Insurance Regulatory Authority Act	Foreign insurance companies could operate subject to a ceiling on ownership of 26%
2002	General Insurance Business (Nationalization) Amendment Act	National Insurance Company Ltd., New India Assurance Company Ltd., Oriental Insurance Company Ltd., and United India Insurance Company Ltd. became autonomous companies

With the opening of the insurance sector to foreign companies, as of 2009 there are 23 companies offering life insurance products and 17 companies underwriting general insurance policies.

List I Seventh Schedule of the Indian Constitution Clause 47—Insurance empowers the central government to legislate exclusively on all matters of insurance. The two primary legislative enactments that govern the insurance business are the Insurance Act, 1938 and Insurance Regulatory & Development Authority Act, 1999.

The Insurance Act, 1938 has undergone several amendments, and it broadly lays down the regulatory aspects that are imposed upon insurance companies with the central government through the Controller of Insurance acting as a watchdog to investigate the operations of the insurance company at any time. Under the Act, a company is required to fulfil the following conditions in order to secure an insurance licence enabling it to operate the insurance business in India.

Registration   Insurance companies are required to register with the controller of insurance and to renew the registration annually.

Accounts and audits   All accounts of income and expenditure have to be maintained as per the class of insurance—motor, marine, fire, and so on.

Investments   Insurance companies have to be in categories approved by the central government.

Limitation on management expenses   The Act prescribes the maximum limit for expenses as percentage of the business generated.

Prohibition on rebates or discounts   Rebates on commission or premiums are not allowed.

In 1999, with the passing of the Insurance Regulatory & Development Act, 1999 the Insurance Regulatory and Development Authority (IRDA) took over all the key regulatory functions of the insurance sector. Besides regulatory aspects the IRDA was responsible for protecting the interests of the consumer; hence, the Institution of Insurance Ombudsman was established in 1999 to listen to grievances of the consumers against any of the insurance companies.

Besides, the Insurance Act, 1938, and Insurance Regulatory & Development Authority Act, 1999—which deal with the functioning of the insurance company—there are other laws that have an impact on the general insurance business. These laws are as follows:

- The Motor Vehicles Act, 1939
- The Inland Steam – Vessels (Amendment) Act, 1977
- Marine Insurance Act, 1963
- Carriage of Goods by Sea Act, 1925
- The Merchant Shipping Act, 1958
- Bill of Lading Act, 1856
- The Indian Ports (Major Ports) Act, 1963

- Indian Railway Act, 1989
- The Carriers Act, 1865
- The Indian Post Office Act, 1898
- The Carriage by Air Act, 1972
- Multi-Modal Transportation Act, 1993
- Public Liability Insurance Act, 1991
- The Indian Stamp Act, 1899
- The Consumer Protection Act, 1986
- Exchange Control Regulations

WHAT IS INSURANCE?

The legal dictionary defines insurance as 'a contract whereby, for specified consideration, one party undertakes to compensate the other for a loss relating to a particular subject as a result of the occurrence of designated hazards'.

Insurance is the transferring of a risk from the insured to the insurer by the payment of a small predictable amount of money called the premium to protect against a larger unpredictable expense or loss.

Insurance is also a business venture like any other business that has to be managed to deliver profits. From the premium collected which is the primary source of income the insurance company has to make provisions to meet its operating costs, meet its statutory obligations, pay for the insurance claims, and so on.

Under the Indian Contracts Act, 1872, insurance is a contract of indemnity between two persons—the indemnifier (insurance company) and the indemnified (insured) towards the reimbursement of a loss. The liability of the indemnifier (insurance company) is primary and arises when the event occurs. Once the insurance company has discharged its liability towards the insured, there are no further legal rights against the third party.

The insurance contract is a legal document, which is legally enforceable as it fulfils all the requirements essential for the formation of a valid contract, that is, there is an offer and acceptance for a consideration to fulfil a legal purpose between two parties that have the capacity to enter into a contract. An insurance contract spells out the coverage, features, conditions, and limitations of an insurance policy. It is important to read the insurance contract carefully as you do not want to pay for that insurance where you later find out that what you thought was covered is not included at all.

Insurance, therefore, can be defined as a business that indemnifies the risk of the insured by transferring the risk from the insured to the insurer.

Salient Features of an Insurance Contract

The following are some of the salient features of an insurance contract:

- The Fortuity Doctrine arises from 'the basic concept that insurance covers risks, rather than losses that were planned, intended, or anticipated by the insured'. The *Collins English Dictionary* defines fortuity as 'a chance or accidental occurrence'.

- All insurance contracts are contracts of adhesion, that is, offered intact to one party by another under circumstances requiring the second party to accept or reject the contract in total without having the opportunity to bargain over the terms and conditions of the contract.
- All insurance contracts are aleatory agreements as they provide for unequal transfer of value between the parties dependent on the happening of an uncertain event. Insurance policies are aleatory contracts because an insured can pay premiums for many years without sustaining a covered loss. On the other hand there have been occasions when the insured has paid a relatively small premium for a short period of time and received compensation for a substantial loss.
- All insurance contracts are unilateral as it is the insurer that makes legally enforceable contracts promising to pay to the insured on the happening of a future event. All insurance claims are payable if the policy is in force and the premiums have been paid.
- All insurance contracts are based upon the principle that the insured as a prudent or sensible person will take all the steps necessary to save the property in the event that there is a mishap. This is commonly referred as the doctrine of 'mitigation of loss'.
- All insurance contracts are for a predetermined well-defined period—normally for a year, or duration of a voyage or journey, for example, travel insurance.

PRINCIPLES OF INSURANCE CONTRACTS

Over and above the application of the principles of contracting under the Indian Contract Act, 1872, there are certain basic principles that apply to all types of insurance contracts irrespective of whether it is a life or general insurance policy. It is important to understand the various principles of insurance as these principles are applied by insurance companies when they have to interpret the terms and conditions stated in the insurance policy on having to process an insurance claim. Some of the most commonly applied principles of insurance contracts are discussed in the following pages.

Principle of Utmost Good Faith

The principle of utmost good faith or *uberrimae fides* states that there is a full disclosure of all the material and relevant information by the insured party to the insurer and vice versa, so that both can take an educated decision on whether they would like to enter into an insurance contract.

Non-disclosure of material facts by the insured to the insurer, whether intentional or not, could compel the insurer agreeing not to cover the risk, as well as may lead to an inaccurate assessment of the premium amount.

For example, when taking a medical insurance 'material facts' are age, income, current health status, residence address, occupation, and type of insurance plan selected. When applying for car insurance it will be the year of make, model, seating capacity, horsepower of the engine, and type of registration—commercial or private.

Principle of Indemnity

Insurance contracts are contracts of indemnity, which implies that the loss shall be paid to the extent of the policy, provided the premiums are fully paid up as on the date of the incident. The purpose of indemnity is to provide for compensation to the insured so as to place him in the same position that he was prior to the loss, and to ensure that he should not enjoy a benefit from the occurrence of the loss.

When computing the value of the property, two methods are used:

Actual cash value   The sum of money required to pay for damages or lost property, computed on the basis of replacement value less its depreciation by obsolescence or general wear.
This is calculated as follows:

Replacement cost − depreciation = Actual cash value

Fair market value   This is defined as the value of a property if it were to be sold in the free market, resulting in a transaction between a willing buyer and a willing seller. This is the actual value at which a transaction takes place irrespective of its actual cash value.

The common methods of indemnifying the insured are as follows:
- By cash payment as per the amount payable under the policy
- Repair of the vehicle
- Replacement of the damaged parts
- Reinstatement or restoring or rebuilding the machinery

A life insurance policy is not based on the principle of indemnity, but is a value-based policy where the amount is payable upon the death of the policyholder.

Example   Neev's car, a Honda city with year of registration 2011, is insured for ₹12 lakh. The car meets with an accident on 17 February 2013, and the cost of repair of the vehicle is assessed at ₹3 lakh. In keeping with the principle of indemnity, the maximum amount payable to Neev is ₹3 lakh. In case the compensation is more than ₹3 lakh he stands to gain a profit from the loss.

However, in case the car is completely destroyed the insurance company will treat the claim as a total loss. A total loss occurs when the insured property is completely destroyed or when the insured is irretrievably deprived of the insured property. In such a case when computing the claim payable, the insurance company will determine the actual cash value which is replacement value less its depreciation.

The actual cash value in this case would be assessed as follows:
  Replacement cost of the car = ₹12 lakh
  Depreciation @ 40% = ₹4.80 lakh (as the car is two years old)
  Actual cash value = Replacement cost − Depreciation
      = ₹12 lakh − ₹4.80 lakh
      = ₹7.20 lakh
Neev will be paid an amount of ₹7.20 lakh towards the settlement of his claim.

Principle of Subrogation

'Subrogation' means the restitution of the rights of an assured in favour of the insurer against the third party for any damages caused by him after the insurer has indemnified the assured for the loss. The principle of subrogation is invoked when a third party is responsible for the loss and can only be applied once the claim has been paid. The principle of subrogation does not apply to life insurance policies.

When an accident happens, the aggrieved party has an option of either making a claim against the person responsible for causing the damage or against the insurance company. In case the aggrieved files a claim with the insurance company and the insurance company settles the claim, then the aggrieved party cannot make another claim against the party causing the damage. This act on the part of the aggrieved would give an opportunity to the aggrieved party to make a profit from the loss.

CASE 6.1	
APPELLANT:	Vasudev Mudaliar
	vs
RESPONDENT:	Caledonian Insurance Co. and Another
DATE:	3 January, 1964 AIR 1965 Mad 159
FACTS:	One G. H. Morley had insured his car MSP 2228 with the Caledonian Insurance Co., the plaintiff, against comprehensive risks for ₹4000. On 6 February 1955, on the Madras–Bangalore road, a lorry MDJ 1099, coming from opposite direction and after overtaking a bus, collided with the car causing serious damage to it. The insurer settled the claim of the assured at ₹3030, treating the case as a total loss and itself taking over the damaged car. The insurer later sold it on 16 April 1955, for ₹1500 and brought the suit to recover the balance of ₹1530 from the second defendant, the owner of the lorry, as loss and damages it had sustained by the wilful, gross, rash, and negligent driving of the lorry. The assured did not figure as a party to the suit either as a plaintiff along with the insurer or as a defendant. The basis of the insurer's claim in the suit was that it was subrogated to the rights of the assured against the defendants, including the right to sue and recover damages from them, and that, in any case, it held an assignment from the assured of all his rights.

The issue which was decided by the court was whether the insurance company could sue the owner of the truck by exercising its right of subrogation. The high court ruled in the affirmative in favour of the insurance company.

Principle of Insurable Interest

'Insurable interest exists when an insured person derives a financial or other kind of benefit from the continuous existence of the insured object. The legal right to insure arising out of a financial relationship is recognized under law between the insured and the subject matter of insurance.'

Without an insurable interest, insurers will not cover the loss. In order to insure something or someone, the insured must provide proof that the loss will have a genuine economic impact in the event the loss occurs. It is worth noting that for property insurance policies, an insurable interest must exist during the underwriting process and at the time of loss. However, for life insurance, an insurable interest must exist at the time of purchase only.

> **Example** Kapil is driving home from office in the evening when he is hit by a speeding car from the rear driven by a drunk driver Rajiv. Kapil files a claim with the insurance company seeking compensation for the damages to his car. The loss is estimated at ₹2,00,000 and the claim is settled by them. The claim was paid by the insurance company as there was an insurable interest between Kapil and the car, both at the time of the accident and also at the time that the car's insurance policy was taken as the car continued to be registered in his name.

Principle of Contribution

As per the doctrine of contribution, the indemnity provided for the loss occurring on the asset, which is insured with several insurers has to be proportionately shared among them according to the rateable proportion of the loss. In other words, the total compensation amount payable to the insured should not exceed the amount of the loss.

The doctrine of contribution enables insurance companies to insure exceptionally high-value assets and to share the risk proportionately. This is normally done with one of the insurance companies being the lead insurer who in turn shares the risk with other insurance companies. When an insurance claim has to be paid each insurance company pays towards the loss in proportion to its contribution.

> **Example** **Insuring the Olympic Games 2012** In 2012, following approximately 12 months of intense negotiations between the International Olympic Committee (IOC) and 26 international insurance entities, the IOC announced that it had officially insured the London 2012 Olympic Games for a sum of £62,000,100. The insurance policy was intended to cover any terrorist attack or outbreaks of hostility which might impact the progression of the Games. The £62 million sum represented the maximum amount insurers were prepared to take on as financial risk with the amount divided among them. The 26 insurance companies would have to share the burden of the loss in proportion to their contributions, in case there were any terrorist attacks or outbreaks of hostility.

Principle of Proximate Cause

The term 'proximate cause' literally means the nearest cause or direct cause. In insurance it relates to the immediate cause of the mishap which has resulted in the loss. It establishes a relationship between the action and the result—typically an injury or a loss. The doctrine of proximate clause plays an important role when deciding (i) claims relating to property insurance and (ii) third-party liability insurance.

Claims related to property insurance

Normally, whenever any insurance policy is purchased, for example, a fire policy for the protection of a house, the reasons are mentioned in the policy for the causes of fire such as electrical short circuit, gas cylinder explosion, leakage of gas, and so on. In case the fire occurs owing to any of these causes the insurance company is liable to pay the claim.

Most insurance companies attempt to absolve themselves from paying insurance claims arising from an Act of God such as floods, earthquakes, or other accidents or events that occur without any human intervention and that could not have been prevented by reasonable care or foresight, but is the result of natural causes (snowstorm is an Act of God; driving is an act of man). This is done by keeping high insurance tariff rates for such contingencies which normally act as a deterrent preventing policyholders from purchasing such insurance cover.

However, when there are multiple events that could have caused a fire, then the primary cause that resulted in the fire has to be established by referring to the doctrine of 'proximate cause'.

In such cases where the first event sets in motion a chain of events that causes a second event that causes the loss, there are three common law tests for ascertaining the 'proximate cause':

(i) The last-cause test   It states that the loss will be covered if the last cause in the chain of events is covered.

(ii) The first-cause test   It states that the loss will be covered if the first cause in the chain of events is covered.

(iii) The predominant-cause test   It states that the loss will be covered if the covered cause of loss is 'predominant' over the non-covered cause of loss.

Example   Sunil has taken a fire insurance policy for his new house that covers the following risks or perils:

- Fire, lightning, explosion, aircraft damage
- Riot/strike, malicious damage
- Storm, cyclone, flood and inundation, landslide and subsidence, rock slide
- Impact damage resulting in bursting and/or overflowing of water tanks, electrical equipment, other apparatus and pipes
- Earthquake
- Terrorism

An earthquake occurs in the city which results in leakage of LPG gas, which gets ignited due to an electrical short circuit. In this example the first test clause and the predominant test clauses both can be applied to determine whether the claim is payable and as the first cause was the earthquake that set in motion the series of events leading to Sunil's house catching fire, the claim is payable.

Claims related to third-party liability

In the context of third-party liability insurance, it is important for the third party or claimant to prove that the actions of the defendant were 'proximate' or close enough to have led to the damages. If this can be proved then the defendant is liable to pay the third-party damages. Here the doctrine of 'proximate cause' is applied to determine if the actions of the defendant sets in motion a series of events that could have foreseeably led to the third-party suffering damages.

CASE 6.2	APPELLANT:	Shri Kumaresh
		vs
	RESPONDENT:	The National Insurance Company Ltd & Another (Supreme Court of India Civil Appeal No. 3784 of 2011)
	DATE:	29 April 2011
	FACTS:	On 1 November 2006, at about 7.15 p.m., the appellant was proceeding on a motorcycle as a pillion rider when a lorry came from behind in high speed and dashed against the motorcycle. The left wheel of the lorry ran over the right leg of the appellant, due to which he sustained grievous injuries. The right leg of the appellant had to be amputated as a result of the accident.

The appellant filed a claim petition under Section 166 of the Motor Vehicles Act, 1988 claiming ₹15 lakh as compensation. At the time of the accident, the appellant was aged 20 years and claimed to be earning ₹6000 per month as salary as a building centring worker. Motor Accidents Claims Tribunal awarded ₹2,81,200 compensation with 6% interest. High Court of Karnataka modified the compensation in various heads and enhanced to ₹5,48,000 with 6% interest. Honourable Supreme Court of India revised the compensation in various heads and enhanced to ₹10,00,000 with 9% interest payable jointly and severally by respondents.

This judgement is based on the doctrine of proximate cause and the reasoning that the grievous injury sustained when the lorry ran over the leg of the appellant led to the amputation of the leg; hence the claim amount was enhanced by the Supreme Court.

PURCHASING AN INSURANCE POLICY OR INSURANCE CONTRACT

'Insurance is a subject matter of solicitation' is the tagline of numerous advertisements marketing all types of insurance products that implies that customer should fully understand the implications of insurance before taking an insurance policy. Before an insurance policy can be issued by the insurance company an application has to be moved by the individual or company desirous of obtaining an insurance cover to the insurance company.

The simplest way to get a life or general insurance cover is to contact an insurance agent or insurance broker.

Insurance Agents

Two types of agents sell insurance: (i) independent agents or brokers who are self-employed business people representing more than one insurance company and are paid on a commission basis and (ii) exclusive agents who may be salaried or working on a commission basis exclusively for business development of a insurance company.

The basic difference between the two is that an insurance agent represents the insurance company and therefore represents the interest of the insurance company, whilst an insurance broker has a legal relationship of trust towards the customer and represents the customer's interest vis-à-vis the insurance company. In both the cases insurance agents and brokers have to be registered with IRDA, which conducts qualifying exam for them before certifying them.

The advantages of taking a policy through an insurance broker is that he or she is familiar with your situation and can empathize with you, he or she is keen to retain you as his or her customer and will go the extra mile. When taking insurance coverage, renewing the policy or filing a claim, or even dealing with the insurance company in routine matters his or her intimate knowledge of the working of insurance companies can expedite matters. It is suggested that a policy should be taken through an insurance broker even though it is convenient to take a policy through an insurance agent or online over the Internet.

Proposal Stage

A *proposer* is the person who is seeking the insurance cover.

An insurance proposal is a request from the proposer seeking an insurance cover, made in writing by filling the insurance company's proposal form.

Proposal forms are by and large similar but questions may vary according to the nature of the insurance cover required. A set of questions that are commonly asked when a property has to be insured is given as follows:

   (i) Name, address, telephone number, and other personal identification details
  (ii) The situation of the property
 (iii) Proposer's profession
  (iv) Previous and present insurance, if any
   (v) Previous loss experience
  (vi) Previous sum insured
 (vii) The contents on the premises in the location
(viii) The type of property mentioning whether hazardous, non-hazardous, and extra hazardous
  (ix) The type of fire protection available—sprinklers, smoke detectors, and others
   (x) The proportion of ownership of others in the property at risk; in other words, whether the property is mortgaged to banks or leased to tenants
  (xi) The nature of adjoining risks, say, the applicant's immediate neighbours in case a commercial property has to be insured
 (xii) The sum proposed for insurance, known as sum insured

The proposal form generally ends with a declaration to be signed by the proposer stating that whatever information has been provided is true to the best of his or her knowledge. Such a declaration becomes the basis of the insurance contract. Every proposal form must also be dated. Once the proposal is accepted by the insurance agent on behalf of the insurance company a cover note is issued.

Cover Note

A *cover note* is a document signifying the acceptance of the proposal and is as good as an insurance policy. It is normally valid for a period of 15 days from the date of issue to enable the insurance company to prepare the insurance policy document and for the premium cheque to be encashed. All cover notes carry a rider that the cover note is 'subject to the encashment of the cheque', which implies that if the cheque is not encashed, then there is no binding insurance cover. Upon encashment of the cheque, the date of commencement of the policy will be the same as the date of issue of the cover note. A cover note expires on the date mentioned on the note or on the issuance of the policy document.

In the case of group health insurance policies taken by companies for their employees, individual policies for each employee are not issued, and only a master group insurance policy is issued which is retained by the employer. Each individual employee is issued a certificate of insurance indicating the number of the master group insurance policy.

Insurance Policy

Insurance policy is a contract between the insured and the insurer which has various sections elucidating the policy.

Heading   It gives the insurance company's name and address of the registered office where communication can be sent.

Declaration   It identifies who is insured, the insured's address, the risks or property covered, the policy limits (sum insured), any applicable deductibles, the policy period, and premium amount. This information is usually provided on the proposal form that is filled out by the proposer and is mentioned in the cover note issued by the insurance company.

Definitions   These are important terms used in the policy.

Operative or insuring clause   This is the essence of the contract. It specifies the perils insured under the policy, and refers to the contractual agreement between the insurance company and the insured. It summarizes the major promises of the insurance company, stating what is covered.

Exclusions   It spells out the perils, hazards, or losses arising out of specific causes that are not covered by the policy.

Add-ons   These include additional coverage provided by the basic policy as opposed to exclusions; similar to endorsements that modify the basic policy.

Terms and conditions   These are the provisions, rules of conduct, duties and obligations required for coverage. If policy conditions are not met, then the insurer can deny the claim. Some of the common conditions that a proposer is required to fulfil are: sharing material information in good faith, the proposer having an insurable interest in the subject matter of insurance, and identification of the subject matter.

Endorsements Additional forms attached to the policy form that modify it in some way, either unconditionally or upon the existence of some condition. Because it is very risky to directly rewrite core policy language, insurers usually modify standard forms by attaching endorsements pre-approved by the insurance company's lawyers for various common modifications. Generally, endorsements are issued for alterations such as the following:

(a) Change in insurable interest
(b) Cancellation of insurance
(c) Change in the value at risk
(d) Change in the location or situation of risk
(e) Reduction or addition to the risk

Schedule Wherein are mentioned the description of the property insured, its location and site map.

Sum insured This clause mentions the sum insured or the value of the risk.

Attestations and signature clause This provides for the signatures of the authorized official of the insurance company.

Period of insurance Normally, an insurance policy is issued for one full year.

Renewal Notice

As the name suggests, renewal notice is sent by the insurance company to the insured advising him of the date of expiry of the policy as well as all the material details of the present insurance cover mentioning the premium amount to be paid to renew the policy.

If any changes are required to be done by the insurance company to the existing policy the insured should inform the insurance company at the earliest to enable it to incorporate the changes and re-quote the premium amount. Some of the common changes that are requested for are: removal of hypothecation in the case of car insurance policies once the loan is fully paid up; change in the value of the sum insured for fire insurance policies; inclusion or exclusions of dependents in health insurance policies, and so on.

TYPES OF INSURANCE POLICIES

Insurance can be classified into four broad categories: (i) life insurance, (ii) general insurance, (iii) fire insurance, and (iv) marine insurance, as illustrated in Fig. 6.1. However, both fire and marine insurance policies are issued by general insurance companies. Under the two classifications of life and general insurance, policies are categorized as per the type of insurance cover that they provide to an individual or a company.

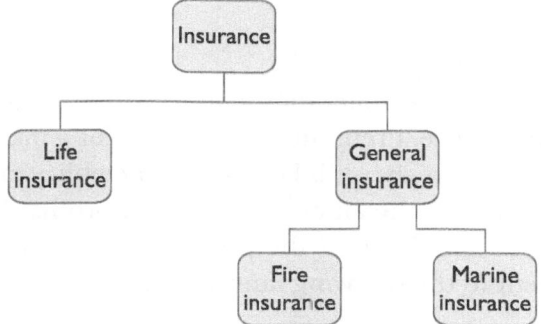

FIGURE 6.1 Types of Insurance Policies

Life Insurance Policies

Various types of life insurance products are defined to enable personnel managers to suggest them to employees, who are keen to invest in life insurance in order to save on taxes. These are illustrated in Fig. 6.2.

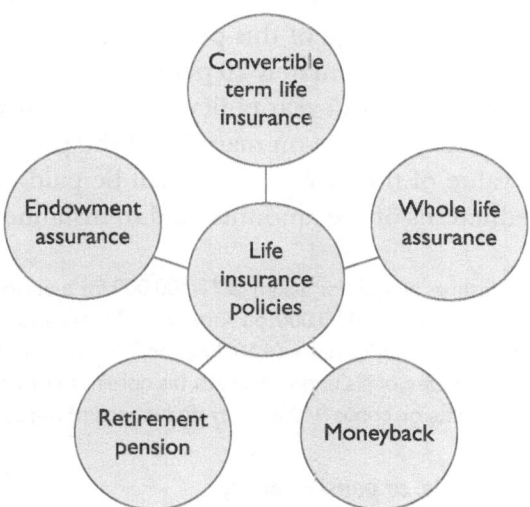

FIGURE 6.2 Types of Life Insurance Policies

Convertible Term Life Insurance

As the name implies, convertible term life insurance policy is for a fixed term not exceeding 35 years with an agreed premium amount, which is lower initially and then increases as per the paying capacity of the policyholder without impacting the sum insured. The premium can be paid annually, half-yearly, quarterly, or monthly. On maturity the amount is paid to the policyholder along with profits. In case of untimely death of the policyholder the amount is paid to the nominees.

> **Example**　Rajiv insures himself for a sum insured of ₹25,00,000 for a period of 25 years. At the end of the term he will receive the amount of ₹25,00,000 plus bonus or profits. In case of his death, his nominees or heirs will receive this amount.

Whole life assurance policy

In a whole life assurance policy for the sum assured a higher premium is payable than for term life insurance. Premiums are payable for a maximum period of 35 years or the age of 80 years, whichever is later. Once the policy matures no amount is payable to the policyholder as the amount along with profits shall be paid to the nominee or legal heirs on the death of the policyholder. This policy ensures a guaranteed financial benefit to the surviving family members.

> **Example**　Rajiv insures himself for a sum of ₹30,00,000 for a period of 35 years. Rajiv survives the 35-year term period; however, as the financial benefits are only payable to his family members after his demise, the amount of ₹30,00,000 plus bonus or profits will be paid only to them.

Moneyback policy

This policy is for a fixed term of 20 or 25 years with an agreed premium amount payable annually, half yearly, quarterly, or monthly. The premium amount in this policy is one of the highest. The advantage of this policy is that the policyholder receives survival benefit equivalent to approximately 20 per cent of the value in case of a 20-year policy and 15 per cent in case of a 25-year policy of the sum insured spread over equal instalments with 40 per cent payable on maturity of the policy. In the event of his untimely death, the full value of the sum assured shall be paid to his nominees or legal heirs without any deductions of the amounts paid in instalments to the policyholder.

> **Example**　Rajiv insures himself for a sum of ₹30,00,000 for a period of 25 years. Rajiv on surviving five years will receive an amount of ₹4,50,000; on surviving 10 years another ₹4,50,000; on surviving 15 years another ₹4,50,000; on surviving 20 years ₹4,50,000; and finally on maturity at the end of 25 years ₹7,00,000 plus bonus or profits. In case of his untimely death, his nominees or heirs will receive the full sum assured of ₹30,00,000 with profits or bonus without any deductions of the survival benefits already paid to Rajiv.

Retirement plan, annuity, or pension policy

As the name suggests, it is a policy designed to give a fixed guaranteed income to the policyholder after his retirement either for life or a fixed term. Insurance companies normally prefer a fixed-term payment plan of 15 or 20 years based upon the retirement age of 60 years, which means that the policyholder will get a guaranteed income till the age of 75 or 80 years.

> **Example**　Rajiv insures himself at the age of 50 years for an amount of ₹3,00,000. As the retirement age is 60 years the policy is taken for 10 years and the premium payable is ₹30,000 per annum. It is estimated that the policyholder will receive an annual income of ₹24,000 for the next 20 years.

Endowment assurance policy

An endowment assurance policy is similar to a term life insurance policy with the added cover of disability due to accident available to the whole family at a moderate premium for the sum assured as compared to other policies. The advantage of this policy is that the assured amount plus bonus or profits payable can be reinvested into a retirement or pension or annuity policy. In case of untimely death, the sum assured with profits will be paid to the nominee or legal heirs.

Example   Rajiv insures himself for a sum insured of ₹30,00,000 for a period of 25 years. At the end of the term he will receive the amount of ₹30,00,000 plus bonus or profits. In case of his untimely death, his nominees or heirs will receive this amount. In case Rajiv meets with an accident, which results in his permanent disability he is entitled to disability benefits under the policy.

General Insurance Policies

All types of insurance policies—other than life insurance policies— are called general insurance policies, which are issued by general insurance companies. These policies offer a wide range of products covering all types of contingencies as illustrated in Fig. 6.3. Types of general insurance policies are given as follows.

FIGURE 6.3   Types of General Insurance Policies

Fire policy—building and contents

Fire policy is by far one of the most important insurance policies taken by any business entity as it provides insurance cover for the building and its contents against the perils of:

- fire, lightening, explosion, aircraft damage
- riot/strike, malicious damage
- storm, cyclone, flood and inundation, landslide and subsidence, rock slide
- impact damage resulting in bursting and/or overflowing of water tanks, electrical equipment, other apparatus and pipes
- earthquake
- terrorism

Marine insurance

Marine insurance deals with insurance of goods in transit through the following modes of transport: sea, rail, road, air, inland waterways, and post parcels. Marine insurance policies have four distinct coverages: (i) marine hull insurance—covers a ship's hull, plant, and machinery; (ii) marine cargo insurance—personal effects of the ship's crew and passengers and cargo; (iii) marine freight insurance—covers loss of freight charges in case goods are lost, stolen, or damaged; (iv) marine liability insurance—covers third-party liability.

Accident and sickness insurance or health insurance

Accident and sickness insurance or health insurance can be individual and corporate health insurance policies, which are commonly referred to as Medicaid policies. For individual Medicaid policy the premium is payable by the individual, whereas for corporate Medicaid policy the premium is paid by the company on behalf of all the employees of the establishment. The objective of the policy is to provide for domiciliary and hospitalization benefits.

Motor or car insurance

Motor or car insurance is mandatory under the Motor Vehicles Act, 1988 to take comprehensive car insurance or third-party car insurance before any car can be registered with the regional transport authority. The policy covers accidental damage to the vehicle as well as damage due to fire, lightning, self-ignition, explosion, riot, strike, malicious act, terrorism, earthquake, flood, cyclone, and third-party liability claims. When third-party car insurance coverage is taken claims on account of accidents resulting in a liability to pay to third parties are entertained. A fleet insurance policy can be taken when there are more than five or more commercial automobiles to be insured.

Travel insurance

As the name suggests, travel insurance is a policy that is valid for the duration of a trip within India or abroad. It normally covers medical contingencies, travel-related issues such as delayed flights, loss of baggage, loss of passport, cancellation of flights, and personal accidents while travelling leading to death or disablement. For frequent travellers multi-trip insurance is also available.

Engineering insurance

The following types of policies are available under engineering insurance:

Machinery breakdown policy   All sorts of industrial and electrical machinery such as pumps, turbines, compressors, generator, transformer, and motor can be insured against accidental breakdown of both mechanical and electrical natures. The policy covers the insured against financial loss, and refunds the expenses incurred in repairing or replacing the machinery.

Boiler and pressure plant policy   This policy affords protection against damage to the boilers and/or pressure vessels or other machinery including the equipment itself, damage to the surrounding property of the insured, or liability of the insured by law to any third party on account of death or bodily injury.

Electronic equipment policy   This policy covers computers, audio-visual equipment, and micro-processors against unforeseen or sudden physical loss from fire and allied perils such as breakdown and short circuiting, resulting in material damage or increased working cost.

Industrial all-risk policy   This policy covers the risks of fire and allied perils, burglary and theft, machinery breakdown, boiler explosion, electronic equipment, machinery loss of profit, and consequential loss due to fire provided that the minimum sum insured is ₹100 crore.

Plate glass insurance policy   This policy covers plate glass, lettering, frames, and ornamentation against accidental breakages to display windows or showcases of commercial establishments.

Neon sign insurance policy   Also called electronic signage insurance, this policy covers loss or damage to the neon sign installation by accidental external means or fire, lightning, external explosion, or theft.

Workmen compensation insurance

Workmen compensation insurance covers an employer under any claims that may arise under the Workmen's Compensation Act, 1923 and the Fatal Accidents Act, 1855 resulting in the payment of compensation to employees not covered under Employees State Insurance Act, 1948 for bodily injury or disease sustained or contracted out of and in the course of employment.

Money insurance

As and when cash is transferred from one place to another there is a risk attached to it. Such risk is covered by the following insurance policies:

Cash in safe   This insures the cash in safe and has normally two limits. A daily cash limit and a higher limit for specified days of the month. A hotel can have a daily cash in safe limit of ₹15,00,000, but from the 4th to 10th day of each month it has a higher limit of ₹25,00,000 as decided by the hotel for days that salary and wages are paid.

Cash in transit This insures cash when it is being taken from the business premises to the bank for depositing or for withdrawing cash. This limit is fixed upon the maximum amount that is ever deposited or withdrawn on any given day.

Cash in counter This insures the cash amount which is given to the restaurant cashiers or front-office cashiers for managing the daily operations; this is a fixed limit and is commonly called an imprest.

Fidelity guarantee policy This covers the employer in respect of any direct financial loss, which he may suffer as a result of dishonesty, theft, loss, and pilferage by employees. In the case of death, dismissal, or retirement of the employee the policy still covers the company and a claim can be filed within 12 calendar months of such death, dismissal, or retirement whichever of these events shall first happen.

Loss of profit insurance

Loss of profit insurance covers loss of gross profit and/or increase in cost of working due to reduction in turnover or output due to the occurrence of any of the perils that have been insured under the fire policy. The policy covers the following:

- Loss of net trading profit
- Standing charges
- Loss in respect of wages other than those covered by the standing charges
- Increased cost of working
- Auditor's fees

Public liability insurance (third-party liability insurance)

This policy commonly known as third-party insurance policy covers the amount which the insured becomes legally liable to pay as damages to third parties as a result of accidental death, bodily injury, loss, or damage to the property belonging to a third party. The legal cost and expenses incurred in defending the case are also payable with prior consent of the insurance company.

When a public liability insurance is taken, two limits are specified in the policy: annual limit and a per-incident limit. For example, a hotel can take an annual limit of ₹2 crore and fix a per-incident limit of ₹20,00,000. In case there is an incident, the maximum coverage for that incident will be ₹20,00,000.

Public liability insurance under the Public Liability Insurance Act, 1991

Public liability insurance under the Public Liability Insurance Act, 1991 covers the statutory liability of the insured arising out of accidents occurring due to handling of hazardous substances as provided under the Public Liability Insurance Act, 1991 and Public Liability Insurance Rules, 1991.

Besides these insurance products there are a host of other products that are tailor-made to suit the insurance requirements of any business.

INSURANCE COVERAGE OFTEN AVAILED BY HOTELS

All modern hotels offer a host of facilities and services to the guests. In order to do so they have an army of employees and array of equipment installed on their premises. Besides the building structure, the lavish interiors of hotel rooms, and public area, there are a host of mechanical and electrical equipment in use all over the premises that have to be insured against fire, earthquake, floods, and other calamities. In guest rooms there are TV sets, mini bars, hot head irons, DVD players, electronically controlled curtains and sheers, mood control lightning fixtures, tea/coffee makers, and so on. 'Back of the house', which is the nerve centre of the hotel, there are air-conditioning plants, boilers, sewage treatment plants, diesel generator sets, telephone exchanges, water desalination filters and purifiers, laundry equipment, kitchen equipment, fire fighting equipment, and so on. All these facilities need to be adequately insured against any type of electrical or mechanical breakdowns, losses due to fire, or any untoward incidents or events.

Besides plant, machinery, and the physical assets, the hotels have to protect themselves from third-party liability claims that arise out of deficiency in service, not delivering upon the promises made, injuries sustained by guests whilst staying or using any of the hotel facilities, and so on. They also have to protect their employees from injuries whilst at work and take adequate health covers for their well-being.

Some of the insurance policies commonly taken by hotels are listed as follows:

(i) Standard fire policy
(ii) Machinery breakdown policy
(iii) Boiler and pressure plant
(iv) Electronic equipment
(v) Plate glass insurance
(vi) Cash in safe
(vii) Cash in transit
(viii) Cash in counter
(ix) Motor insurance or fleet insurance policy
(x) Group health insurance
(xi) Fidelity guarantees policy
(xii) Workmen compensation insurance
(xiii) Loss of profit insurance
(xiv) Public liability insurance
(xv) Neon sign insurance

Besides taking out adequate insurance covers for the hotels as per their individual requirements, it is important for the hotel managements to understand the process of insurance claim settlement. Understanding the process is critical for any hotelier, as it will help the hotel management to plan out the timelines for the reinstatement of the property.

FILING AN INSURANCE CLAIM

When a fire or any other untoward incident occurs, the first attempt is to secure the area where the incident occurred so as to reduce its impact; the second is to protect the lives of those around; and the third measure is to preserve whatever best possible from being destroyed.

> **Example**   Centaur Hotel Juhu Beach, located on the Juhu beach strip in Mumbai was the victim of a bomb explosion on 12 March 1993, which was a part of a series of explosions that rocked the city. The explosion left a gaping hole in the building wall on the south destroying approximately 70 guest rooms, ripping through the electrical, plumbing, water, and sanitation systems. It was left to the hotel team to contain the fire, to suture the water and electrical lines so as to prevent electrical short-circuiting.
>
> A central command and control point was established in the lobby to coordinate the various activities, whilst engineering and security teams were involved in securing the affected area. The second team led by the housekeeper was busy evacuating guests from the guest rooms and guiding them to the lobby. Smaller teams consisting of other department heads searched the rest of the hotel for survivors and rendered them first aid. The food and beverage department was entrusted to serve hot or cold beverages to the shocked guests in order to calm them. The lobby manager was delegated the task of informing the police, fire brigade, and the insurance company officials.
>
> The general manager on the basis of his own observations and inputs from his other team members was required to submit an unusual incident report, which had to be carefully written as it is a first-hand account of the incident. Insurance companies give much importance to such a report; in case of fire-related claims, both the fire department and police department need to be informed so as to obtain the first information report from them documenting the fire incident.
>
> Once the incident had been contained, follow-up was done with the insurance company in order to expedite the insurance claim process.

There are three stages to the processing of a fire or any type of insurance claim—initial stage, investigative stage, and settlement stage.

The initial stage   It involves informing the insurance company at the earliest of the incident. The purpose of informing the insurance company as soon as possible is to allow the insurance company to investigate the loss at its early stages. Once the information is received by the insurance company, it internally initiates the claim procedure, which involves scrutiny of the policy's terms and conditions. The following points are considered:

- The policy is in force on the date of occurrence of the loss or damage.
- The loss or damage is by a peril insured by the policy.
- The subject matter affected by the loss is the same as is insured under the policy.
- Notice of loss has been received without undue delay.

Once the scrutiny has been completed the insurance company allots a claim number and enters it in their Claims Register. A separate claim file is opened containing a copy of the policy and any other relevant papers, and a claim form is issued to the insured without prejudice or admission of its liability.

The hotel on receiving the claim form is required to complete the form and return it back to the insurance company at the earliest. The submission of the claim form to the insurance company completes the initial process.

The investigative stage   It involves the appointment of a surveyor or loss assessor by the insurance company. The loss assessor or surveyor is a professional who is certified by the IRDA and trained to give his independent assessment of the loss. The practice of appointing independent loss surveyors is to ensure a fair assessment of the loss and is based on the principle that since both the insurers and insured are interested parties, the opinion of an independent professional person should be acceptable to both the parties as well as to a court of law in the event of any dispute. However, often, the surveyor is appointed immediately and the survey carried out on receiving the communication of a loss, that is, even before the claim form could be issued. The Insurance Act, 1938 under Section 64 UM specifies that no loss exceeding ₹20,000 can be paid unless certified by the loss assessor or surveyor.

The claim is processed on the basis of:

(i) the completed claim form;
(ii) independent report from surveyors, legal and/or medical opinion, as the case may be; and
(iii) various documents furnished by the insured; and any other evidence secured by the insurers.

Settlement stage   If the claim is in order, settlement is effected by cheque. The payment is entered in the claims register as well as in the relevant policy record. Settlement of the claim involves securing a full and final settlement receipt from the insured.

Once the insurance claim amount has been finalized, a hotel can commence the repair and restoration work subject to final disbursement by the insurance company. Payment of a claim reduces the value of the sum insured and to restore the sum insured of the fire policy back to its original value a pro-rata premium is paid to the insurance company.

For claims that are made under other types of policies the claim procedure remains the same. However, there is a difference in the case of fidelity guarantee policy where a payout is made, and a motor insurance policy where there is a total loss claim. The insurance policy in both cases cannot be renewed by payment of a premium. In case of a medical insurance claim that exhausts the entire amount of the sum insured and the full capital value is paid, the policy stands terminated; but if the claim does not exhaust the full capital value the insurance policy continues with a reduced sum insured.

GRIEVANCE REDRESSAL MACHINERY

In the event that the insurance company fails to deliver on its promise, consumers or policyholders can approach certain institutions for the redressal of their complaints, which are discussed subsequently.

Consumer Protection Act, 1986

The holder of an insurance policy is defined as a consumer under Section 2(d)(ii) of the Consumer Protection Act, 1986 and is entitled to lodge a complaint against the insurance company with the consumer courts. Insurance is regarded as a service and complaints of any deficiency in service (Section 2(g)) can be entertained by the consumer courts.

According to Section 2(d), 'consumer means any person who—

(i) *buys any goods for a consideration which has been paid or promised or partly paid and partly promised, or under any system of deferred payment and includes any user of such goods other than the person who buys such goods for consideration paid or promised or partly paid or partly promised, or under any system of deferred payment when such use is made with the approval of such person, but does not include a person who obtains such goods for resale or for any commercial purpose; or*

(ii) *hires or avails of any services for a consideration which has been paid or promised or partly paid and partly promised, or under any system of deferred payment and includes any beneficiary of such services other than the person who hires or avails of the services for consideration paid or promised, or partly paid and partly promised, or under any system of deferred payments, when such services are availed of with the approval of the first-mentioned person.*

Section 2(e) defines a consumer dispute as one where the person against whom the complaint is being made denies or disputes the allegations contained in the complaint.

According to Section 2(g), deficiency means any fault, imperfection, shortcoming, or inadequacy in the quality, nature, and manner of performance which is required to be maintained by or under any law for the time being in force, or has been undertaken to be performed by a person in pursuance of a contract or otherwise in relation to any service.

Under the Consumer Protection Act, 1986, consumer courts that have been established at the district, state, or national level enjoy the powers of the civil courts. The district consumer forum can entertain a complaint up to a value of ₹5,00,000, the state commission can entertain a complaint up to a value of ₹20,00,000, and the national commission is the final authority and can entertain complaint above the value of ₹20,00,000.

In case the customer is dissatisfied with the judgement of the national commission he can approach the courts for the redressal of his complaint. In *Secretary, Thirumurugan Co-operative Agricultural Credit Society vs M. Lalitha, [(2004) 1 SCC 305]* has interpreted Section 3 of the Consumer Protection Act, 1986 to mean that the remedies provided under the Consumer Protection Act, 1986 are in addition to the remedies provided under other statutes.

Under Section 14 of the Consumer Protection Act, 1986, the consumer court can issue orders to the opposite party to do any of the following acts:

   (i) *To remove the defect*
  (ii) *To replace the goods with new goods of similar description which shall be free from any defect*
 (iii) *To return to the complainant the price*
 (iv) *To pay such amount as may be awarded as compensation to the consumer for the loss or injury suffered by the consumer due to the negligence of the opposite party*
  (v) *To discontinue the unfair trade practice or the restrictive trade practice or not to repeat them*
 (vi) *To cease and desist manufacture of hazardous goods*
 (vii) *To pay such sums as orders if injury/loss is suffered by a large number of consumers not identifiable conveniently*
(viii) *To issue corrective advertisement for neutralizing effect of misleading advertisement*
 (ix) *Not to offer the hazardous goods for sale*
  (x) *To withdraw the hazardous goods from being offered for sale*
 (xi) *To provide for adequate costs to parties (the Complainant)*

Most of the insurance complaints filed with the consumer courts deal with the following issues:

- Delay in settlement of claims
- Rejection of insurance claims
- Partial settlement of claims
- Non-settlement of a claim

Institution of Insurance Ombudsman

The Institution of Insurance Ombudsman was set up in 1999 under Section 114(1) of Insurance Act, 1938 when they framed the 'Redressal of Public Grievances Rules, 1998'. The insurance ombudsman entertains complaints up to a maximum limit of ₹20,00,000 from individuals on all policies taken by an individual on a personal basis; for example, life insurance, personal accident insurance, medical insurance, personal motor vehicle insurance, and comprehensive household articles insurance.

Prior to approaching the insurance ombudsman for redressal of his or her grievance a policyholder has to lodge a complaint with the Grievance Redressal Officer of the insurance company. If there is no response from the company's Grievance Redressal Officer the policyholder can escalate the complaint to the ombudsman.

The ombudsman is competent to hear complaints related to the following:

- Delay in settlement of claims
- Rejection of insurance claims
- Partial settlement of claims
- Non-settlement of a claim

Grievance Cell of the Insurance Regulatory and Development Authority

The Grievance Cell of the IRDA has no judicial authority like the Insurance Ombudsman or the Consumer Forum and plays the role of an arbitrator between the policyholder and the insurance company.

Only cases of delay in issuing the policies and non-processing of claims pertaining to life and general insurance are taken up by the grievance cell with the insurance companies.

LOSS PREVENTION ASSOCIATION OF INDIA

The Loss Prevention Association of India was set up under the aegis of the General Insurance Corporation of India with the aim of promoting safety and loss prevention through education, training, dissemination of information through advertisements, and so on.

- It conducts training programmes and provides educational material to corporates on fire safety and hazardous material handling.
- It carries out risk analysis of large industries and recommends the best safety and loss prevention standards specific to that industry.
- It educates workers and the general public on loss prevention techniques.
- It is one of the foremost agencies for inspecting and certifying fire safety standards as per guidelines given by the Insurance Tariff Advisory Committee.

SUMMARY

This chapter gave an overview of the insurance industry and the various steps taken by the government to regulate this business: moving from privatization to nationalization to privatization, the industry has gone a full circle. The chapter discussed various types of insurance products available in the market that address individual needs as well as fulfil the requirements of businesses under life and general insurance coverage. The salient principles of insurance which are common to all types of insurance policies were also discussed. The first step towards securing adequate insurance coverage is based upon the suitability and usefulness of the policy for the hotel, which commences from the application process till the policy document is issued. Finally, the chapter discussed how to file a claim; understanding the claim settlement process which in general goes through three stages—the initial stage, investigative, and settlement stages where the principles of insurance are applied to settle the claims. Specific types of policies may have different requirements towards settlement of claims notably health and motor insurance claims. The chapter highlights where to file for redressal of the grievances in case of any grievance with the insurance company or the settlement of a claim. The proactive approach of the Loss Prevention Association of India that promotes loss prevention through training seminars, brochures and advertisements, and so on has also been highlighted.

KEY TERMS

Insurance A business that indemnifies the risk of the insured by transferring the risk from the insured to the insurer.

Fortuity doctrine States that the basic concept of insurance is to cover risks, rather than losses that were planned, intended, or anticipated by the insured.

Doctrine of mitigation of loss Based upon the principle that the insured as a prudent or sensible person will take all the steps necessary to save the property in the event that there is a mishap.

Principle of utmost good faith or uberrimae fides States that there is a full disclosure of all the material and relevant information by the insured party to the insurer and vice versa so that both can take an educated decision on whether they would like to enter into an insurance contract.

Principle of indemnity To provide for compensation to the insured so as to place him or her in the same position that he or she was prior to the loss, and that he or she should not enjoy a benefit from the occurrence of the loss.

Subrogation The restitution of the rights of an assured in favour of the insurer against the third party for any damages caused by him in place of the assured after the insurer has indemnified him for the loss.

Insurable interest Exists when an insured person derives a financial or other kind of benefit from the continuous existence of the insured object, and the legal right to insure arises out of a financial relationship recognized under law between the insured and the subject matter of insurance.

Doctrine of proximate cause Nearest cause or direct cause and relates to the immediate cause of the mishap, which has resulted in the loss establishing a relationship between the action and the result.

Proposer Person who is seeking the insurance cover.

Proposal A request from the proposer seeking an insurance cover, made in writing by filling the insurance company's proposal form.

Cover note A document signifying the acceptance of the proposal and is as good as an insurance policy valid for a period of 15 days from the date of issue to enable the insurance company to prepare the insurance policy document and for the premium cheque to be encashed. It lapses once the policy is issued or 15 days whichever is earlier.

Insurance policy A contract between the insured and the insurer which has various sections that define the policy.

Renewal notice Sent by the insurance company to the insured advising him of the date of the expiry of the policy as well as all the material details of the present insurance cover mentioning the premium amount to be paid to renew the policy.

Act of God A flood, an earthquake, or other accidents or events that occur without any human intervention and that could not have been prevented by reasonable care or foresight, but is the result of natural causes (a snowstorm is an Act of God; driving is an act of man).

Actual cash value The sum of money required to pay for damages or lost property, computed on the basis of replacement value less its depreciation by obsolescence or general wear.

Total loss Occurs when the insured property is completely destroyed or when the insured is irretrievably deprived of the insured property.

Add-ons Additional coverage to the basic policy.

Insurance agents Two types of agents sell insurance: (i) independent agents or brokers who are self-employed business people representing more than one insurance company and are paid on a commission basis and (ii) exclusive agents who may be salaried or working on a commission basis exclusively for business development of an insurance company.

All risk Insurance against loss or damage to property arising from any fortuitous cause, except such as may be specifically excluded.

Annuity A life insurance company contract that pays a periodic income benefit for a specified period of time.

Appraisal A survey of property made for determining its insurable value or the amount of loss sustained.

Beneficiary or nominee Person to whom the proceeds of the insurance are to be paid upon the insured's death or when an endowment matures as nominated by the owner of the life insurance policy.

Insurance claim A formal request for payment of a loss under an insurance policy

Claimant One who seeks reimbursement for loss under the terms and conditions of the insurance contract.

Comprehensive coverage Traditional name for physical damage coverage for losses by fire, theft, vandalism, falling objects, and various other perils.

Consequential loss A loss arising indirectly from an insured peril.

Contribution Circumstances where more than one party covers the risk with each party deemed to be liable for his or her proportion of the loss.

Fire Combustion sufficient to product a spark, flame, or glow, which is hostile (as opposed to friendly—i.e., not in the place where it is intended to be as in a furnace or fireplace).

Hazard A specific situation that increases the probability of the occurrence of loss arising from a peril, or that may influence the extent of the loss. For example, slippery floors, unsanitary conditions, shingled roofs, congested traffic, unguarded premises, and uninspected boilers are hazards.

Insured The person signing the insurance agreement with the insurer who agrees to provide the insurance coverage.

Material fact   Anything affecting an insurance contract significant enough to change the agreement between the insurance company and the policyholder.

Insurer   The insurance company offering an insurance policy to an insured and willing to indemnify for losses, provide pecuniary benefits, or render services.

Negligence   Failure to use the degree of care expected from a reasonable and prudent person.

Pre-existing conditions   The physical condition of an insured person prior to the issuance of the policy.

Premium   The amount payable for an insurance policy paid periodically (annually, semi-annually, quarterly, or monthly).

Underwriting   The process of examining, accepting, or rejecting insurance risks, and classifying those selected in order to charge the proper premium for each.

Consumer dispute   Where the person against whom the complaint is being made denies or disputes the allegations contained in the complaint.

EXERCISES

Define the Following

1. Insurance agent
2. Contribution
3. Underwriting
4. Beneficiary
5. Actual cash value
6. Cover note
7. Subrogation
8. Insurance policy
9. Consequential loss
10. Annuity

Concept Review Questions

1. Explain the application process for securing an insurance policy.
2. Discuss the historical evolution of insurance business in India.
3. Describe the process of settlement of a claim.
4. Explain the importance of the application of the doctrine of proximate cause and subrogation in settling claims.

5. Define the important features of an insurance contract.

Critical Thinking Questions

1. It has been said that 'Insurance is the subject matter of solicitation'. Recommend insurance policies that a hotel should take to protect its assets.
2. What is the role of the consumer courts and the insurance companies' grievance officers in addressing customer grievances?
3. Insurance contracts are 'contingent contracts'. Explain this statement.

Research Question

1. Does the insurance ombudsman ensure a fair hearing and settlement of insurance claims?

Project

1. The Loss Prevention Association of India has played a stellar role in educating consumers and promoting transparency in the marketing of insurance products to clients. Has the Association outlived its usefulness? Comment.

REFERENCES

<http://www.irda.gov.in/ADMINCMS/cms/NormalData_Layout.aspx?page=PageNo4&mid=2> accessed on 1 August 2012.

<http://en.wikipedia.org/wiki/History_of_insurance> accessed on 1 August 2012.

<http://www.iran-law.com/article.php3?id_article=61> accessed on 1 August 2012.

<http://www.ssa.gov/history/ottob.html> accessed on 2 August 2012.

<http://www.futuregenerali.in/GeneralInsurance/CorporateProducts/LossofProfitsPolicy/LossOfProfitsPolicy.aspx> accessed on 2 August 2012.

<http://www.futuregenerali.in/GeneralInsurance/CorporateProducts/MarineCargoInsurance/MarineCargoInsurance.aspx> accessed on 2 August 2012.

<http://www.futuregenerali.in/GeneralInsurance/CorporateProducts/EngineeringInsurance/MachineryBreakdown.aspx> accessed on 2 August 2012.

<http://www.futuregenerali.in/GeneralInsurance/CorporateProducts/IndustrialAllRisk/IndustrialAllRisk.aspx> accessed on 2 August 2012.

<http://newindia.co.in/Content.aspx?pageid=50> accessed on 2 August 2012.

<http://www.thefreedictionary.com/fortuity> accessed on 2 August 2012.

<http://encyclopedia.thefreedictionary.com/insurable+interest> accessed on 2 August 2012.

<http://www.californiaautoinsurance.in/2012/07/risk-management-of-olympic-proportions-crunching-the-numbers-and-insuring-the-london-2012-games/> accessed on 2 August 2012.

<http://ekikrat.in/Machinery-Breakdown-Policy-United-India-Insurance> accessed on 6 August 2012.

<http://www.scribd.com/doc/3630312/Project-Report-on-United-India-Insurance-Co> accessed on 6 August 2012.

<http://newindia.co.in/Content.aspx?pageid=15> accessed on 6 August 2012.

<http://www.gbic.co.in/faq.html> accessed on 6 August 2012.

<http://www.irda.gov.in/ADMINCMS/cms/NormalData_Layout.aspx?page=PageNo225&mid=14.2> accessed on 6 August 2012.

<http://www.sethassociates.com/consumer-protection-act-in-india.html> accessed on 6 August 2012.

<http://www.vakilno1.com/bareacts/consumerprotectionact/consumerprotectionact.htm> accessed on 7 August 2012.

<http://www.indiastudychannel.com/resources/138535-Types-insurance-methods-settlement.aspx> accessed on 7 August 2012.

Part III

Laws Related to Employees and Guests

Chapter 7   Labour Laws

Chapter 8   Hospitality Law

Labour Laws

LEARNING OBJECTIVES

After going through this chapter, the reader will be familiar with the following:

- History of labour legislation and formulation of India's labour policy
- Formation of trade unions and the mechanics of dispute settlement
- Process of selection, recruitment, appointment, and discharge of employees
- Laws related to social security, employee welfare, and benefits
- Laws guaranteeing special status to women and persons with special needs

INTRODUCTION

In *Wealth of Nations,* Adam Smith (1776) stated, 'Labour was the first price, the original purchase—money that was paid for all things. It was not by gold or by silver, but by labour, that all wealth of the world was originally purchased'.

In his speech to the Madras Central Labour Board in Madras (1920), Mahatma Gandhi remarked, 'A nation may do without its millionaires and without its capitalists, but a nation can never do without its labour.'

These two statements centuries apart, signify the importance of labour as society transited from being agriculture based to an industrialized one. The 18th and 19th centuries witnessed the mechanization of the textile industry in England which ushered in the Industrial Revolution.

During this period, India had a strong agrarian economic base and its textiles were renowned all over the world being exported primarily to England and other parts of Europe. However, the Industrial Revolution would have a direct impact on India, as the British in order to support their growing textile industry took measures to discourage Indian textile manufacturing.

During the late 19th and early 20th centuries, the British passed various pieces of legislation to regulate labour in India. Indentured labour or bonded labour was supplied to the plantation owners by contractors who, in turn, provided food and accommodation to the labourers. This practice of providing indentured labour to the indigo plantation industry in Bengal and the tea industry in Assam was the first to attract legislation by the British. A person willing to become a coolie, that is, a labourer doing menial tasks to escape poverty in exchange for food and accommodation, was known as indentured labourer.

Most of the laws that were enacted during the British rule of India were overtly labour oriented but designed to favour business owners in the long run. The largest employer during the 19th century was the Indian Railways, which was developing its network throughout the length and breadth of the country. The laws enacted were designed to preserve British control over the Indian workforce by ensuring benefits such as prompt payment of wages, weekly holidays, compensation in case of accidents and redressal of industrial disputes, and so on.

Some of the laws that were enacted were as follows:

- The Bengal Indigo Contracts Act, 1836
- The Fatal Accidents Act, 1855
- The Workmen's Compensation Act, 1923
- The Mines Act, 1923
- Trade Unions Act, 1926
- Trade Dispute Act, 1929
- The Children (Pledging of Labour) Act, 1933
- The Payment of Wages Act, 1936
- The Payment of Wages Rules, 1937
- The Weekly Holiday Act, 1942
- The War Injuries Ordinance Act, 1943
- The War Injuries (Insurance Compensation) Act, 1943
- The Industrial Employment Standing Orders Act, 1946
- The Industrial Employment Standing Orders Rules, 1946
- The Mica Mines Labour Funds Act, 1946
- The Industrial Disputes Act, 1947

Post Independence, India inherited an economy that was deficient in capital. The formulation of the Five Year Plans, the first one being adopted in 1951, was the route adopted by the central and state governments to support and encourage planned economic growth.

CONSTITUTIONAL PROVISIONS

The adoption of the Indian Constitution by the Constituent Assembly on 26 January 1950 gave to all citizens of India fundamental rights, which would coexist with the directive principles of state policy. Certain key items were placed in the concurrent list to enable the centre and the state to enact suitable legislation.

Fundamental Rights (Part III Articles 12–35)

Fundamental rights guarantee that the residents of India can lead a peaceful life with the Supreme Court and the high courts empowered to enforce these rights. The six fundamental rights are (Fig. 7.1): right to equality; right to freedom; right against exploitation; right to freedom of religion; cultural and educational rights; and right to constitutional remedies.

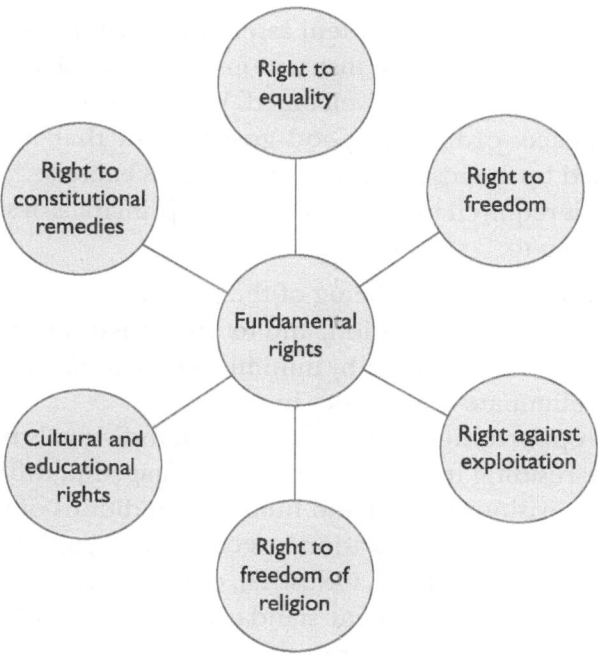

FIGURE 7.1 Fundamental Rights

Articles 14–16 Right to Equality   It guarantees to all citizens equality before the law, prohibition of discrimination on the grounds of religion, race, caste, sex or place of birth, and equality of opportunity in matters of public employment.

Articles 19–22 Right to Freedom   It guarantees protection of freedom of speech, life, and liberty, and protection against conviction for offences and against arrest and detention.

Articles 23 and 24 Right against Exploitation   It prohibits forced labour and employment of children in factories and industries.

Articles 25–28 Right to Freedom of Religion   It guarantees the right to practise any faith, freedom of conscience, and to practise any profession freely.

Articles 29 and 30 Cultural and Educational Rights   They protect the interest of minorities to attend any educational institute.

Articles 32–35 Right to Constitutional Remedies   It confers the right to every citizen to approach the Supreme Court or the high courts for the enforcement of their fundamental rights.

Under the Indian Constitution, the *Directive Principles of State Policy (Part IV—Articles 36–51)*, though not enforceable by any court 'are nevertheless fundamental in the governance of the country and it shall be the duty of the State to apply these principles in making laws'.

In his speech to the constituent assembly, Dr Ambedkar remarked that 'directive principles of state policy are instructions to the legislature and the executive. Such a thing, to my mind, is to be welcomed. Wherever there is grant or power in general terms for peace, order and good government that it is necessary, it should be accompanied by the instructions regulating its exercise.'

The state is required to apply the directive principles of state policy while legislating laws pertaining to:

(i) the promotion of well-being of the people;

(ii) right to work, to education, and to public assistance in certain cases;

(iii) secure a just social order by minimizing the inequalities in income, and endeavour to eliminate inequalities in status;

(iv) create opportunities, not only amongst individuals but also amongst groups of people residing in different areas or engaged in different vocations;

(v) make provisions for just and humane conditions of work and maternity relief;

(vi) secure, by suitable legislation or economic organisation or in any other way, to all workers, agricultural, industrial, or otherwise, work, a living wage, conditions of work ensuring a decent standard of life and full enjoyment of leisure and social and cultural opportunities;

(vii) secure the participation of workers in the management of undertakings, establishments or other organizations engaged in any industry; and

(viii) within the limits of its economic capacity and development, make effective provision for securing the right to work, to education, and to public assistance in cases of unemployment, old age, sickness and disablement, and in other cases of undeserved want.

Concurrent List (Article 246 List III of the Seventh Schedule)

Concurrent List under the Indian Constitution gives both the centre and the states legislative powers to enact laws on the items that are listed in the Concurrent List. These are listed in items 22–24 which are given as follows:

(i) Item 22. Trade unions; industrial and labour disputes.

(ii) Item 23. Social security and social insurance; employment and unemployment.

(iii) Item 24. Welfare of labour including conditions of work, provident funds, employers' liability, workmen's compensation, invalidity and old age pensions and maternity benefits.

However, if any piece of legislation passed by the state conflicts in any manner with a central law passed on the same subject, the provisions of the central act shall take precedence.

Fundamental rights and directive principles of state policy formed the cornerstone of India's labour policy, which emphasize the twofold objective maintaining industrial peace and promoting the welfare of labour. The Concurrent List ensures that whilst legislating the state should make effective provision for securing the right to work under just and humane conditions, ensuring a living wage that secures a decent standard of life, full enjoyment of leisure, and social and cultural opportunities keeping in mind the welfare of employees. The state shall further enact laws for the empowerment and equality of women at the workplace.

CATEGORIZATION OF LABOUR LAWS

Labour laws have been categorized by the Ministry of Labour according to the purpose that they have been enacted for, such as the following:

(i) Laws related to industrial relations
   (a) The Trade Unions Act, 1926
   (b) The Industrial Employment (Standing Orders) Act, 1946
   (c) The Industrial Employment (Standing Orders) Rules, 1946
   (d) The Industrial Disputes Act, 1947
   (e) The Trade Unions (Amendments) Act, 2001

(ii) Laws related to wages
   (a) The Payment of Wages Act, 1936
   (b) The Payment of Wages Rules, 1937
   (c) The Minimum Wages Act, 1948
   (d) The Minimum Wages (Central) Rules, 1950
   (e) The Payment of Bonus Act, 1965
   (f) The Payment of Bonus Rules, 1975
   (g) The Payment of Wages (Amendment) Act, 2005

(iii) Laws related to working hours, conditions of services, and employment
   (a) The Factories Act, 1948
   (b) The Contract Labour (Regulation & Abolition) Act, 1970
   (c) The Contract Labour(Regulation & Abolition) Rules, 1971
   (d) The Shops and Establishments Act, 1948

(iv) Laws related to equality and empowerment of women
   (a) The Maternity Benefit Act, 1961
   (b) The Equal Remuneration Act, 1976

(v) Laws related to social security
   (a) The Workmen's Compensation Act, 1923
   (b) The Employees' State Insurance Act, 1948
   (c) The Employees' Provident Fund & Miscellaneous Provisions Act, 1952
   (d) The Payment of Gratuity Act, 1972
   (e) The Payment of Gratuity Rules, 1972

(f) The Employees' Provident Fund & Miscellaneous Provisions (Amendment) Act, 1996

(g) The Workmen's Compensation (Amendments) Act, 2000

(h) The Payment of Gratuity (Amendment) Act, 2010

(vi) Laws related to employment and training

(a) The Employment Exchanges (Compulsory Notification of Vacancies) Act, 1959

(b) The Employment Exchanges (Compulsory Notification of Vacancies) Rules, 1959

(c) The Apprentices Act, 1961

(vii) Others

(a) The Fatal Accidents Act, 1855

(b) The Weekly Holiday Act, 1942

(c) The National and Festival Holidays Act

(d) The Personal Injuries (Emergency) Provisions Act, 1962

(e) The Personal Injuries (Compensation Insurance) Act, 1963

(f) The Public Liability Insurance Act, 1991

This exhaustive list can be divided into two parts: labour laws defining the relationship between employers, employees, and trade unions and those that provide for rights of employees at workplace such as wages, working hours, working conditions, welfare measures, and so on.

CATEGORIZATION OF INDUSTRY

Indian labour law divides industry into two broad categories—shops and commercial establishments and factories as illustrated in Fig. 7.2.

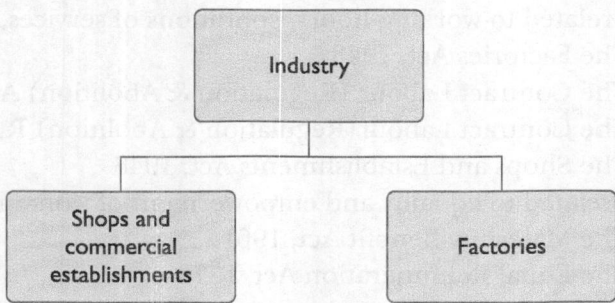

FIGURE 7.2 Categorization of Industry

Every state has its own Shops and Establishments Act that regulates the activities of shops and commercial establishments; however, broadly the definition of a shop or commercial establishment is the same in all the states. For the purpose of this chapter, the definition as mentioned in the Delhi Shops and Establishments Act, 1954 has been considered.

TEXT

Delhi Shops and Establishments Act, 1954—Definitions Section 2, Paras (5) and (9):

(5) 'commercial establishment' means any premises wherein any trade, business or profession or any work in connection with, or incidental or ancillary thereto, is carried on and includes a society registered under the Societies registration Act 1860 (XXI of 1860) and charitable or other trust, whether registered or not, which carries on any business, trade or profession or work in connection with or incidental or ancillary thereto, journalistic and printing establishments, contractors and auditors establishments quarries, and mines not governed by the Mines Act, 1952 (XXXV of 1952), educational or other institution run for private gain and premises in which business of banking, insurance, stocks and shares, brokerage or produce exchange is carried on, but does not include a shop or a factory registered under the Factories Act, 1948 (LXIII of 1948), or theatres, cinemas, restaurants, eating houses, residential hotels, clubs or other places of public amusement or entertainment;

(9) 'establishment' means a shop, a commercial establishment, residential hotel, restaurant, eating-house, theatre or other places of public amusement or entertainment to which this Act applies and includes such other establishment as Government may, by notification in the Official Gazette, declare to be an establishment for the purpose of this Act;

Interpretation clause under The Factories Act, 1948 defines a factory:

TEXT

(m) 'Factory' means any premises including the precincts thereof—

(i) As 'an industrial establishment employing 10 or more persons and carrying manufacturing activities with the aid of power.'

(ii) An industrial establishment employing 20 or more persons and carrying manufacturing activities without the aid of power.

It is clear from the above definitions that hotels are required to register themselves under the Shops and Establishment Acts and do not fall in the category of an industry under the Factories Act, 1948. The Act further regulates the opening and closing hours of the establishment, appointment of employees, and mode of payment of wages, leave records, weekly offs, and so on.

CLASSIFICATION OF EMPLOYEES

Employees are broadly classified into three categories as illustrated in Fig. 7.3.

- Government servants, civil servants, and public servants are governed by the service conditions and rules that stem from the Indian Constitution. These employees enjoy statutory protection of tenure and automatic salary increases.
- Public sector employees serving in government controlled organizations are governed by the service conditions of their organizations.
- Private sector employees are divided into two categories—management and staff, or management and workmen. Employees drawing a basic salary of ₹6500 per month are considered as managerial or supervisory employees and their service conditions are determined as per the terms and conditions of the service contract. Workmen or staff, on the other hand, are governed by the service conditions framed and adopted by the establishment based upon the guidelines mentioned in the various acts such as Industrial Disputes Act, 1947 and Delhi Shops and Establishment Act, 1954.

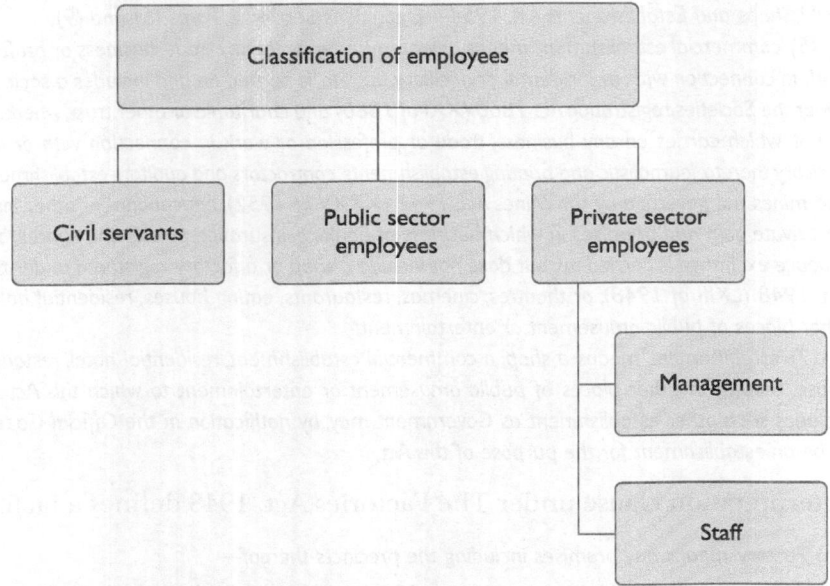

FIGURE 7.3   Classification of Employees

Our study of labour laws will pursue the following broader categorization:

(i) Labour laws defining the relationship between employers, employees, and trade unions

(ii) Labour laws that provide for rights of employees at workplace such as wages, working hours, working conditions, welfare measures, and so on

Labour Laws Defining the Relationship Between Employers, Employees, and Trade Unions

Labour laws that define the relationship between employers, employees, and trade unions are the Industrial Disputes Act, 1947, The Trade Unions Act, 1926, The Trade Unions (Amendment) Act, 2001, and The Factories Act, 1948.

The Industrial Disputes Act, 1947

Introduction   A few provisions of this Act are derived from the Trade Dispute Act, 1929, such as settlement of disputes by negotiations, conciliation, mediation, voluntary arbitration, and compulsory adjudication instead of by trial of strength through strikes and lockouts to ensure industrial peace.

Although a hotel requires to be registered under the State's Shops and Establishments Act as a 'commercial establishment' and has not been classified as an industry, it is important to understand what is an industry, who is a workman, and what constitutes an industrial dispute and the dispute settlement machinery.

The Act provides for the creation of an institutional framework for the settlement of industrial disputes, namely the grievance redressal committee, the works committee, and the adjudication machinery consisting of labour courts, industrial tribunals, and national tribunals. The grievance redressal committee and the works committee comprise the representatives of workers and employers. Labour courts and state industrial tribunals are set up by the state governments, whereas the national tribunal is set up by the central government.

Industry

Section 2 Clause (j) Industry means any systematic activity carried on by co-operation between an employer and his workmen for the production, supply or distribution of goods or services with a view to satisfy human wants or wishes. Workmen may be employed by such employer directly or by or through any agency, including a contractor. (Section 2(j)); whether or not,

(i) *any capital has been invested for the purpose of carrying on such activity; or*
(ii) *such activity is carried on with a motive to make any gain or profit, and includes*
    (a) *any activity of the Dock Labour Board established under section 5-A of the Dock Workers (Regulation of Employment) Act, 1948 (9 of 1948);*
    (b) *any activity relating to the promotion of sales or business or both carried on by an establishment,*

But does not include
    (1) *Any agricultural operation except where such agricultural operation is carried on in an integrated manner with any other activity (being any such activity as is referred to in the foregoing provisions of this clause) and such other activity is the predominant one.*

        Explanation *For the purposes of this sub-clause, 'agricultural operation' does not include any activity carried on in a plantation as defined in clause (f) of section 2 of the Plantation Labour Act, 1951; or*

    (2) *hospitals or dispensaries; or*
    (3) *educational, scientific, research to training institutions; or*
    (4) *institutions owned or managed by organizations wholly or substantially engaged in any charitable, social or philanthropic service; or*
    (5) *khadi or village industries; or*
    (6) *any activity of the Government relatable to the sovereign functions of the Government including all the activities carried on by the departments of the Central Governments dealing with defense research, atomic energy and space; or*
    (7) *any domestic service; or*
    (8) *any activity, being a profession practiced by an individual or body of individuals, if the number of persons employed by the individuals or body of individuals in relation to such profession is less than ten; or*
    (9) *any activity, being an activity carried on by a co-operative society or a club or any other like body of individuals, if the number of persons employed by the co-operative society, club or other like body of individuals in relation to such activity is less than ten.*

Workman

Section 2 clause (s) a 'Workman' means any person (including an apprentice) employed in any industry to do any manual, unskilled, skilled, technical, operational, clerical or supervisory work for hire or reward, whether the terms of employment be express or implied, and for the purposes of any proceeding under this Act in relation to an industrial dispute, includes any such person who has been dismissed, discharged or retrenched in connection with, or as a consequence of, that dispute, or whose dismissal, discharge or retrenchment has led to that dispute, but does not include any such person:

(i) who is subject to the Air Force Act, 1950 (45 of 1950), or the Army Act, 1950 (46 of 1950), or the Navy Act, 1957 (62 of 1957); or

(ii) who is employed in the police service or as an officer or other employee of a prison; or

(iii) who is employed mainly in a managerial or administrative capacity; or

(iv) who, being employed in a supervisory capacity, draws wages exceeding one thousand six hundred rupees per month or exercises, either by the nature of the duties attached to the office or by reason of the powers vested in him, functions mainly of a managerial nature-Section 2(s).

The hotel business is a systematic activity carried out by the cooperation between the hotel management (employer) and its employees (workmen) for the production, supply, or distribution of goods or services with a view to satisfy human desires and wishes. The hotel hires various categories of employees to engage in manual, unskilled, skilled, technical, operational, clerical, or supervisory works directly or through contractors. This definition makes it clear that managerial employees as well as supervisors who exercise managerial functions are not covered by this Act.

Industrial dispute

Section 2 Clause (k) an 'industrial dispute' means any dispute or difference between employers and employers, or between employers and workmen, or between workmen and workmen, the subject matter of which is connected with the employment or non-employment or the terms of employment or with the conditions of labour, of any person.

An industrial dispute is one that is (i) between employers and employers, (ii) between employers and workmen, or (iii) between workmen and workmen, the subject matter of which is connected with the employment or non-employment of any person, who has been dismissed, discharged, or retrenched in connection with, or as a consequence of that dispute, or whose dismissal, discharge, or retrenchment has led to that dispute.

Example 1.   Between employers and employers   The vice-president (operations) has appointed Rajesh as a general manager, sales and marketing to market Choice Hotels to corporate clients. As per the terms of the appointment letter, Rajesh will be given a performance bonus of ₹30,000 provided his team achieves the room nights and revenue targets agreed upon for the financial year. During the year-end performance review it is observed that the room night goals have been met; however, the team has not achieved its revenue targets. Under these circumstances the bonus is withheld by the vice-president (operations) and Rajesh approaches the company's grievance redressal committee to resolve the issue. The committee gives a decision in favour of the vice-president as the appointment letter clearly stipulates that the bonus is payable provided both the room night and revenue targets are met by Rajesh.

Example 2. Between employers and workmen   The housekeeping and engineering employees of a hotel have been caught sleeping on duty by the lobby manager and the hotel security. This act of misconduct is an area of concern that requires to be addressed on an urgent basis by the management.

Eight employees who are habitual offenders are suspended and served show-cause notices by the management on the grounds that they were sleeping on duty. The contention of the hotel management was that they had a right to terminate their services in keeping with the service rules and regulations that were in place at the hotel. The workmen's union took up the matter on behalf of the affected employees suggesting that the management was victimizing the concerned employees as there was insufficient evidence to warrant the termination of their services.

The enquiry officer concluded though sleeping on duty is an act of misconduct, they should be given another opportunity and be allowed to resume their duties, after a final severe warning letter is placed on their personal files.

Example 3. Between workmen and workmen   It is the responsibility of the personnel department and the kitchen to ensure that wholesome meals are provided to employees at the staff cafeteria whilst they are on duty. On 15 May 2010, it was reported that a section of employees who were dissatisfied with the food quality and the repetitive nature of the menu being served entered into a brawl with the cooks in the cafeteria. The workmen's union escalated the matter and approached the general manager informing him that the quality of food had been deteriorating over the past few weeks in spite of the best quality of ingredients being purchased.

An enquiry committee consisting of the personnel manager, executive chef, and members of the union was constituted to examine the various issues. Its recommendations were as follows:

 (i) Employees who had participated in the brawl should be issued warning letters and an unqualified apology taken on record stating that if the offence is repeated the management has a right to terminate both sections of the employees.
 (ii) The cafeteria cooks should undergo training to improve their culinary skills.
 (iii) The quality of ingredients that were being purchased required to be monitored as vendors would on occasions provide sub-standard material that would be handed over to the cafeteria for preparing staff meals.
 (iv) A cafeteria committee is instituted to manage the affairs of the staff cafeteria consisting of representatives of the management and the workmen's unions and would be responsible for maintaining the costs and quality of the meals being served.

Dispute settlement mechanism   Sections 3 to 9C of the Act propose the setting up of a grievance redressal committee, works committee, board of conciliation, labour courts, and state and national tribunals for the redressal of disputes.

Section 9 C—Grievance Redressal Committee

The Industrial Disputes (Amendment) Act, 2010 (effective 15 September 2010) envisages the setting up of a grievance redressal machinery to address individual grievances in any establishment that has more than 20 employees. The committee shall have six members equally divided between employer and employees with a suitable mix of men and women members. The chairman of the committee will be appointed by rotation between the employer and the employees' representatives. Upon receipt of a grievance from an individual member, the committee is required to give its decision within a month and the aggrieved party can appeal to the employer in case he or she is dissatisfied with the committee's decision; in such cases, the employer has to communicate his decision within 30 days to the employee. As a last resort, if the employee continues to be dissatisfied with the decisions he can raise an industrial dispute under the Act.

> **Example**   Ramada Hotels has appointed Sumit Singh as head of corporate relations to look after owner–operator relations at their corporate headquarters. Upon joining the company, he is issued an appointment letter, undergoes an induction programme briefing him on the companies policies and procedures, and given his job profile enlisting his duties and responsibilities.
>
> As per the terms of his appointment he shall be on probation for a period of six months, which can be extended for a further period of three months. Upon confirmation at the end of the probation period he is entitled to an increment.
>
> At the end of one year Sumit is yet to receive his confirmation letter and his annual increment. He approaches the personnel manager to redress his grievance. The personnel department has not received his performance appraisal; hence they are not confirming or processing his annual increment. A disgruntled Sumit approaches the grievance redressal committee consisting of the personnel manager and his department head. The matter is resolved when the head of department completes Sumit's performance appraisal recommending his confirmation, thereby enabling the personnel department to issue Sumit his confirmation and annual increment letter.

Section 3 Works Committee

Section 3, Clause (2) enunciates the role of the works committee as follows: 'to promote measures for securing and preserving amity and good relations between the employer and workmen and, to that end, to comment upon matters of their common interest or concern and endeavour to compose any material difference of opinion in respect of such matters'.

It is mandatory to have a works committee look into the grievances of employees in industries employing more than 100 employees. The committee shall consist of an equal number divided between employer and employees with a mix of male and female members. The chairman of the committee shall be appointed by rotation between the employer and the employees' representatives. The employees' representatives can be selected from any department, but shall be appointed after consultations with the representatives of the registered trade union as elected under the Trade Unions Act, 1926. If the works committee fails to resolve the differences the dispute shall be referred for conciliation.

Sections 4 and 5—Board of Conciliation

Conciliation has been defined by the legal dictionary as follows: 'The process of adjusting or settling disputes in a friendly manner through extra judicial means. Conciliation means bringing two opposing sides together to reach a compromise in an attempt to avoid taking a case to trial. A court of conciliation is one that suggests the manner in which two opposing parties may avoid trial by proposing mutually acceptable terms.'

The government under Sections 4 and 5 can appoint a board of conciliation with a conciliation officer as its chairman presiding over a quorum of four members equally representing both the parties to the dispute. As is the established practice, labour commissioners or assistant labour inspectors of the area are designated as conciliation officers; they may be appointed for a specified area or location or for a specified industry, for example, automobiles, hospitality, and so on.

The powers, duties, responsibilities, and procedure to be followed by a conciliation officer are defined in Sections 11 and 12. The conciliation officer can 'inquire into an existing or apprehended industrial dispute and after giving reasonable notice enter the premises occupied by an industrial establishment to which the dispute relates.' All conciliation officers are vested with power of a court when presiding over the hearings and can summon any person or examine any document or initiate investigation proceedings which in their opinion can help in resolving the dispute. During conciliation proceedings, 'in respect of any dispute, no employer can alter the conditions of service to the prejudice of the workmen concerned with the dispute or dismiss or punish any such workmen without obtaining written permission of the authority concerned.'

TEXT

The conciliation officer shall, for the purpose of bringing about a settlement of dispute, without delay, investigate the dispute and all matters affecting the merits and the right settlement thereof and may do all such things as he thinks fit for the purpose of inducing the parties to come to a fair and amicable settlement of the dispute.

If the employer and the workmen fail to arrive at a settlement through negotiations, the conciliation officer may intervene as a mediator, endeavour to reconcile the differences of opinion and help the labour and management in achieving a successful settlement. Intervention by the conciliation officer is mandatory in case an industrial dispute has arisen in a public utility service and a notice of strike or lockout (under section 22) has been served.

The conciliation officer shall send a report of proceedings to the government, as to whether the settlement has been achieved or not, within fourteen days of the commencement of the conciliation proceedings or within such extended time as may be allowed and in the prescribed manner. If a settlement is arrived at as a result of conciliation proceedings a memorandum of settlement is worked out and it becomes binding on all the parties concerned for a period agreed upon. If no settlement is arrived at, the conciliation officer shall, as soon as practicable after the close of investigation, send a full report to the government, setting forth the steps taken by him for ascertaining the facts and circumstances relating to the dispute and for bringing about a settlement thereof, and the reasons on account of which a settlement could not be reached.

After receiving the report if the government is satisfied that it should be referred to a labour court, state tribunal, or national tribunal the government can refer the matter within 14 days. In Puducherry, the government has fixed the time limit of 60 days from the commencement of the conciliation proceedings.

TEXT

A settlement arrived at, in the course of conciliation proceedings comes into operation - on such date as is agreed upon by the parties to the dispute: or where no such date is agreed upon, on the date on which the memorandum of settlement is signed by both the parties to the dispute. The settlement shall be binding -for the period agreed upon by the parties: and where no such period is agreed upon, for a period of six months from the date on which the memorandum of settlement is signed.

The settlement shall remain binding for a further period until the expiry of two months from the date on which a notice in writing for termination of the settlement is given by any one party to the other party or parties.

Under Sections 18(3) and 18(1), two types of settlement have been recognized:

(i) Settlement arrived in the course of conciliation proceeding before the authority. Such settlements not only bind the member of the signatory union but also non-members as well as all the present and future employees of the management.

(ii) Settlement not arrived in the course of conciliation proceedings but signed independently by the parties to the settlement and binds only such members who are signatory or party to the settlement.

Under Section 19(2), all settlements are binding during the period mentioned in it and after the period has expired it continues to be binding, unless a two-month notice of termination is given by one party to another. If no period has been specified, settlement is valid for six months and an award is valid for one year.

Section 10 (a) Arbitration

Arbitration is the submission of a dispute to an unbiased third person designated by the parties to the controversy, who agree in advance to comply with the award—a decision to be issued after a hearing at which both parties have an opportunity to be heard.

This Section recommends arbitration or voluntary arbitration as an alternative method to resolve an industrial dispute which leads to a binding arbitral award. Arbitration proceedings are carried out under the procedures framed under the Indian Arbitration Act, 1940. This Act was subsequently amended in 1996 with 'the objective of amending the law relating to domestic arbitration, international commercial arbitration and enforcement of foreign arbitral awards as also to define the law relating to conciliation'.

Under Indian Arbitration and Conciliation Act, 1996, there has to be an 'arbitral agreement' under Chapter II, Section 7 which:

means an agreement by the parties to submit to arbitration all or certain disputes which have arisen or which may arise between them in respect of a defined legal relationship, whether contractual or not.

(2) An arbitration agreement may be in the form of an arbitration clause in a contract or in the form of a separate agreement.

Mutual consent from both the parties is essential prior to the appointment of an arbitration officer well versed in legal matters. The tribunal normally has three arbitrators, one each being appointed by the respective parties with the third arbitrator being appointed by the two to head the tribunal. A sole arbitrator can also be appointed if both the parties are in agreement.

The appointment of an arbitrator can be challenged and his or her removal can be done under the following circumstances:

Under section 12. Grounds for challenge.

(1) *When a person is approached in connection with his possible appointment as an arbitrator, he shall disclose in writing any circumstances likely to give rise to justifiable doubts as to his independence or impartiality.*

(2) *An arbitrator, from the time of his appointment and throughout the arbitral proceedings, shall, without delay, disclose to the parties in writing any circumstances referred to in sub-section (1) unless they have already been informed of them by him.*

(3) *An arbitrator may be challenged only if*
   (a) *Circumstances exist that give rise to justifiable doubts as to his independence or impartiality, or*
   (b) *He does not possess the qualifications agreed to by the parties.*

Under section 14 Failure or impossibility to act.

The mandate of an arbitrator shall terminate if
   (a) *He becomes de jure or de facto unable to perform his functions or for other reasons fails to act without undue delay; and*
   (b) *He withdraws from his office or the parties agree to the termination of his mandate.*

These two sections along with Section 15 clarify that the arbitrator can only be removed if he or she is known to be partial towards one party, resigns from the post, or is removed from the post by the consent of both the parties, is not suitably qualified to hold the post, is unable to perform his or her functions, or is substituted by the appointment of another arbitrator.

Chapters IV, V, and VI spell out the jurisdiction of the arbitral tribunal, the manner of conducting its proceedings and the basic principal of making an arbitral award or settlement. The arbitral tribunal should decide applying the principle of *ex aequo et bono*, which in Latin means 'just and fair' or based 'on inequity and good conscience' or as *amiable compositeur* French term for 'an unbiased third party' that acts as an conciliator between two parties to a dispute.

An arbitral award is similar to conciliation settlement for if both the parties agree during the arbitration proceedings to a settlement, it will be recorded as an arbitral settlement on agreed terms. On the other hand, if the arbitral award is given by the tribunal, it shall state the reasons upon which the award is based.

Any arbitral award can be challenged within three months from the date of the award or the receipt of the copy of the award by the party by moving an application to the high court.

Section 7 Adjudication

Adjudication is the legal process of resolving a dispute and implies a hearing by a court, after notice, of legal evidence on the factual issue(s) involved prior to pronouncing of a judgement or decree in a court proceeding. It indicates that the claims of all the parties thereto have been considered and set at rest.

Adjudication means a mandatory settlement of an industrial dispute by a labour court, industrial tribunal, or national tribunal. The final solution to any unsettled dispute is for the appropriate government to refer the dispute to either of the adjudicatory authorities for adjudication.

There is a three-tier system of adjudication to address any unsettled disputes:

  (i) Labour courts
 (ii) Industrial tribunal
(iii) National tribunal

The adjudicatory authorities resolve the industrial dispute by passing an award, which is binding on the parties. Currently, no provision for appeal against an award exists and it can only be challenged by way of a writ petition under Articles 226 and 227 of the Indian Constitution before the high court or under a special leave petition under Article 136 of the Constitution of India before the Supreme Court.

Labour courts: Under Section 7, the state government is empowered to constitute labour courts which shall be presided by the presiding officer. Labour courts have powers to adjudicate on the following matters:

  (i) Interpretation of standing orders
 (ii) Violation of standing orders
(iii) Discharge or dismissal of a workman
 (iv) Withdrawal of any customary concession or privilege
  (v) Illegality or otherwise of a strike or lock-out
 (vi) Other matters which are not under Industrial Tribunal as mentioned in the Second Schedule of the Act.

Industrial tribunal: Industrial tribunals are also presided by the presiding officer and are constituted by state government under Section 7A. Industrial tribunals have powers in respect of:

   (i) Wages, including period and mode of payment
  (ii) Compensatory and other allowances
 (iii) Hours of work and rest intervals
 (iv) Leave with wages and holidays
  (v) Bonus, profit-sharing, provident fund, and gratuity
 (vi) Shift working changes
(vii) Classification by grades
(viii) Rules of discipline
 (ix) Rationalization and retrenchment of workmen. [Third Schedule to the Act].

National tribunal: Adjudication of industrial disputes of national importance or to handle disputes involving large industrial establishments situated in more than one state (Section 7B) are handled by national tribunals. The government can refer any dispute under Section 10(1) to a board of conciliation, court of enquiry, labour court, or industrial tribunal.

The labour court and the tribunal have wide ranging powers:

(i) After re-evaluating the evidence they can reduce the quantum of punishment if it is disproportionate to the gravity of the misconduct.

(ii) They can set aside the termination and order reinstatement of an employee. If the court orders reinstatement and the employer files an appeal in the higher court, the employer is required to pay full wages to the employee during the period of pendency of proceedings with the high court or Supreme Court. However, if the workman was gainfully employed elsewhere, the court can withhold the payment of such wages under Section 17B.

Any interim or final decision given by the labour court, industrial tribunal, or national tribunal including an arbitration decision is called an award and it is required to be published (Section 17) by the state or central government within 30 days of the award. The award becomes effective 30 days after its publication as stipulated under Section 17(a).

It is important to understand the meaning of important terms that have been defined in the Act, which are discussed as follows.

Lay-off

Lay-off means failure, refusal, or inability of an employer on account of shortage of coal, power, or raw materials or accumulation of stock or breakdown of machinery or natural calamity, to give employment to a workman on muster roll within two hours after reporting to work. Lay-off can be for half day also. In such case, worker can be asked to come in the second half of the shift. (Section2, Clause KKK)

The employer can offer alternate employment if it does not call for any special skill or previous experience, and lay-off compensation will not be payable if the employee refuses to accept the alternate employment (Section 25E). Compensation payable on account of lay-off works out to 50 per cent of salary (basic + dearness allowance) for employees who have completed one year of service in an establishment that employs more than 50 but less than 100 employees (Section 25C).

The above provisions of compensation for lay-off do not apply to the following:

(i) Industrial establishments employing less than 50 workmen
(ii) Seasonal industry
(iii) Establishments employing 100 or more workmen, where approval of the government is required under Section 25M(1)

Retrenchment

Retrenchment means the reduction in the company's workforce by way of termination by the employer of surplus labour or staff not by way of punishment, but for any reason on the basis of last in first out in respect of each category; for example, the junior-most employee should be retrenched first (Section 25G), however, if the employer wishes to rehire then he must first give an opportunity to retrenched employees (Section 25 H).

However, 'retrenchment' does not include voluntary retirement or retirement on reaching the age of superannuation or termination on account of non-renewal of contract or termination on account of continued ill-health of a workman (Section 2(OO)).

A worker who has completed one year of service can be retrenched by giving one month's notice or paying one month's salary plus retrenchment compensation, which is equivalent to 15 days' average wages for every completed year of service (Section 25F).

In *Parry's Employees Union vs Third Industrial Tribunal 2001 LLR 462 (Cal HC)*, it was held that for purposes of retrenchment compensation under the Act, the monthly salary should be divided by 30 days and not 26 days as required under the Gratuity Act.

An employee who has completed one year of continuous service is eligible for lay-off and retrenchment compensation as per Section 25B, which clarifies 'continuous service' as service interrupted by sickness, authorized leave, accident or strike which is not illegal, or lockout or cessation of work which is not due to fault of workman.

In *Workmen vs Management of American Express AIR 1986 SC 548= 1985(4) SCC 71*, it was held that 'actually worked' cannot mean only those days where workman worked with hammer, sickle, or pen, but must necessarily comprehend all those days during which he was in the employment of the employer and for which has been paid wages either under express of implied contract of service or by compulsion of statute, standing orders, and upheld the definition of continuous service as per Section 25B.

Closure

Closure refers to the permanent closing of an establishment or a part of the establishment—Section 2 (cc). However, if the number of persons employed is 50 or more, two months' notice is required to be given but if the number of employees is less than 50, a two months' notice is not required to be given by the employer to the government or employee (Section 25FFA). In the event of closure compensation has to be given to the employee, which will be calculated on the basis that the employee has been retrenched (Section 25FFF(1)).

In large industrial corporations or government undertakings, the Act envisages that prior approval has to be taken from the government under Sections 25M and 25O to lay off, retrench, or close operations of the company. This was a draconian measure that was incorporated in the Act to safeguard the workers' interests and permission was rarely given.

In *Papnasan Labour Union vs Madura Coats AIR 1995 SC 2200,* the provisions of Section 25M for permission to lay off workers with prior approval of the government was upheld by the court.

In *Workmen vs Meenakshi Mills Ltd. AIR 1994 SC 2696 (5-member bench),* it was held that powers to give prior permission are quasi-judicial under Section 25N, and hence opportunity of hearing must be given and the order giving permission or refusing permission is subject to judicial review.

In *Bharatia Electric Steel Co. Ltd. vs State of Haryana 1998 LLR 322 (P&H HC DB)*, under Section 25O requires the management to seek prior permission from the government to close operations. The court held that permission cannot be refused if the reasons given by the employer are genuine and adequate. It further clarified that application of this Section should be limited to cases where the employer is acting arbitrarily or unfairly.

Strike

Strike is defined under Section 2(q) and refers to a cessation of work by a body of persons employed in any industry, acting in combination, or a concerted refusal, or a refusal under a common understanding, of any number of persons who are or have been so employed to continue to work or to accept employment.

Under Section 23 employees cannot go on strike:

(i) During pendency of any conciliation or arbitration proceedings and seven days thereafter

(ii) During the period when proceedings are pending before a labour court, industrial tribunal, or national tribunal

(iii) During the period when settlement or award is in operation in respect of the matters covered by award or settlement

Lockout

Section 2(i) defines a lockout as a temporary closing of a place of employment or the suspension of work, or the refusal by an employer to continue to employ any number of persons employed by him.

In case of a strike or lockout either party is required to give a 14-day notice to the other party for example before employees proceed on a strike or an employer declares a lockout.

Wages during strike and lockouts

Wages during a strike period are payable only if the strike is both legal and justified; on the other hand, if the lockout by employer is legal and justified workmen are not entitled to payment of wages for the period during which the lockout continues to be in force.

Unfair labour practices

During the pendency of any dispute the management cannot take any measures that would adversely affect the rights of the employee or impact the outcome of the award. In case either party commits an offence under the Industrial Disputes Act, 1947, they can be punished. Section 25T prohibits unfair labour practices by employer or workmen or a trade union, whilst Section 25U spells out the punishment that should be meted out to a person who commits an unfair labour practice.

Offences and punishment under the industrial disputes are tabulated in Table 7.1 for easy reference.

TABLE 7.1 Offences and Penalties under the Industrial Disputes Act, 1947

Offences	Penalties
Any employer who resorts to lay-off or retrenches workmen without obtaining prior permission from the government.	Imprisonment up to one month or fine up to ₹1000 or both.
Closure of an undertaking without obtaining prior approval of the government.	Imprisonment up to six months or fine up to ₹5000 or both.
Closure of an undertaking in contravention of an order refusing to grant permission for closure, or non-compliance of an order to reopen a closed undertaking.	Imprisonment up to one year or fine up to ₹5000 or both. In case of a continuing offence a further fine up to ₹2000 per day.
Closure of an undertaking without giving a notice to the workman under Section 25-FFA.	Imprisonment up to six months or fine up to ₹5000 or both.
Any workman who participates or acts in furtherance of an illegal strike.	Imprisonment up to one month or fine up to ₹50 or both.
An employer who declares an illegal lockout or acts in furtherance of the same.	Imprisonment up to one month or fine up to ₹1000 or both.
Any person who instigates or incites another person to take part in or finances any illegal strike or lockout, or commits any unfair labour practice.	Imprisonment up to six months or fine up to ₹1000 or both.
Any person who commits a breach of any settlement or award binding on him.	Imprisonment up to six months or fine or both. In case of a continuing breach an additional fine up to ₹200 per day.
Any person who wilfully discloses any information which is declared to be confidential under Section 21.	Imprisonment up to six months or fine up to ₹1000 or both.
Contravention of any other provision of the Act or the rules made there under.	Fine up to ₹100.

Schedule 5 to to the Act gives a list of what constitutes unfair labour practices by employers and employees.

In case of employer

  (i) Interfering in trade union activities
 (ii) Threatening workmen to refrain them from trade union activities
(iii) Establish employer sponsored trade union
 (iv) Discourage trade union activities by various means
  (v) Discharge or dismiss by way of victimization or falsely implicating workmen
 (vi) Abolish work of regular nature and to give that work to contractors
(vii) Mala fide transfer of workman under guise of management policy
(viii) Employ badli or casuals and continue them for years
 (ix) Recruitment workmen during strike which is not illegal
  (x) Acts of force and violence

(xi) Not implementing settlement or agreement or award

(xii) Refuse collective bargaining

(xiii) Continue illegal lockout

In case of workmen and trade unions

(i) Support or instigate illegal strike

(ii) Coerce workmen to join or not to join a particular trade union

(iii) Threaten or intimidate workmen who do not join strike

(iv) Refuse collective bargaining in good faith

(v) Coercive actions including 'go slow', 'gherao', 'squatting on work premises after working hours', and so on

(vi) Wilful damage to employer's property

(vii) Acts of force or violence or intimidation

The Trade Unions Act, 1926 and the Trade Unions (Amendments) Act, 2001

When a new hotel property commences operation, there are no trade unions as majority of the staff is freshly recruited. As in any new organization in infancy, the objective of the management should be to match the personal growth aspirations of the employees with the growth of the hotel, which is a difficult task in itself. It is when a mismatch occurs that the employees start thinking in terms of forming a trade union.

It is important for hotel operators and owners to understand the laws that govern the formation, amalgamation, and dissolution of trade unions, and the privileges of the office-bearers and its members.

In India, the first organized trade union was formed in 1918.The Indian Trade Unions Act, 1926, along with the Trade Unions (Amendment) Act, 2001, deals with the registration of trade unions, their rights, liabilities, responsibilities, and lays down the ground rules for the utilization of the union's funds. A registered trade union enjoys a legal and corporate status and if it is registered under any other Act, such as The Society's Registration Act, 1850, The Co-operative Society's Act, 1912, or The Companies Act, 1956, then the registration is void.

The administration of the Act is entrusted with the Ministry of Labour and its primary task is to monitor industrial relations at the central level which involves the following:

- Intervention, mediation, and conciliation in industrial disputes in order to bring about settlement of disputes
- Intervention in situations of threatened strikes and lockouts with a view to avert the strikes and lockouts
- Implementation of settlements and awards

What is a trade union? According to the Trade Unions Act, 1926, *'trade union' means 'any combination, whether temporary or permanent, formed primarily for the purpose of regulating the relations between workmen and employers or between workmen and workmen or between employers and employers, or for imposing restrictive conditions on the conduct of any trade or business, and includes any federation of two or more trade unions'.*

A trade union is a voluntary organization of workers pertaining to a particular industry formed to balance and improve the relations between the employer and the employees by promoting and protecting the welfare and interests of workers by collective action. Besides representing the legitimate demands of the workers to the management, they are required to inculcate a sense of discipline and responsibility in the workers.

The aim of a trade union is to:

(i) secure fair wages for workers and improve their opportunities for promotion and training;

(ii) safeguard security of tenure and improve their conditions of service;

(iii) improve working and living conditions of workers;

(iv) provide them educational, cultural, and recreational facilities;

(v) facilitate technological advancement by broadening the understanding of the workers;

(vi) help them in improving the levels of production, productivity, discipline, and high standard of living; and

(vii) promote individual and collective welfare and thus correlate the workers' interests with that of their industry.

Registration, change of name, amalgamation, and dissolution of trade union
Registration of a union   In order to register a trade union with the registrar of trade union, at least 10 per cent or 100 workmen, whichever is less, subject to a minimum of seven workmen employed in the establishment or industry with which it is connected, should be members of such a trade union on the date of making an application for registration. Furthermore, at all times the union will continue to have a minimum of 10 per cent or 100 workmen, whichever is less, subject to a minimum of seven persons employed in the establishment or industry as its members.

The application shall be accompanied by a copy of the 'rules of the trade union' and a statement giving the following particulars:

(i) Names, occupations, and addresses of the members making the application.

(ii) The name of the trade union and the address of its head office.

(iii) The titles, names, ages, addresses, and occupations of the office bearers of the trade union in the prescribed format. However, for being a member of the executive or any other office-bearer of a registered trade union, he or she should be above the age of 18 years, and if he has been convicted by a court in India for any offence involving moral turpitude and sentenced to imprisonment, five years should have elapsed since his or her release.

The registrar, on being satisfied that the union has complied with all the requirements of the Act, shall register the trade union and issue a certificate of registration.

Change of name of the union   The registrar of unions can approve a change in name of the union provided the application is accompanied with a consent letter signed by two-thirds of the registered members of the union.

Amalgamation of unions   Two or more registered trade unions can be amalgamated to form a single trade union provided 50 per cent of the registered members of each of the individual trade unions that are seeking to amalgamate agree to the amalgamation. At least 60 per cent votes should be cast in favour of amalgamation of the combined strength of all the unions wishing to amalgamate. After the amalgamation, the funds of the unions can be maintained separately if the unions so desire.

Dissolution of unions   A registered trade union can be dissolved, if a notice is sent within 14 days of the dissolution, signed by seven members and the secretary of the trade union to the registrar. If the registrar is satisfied that the dissolution is in accordance with the rules of the trade union, the dissolution shall take effect from the date of such registration.

Statutory compliances to be met by trade unions   Statutory compliances that have to be met by the trade unions are as follows:

  (i) Registration of membership;
 (ii) Income and expense statement;
(iii) Details of all assets and liabilities;
 (iv) Statement of the general fund and the political fund accounts;
  (v) Statement of expenses made from the general fund;
 (vi) Availability of the register of membership and its books of accounts for inspection by the members of the union; and
(vii) No member of the union forced to pay a contribution to a political fund; non-contribution by a member to such a fund (political fund) should not disqualify him from any of the benefits of membership of the union.

Offences for which a trade union office bearers can be penalized   Every office-bearer or other person who is bound by the rules of the trade union shall be punishable with a payment of a fine, if:

  (i) There is a default on the part of any registered trade union in giving any notice or sending any statement or other document as required by or under any provision of this Act.
 (ii) Any person wilfully makes, or causes to be made, any false entry in, or any omission from, the general statement or in or from any copy of rules or of alterations of rules sent to the registrar.

(iii) Any person who, with intent to deceive, gives to any member of a registered trade union or to any person intending or applying to become a member of such trade union any document purporting to be a copy of the rules of the trade union or of any alterations to the same which he or she knows, or has reason to believe, is not a correct copy of such rules or alterations as are for the time being in force, or any person who, with the like intent, gives a copy of any rules of an unregistered trade union to any person on the pretence that such rules are the rules of a registered trade union.

TEXT

Legal safeguards provided to a registered union office bearers and members   *No office-bearer or member of a registered trade union shall be liable to punishment under the Indian Penal Code, 1860 in respect of any agreement made between the members for the purpose of furthering any such object of the trade union as specified in the Act, unless the agreement is an agreement to commit an offence.*

No suit or other legal proceeding shall be maintainable in any civil court against any registered trade union or any office-bearer or member thereof in respect of any act done in contemplation or furtherance of a trade dispute to which a member of the trade union is a party on the ground only that such an act induces some other person to break a contract of employment, or that it is in interference with the trade, business, or employment of some other person or with the right of some other person to dispose of his capital of his labour as he wills.

Factories Act, 1948   The Factories Act, 1948 is comprehensive and is based on the provisions of the Factories Act of Great Britain, 1937. It contains detailed provisions regarding the health, safety, and welfare of workers inside factories, the hours of work, the minimum age of workers, leave rules, and so on. The Act envisages periodic inspections by the chief inspector or any other person to undertake safety and occupational health surveys. The management and all other persons shall afford all facilities for such survey, including examination, testing of plant and machinery, collection of samples, other data, and medical examination.

The term factory is defined in Section 2(m) of the Act as follows:

TEXT

Factory means any premises including the precincts thereof:

(i) *whereon ten or more workers are working, or were working on any day of the preceding twelve months, and in any part of which a manufacturing process is being carried on with the aid of power or is ordinarily so carried on, or*

(ii) *whereon twenty or more workers are working, or were working on any day of the preceding twelve months, and in any part of which a manufacturing process is being carried on without the aid of power, or is ordinarily so carried on, but does not include a mine subject to the operation of the Indian Mines Act, 1952 (Act XXXV of 1952), or a mobile unit belonging to the armed forces of the Union, a railway running shed or a hotel, restaurant or eating place.*

From the above definition it is clear that hotels, restaurants, or eating places do not come under the ambit of The Factories Act, 1948, but are governed by the Shops and Establishments Act.

Labour Laws that Provide for Rights of Employees at Workplace

In this section, we will review those pieces of legislation that provide for rights of employees at workplace, such as wages, working hours, working conditions, welfare measures, and so on. Although there is a long list of enactments that covers all these aspects, a few important laws are as follows:

    (i) Employment Exchanges (Compulsory Notification of Vacancies) Act, 1959
    (ii) The Apprentices Act, 1961
    (iii) Shops & Establishments Act, 1948
    (iv) The Minimum Wages Act, 1948 and Minimum Wages (Central) Rules, 1950
    (v) The Payment of Wages Act, 1936 and Payment of Wages Rules, 1937
    (vi) The Payment of Wages (Amendment) Act, 2005
    (vii) Equal Remuneration Act, 1976
    (viii) The Payment of Bonus Act, 1965
    (ix) The Payment of Bonus Rules, 1965
    (x) The Payment of Bonus Rules, 1975
    (xi) Payment of Gratuity Act, 1972
    (xii) Employees Provident Fund Scheme, 1952 (EPF)
    (xiii) Employees' Deposit Linked Insurance Scheme, 1976
    (xiv) Employees' Pension Scheme, 1995
    (xv) The Employees' Family Pension Scheme, 1971
    (xvi) The Public Provident Act, 1968
    (xvii) Weekly Holidays Act, 1942
    (xviii) The Maternity Benefit Act, 1961
    (xix) The Workmen's Compensation Act, 1923
    (xx) The Workmen's Compensation (Amendments) Act, 2000

Recruitment of employees

In order to encourage a systematic process of resettlement and recruitment post Independence, the central government established the Directorate General of Resettlement and Employment in 1945 and by 1948 Employment Exchanges were opened to assist displaced persons from across the border.

The Directorate General of Resettlement and Employment underwent a change with the government promulgating the Employment Exchanges (Compulsory Notification of Vacancies) Act, 1959. The threefold objective of the Act was to (i) maintain a list of people seeking employment, (ii) secure information from companies wishing to recruit people, and (iii) post vacancies that were being advertised. In keeping with this stated objective the government began publishing a weekly newspaper *Rozgaar Samachar* or *Employment News* listing all the advertised vacancies.

The Act made it mandatory for all 'establishments', which were defined as:

TEXT

(a) *any office,*
(b) *any place where any industry, trade, business, or occupation is carried on*
(c) *'establishment in public sector' means*
  (i) *the government or government controlled department,*
  (ii) *a government company as defined in Section 617 of the Companies Act, 1956 (1 of 1956);*
  (iii) *a corporation established by the centre or the state (including a co-operative society) established by or under a Central, Provincial or State Act, which is owned, controlled, or managed by the government;*
  (iv) *a local government authority*
(d) *'establishments in the private sector' as an establishment not in the public sector where ordinarily 25 or more persons are employed against remuneration to notify the government of vacancies in their organizations.*

Although the law makes it mandatory for private-sector establishments to post their existing vacancies in the employment news bulletin, most of the hotel chains prefer to post vacancies in the national newspapers, on the recruitment pages of their websites, Facebook, or LinkedIn. Irrespective of the means of communication, an employment advertisement must accurately describe the position or job that is being advertised in order to attract the best talent from the market.

In order to meet the skilled labour requirements of the various industries, the government decided to utilize the facilities available in the various industries for training technicians and vocational trainees and promulgated. The Apprentices Act, 1961.The Act gives an opportunity to graduates, diploma holders in engineering, and higher secondary (10+2) students. Training is imparted to the apprentices as per the contracts entered into between the apprentices and the establishments that they are employed in. Under the apprenticeship scheme, 50 per cent of stipendiary amount is reimbursed to the training establishments, however, the organization is free to pay stipend at higher rates. Successful candidates are awarded the National Apprenticeship Certificate from the Board in the trade that they have learnt.

The Federation of Hotels and Restaurants Association of India (FHRAI), Travel Agents Association of India (TAAI), Indian Association of Tour Operators (IATO) has initialled agreements with the government under the 'Hunar Se Rozgaar Scheme' to provide training and employment to the trainees on merit.

Recruitment is done by hotels through campus recruitments for interns and management trainees. In certain cases, especially for senior executive positions, qualified head hunters are approached by the hotels, or recruitment is done directly by placing advertisements in leading newspapers as illustrated in Fig. 7.4.

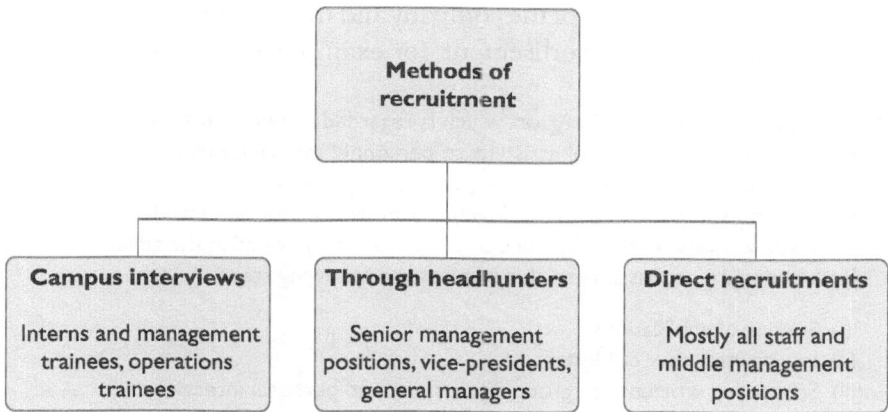

FIGURE 7.4 Methods of Recruitment

For campus recruitments, recruiters from all prestigious hotel companies visit hotel management schools for recruiting passing-out graduates. Campus recruitment is one of the most awaited events for the graduating class of Institute of Hotel Management students. For the lucky few, a campus interview is the first step that an individual takes towards fulfilling his or her ambition of pursuing a rewarding career in the hospitality industry.

Headhunters assist hotels in sourcing senior executives against the hotel's requirements that have been given to them; in this case, the headhunter is responsible for vetting, screening the candidate application, and if he or she is considered suitable his or her name is recommended to the hotel company.

Direct recruitment is for those who apply against advertised vacancies directly to hotel companies or individual hotel properties. The employment process starts with an employment advertisement followed by issuing of appointment letters. Upon joining the company, the employees go through induction process and in case the employees decide to leave the company at a future date, the resignation process is outlined.

Employment advertisements   The essential elements of an employment advertisement that enable the applicants to take an educated call are as follows:

(i) A brief but accurate description of the job position detailing the educational qualifications, work experience, and any special skills that are an essential requirement, for the job.
(ii) A brief description of the company's activities by providing links to the company's websites.
(iii) Salary details and whether it is negotiable or not.
(iv) Will the job involve relocation to a new city?
(v) The company is an equal opportunity employer and encourages women and people with disabilities to apply.

(vi) The contact details of the company and the manner in which the applicants should respond to the advertisement, for example, by e-mail, fax, post, and so on.

> **Example**   The Westin, Gurgaon, which is regarded as one of the best in the region has advertised for a supervisory position of assistant to personnel manager. Ruchi is one of the applicants for this post after completing her hotel management programme from the Institute of Hotel Management, Mumbai, and she is looking forward to being shortlisted for an interview.
>
> All applications received by the closed-out date mentioned in the advertisement by the personnel department are processed and this involves the following steps:
>
> (i) Sorting of applications
> (ii) Issuing interview call letters
> (iii) Scheduling written test, group discussions, and personal interviews
> (iv) Shortlisting potential candidates
> (v) Final round of interviews
> (vi) Issuing appointment letters
>
> After going through the written tests, group discussion, and finally a personal interview, Ruchi is selected. She is advised that the appointment letter shall be issued shortly and should consider joining within 15 days of receiving the appointment letter.

Appointment letters   Three important pieces of legislation make it mandatory for any organization to define the companies' working conditions. These are encapsulated in the standing orders and all appointment letters have to conform to these:

(i) The Factories Act, 1948 has provisions related to the employment, wages, health, safety, welfare, working hours, employment of women, annual leave, and so on.

(ii) Similarly, the Shops & Establishments Act, 1948 lists the important provisions that any employer has to adhere to, which are as follows:

    (a) *Laying down the hours of work per day and week.*
    (b) *Laying down guidelines for spread-over, rest interval, opening and closing hours, closed days, national and religious holidays and overtime work.*
    (c) *Rules for employment of children, young persons and women.*
    (d) *Rules for annual leave, maternity leave, sickness and casual leave.*
    (e) *Rules for employment and termination of service.*
    (f) *Maintenance of registers and records and display of notices.*
    (g) *Obligations of employers.*
    (h) *Obligations of employee.*

(iii) The objective of the Industrial Employment (Standing Orders) Act, 1947 is to provide service rules for workmen.

Standing orders are rules of conduct for workmen employed in industries, factories, or shops and establishments.

Section 2(g) The schedule of the Industrial Employment (Standing Orders) Act 1946 requires that the following should be specified in Standing Orders:

(a) *Classification of workmen i.e. temporary, badli, casual, permanent, skilled etc.*
(b) *Manner of intimating to workmen working hours, shift working, transfers etc.*
(c) *Holidays*
(d) *Attendance and late coming rules*
(e) *Leave rules*
(f) *Leave eligibility and leave conditions*
(g) *Closing and reopening of sections of industrial establishment*
(h) *Termination of employment, suspension, dismissal etc. for misconduct and acts or omissions which constitute misconduct*
(i) *Retirement age*
(j) *Means of redressal of workmen against unfair treatment or wrongful exactions by employer*
(k) *any other matter that may be prescribed*

All the above three pieces of legislation have common reference points that an employer is required to adhere to when defining the establishment's model standing orders related to service conditions such as attendance, leave rules, termination, resignation, and so on, and of acts that constitute misconduct that will invite disciplinary action.

Till such time that a company's model standing orders are not approved (certified) by the Labour Commissioner (certifying officer), the model standing orders specified by the Act shall automatically apply to the business (Section 12A). Prior to certification the Labour Commissioner is required to listen to any objections that the unions may have, and if no objections are received the standing orders for an establishment will be certified. Certified standing orders have to be displayed in English and the local language at a prominent location in the establishment or near entrance of the establishment. Standing orders are binding on employers and employees.

In *Eicher Goodearth Ltd. vs R K Soni (1993) XXIV LLR 524, 1993 LLR 524 (Raj HC)*, the Rajasthan High Court ruled that if there is inconsistency between standing order and appointment letter, the provisions of standing order will supersede any terms and conditions of employment, contained in the appointment letter. However, these conditions of service do not override the statutory laws of the country.

Defining 'misconduct' is one of the most important aspects of the standing order as disciplinary action can only be initiated by the management if an employee commits a misconduct that has been defined in the standing order. Normally standing orders contain such acts like insubordination, disobedience, fraud, dishonesty, damage to employer's property, taking bribe, habitual absence or habitual late attendance, riotous behaviour, habitual neglect of work, strike in contravention of rules, and so on, as misconducts. The certified standing orders may cover other acts such as misuse of the Internet, suggestive gestures towards female employees as 'misconduct', if approved by the certifying officer. Any modifications of a standing order is possible by following the same procedure as is required to be followed for the approval of a standing order.

Once the recruitment process is over, employee appointment letters are issued keeping in mind the certified standing order applicable to the company. The personnel manager has to incorporate the following points when issuing an appointment letter:

(i) It should be addressed to the person being offered the job.

(ii) It should indicate the job position for which the company is making the offer with a brief nature of the assignment.

(iii) It should communicate salary details in unambiguous terms whether it is gross salary or cost to company.

(iv) It should indicate details of allowances, benefits, or other perks being offered.

(v) It should indicate leave entitlements during the year—privilege, casual, medical, and others.

(vi) It should indicate that confirmation will be subject to performance appraisal upon completion of the period of probation, if any, for example, six months.

(vii) It should give the name of the person to whom the selected person has to report on the date of joining.

(viii) It should mention the date by which the offer letter should be accepted by the candidate after which the offer stands closed.

(ix) It should indicate the manner of acceptance of the offer letter, for example, kindly return the duplicate copy of the offer letter duly signed by post or courier.

Example   It was a red letter day for Ruchi when she received the appointment letter from Westin, Gurgaon appointing her as the assistant to the personnel manager. Ruchi was required to respond to the offer letter within 15 days of receiving the offer by:

(i) Sending the duplicate copy of the appointment letter duly signed by her by post or courier to the company indicating her date of joining; or

(ii) Reporting on duty on or by 15 June 2011 to the personnel manager.

Ruchi opted for option (i) by indicating her date of joining as 21 June 2011, however, her acceptance letter was received by the personnel manager three days after the mandatory 15 days. On receiving no communication from Ruchi within the stipulated 15 days, the personnel manager went ahead and appointed the next suitable candidate to the post.

Ruchi reported for duty on 21 June 2011 to the personnel manager, who regretted that the management was not in a position to accommodate her as they had given Ruchi a reasonable period of time to respond to the offer. In such cases, where time is of the essence, it is important to respond within the time limit specified, as it can result in the loss of an excellent opportunity.

If, on the other hand, Ruchi would have responded on time then she would have joined the company and would have been taken through the induction process. During the induction process, Ruchi would have been apprised of the various important issues that are part of the standing orders.

Induction   The induction process of any hotel for an employee comprises the following steps:

(i) Brief on the company's profile, its vision and mission statements, and the employee's role in achieving these goals.

(ii) Job description or job profile and the reporting pattern to be followed by the employee.

(iii) Giving a copy of the company's certified standing orders listing all the dos and don'ts applicable to all employees, which has to be countersigned by the employee and returned to the personnel department.

(iv) Completion of all required documentation, for example, filling up the employee application form and history card, opening of a salary account with the hotel's bank, opening of the Provident Fund and Employee State Insurance accounts, completing the employee medical insurance form, and income tax declaration form.

(v) Hotel orientation programme that introduces the employee to all the departments and finally once the induction process is over the employee reports to his department head.

Wages/salary It is important to understand the legal definition of 'wages' and the rules that govern the payment of wages. The Minimum Wages Act, 1948 and Minimum Wages (Central) Rules, 1950, the Payment of Wages Act, 1936, the Payment of Wages Rules, 1937, The Payment of Wages (Amendment) Act, 2005 and The Industrial Disputes Act, 1948 define wages, and stipulate fines to ensure regular and prompt payment of wages by the employer after making the statutory deductions from the employees' salaries. The Payment of Wages Act, 1936 and the Payment of Wages (Amendment) Act, 2005 specifically prohibits arbitrary fines and deductions from an employee wages.

Both male and female employees have to be paid same salaries for same job positions, and no discrimination can be made between them at the time of recruitment. (Sections 4(1) and (5) of the Equal Remuneration Act, 1976).

TEXT

'Wages' means all remuneration capable of being expressed in terms of money, which would, if the terms of employment, expressed or implied, were fulfilled, be payable to a workman in respect of his employment or of work done in such employment, and includes
- *such allowances (including dearness allowance) as the workman is for the time being entitled to;*
- *the value of any house accommodation, or of supply of light, water, medical attendance or other amenity or of any service or of any concessional supply of food-grains or other articles;*
- *any travelling concession;*
- *any commission payable on the promotion of sales or business or both;*

But does not include
- *Any bonus;*
- *Any contribution paid or payable by the employer to any pension fund or provident fund or for the benefit of the workman under any law for the time being in force;*
- *Any gratuity payable on the termination of his service;*

Evolving a wage policy assumed great importance as a majority of the workforce was employed in the unorganized sector and was vulnerable to exploitation by their employers, which made the government enact the Minimum Wages Act, 1948 and Minimum Wages (Central) Rules, 1950. The Act defines minimum wages as basic pay plus any applicable allowances that are or shall be recommended by the central advisory board of the central or the state governments, which can be revised by the respective governments from time to time. All wages are required to be paid in cash; however, wages can be paid in kind if the government so desires after notifying it in the official gazette.

The Act specifies that all employers are required to pay their employees, wages that are above the minimum rate of wages notified for that class of employees with applicable deduction by the seventh or 10th day of the month.

For calculation of wages a day will consist of 24 hours and a normal working day for an adult employee will be nine hours. A weekly off shall be given after every six days of work normally on a Sunday. In case an employee is required to work overtime he shall be compensated at one-and-a-half time or double the daily basic rate of pay. In case of night shifts he shall be entitled to a 24 hours' rest before being rotated to another shift pattern.

Even though the government had enacted The Minimum Wages Act, 1948, it was left to the Payment of Wages Act, 1936, Payment of Wages Rules, 1937, and Payment of Wages (Amendment) Act, 2005 to ensure regular and prompt payment of wages.

The Act applies to all establishments that employ 20 or more employees who draw a basic pay of less than ₹6500 per month directly or indirectly through a contractor. The manager responsible for the supervision of the establishment shall be responsible for paying the salary of all the employees, whether employed directly or through a contractor. Every manager has to ensure that there is no discrimination in wages between men and women for the same nature of duties or work.

The definition of wages is further elaborated to:

TEXT

Include all remuneration, bonus, or sums payable for termination of service, but do not include house rent reimbursement, light vehicle charges, medical expenses, travel allowance, and so on, and should be paid in currency or by cheque after taking the consent from the employee on the notified date, for example, seventh or tenth of every month. Every employee is required to nominate his or her beneficiary who is entitled to receive the wages due to him or her in the event of his or her death.

The Act places the responsibility on the employer to ensure that wages are paid after making the statutory deductions such as provident fund, family pension, income tax, and any other deductions such as:

(i) Fines: The quantum of fine cannot be in excess of 3 per cent of one month's wages and has to be collected within 60 days. All amounts collected as fines shall be deposited into the Employee Welfare Fund.

(ii) Deduction for absence from duty.

(iii) Deduction for damage to or loss of goods expressly entrusted to the employed person for custody, or for loss of money for which he is required to account where such damage or loss is directly attributable to his neglect or default.

(iv) Deduction for house accommodation supplied by the employer.

(v) Deduction for such amenities and services supplied by the employer.

The Act makes it mandatory for all employers to pay wages to discharged or terminated employees or to employees that have resigned all terminal benefits that are applicable and payable under the Act.

Payment of ex-gratia, bonus Ex-gratia, bonus, and gratuity are distinct from wages as ex-gratia and bonus are incentives or rewards for work done, whilst gratuity is a lump-sum payment which constitutes a retirement benefit. It is important to briefly elaborate upon these three important concepts that are directly linked to wages.

Ex-gratia and bonus Textile owners of Ahmadabad used to give 'ex-gratia' incentives, which in Latin means 'out of kindness', to their employees in cash or kind in the years that they made profits. By the 1930s, payment of 'ex-gratia' had become an established practice. This led employees to believe that as they were responsible for the profits of the company and it was their inherent right to demand a share in the profits of the company. Thus, the concept of ex-gratia changed to one of profit-sharing.

As computation of profits was a dilemma for the managements post Independence, the Government of India constituted the Bonus Commission in 1961 to determine a just and equitable manner for computing profits. The trade unions were aware that computing profits would always be a grey area and suggested the concept of deferred wages which should be paid to all employees. The concept of deferred wages propounded was to pay 13 months' salary for 12 months of work, payable during the festival holidays which used to be normally around the Hindu festival of Diwali.

The Payment of Bonus Act, 1965, the Payment of Bonus Rules, 1965, and the Payment of Bonus Rules, 1975 integrated the concept of profit-sharing and deferred wages reiterating the main concept of bonus as profit-sharing. The Act makes it mandatory for all establishments having more than 20 employees to pay bonus annually, laying down the criteria for the calculation and disbursement of bonus to all employees eligible to receive bonus from the allocable surplus.

Eligibility criteria for bonus are as follows:

(i) *An employee will be entitled for bonus only when he has worked for 30 working days in that year and is drawing wages up to ₹10,000 per month or less. The Payment of Bonus (Amendment) Act 2012 stipulates that for calculation purposes ₹3500 per month maximum will be taken even if an employee is drawing up to ₹3500 per month (Section 12).*

(ii) *However, an employee can be disqualified from receiving bonus in any accounting year on the following grounds:*

    (a) *on dismissal of an employee for fraud, or riotous or violent behaviour while on the premises of the establishment;*

    (b) *theft, misappropriation, or sabotage of any property of the establishment; or*

    (c) *misconduct of causing financial loss to the employer to the extent that bonus can be deducted for that year.*

TEXT

Calculation of bonus   The minimum bonus payable is 8.33 per cent and the maximum 20 per cent by those establishments that have an allocable surplus available after deducting from the gross profits depreciation, direct tax payable on the profits, development rebate or investment allowance or development allowance under the Income Tax Act, 1961. In case the establishment is not making profits, the payment of bonus can be deferred for a maximum period of five years since the commencement of business; upon completion of five years, minimum bonus at the rate of 8.33 per cent is payable even when there are no profits.

As illustrated in Table 7. 2, the calculation of bonus is based upon the basic salary consisting of basic plus dearness allowance excluding all other perks.

TABLE 7.2   Calculation of Bonus

Heading	₹
Net profit	10,00,000
Add back charges to P&L account as per balance sheet	5,00,000
Gross profit	15,00,000
Less deductions like tax, depreciation, and others	7,50,000
Available surplus	7,50,000
Allocable surplus 60% of available surplus	4,50,000
Total wage bill	45,00,000
Available surplus is 10% of wage bill	4,50,000

Hence, 10 per cent of the wage bill will be paid as bonus to employees who draw up to ₹3500 per month.

The distribution of the allocable surplus to the individual employees is shown in Table 7.3.

TABLE 7.3   Distribution of Allocable Surplus

Employee	Annual salary	Bonus @ 10%
Employee A	30,000	3000
Employee B	45,000	4500
Employee C	20,000	2000

Set-off   In case the wage bill is ₹90,00,000 then ₹4,50,000 is only 5 per cent of the wage bill which is less than the minimum bonus payable which at the rate of 8.33 per cent of ₹90,00,000 is ₹7,50,000. Hence there is a shortfall between the minimum bonus payable and allocable surplus (7,50,000 − 4,50,000 = 3,00,000).

This amount of ₹3,00,000 will be set off against the allocable surplus for the next financial year.

A *set-off* can be defined as when allocable surplus is insufficient to pay the minimum bonus in any one financial year then the shortfall that will be carried over or set off against the next financial year up to a maximum of four years.

Set-on   In case the wage bill is ₹9,00,000 then ₹4,50,000 constitutes 50 per cent of the wage bill which is more than the maximum bonus payable at the rate of 20 per cent of ₹1,80,000. Hence, the excess between the maximum bonus payable and allocable surplus is (1,80,000 − 4,50,000 = 2,70,000). This amount of ₹2,70,000 will be set on against the allocable surplus of the next financial year, up to a maximum of four years subject to a maximum of 20 per cent of the wages which is ₹1,80,000 the balance ₹90,000 shall be written off.

Gratuity, employees' provident fund, employees' deposit linked insurance, public provident fund, and employee pension scheme   *Gratuity* is intended to be a retirement benefit, just like provident fund (PF), public provident fund (PPF), and pension. Under the Payment of Gratuity Act, 1972 and the Payment of Gratuity Rules, gratuity cannot be attached in execution of any decree or order of any civil, revenue, or criminal court.

All employees who have completed five years of continuous service in an organization that employs 10 or more employees are eligible for gratuity:

(i) on the termination of their employment;
(ii) on their superannuation;
(iii) on their retirement or resignation, or
(iv) on their death or disablement due to accident or disease, continuous service of five years is not required, and gratuity shall be paid to the nominee or to his heirs. If the heir is a minor, the monies shall be invested for the benefit of the minor till he attains majority.

Disablement   Disablement means such incapacity of an employee for the work which he was capable of performing before the accident or disease resulting in such disablement.

Family   For a male employee, a family is defined as himself, his wife, his children, whether married or unmarried, his dependent parents and the dependent parents of his wife, and the widow and children of his predeceased son, if any.

In case of a female employee, a family is defined as herself, her husband, her children, whether married or unmarried, her dependent parents and the dependent parents of her husband, and the widow and children of her predeceased son, if any.

Continuous service   An employee shall be said to be in continuous service for a period if he has, for that period, been in uninterrupted service, including service which may be interrupted on account of sickness, accident, leave, absence from duty without leave (not being absence in respect of which an order treating the absence as break in service has been passed in accordance with the standing orders, rules or regulations governing the employees of the establishment), lay-off, strike, or a lock-out or cessation of work not due to any fault of the employee for a period of one year.

The Act envisages forfeiture of gratuity only in extreme cases even though five years of continuous service have been completed:

(i)   where such termination has been as a result of his or her wilful omission or negligence resulting in damage or loss of the employer's property, in which case the gratuity is forfeited to the extent of the damage caused;

(ii)   where the employee has been dismissed on account of his or her riotous, violent or disorderly conduct; or

(iii)   for an offence involving moral turpitude committed in the course of employment, the gratuity shall be wholly or partly forfeited.

Historically, employers would default on the payment of gratuity as they would fail to make provisions for it. To ensure that employers would not default in their payments the Act laid stringent stipulations such as obtaining an insurance cover for the employer's liability for payment of gratuity from Life Insurance Corporation or any other insurer. Large organizations employing more than 500 employees could establish an approved company gratuity fund. If an employer failed to pay the insurance premium or the contribution to an approved gratuity fund he would have to deposit the amount due including interest, if any, for delayed payments to the central/state governments.

For example, to claim gratuity, Ruchi would be required to move an application for the payment of gratuity to the personnel department; however, if for any reason Ruchi forgets to move the application, the employer has to inform Ruchi the gratuity amount payable and release the payment within 30 days of her leaving service. Where there is an inordinate delay by the employer to release the gratuity, the district collector is empowered to make the payment from the treasury and have the amount recovered from the employer with interest.

Here there is a disconnect between the IT Act and the Gratuity Act as the tax-free exemption limit for gratuity is ₹3,50,000: however, the maximum gratuity payable with effect from 17 May 2010 is ₹10,00,000 under the Gratuity Act and the amount in excess of ₹3,50,000 is taxable.

Calculation of gratuity is based upon the following formula:

Gratuity = Last average salary drawn for 15 days (basic + dearness allowance)
       × number of completed years of service

Example Ruchi has completed 9 years of service with Westin Hotels, and is eligible to claim gratuity as she has completed the mandatory 5 years cf service as required under the Act. Her gratuity calculation will be as follows:

Basic salary: ₹50,000 per month

Dearness allowance (DA): ₹10,000 per month

Total basic + DA: ₹60,000

Average salary per day: ₹2,000

Average salary for 15 days: ₹30,000

Number of years of service: 9 years

Gratuity payable: ₹30,000 × 9 = ₹2,70,000

There will be no tax payable by Ruchi on this amount as it is within the tax exemption limit of ₹3,50,000.

Provident fund, under the Employees' Provident Funds & Miscellaneous Provisions Act, 1952 (EPF & MP Act), is a contributory fund that provides benefits to the employees who are members of the fund upon their retirement and for their dependents in case of death. A board of trustees is responsible for administering the fund through the employee provident fund organization which is responsible for managing it under the aegis of the ministry of labour.

Today, there are three schemes in operation under the Act:

(i) Employees Provident Fund Scheme 1952 (EPF): Both the employee and the employer are required to make equal contributions to the fund at the rate of 8.33 per cent of the basic wage plus dearness allowances. To be eligible for membership of the fund, an employee must have completed one year's continuous service or have worked for 240 days during a period of 12 months and drawing a salary up to ₹6,500 per month. The employer's contribution will be restricted to 12 per cent of ₹6500; however, the employee can contribute a higher percentage up to 20 per cent. It is applicable to every establishment which employs 20 or more persons.

Members are eligible to take loans against their provident fund savings to meet medical expenses, family obligation, and education expenses of children.

(ii) Employees' Deposit Linked Insurance Scheme, 1976: Under this Scheme, on the death of an employee, while in service, the employees' dependents are entitled to receive the provident fund accumulations plus an additional amount equal to the average balance in the provident fund account of the deceased during the preceding 12 months.

(iii) Employees' Pension Scheme, 1995: The Employees' Family Pension Scheme, 1971 was replaced by the Employee Pension Scheme in 1995, which is commonly known as the superannuation scheme. This Scheme is a retirement plan intended to provide a person with a defined income for life. A portion of the contribution made by both the employer and the employee is diverted into the pension fund with an additional contribution by the central government.

To be eligible for pension, an employee has to complete 10 years of service. Upon completion of 33 years of contributory service, the pension amount payable is at the rate of 50 per cent of the salary. In case of death of the employee, the family members will receive the pension on the basis of the salary and number of years of service.

Public Provident Fund Account (PPF) is an account that an individual can maintain with any public sector bank or the post office and the scheme is for a minimum period of 15 years, where the maximum amount that can be deposited is ₹1,00,000 in a financial year with effect from Financial Year 2011–12; the earlier limit was ₹70,000. Upon completion of 15 years, the individual can extend it for a further period of five years. The PPF scheme became operational in 1968 with the passing of The Public Provident Act, 1968.

Computation of salary   Wages can be gross salary or cost to company. For example, in the case of Ruchi, the hotel accounts department in order to make a fair assessment of Ruchi's salary deductions and income tax liability, requires Ruchi to furnish details of her savings, investments, and so on permitted under the Income Tax Act, 1961.

Income Tax Rebates
Currently, the tax benefits that are permitted by the government are as follows, an overall tax exemption limit: ₹2,00,000 for men and women (FY 2012–13). Certain investments and expenses that are tax exempted up to ₹1,00,000 under Section 80-C are as follows:

(i) Payment of life insurance premiums.
(ii) Contribution to provident fund, public provident fund, national pension schemes, equity linked savings schemes, post office saving schemes, national saving certificates, and so on.
(iii) Tax saving fixed deposits with nationalized banks.

Further income tax can be saved by Ruchi if she invests up to ₹20,000 in infrastructure bonds (Section 80-CCF), payment of medical insurance premiums up to ₹15,000 (Section 80-D), 50 per cent of the donations to charitable institutions and charitable bodies working on road safety programmes (Section 80-G), or interest paid on housing loan up to ₹1,50,000 per annum.

This is not an exhaustive list but only indicative. Once Ruchi furnishes these details to the personnel department, it will be able to compute her salary efficiently.

Deductions from Salary Other Than Statutory Deductions
Besides the statutory deductions, the other types of deductions that the company can make from Ruchi's salary are as follows:

(i) Fines: The quantum of fine cannot be in excess of 3 per cent of one month's wages and has to be collected within 60 days. All amounts collected as fines shall be deposited into the Employee Welfare Fund.

(ii) Deduction for absence from duty.

(iii) Deduction for damage to or loss of goods expressly entrusted to the employed person for custody, or for loss of money for which he is required to account where such damage or loss is directly attributable to his neglect or default.

(iv) Deduction for house accommodation supplied by the employer.

(v) Deduction for such amenities and services supplied by the employer.

Ruchi upon completion of one month receives her salary slip showing all the deductions as per the details furnished by her to the accounts department. The salary amount that is paid to Ruchi after deductions is known as cash in hand or take-home salary, whilst the figure without deductions is known as gross salary.

When the salary is cost to company, salary is computed keeping in mind the direct and indirect costs that the company has to bear on retaining the employee, which includes basic salary, all allowances, perks, contributions to various PF funds plus any other miscellaneous expenses the company incurs on its employee.

Discharge of employees   An employee can be discharged from his services in any of the following manner:

Termination   The legal dictionary defines to terminate as 'to discontinue, bring to completion, release, and bring an end to'. It implies the release from employment against the employees will at the behest of the management.

Resignation   Defined as giving up, leaving, and quitting voluntarily from employment by an employee by giving a notice to the employer.

Retirement   Defined as 'to withdraw from one's occupation, business or office, having finished one's active working life' voluntarily or involuntarily.

Superannuation   The act of discharging an employee because of age.

Disablement   Such incapacity of an employee for the work which he or she was capable of performing before the accident or disease resulting in such disablement.

Once an employee has been discharged from service depending on the manner of discharge, the personnel department will initiate the employee exit procedure. The employee shall obtain a clearance certificate from all the departments that he or she has no company property that is returnable to the company and no financial dues pending. The employee will formally hand over charge of his or her job position to the person who has been designated to take charge from him or her. The employee will face an exit interview with his or her superiors and will finally receive his or her employment certificate giving details of his or her tenure in the company.

- In case of termination, the management will pay 30 days' salary in lieu of notice period, any terminal benefits due to him such as PF and gratuity.
- In case of resignation, the employee will give a month's notice to the employer before the company will relieve him or her of his or her duties.

- In the event of retirement and superannuation, the company will discharge the employee with full benefits and no notice period is required to be given by either side to each other.
- In case of disablement due to accident or disease the employee will stand relieved from the date of disablement and all the disablement benefits that an employee is entitled to shall be payable by the company besides his or her other terminal benefits.

Types of leaves and leave rules   As mentioned earlier the model standing order describes the type of leave that an employee is permitted as defined under the various acts such as the Weekly Holidays Act, 1942, Factories Act, 1947, Shops and Establishments Act, The Sales Promotion Employees (Conditions of Service) Act, 1976, or The Sales Promotion Employees (Conditions of Service) Rules, 1976. All leaves are calculated on a calendar year basis and recorded on financial year basis.

Weekly offs   These can be availed by an employee after he has worked for six days and each working day is of nine hours. It is normally a Sunday, but in organizations that follow different shift systems weekly offs can be changed provided the basic principle is followed of The Weekly Holidays Act, 1942 (Section 3).

Privilege leave or earned leave or annual leave   As per the Factories Act, 1948, an employee is entitled to one day's leave for every 20 days worked, and he or she should have worked for a minimum of 240 days in a calendar year to be entitled to annual leave which will be credited to his or her leave account upon completion of one year of service at the beginning of the calendar year. This works out to 18 days' leave in a calendar year. However, as per the prevailing practice, most organizations give 21 to 30 days earned leave to their employees for which they take approval from the labour commissioner when getting their model standing orders certified.

Casual leave   A 15 days' casual leave is credited to an employee's leave account at the commencement of the calendar year to enable him to attend to personal obligations. Leave not availed during the calendar year automatically lapses.

Medical or sick leave   As per the act, 14 days' sick leave can be availed by an employee in a calendar year upon producing a medical certificate. Certain organizations have no provisions for medical leave but grant medical leave provided it is certified by the company medical officer.

Extraordinary leave   This is discretionary in nature and in common parlance known as leave without pay, it can be availed anytime to attend to emergencies.

Study leave   In order to encourage employees to enhance their professional skills and knowledge, companies grant study leave to their employees for the duration of the study programme.

Leave not due   When there is no leave to the credit of the employee and the employee desires to proceed on leave owing to personal circumstances, he can apply for leave not due. This type of leave is discretionary and if granted will be treated as extraordinary leave which is leave without pay.

Procedure for availing leave *Privilege leave* normally has to be applied for 30 days in advance and in case it is not granted by the management, the employee can get his leave encashed in case he or she so desires. Most hotel companies prefer to give a maximum of 21 days leave in a calendar year, the minimum privilege leave that can be granted is five days.

Casual leave can be availed at short notice for personal emergencies; however, the maximum casual leave that can be taken at any one time is three days. In case, additional days are taken and exceed five days, then casual leave is converted to privilege leave.

National and festival holidays An employee can avail a holiday on national and festival holidays which are announced by the government.

Most organizations restrict these to 10 days in a calendar year.

Annexure I The 14 national and festival holidays are gazetted holidays. The three national holidays are: 26 January–Republic Day, 15 August–Independence Day, and 02 October–Mahatma Gandhi's Birthday, which are included in this list along with 11 festival holidays such as Buddha Purnima, Christmas Day, Dussehra (Vijay Dashmi), Diwali (Deepavali), Good Friday, Guru Nanak's Birthday, Idu'l Fitr, Idu'l Zuha, Mahavir Jayanti, Muharram, Prophet Mohammad's Birthday (Id-e-Milad).

Annexure II lists additional festival holidays which are regarded as restricted holidays or optional holidays as every state has its own set of festivals; however, a maximum of two such holidays can be availed by an employee.

Holiday on account of elections to the Lok Sabha and Vidhan Sabha In case of general elections to the Lok Sabha and Vidhana Sabha, the chief election commissioner can declare a holiday on the day of the polling to enable employees to cast their votes.

Hiring of contractual employees

We have discussed the hiring of employees who are directly recruited by the hotel but there are certain positions for which hoteliers recruit indirectly through contractors. This trend of outsourcing certain operational functions to contractors is fairly recent, and has evolved out of a need to reduce manpower which constitutes a fairly high operational cost. If the hotel intends to hire 20 or more contract labourers for a period of 12 months or more it is required to register itself with the labour department.

The legal dictionary defines 'a contractor is an individual or a firm, corporation or association contracted to carry out some business activity under a contractual agreement or licence to perform the commercial activities'.

A contractor is required to register himself or herself with the labour department (Section 12, Rule 21); to maintain a register of workers for each registered establishment; to issue an employment card to each worker and to issue a service certificate upon their termination (Rule 75, 76, and 77).

A contractor's duties and liabilities under the Act are as follows:

(i) To maintain the employees' Muster Roll, Register of Wages, Register of Deductions, Register of Overtime, Register of Fines, Register of Advances, and issue Wage Slip {Rule 79}

(ii) To display an abstract of the contract labour act and rules in English & Hindi and in the language spoken by the majority of workers {Rule 80}

(iii) To display notices showing rates of wages, hours of work, wage period, dates of payment, names and address of the inspector and to send copy to the inspector and any change for with {Rule 81}

A contractor's licence can be suspended, revoked, or amended if the contractor fails to comply with the conditions of the Act (Sections 9 and 14).

Duties and Liabilities of the Hoteliers Under the Act

The hotel should check that the contractor is registered and licensed to engage manpower under the Contract Labour (Regulation & Abolition) Act, 1970 and the Contract Labour Regulation Rules before awarding him the contract.

A hotelier is required to provide canteen, restrooms, sufficient supply of drinking water, latrines and urinals, washing facilities, first-aid facilities to the employees of the contractor.

For the facilities offered by the hotel to the contractor's labourers the hotel can make deductions from the payment being made to the contractor.

Laws Related to Equality and Empowerment of Women

'Enable every woman who can work to take her place on the labour front, under the principle of equal pay for equal work.'

—Mao Tse Tung

The Equal Remuneration Act, 1976

It was enacted to give effect to Article 39 of the Constitution of India, which contains the directive principle of equal pay for equal work for both men and women. The Act provides for the payment of equal remuneration to men and women employees for the same work or work of a similar nature and for the prevention of discrimination on the ground of sex against women in the matter of employment. The main provisions of the Act are as follows.

Equal pay for equal work   No employer shall pay to any worker employed by him remuneration at rates less favourable than those at which remuneration is paid by him to the workers of the opposite sex for performing the same work or work of similar nature. {Section 4(1)}

No discrimination to be made while recruiting men and women   *No employer shall make any discrimination against women while making recruiting for the same work or work of a similar nature. {Section 5}*

Exceptions   *The provisions of the Act shall be inapplicable when special treatment is given to women under any law or when special treatment is accorded to women in connection with the birth of a child. {Section 15}*

Any complaints arising out of non-payment of wages at equal rates to men and women employees for the same work or work of similar nature or any discrimination between men and women in matters of recruitment or if an employer makes any recruitment in violation of the Act shall attract penalties with a fine up to ₹10,000 (Section 10).

What is meant by equality of work?
The equality of work is not based on the designation or the nature of work alone. There are several other factors, which are equally relevant. They are qualifications, responsibilities, reliabilities, experience, confidentiality, functional need and requirements commensurate with the position in the hierarchy.

The Maternity Benefit Act of 1961

This Act was passed to provide uniform maternity benefit for women employees in industries not covered by the Employees State Insurance Act. The objective was to protect the dignity of motherhood and the baby by providing for the full and healthy maintenance of a woman and her child at this important time when she is not working.

Maternity leave   A female employee is entitled to maternity leave of 12 weeks of which six weeks have to be availed of prior to delivery and six weeks after the birth of a child. An additional leave of four weeks will be granted on full pay in case of illness due to the pregnancy, delivery, miscarriage, or premature birth.

Eligibility of benefits   These benefits have been have been categorized as non-cash and cash benefits. To be eligible for benefits envisaged under the Act, a woman employee employed directly or through a contractor, including temporary employees; or unmarried are eligible for maternity benefit when she is expecting a child and has worked for her employer for at least 80 days in the 12 months immediately preceding the date of her expected delivery (Section 5).

Non-cash benefits

   (i) Light work for 10 weeks (six weeks plus one month) before the date of her expected delivery, if she asks for it.
   (ii) Two nursing breaks in the course of her daily work until the child is 15 months old.
   (iii) No discharge or dismissal while she is on maternity leave.
   (iv) No change to her disadvantage in any of the conditions of her employment while on maternity leave (Section 5).

(v) Pregnant women discharged or dismissed may still claim maternity benefit from the employer.

Cash benefits (Maximum limit ₹ 20,000)

(i) She should give written notice to the employer about seven weeks before the date of her delivery that she will be absent for six weeks before and after her delivery. She should also name the person to whom payment will be made in case she cannot take it herself.

(ii) Leave with average pay for six weeks before the delivery should be collected by her before proceeding on leave.

(iii) Leave with average pay for six weeks after the delivery within 48 hours of giving proof that she has had a child.

(iv) A medical bonus of ₹1000 if the employer does not provide free medical care to the woman.

(v) An additional leave with pay up to one month if the woman shows proof of illness due to the pregnancy, delivery, miscarriage, or premature birth.

(vi) In case of miscarriage, six weeks leave with average pay from the date of miscarriage.

(vii) A woman can be dismissed for gross misconduct and loses the maternity benefit under the Act.

On the other hand, in case of discharge or dismissal of a woman employee during or on account of her absence from work, the employer shall be punishable with imprisonment which shall not be less than three months, but it will extend to one year and will fine, but not exceeding ₹5000 (Section 18).

Protection of women against sexual harassment at workplace bill, 2010

As there is no law to protect working women from sexual harassment at the workplace, the Supreme Court has laid down strict guidelines for all employers to follow by delivering its judgement in the case of *Vishakha vs State of Rajasthan AIR 1997 (7) SCC323.*

A gang rape of a social worker in Rajasthan prompted Vishaka, an NGO, file a writ petition seeking the enforcement of fundamental rights of working women under Articles 14.15.19 (1)(a)(g) and 21 of the Indian constitution which are quoted as follows.

Article 14—Equality before law. The State shall not deny to any person equality before the law or the equal protection of the laws within the territory of India.

Article 15—Prohibition of discrimination on grounds of religion, race, caste, sex or place of birth.

(1) *The State shall not discriminate against any citizen on grounds only of religion, race, caste, sex, and place of birth or any of them.*

(2) *No citizen shall, on grounds only of religion, race, caste, sex, place of birth or any of them, be subject to any disability, liability, restriction or condition with regard to—*

(a) *Access to shops, public restaurants, hotels and places of public entertainment; or*

(b) *The use of wells, tanks, bathing ghats, roads and places of public resort maintained wholly or partly out of State funds or dedicated to the use of the general public.*

(3) *Nothing in this article shall prevent the State from making any special provision for women and children.*

(4) *Nothing in this article or in clause (2) of article 29 shall prevent the State from making any special provision for the advancement of any socially and educationally backward classes of citizens or for the Scheduled Castes and the Scheduled Tribes.*

Article 19—Protection of certain rights regarding freedom of speech, etc.

(1) **All citizens shall have the right:**

(a) *To freedom of speech and expression;*

(g) *To practice any profession, or to carry on any occupation, trade or business.*

Article 21—Protection of life and personal liberty. No person shall be deprived of his life or personal liberty except according to procedure established by law.

The guidelines that were enunciated in the Supreme Court judgement are given as follows:

(i) Express prohibition of sexual harassment includes physical contact and advances, demand or request for sexual favours, sexually coloured remarks, showing pornographic or any unwelcome conduct of sexual nature including physical, non-verbal, or verbal conduct.

(ii) Regulation of government and public-sector bodies must include rules to provide for appropriate penalties against the offender.

(iii) Private employers should take steps to include the mentioned prohibitions in the standing orders under the Industrial Employment (Standing Orders) Act, 1946.

(iv) Appropriate work conditions should be provided to ensure that there is no hostile environment towards women.

(v) No woman should have reasonable grounds to believe that she is in a disadvantaged position with her employment.

(vi) Victims can seek the transfer of the perpetrator or their own transfer.

Till the Act on The Prohibition of Sexual Harassment of Women at Workplace Bill, 2010 gets parliamentary sanction the Supreme Court ruling defining sexual harassment and the preventive steps that an employer has to take are applicable.

The Protection of Women against Sexual Harassment at Workplace Bill, 2010 describes sexual harassment at the workplace under Section 3:

TEXT

At any workplace, no women, shall be subjected to sexual harassment, including unwelcome sexually determined behaviour, physical contact, advances, sexually coloured remarks, showing pornography, sexual demand, request for sexual favours or any other unwelcome conduct of sexual nature whether verbal, textual, physical, graphic or electronic or by any other actions, which may include, but is not limited to:

(a) *Implied or overt promise of preferential treatment in employment; or*
(b) *Implied or overt threat of detrimental treatment in employment; or*
(c) *Implied or overt threat about the present or future employment status*
(d) *Conduct which interferes with work or creates an intimidating or offensive or hostile work environment; or*
(e) *Humiliating conduct constituting health and safety problems.*

Chapter 5, Section 20 states the duties of the employer:

The employer shall:

(a) *Provide a safe working environment at the workplace which will include safety from the employees of the establishment as well as third parties coming into contact at the workplace:*
(b) *Display at any conspicuous place in the workplace the office order made under subsection (1) of section 4:*
(c) *Undertake workshops and training programs at regular intervals for sensitizing members*
(d) *Provide necessary facilities to the Committee or local committee, as the case may be, to deal with the complaint and conduct enquiry;*
(e) *Ensure the attendance of respondent and witness before the committee or the local committee as the case maybe*
(f) *Make available such information to the committee or the local committee as the case may be, as it may require with regard to the complaint made under sub section (1) of section 7;*
(g) *Assist the women if she so chooses in the filing of a criminal complaint in relation to the offence;*
(h) *Initiate criminal action under the penal code or any other law for the time being in force against the perpetrator after the conclusion of the enquiry, or without waiting for the enquiry, where the perpetrator is not an employee in the work place where the incident of sexual harassment has taken place.*

Chapter 5, Section 20, Clause (a) clearly stipulates that the employer shall be held responsible in case any guest staying in the hotel by his or her action or conduct requests for sexual favours from women employees. Hence, it is imperative for the hotel management to formulate suitable policies as well as conduct training programmes to educate women employees.

Furthermore, the hotel management is required to initiate action in cases where there are complaints against guests by women employees. Daniel E. Eaton in his research paper titled 'Beyond room service – legal consequences of sexual harassment of staff by hotel guests', published by the *Cornell Hotel and Restaurant Administration Quarterly*, November 2004, refers to the legal case *Flower vs Mayfair Joint Venture, 2000 WL 272187 (S.N.D.Y. 2000)* wherein the court observed that 'the employer is required only to take prompt and adequate measures to remedy the situation'. In this case, the Mayfair Hotel took steps to ensure that the employee is not required to service that particular guest.

A hotel is required under Section 4, Clause (1) to constitute an internal complaint committee consisting of 50 per cent women members of which the chairperson shall always be a women employee who is senior to the aggrieved women employee. Two other employees shall also be members along with one member representing an NGO or association committed to women's causes.

Complaints can be filed under Section 7, Clause (1) with the internal complaint committee in the first instance. It shall be the responsibility of the management to assist the committee in every manner possible to ensure that an impartial enquiry is conducted.

Other legal remedies available to a victim are as follows:

(i) A civil suit may be filed for causing mental anguish, physical harassment, and so on.

(ii) A criminal suit may be filed, citing Section 354 (assault or criminal force to a woman), Section 509 (word, gesture, or act insulting a woman's modesty), and Section 294 (doing an obscene act or song to cause annoyance in a public place) of the Indian Penal Code, 1860.

(iii) A complaint based on Indecent Representation of Women (Prohibition) Act, 1986, if an individual harasses another with books, films, pamphlets, and paintings depicting women badly, the accused persons are liable for a minimal sentence spanning two years.

Some of the high-profile cases that have resulted in highlighting this issue are discussed as follows.

Rupan Deol Bajaj vs KPS Gill 1998 SC, A senior IAS officer, Rupan Bajaj was slapped on the posterior by the then Chief of Police, Punjab, K. P. S. Gill at a dinner party in July 1988. Rupan Bajaj filed a suit against him, despite the public opinion that she was blowing it out of proportion, along with the attempts by all the senior officials of the state to suppress the matter. The Supreme Court in January 1998 fined K P S. Gill for ₹2.5 lakh in lieu of three months' rigorous imprisonment under Sections 294 and 509 of the Indian Penal Code, 1860.

N Radhabai vs D. Ramchandran When Radhabai, Secretary to D. Ramchandran, the then Social Minister for State protested against his abuse of girls in the welfare institutions, he attempted to molest her, which was followed by her dismissal. The Supreme Court in 1995 passed the judgement in her favour, with back pay and perks from the date of dismissal.

The International Union of Food, Agricultural, Hotel, Restaurant, Catering, Tobacco and Allied Workers' Associations (IUF) is an international federation of trade unions representing workers employed in:

(i) agriculture and plantations;
(ii) the preparation and manufacture of food and beverages;
(iii) hotels, restaurants, and catering services; and
(iv) all stages of tobacco processing.

The IUF was motivated by the 'the recent highly publicized events at the Sofitel New York', a reference to the arrest of former International Monetary Fund Managing Director Dominique Strauss-Kahn, and designed 'to highlight the vulnerable situation of hotel housekeepers'.

IUF specifically directed its inquiry at the Marriott, Intercontinental, Wyndham Hotels, Hilton, Accor, Hyatt, Rezidor, Starwood, Carlson Hotels, and Melia hotel chains to formulate policies to prevent sexual harassment at work.

The Indian hotel operators should formulate their policies in good time as parliamentary approval for the Bill is awaited. The stringent law will make it mandatory for every establishment to display its policy at prominent places in the hotel as well as to have sexual harassment incorporated into their standing orders as an act of misconduct.

Employees with Special Needs

The passing of The Persons with Disabilities (Equal Opportunities, Protection of Rights and Full Participation) Act, (PWD Act) of 1995 has been a landmark legislation for India. It marks a shift in the attitude towards people with disabilities. It recognizes for the first time that people with disabilities should be given opportunities that will enable them to integrate into the mainstream society.

Chapter I, Clause 2 of the Act defines 'Disability' as:

   (i) blindness
   (ii) low vision
   (iii) leprosy-cured
   (iv) hearing impairment
   (v) loco-motor disability
   (vi) mental retardation
   (vii) mental illness

and further clarifies:

   (j) *'hearing impairment' means loss of sixty decibels or more in the better ear in the conversational range of frequencies;*
   (k) *'leprosy cured person' means any person who has been cured of leprosy but is suffering from—*
      (i) *loss of sensation in hands or feet as well as loss of sensation and paresis in the eye and eye-lid but with no manifest deformity;*
      (ii) *manifest deformity and paresis but having sufficient mobility in their hands and feet to enable them to engage in normal economic activity;*
      (iii) *Extreme physical deformity as well as advanced age which prevents him from undertaking any gainful occupation, and the expression 'leprosy cured' shall be construed accordingly;*
   (l) *'loco motor disability' means disability of the bones, joints or muscles leading to substantial restriction of the movement of the limbs or any form of cerebral palsy;*
   (m) *'mental illness' means any mental disorder other than mental retardation;*
   (n) *'mental retardation' means a condition of arrested or incomplete development of mind of a person which is specially characterized by sub normality of intelligence;*
   (o) *'person with low vision' means a person with impairment of visual functioning even after treatment or standard refractive correction but who uses or is potentially capable of using vision for the planning or execution of a task with appropriate assistive device.*

Chapter 8 of the Act stipulates that affirmative action should be taken to ensure that people with disabilities are not discriminated in any manner and have access to education, employment, public transportation system, and private and public buildings.

If 5 per cent of the workforce in public and private sectors comprises people with disabilities, the Act has a provision of giving incentives in the way the central or state governments think appropriate.

Employee Safety at the Workplace

The Workmen's Compensation Act, 1923 and The Workmen's Compensation (Amendments) Act, 2000 aim 'to provide workmen and their dependents relief in case of accidents causing death or disablement in the course of their employment'.

Disablement

Under the Workmen's Compensation Act, 1923 an accident arising out of employment implies a casual connection between the injury and the accident and the work done in the course of employment. Employment should be the distinctive and the proximate cause of the injury.

The three tests for determining whether an accident arose out of employment are as follows:

(i) At the time of injury workman must have been engaged in the business of the employer and must not be doing something for his personal benefit.
(ii) Accident occurred at the place where he was performing his duties.
(iii) Injury must have resulted from some risk incidental to the duties of the service, or inherent in the nature or condition of employment.

The Act draws a distinction between the various types of disablement resulting in the loss of the earning capacity of a workman that can occur on account of injury sustained at the workplace. Disablement, whether permanent or temporary, is said to be total when it incapacitates a worker for all work he was capable of doing prior to the time of the accident resulting in such disablement.

Accident compensation becomes payable by an employer when:

(i) A workman who has suffered an accident arising out of and in the course of his employment, resulting in:
    (a) permanent total disablement;
    (b) permanent partial disablement;
    (c) temporary disablement whether total or partial; or
    (d) death.
(ii) A workman has contracted an occupational disease.

Disablements can be classified into (i) total or (ii) partial which can be either (a) permanent or (b) temporary—permanent total disablement, permanent partial disablement, or temporary partial disablement.

Permanent total disablement is considered to be permanent if a workman, as a result of an accident, suffers from an injury or a combination of injuries that would lead to the loss of earning capacity when totalled comes to 100 per cent or more. The injuries are specified in Part I of Schedule I and in Part II of Schedule I of the Act.

> **Example**   Rakesh is a boiler operator at a hotel, and it is his responsibility to ensure that a steady temperature of hot water being circulated in the hotel is maintained at all times. On 15 June 2010, when Rakesh reports on duty he goes through the boiler log and observes that the temperature readings show an abnormality as they are on the high side. Rakesh immediately informs the chief engineer who is of the opinion that the boiler should be temporarily shut down to assess the situation.
>
> The chief engineer tells Rakesh to go back to the boiler room to monitor the temperatures while he goes about informing all the executives of the boiler shutdown. The front-office manager, housekeeper, and the laundry manager would like the shutdown to be delayed by six hours as they are running a full house and this would give them adequate time to plan. This delay results in the boiler bursting with a deafening noise resulting in Rakesh sustaining injuries all over his body.
>
> Rakesh is rushed to the hospital where his injuries are attended to. Further tests reveal that the explosion of the boiler resulted in Rakesh becoming deaf.
>
> Under the Workmen's Compensation Act, 1923 'absolute deafness' is categorized as 100% loss of earning capacity which is a permanent total disability and the hotel will have to pay compensation to Rakesh.

Permanent partial disablement is when the earning capacity of a workman is reduced for all times, which he was capable of undertaking at the time of the accident.

The workman should have suffered injuries specified in Part II of Schedule I of the Act the time of the accident.

> **Example**   Sunil is a trainee chef who is given the task of preparing minced meat by using the meat mincing machine. He is engaged in a conversation with his fellow colleague and trainee, which results in Sunil losing his concentration and instead of using the spatula to force the meat into the mincer he uses his bare hands resulting in the thumb and index finger being chopped off by the blades of the machine.
>
> Under the Act, the percentage loss of earning capacity on account of loss of the thumb is 30% and the index finger is 14%, that is, a total of 44%. The hotel will have to compensate Sunil 44% of his wages on account of his permanent partial disablement.

Temporary partial or total disablement is disablement of a temporary nature and reduces the earning capacity of a workman in the employment in which he was engaged at the time of the accident. This benefit is available only for a limited period of time as the employee shall fully recover in the future and will be able to resume his duties without loss of wages.

> **Example**   Akshay is employed as a valet with Sun & Sand Hotel and his primary responsibility is to handle VIP guests' pick up and drop to and from the hotel. On 17 April 2010 Akshay is en-route to the airport from the hotel, when he meets with an accident in which he breaks his shinbone. His leg is put in a plaster cast, and he is advised complete bed rest for 12 weeks after which Akshay will be permitted to resume his duties. During this period Akshay is temporarily totally disabled, and the hotel is required to pay him disability benefits.

Occupational disease

The legal dictionary defines occupational disease as 'a disease resulting from exposure during employment to conditions or substances that are detrimental to health (such as black lung disease contracted by miners)'. A worker contracting an occupational disease is deemed to have suffered an accident out of and in the course of employment and the employer is liable to pay compensation for the same. Compensation for the same is payable to the worker as per the categorization of the disease as Category A, B, and C under the Act.

The list of occupational diseases under the Act is exhaustive; however, the European Agency for Safety and Health at Work has conducted a research on the working environment in hotels and its findings are listed in Table 7.4.

TABLE 7.4 Impact of Physical Environment on Health

Risk	Physical work environment	Health outcome
Noise and high sound levels	Discotheques, nightclubs, kitchens, restaurants	Hearing loss and mental fatigue
Temperature and breathing problems	High temperatures and steam in laundry, kitchens' warm, humid environment	Muscle cramps, heat exhaustion, headaches, extreme cases of heat stroke
Contact with dangerous substances	Housekeeping and kitchen's exposure to oven and floor cleaners, disinfectants, soaps and detergents, pesticides, and so on.	Eczema, skin infections, allergies, eye and nose irritations, respiratory diseases
	Working extensively in wet areas—kitchen stewarding	Dermatitis
Smoking and alcohol consumption	Passive smoking in discotheques, nightclubs, bars	Respiratory problems, lower life expectancy

From the examples in Table 7.4, it is evident that hotels will have to take steps to ensure that employees are adequately protected against the hazards of occupational diseases.

The Fatal Accidents Act, 1885, on the other hand, 'aims at providing compensation to families for loss occasioned by the death of a person caused by an actionable wrong against a person who, by his wrongful act, neglect or default, may have caused the death of another person, and it is often-times right and expedient that the wrong-doer in such case should be answerable in damages for the injury so caused by him by moving a plaint in any court'.

This is based upon the legal principle, *ubicunque est injuria, ibi damnum sequitur*, and when translated from the Latin means 'whenever there is a wrong, there damage follows'. When facts and circumstances exit and meet the legal requirements to file a legitimate suit for a wrongful death, a law suit can be brought on behalf of the beneficiaries of the deceased person on the grounds that death was attributable to the wilful or negligent conduct of another.

> **Example**　A large number of modern hotels which are being built are tall skyscrapers having glass facades, which require to be cleaned periodically. Glass cleaning of such tall structures requires specialized skills and equipment, and hotels outsource this activity to contractors. ABC contractors have the required expertise in executing assignment of this nature and are awarded the contract by a hotel.
>
> A trolley is suspended from the roof which runs alongside the glass facade from which the glass cleaner operates with his supplies. The glass cleaner wears an additional lifeline, should any mishap occur while he is working and he can be pulled up to safety. The movement of the trolley is the responsibility of the trolley operator who has to ensure that the movement is smooth and gentle as hasty and rushed movement can result in the glass cleaner positioned in the trolley loose his balance and fall off the trolley.
>
> Ramesh has recently joined the company and is the trolley operator on duty along with Suresh, the glass cleaner positioned in the suspended trolley. Whilst the trolley is being moved erratically by Ramesh, Suresh loses his balance and goes overboard and the lifeline snaps and he plunges to death.
>
> Due to the company's negligence, Suresh meets with a fatal accident resulting in his death. The dependents of Suresh move a plaint against the company claiming for compensation under the provision of the Fatal Accidents Act, 1885.

SUMMARY

This chapter examined two salient aspects of labour laws that provide for the rights of employees at workplace such as wages, working hours, working conditions, and define the relationship between employers, employees, and trade unions. Furthermore, the chapter discussed constitutional provisions that ensure the rights of individuals at the workplace, and how the companies' standing orders play a pivotal role in maintaining employers' and employees' relations. The chapter highlighted the requirements that are mandatory for an employer to fulfil pertaining to social security and welfare and also empowerment of women and the steps being taken to prevent sexual harassment at the workplace. The chapter pointed out the need for maintaining, safety standards at the workplace as disregard of workers' safety could lead to injuries that result in compensations being paid to employees as well as give rise to situations where employees could sue for compensations.

KEY TERMS

Fundamental rights　Guarantee that the residents of India can lead a peaceful life with the Supreme Court and the high courts empowered to enforce these rights. The six fundamental rights are: right to equality; right to freedom of speech; right against exploitation; right to freedom of religion; cultural and educational rights; and right to constitutional remedies.

Directive principles of state policy　Not enforceable by any court, these are instructions to the legislature and the executive fundamental to the governance of the country, and it shall be the duty of the state to apply these principles in making laws.

Concurrent list　Under the Indian Constitution gives both the centre and the states legislative powers to enact laws on the items that are listed in this list. However, if any piece of legislation passed by the state conflicts in any manner with a central law passed on the same subject, the provisions of the central act shall take precedence.

Industry Any systematic activity carried on by cooperation between an employer and his or her workmen for the production, supply, or distribution of goods or services with a view to satisfy human wants or wishes, irrespective of any capital that has been invested for the purpose of carrying on such activity; or such activity is carried on with a motive to make any gain or profit; or any activity relating to the promotion of sales or business or both carried on by an establishment.

Workman Any person (including an apprentice) employed in any industry to do any manual, unskilled, skilled, technical, operational, clerical, or supervisory work for hire or reward, whether the terms of employment are express or implied.

Industrial dispute One that is (i) between employers and employers, (ii) between employers and workmen, (iii) between workmen and workmen, the subject matter of which is connected with the employment or non-employment of any person, who has been dismissed, discharged, or retrenched in connection with, or as a consequence of that dispute, or whose dismissal, discharge, or retrenchment has led to that dispute.

Conciliation The process of adjusting or settling disputes in a friendly manner through extra-judicial means. Conciliation means bringing two opposing sides together to reach a compromise in an attempt to avoid taking a case to trial. A court of conciliation is one that suggests the manner in which two opposing parties may avoid trial by proposing mutually acceptable terms.

Arbitration The submission of a dispute to an unbiased third person designated by the parties to the controversy, who agree in advance to comply with the award—a decision to be issued after a hearing at which both parties have an opportunity to be heard.

Adjudication The legal process of resolving a dispute and implies a hearing by a court, after notice, of legal evidence on the factual issue(s) involved prior to pronouncing of a judgement or decree in a court proceeding. It indicates that the claims of all the parties thereto have been considered and set at rest.

Lay-off Failure, refusal, or inability of an employer on account of shortage of coal, power, or raw materials or accumulation of stock or breakdown of machinery or natural calamity, to give employment to a workman on muster roll within two hours after reporting to work.

Retrenchment The reduction in the company's workforce by way of termination by the employer of surplus labour or staff not as a punishment but for any reason on the basis of last in first out in respect of each category.

Closure The permanent closing of an establishment or a part of the establishment—if the number of persons employed is 50 or more, two months' notice is required to be given, but if the number of employees is less than 50, two months' notice is not required to be given by the employer to the government or the employees.

Strike A temporary stoppage of normal activity in any industry undertaken as a protest or a cessation of work by a body of persons employed in that industry, acting in combination, a concerted refusal, or a refusal under a common understanding, of any number of persons who are or have been so employed to continue to work or to accept employment.

Lockout A temporary closing of a place of employment or the suspension of work, or the refusal by an employer to continue to employ any number of persons employed by him.

Trade union A voluntary organization of workers pertaining to a particular industry formed to balance and improve the relations between the employer and the employees by promoting and protecting the welfare and interests of workers by collective action.

Standing orders Rules of conduct for workmen employed in industries, factories, or shops and establishments to regulate service conditions such as attendance, leave rules, termination, resignation, and others; and of acts that constitute misconduct that will invite disciplinary action.

Misconduct Such acts like insubordination, disobedience, fraud, dishonesty, damage to employer's property, taking bribe, habitual absence or habitual late attendance, riotous behaviour, habitual neglect of work, strike in contravention of rules, misuse of the Internet, and suggestive gestures towards female employees.

Wages All remuneration capable of being expressed in terms of money, which would be payable to an employee for work done in the course of his or her employment whether express or implied inclusive of such allowances (including dearness allowance), the value of any house accommodation, or of supply of light, water, medical attendance, or other amenities, or of any service, or of any concessional supply of food grains or other articles. These also include any travelling concession, any commission payable on the promotion of sales or business, or both; exclusive of bonus, contributions paid or payable by the employer to any pension fund or provident fund, and any gratuity payable on the termination of his or her service.

Minimum wages Basic pay plus any applicable allowances such as dearness allowance.

Ex-gratia In Latin means 'out of kindness'. This includes cash benefit or something given as a favour when no legal obligation exists.

Deferred wages   This concept was to pay 13 months' salary for 12 months of work, payable during the festival holidays which was normally around the Hindu festival of Diwali.

Bonus   An incentive based upon the concept of profit-sharing and deferred wages reiterating the main concept of bonus as profit-sharing. The Payment of Bonus Act, 1965 makes it mandatory for all establishments having more than 20 employees to pay bonus annually, laying down the criteria for the calculation and disbursement of bonus to all employees eligible to receive bonus from the allocable surplus.

Disablement   Such incapacity of an employee for the work which he was capable of performing before the accident or disease resulting in such disablement.

Family   For a male employee, a family is defined as himself, his wife, his children, whether married or unmarried, his dependent parents and the dependent parents of his wife and the widow and children of his predeceased son, if any. In case of a female employee, a family is defined as herself, her husband, her children, whether married or unmarried, her dependent parents and the dependent parents of her husband and the widow and children of her predeceased son, if any.

Continuous service   For an employee shall be the period in which he has been in uninterrupted service, including service which may be interrupted on account of sickness, accident, leave, or absence from duty without leave (not being absence in respect of which an order treating the absence as break in service has been passed in accordance with the standing orders, rules or regulations governing the employees of the establishment), lay-off, strike or a lockout, or cessation of work not due to any fault of the employee for a period of one year.

Gratuity   A lump sum payment payable to an employee who has completed a minimum of five years of service prior to his discharge from the company, and the amount payable is equivalent to the last average salary drawn for 15 days (basic +dearness allowance) multiplied by the number of completed years of service.

Termination   The legal dictionary defines to terminate as 'to discontinue, bring to completion, release, and bring an end to'. It implies the release from employment against the employees will at the behest of the management.

Resignation   Giving up, leaving, and quitting voluntarily from employment by an employee after giving a notice to the employer.

Retirement   To withdraw from one's occupation, business or office, having finished one's active working life voluntarily or involuntarily.

Superannuation   The act of discharging an employee because of age.

Weekly offs   Availed by an employee after he has worked for 6 days and each working day is of 9 hours. It is normally a Sunday, but in organizations that follow different shift systems, weekly offs can be changed provided the basic principle is followed.

Privilege leave or earned leave or annual leave   As per the Factories Act, 1948 an employee is entitled to one day's leave for every 20 days worked and he should have worked for a minimum of 240 days in a calendar year to be entitled to annual leave which will be credited to his leave account upon completion of one year of service at the beginning of the calendar year. This works out to 18 days leave in a calendar year. However, as per the prevailing practice most of the organizations give 21 to 30 days earned leave to their employees for which they take approval from the labour commissioner when getting their model standing orders certified.

Casual leave   Casual leave of 15 days is credited to an employee leave account at the commencement of the calendar year to enable him to attend to personal obligations. Leave not availed during the calendar year automatically lapses.

Medical or sick leave   As per the Act, 14 days' sick leave can be availed by an employee in a calendar year upon production of a medical certificate. Certain organizations have no provisions for medical leave but grant medical leave provided it is certified by the company medical officer.

Extraordinary leave   Discretionary in nature and in common a parlance known as leave without pay it can be availed anytime to attend to emergencies.

Study leave   In order to encourage employees to enhance their professional skills and knowledge, companies grant study leave to their employees for the duration of their study programmes.

Leave not due   When there is no leave to the credit of the employee and the employee desires to proceed on leave owing to personal circumstances he can apply for leave not due. This type of leave is discretionary and if granted will be treated as extraordinary leave which is leave without pay.

Maternity leave   A female employee is entitled to maternity leave of 12 weeks of which 6 weeks have to be availed of prior to delivery and 6 weeks after the birth of a child. Additional leave of 4 weeks will be granted on full pay in case of illness due to the pregnancy, delivery, miscarriage, or premature birth.

Contractor An individual or a firm, corporation, or an association contracted to carry out some business activity under a contractual agreement or licence to perform the commercial activities.

EXERCISES

Define the Following

1. Retrenchment
2. Directive principles of state policy
3. Extraordinary leave
4. Industrial dispute
5. Appointment letters
6. Wages
7. Trade unions
8. Misconduct
9. Employee pension scheme
10. Public provident fund

Concept Review Questions

1. Define the role of a conciliation officer in settling disputes.
2. What are wages? Explain the method of computing wages by giving examples.
3. What is allocable surplus and how does it impact bonus calculations?
4. Describe the induction process for a new employee in a hotel.

5. Write a brief on the constitutional provisions that guarantee the welfare of employees.
6. What is the difference between arbitration and conciliation under the Indian Arbitration and Conciliation Act, 1996?

Critical Thinking Questions

1. Study the welfare measures that are implemented by at least three different hotels and their impact on employee morale and productivity.
2. Elaborate on this statement 'government has enacted laws providing for social security for employees on their discharge'.

Research Question

1. Model standing orders are the basis on which disciplinary action can be initiated against an errant employee. How can these be made more relevant?

Project

1. The Supreme Court gave a landmark judgement in *Vishaka vs State of Rajasthan*. What was the impact of this judgement?

REFERENCES

Daniel E. Eaton, 'Beyond room service – legal consequences of sexual harassment of staff by hotel guests', *Cornell Hotel and Restaurant Administration Quarterly*, November 2004, 347–361.

<http://en.wikisource.org/wiki/Page:Speeches_And_Writings_MKGandhi.djvu/874> accessed on 22 May 2012.

<http://www.brainyquote.com/quotes/keywords/labour_4.html#ZzL03CP4Zd1Kf23U.99> accessed on 22 May 2012.

<http://www.brainyquote.com/quotes/keywords/labour_2.html#AkYkzxlg5Dv3Hrlh.99> accessed on 22 May 2012.

<http://www.constitution.org/cons/india/p03019.html> accessed on 22 May 2012.

<http://www.civilserviceindia.com/subject/Law/notes/fundamental-right-principles.html> accessed on 22 May 2012.

<http://labour.nic.in/act/welcome.html> accessed on 14 May 2012.

<http://www.lawzonline.com/bareacts/delhi-shops-and-establishments-act/Section2-delhi-shops-and-establishments-act.html> accessed on 14 May 2012.

<http://www.lawzonline.com/bareacts/delhi-shops-and-establishments-act/Section 5-delhi-shops-and-establishments-act.html> accessed on 14 May 2012.

<http://labour.nic.in/cgit/> accessed on 18 May 2012.

<http://legal-dictionary.thefreedictionary.com/conciliation> accessed on 16 May 2012. <http://definitions.uslegal.com/e/ex-aequo-et-bono/> accessed on 16 May 2012.

<http://www.ehow.com/how_5032397_write-employment-ads.html> accessed on 26 May 2012

<http://www.thefreedictionary.com/superannuation> accessed on 19 May 2012.

<http://www.incometaxindia.gov.in/archive/taxation_of_
   salaried_employees.pdf> accessed on 25 May 2012.

<http://definitions.uslegal.com/e/employee-termination/>
   accessed on 19 May 2012.

<http://definitions.uslegal.com/e/employee-resignation/>
   accessed on 19 May 2012.

<http://www.excelconsultancyservices.co.in/Glossary.
   htm#gContractor> accessed on 19 May 2012.

<http://www.indiapost.gov.in/POSBActs/PPFRules1968.
   pdf> accessed on 19 May 2012.

<http://legal-dictionary.thefreedictionary.com/arbitration>
   accessed on 16 May 2012.

<http://legal-dictionary.thefreedictionary.com/
   adjudication> accessed on 16 May 2012.

<http://www.thefreedictionary.com/ex+gratia> accessed
   on 16 May 2012.

<http://www.legalserviceindia.com/articles/rape_laws.htm>
   accessed on 16 May 2012.

<http://www.travel-impact-newswire.com/2011/06/unions-
   seek-anti-sexual-harassment-policy-disclosure-by-hotel-
   chains/#axzz1zx8LPmsi> accessed on 01 June 2012.

<http://www.iuf.org/www/en/index_archive.shtml>
   accessed on 01 June 2012.

<http://legal-dictionary.thefreedictionary.com/
   Occupational+Disease> accessed on 17 May 2012.

<http://osha.europa.eu/en/publications/reports/
   TE7007132ENC_horeca> accessed on 16 May 2012.

Hospitality Law

LEARNING OBJECTIVES

After going through this chapter, the reader will be familiar with the following:

- Basics of hospitality and hoteliering
- Application of law of torts or common law to the hotel industry
- Legal obligations of providing for accommodation, safety, and security of guests and their belongings
- Preventing fraud committed by guests
- Developing a standard operating procedure for handling emergencies
- Defining operational standards keeping the law in mind

INTRODUCTION

Hospitality is the key to a hotel's success and the *Oxford Dictionary* defines it as 'the friendly and generous reception and entertainment of guests, visitors and strangers'. The word has its origins from the Latin word *hospes*, which literally means *hostis* or host and the old French word *hospitalite*.

The story of the friendship between Lord Krishna, the King of Dwarka, and Sudama, a poor and humble villager, has been told in the *Bhagwat Purana*. Both of them were the disciples of Sage Sandipani and it was in his ashram where their friendship matured. When poverty and difficult times engulfed Sudama, his wife suggested that he should go and meet Lord Krishna. Sudama carried for Lord Krishna the gift of *Poha* or flattened rice, which he knew Lord Krishna liked.

Lord Krishna was delighted to meet Sudama and was the perfect host aware of his duties and responsibilities and welcomed Sudama by washing his feet. It was a gesture that established that in a host–guest relationship, the professional status or economic standing of the guest is of no importance; what is paramount is that the guest is made to feel welcome with great humility and is made comfortable.

Sudama was so overwhelmed that he was hesitant to give Lord Krishna the *Poha*, which he had brought as a gift, thinking what Lord Krishna will feel after receiving such a trivial gift. However, Lord Krishna snatched the *Poha* from him and accepted it gracefully. Next day, Sudama bid farewell to Lord Krishna and his wife Rukmani.

Upon arrival at his village, he was surprised to find that he had been blessed with a palatial house and his family was no longer in poverty.

This short anecdote encapsulates all the qualities that a good hotelier should have: a sense of concern towards guests executed dutifully and responsibly with care, humility, and graciousness.

In the modern context, to play the perfect host at all times, a hotel general manager has to be fully aware of his or her duties and responsibilities towards the guests as the Law 'recognizes him as the person responsible for managing the affairs of the hotel' (Hotel Proprietors Act, 1956 (UK)). In India, the Sarais Act, 1867 defines a hotel general manager's role in the form of a keeper of a *sarai*: '"Keeper of a sarai" includes the owner and any person having or acting in the care or management thereof'.

WHAT IS A HOTEL?

A hotel general manager is also required to fully understand the legal definition of the hotel of which he is in charge. Legal definitions of a hotel under various laws are cited in the following paragraphs.

The Hotel Proprietors Act, 1956 (UK) defines an inn or a hotel as 'an establishment held out by the proprietor as offering food, drink and, if so required, sleeping accommodation, without special contract, to any traveller presenting himself who appears able and willing to pay a reasonable sum for the services and facilities provided, and, who is a in a fit state to be received'.

Under the Sarais Act, 1867, *Sarai* or *Purao* is defined as 'any building used for the shelter and accommodation of travellers, and includes, in any case in which only part of a building is used as a Sarai, the part so used of such building. It also includes a Purao so far as the provisions of this Act are applicable thereto'.

As per the Delhi Municipal Corporation Bye-Law Order, 1964 (Regulation of Hotels, Lodging Houses, and Similar Places), a lodging facility is defined as 'any sarai, hotel, boarding house for the general public, rest house or unlicenced immigration depot, or any other place where visitors are received and provided sleeping accommodation on payment and shall include religious and charitable institutions or *Raen Baseras* [night shelters] maintained or supervised by the Government or the corporation'.

According to the Delhi Rent Control Act, 1958, 'hotel or lodging house means a building or a part of a building where lodging with or without board or other services is provided for a monetary gain'. The Hotel Rate and Structure Committee formed in 1958 further amplified that 'no establishment that does not primarily offer residential accommodation and is not so used should be permitted to use the word Hotel'.

A hotel is a building or part of a building where the owner offers to travellers or general public willingness and ability to pay primary sleeping accommodation with or without food and drink and other services and facilities without any prior or special contract.

THE SARAIS ACT, 1867

The Sarais Act, 1867 is the first attempt in India to spell out the duties and responsibilities of a hotelier or an innkeeper. The Act states that no one can operate a *sarai* if it is not registered and licenced by the local administration, and stipulates that an innkeeper or a general manager is required to produce a character certificate in order to manage the affairs of a *sarai* (Clauses 5 and 6). A general manager is required to register himself or herself under this Act with the authorities, and this is normally done by the human resources division of the hotel.

A general manager is further required to maintain a record of all guests staying at the *sarai* and furnish the details to the local administration from time to time (Clause 8). This record in common hotel parlance is called Guest Arrival and Departure Register listing the details of all registered guests and is maintained by all hotels in the format as required by law and shown to the authorities, as and when required.

Clause 7 of the Sarais Act, 1867 defines the following duties of a hotelier:

(1) *When any person in such sarai is ill of any infectious or contagious disease, or dies of such disease, to give immediate notice thereof to the nearest police station.*

(2) *At all times when required by any Magistrate or any other person duty authorized by the Magistrate of the District in this behalf, to give him free access to the sarai and allow him to inspect the same or any part thereof.*

(3) *To thoroughly cleanse the rooms and verandahs, and drains of the sarai, and the wells, tanks, or other sources from which water is obtained for the persons or animals using it, to the satisfaction of, and so often as shall be required by, the Magistrate of the District, or such person as he shall appoint in this behalf.*

(4) *To remove all noxious vegetation on or near the sarai, and all trees and branches of trees capable of affording to thieves means of entering or leaving the sarai.*

(5) *To keep the gates, walls, fences, roofs, and drains of the sarai in repair.*

(6) *To provide such number of watchmen as may, in the opinion of the Magistrate of the District, subject to such rules as the State Government may prescribe in this behalf, be necessary for the safety and protection of persons and animals or vehicles lodging in, halting at, or placed in the sarai.*

(7) *To exhibit a list of charges for the use of the sarai at such place and in such form and languages as the Magistrate of the District shall from time to time direct.*

The Act requires the hotelier to display the room charges being levied and focuses on the safety and security of guests, proper maintenance of the property, hygiene, sanitation, and cleanliness of the premises. In case the above requirements are not met, the local administration has the powers to impose fines and penalties, and in extreme cases, can withdraw a hotel's operating licence. If the sarai is in a state of disrepair, the premises can be temporarily sealed till the repairs are carried out (Clauses 9 and 10 of the Sarais Act, 1867). All these aspects of hoteliering are followed even today.

Hotel laws defining the relationship between the hotelier and the guests have been evolving with changing guest requirements. The issues that require attention are related to who is a guest, duties of a hotelier towards guests, a hotel's liability towards guests, damage or loss of guest property, the circumstances under which a hotelier can refuse accommodation as well as evict a guest, and the responsibilities of a guest towards a hotelier, for example, not committing fraud, damaging or stealing hotel property, and so on.

WHO IS A GUEST?

The commonly accepted description of a guest is 'any traveller or person who is a recipient of hospitality or entertainment extended by another in the role of a host at a restaurant, hotel, or other establishment and pays for meals or accommodations offered'.

According to the Australian Carriers and Innkeepers Act, 1958, 'a traveller shall be deemed to be a guest at an inn only on days during which he is entitled to use a room at the inn that has been engaged by or for him for sleeping'. Under The Hotel Proprietors Act, 1956 (UK), a further qualification was introduced that a traveller shall be a guest 'during the period commencing with the midnight immediately preceding, and ending with the midnight immediately following, a period for which the traveller was a guest at the hotel and entitled to use the accommodation so engaged'.

As illustrated in Fig. 8.1, there are various types of guests and visitors. Guests are of two types: resident visitors (in-house guests) who hire accommodation and use the various facilities of the hotel, and non-resident visitors (also called patrons).

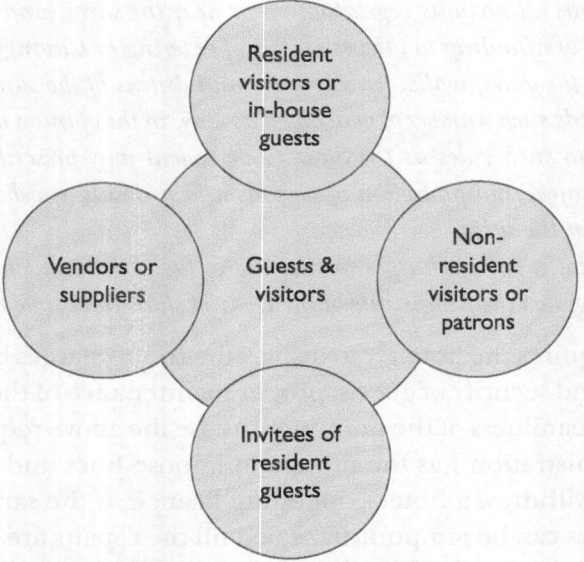

FIGURE 8.1 Types of Guests and Visitors

To qualify as a resident guest or in-house guest, a person has to stay for a minimum period of 24 hours in a hotel room for which he has paid and is therefore entitled to the use of the facilities offered by the hotel.

Non-resident visitors (also called patrons) are visitors who enjoy the facilities located in the public areas such as restaurants and bars, health club and spas, banquets, business centres upon payment for the services utilized.

There are two types of visitors to a hotel: (i) guests who are invitees of resident visitors or in-house guests for social meetings or meals to the resident visitor's room or hotel's restaurants, and (ii) vendors or suppliers of goods and services to the hotel attending meetings with various members of the management team.

LAW OF TORTS OR TORTS LAW OR COMMON LAW

The legal difference between duty of care and negligence is defined under the law of torts. It is an intrinsic part of 'public duty', which the law recognizes to be the foremost duty of a hotelier. In a hotel, the most common reasons that can lead to litigation are negligence, assault and battery, private nuisance, invasion of privacy, false imprisonment, theft, and trespass.

Tort is French for wrong, a civil wrong, or wrongful act, whether intentional or unintentional (accidental), from which injury occurs to another. Torts include all negligence cases as well as intentional wrongs that result in harm. Negligence is unintentional tort, whereas assault and battery, trespass, false imprisonment, defamation, (libel or slander) invasion of privacy, and private nuisance are examples of intentional tort. The person responsible for the wrongdoing is called a tortfeasor.

According to J. W. Salmond (1977), 'a tort is a civil wrong for which the remedy is an action for unliquidated damages and which is not exclusively the breach of a contract, or the breach of trust, or the breach of other merely equitable obligation.'.

For a better understanding of the laws of torts, a hotelier must understand the following important legal terms of torts law.

Assault The act or instance of unlawfully threatening or attempting to injure another person without physically touching the person.

Battery The unlawful and unwanted touching or striking of one person by another directly or indirectly with the intention of bringing about a harmful or offensive contact.

Private nuisance A broad legal concept including anything that disturbs the reasonable use of a property or endangers life and health or is offensive.

Invasion of privacy The wrongful intrusion by individuals or the government into the private affairs of individuals with which the public has no concern or any wrongdoing for which an action for damages may be brought.

Theft   The dishonest taking of property belonging to another person with the intention of depriving the owner permanently of its possession.

Trespass   Committing an unlawful injury to the person, property, or rights of another, with actual or implied force or violence, especially to enter onto another's land wrongfully or to infringe on the privacy, time, or attention of another person.

False imprisonment   Restraining a person without lawful authority.

Liability   Defined by the *Oxford Dictionary* as 'the state of being legally responsible for something' and by the *Online Legal Dictionary* as: 'one of the most significant words in the field of law, liability means legal responsibility for one's acts or omissions. Failure of a person or entity to meet that responsibility leaves him/her open to a lawsuit for any resulting damages or a court order to perform'.

Vicarious liability   Based on the doctrine of 'Respondent Superior' (Latin for 'let the master answer'), imposes responsibility upon one person for the failure of another, with whom the person has a special relationship (such as an employer and an employee, or owner of a vehicle and a driver), to exercise such care as a reasonably prudent person would use under similar circumstances.

Strict liability   Sometimes called absolute liability, is the legal responsibility for damages or injury, even if the person found strictly liable was not at fault or negligent. Strict liability has been applied to certain activities in tort, such as holding an employer absolutely liable for the torts of their employees, but today it is most commonly associated with defectively manufactured products.

Due care   Means all employees are well trained and knowledgeable of the industry standards and the standards of the hotel that they are required to follow when interacting with guests and in their interactions they exercise reasonable care that would be expected of any prudent person in a similar situation ensuring that their actions or inactions will not result in injury, loss, or damage to the guest.

Due care is the conduct that a reasonable man or woman will exercise in a particular situation, in looking out for the safety of others. If one uses due care then an injured party cannot prove negligence. It is important to establish that the inaction or action leading to the negligence is directly attributable to the hotel.

Negligence   The failure to exercise reasonable care resulting in injury, loss, or damage to the guests. Negligence is also referred to unintentional tort and can be gross negligence, contributory negligence, or comparative negligence.

Gross negligence   A conscious and voluntary disregard of the need to use reasonable care, which is likely to cause foreseeable grave injury or harm to persons, property, or both.

Contributory negligence A doctrine of common law that if a person was injured in part due to his or her own negligence (his or her negligence 'contributed' to the accident), the injured party would not be entitled to collect any damages (money) from another party who supposedly caused the accident.

Comparative negligence A rule of law applied in accident cases to determine responsibility and damages based on the negligence of every party directly involved in the accident.

Hotels in India are fortunate that they have not been held liable on grounds of negligence stemming from the decisions taken by the managers and employees, as there is lack of awareness of the laws, and Indians by nature are not as litigious when compared to western standards.

DUTIES OF A HOTELIER TOWARDS GUESTS

The Australian Carriers & Innkeepers Act, 1958 (incorporating amendments as on 1 August 2010), The Hotel Proprietors Act, 1956 (UK), and Irish Hotel Proprietors Act, 1963, recognize that one of the foremost duties of a hotelier is to receive guests at the hotel with certain exceptions. The Irish Hotel Proprietors Act, 1963 defines the 'public duty' of a hotelier in Clause 3 as follows:

TEXT

(1) *The proprietor of a hotel is under a duty to receive at the hotel as guests all persons who, whether or not under special contract, present themselves and require sleeping accommodation, food or drink and to provide them therewith, unless he has reasonable grounds of refusal.*
(2) *Subject to the terms of any special contract, the proprietor is under a duty to provide such accommodation, food or drink at the charges for the time being current at the hotel.*

The primary 'public duty' is to welcome guests as per the standards of the hotel while exercising due care. A hotelier is duty bound to:

(i) Provide accommodation against confirmed room reservations.
(ii) Provide safety and security to guests and their belongings, which involves exercising 'duty of care' as follows:
   (a) maintaining guest privacy;
   (b) preventing personal injury and subsequent law suits;
   (c) liability for loss or damage to guest property;
   (d) bailment;
   (e) responsibility for guests' lost and found items;
   (f) handling unusual incidents;
   (g) establishing and maintaining service standards;
   (h) warning guests of any unsafe conditions or areas of the hotel;
   (i) hiring employees who are qualified and well trained in hotel operations; and
   (j) handling guests with disabilities.
(iii) Circumstances under which he or she can deny accommodation to a guest.

(iv) Circumstances under which he or she can evict a guest.
(v) Serve food and beverage responsibly.
(vi) Handle fraud committed by guests.

To Provide Accommodation against Confirmed Room Reservations

Guest room reservation policies for booking, confirming, and reserving accommodation are well established in all hotels.

A confirmed room reservation is one that is held without taking a deposit, whilst a guaranteed room reservation is one that has been confirmed against a deposit of one night's room charges collected at the time of processing the reservation request. The essentials of a room reservation are: names of the guests, number of persons, number of rooms, the type of accommodation requested—single or double room, the rates, period of stay, and the mode of payment. If the guest fails to register with the hotel on the specified date, he or she is regarded as a no show guest, and the guest generally forfeits the deposit collected earlier as damages.

Overbooking

Overbooking is a practice that hoteliers follow to maximize occupancy and revenue by overselling up to 10 per cent of the available room inventory, and is based upon educated calculations of no show reservations. Hotels are generally liable for damages, if they cannot honour a confirmed reservation because of 'overbooking' and the guests can sue the hotel for damage in case the hotel actually has accommodation available but fails to provide it.

Overbooking by hotels has always posed a problem: Turn-away guest is a guest holding a confirmed reservation but has been refused accommodation on arrival at the hotel, and is subsequently being accommodated in another hotel of equal or comparable standards for one night. Generally, many hotels have adopted a policy towards turn-away guests that requires them to secure comparable accommodation for one night and to bear the cost of transportation to the hotel that he or she is shifted to with the difference in room charges, if any, being paid by the hotel. It is also the responsibility of the hotel turning away the guest to bring back the guest to the hotel at its cost the next day.

To address the issue of room reservations and overbooking, the Federation of Hotel and Restaurant Association of India (FHRAI) and Indian Association of Tour Operators (IATO) have entered into an '*Agreement on Code of Practice between FHRAI & IATO*'.

Articles 8 to 13 outline what constitutes a reservation agreement—which must stipulate the type of accommodation, rate offered advance deposits collected and the balance due to the hotel:

TEXT

Article 25—mentions the obligations of the hotel towards the Client-in the event of Overbooking.
For any reservation accepted and confirmed the hotel shall respect its contractual commitments.
Failing this it shall compensate the tour operator or the client for the loss actually suffered.

Should the hotel not provide the client with the reserved accommodation it has confirmed, it will at its own expenses:

Secure accommodation for the client at the nearest equivalent hotel and pay, where applicable, for any difference of price.

Notify the client or the Tour Operator in advance of the clients arrival and where applicable eventually pay for the clients communication costs to notify his/her home or office of the change of hotel. The hotel will also pay for the client's transportation to the hotel.

Pay for the client's transportation back to the original hotel, if the client wishes to return to the hotel he/she had originally reserved when space becomes available.'

Secure accommodation for the client at the nearest equivalent hotel and pay, where applicable, for any difference of price.

Notify the client or the Tour Operator in advance of the clients arrival and where applicable eventually pay for the clients communication costs to notify his/her home or office of the change of hotel. The hotel will also pay for the client's transportation to the hotel.

Pay for the client's transportation back to the original hotel, if the client wishes to return to the hotel he/she had originally reserved when space becomes available.

Example STIC Travels, New Delhi, has made a guaranteed reservation for a single room for Sanjiv Khanna at Hotel Le Méridien, New Delhi.

The details of Sanjiv Khanna's room reservation are given as follows:

- Check in 15 June 2012, arrival by AI-101 from New York at 17:00 hrs.
- Check out 18 June 2012, departure by A-102 from New Delhi at 01:30 hrs.
- Room rate ₹10,500 per night inclusive of breakfast and taxes.

Other instructions

- Complimentary airport pick-up and drop.
- One night's deposit of ₹10,500 paid by Visa credit card.
- Late checkout 19:00 hrs at no extra charge.
- Guest will settle the hotel bill directly.

Upon arrival at the airport, Sanjiv Khanna is informed by the hotel's airport representative that there are no rooms available at the hotel, and the hotel management is shifting him to the hotel Shangri-La located opposite to Le Méridien. The hotel management will be shifting him back to the hotel the next day. Sanjiv Khanna is very agitated and insists that he will complain against the hotel to his travel agent.

Impact

In keeping with the agreement on code of practice, the hotel has fulfilled all its obligations and is well within its right to shift Sanjiv Khanna to an alternative hotel for one night and to bring him back the next day. In this case, both the travel agent and the hotel will be responding to the guest complaint.

To Provide Safety and Security—Exercising 'Duty of Care'

Maintaining guest privacy

Guest privacy is of paramount importance for a guest when he registers in a hotel. All hotels are duty bound to ensure that this is respected by employees as well as other visitors. A guest's right to privacy is based upon the principle that once the room is allotted to a guest, it is akin to the guest staying in his home where he is the lord and master and any intrusion or visit to his room would require his express approval. This is based upon the following concept of law of torts—private nuisance and invasion of privacy which has been defined earlier.

Guest key control is the first step that is taken by the hotel to ensure guest safety and privacy. Some of the important elements of key control which are followed by hotels are as follows:

- Regularly inspecting room locks for damage, wear, and tear
- Changing locks when a room key is missing
- Not displaying room numbers on the key or the key tags
- Requiring guests to identify themselves when requesting for a replacement or additional key
- Refusing to give out room information to visitors who inquire at the front desk or telephonically
- Locating key drop boxes behind the front-desk counter not on the front-desk counter

Advances in technology have led to the introduction of electronic locks that have computerized guest room keys. These locks come with a host of features such as tracking the number of times the lock has been opened and by which type of key—hotel master, floor master, maintenance or housekeeping key, or the guest key. These features enable the hotel management to identify if any of the keys has been misused. Hotels have provided additional devices to ensure room safety of guests such as dead-bolt locks, magic eye or door viewers, chain locks, and multiple telephones in the room and bathrooms for communicating in case of an emergency.

Guest elevators have floor access keys that ensure that only the guest or the concerned staff has access to the guest floors. This measure ensures that no undesirable visitor can access the floors.

Some of the well-established procedures adopted by hotels to ensure guest privacy are as follows:

- Checking with the guest before permitting visitors to the guest's room
- Housekeeping to announce themselves prior to servicing the room
- Unscheduled maintenance carried out in the presence of the guest, if they so desire
- Routine or major maintenance carried out by taking rooms or public areas under temporary maintenance and released once the activity has been completed
- Room service personnel to do clearance of guest rooms only when they are requested to do so by the guests
- Respecting the 'Do Not Disturb Sign' posted by the guests on their room doors

- Not issuing a duplicate room key to any person without the express permission of the guest
- Ensuring that all the entries to the room are secured to prevent outsiders from entering

CASE 8.1   APPELLANT: Connie Francis Garzilli and Joseph Garzilli, Plaintiffs
vs
RESPONDENT: Howard Johnson's Motor Lodges, Inc., Defendant

FACTS: Connie Francis is an internationally known singer, recording artist, and professional entertainer who, prior to her partial retirement in 1971, was earning substantial sums for her personal appearances as an entertainer, for example, in 1968 $163,000, in 1969 $325,000, and in 1970 $287,500. Her average fee for an eight-performance engagement at a night club or theatre during those years was approximately $35,000. It was undisputed that in the course of her career, which commenced when she was 10 years old, she had sold approximately 80 million records, had performed in innumerable theatres and night clubs throughout the world, and had made some five motion pictures to her credit.

Following her marriage to the plaintiff, Mr. Garzilli, in September 1973 and the loss of her child in July 1974, Connie Francis decided to resume her professional career. Her first engagement was at the Westbury Music Fair in Westbury, Long Island, for which she was to receive a guaranteed minimum of $20,000 plus a percentage ranging between 50% and 60% of the gross box-office receipts for a series of eight performances beginning on November 6, 1974. The testimony was that her return to the entertainment field was very much a success, and she was well received by capacity audiences for her first two evening performances.

In connection with this engagement, Connie Francis and her husband took rooms at the defendant's Motor Lodge in Westbury. In the early morning hours of November 8, 1974, after her second performance, she was criminally assaulted by an unknown man who came through one of the sliding glass doors of her rooms. The doors gave the appearance of being locked, but the testimony showed they were capable of being unsecured from outside without much difficulty.

In addition to the pain and suffering which accompanied and immediately followed the assault, and the fear, anxiety, and depression which ensued thereafter, the proof showed that Connie Francis continued to suffer from a significant depressive reaction and a traumatic neurosis which was manifested by depression, social and sexual withdrawal, and traumatic phobia. It was the opinion of one of her psychiatrists who testified that she would have significant difficulty in ever trying to resume her professional career for at least the next 10 years. Connie Francis herself testified that she could no longer appear before an audience because of her feeling of shame and humiliation, and she could no longer stay in a hotel or a motel room which would be necessary for her to do if she were to fulfil her engagements.

DECISION: The jury gave the verdict in favour of the plaintiffs, Connie Francis Garzilli ('Connie Francis') and her husband, Joseph Garzilli, for $2.5 million and $150,000, respectively. The hotel repealed against this judgement; however, the appellate court upheld the decision of the lower court except for reducing the compensation payable to Joseph Garzilli to $25,000.

This case is based upon the concept in tort law of criminal assault, battery, and trespass which have been defined earlier in this chapter.

IMPACT: It imposed an affirmative duty on the hotel to protect guests against third-party criminal conduct on their premises. It compelled hotels to review the entire gamut of security procedures being followed. This is one of the few early civil-liability cases where a hotel company had to pay compensation to a guest of a substantial value. This made insurance company's enhance the premium rates for providing public liability insurance cover to hotels.

Preventing personal injury and subsequent law suits

Generally, hotels are not liable for every accident or loss that occurs on the premises, nor do they insure the absolute safety of every guest, and are generally not liable for harm to guests unless 'fault' can be established against them.

It is important for hotels to ensure that guests do not suffer personal injuries during their stay, as this can lead to prolonged litigations and claims against them. Personal injury has been defined as a damage or harm inflicted upon the body, mind, or emotions of an individual. If negligence on the part of hotel can be proved, it can result in a compensation being paid by the defendant.

CASE 8.2

APPELLANT: Frummer

vs

RESPONDENT: Hilton Hotels International, Inc., 304 N.Y.S.2d 335 (1969)

FACTS: While staying as a guest at the Hilton Hotel in London, Frummer (Plaintiff) slipped and fell in the shower and sustained serious injuries. Frummer brought a suit against Hilton Hotels (defendant) under three issues:

(i) failure to provide a rubber shower mat after a specific request;
(ii) failure to install grab bars in the shower; and
(iii) not constructing the bathtub to minimize the risk of falling.

Hilton Hotels claimed in its defence that Frummer's injuries were due to his own carelessness and offered expert testimony that it had done everything required under a reasonable standard of care that the Hilton Chain adhered to.

The trial court briefed the jury that Frummer could not recover if it is determined that there had been contributory negligence by Frummer. English law recognizes comparative negligence while New York law does not. Frummer presented significant evidence of negligence on the part of Hilton Hotels and would have recovered under the correct English law on grounds of comparative negligence. Hilton Hotels was keen to apply the New York law in their interest because if the English rule was applied to the case, the verdict would have been against Hilton Hotels.

After the jury returned a verdict for Hilton Hotels, the court discovered *sua sponte* (Latin: of their own accord) that English law recognizes comparative negligence, whereby a plaintiff who is found contributorily negligent may recover a judgement reduced compensation in proportion to the plaintiff's fault.

Frummer appealed against the verdict of the New York court and sought a new trial on the grounds that the accident had occurred at the Hilton Hotel in London, and therefore it should have been tried under English law. The court on the other hand having discovered *sua sponte* that a foreign law should have been used at trial but was not, decided to order a new trial as it were of the opinion that a mis-trial had occurred as the use of that law (English) would have affected the outcome of the case.

DECISION: The case was retried and the earlier judgement of the jury was reversed by the jury, and the revised judgement was given in the plaintiff's favour. The judgement upheld the concept of strict liability and due care.

IMPACT: Bathroom service standards were redefined by hotel operators. Grab bars and anti-skid mats have been implemented as standard features in guest bathrooms. Shower cubicles are gradually replacing bathtubs in hotels over the years.

CASE 8.3

APPELLANT: Klaus Mittelbachert

vs

RESPONDENT: East India Hotels Ltd. (3rd January 1997)

FACTS: Klaus Mittelbachert, the plaintiff, was a German national born on 2 September 1942, employed as a co-pilot in Lufthansa. He piloted the flight from Bangkok to New Delhi on 11 August 1972, and was scheduled to continue the flight to Frankfurt on 14 August 1972. For the intervening time, designated in the airline terminology as lay-over period, he checked into and stayed at Hotel Oberoi Intercontinental.

The four defendants were Defendant No. 1 East India Hotels; Defendant No. 2 General Manager of the Hotel Oberoi Intercontinental, a five-star hotel located at Dr. Zakir Hussain Marg, New Delhi; Defendant No. 3 Hotel Oberoi Intercontinental; and Defendant No. 4 the Chairman. The hotel was allegedly being managed by the Defendant No. 2 at the material time.

The hotel had a swimming pool equipped with a diving board. In the afternoon of 13 August 1972, the plaintiff visited the swimming pool and at about 6.00 p.m., while diving the plaintiff met with an accident. He hit his head on the bottom of the swimming pool. He was taken out bleeding from the right ear and appearing to have been paralysed in the arms and the legs. He was taken to Holy Family Hospital, situated nearby, where he was admitted and remained under treatment until 21 August 1972, on which date he was flown to Germany under medical escort.

On 22 August 1972, he was admitted for treatment at the Orthopedic Clinic and Polyclinic of the University of Heidelberg. The condition of the plaintiff did not improve and he went on deteriorating from bad to worse till his discharge from the clinic on 24 March 1973, when he was shifted back to his residence where his treatment continued.

On 11 August 1975, the present suit was filed for recovery of an amount of ₹50,00,000 by way of damages with interest calculated at the rate of 12% from the date of the filing of the suit until payment and costs.

According to the plaintiff, the accident was caused by what in the circumstances amounted to a trap. The diving board placed at the swimming pool suggested a proper depth of water into which a swimmer could dive. The defendant hotel owed the plaintiff a duty to take care and ensure his safety. Having failed therein, the defendants are guilty of negligence and are, therefore, liable to compensate the plaintiff for the consequences resulting from the accident.

The defendants have denied their liability. It is submitted that the general manager and the chairman have been unnecessarily joined as parties to the suit as none of them can be held liable or personally liable. The defendants admit that East India Hotels Ltd is the owner of The Oberoi Intercontinental Hotel and is solely responsible for the acts of The Oberoi Intercontinental Hotel.

All other material averments in the plaint to the extent to which liability flowing from the accident is sought to be fixed on the defendants have been denied. It is submitted that there was no negligence on the part of the hotel, and that it was the plaintiff who was negligent; and that, in any case, the plaintiff was equally negligent and, under the doctrine of contributory negligence, the plaintiff was entitled to no damages at all.

On 4 January 1977, issues that required to be decided by the Court were framed.

A material event occurred during the pendency of the suit. On 27 September 1985 at 9.55 p.m., the plaintiff died of acute cardiac arrest.

DECISION: It was established that the general manager and the chairman were not in control of the hotel and not liable or personally liable. Furthermore, the plaintiff agreed that in case of a decree in favour of the plaintiff, it will be against East India Hotels Ltd and Hotel Oberoi Intercontinental, New Delhi.

The contending pleas raised by the plaintiff and the defendants as to whether the negligence was on the part of the defendants or on the part of the plaintiff or whether it was a case of contributory negligence as suggested by the defendants. The court upon hearing the defendants and the plaintiff arguments concluded that the plaintiff was not negligent or careless and contributory negligence was not established.

It further examined if the hotel had implemented the doctrine of due care as established in torts law effectively and efficiently, not only the building structure but the services offered there also have to be safe and immune from any danger inherent or otherwise. A hotel owner holds himself out as willing and also as capable to accommodate and entertain the guests.

The fact that a diving board was provided by the hotel implies that the hotel desired the guest should use it. The structure and the design of the pool were examined as the defendants had claimed that it was designed as per the prevalent architectural standards. Having arrived at a finding that the design of the swimming pool was defective, adequate depth had not been provided to facilitate diving, the conclusion which necessarily emerges is that the swimming pool of the defendant's hotel was a trap. It was a 'hazardous premise' in the sense in which the term is used in the law of torts. The liability of the defendants for adverse consequences flowing from the use of the swimming pool—a hazardous premise—would be absolute.

The court relied upon the doctrine of *res ipsa loquitur* (Latin: the thing speaks for itself). The evidence proves that the disabilities were a direct result of the accident which is attributable to the hotel and the plaintiff should be compensated by the defendant.

Personal injury may cause non-pecuniary as well as pecuniary loss to the plaintiff. Non-pecuniary loss includes damages on the heads of (i) pain and suffering; (ii) loss of amenities; and (iii) loss of expectation of life. Pecuniary loss may cover damages calculable on the heads of (i) consequential expenses; (ii) cost of care; and (iii) loss of earnings.

Broadly speaking, while fixing an amount of compensation payable to a victim of an accident, the damages have to be assessed separately as pecuniary damages and special damages. Pecuniary damages are those which the victim has actually incurred and which are capable of being calculated in terms of money, whereas non-pecuniary damages are those which are incapable of being assessed by arithmetical calculations. The court relied on the concept of exemplary damages by reference to the paying capacity of the wrongdoer which had been recognized in *M. C. Mehta vs Union of India*:

TEXT

The measure of compensation in these kinds of cases must be correlated to the magnitude and capacity of the enterprise because such compensation must have a deterrent effect. The larger and more prosperous the enterprise, the greater must be the amount of compensation payable by it for the harm caused on account of an accident in the carrying on of the hazardous or inherently dangerous activity by the enterprise.

The court took cognize of the affidavit dated 3 March 1986 sworn in by Dr, Horst Brandt, family physician of the plaintiff, who had treated him continuously since the year 1974 until his death. He had narrated in brief the history of the physical and nervous condition of the plaintiff. He had also carried out an inspection of the dead body of the plaintiff. He had summed up his conclusions vide para 5 of the affidavit in the following words:

TEXT

Taking into consideration Mr Mittelbachert's overall condition as well as history, I am of the opinion that the cause of cardiac arrest was pulmonary embolism which was connected with the recurring thrombosis of the veins I have above referred to and it was caused by his tatraplegic condition. I, therefore, say that Mr Mittelbachert's death was caused by the accident above referred to.

For the foregoing reasons, it is held that the injuries sustained by the plaintiff on 13 August 1972 have caused his death on 27 September 1985. The cause of action survives to the legal heirs under Section 306 of the Indian Succession Act, 1925.

The court awarded a decree of Dm 4,59,921.87, which was equivalent to ₹1,02,71,365.98. The plaintiff had thus proved his entitlement to damages quantified at ₹1,03,25,245.98. The decree shall however, remain confined to ₹50,00,000.00 as prayed for by the plaintiff. The court deemed it proper to allow interest on the decretal amount not from the date of institution of suit but from the date of the death of the plaintiff (i.e., 27 September 1985) at the rate of 6% per annum.

CASE
SUMMARY:　The following issues were examined in this case:
- Doctrine of duty of care and standards of care.
- Contributory negligence on behalf of the plaintiff.
- Doctrine of *res ipsa loquitur* (Latin: The thing speaks for itself). The evidence speaks for itself.
- Judgement was based on torts and statutory law.

IMPACT:　The design of forthcoming pools in hotels underwent following changes:
- Hotels began displaying prominently all the rules, dos and don'ts that guests were expected to follow when using the facility.
- Hotels were required to ensure a uniform depth which had to be clearly marked on the walls of the pool.
- Diving boards were prohibited unless the pool had been built keeping the maximum plummet depth required at the point of entry for diving.
- It became mandatory for hotels to have life guards on duty during the operating hours of the pool.

Liability for loss or theft or damage to guest property

Section 6 of the Irish Hotel Proprietors Act, 1963 states the circumstances under which an innkeeper is liable for guest property:

TEXT

(1) *Where sleeping accommodation is engaged for a person as a guest at a hotel, whether or not under special contract, the proprietor is liable for any damage to, or loss or destruction of, property received by him from that person or from some other person on his behalf.*

(2) *A motor vehicle shall be deemed to have been received by the proprietor where it has been placed within the premises of the hotel or in any garage, car park or other premises provided by the proprietor of the hotel for this purpose.*

(3) *The liability imposed by this section does not apply to a motor vehicle or to any property left therein unless the proprietor of the hotel or some servant of his authorized, or appearing to be authorized, for the purpose has been previously notified that the motor vehicle has been brought to the hotel.*

(4) *The liability imposed by this section:*
　　(a) *Applies only where the damage, loss or destruction occurs during the time for which the sleeping accommodation is engaged or during a reasonable period before or after that time;*
　　(b) *Extends to property of which the proprietor of the hotel takes charge, whether at the hotel or outside it, during that time or period.*

(5) *The proprietor is exempt from liability under this section to the extent that the damage, loss or destruction is due to an unforeseeable and irresistible act of nature or an act of war or is due to the guest himself or to any person accompanying him or in his employment or visiting him.*

The Hotel Proprietors Act, 1956 (UK) further qualifies that 'at the time of the loss or damage sleeping accommodation at the hotel had been engaged for the traveler; and the loss or damage occurred during the period commencing with the midnight immediately preceding, and ending with the midnight immediately following, a period for which the traveler was a guest at the hotel and entitled to use the accommodation so engaged'.

These laws clarify that for the hotel to be liable for the damage, loss or destruction of guest property, it should occur whilst he is a registered guest at the hotel and the property is in the custody of the hotel. It further stipulates that damage to guest property due to unforeseen natural circumstances, act of war, or on account of the guest's own negligence, the hotel shall not be held liable.

Clauses 28, 29, and 30 of The Australian Carriers & Innkeepers Act, 1958 (incorporating amendments till 1 August 2010) impose a limitation on liability under certain circumstances 'with respect to property that, while at the inn, is lost, whether by theft or otherwise, or damaged shall not exceed—(a) In the case of property that is so lost or damaged—is being held for safe custody after being deposited by or on behalf of the traveler with the innkeeper or a servant authorized or appearing to be authorized for the purpose; or after the traveler or some person on his behalf was unable to deposit it because the innkeeper or such a servant failed or refused without reasonable excuse to receive it—$2000; and (b) in the case of any other property that is so lost or damaged but not under safe custody of the innkeeper—$100.'

The law draws a distinction between property that is lost or damaged belonging to a resident guest, and property that is lost and damaged belonging to a patron or visitor and sets the compensation limits accordingly. In India, there is no such law to protect the interest of the hotelier; hence, there are exculpatory notices or disclaimers that are printed on the reverse of most of the guest documents fixing the limits of compensation available to guests, for example, laundry list, left luggage dockets, and so on.

A hotel's liability for loss or damage to a non-resident guest's property is limited, as it is for the guest to prove that the loss or damage occurred in the hotel's premises and that the fault was the hotel's. If it gets established beyond reasonable doubt, then the hotel's liability gets limited to a maximum of $100 under Australian law.

Patrons and visitors when parking their vehicles in the hotel premises are given an acknowledgment receipt by the hotel valet that is required to be signed by the patron or visitor. By appending his signature to the vehicle parking ticket, the guest acknowledges that he or she shall not hold the hotel management for any loss or theft or damage to his or her vehicle even though the hotel is taking responsibility for parking the vehicle in a secure area, whether inside the hotel premises or outside in a location where the hotel exercises control.

CASE 8.4

APPELLANT: Anil Virmani

vs

RESPONDENT: Hyatt Hotels, First Appeal No. 102 of 2004 National Consumer Disputes Redressal Commission, New Delhi

FACTS: Atul Virmani (plaintiff) came to Delhi by his Maruti Gypsy, which he had purchased from M/s Rohan Motors, Dehradun for ₹2,86,395. It is the say of the complainant that accessories worth ₹50,000 were installed in the said vehicle, which was insured against third-party claim but the peril of theft was not included in the policy.

The case of the complainant was that on 18 September 1996 at about 11.15 p.m. he visited the Hyatt Regency (the Hotel) by paying a fee of ₹900. According to the complainant, this fee included the entrance fee as well as for the safe parking of the vehicle. On arrival at the hotel, the representative of the hotel demanded the key of the vehicle for parking the vehicle at the parking lot in safe custody. Therefore, the complainant delivered the possession of the vehicle to the representative of the hotel who drove the car to the parking lot. The valet had issued a docket as receipt for delivery of the vehicle to the complainant, which he had to produce while checking out of the hotel. When the complainant came out of the hotel at 1.40 a.m. on 19 September 1996 and presented the docket to the valet who had the key of the car, the latter informed him after half an hour that the car of the complainant was missing from the parking place. The hotel staff also informed that the vehicle of the complainant was permitted to go from the parking place between 12.20 a.m. and 12.40 a.m. on 19 September 1996 and there is an entry in the register regarding the checking in and checking out of the vehicle. The hotel staff called the police and a report was dictated by the staff of the hotel and was signed by the complainant. According to complainant, vehicle contained ₹2,500 in cash apart from the driving licence of the complainant.

The case was contested by the hotel (defendant) stating that valet service rendered was a free service and the complainant is not a consumer under the Consumer Protection Act, 1986. The hotel authorities admitted that the complainant had visited on 18 September 1996 and handed over the keys of his Maruti Gypsy to the valet on duty for the purpose of getting the vehicle parked. The valet had handed over the docket to the complainant, but no monetary consideration or parking fee was charged. Hotel authorities were not legally bound to keep the vehicle in the hotel premises. It was also stated that on the reverse of every car docket issued to the visitors, a disclaimer notice is printed through which the visitors were informed that the vehicle could be parked within the hotel premises at their own risk and that the hotel would not be liable for the loss or damage to the vehicle parked. It was further submitted that the complainant had gone to the discotheque by paying entry free of ₹900, which was charged only for the use of discotheque and did not include any parking fee.

The learned counsel for the hotel brought to the judge's notice a copy of the token or car docket issued to those who use the valet facilities wherein on the reverse of the docket, a notice or disclaimer is printed wherein it is mentioned as follows:

(i) Parking of vehicle is entirely at owner's risk. Hotel Hyatt Regency Delhi/Asian Hotels Limited disclaim all responsibility for any theft/damage or destruction of the vehicle/its contents caused by fire, third party acts, force majeure or any other cause whatsoever.

(ii) Vehicle owners are advised not to leave any valuable items in the vehicle at the time of parking.

(iii) The vehicle is being permitted to be parked in the hotel area on the premise that the vehicle does not contain any firearms, explosive or narcotics substances.

The State Commission after going through records and hearing the counsel for the parties held that there was deficiency in service by the hotel in not ensuring the safety of the car entrusted to their custody. Accordingly, the hotel was directed to pay the complainant a sum of ₹2,00,000 along with 10% interest from the date of the theft till the date of the payment with ₹5,000 as cost.

Aggrieved and dissatisfied by the order of the State Commission, the hotel has filed appeal before the National Consumer Disputes Redressal Commission in 2004.

FINDINGS: Hotel Hyatt Regency is currently known as Hyatt. This hotel is a part of the chain of hotels run in different countries. In fact, the name board does not mention that it is a 'hotel'; it is only called Hyatt because of its fame and popularity. The five-star hotels provide several facilities as customers pay heavy price for room rent, meals, and other amenities. Hotels provide some facilities free of cost like providing newspapers in the hotel rooms, complimentary fruit baskets, and mineral water bottles. Similarly, left luggage facility for a few hours after early checkout and valet parking facilities are also provided. These so-called free services are not actually free because they are more than made up by the exorbitant rental charges, very high charges for food, and very high entrance fees for discotheques.

It is not in dispute that the complainant had used the hotel facilities by paying ₹900 as entry fee to discotheque; in addition, he must have spent money for his food. The hotel did not dispute that the car key was taken by the valet of the hotel and vehicle was not delivered to the owner who had the docket. It is due to sheer negligence of the hotel staff that they had allowed the car to be stolen and taken out by some unauthorized person for whom there was an entry in their register.

We have only perused copy of the sample docket wherein disclaimer is written in small letters. Those who visit five-star hotels and use the car parking facilities are aware that after the car keys are given to the valet, there is hardly any time for the consumer to read docket conditions written on the reverse of the docket because there would be a fleet of cars entering and exiting from the hotel. When a uniformed liveried valet with his imposing figure asks for the car keys, he exudes confidence in the consumer. Therefore, for the management of a five-star hotel to shirk the responsibility of the safety of the car parked in their premises does not augur well. The hotel is liable for the negligence of its staff.

This view is fortified by the decision of this Commission in *Mahesh Enterprises vs Arun Kumar Gumber & Others. 11 (2001) CPJ (NC) 1* wherein it was held that:

TEXT

In our opinion, in the facts and circumstances of the case, the State Commission was legally right in holding that the facts and the circumstances would constitute bailment and the person responsible for the management of the parking area was liable to make good the loss.

IMPACT: Pursuant to this judgement, most of the luxury hotels have opted to outsource their car-parking valet services. The concessionaire entrusted with the car valet service can charge guests for parking their vehicles. By adopting this route, the hotel has reduced its liability, as the bailment contract is now between the guest and the concessionaire company.

Most hotels customarily inform their guests to place their valuables in the hotel's safe located at the front desk or in electronic safes that are provided in the guest rooms. Additional steps are taken by the hotel to further limit their liability for losses, by posting notices on the reverse of the guest registration cards, as part of house rules posted on the reverse of the room entrance doors, and as flyers in the hotel's service directories.

With the introduction of electronic safes in guest rooms, the liability of hotels for theft of valuables from the rooms has been limited though not completely eliminated, as the password for operating the electronic safes are fed by the guest himself.

CASE 8.5	APPELLANT:	Renate K. and Heinz K.
		vs
	RESPONDENT:	Hotel "T" Liable for Theft from Safe in Hotel Room, Austrian Supreme Court (1 Ob 119/11 of July 21)

FACTS: The plaintiffs (a German couple) sued a Vienna four-star hotel company for compensation of more than €160,000 of valuables stolen from the safe in their hotel room. When they had asked at the reception where to keep their valuables, the receptionist had told them to use the safe in their room. This safe had to be locked and unlocked by a code of four numbers chosen by the plaintiffs. However, the safe could also be opened using a 'master code'. This master code for emergency cases had not been changed by the hotel management for almost two years and was known by no less than 16 of the current employees and an unclear number of former employees. Because of earlier thefts from hotel rooms, police had already urged the hotel manager to increase safety standards.

As guests of a four-star hotel who had explicitly asked for a way to safely store their valuables, they could have expected that an emergency code would not be known to a vast number of current and former employees.

DECISION: As regards potential contributory negligence of the plaintiffs who—as the hotel stated—had not mentioned the extraordinary value of the items to be stored, the Supreme Court held that the hotel had not explained which safety measures would have been taken if the actual value had been known. Thus, there was no causal connection between the potential failure and the damage. Dismissing the hotel's appeal, the Austrian Supreme Court upheld the judgements of the lower courts, holding the hotel company liable for the theft.

IMPACT: Although the hotel had been warned to take corrective action by the authorities owing to a large number of thefts, the hotel failed to take corrective steps to change the master code of the safe that had been compromised, resulting in the hotel losing the case. Keeping this case in mind, hoteliers have devised operating procedures to prevent non-occurrence of such events.

Bailment

The French term 'bailor' means to deliver, which implies that the possession of the property changes hands upon delivery without a change in ownership.

The Indian Contract Act, 1872 defines this transaction as bailment:

TEXT
Chapter 9—Section 148. 'Bailment', 'bailor', and 'bailee' defined. A 'bailment' is the delivery of goods by one person to another for some purpose, upon a contract that they shall, when the purpose is accomplished, be returned or otherwise disposed of according to the directions of the person delivering them. The person delivering the goods is called the 'bailor'. The person to whom they are delivered is called, the 'bailee'.

The hotel is at liberty to levy a charge for keeping the goods (non-gratuitous bailment) or agree to keep it without levying a charge (gratuitous bailment). Voluntary bailment is when a guest voluntarily hands over possession of his or her goods to the hotelier for custody, whereas when the hotel finds misplaced, lost, or abandoned guest property, the hotel involuntarily comes into possession of the guest property.

When accepting any guest property for custody, the hotelier should ensure that the same is shown to him or her prior to it being placed in a container. The same should be sealed by the guest in the presence of the hotelier. It is the duty of the 'bailee', in this case the hotel, to return the property to the guest 'bailor' in the same condition that it was received. Once the property is restored to the guest or to his or her representative, the hotel has discharged its duty as a bailee.

> **Example**   Andrews is staying in Room No.203 at the Courtyard by Marriott and approaches the lobby manager of the hotel for the safekeeping of his valuable laptop, which does not fit into the guest safe provided by the hotel in his room, while he is going for a sightseeing tour. The lobby manager agrees to keep the laptop in the hotel safe and issues a receipt acknowledging it and advises Andrews that the laptop will be handed over to the person who presents this receipt to the front desk. On his return from the sightseeing tour, Andrews approaches the front desk and collects his laptop after handing over the receipt.
>
> In this example, Andrews is the bailor while the lobby manager accepting the laptop is the bailee, and the transaction between them is called "voluntary gratuitous bailment.

Under Section 162, a gratuitous bailment can also get discharged by death of either the bailee or the bailor, thereby terminating the contract.

The concept of allowing guests to keep their luggage in the left luggage room after they have checked out of the hotel against the issue of a left luggage receipt is based on the principle of gratuitous bailment. In the event of the bag being damaged or not retrievable, the hotel will be liable to make good the loss. Most countries have enacted laws limiting the amount of compensation payable by a hotel in the event of a loss.

Responsibility for guest lost and found items

Guest property can be classified as either valuable or invaluable items. Generally, hotels are not liable for valuables that are not secured in the hotel safe.

Here it is suggested that hoteliers follow the definition of valuables under Section 2 of the Wealth Tax Act, 1957, as 'jewellery, bullion and furniture, utensils or any other article made wholly or partly of gold, silver, platinum or any other precious metal or any alloy containing one or more of such precious metals'.

Jewellery is further explained in the Act:

(a) *'jewellery' includes:*
　　(i) *ornaments made of gold, silver, platinum or any other precious metal or any alloy containing one or more of such precious metals, whether or not containing any precious or semi-precious stones and whether or not worked or sewn into any wearing apparel;*
　　(ii) *Precious or semi-precious stones, whether or not set in any furniture, utensils or other article or worked or sewn into any wearing apparel.*

From a hotelier's perspective, it also includes items such as expensive electronic items—laptops, cell phones, music players, important legal documents, cash, watches, fine writing instruments, art and artefacts, and so on. Invaluable items are normally items of personal use—apparel, toiletries, food and beverage items, and so on.

It is the responsibility of the housekeeping department to record accurately all misplaced, lost, or abandoned items in the lost and found register maintained by them, and the duty of the front office to inform the guests and seek their directions as to how they would like the hotel to arrange for return of the items. Returning the property to the rightful owner is one of the most important duties of a hotelier.

Misplaced property is property that has been carefully placed by the owner, who has then forgotten where he kept it.

Example Satish kept his expensive watch carefully in the third drawer of the hotel closet in his room; however, whilst checking out he forgot where he had placed it.

Lost property is property that the rightful owner has inadvertently kept and then forgotten where he kept it.

Example Arun kept his expensive watch in the hotel room; however, whilst checking out he forgot where he had placed it in the room.

Abandoned property is one that the owner has deliberately kept aside with no intention of retrieving it.

Example Arun left his old watch, which was broken, in the wastepaper bin of the hotel room.

Hotels accept involuntarily to act as bailees in respect of misplaced, lost, or abandoned property of guests found in the hotel premises. Hotels should make every effort to locate the rightful owners. When restoring a property to the rightful owner, care should be taken by the hotel to secure a delivery receipt from the guest stating that the property has been received in good condition and there are no further claims against the hotel.

As a general practice, all guest property found in the hotel premises is the property of the hotel irrespective of which employee found it. Only after due diligence when it is confirmed that the rightful owner cannot be found, the hotel can dispose of the property as it thinks fit. Normally, the hotel hands over the property to the finder after recording the reason for disposing it in the lost and found register after a reasonable period of time based upon Section 169 of the Indian Contract Act, 1872.

Under Section 169 of the Indian Contract Act, 1872, 'if after due diligence the rightful owner cannot be traced and the property in question is in the danger of perishing or of losing the greater part of its value or when the lawful charges of the finder amount to two-thirds of its value'.

Handling unusual incidents

Unusual incidents faced by hotels are fire, natural disasters, terrorist attacks, war, pestilence and other acts of god, death of a guest under natural or unnatural circumstances, for example, a suicide or a murder.

Fire, natural disasters, terrorist attacks, war, pestilence, and other acts of god Fire, natural disasters, terrorist attacks, war, pestilence, and other acts of god have resulted in considerable loss of life besides damage to property costing millions of rupees. Hotels worldwide have been ravaged by natural disasters and have been targets of terrorist attacks.

In order to protect their guests and properties against terror attacks, hotels and restaurants have enhanced their security measures with CCTVs (closed circuit televisions) being installed in corridors and public areas; traffic control barriers; X-ray scanners to screen guest baggage; and training of staff in fire fighting and first-aid procedures.

Some of the significant natural disasters and terrorist acts that have affected hotels are listed as follows:

  (i) 13 March 1993, Mumbai, India: A series of 13 bomb blasts rocked Mumbai including the Searock Hotel, Centaur Hotels at Juhu Beach, and Mumbai Airport

 (ii) 26 January 2001, Gujarat: An earthquake measuring 7.6 on the Richter scale with epicentre Kutch, Gujarat rocked Gujarat.

(iii) 27 March 2002, Netanya, Israel: Palestinian Islamic socio-political organization Hamas carried out a suicide bombing at the Park Hotel.

 (iv) 19 August 2003, Baghdad, Iraq: The Iranian UN headquarters in the Canal Hotel was the target of a terrorist attack by a suicide bomber who drove a truck full of explosives.

  (v) 26 December 2004, India: Indian Ocean tsunami affected India, Sri Lanka, Indonesia, Bangladesh, Thailand, and Maldives.

 (vi) 08 October 2005, Kashmir: An earthquake 7.6 on the Richter scale with epicenter Muzzafarabad, Azad Kashmir rocked Kashmir.

(vii) 09 November 2005 Amman, Jordan: A series of bomb attacks carried out on three famous hotels: the Grand Hyatt Hotel, the Radisson SAS Hotel, and the Days Inn.

(viii) 20 September 2008 Islamabad, Pakistan: Dump truck filled with explosives was detonated in front of the Marriott Hotel. The explosion caused a natural gas leak that set the top floor of the hotel on fire and slowly spread to the entire hotel.

 (ix) 26–29 November 2008, Mumbai, India: Terrorists attacked and seized two hotels: the Taj Mahal Palace & Tower and the Oberoi Trident. The siege lasted for over three days.

  (x) 17 July 2009, Jakarta, Indonesia: Two suicide bombers checked into the JW Marriott and the Ritz-Carlton Hotel.

(xi) 12 January 2010 Haiti: An earthquake with 7.0 Richter scale magnitude and epicentre Port Au Prince, Haiti rocked Haiti.

(xii) 11 March 2011 Tohoku, Japan: Earthquake and tsunami rocked Japan.

(xiii) July – December 2011: Floods in Thailand caused by monsoons and the swelling of the rivers Chao Phraya and Mekong affected North and Central Thailand.

These are all exceptions when a hotel is absolved from liability arising from injuries or death. Notwithstanding these exceptions, hoteliers are bound to protect and evacuate their guests as speedily as possible to a safer location. Due care has to be exercised by hotels to ensure that guests are protected from any further harm once the disaster has occurred and to attend to any special guest needs arising from the incident.

Death of a guest   Suicide or the right to take one's life is a punishable offence under Section 309 of the Indian Criminal Procedure Code, punishable with imprisonment for a period of one year. Murder under Section 300 and culpable homicides under Section 299 are two offences defined under the Indian Penal Code that carry life imprisonment or capital punishment. Death of celebrities in hotels has always fascinated writers, film producers have woven murder mysteries, fictional stories, and movies that have thrilled audience's world over. The following are some of the incidents:

- On 4 April 1968, American leader of the African American civil rights movement and Nobel Peace Prize laureate, Martin Luther King, Jr., was gunned down on the balcony of his hotel room at the Lorraine Motel in Memphis, Tennessee.
- On 5 June 1968, Robert F. Kennedy, brother of assassinated US President John F. Kennedy was fatally shot in the kitchen of the Ambassador Hotel just after midnight.
- On 10 January 1971, style icon Coco Chanel creator of the popular perfume fragrances, Chanel No. 5, passed away at the age of 87 at the Ritz Carlton Hotel, Paris.
- On 5 March 1982, actor/comedian John Belushi died of an accidental drug overdose while staying in one of the bungalows at the famous Chateau Marmont on the Sunset Strip in Hollywood.
- On 26 May 2009, Polish millionairess Kinga Legg was murdered at the Le Bristol Hotel, Paris.
- On 11 February 2012, Pop superstar Whitney Houston died on the eve of the Grammy Awards in Los Angeles at the Beverly Hilton Hotel.

From a hotelier's perspective, in all cases of death, steps have to be taken to ensure normalcy in hotel operations as soon as possible. This involves establishing well-defined procedures that are meticulously followed by all employees:

Suggested procedures to be followed in the event of a death in the hotel are as follows:

- Senior management to immediately step in to control the situation
- Cordoning off the location from public view
- Not touching or tampering with evidence on site
- Preventing any kind of gossip or rumour mongering amongst employees

- Informing the local police station immediately and assisting the police in its investigation
- Once the police have given their consent, relocating the body to the hotel dispensary
- Calling the hotel doctor and obtaining a death certificate certifying the cause and time of death
- In case he or she is a hotel resident, contacting his or her relatives and offering all assistance to the members of the family
- Be guided by the administration and facilitating its proceedings
- Recording the facts of the incident in the log book without colouring them with any hypothesis or conclusions

Establishing and maintaining service standards

Maintaining service standards of the highest order is an essential requirement of all hotels and especially branded properties. There are a host of facilities that are available for guest use in a hotel. They range from in-room facilities such as tea/coffee-makers, Jacuzzi in bathrooms, Wi-Fi connectivity or Internet connectivity, electronic safes, mini-bars, iron and ironing boards, electronically controlled blinds, TV sets, DVD players, and so on.

It is imperative that as and when a facility is introduced or upgraded, the service standards should be re-defined by the hotel and all employees must be trained on the revised upgraded standards.

Example   Ian Smith and Janet Smith are staying at the InterContinental Hotel, Mumbai and have been allotted room no. 707. Ian desires to have a cup of tea upon arrival and decides to use the tea/coffee kettle to heat the water to brew the tea. When he switches the power ON to start the machine, he gets an electrical shock. Janet quickly pushes the power switch to OFF and is able to prevent any further harm.

Janet is aghast and calls for assistance from the lobby manager. The lobby manager arrives with the electrical maintenance person and they discover that the plug of the kettle had a naked wire that was loosely connected to the main electrical socket that powers the kettle resulting in Ian receiving an electrical shock.

In this example, two departments have been negligent in preparing the room for a guest arrival resulting in Ian receiving an electrical shock:

(i) Maintenance department, which is responsible for ensuring that all appliances in the guest room should be properly wired and in working condition.
(ii) Housekeeping department, which is responsible to prepare and finally check the room before giving it as a clear vacant room to the front desk for allotting it to a guest.

Impact
Both departments have faulted by not adhering to the service standards laid out by the hotel. In case Ian and Janet had decided to sue the hotel the court would have examined the applicability of the doctrine of vicarious liability in this case.

Warn guest of any unsafe conditions or areas of the hotel

Hoteliers have a twofold duty either to correct a hazardous or dangerous condition, and eliminate or warn of its existence. 'In the law of torts or common law, a visitor to the hotel is like an invitee and this defines the legal rights of the visitor if they are injured due to negligence of the hotelier. The Hotelier has a duty to make the property safe for the guests which includes conducting a reasonable inspection of the premises to uncover hidden dangers. Furthermore, hotelier assumes a duty to rescue a guest who falls into peril while visiting the property.'

Appropriate signage should be put in hotels indicating areas where repairs are in progress or areas that have been temporarily closed for renovations and such locations should be cordoned off to ensure that no guests accidently stray into it.

> **Example**   When members of housekeeping mop the floors, they must put up a signage stating 'Danger slippery surface'. When maintenance staff attends to the lifts, proper signage should be placed at the entrance of the lift doors indicating 'Lift under maintenance'. When cleaning takes place in restaurants, an appropriate signage indicating 'This section is closed for service' should be placed. When walls are being painted, 'Wet paint' signage should be displayed on the site. These are examples of visible hazards or dangers that are required to be pointed out to guests.

Besides visible hazards or dangers, hotels must warn guests of hidden dangers or hazards unknown to guests. For example, the shallow ends of pools must carry the signage—'Shallow water—no diving'. The case of *Klaus Mittelbachert vs East India Hotels Ltd.* is a significant case that has had a lasting impact on design and safety standards in and around swimming pools. Hotels that have no lifeguard on duty should display the signage 'Swim at your own risk'. On occasions when repair works involving welding are in progress on a higher floor, it is the duty of the hotel management to display appropriate signage like 'Work in progress', which warns the guests of the apparent danger that exists due to the welding work in progress.

Hire employees who are qualified and well trained in hotel operations

It is the primary function of the personnel department of a hotel to ensure that it employs individuals who match the requirements of the job description. Care should be taken by the department that the prospective employee has the education, experience, and qualifications that fit the position.

> **Example**
>
> ### Advertisement for the Position of a Lifeguard (The Loews Hotel)
>
> #### Sample Job Description for the Position of a Lifeguard
>
> **Company:** Loews Hotels
> **Property:** Loews Hotels at Universal Orlando
> **Location:** Florida-Orlando Management
> **Position:** No
> **Position:** Lifeguard
>
> **Entry-level Position:** No
> **Industry Categories:** Hotel/Resort
> **Position Categories:** Sports/Golf/Fitness
> **Job Availability:**

Position Summary

Responsible for the safety of all guests in the pool area. Assists in providing exceptional service to guests at the pool commensurate with the demands and expectations of a world-class hotel. Greets guests at the pool area, provides pool towels to guests, escort guests and positions chairs, sets up, refreshes, and tears down cabanas. Maintains the cleanliness and physical appearance of pool area.

- Greets guests arriving at the pool.
- Responsible for keeping current with all licences and training required to comply with the Ellis and Associates International Lifeguard Training Program.
- Responsible for maintaining guest safety in all pool areas, demonstrating professional and consistent adherence to all pool safety standards.
- Maintains safe use of the pool slide and does not allow dangerous activities.
- Responsible for maintaining proper positioning, visibility, and condition of pool safety and rescue equipment.
- Performs daily safety checks of pool area and slide for potential hazards.
- Knows the location and contents of first-aid kits.
- Adheres to all pool safety standards, including safety procedures for adverse weather conditions.
- Executes all water safety and rescue procedures in accordance with current Ellis and Associates standards.
- Performs all duties in a timely and professional manner.
- Turns in lost and found items throughout shift according to hotel procedures.
- Performs proper opening and closing procedures.
- Knowledgeable of and able to communicate all hotel recreational offerings.
- Assists in the performance of all pool attendant activities.
- Performs other duties as assigned.

General

- Promotes and applies teamwork skills at all times.
- Notifies appropriate individual promptly and fully of problems and/or unusual matters of significance.
- Is polite, friendly, and helpful to guests, management, and fellow employees.
- Executes emergency procedures in accordance with hotel standards.
- Complies with required safety regulations and procedures.
- Attends appropriate hotel meetings and training sessions.
- Maintains cleanliness and excellent condition of equipment and work area.
- Complies with hotel standards, policies, and rules.
- Recycles whenever possible.
- Remains current with hotel information and changes.
- Complies with hotel uniform and grooming standards.

Required Skills and Experience

- Must possess current Ellis and Associates Lifeguard Licence or have the ability to obtain one.
- Excellent guest service skills.
- Excellent oral communication skills.
- Able to work a flexible schedule to include weekends and holidays.
- Preferred skills and abilities.
- Previous lifeguard experience preferred but not required.

The above advertisement clearly spells out that the potential candidate shall have to work flexible hours, should be licenced and trained as a lifeguard, have good communication and guest handling skills, should be familiar with basic first-aid techniques, and should maintain safety standards as required by the management.

Handling guests with disabilities

In Chapter 7 we discussed disability as defined by the Persons with Disabilities (Equal Opportunities, Protection of Rights and Full Participation) Act, 1995. This definition of disability is important as it helps the hotel to prepare itself to handle guests with special requirements.

Chapter 8 of the Act stipulates that affirmative action should be taken to ensure that people with disabilities are not discriminated in any manner and have access to education, employment, public transportation system, and private and public buildings.

Sections 45 and 46 recommend that the environment be made user-friendly for the disabled by:

- installing ramps in public buildings
- adaptation of toilets for wheel-chair users
- providing braille symbols and auditory signals in elevators or lifts
- installing ramps in hospitals, primary health centres, and other medical care and rehabilitation institutions
- devising appropriate symbols of disability
- placing warning signals at appropriate places

Hotel operators have developed policies for handling guests with disabilities.

Suggested hotel features to handle physically challenged guests

Entry to the hotel building
- All disabled guests should use the main entrance to the hotel which has a gentle ramp leading into the lobby.
- Car parking bays for the disabled are provided in the front of the hotel. Valet assistance is available 24 hours in the main porch of the hotel.

Inside the hotel
- Ramps are provided for wheelchair access from one part of the floor to the other.
- The floor surfaces throughout the ground floor are marble, wood, and short pile carpet depending on the material used.
- Lobby lifts have wide doors to facilitate wheelchair access.
- Toilets for the disabled have wheelchair access and are provided with grab bars.
- All restaurants have provisions to accommodate guests that have special needs: wheelchair access, large print menus, chairs with and without back support and armrests, menus in Braille for the visually handicapped, and so on.
- Hotel's staff is available to advise any person who requires assistance.
- All guest rooms on all floors can be accessed by the lobby lift.

- Corridors on all floors have short pile carpets.
- Fire doors are held open on automatic magnets connected to the hotel's fire alarm system.
- In an emergency, wheelchair is available at the bell desk.
- Handicapped guest rooms are located on the lower floors.

In-room features
- Bedroom doors open inwards allowing ample space for a disabled person to pass through.
- Low-mounted electronic door locks are opened by a key card.
- Bedside control panels allow for operation of the room lights, TV, DVDs, heating, and cooling control.
- Emergency call can be made from the bedside telephones and the bathroom phones.
- All rooms have fire sprinklers and smoke detection systems.
- Adjoining standard rooms are linked to adapted rooms by intercom and connecting doors.
- Bedside emergency call button.
- Closet with low mounted hangers.

Bathroom features
- Bathroom door permits easy wheelchair access.
- Low-mounted towel rail.
- Floor-mounted commodes with no obstructions.
- Grab bars along left and right side of commodes.
- Lever type taps on shower, bath tub, and sinks.
- Wall-mounted and hand-held shower units in bath tubs.
- Bathtubs and shower stalls with grab bars mounted on the sides.
- Emergency call buttons.
- Hard plastic stools provided for bathing.

Circumstances under which a Hotelier can Refuse Admission or Deny Accommodation to a Guest

We are all familiar with the signage located at the entrance of all hotels 'Rights of Admission Reserved'. Under torts law it gives the right to the hotelier to prevent a guest from entering the hotel in case he or she is of the considered opinion that the guest is not in a fit condition to be received. In the event that the guest insists on entering the hotel property, he or she can be sued by the hotel as a trespasser and evicted by the hotel.

What is a 'fit condition to be received' has been debated by the courts from time to time; however, over and above the torts law, various countries have further legislated on this subject to ensure that there is no ambiguity in denying admission or accommodation to guests.

According to Kansas State Law Chapter 36 Article 602, -

a hotelier can refuse admission to the premises or deny accommodation to a prospective guest if the hotelier is of the opinion that the prospective guest is:

(a) *unwilling or unable to pay for a room or other establishment privileges such as food and beverage outlets, business centre, recreation, and health facilities.*

(b) *visibly under the influence of alcohol or other drugs or creating a public nuisance by engaging in fighting or disorderly conduct—such as using offensive, abusive, or obscene language*

(c) *if the person's use of a room or accommodation would violate the facility's maximum capacity.*

(d) *if the innkeeper reasonably believes the person will use the room or facility for an unlawful purpose.*

(e) *if the innkeeper reasonably believes the person will bring in something that would create an unreasonable danger or risk to others such as firearms and other types of weapons.*

(f) *any Minor below the age of 18 years who is unaccompanied by his or her legal guardian.*

Chapter 36, Article 604 of the Kansas State Law further clarifies that if under the above circumstances a hotelier denies accommodation to a prospective guest the hotelier cannot be prosecuted on the grounds of denial. 'Any innkeeper who refuses or denies such accommodations, facilities or privileges of a hotel for any of the reasons specified in subsections (a) through (f) shall not be liable in any civil or criminal action or for any fine or penalty based upon such refusal or denial, except that such accommodation, facilities or privilege of a hotel shall not be refused or denied based upon the person's race, religion, color, sex, disability, origin or ancestry.'

Broadly speaking, a hotelier can deny accommodation on the grounds of health, safety, and security and on the grounds that the person is a minor. However, denial of accommodation cannot be done on the basis of a person's race, religion, colour, sex, disability, origin, or ancestry.

CASE 8.6

APPELLANT: Saunders

VS

RESPONDENT: Patricia Hotel

In *Saunders vs Patricia Hotel*, a guest at the hotel's tavern was asked to leave because of hearsay that he had a knife. Saunders argued with the bouncer that he did not have a knife and finally refused to leave and defiantly slumped into his tavern chair. Bouncers picked him up and threw him out. He was given a reasonable opportunity by the hotel to leave but declined, hence he was forcibly removed from the premises by the bouncers. *Court found that Saunders was a visitor but became a trespasser once asked to leave.* Saunders' claim was dismissed by the court.

CASE 8.7

APPELLANT: Johnston

vs

RESPONDENT: Levin and Midtown Hotel Limited (1996), 25 C.H.R.R.D/82 (Ontario Board of Inquiry)

As a result of childhood polio, Harold Johnston was unsteady on his feet and required a leg brace. He also suffered from brain damage after childhood surgery, leaving him with slurred speech. Johnston was refused entry into a restaurant because the owner thought he was intoxicated. While the owner had a statutory duty to refuse service to an intoxicated person, he was found liable for discrimination because he failed to make reasonable efforts to determine whether Johnston was intoxicated. At the time of the refusal of service, Johnston's leg brace was easily visible and the reason for his slurred speech was explained to the restaurant owner. *The Ontario Board of inquiry ruled that refusal to serve a patron because of the patron's apparent intoxication must be based on reasonable evidence and belief.*

CASE 8.8

APPELLANT: Randhwa

vs

RESPONDENT: Tequila Bar and Grill Ltd. (2008), 62 C.H.R.R.D/350

Randhawa made a human rights complaint alleging discrimination on the grounds of race, colour, ancestry, place of origin, and religious beliefs when he was denied entry to the Tequila Nightclub. He alleged that when he and some friends tried to enter the nightclub, a doorman told them that the line-up was under surveillance by management, and that when they reached the entrance, another doorman would be instructed to ask them for several pieces of identification. Even though the complainant and his friends responded that they had appropriate identification, the doorman asked for additional identification which Randhawa and his friends could not meet. The doorman stated that management had a certain image for the bar and did not want the clients to say that there were a lot of 'brown people' inside. The respondent nightclub denied using racist policies to determine entrance to the club. *The panel found merit to the complaint, ordering the respondent to implement a specific anti-racism policy and to participate in a commission human rights education workshop. The panel awarded $5,000 in general damages for injury to dignity and self respect, as well as travel expenses and interest.*

Circumstances under which a Hotelier can Evict a Guest

Under certain exceptional circumstances, the hotelier is vested with the power to evict persons who are registered as guests. These exceptions have been validated under English Common Law and the precedents set are followed in India.

According to Kansas State Law Chapter 36, Article 604,

Ejection of person from hotel premises:
- *Disorderly conduct*
- *Non-payment of dues*

- *Using the premises for an unlawful purpose or act*
- *Bringing property onto the premises that may be dangerous to others*
- *Failing to register as a guest*
- *Using false pretense to obtain accommodations*
- *Being a minor unaccompanied by an adult registered guest*
- *Violating central, state, or local hotel laws or regulations*
- *Violating a conspicuously posted hotel or motel rule*
- *Failing to vacate a room at the agreed checkout time*

In order not to attract any liability and contentious litigation for evicting a guest, hoteliers are cautious and conservative. They can evict guests who have refused to pay; or when they are convinced that the person used the room or premises for an unlawful purpose or brought a potentially dangerous object onto the premises, or failed to check out at the appointed day and time.

The above circumstances have been validated by statute law in various countries and some of these have been incorporated in the *Code of Conduct for Safe and Honourable Tourism* applicable in India:

Clause 3—Regulated use of Premises and Official Equipment:

Tourism service providers shall verify and maintain a record of details pertaining to tourists, personnel and service providers like address, contact details etc. and also commit themselves to confidentiality. (Form-C (Rule-14, Registration of Foreigners Rules, 1992)

Management/Owners are encouraged to prohibit the use of the organizations premises for use or abuse of illicit substances, sexual violations and of company equipment for the viewing, storage, distribution, promotion or use of material which could increase vulnerability to exploitation. (Narcotics Drugs and Psychotropic Substances Act & Immoral Traffic Prevention Act 1956 Sections 5 & 7)

Internet usage that promotes, seeks any contacts for sex tourism and other sexual services, for search of pornographic material and/or to solicit the sale and purchase of illicit substances shall be prohibited. (Section 67 (b) Information Technology (Amendment) Act 2008)

Clause 4—Ethical Business practices and marketing:

Management and Owners shall ensure that all contracts with business partners, suppliers and franchisee agreements bear a clause seeking commitments to provisions of the 'Code of Conduct for Safe and Honorable Tourism' in their businesses.

Tourists are encouraged to understand local social, cultural norms and beliefs and encouraged to conduct themselves in a manner that respects these beliefs.

Like in many places in the rest of the world tourists are encouraged to follow some basic and practical safety tips such as to remain with a group or meet new people in public places, not to accept items from persons whom they have befriended recently, be wary of unexpected, unknown persons coming to their hotel room, never open the door to unsolicited room service or maintenance people etc.

Any tourism enterprise or service provider found to act in a manner that undermines the safety of persons as outlined in this code may be black listed.'

Serving Food and Beverage Responsibly

Truth in menu broadly means that the offerings on the food menu and beverage list display accurate information as to the description and nature of the food and beverage product and the price that is being charged.

> **Example** *Grilled chicken salad with seasonal fruits:* Grilled boneless slices of chicken breasts served on a bed of lettuce with segments of freshly peeled oranges, blueberries masked with red wine vinaigrette sauce.

The description of the dish as mentioned in the menu should be an accurate description of the dish on offer and should have the ingredients that have been mentioned in the menu. Serving food and beverages responsibly also involves that laws pertaining to service of alcoholic beverages and restrictions on smoking in public places such as bars, restaurants, hotel lobbies are strictly implemented.

Smoking in public places such as bars, restaurants, hotel lobbies is regulated by The Cigarettes and Other Tobacco Products (Prohibition of Advertisement and Regulation of Trade and Commerce, Production, Supply and Distribution) Act, 2003 (COTPA). There is a specific provision under Sections 4 and 6:

Section 4—No person shall smoke in any Public Place: Provided that in a hotel having thirty rooms or a restaurant having a seating capacity of thirty persons or more and in the airports, a separate provision for smoking area or space maybe made.'

Section 6—No Person shall sell or offer for sale, or permit sale of, cigarettes or any other tobacco products: To any person who is under eighteen years of age, and in an area within a radius of one hundred yards of any educational institute.

These Sections become applicable with the passing of the Prohibition of Smoking in Public Places Rules, 2008. The fine for smoking in a public place is currently ₹200.

Clause 3 of *Code of Conduct for Safe and Honourable Tourism*—regulated use of premises—emphasizes that the excise policy applicable to the state should be followed. For example, individuals under the permitted age shall not be allowed permission into restricted areas as bars and pubs (Goa 18 years, Delhi 25 years, Karnataka, Uttarakhand, and Maharashtra 21 years).

Handling Fraud Committed by Guests

Some of the frauds and misdemeanours committed by guests on hotels are as follows:

- Non-payment of charges
- Skippers
- Credit-card frauds
- Theft of hotel property from guest rooms
- Food and beverage complaints in order to secure waiver of charges

Non-payment by guests

Non-payment by guests who are not on the hotel's approved credit list amounts to a fraud. The remedy available to hoteliers is to detain the property of the guests till such time that the payment is received from them. This is permitted under the Indian Contract Act, 1872 and is called the pledging of goods under Section 172, which is the bailment of goods as security for payment of a debt. The bailor or the guest is the pawnor and the bailee or the hotel is the pawnee. Whilst detaining the guest property, care should be exercised by the hotel that the guest signs a document pledging his property to the hotel till he or she clears the bill.

Upon receipt of the payment from the guest, the hotel is obliged to return the goods in the same condition in which they were received by it and whilst the goods are in the hotel's custody, due care has to be exercised that they are not damaged or destroyed.

In the event that the guest does not settle his bills upon expiry of the period agreed upon, the hotel can dispose of the goods in order to settle its dues.

Skippers

These are guest who have no previous record of stay at the hotel and have no intention of paying the hotel's charges and vacate the hotel premises surreptitiously without the knowledge of the hotel management. As a general rule, hotels cover their charges by insisting on a deposit from them on a continuing basis. However, once it is established that a guest has skipped, the hotel informs the hotel federation so that the details of the guest can be circulated to all member hotels. By taking these measures, the hotel ensures that fellow hoteliers do not become victims of the skipper intentions. Furthermore, in case he or she is registered in any of the member hotels, he or she can be apprehended with the help of the police.

Credit-card frauds

Most of the credit-card frauds that are committed by guests on hotels is by using credit cards that have been cloned based upon the information that is provided by the credit-card owner inadvertently. These duplicate cards are difficult to identify by the hotel and can only be detected by vigilant cashiers. Often, hotels get to know of this once the payment gets declined by the merchant banker or the original owner of the card disputes the charges. The only way to prevent it is for the original credit-card owner to not disclose personal information to any individual who seeks it. Details such ascard number, CVV number, date of birth, card limit, card PIN number, and residential address.

Theft of hotel property from guest rooms

It requires housekeeping to be vigilant to curb any theft of hotel property from guest rooms. When servicing the rooms, housekeepers should keep a close watch on the amenities that are placed in the rooms: toiletries, extra blankets, towels, tea/coffee sachets, sugar, mini-bar items, as well as track the additional amenities that are placed in the room upon guest request. Although a policy exists that upon check-out, the front-office informs housekeeping to check the departure room to ascertain if there are any items that are missing, regretfully lack of co-ordination between these departments on occasions has resulted in guests successfully walking away with items stolen from the room.

Food and beverage complaints to secure waiver of charges

We are all familiar with guest complaints related to food and beverage items in the hotel's restaurants and bars. Some of the common ones are as follows:

- Food being served was cold, for example, cold soup.
- The oil used was rancid.
- The meats were not cooked properly and tasted raw.
- The meat pieces were stringy and rubbery.
- Stale food was served (mostly in banquets).
- The whiskey tastes adulterated. For example, it is not black label.
- The dish does not match the menu description.

In such circumstances, the restaurant managers resort to waiving the charges for the item that was the cause of the complaint or get the item replaced. By his actions, the guest has deprived the hotel of revenue that the hotel would have legitimately earned.

The forthcoming chapters will discuss the laws related to food and beverage licensing and operations in more detail.

SUMMARY

This chapter highlighted the duties and responsibilities of a hotelier towards guests and defined the legal relationship between the two. The chapter gave an understanding of the law of torts or common law and its application to the hotel industry. It discussed the types of guests and visitors to the hotels, and the way they should be received by the hotel. The chapter mentioned that the public duty of a hotelier is to receive guests whilst exercising the duty of care which involves maintaining guest safety, security, and privacy.

Coping with unusual incidents and accidents on hotel premises is discussed and establishing standards that are easy to implement in order to prevent reoccurrence in the future.

The chapter also discussed the ways to handle frauds committed by guests.

KEY TERMS

Hotel A building or part of a building which an owner offers to travellers or general public willing and able to pay primarily for the sleeping accommodation with or without food and drink for the services and facilities provided without any special contract.

Hospitality The friendly and generous reception and entertainment of guests, visitors, and strangers. The word has its origins from the Latin word *hospes* which literally means 'hostis' or 'host' and the old French word 'hospitalite'.

Resident guest or in-house guest A person who stays for a minimum period of 24 hours in a hotel room for which he has paid and is therefore entitled to the use of the facilities offered by the hotel.

Non-resident visitors (or patrons) Visitors who enjoy the facilities located in the public areas such as restaurants and bars, health club and spas, banquets, and business centres upon payment for the services utilized.

Confirmed or guaranteed room reservation That has been confirmed against a deposit of one night's room charges which are collected at the time of requesting for a room reservation. The essentials of a room reservation are names of the guests, number of persons, the type of accommodation requested, the rates, the period of stay, and the mode of payment.

Overbooking A practice that hoteliers follow in order to maximize occupancies and revenues by overselling the available rooms and is based upon educated calculation of no-show reservations. As a practice it may constitute up to 10 per cent of the available room inventory.

No show guest   A guest holding a confirmed or guaranteed reservation fails to register with the hotel. The hotel is generally entitled to damages and the deposit collected from the guest stands forfeited.

Turn-away guests   A hotel is required to secure comparable accommodation, if, for any reason, a room should not be available for a guest who holds a valid confirmed reservation and to bear the cost of transportation to the hotel that he is shifted to.

Bailment   The delivery of goods by one person to another for some purpose, upon a contract that they shall, when the purpose is accomplished, be returned or otherwise disposed of according to the directions of the person delivering them.

Bailor   The person delivering the goods for safekeeping.

Bailee   The person accepting the goods for safekeeping.

Non-gratuitous bailment   When a charge for keeping the goods is levied.

Gratuitous bailment   When goods are kept without levying a charge.

Voluntary bailment   When a guest voluntarily hands over possession of his goods to the hotelier for custody.

Involuntary bailment   When the hotel comes into possession of misplaced, lost, or abandoned guest property as it has been found on the hotel premises.

Tort   French for wrong, a civil wrong, or wrongful act, whether intentional or unintentional (accidental), from which injury occurs to another. Torts include all negligence cases as well as intentional wrongs that result in harm.

Sua sponte   Latin term meaning 'of one's own accord'. It refers to when the court addresses an issue that has not been presented for consideration by the litigants.

Personal injury   Damage or harm inflicted upon the body, mind, or emotions of an individual.

Misplaced property   One that has been carefully placed by the owner who has then forgotten where he kept it.

Lost property   One that the rightful owner has inadvertently kept and then forgotten where he kept it.

Abandoned property   One that the owner has deliberately kept aside with no intention of retrieving it.

Jewellery   includes—(i) ornaments made of gold, silver, platinum or any other precious metal or any alloy containing one or more of such precious metals, whether or not containing any precious or semi-precious stones and whether or not worked or sewn into any wearing apparel; (ii) Precious or semi-precious stones, whether or not set in any furniture, utensils or other article or worked or sewn into any wearing apparel.

EXERCISES

Define the Following

1. Assault
2. Battery
3. Negligence
4. Theft
5. Misplaced property
6. Patron
7. Turn-away guest
8. Jewellery
9. Vicarious liability
10. Invasion of privacy

Concept Review Questions

1. Draw a comparison between bailment and pledge by giving examples from the hotel industry.
2. Write a brief on the Sarais Act 1867.
3. Overbooking is an issue that can impact a hotel's business resulting in turnaway guests. How do hotels handle this?

4. Explain the term 'duty of care' with examples.
5. Most legal cases filed against hotels are based on the law of torts. Write a brief note on it.

Critical Thinking Questions

1. What steps can a hotelier take to ensure that legal cases are not filed by guests for deficiency of service?
2. Prepare a standard operating procedure to deal with unusual incidents such as fire, death of a guest in the hotel, and so on.
3. What is the impact of *Connie Francis Garzilli and Joseph Garzelli vs Howard Johnson Motor Lodges, Inc* case on the hospitality industry?

Research Question

1. With rapid technological changes in every sphere of hotel operations, how will adopting newer technology improve guest service delivery?

Projects

1. Should a comprehensive law be passed by the legislature limiting the liability of a hotelier towards guests against loss or theft of guest property, deficiency in services, etc.? Would such a law benefit the hotel industry?

2. Prepare a list of special features or facilities that a hotel should have to make physically challenged guests feel more welcome.

REFERENCES

<http://oxforddictionaries.com/definition/hospitality accessed on 20 March 2012.

<http://en.wikipedia.org/wiki/Taittiriya_Upanishad accessed on 20 March 2012.

<http://en.wikipedia.org/wiki/Sudama#The_story accessed on 20 March 2012.

<http://kansasstatutes.lesterama.org/Chapter_36/Article_6/ accessed on 21 March 2012.

<http://www.enotes.com/travel-reference/hotel-liability accessed on 21 March 2012.

<http://legal-dictionary.thefreedictionary.com/due+care > accessed on 24 March 2012.

<http://legal-dictionary.thefreedictionary.com/Gross+negligence > accessed on 24 March 2012.

<http://legal-dictionary.thefreedictionary.com/contributory+negligence > accessed on 24 March 2012.

<http://legal-dictionary.thefreedictionary.com/comparative+negligence > accessed on 24 March 2012.

<http://www.legalserviceindia.com/article/1129-Torts-In-India.html> accessed on 25 March 2012.

<http://legal-dictionary.thefreedictionary.com/tort> accessed on 25 March 2012.

R. F. V. Heuston and John William Salmond, *Salmond On the Law of Torts*. 17th ed. London: Sweet & Maxwell, 1977.

<http://library.jcsc.edu.jm/search/Record/825/Cite> accessed on 25 March 2012.

<http://oxforddictionaries.com/definition/liability> accessed on 25 March 2012.

<http://legal-dictionary.thefreedictionary.com/liability> accessed on 25 March 2012.

<http://legal-dictionary.thefreedictionary.com/Vicarious+Liability> accessed on 25 March 2012.

<http://www.thefreedictionary.com/Tort+feasor> accessed on 25 March 2012.

<http://www.thefreedictionary.com/Private+Nuisance> accessed on 25 March 2012.

<http://www.thefreedictionary.com/Battery> accessed on 25 March 2012.

<http://www.thefreedictionary.com/assualt> accessed on 25 March 2012.

The Australian Carriers & Innkeepers Act 1958 <www.legislation.vic.gov.au/domino/Web_notes/LDMS/LTObject_Store/LTObjSt1.nsf/d1a8d8a9bed958efca25761600042ef5/12f6ad7ad4a2a9b9ca25776100192ad0/$FILE/58-6214a031doc.doc> accessed on 25 March 2012.

<http://en.wikipedia.org/wiki/Tort> accessed on 25 March 2012.

The Indian Contract Act, 1872, Chapter 9, Section 148 <http://www.vakilno1.com/bareacts/indiancontractact/indiancontractact.html> accessed on 7 April 2012.

Klaus Mittelbachert vs East India Hotels Ltd. on 3 January, 1997 (1999 ACJ 287, 1997 IIAD Delhi 23, AIR 1997 Delhi 201) <http://indiankanoon.org/doc/1090050/> accessed on 7 April 2012.

<http://www.lawnix.com/cases/frummer-hilton-hotels.htm > accessed on 27 March 2012.

<http://definitions.uslegal.com/s/sua-sponte/> accessed on 26 March 2012.

<http://en.wikipedia.org/wiki/List_of_natural_disasters_by_death_> accessed on 26 March 2012.

National Consumer Disputes Redressal Commission, New Delhi First appeal no. 102 of 2004 (Against the order dated 24.1.2004 in complaint no. 147/97 of The State Commission, New Delhi) <http://ncdrc.nic.in/FA10204.htm> accessed on 21 March 2012.

<http://iftta.org/content/austrian-supreme-court-hotel-liable-theft-safe-hotel-room> accessed on 23 March 2012.

Connie Francis Garzilli and Joseph Garzilli, Plaintiffs, vs Howard Johnson's Motor Lodges, Inc., Defendant <http://ny.findacase.com/research/wfrmDocViewer.aspx/xq/fac.19760920_0000092.ENY.htm/qx> accessed on 26 March 2012.

<http://articles.timesofindia.indiatimes.com/2008-06-29/ahmedabad/27779787_1_hotel-staff-room-service-sardarnagar-police> accessed on 6 April 2012.

<http://www.lawisgreek.com/indian-laws-for-suicide-legal-rights-and-social-issues> accessed on 6 April 2012.

<http://www.indianexpress.com/Storyold/62540/> accessed on 6 April 2012.

<http://www.hcareers.com/seeker/search/view?jobAdId=778A3AD1B8B7AF0C> accessed on 7 April 2012.

<http://indiatoday.intoday.in/story/whitney-houston-died-from-drowning-says-coroner/1/178946.html> accessed on 7 April 2012.

<http://abcnews.go.com/Travel/celebrity-hotel-deaths/story?id=15585904> accessed on 7 April 2012.

<http://socialjustice.nic.in/pwdact1995.php?> accessed on 6 April 2012.

<http://kansasstatutes.lesterama.org/Chapter_36/Article_6/> accessed on 14 April 2012.

<http://www.pctools.com/security-news/vacation-credit-fraud/> accessed on 16 April 2012.

Part IV

Laws Related to Food and Beverage

Chapter 9   Food Legislation

Chapter 10   Liquor Licensing

Food Legislation

LEARNING OBJECTIVES

After going through this chapter, the reader will be familiar with the following:

- Laws governing the food business with special emphasis on Prevention of Food Adulteration Act, 1954 and the Food Safety and Standards Act, 2006
- Food, adulterants, food adulteration, contaminants, extraneous substances, and misbranding
- Role of food safety officers and food analysts in upholding food standards
- Process of securing food business operator's licence and the penal provisions for operating a business without a licence
- A model food safety management programme

INTRODUCTION

Throughout history, man has been involved in cultivating and sourcing varieties of food—a basic dietary requirement that provides for nourishment and growth of the body. As civilizations evolved, so did cuisines catering to a variety of tastes and requirements. Man experimented with different cooking methods, such as baking, boiling, roasting, and frying with a combination of aromatic spices and condiments that would magically impart flavour to food, making it palatable and appealing whilst retaining its nutritional qualities. These were preliminary attempts to enhance the appearance, texture, and taste of food items.

Over centuries, ambitious rulers with territorial designs, explorers thirsty of adventure, and traders travelling for profit required foods that could be preserved with ease to enhance their shelf life. The earliest attempt to preserve food was to pickle it using a combination of salt, vinegar, and oil. Certain meats such as bacon were preserved by salting it. Smoking was another popular method of curing and preserving meats and poultry and this process imparted a smokey flavour to the meat.

In Gujarat, *Khakras* and *Theplas*, which are, respectively, roasted and pan-fried Indian breads made from wheat, flavoured with fenugreek, were given to soldiers on their march during battles as these provided for nourishment and could be easily eaten with pickled vegetables, yogurt, and so on.

Globalization of food made people pick up the good and bad practices of food preservation and enhancement. Examples are enhancing the appearance of breads by adding chalk and mashed potatoes; mixing red brick powder with red chilli powder to add colour and volume; adding caramelized sugar syrup to give honey a rich golden colour; and blending old or stale tea leaves with fresh tea leaves to add weight.

It was only during the 18th and 19th centuries that a scientific attempt was made to determine the difference between food additives and preservatives that are beneficial and adulterants that are harmful.

A pioneer in this field was the German chemist Friedrich Accum whose book *A Treatise on Adulterations of Food and Culinary Poisons,* published in the UK in 1820, outlined the harmful effects of food adulteration. The practice of adulterating food was rampant in London with people developing a taste for adulterated food items. His endeavours earned him the wrath of powerful people whom he had exposed, and he finally had to return to Germany.

Between 1851 and 1854, Arthur Hill Hassall did extensive research in London by collecting over 2500 samples of food and drinks for analysis, and his detailed findings were published as reports of the Analytical Sanitary Commission in the renowned medical journal *The Lancet* published by Thomas Wakley, a surgeon and Member of Parliament. In 1855, Arthur Hill Hassall published a book by collating his various articles. This book grabbed the attention of parliamentarians who set up a Parliamentary Committee of Inquiry to investigate the veracity of Hassall's findings. Hassall's investigations resulted in the passing of the Food Adulteration Act, 1860, which recognized that the state was responsible for protecting the interests of the consumer. The law was a compromise, as it battled to serve conflicting interests, and its inherent weaknesses lay in the fact that criminal intent or *Mens Rea* had to be established before any prosecution proceedings could commence against the offender.

The Food Adulteration Act, 1872 (UK)

The Food Adulteration Act, 1872 (UK) was an improvement and attempted to address some of the anomalies of the previous legislation by recommending the appointment of food inspectors and public analysts. Food inspectors were responsible for the collection of samples whilst the public analysts would study the samples taken and submit their reports to the inspectors. Based upon the findings mentioned in the reports, the inspectors would initiate proceedings to serve notices through the magistrate. However, the Act still required criminal intent or *Mens Rea* to be established before any prosecution could be initiated.

In 1874, the Society of Public Analysts was founded with Hassall as its first president, and a select committee was set up to examine the working of the 1872 Act.

The report of this committee prepared under the guidance of Hassall provided the basis for the Sale of Food and Drugs Act, 1875.

The Sale of Food and Drugs Act, 1875 (UK)

The Sale of Food and Drugs Act, 1875 (UK) was a marked improvement on the Food Adulteration Act, 1872, as it:

  (i) defined the various offences of food adulteration extending the scope to the entire supply chain—from the manufacturer to the retailer
 (ii) vested food inspectors with magisterial power of search and collection of samples
(iii) elaborated on the appointment and duties of the public analyst
 (iv) empowered the general public of getting food articles analysed by paying fee to the public analysts
  (v) treated the certificates given by the public analysts as conclusive evidence by the magistrates
 (vi) stipulated that criminal intention or *Mens Rea* was not necessary to establish in order to initiate legal proceedings

London, being the nerve centre of government, trade, and commerce, attracted talents from other parts of the island and Europe. These waves of migration into the city stretched the food supply chain to the limit and resulted in non-availability of food items. Salted and unsalted butter was in great demand, and in order to meet the demands, unscrupulous manufactures and traders adulterated it with animal fat.

The Margarine Act, 1887 (UK)

The introduction of The Margarine Act, 1887 (UK) was the first attempt to define and standardize a manufactured food product. In this case, addition of animal fat to butter was prohibited and water content was limited to 12–14 per cent. This legislation would pave the way for future pieces of legislations that would impact the packaged food industry.

It was only in 1990 that a comprehensive Food & Safety Act was passed in the UK. The various efforts made by individuals and the legislative measures initiated by the government in the UK, which have been discussed earlier, are illustrated in Fig. 9.1.

INDIAN SCENARIO

During the stewardship of Lord Curzon, Viceroy of India (1899–1905), the severe famine of 1899–1900 resulted in an estimated death of 7.5 million to 9.0 million people. In order to deal with food shortage, the administration was forced to take measures against the availability of contaminated and adulterated food items leading to malnutrition and hoarding of food articles.

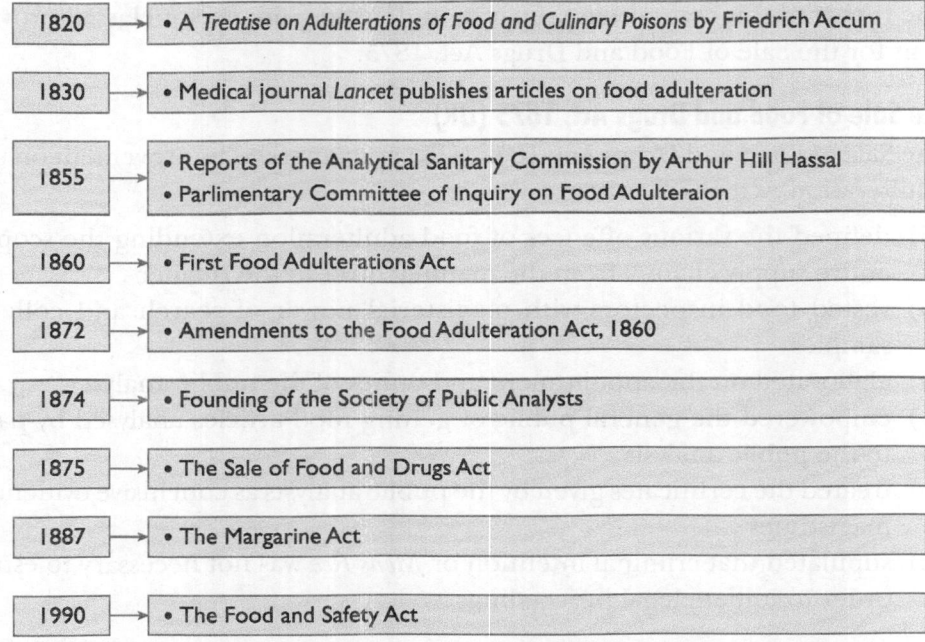

1820	• A *Treatise on Adulterations of Food and Culinary Poisons* by Friedrich Accum
1830	• Medical journal *Lancet* publishes articles on food adulteration
1855	• Reports of the Analytical Sanitary Commission by Arthur Hill Hassal • Parlimentary Committee of Inquiry on Food Adulteraion
1860	• First Food Adulterations Act
1872	• Amendments to the Food Adulteration Act, 1860
1874	• Founding of the Society of Public Analysts
1875	• The Sale of Food and Drugs Act
1887	• The Margarine Act
1990	• The Food and Safety Act

FIGURE 9.1   Timeline: Fight against Food Adulteration (in UK)

During the British rule, various states took individual legislative measures to fight food adulteration, and numerous laws were promulgated between 1912 and 1954. These Acts were not uniform and fulfilled local state requirements, leading to conflict of interest between states as items that were considered adulterated in one state were not necessarily regarded as adulterated in another state. This hampered inter-state trade of food items, resulting in artificial food shortages.

These state laws were not designed to curb the menace of food adulteration and misbranding, did not address the complete food supply chain from farm to fork, and were ineffective in controlling the use of additives for food preservation and in packaged foods. These state enactments were not comprehensive as they did not define standards of what constituted healthy foods.

To effectively deal with these issues, the Government of India constituted a Central Advisory Board of Health in 1937 and the Food Adulteration Committee in 1943. These two bodies recommended that a Central Act be enacted, which was passed after India attained its independence.

Enabling provisions were made in The Constitution of India, List—III of the Seventh Schedule, also known as the Concurrent List—'Clause 18—Adulteration of Foodstuff and Other Goods,' whereby both the centre and the states enjoyed concurrent legislative powers to enact laws.

Furthermore, Part IV—Directive Principles of State Policy, Clause 47 states—'Duty of the State to raise the level of nutrition and the standard of living and to improve public health. The State shall regard the raising of the level of nutrition and the standard of living of its people and the improvement of public health as among its primary duties and, in particular, the State shall endeavour to bring about prohibition of the consumption except for medicinal purposes of intoxicating drinks and of drugs which are injurious to health.'

By enshrining these values in the Constitution, the lawmakers acknowledged that the state was responsible for protecting the health and well-being of its citizens.

The Prevention of Food Adulteration Act, 1954 incorporated various suggestions made by the Central Advisory Board of Health and came into force on 1 June 1955.

THE PREVENTION OF FOOD ADULTERATION ACT, 1954

The objectives and purposes of the Prevention of Food Adulteration Act, 1954 were threefold:

  (i) To protect the public from poisonous and harmful food
 (ii) To prevent the sale of substandard food
(iii) To eliminate fraudulent practices in the interest of consumers

Section 7 of the Act states the following:

TEXT

No person shall himself or by any person on his behalf manufacture for sale, or store, sell or distribute:

   (i) *Any adulterated food*
  (ii) *Any misbranded food*
 (iii) *Any article of food for the sale of which a licence is prescribed, except in accordance with the conditions or the licence*
 (iv) *Any article of food the sale of which is for the time being prohibited by the Food (Health) Authority in the interest of public health*
  (v) *Any article of food in contravention of any other provision of' this Act or of any rule made there under*
 (vi) *Any adulterant.*

Section 7 along with the 'validity of the report submitted by the public analysts' under Section 13 of the Prevention of Food Adulteration Act, 1954 was challenged in the courts.

These operative sections of the Act, namely Sections 7 and 13, were challenged on the grounds that these violated an individual's 'fundamental right' to practice any profession or to carry on any occupation, trade or business (Clause 19(g)). Furthermore, the Act was discriminatory in nature as it violated Article 14 of the Constitution 'Equality before law—The State shall not deny to any person equality before the law or the equal protection of the laws within the territory of India'

To protect the interests of the general public, the Constitution placed reasonable restrictions on the fundamental rights. These were embodied in Article 19(6), which allows the State to make any law imposing, in the interests of the general public, reasonable restrictions. This clause effectively overrode Clause 19 (g).

In *Andhra Pradesh Grain and Seed Merchants Association vs Union of India A.I.R. 1971 S.C. 2346,* the Supreme Court held that the Prevention of Food Adulteration Act, 1954 was not unconstitutional and that a report submitted under 'Section 13' cannot be challenged. In *Municipal Corporation of Delhi vs Surja Ram,* the object and the purpose of the Act was upheld by the Court. The salient features of the Act were as follows:

(i) The Act replaced all local laws enacted by various states on the subject of food adulteration.

(ii) The Act applied uniformly to the whole of India.

(iii) It recognized that both the centre and the states were responsible for protecting the interests of the consumer.

(iv) It established Central Food Laboratories where samples could be sent for analysis. It instituted a coordinating committee between the centre and the states to administer the Act.

(v) It vested powers in the centre to set quality standards for various food articles that were not arbitrary or discriminatory (*State of Uttar Pradesh vs Kartar Singh A.I.R. 1964 S.C. 1135*).

(vi) The Act made it clear that in order to prosecute, the doctrine of *Mens Rea* or criminal intent need not be established. This was upheld by the courts in the following cases: *Sarjoo Prasad vs State of Uttar Pradesh A.I.R. 1961 S.C. 631* and *Andhra Pradesh Grain and Seed Merchants Association vs Union of India A.I.R. 1971 S.C. 2346.*

The legislative measures initiated by the Indian government in fighting the menace of food adulteration are illustrated in Fig. 9.2.

The purpose and objectives of these Acts are as follows:

Food Products Order, 1955 This Order laid down the Food Products Order standards and quality specifications regarding the production and marketing of processed fruits vegetables, sweetened aerated water, vinegar, synthetic syrups, and imported processed foods and vegetables.

Meat Foods Products Order, 1973 This Order regulates the production of meat products by manufacturers by (1) specifying the sanitation and hygiene requirements for slaughterhouses; (2) defining the permissible limit of heavy metals, preservatives, and insecticide residues in meat products; and (3) specifying the packing, marking, and labelling provisions for containers of meat products.

Livestock Importation Act, 1898 This Act regulates the import of meat products, eggs and egg powder, and milk products into the country.

Milk and Milk Products Order, 1992 (MPO) This Order regulates the production, distribution, and supply of milk and sets the hygiene and sanitary requirements for dairy plants, including quality control, and packing; marking and labelling standards for milk and milk products. MPO standards apply to imported milk products as well.

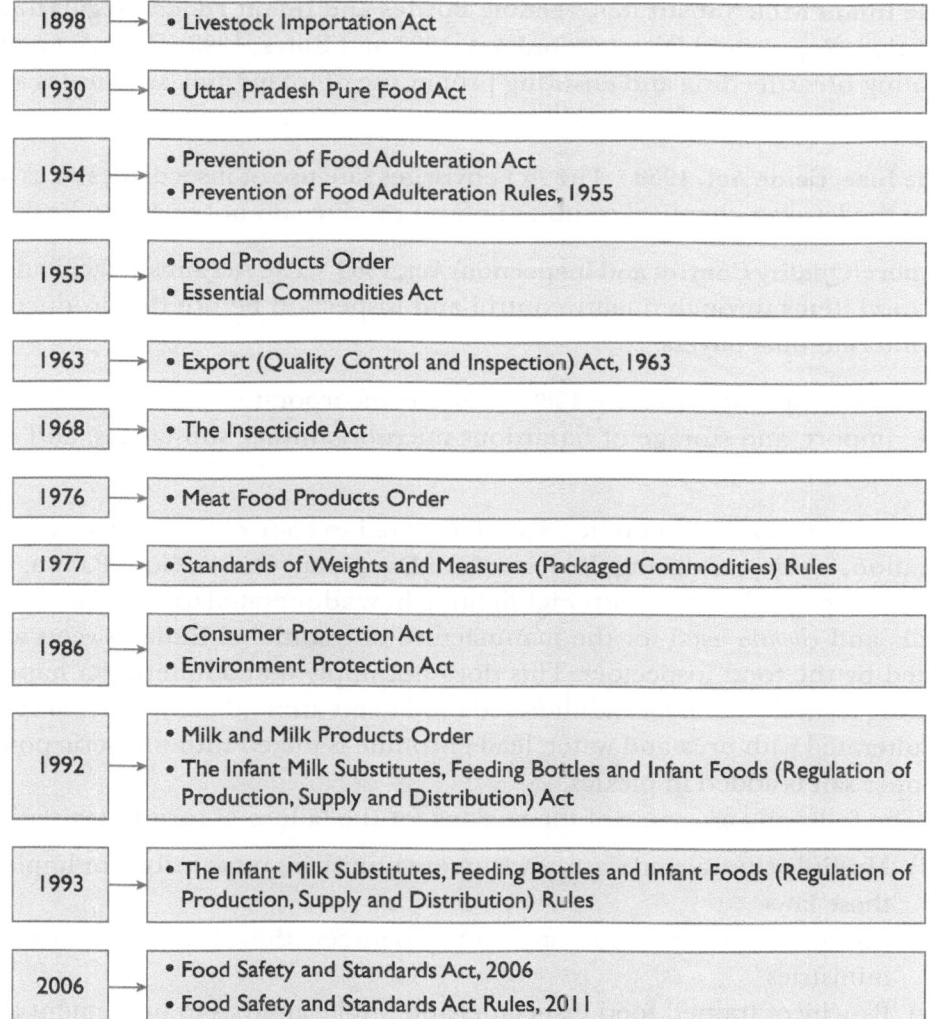

FIGURE 9.2 Timeline: Fight against Food Adulteration (in India)

Essential Commodities Act, 1955 A large number of control orders have been issued from time to time in order to regulate the manufacture, commerce, and distribution of essential commodities, including food, under the provisions of this Act.

Standards of Weights and Measures Act, 1976 and the Standards of Weights and Measures (Packaged Commodities) Rules, 1977 This Act standardizes the weight of various packaged articles and governs the sale of packaged commodities. It is mandatory to register all packaged products in the country.

Consumer Protection Act, 1986 This Act provides for constitution of district forums and state and national commissions for settlement of disputes between the seller/ service provider and the consumer.

The Infant Milk Substitutes, Feeding Bottles and Infant Foods (Regulation of Production, Supply and Distribution) Act, 1992 and Rules, 1993 This Act aims at promoting breastfeeding and ensuring proper use of infant milk substitutes and infant food.

The Insecticide Act, 1968 The Act envisages safe use of insecticides so as to ensure that the leftover chemical residues in farm produce do not pose any health hazard.

Export (Quality Control and Inspection) Act, 1963 The Act aims at facilitating export of food items through quality control and inspection before the products are sold to international buyers.

Environment Protection Act, 1986 This Act incorporates rules for the manufacture, use, import, and storage of hazardous microorganisms, substances, and cells used as foodstuff.

In spite of various pieces of legislation enacted to control the menace of food adulteration, every year during the festivals of Deepavali, Onam, Gudi Padwa, Holi, and Eid, newspapers carry reports highlighting how adulterated food items such as *khoya*, milk, and *chenna* used for the manufacture of traditional Indian sweets are confiscated by the food inspectors. This does not imply that adulteration happens only during festivals but in fact adulterated food items are sold daily; for example, milk is adulterated with urea and water, lead chromite is mixed with turmeric powder, and copper salt is added in pickles.

The following are some of the reasons for the failure of various legislations:

(i) Multiple central and state government ministries responsible for implementing these laws
(ii) Ineffective coordination and rivalry between the centre, the states, and the ministries
(iii) Paucity of trained food inspectors and public analysts to implement the laws
(iv) Lack of public awareness on the dangers of food adulteration
(v) Multiple laws dealing with similar issues leading to unnecessary and prolonged litigations

For the next 50 years, the Prevention of Food Adulteration Act, 1954, along with other legislative enactments, was the government's main weapon to fight food adulteration.

IMPORTANT LEGAL TERMS

It is important for hoteliers and restaurant operators to understand the latest licensing procedure, how the law defines food, food adulteration, food adulterants, impact of food poisoning, misbranding, and food additives.

What is Food?

Food has been legally defined for the first time in the Uttar Pradesh Pure Food Act, 1950 as follows:

TEXT

'Food' means any article of food or drink, other than drug, water, wine, liquor or excisable articles (Intoxicants) used for human consumption including:

(i) any substance which is ordinarily mixed in the preparation of food;
(ii) any flavouring matter or condiment;
(iii) and any colouring matter used or intended to be used:

Provided that, notwithstanding anything contained in this definition, the addition of any colouring or flavouring matter or condiment to an article used as food or drink shall be deemed to be the addition of substance of food.

Uttar Pradesh Pure Food Act, 1950 was subsequently repealed with the passing of the Prevention of Food Adulteration Act, 1954. The Prevention of Food Adulteration Act, 1954 improved upon the definition of 'food' as defined in the Uttar Pradesh Pure Food Act, 1950 by inserting Clause7(v)(c). The complete text of the clause is given as follows:

TEXT

7 (v) 'Food' means any article used as food or drink for human consumption other than drugs and water and includes,

(a) Any article, which ordinarily enters into, or is used in the composition or preparation of, human food,
(b) Any flavouring matter or condiments, and
(c) Any other article which the central government may, having regard to its use, nature, substance or quality declare, by notification in the official gazette, as food for the purposes of this Act.

These definitions were open to interpretation and in *State of Tamil Nadu vs R. Krishnamurthy A.I.R. 1980 S.C. 538*, the Supreme Court ruled that for any article to be termed as 'food', it was not essential that it be sold as food or used in the preparation or composition of food; it may not even be fit for human consumption or described or exhibited as intended for human consumption. It is enough if it is generally or commonly used for human consumption or in the preparation of human food.

Under the Food Safety and Standards Act, 2006,

TEXT

'Food' means any substance, whether processed, partially processed or unprocessed, which is intended for human consumption and includes primary food, genetically modified or engineered food or food containing such ingredients, infant food, packaged drinking water, alcoholic drink, chewing gum, and any substance, including water used into the food during its manufacture, preparation or treatment but does not include any animal feed, live animals unless they are prepared or processed for placing on the market for human consumption, plants prior to harvesting, drugs and medicinal products, cosmetics, narcotic or psychotropic substances.

The Prevention of Food Adulteration Act, 1954 defines 'primary food' as 'any article of food, being a produce of agriculture or horticulture in its natural form'. Food Safety and Standards Act, 2006 further elaborates on this definition under Clause 3(zk)—'"primary food" means an article of food, being a produce of agriculture or horticulture or animal husbandry and dairying or aquaculture in its natural form, resulting from the growing, raising, cultivation, picking, harvesting, collection or catching in the hands of a person other than a farmer or fisherman.' This definition was an important one as it drew a distinction between processed and partially processed foods and primary foods.

The concept behind genetically modified or engineered foods was to harness the knowledge gained in the field of biotechnology and its application to agriculture, so as to enhance agricultural yield and productivity to feed the growing population. Initially, in India, there was resistance towards growing genetically modified food grains, cotton, fruits, and vegetables as it was believed that genetically modified foods were injurious and harmful for health as opposed to organic foods. This was widely reported in the press. The only successfully grown genetically modified item in India has been Bt cotton. Some of the genetically modified food articles are brinjal (eggplant), rice, corn, soybean, sugarcane, tomatoes, potatoes, and beetroot, which are grown mostly in the US.

Imported fruits and vegetables are available in India, which may or may not be genetically modified; however, The Food Safety and Standards Act, 2006 takes cognizance of these worldwide developments and recognizes that India will have to legislate to make genetically modified foods acceptable even though currently the government's stand is ambivalent.

Interpretation of these definitions helps us define food as a substance or article of human consumption other than water or drugs that is of plant or animal origin; that may be grown organically, genetically modified or engineered; and that may be processed, partially processed, or unprocessed, containing ingredients, flavouring materials, or condiments used in the preparation of human food that provides nutrition to the body, stimulates growth, and maintains life.

What is an Adulterant and Adulterated Food?

For a better understanding, it is important to read the definition of 'adulterant' in the context of the meaning of 'adulterated food', 'unsafe food', 'contamination', and 'extraneous matter' as mentioned in the Acts.

Prevention of Food Adulteration Act, 1954—'1(i) "Adulterant" means any material which is or could be employed for the purpose of adulteration.'

Food Safety and Standards Act, 2006—'3(1)(a) Adulterant means any material which is or could be employed for making the food unsafe or sub-standard, misbranded or containing extraneous matter.'

Both the Acts define an adulterant. The definition under Food Safety and Standards Act, 2006 is wider in its reach, scope, and application, as it defines an adulterated food product as 'unsafe or sub-standard, misbranded, or containing extraneous matter'. In order to understand what an adulterant is, it is important to understand what food is unsafe or sub-standard, misbranded, or contains extraneous matter.

Whereas the Food Safety and Standards Act, 2006, Clause 3(zz) defines:

TEXT

'*unsafe food*' *as an article of food whose nature, substance, or quality is so affected as to render it injurious to health:*

(i) *by the article itself, or its package thereof, which is composed, whether wholly or in part, of poisonous or deleterious substances; or*

(ii) *by the article consisting, wholly or in part, of any filthy, putrid, rotten, decomposed or diseased animal substance or vegetable substance; or*

(iii) *by virtue of its unhygienic processing or the presence in that article of any harmful substance; or*

(iv) *by the substitution of any inferior or cheaper substance whether wholly or in part; or*

(v) *by addition of a substance directly or as an ingredient which is not permitted; or*

(vi) *by the abstraction, wholly or in part, of any of its constituents; or*

(vii) *by the article being so coloured, flavoured or coated, powdered or polished, as to damage or conceal the article or to make it appear better or of greater value than it really is; or*

(viii) *by the presence of any colouring matter or preservatives other than that specified in respect thereof; or*

(ix) *by the article having been infected or infested with worms, weevils or insects; or*

(x) *by virtue of its being prepared, packed or kept under insanitary conditions; or*

(xi) *by virtue of its being misbranded or sub-standard or food containing extraneous matter; or*

(xii) *by virtue of containing pesticides and other contaminants' in excess of quantities specified by regulations.*

Clause 3(g) states:

TEXT

'*contaminant*' *means any substance, whether or not added to food, but which is present in such food as a result of the production (including operations carried out in crop husbandry, animal husbandry, or veterinary medicine), manufacture, processing, preparation, treatment, packing, packaging, transport, or holding of such food or as a result of environmental contamination and does not include insect fragments, rodent hairs, and other extraneous matter.*

Clause 3(i) states:

TEXT

'*extraneous matter*' *means any matter contained in an article of food which may be carried from the raw materials, packaging materials or process systems used for its manufacture or which is added to it, but such matter does not render such article of food unsafe.*

Clause 3(zf) states:

TEXT

'*misbranded food*' *means an article of food:*

(A) *if it is purported, or is represented to be, or is being:*

    (i) *offered or promoted for sale with false, misleading or deceptive claims either;*

        (a) *upon the label of the package, or*

        (b) *through advertisement, or*

(ii) *sold by a name which belongs to another article of food; or*

(iii) *offered or promoted for sale under the name of a fictitious individual or company as the manufacturer or producer of the article as borne on the package or containing the article or the label on such package; or*

(B) *if the article is sold in packages which have been sealed or prepared by or at the instance of the manufacturer or producer bearing his name and address but:*

  (i) *the article is an imitation of, or is a substitute for, or resembles in a manner likely to deceive, another article of food under the name of which it is sold, and is not plainly and conspicuously labelled so as to indicate its true character; or*

  (ii) *the package containing the article or the label on the package bears any statement, design or device regarding the ingredients or the substances contained therein, which is false or misleading in any material particular, or if the package is otherwise deceptive with respect to its contents; or*

  (iii) *the article is offered for sale as the product of any place or country which is false; or*

(C) *if the article contained in the package—*

  (i) *contains any artificial flavouring, colouring or chemical preservative and the package is without a declaratory label stating that fact or is not labelled in accordance with the requirements of this Act or regulations made there under or is in contravention thereof; or*

  (ii) *is offered for sale for special dietary uses, unless its label bears such information as may be specified by regulation, concerning its vitamins, minerals or other dietary properties in order sufficiently to inform its purchaser as to its value for such use; or*

  (iii) *is not conspicuously or correctly stated on the outside thereof within the limits of variability laid down under this Act.*

The definition of a food article being misbranded is wide in its application and the best definition of misbranding has been given by the Federal Drug Authority of USA, which surmises the Indian definition: 'if the label, brand, tag or notice under which it is sold is false or misleading in any particular as to the kind, grade or quality or composition; or if it is sold as the product of one manufacturer when in reality it is the product of another manufacturer; or if on the label, brand, tag or notice under which it is sold, there is any false statement concerning the sanitary conditions under which it is manufactured'.

On reviewing these legal provisions, unsafe food or food that is injurious to health is one that is adulterated by any material or substance that is or can be used by substitution, addition, or abstraction to or from food, so that the natural composition and quality of the original food substance is affected, thereby making the food article unsafe and injurious to health.

What is Adulteration?

The Prevention of Food Adulteration Act, 1954 defines an article of food as 'adulterated' if it meets the following requirements:

Clause 2(ia):

(a) *If the article sold by vendor is not of the nature, substance or quality demanded by the purchaser.*

(b) *If the article contains any other substance which affects the substance or quality thereof.*

(c) *If any inferior or cheaper substance has been substituted wholly or in part for the article so as to affect the nature, substance or quality of the product.*

(d) *If any constituent of the article has been wholly or in part extracted to affect the quality thereof.*

(e) *If the article has been prepared, packed or kept under unsanitary conditions whereby it has become contaminated or injurious to health.*

(f) *If the article consists wholly or in part of any filthy, putrefied, rotten decomposed or diseased animal or vegetable substance or is insect-infested or is otherwise unfit for human consumption.*

(g) *If the article is obtained from a diseased animal.*

(h) *If the article contains any poisonous or other ingredient which renders it injurious to health.*

(i) *If the container of the article is composed, whether, wholly or in part of any poisonous or deleterious substance which renders sits contents injurious to health.*

(j) *If any colouring matter other than that prescribed in respect thereof is present in the article or if the amounts of the prescribed colouring matter which is present in the article are not within the prescribed limits.*

(k) *If the article contains any prohibited preservative or permitted preservative in excess of the prescribed limits.*

(l) *If the quality or purity of the Article falls below the prescribed limits of variability which renders it injurious to health.*

(m) *If the quality or purity of the article falls below the prescribed standard or its constituents are present in quantities not within the prescribed limits of variability which renders it injurious to health.*

Normally, adulteration refers to the mixing of substances of an inferior quality, which makes the food or beverage articles unsafe and injurious to health or affects the quality of the original food by altering its natural composition.

Adulteration can be of various types such as intentional, unintentional, or natural as illustrated in Fig. 9.3.

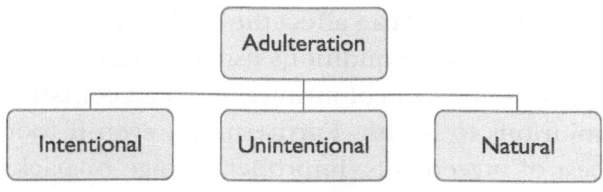

FIGURE 9.3 Types of Adulteration

Intentional adulteration

Intentional adulteration is the act of knowingly adding, removing, or altering the existing natural properties of food. Studies on food adulteration conducted by the Food Safety and Standards Authority of India reveal that food adulteration has been increasing since 2008. In 2008, 94,000 samples were examined of which over 8,300 were found to be adulterated (8.79%). In 2009, 1.13 lakh samples were examined of which 11.14% were found to be adulterated. In 2010, 1.17 lakh samples were examined of which over 14,000 samples (12.65%) were found to be adulterated.

The most commonly used adulterants are water to dilute milk; sand, small stones in pulses and food grains; used tea leaves or sawdust in tea; rancid oil in fresh oil; brick powder in red chilli powder; and sugar and water in honey. The use of these adulterants in food items can result in damage to the digestive system, paralysis, deficiency of vitamins A and E, and cancer, if taken over a prolonged period of time.

Unintentional adulteration

Unintentional adulteration is usually attributed to ignorance, carelessness, or lack of facilities for maintaining food quality. This kind of adulteration results from pesticide and insect residues or microorganisms entering the food right from the farm through various stages of the food chain reaching to the customer.

Natural adulteration

Natural adulteration occurs due to the presence of certain toxic chemicals and organic compounds naturally occurring in foods, which are injurious to health and are not added to the foods intentionally or unintentionally. These natural toxins protect these foods against bacteria, insects, strong sunlight, and so on. Some of the examples are toxic varieties of pulses, mushrooms, green and other vegetables, fish and other sea foods. About 5000 species of marine fish are known to be poisonous and many of these are among edible varieties.

The most commonly eaten potato contains a natural toxin, solanine, which is present in the potato peels and in the eyes of the potato. Herbal teas, which are mostly marketed as health foods that assist in weight loss or as stimulants, contain a natural toxin called Ma Huang. Seafood products such as oysters, clams, scallops, and prawns have natural toxins that they get from feeding on algae.

Besides adulterants that can affect the quality of the food, food preparation under unhygienic or unsanitary conditions using substandard or rotten putrid materials, prohibited preservatives, or colouring agents can contaminate the quality of the food making it injurious to health. Furthermore, even if food is prepared hygienically using the best of ingredients, improper storage or packing can result in the food article deteriorating, making it unfit for human consumption, which is commonly referred to as food poisoning.

What is Food Poisoning?

Hotels and restaurateurs are familiar with the term food poisoning, an unpleasant illness caused by eating contaminated foods. Figure 9.4 illustrates the various groups and types of food poisoning and their sub-categorization. Food poisoning can be categorized into two broad groups: infectious and toxic. Infectious food poisoning can be bacterial, viral, or caused by parasites, whereas toxic food poisoning can be natural or caused by pesticide residue in primary foods.

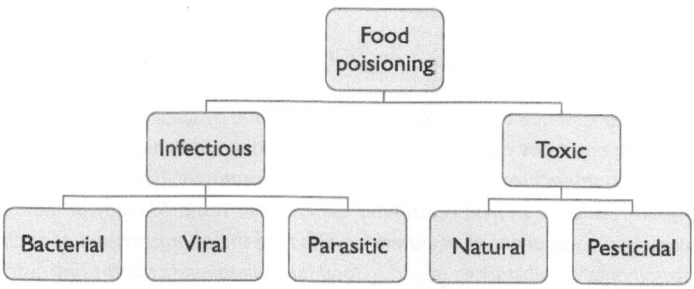

FIGURE 9.4 Groups and Types of Food Poisoning

Improper storage or storage of food items at wrong temperatures can result in contamination, which encourages bacteria, virus, or parasites to grow, and affects raw vegetables and fruits, moist food grains or pulses, baked breads and confectionary items causing amoebic dysentery, hepatitis, fever, and vomiting.

Bacterial food poisoning is the biggest cause of food-related infections—the most common being the Salmonella bacteria, which mostly occur in meat and meat products, raw vegetables, salads, shell-fish, eggs and egg products, and warmed-up leftovers, causing food infection resulting in high fever and burning sensation. Dairy products, baked foods, especially custard or cream-filled foods, meat and meat products, low-acid frozen foods, salads, and cream sauces are affected by the Staphylococcus bacterium, which causes vomiting, abdominal cramps, diarrhoea, severe thirst, and cold sweats.

Viral food poisoning is caused by viruses that invade any organism including the human body and multiply rapidly by feeding on the host cells of the human body. Food poisoning is caused by coming into contact with a person who is already infected, sharing food with an infected individual, and inadequate washing of the hands after contact with food or water contaminated by infected faeces. In extreme cases, this can cause cancer.

Food poisoning caused by parasites is rare. The main cause of transmission is through drinking untreated water or eating contaminated food. A parasite is a type of germ (or microbe), which lives on or within any living thing and is often found in the digestive systems of many animals, for example, pigs and cattle. These parasites are a type of tapeworm, which consumes blood or other nutrients within the small intestine, resulting in an inflammation within that area. The common symptoms are mild diarrhoea, bloating, weight loss, abdominal cramps, tiredness, flu, and blood in the faeces.

A toxin is defined as 'a poisonous substance produced by a living organism' although it can also include 'man-made' substances, Toxic food poisoning is caused by highly potent toxins that are found within food and, once eaten, attack the body overwhelming the immune system. The presence of natural toxin results in natural food adulteration, whereas the presence of pesticide residue in foods that is sprayed over crops in the fields results in unintentional food adulteration.

This type of food poisoning affects the entire body, the symptoms of which include dizziness, rapid heartbeat, and skin rash. If illness is caused by toxins, then it is usually due to inadequate food preparation methods.

What are Food Additives?

The Food Safety and Standards Act, 2006, Clause 3(k) defines:

'Food additive' as any substance not normally consumed as food by itself or used as a typical ingredient of the food, whether or not it has nutritive value, the intentional addition of which to food for a technological purpose in the manufacture, processing, preparation, treatment, packing, packaging, transport or holding of such food results, or maybe reasonably expected to result (directly or indirectly), in it or its by-products becoming a component of or otherwise effecting the characteristics of such food but does not include 'Contaminants' or substances added to food for maintaining or improving nutritional qualities.

Food additives are generally used by the food industry to preserve the freshness of foods by slowing down spoilage caused by exposure to air, bacteria fungus, and so on and to improve or maintain nutritional value, taste, texture, flavour, colour, and appearance without affecting the characteristics of food.

Types of Food Additives

The Prevention of Food Adulteration Rules, 1955, Appendix 'C' gives an exhaustive list of food additives arranged according to their International Numbering System, which are classified as follows:

(i) According to the function that they perform during the processing, preparation, treatment, and packaging stages when added to food, for example, anti-caking agents, acidity regulators, and so on:

Acids   Food acids are added to make flavours 'sharper'; they also act as preservatives and antioxidants. Common food acids include vinegar, citric acid, tartaric acid, malic acid, fumaric acid, and lactic acid.

Acidity regulators   These are used to modify the acidity and alkalinity of foods.

Anti-caking agents   These are used to keep powders such as milk powder from caking or sticking.

Antifoaming agents   These are used to reduce or prevent foaming in foods.

Antioxidants   Antioxidants such as vitamin C act as preservatives by inhibiting the effects of oxygen on food; they are also beneficial for health.

Bulking agents   Bulking agents such as starch are added to increase the bulk of a food without affecting its nutritional value.

Food colouring   These are added to food to replace colours lost during preparation or to make food look more attractive.

Colour retention agents   In contrast to colourings, colour retention agents are used to preserve a food's existing colour.

Emulsifiers These allow water and oils to remain mixed together in an emulsion, as in mayonnaise, ice cream, and homogenized milk.

Flavour enhancers These enhance a food's existing flavours or give food a particular taste or smell. These may be extracted from natural sources (through distillation, solvent extraction, maceration, among other methods) or created artificially.

Flour treatment agents These are added to flour to improve its colour or its use in baking.

Glazing agents These provide a shiny appearance or protective coating to foods.

Humectants These prevent foods from drying out.

Tracer gas This allows for package integrity by preventing foods from being exposed to atmosphere, thus guaranteeing shelf life.

Stabilizers Stabilizers, thickeners, and gelling agents, such as agar or pectin (used in jam, for example) give foods a firmer texture by stabilizing emulsions.

Sweeteners These are added to foods for flavouring. Sweeteners other than sugar are added to keep the food energy (calories) low.

Thickeners These are substances that, when added to a mixture, increase its viscosity without substantially modifying other properties.

(ii) According to the quantity of food additives that can be added during the various stages of preparation depending on the type of food being prepared, for example, bread, biscuits, chocolate, confectionery, cocoa, edible oils, milk products, fruits and vegetables, and fish and fish products.

The basic differences between preservatives and food additives are illustrated in Table 9.1.

TABLE 9.1 Differences Between Food Additives and Food Preservatives

Food additives	Food preservatives
These are added to retain nutritional values, taste, texture, flavour, colour, and appearance of food.	These are added to increase the shelf life of processed food items by slowing down or stopping the natural process of decomposition.
These are an integral part of food processing.	These are not an integral part of the food processing.
These are mentioned as part of the ingredients on the food label.	These are mentioned separately on food labels printed on packaged foods.

What are Food Preservatives?

According to Rule 52 of Prevention of Food Adulteration Rules, 1955, 'Food Preservative is a substance which when added to food, is capable of inhibiting, retarding or arresting the process of fermentation, acidification or other decomposition of food'. These preservatives are further classified as Class I and Class II.

Class I preservatives are common salt, sugar, dextrose, spices, vinegar, honey, glucose syrup, and edible oils, and their use is not restricted by the Act.

Class II preservatives are listed under Rule 53 of Prevention of Food Adulteration Rules, 1955, which states 'benzoic acid including salts thereof, sulphurous acid including salts thereof, nitrates of sodium and potassium, in respect of foods likes jams, pickled meat; sorbic acid including sodium, potassium and calcium salts, etc.'. However, their use is restricted as use of these preservative beyond its permitted limit as mentioned in the Act results in the decomposition of the food item.

Defining Food Quality and Standards

Appendix 'B' of Prevention of Food Adulteration Rules, 1955 forms a part of the Food Safety and Standards Rules, 2011, which defines the standards of quality of various articles of food items that are commercially marketed and classified as shown in Table 9.2.

TABLE 9.2 Categories of Food Items

Category	Food items
Beverages—non-alcoholic	Carbonated water
Baking powder	Consists of sodium bicarbonate or a combination capable of yielding carbon dioxide while baking
Starchy foods	Arrowroot
Asafoetida (*Hing*)	Asafoetida (*Hing*)
Spices and condiments	Caraway, caraway black, cardamom (*chhoti elachi*) cardamom amomum (*badi elaichi*) chillies, cinnamon (*dalchini*) cloves (*laung*), coriander (*dhania*), cumin *safed zeera*), cumin black (*kalonji*) fennel (*saunf*), fenugreek (*methi*), ginger (*sonth, adrakh*), mace (*jaepatri*), mustard (*rai, sarson*), nutmeg (*jaiphal*), pepper black (*kalimirch*), poppy (*khas-khas*), saffron (*kesar*), turmeric (*haldi*), curry powder, mixed masala, bishop's weed (*ajowan*), and dried mango powder (*amchur*)
Beans	Dry kidney-shaped or flattened seeds of the leguminous varieties used as food
Sweetening agents	Plantation white sugar, *Misri* refined sugar, *Khandsari* sugar (Sulphur), *Bura* sugar, honey, *Gur* or jaggery, cube sugar, dextrose, glucose, golden syrup, icing sugar, aspartame, saccharin
Coffee	*Coffea liberica*, *Coffea excelsa*, and *Coffea robusta*

(Contd)

TABLE 9.2 (Contd)

Category	Food items
Edible fats	Suet, lard, cocoa butter, refined salseed fat, *Kokum* fat, *Dhupa* fat, *Phulwara* fat
Milk and milk products	Milk, pasteurized milk, sterilized milk, flavoured milk, mixed milk, standardized milk, toned milk, double-toned milk, skimmed milk, full-cream milk Milk products such as cream, *malai*, skimmed milk, curd, *chhenna*, cheese, processed cheese, ice-cream, milk ices, condensed milk, sweetened and unsweetened milk powder, partly skimmed milk powder, *khoya*, infant milk food, table butter, and white butter
Table margarine	Emulsion of edible oils and fats with water
Bakery and industrial margarine	Emulsion of edible oils and fats with water
Tea	Tea, *Kangra* tea
Edible common salt	Sodium chloride (NaCl), iodized salt, rock salt which is crystalline solid, white or pale, pink or light grey in colour
Fruit products	Fruit juice, tomato juice, fruit syrup, fruit squash, fruit beverage or fruit drink, fruit jelly, tomato sauce, tomato ketchup, tomato relish, jam, marmalade, fruit chutney, tomato puree, tomato paste
Edible oils	Coconut oil, groundnut oil, cotton seed oil, linseed oil, *mahua* oil, rapeseed oil, olive oil, poppy oil, sunflower oil, soybean oil, maize oil, sesame or *til* oil, refined vegetable oil, palm oil, blended edible vegetable oil
Cereals	Wheat *atta*, fortified wheat *atta*, wheat flour (maida), semolina (*suji* or *rawa*), besan, pearl barley or barley (*jou*), maize *atta*, jowar and bajra, rice, *urad, masoor, moong, channa, arhar dal*
Bakery shortening	Hydrogenated refined edible vegetable oil
Brewed vinegar	Liquid derived from alcoholic and acetous fermentation of any suitable medium, such as fruits, malt, molasses, sugarcane juice, synthetic vinegar
Gelatine	Purified product obtained by partial hydrolysis of collagen, derived from the skin, white connective tissues, and bones of animals
Sweets and confectionery	Sugar boiled confectionery, lozenges, chewing gum and bubble gum, chocolate, milk chocolates, milk covering chocolate, plain, blended chocolate, white chocolate, filled chocolate
Food colours	Chlorophyll, caramel, riboflavin, Ponceau 4R, carnitosine

(Contd)

TABLE 9.2 (Contd)

Category	Food items
Silver leaf	*Chandi ka warq* shall contain not less than 99.9% of silver
Dry fruits and nuts	Chestnuts, almonds, cashew nuts, walnuts, hazelnuts, peanuts, macadamia nuts, pistachio, prunes, raisins, cherries, figs, dates, sultanas, currents
Beverages—alcoholic	Toddy
Pan masala	Food generally taken with pan
Fat spread	Water in oil emulsion
Mineral water	Natural or fortified mineral water

Besides standards that are codified by the Food Safety and Standards Act, 2006, there are two other accreditation agencies in India which voluntarily require that processing, preparation, treatment, packing, and packaging of processed foods and agricultural produce should be certified. These two agencies are the Bureau of Indian Standards (BIS), earlier known as the Indian Standards Institute (ISI), and Directorate of Marketing and Inspection (DMI) under the Agricultural Produce (Grading & Marking) Act, 1937 (AGMARK). Both ISI or BIS and AGMARK are well-accepted certifications that are awarded to manufacturers who have met high standards of food processing that are internationally recognized.

Bureau of Indian Standards or Indian Standards Institute   Bureau of Indian Standards is an organization that was formed under The Bureau of Indian Standards Act, 1986.

The organization's responsibility is to set the standards for the Indian food processing industry. These standards cover the hygienic conditions under which products are manufactured, packaged, and labelled including raw materials that are permitted and their quality parameters. Packaged food manufacturers that fulfil the standards laid down by the BIS can voluntarily apply for certification to the Bureau to obtain the 'ISI' mark, which can then be displayed on their products packaging. If a manufacturer has a variety of food products then each one shall require individual certification. Compulsory certification is required under the Bureau of Indian Standards Act, 1986 for the following products: food colours/additives, vegetable oils (*vanaspati*), and containers for packing, milk powder and condensed milk, and packaged drinking water.

The Bureau encourages manufacturers of food products to apply for certification through awareness campaigns highlighting the benefits of certification and relies on third-party accreditation agencies to do the evaluation process before awarding the ISI mark.

Directorate of Marketing and Inspection   Directorate of Marketing and Inspection enforces the AGMARK through its network of five regional offices and 22 laboratories located across India.

The Act specifies the compulsory grading and standardization of agricultural and agricultural commodities, which are prone to adulteration such as butter, ghee, vegetable oils, ground-spices, honey, wheat flour (*atta*), blended edible vegetable oils, and fat spread.

Manufacturers can apply for grading voluntarily and those who meet the standards laid down by the DMI are allowed to use 'Agmark' labels on their products.

FOOD SAFETY AND STANDARDS ACT, 2006

The Parliament of India passed the Food Safety and Standards Act in 2006, which became operational on 5 August 2011. The Act builds upon the existing Prevention of Food Adulteration Act, 1954 and the Prevention of Food Adulteration Rules, 1955 and consolidates the various enactments governing food adulteration. The Food Safety and Standards Act, 2006, along with the Food Safety and Standards Regulations, 2011, provide the legislative framework for the implementation of the law.

The main objectives of the Act are as follows:

(i) To introduce a single statute relating to food
(ii) To provide for scientific development of the food processing industry

The Food Safety and Standards Regulations, 2011 are divided into seven sections covering various aspects of the food operator's business:

(i) Food Safety and Standards (Licensing and Registration of Food businesses) Regulations, 2011
(ii) Food Safety and Standards (Packaging and Labelling) Regulations, 2011
(iii) Food Safety and Standards (Food Products Standards and Food Additives) Regulations, 2011
(iv) Food Safety and Standards (Food Product Standards and Food Additives Part II) Regulations, 2011
(v) Food Safety and Standards (Prohibition and Restriction on Sales) Regulations, 2011
(vi) Food Safety and Standards (Contaminants, Toxins and Residues) Regulations, 2011
(vii) Food Safety and Standards (Laboratory and Sample Analysis) Regulations, 2011

The salient features of the Food Safety and Standards Act, 2006 are as follows:

(i) It consolidated the following legislative enactments being administered by various Ministries by integrating them into the new Food Safety and Standards Act, 2006:
   (a) Prevention of Food Adulteration Act, 1954 (Ministry of Health and Family Welfare)
   (b) Food Products Order, 1955 (Ministry of Food Processing Industries)
   (c) Meat Foods Product Order, 1973 (Ministry of Food Processing Industries)

    (d) Vegetable Oil Products (Control) Order, 1947 (Ministry of Consumer Affairs, Food, and Public Distribution)

    (e) Edible Oils Packaging (Regulation) Order, 1998 (Ministry of Consumer Affairs, Food, and Public Distribution)

    (f) Solvent Extracted Oil, De-Oiled, Meal and Edible Flour (Control) Order, 1967 (Ministry of Consumer Affairs, Food, and Public Distribution)

    (g) The Milk and Milk Products Order, 1992 (Ministry of Agriculture)

    (h) Essential Commodities Act and Orders, 1955 (Inter Ministerial Group)

    (i) The Standards & Weights and Measures Act, 1976 (Ministry of Consumer Affairs, Food, and Public Distribution)

    (j) Standards of Weights & Measures (Packaged Commodities) Rules, 1977 (Ministry of Consumer Affairs, Food, and Public Distribution)

    (k) Livestock Importation Act, 1898 (Ministry of Agriculture)

    (l) Plant Quarantine (Regulation of Import into India) Order, 2003 (Ministry of Agriculture)

    (m) The Infant Milk Substitutes, Feeding Bottles and Infant Foods (Regulation of Production, Supply and Distribution) Act, 1992 (Ministry of Women and Child development)

(ii) It creates a statutory body with a unified command structure called the Food Safety and Standards Authority of India (FSSAI).

The FSSAI Board consists of 22 board members headed by the Chairman; the Chief Executive Officer (CEO) reporting to the Board is the administrative head responsible for the implementation of the Act. FSSAI has been created as a body corporate to enable the FSSAI Board to function without any pressures from the central or state governments.

(iii) The Act defines the duties and functions of the FSSAI in Chapter 2, Section 16 Clause (1):

TEXT

It shall be the duty of the Food Authority to regulate and monitor the manufacture, processing, distribution, sale and import of food so as to ensure safe and wholesome food.

The Act vests wide ranging powers to the FSSAI:

(a) Defining food standards

(b) Providing guidelines for the setting up of food accreditation bodies, laboratories

(c) Licensing of food business operators (FBOs)

(d) Setting standards of hygiene and sanitation for the food processing and packaging business

(iv) The Act envisages a scientific approach for the establishing of food standards by instituting a scientific committee with various scientific panels to look into the different aspects of the food industry.

Earlier, food standards were being challenged in the courts time and again on the grounds that the standards and quality parameters were established in an arbitrary and unscientific manner. To address this lacuna in the implementation of the Act, scientific panels would deliberate and recommend standards pertaining to various articles of food.

The classic case is of '*haldi powder*' where in two different cases the judges passed differing judgements.

The dried bulbous roots of turmeric rhizome (*haldi*) can be grounded into powder form and it is then very difficult to ascertain whether it is for external use or for human consumption. In two different cases, samples of the bulbous roots of turmeric rhizome were taken. In the first case *Public Prosecutor vs Satyanarayana A.I.R. 1958 A.P.681; 1958 Cr L.J. pp 1375*, the accused had contended that it was for external use and was able to produce a bill proving that he had purchased the same for this purpose and was acquitted.

However, in the case of *State vs T.R.M. Subramanium, 1976 Cr L.J. 1982 pp 1983*, the High Court held that ground turmeric obtained by grinding the bulbous roots of turmeric rhizome was for human consumption and hence adulterated as per the Prevention of Food Adulteration Act, 1954.

This definition of what constitutes adulteration was laid to rest in *Sohan Singh vs State of UP, 2000 Cr L.J. 3929 pp 3936* wherein the Court adjudged that a sample is adulterated if it does not meet the prescribed standard.

Food Safety and Standards Act of India 2006 addresses these concerns by attempting to define the food standards that are internationally accepted whilst preparing the 'Codex India', and in this respect, it relies on the internationally accepted Codex Alimentarius Commission's recommendations. Codex India once prepared will become the bible for all FBOs, setting standards for food processing, packaging and labelling, food product standards and defining food additives, adulterants and preservatives.

The Codex Alimentarius Commission was created in 1963 by the Food and Agriculture Organization (FAO) and the World Health Organization (WHO) of the United Nations, to develop food standards, guidelines, and related texts such as codes of practice under the Joint FAO/WHO Food Standards Programme. The main purpose of this programme is to protect the health of consumers, ensure fair practices in the food trade, and promote coordination of all food standards work undertaken by international governmental and non-governmental organizations.

(v) Implementation is through the state food safety commissioners.

Under the Prevention of Food Adulteration Act, 1954, implementation was left to the food inspectors and the public analyst who would initiate the process and for its effective enforcement had to rely on the local administrative machinery headed by the subdivisional magistrates and district magistrates. Figure 9.5 outlines the hierarchy of the implementation machinery at the state level, which is through the designated officer posted in each district with his or her team consisting of the food safety officer who coordinates with the food analyst for the food analysis reports.

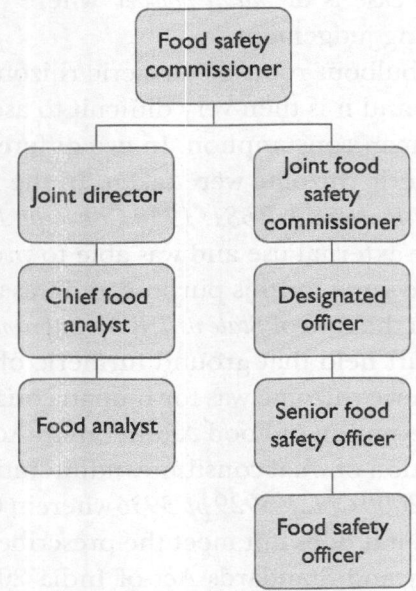

FIGURE 9.5 Implementation Machinery at the State Level

(vi) Chapter IX defines the various offences and provides for penalties by way of fines, punishment by way of imprisonment, and compensation in case of injury or death.

Earlier offences under the Prevention of Food Adulteration Act, 1954 were processed under the Indian Penal Code (IPC) Sections 272 and 273:

Section 272. 'Adulteration of food or drink intended for sale... shall be punished with imprisonment of either description for a term which may extend to six months, or with fine which may extend to one thousand rupees, or with both.'

Section 273. 'Sale of noxious food or drink... shall be punished with imprisonment of either description for a term which may extend to six months, or with fine which may extend to one thousand rupees, or with both.'

A few states such as Uttar Pradesh exercising their legislative powers under the Indian Constitution have enhanced the maximum punishment to life imprisonment plus a fine by amending the appropriate sections of the IPC applicable to food adulteration.

Food Safety and Standards Act, 2006 is an improvement upon the Prevention of Food Adulteration Act, 1954 as it provides for a graded penalty structure where the punishment depends on the severity of the violation. Offences related to manufacturing, selling, storing, or importing sub-standard or misbranded food could incur a fine. In case of grievous injury or death, the punishment consists of both a fine and imprisonment.

Moreover, it provides for the first time an opportunity for the aggrieved person to seek compensation in the event of injury or death. In the event of death the minimum compensation will be ₹5,00,000, for a grievous injury it will be ₹3,00,000, and for all other cases of injury, it will be ₹1,00,000. Prior to the Food Safety and Standards Act, 2006, an aggrieved person could only make a claim under the Consumer Protection Act, 1986. Under the Consumer Protection Act, 1986, depending upon the quantum of the claim, the person can file his or her complaint with the district consumer forum for a complaint up to value of ₹5,00,000, the state commission for a complaint up to value of ₹20,00,000, and the national commission is the final authority and can entertain complaints above the value of ₹20,00,000.

(vii) The Act prohibits advertisements that are misleading, deceiving, or falsely describing an article of food, even if the labelling of the article of food is accurate; such advertisements shall attract a fine.

'Misleading advertising' is defined as any advertisement that falsely describes any food article, gives an inaccurate statement on the nature, substance, and quality, or falsely guarantees any beneficial aspects of the food article being sold through audio or visual publicity, print, electronic media, internet, or website, including any notice, circular, label, wrapper, invoice, or other document.

This is of concern to hoteliers and restaurateurs, as it makes it mandatory for them to give accurate description of dishes that are listed in the menu card and the presentation of the dish should be an authentic representation of the dish as described. A basic requirement is putting a green dot for vegetarian dishes and a red dot for non-vegetarian dishes listed in the menu.

(viii) The Act lays emphasis on food safety and hygiene and mandates that food articles that are being sold by the FBO be produced using materials that meet all the quality parameters during the production, distribution, and sale of that food article.

The Act envisages that FBO shall implement good hygiene practices (GHP), which involve identifying the essential principles of food hygiene applicable throughout the food chain.

(ix) Developing an effective Food Safety Management System is a requirement under the Act, the FBO will have to evolve GHP by identifying areas of concern and then taking remedial steps to rectify the problems, setting up a monitoring procedure to ensure production of safe foods for human consumption. It is suggested that FBOs follow the well-established Hazard Analysis and Critical Control Points (HACCP) system while developing their GHPs.

HACCP is the best system currently available to reduce and prevent food-borne illness and is fully supported by the food service industry. HACCP was first developed and used by the Pillsbury Company in the late 1950s to provide safe food for America's space programme.

(x) The Food Safety and Standards Act, 2006 makes it compulsory for all FBOs to register their business and to obtain licences.

Under the Prevention of Food Adulteration Act, 1954, registration and licensing of the food business was carried out under the various state laws. An FBO desirous of opening a chain of restaurants across India would have to fulfil the different registration and licensing requirements as spelt out by the respective states. The Food Safety and Standards Act, 2006 attempts to address this issue by creating a uniform application for registration or licensing of a food business. The Act provides for the migration from the existing food licensing procedures to the new scheme over a period of one year.

Table 9.3 gives a comparison between the Prevention of Food Adulteration Act, 1954 and the Food Safety and Standards Act, 2006.

TABLE 9.3   Comparison between the Prevention of Food Adulteration Act, 1954 and the Food Safety and Standards Act, 2006

Prevention of Food Adulteration Act, 1954	Food Standards and Safety Act, 2006
The state is responsible for the health and well-being of the citizens.	The state is responsible for the health and well-being of the citizens.
It consists of various pieces of legislations along with the Act.	It consists of a single law incorporating all the previous pieces of legislation.
Multiple ministries responsible for its implementation.	It has a unified command structure for implementation called the FSSAI, under the Ministry of Health & Family Welfare.
It has an arbitrary and unscientific approach towards food standards.	It has a scientific approach for establishing food standards.
Prosecution could be done under IPC.	It has established a judicial redressal system.
There is no provision for compensation for injury or death.	There is provision for compensation for injury and death.
There is lack of public awareness on the harmful effects of food adulteration.	The government is to spend on creating awareness on the harmful effects of food adulteration by advertisements in newspapers, TV campaigns, and other publicity materials such as brochures and pamphlets.
There is a paucity of trained food inspectors and public analysts to implement the laws.	The government is to address the paucity of trained food inspectors and public analysts to implement the laws through recruitment and training.
Registration and licensing of FBOs to be done as per laws prevailing in the various states.	Uniform registration and licensing policy is advocated across the country.

Who is a Food Business Operator?

Clauses 3(n) and (o) define a food business and FBO—'a food business operator is a person or organization that is involved in running a food business whether for profit or loss and is responsibly carrying out the activities related to any stage of manufacture, processing, packaging, storage, transportation, distribution of food, import of food including food services, catering services, sale of food or food ingredients. He is required to operate his business after registering his business and/or obtaining the required licence.'

Licensing

Hotels as a general practice entrust the responsibility of securing eating house, restaurant, and FBO licences to their Food and Beverage Controllers. The chefs or the food and beverage managers are normally nominated as individuals responsible for the day-to-day operations of the facilities as required.

Under the Prevention of Food Adulteration Act, 1954, application for running a restaurant or eating house vested with the state governments, which required registration to be done with multiple government agencies:

 (i)   Trade Health Licence authorities
 (ii) Police department
 (iii) Fire department
 (iv) Excise authorities
 (v)   Municipal Corporation for registration under the Shops and Establishment Act

The other requirements under the Prevention of Food Adulteration Act, 1954 were as follows:

Nomination   The owners or the company is required to file a nomination under Section 17(2) and Rule 12-B of the Prevention of Food Adulteration Act Rules, 1955 with the local health authorities nominating the manager or supervisor responsible for the day-to-day operations of the facility. The purpose of the nomination is to hold accountable an individual in the event of any offences that may happen during the operations of the facility.

Signage   Hoteliers are required to display a notice indicating the medium of oil that is used for cooking the various items, whether it is edible oil, ghee, or vegetable oils (*vanaspati*) (Section 50(7)); for example, 'Only vegetable oil used for cooking'. Normally, such signages are prominently displayed in the kitchens.

Another such signage is 'Milk not for sale'. The licence granted to a hotelier or a restaurateur prohibits them from selling milk directly to guests, but allows them to offer milk-based products such as cold coffee, ice creams, tea or coffee with milk, and Indian sweets made from milk derivatives such as *rasgullas and burfis*.

Supervision of the operations Where a restaurant has more than 20 employees working full time during a calendar year, it is mandatory for the operations to be supervised by a manager who is a catering college diploma holder vide Rule 50 Clause 16(b).

(a) No employee can be hired who is suffering from infectious or, contagious disease per Rule 50 Clause 9.
(b) Food or beverage items being offered to guests will be prominently displayed on a notice board. This aspect of the law is addressed by printing menu cards, which give a list of items available along with the prices per Rule 50 Clause (15).
(c) There will be a clear demarcation between food production and service areas as well as public facilities for ladies and gents per Rule 50 Clause (10).

Licensing process

Figure 9.6 illustrates the licensing process that is required to be followed by an FBO under the Food Safety and Standards Act, 2006.

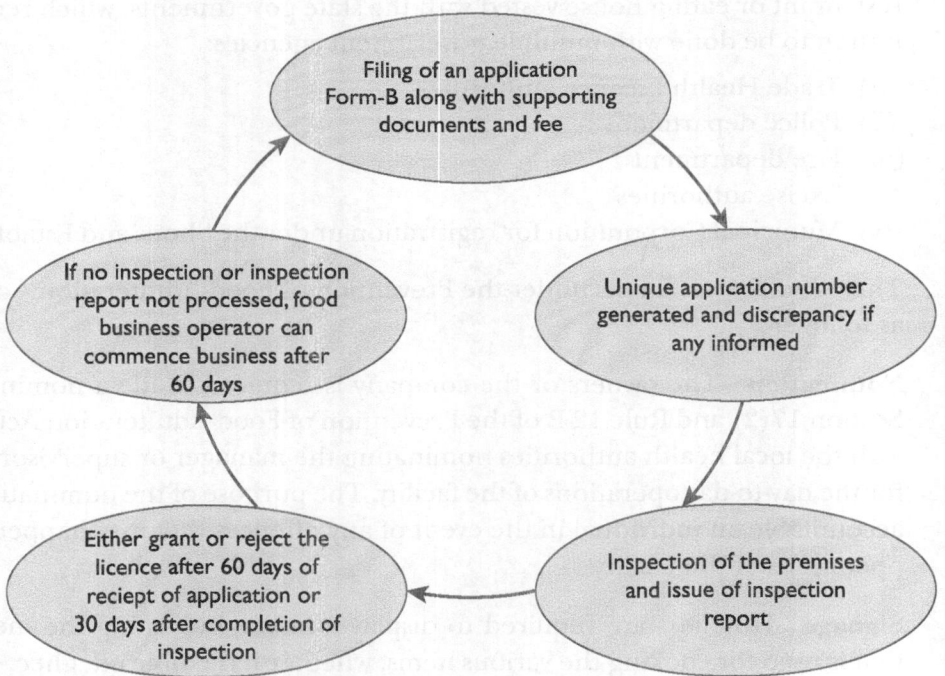

FIGURE 9.6 The Licensing Process

For three- to five-star hotels, restaurants in hotels, and standalone restaurants, applications in duplicate under 'Form B' have to be submitted to the state FSSAI for a licence as opposed to registration under the previous law. However, for retail food chains such as McDonalds and KFC, applications will have to be moved to the Central

Licensing Authority of the FSSAI in 'Form A'. The documentations that need to be attached to the application, however, remain the same as earlier:

(i) Partnership deed/affidavit/memorandum and articles of association of the firm

(ii) List of directors with full address and contact details of the firm

(iii) List of proprietor/partner/director(s)/authorized signatory with full address and contact details with their photo identification and address proof issued by the government

(iv) Proof of possession of premises (sale deed/rent agreement/electricity bill, etc.)

(v) Blueprint/layout plan of the restaurant showing the dimensions in metres/square metres and operation-wise area allocation

(vi) No objection certificates from the municipality or local body, state pollution control board, fire department, and health department

(vii) Nomination form of the person responsible along with alternative responsible person indicating the powers vested with them, for example, assisting the officers in inspections, collection of samples, packing, and dispatch

(viii) List of equipment and machinery along with the number, installed capacity, and horse powers used

(ix) Water analysis report (chemical and bacteriological) including pesticide residue of water to be used as ingredient in food from a recognized/public health laboratory to confirm the potability

(x) Food safety management system plan or certificate, if any, from accredited agencies

(xi) Fee payable by hoteliers—₹5000 per annum; for restaurants—₹2000 per annum

The state food commissioner is responsible for issuing the FBO licence as against registering the business in a time bound manner within 60 days upon receipt of the application. Nomination of the manager/supervisor, signage, and guidelines for general supervision of the facility remain unchanged as mentioned in the Prevention of Food Adulteration Act, 1954. Other requirements of the licence that have to be met are given as follows:

(i) A food safety management plan has to be developed for the operations of the restaurant based on guidelines spelt out in Schedule 4 Parts II & V of the Food Safety and Standards Rules 2011 From an implementation point of view, hoteliers and restaurateurs should face no difficulties as they already have standard operating procedures (SOPs) in place covering most of the guidelines.

(ii) In the event of the food article or facility not meeting the standards laid down by the Act, the licensing authority will send an improvement notice giving the

FBO time to rectify the mistake. In case the FBO fails to comply within the time limit, the licence will be cancelled.

(iii) In case an FBO feels that the food article is not in compliance with the Act, he or she shall initiate procedures for the recall of the food item from the market and will inform the FSSAI accordingly.

Administration of the Food Safety & Standards Act, 2006

The FSSAI has a three-tier administrative structure for the implementation of the Act as illustrated in Fig. 9.7.

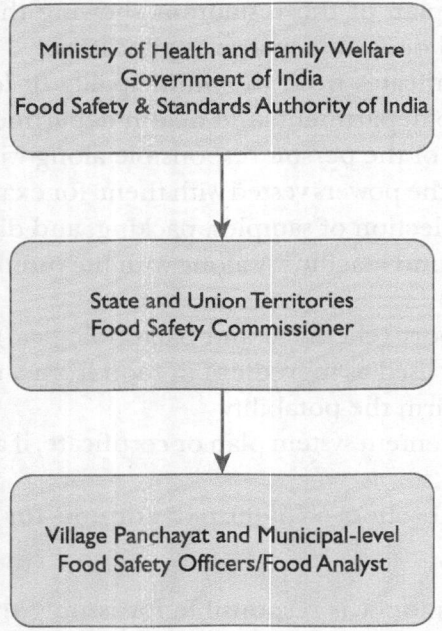

FIGURE 9.7 Administrative Structure of the FSSAI

The FSSAI, consisting of 22 members and a CEO, has a pivotal role as it is responsible for coordinating the following activities at the centre:

(i) Constituting the Central Advisory Committee responsible for advising the FSSAI on issues that need to be prioritized and creation of a knowledge pool

(ii) Constituting the statutory scientific panels and scientific committees and coordinating their activities

(iii) Setting up of a scientific division, which will build upon the existing infrastructure of the central and state laboratories and food testing laboratories and monitoring their activities

(iv) Setting up surveillance, regulatory, and quality assurance divisions

(v) Monitoring the activities of the Codex cell to handle international matters with the Codex Alimentarius Commission

(vi) Setting safety standards for the import of food items
(vii) Granting of approvals for functional foods, dietary products, novel foods, nutraceuticals, and genetically modified foods
(viii) Fixing standards and guidelines for food
(ix) Determining the labelling and advertising norms

At the state level, the state food safety commissioner is responsible for the following:

(i) Appointing the designated officer for each district with the food safety officers and the food analysts reporting to the designated officer
(ii) Ensuring the uniform and efficient implementation of the Act
(iii) Sanctioning the prosecution for offences punishable with imprisonment under the Act
(iv) Conducting and organizing training programmes for the officers

The food safety officer and the food analyst are required to implement the Act while reporting to the designated officer of the district (Fig. 9.8).

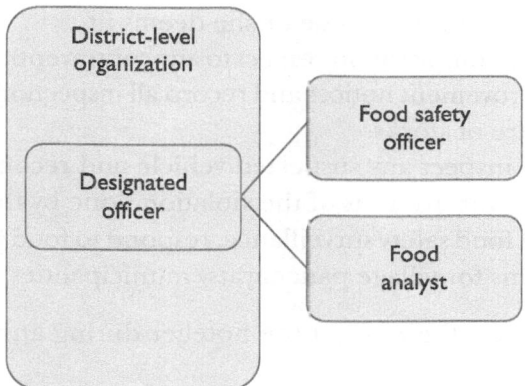

FIGURE 9.8 District-level Organization

Role of Food Safety Officers

Under the Prevention of Food Adulteration Act, 1954, the implementing officer was designated Food Inspector—a title that suggested that he or she was more of a policeman concerned with the violations of the law with scant regard for the safety and health of the public. The new legislation re-designates him or her as a food safety offer, implying thereby that he or she has a more onerous responsibility for looking after the health of the public besides his or her regular policing functions. An additional feature is that the officer can issue an improvement notice to the FBO in case he or she finds something amiss, which is a positive step to ensure compliance by the FBO. It is only in extreme cases that the food safety officer would recommend to the designated officer that the licence be withdrawn if the FBO fails to correct himself or herself after an improvement notice was served upon him or her.

His or her functions in brief are as follows:

(i) Maintain a database of FBOs in the area assigned.

(ii) Frequently inspect FBOs to ensure that they are conducting their business as per the licence granted to them.

(iii) Whilst conducting an inspection of a premise the food safety officer shall be invested with the powers relating to search or inspection by a police officer executing a search warrant issued under the Code of Criminal Procedure, 1973.

(iv) Enter and inspect any place where food articles are stored for sale or for manufacture or exhibited for sale and where any adulterant is manufactured or stored and take samples for analysis. If the article is of perishable nature and the food safety officer feels that it is unfit for human consumption, he can, after giving notice in writing to the FBO, destroy the same.

(v) If the food safety officer desires to take a food sample or other substances intended for human consumption for analysis, he or she is required to give a notice to the FBO of his or her intention. The officer may require the FBO to execute a bond for a sum of money equal to the value of the article seized with one or more sureties as he or she deems fit.

(vi) Investigate complaints in respect to any contravention of the provisions of the Act.

(vii) Issue improvement notices and record all inspections including taking of samples and seizure of stocks.

(viii) Stop and inspect any suspected vehicle and recommend to designated officer giving specific grounds of the violation done by the licensee.

(ix) Carry out food safety surveillance, respond to food poisoning, and facilitate food safety plans for village panchayats/municipalities.

The following are the roles of the hotelier during an inspection and in the subsequent processes:

(i) Extend the maximum cooperation to the food safety officer. If the hotelier fails to cooperate the food safety officer can still take a sample (*Sukhdeo Krishna Kadam vs State of Maharashtra 1979 F.A.J pp 110–114*).

(ii) The food safety officer is permitted to takes samples of any item that is available for sale (*Ram Lal vs State of Rajasthan A.I.R. 2001 S.C.47 pp 48–49*).

(iii) The food safety officer is permitted to takes samples of any food item that is in transit and is being delivered to a purchaser or from a consignee after an article has been delivered to him or her.

(iv) The food safety officer should take the sample in the presence of witnesses and properly seal it. However, if a witness is not forthcoming the sample can still be taken (*Babulal Hargovindass vs State of Gujarat 1980 F.A.J. 40*).

(v) The food safety officer shall make four parts of the sample taken—after sealing each sample, he or she shall send one sample to the food analyst, two samples to the designated officer, and the fourth to the hotelier for independent analysis.

(vi) A portion of the sample taken for analysis is made available to the hotelier after it has been sealed by the food safety officer to enable the hotelier to get the sample analysed independently from accredited laboratories under intimation to the designated officer (Section 47(1)c(iii) of Food Safety and Standards Act, 2006).

(vii) A hotelier has to obtain a receipt from the food safety officer for the sample being taken by him, its cost being calculated at the price that it is normally sold to the public (Section 38(3)).

(viii) The food safety officer is required to send the food sample to the food analyst within the next working day; however, a marginal delay does not render the food analyst's report invalid (*Gopal Dutt vs State of Haryana 1983 Cr L.J pp 303 at 304 (P&H)*).

(ix) A hotelier has to accept any communication from the designated officer in case the sample is found adulterated intimating that proceedings against the hotelier have been initiated.

(x) A hotelier has to accept any communication from the designated officer serving an improvement notice on the establishment and has to ensure that it is complied with during the compliance period.

Role of Food Analysts

The food analyst used to be called a public analyst under the Prevention of Food Adulteration Act, 1954 and was required to have a postgraduate degree in chemistry, biochemistry, or food technology. The food analyst is responsible for analysing the samples received from the food safety officer.

The various steps to be taken by a food analyst are as follows:

(i) Compare and note down the conditions of the container seal and the outer cover containing the sample.

(ii) In case the sample received is found to be unfit for analysis or that the seal is broken, he or she is required to inform the designated officer within seven days and can request for a second sample, which lies with the designated officer.

(iii) Upon analysis, prepare a report indicating the various types of tests undertaken to arrive at a conclusion and send to the designated officer four copies of report within 14 days (Section 46(3)(i)).

(iv) Where the hotelier has also requested for the food sample to be analysed, a copy of the report shall be sent along with a copy to the designated officer (Section 46(3)(ii)).

Any report signed by the food analyst will be used in court proceedings unless it is superseded by a certificate from the Director of the Central Food Laboratory. In the first instance, appeal against the food analyst's report lies with the designated officer; however, a subsequent appeal can be made to the Central Food Laboratories by requesting them to analyse a portion of the sample taken. The certificate issued by the Director of the Central Food Laboratory supersedes the report given by the food analyst, and where such a certificate is produced in any court where proceedings are in progress, there cannot be any further appeal on the validity of the analysis report and it shall be binding on the courts.

Central Food Laboratories

Four Central Food Laboratories were established under the Prevention of Food Adulteration Act, 1954, where appeals can be made for the purpose of getting samples analysed of food articles collected by the food safety officers of states/union territories and local bodies. These laboratories are located at Ghaziabad, Kolkata, Pune, and Mysore.

Besides the Central Food Laboratories, the FSSAI has access to food testing laboratories, which are attached to the DMI that enforces the AGMARK through its network of five regional offices and 22 laboratories located across India.

Enforcement of the Food Safety & Standards Act, 2006

A three-tier enforcement procedure is envisaged by the Act as illustrated in Fig. 9.9, and the same is defined under Section 42. In case the offence is punishable with a fine, the designated officer can initiate the prosecution proceedings by referring the matter to the adjudicating officer. If the offence is punishable with imprisonment and a fine, then the decision is taken by the state food safety commissioner to prosecute

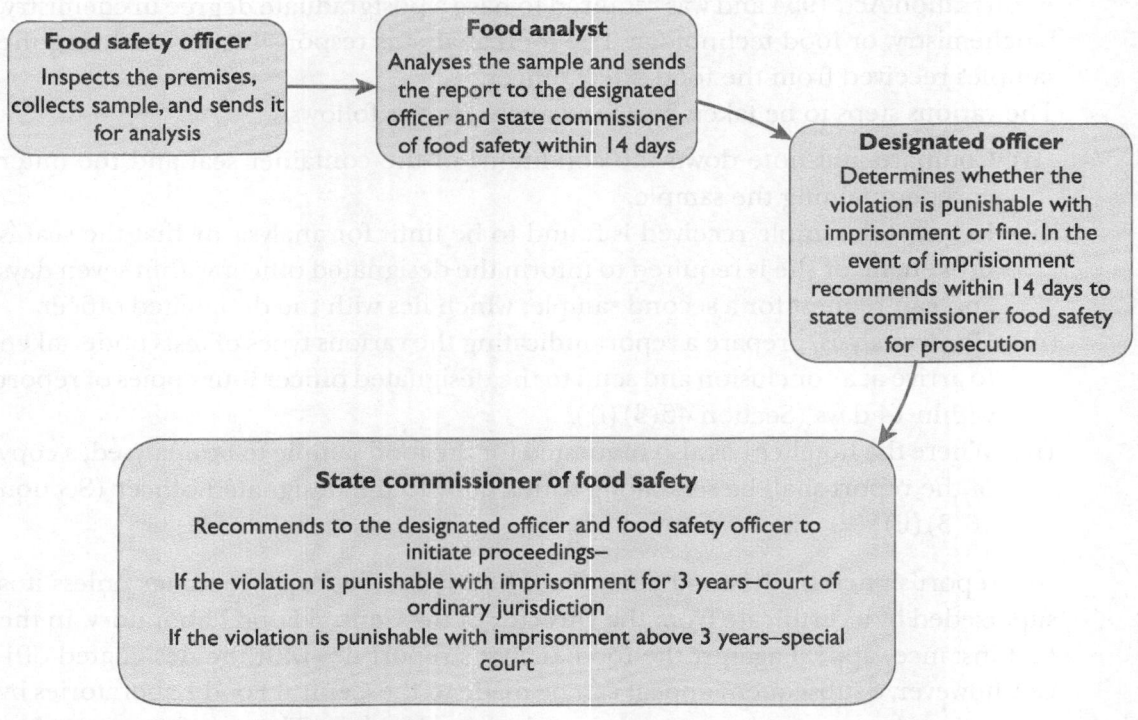

Food safety officer
Inspects the premises, collects sample, and sends it for analysis

Food analyst
Analyses the sample and sends the report to the designated officer and state commissioner of food safety within 14 days

Designated officer
Determines whether the violation is punishable with imprisonment or fine. In the event of imprisonment recommends within 14 days to state commissioner food safety for prosecution

State commissioner of food safety
Recommends to the designated officer and food safety officer to initiate proceedings—
If the violation is punishable with imprisonment for 3 years—court of ordinary jurisdiction
If the violation is punishable with imprisonment above 3 years—special court

FIGURE 9.9 Enforcement Procedure

the offender and the file is sent to the designated officer to have it processed through the adjudicating officer.

Role of the Adjudicating Officer

The judicial proceedings that are held in the Court of the Adjudicating Officer are similar to the proceedings that take place in a civil court under Sections 193 and 228 of the IPC. The adjudicating officer is vested with the powers of a civil judge and is required by law to ascertain the facts of the case on the merits of the evidence placed before him or her before giving any decision.

Some of the criteria that he or she may be required to consider are whether the offence was committed knowingly or not, whether it resulted in a financial gain or gave an unfair advantage to the offender, whether the offence caused any financial loss to the aggrieved person, and whether he qualifies for compensation or not.

If the person is found guilty, an adjudicating officer can take any of the following steps:

(i) Issue direction to the person found guilty of an offence, for taking corrective action to rectify the mistake.
(ii) Order the destruction of such article of food.
(iii) Direct the offender to pay compensation to the victim or representative of the victim in case of injury or death of the consumer.
(iv) Order for cancellation of licence, recall of food from market, or forfeiture of establishment and property.
(v) Issue prohibitory orders.

Table 9.4 illustrate offences that attract a fine, and the adjudicating officer shall be bound by these guidelines whilst awarding the punishment.

TABLE 9.4   Offences that Attract a Fine

Section	Penalty	Fine
50	Selling food not of the nature or substance or quality demanded by the purchaser	Not exceeding ₹2,00,000 in case of petty manufacturer, not exceeding ₹25,000
51	Penalty for manufacturing, storing, selling, distributing, or importing sub-standard food	Up to a maximum of ₹5,00,000
52	Penalty for manufacturing, storing, selling, distributing or importing misbranded food the adjudicating officer can issue instructions have the food item destroyed	Up to a maximum of ₹3,00,000
53	Penalty for misleading advertising	₹10,00,000

(Contd)

TABLE 9.4   (Contd)

Section	Penalty	Fine
54	Penalty for manufacturing, storing, selling, distributing or importing food containing extraneous matter	Not exceeding ₹1,00,000
55	Penalty for failure to comply with the directions of the food safety officer	Up to a maximum of ₹2,00,000
56	Penalty for unsanitary processing or manufacturing of food	Up to a maximum of ₹1,00,000
57	Penalty for manufacturing, storing, selling, distributing an adulterant.	If it is injurious to health fine not to exceed ₹10,00,000 If it is not injurious to health fine not to exceed ₹2,00,000

The adjudicating officer can also award the punishment of imprisonment and a fine for selling unsafe food (Fig. 9.10) as well as award punishment for various offences as indicated in Fig. 9.11.

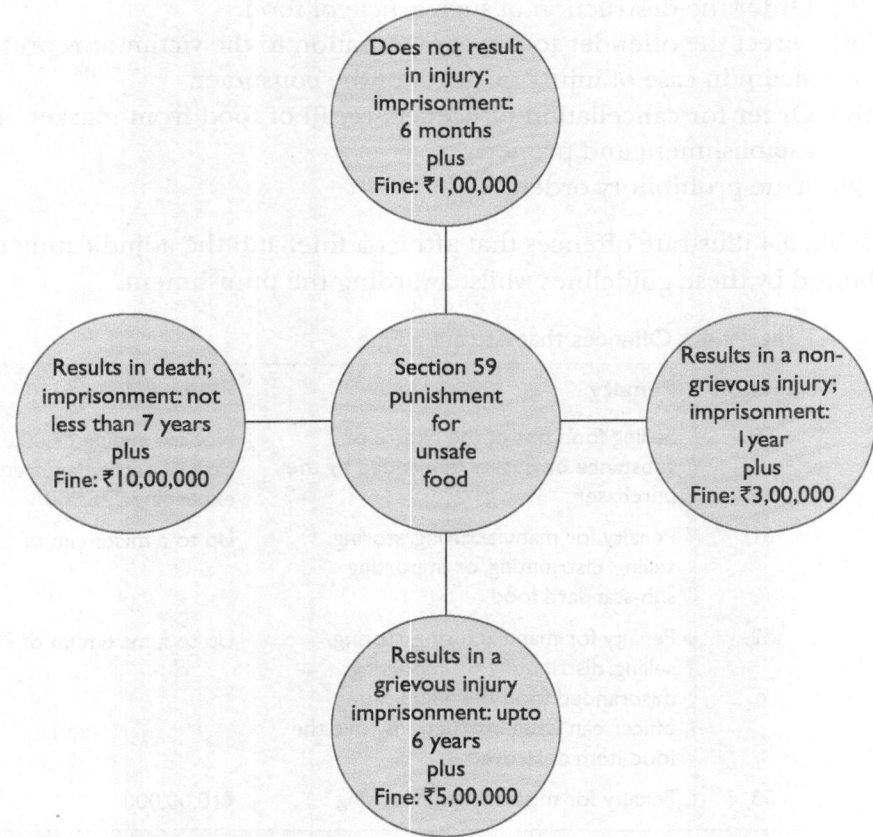

FIGURE 9.10   Punishment for Unsafe Food

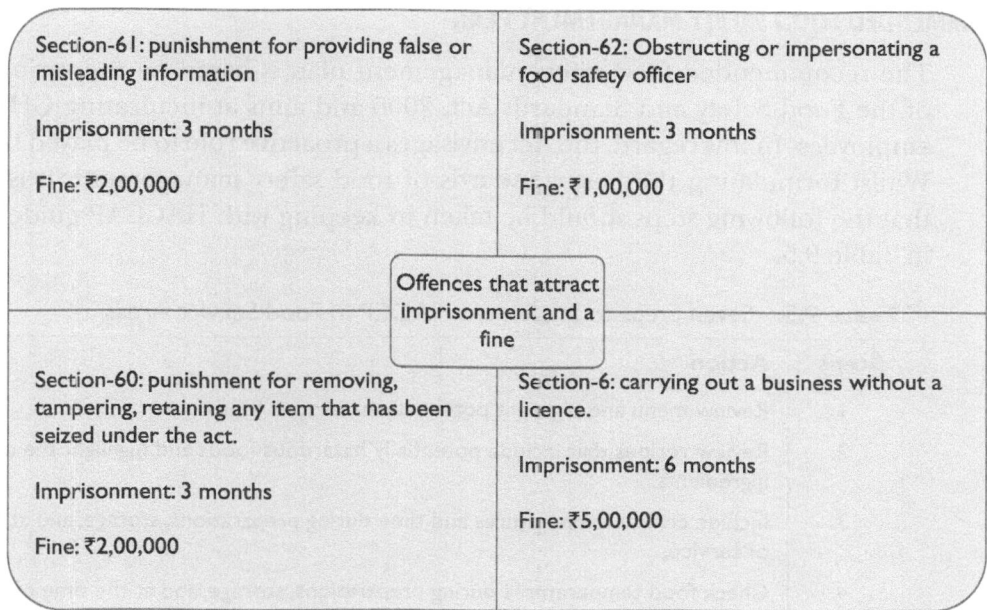

FIGURE 9.11   Offences that Attract Imprisonment and a Fine

As mentioned earlier, the adjudicating officer can award compensation in the event of death or injury. The Act has now fixed the monetary compensation limits as follows:

(i)   ₹5,00,000 in case of death
(ii) ₹3,00,000 in case of grievous injury
(iii) ₹1,00,000 in all other cases of injury

Besides the award of compensation, the adjudicating officer can also order for the cancellation of the licence, forfeiture of the property, and recall of the food item from the market.

The aggrieved party can appeal against the decision of the adjudicating officer to the Food Safety Appellate Tribunal of the respective state within 30 days to review the case. The Food Safety Appellate Tribunal is vested with powers of a civil court and the Food Safety and Standards Act 2006 debars the civil courts from entertaining appeals against the judgements of the adjudicating officer.

Where the adjudicating officer has meted out the punishment of imprisonment for more than three years and a fine plus compensation to the victim on grounds of injury or death, the Food Safety Appellate Tribunal has the right to conduct a summary trial before giving its decision. Appeals against the decision of the Food Safety Appellate Tribunal can be made to the high court within a period of 60 days.

RECOMMENDED FOOD SAFETY MANAGEMENT PLAN

The recommended food safety management plan is based on the various sections of the Food Safety and Standards Act, 2006 and aims at inculcating GHP amongst employees. In this regard, the Act envisages a proactive role to be played by the FBO. Whilst formulating the best standards of food safety management, it is suggested that the following steps should be taken in keeping with HACCAP guidelines listed in Table 9.5.

TABLE 9.5   Seven Steps to Implement HACCP in Food Service Areas

Steps	Action
1.	Review menu and highlight potentially hazardous foods.
2.	Review recipes that include potentially hazardous foods and highlight the problem ingredients.
3.	Include critical temperatures and time during preparations, storage, and at the time of service.
4.	Check food temperatures during preparations, storage, and at the time of service.
5.	Correct required temperatures if they are not being met.
6.	Verify that the steps have been followed by reviewing the process and deviations, if any.
7.	Record the temperature and time actually taken during preparations, storage, and at the time of service.

Once formulated these are then written as SOPs, which all employees are required to follow. Employees are trained on these SOPs for their effective implementation and improving upon them based on feedback. The unit head or the owner will implement the SOPs through the key department heads who will be responsible for implementing them in their respective departments:

(i) Purchasing
(ii) Receiving
(iii) Stores
(iv) Kitchen
(v) Kitchen stewarding
(vi) Respective food and beverage outlets—restaurants, banquets, or rooms service
(vii) Personnel

Purchasing

The primary function of the purchase department is to ensure availability of a product of the right quality and specifications at the negotiated price at the right time as per the requirements of the concerned user department. The product quality and specifications are given by the user department in this case by the chef to the purchase department to enable them to source the product accordingly:

(i) Raw materials shall be purchased from reliable and known vendors.

(ii) Raw materials should be purchased in quantities that can be stored easily.

(iii) Proper records should be maintained of all purchases that are done by the hotel.

(iv) Purchases should be made as per the quality and product specifications (Tables 9.6 and 9.7).

(v) Items should be ordered keeping in mind the shelf life of the product.

(vi) Under the Legal Metrological Act, 2009 and Legal Metrological (Packaged Commodities) Rules, 2011, it is mandatory to sell products such as breads, biscuits, tea, coffee, and soaps only in specified standard weights and sizes. In case of propriety products, branded products or pre-packaged food items, care should be taken that they display accurate information on the package such as the following:

(a) Name of the food article

(b) Name and complete address of the manufacturer

(c) Net quantity/net content/net weight

(d) Lot code and batch number

(e) List of ingredients (inclusive of additives) in descending order

(f) Nutritional information

(g) Date of manufacture

(h) Best before date/expiry date/use by date

(i) Vegetarian (green dot) or non-vegetarian (brown dot) product

(j) Legible, prominent, and unambiguous declaration

(vii) From a practical point of view, the date of manufacture, which is an indication of the freshness of the product, and the date of expiry or use by date after which the food item requires to be discarded are important. Hoteliers can underwrite into their purchase contracts that the manufacturer will exchange the expired goods in case they are not consumed by the expiry date or use by date.

TABLE 9.6 General Specification of Vegetables Followed by Hoteliers

Item	Specifications
Eggplant (Brinjal)	Round or long dark purple colour; the skin should be tight and shining with no holes on the surface.
Beetroot	Smooth round shape and hard to touch; should have no damaged skin and should be free of dirt; dark purple in colour with no leaves or stem.
Beans	Long and crisp; light green in colour; should snap when bent; should not be stringy.
Cauliflower	Round milky white florets without any black or grey tinge with less green stem; should snap when bent.
Carrot	Conical shape with smooth skin; no hair roots; garden fresh; light pink colour or rusty red if frozen.

(Contd)

TABLE 9.6 (Contd)

Item	Specifications
Cucumber	Hard to touch with smooth shiny surface; green in colour; tender from inside when broken.
Curry leaves	Garden fresh; olive green in colour with high aroma.
Cabbage	Light green with firm leaves with stem extending from the base; no holes and worm blemishes.
Capsicum	Tender and crisp with dark shiny green skin; even shape with soft white seeds when cut; no discolouration, bruises, or patches.
Cooking tomatoes	Firm to touch, no cuts or crevasses; red in colour; should not be over-ripe.
Table tomatoes	Red in colour with uniform shape and clear smooth skin; no holes and not over-ripe.
Green coriander	Garden-fresh, bright green with wide leaves; no roots or rotten leaves; free of moisture with a strong aroma.
Green bananas	Bright green in colour with no cuts, damages, or patches.
Green chillies	Olive green or dark green in colour; smooth shiny skin; long and even shape with soft white seeds.
Green peas	Dark green in colour; pods should be full and heavy; split easily along the stem when pressure is applied; peas should be crisp, soft and sweet, free of all moisture.
Ginger	Outer skin should be smooth and shiny and free of dirt; pulp should not be stringy or dry.
Lemon	Thick skin that is bright yellow in colour without bruises or patches; even sized; soft to touch but not pulpy.
Onion	Firm and evenly round bulb with dry and pink coloured skin; tender white and pulpy internal leaves with a sharp taste; no roots and no fungus growth on the skin.
Potatoes	Firm with a smooth skin; as evenly shaped as possible with no mud or dry dirt in the eyes or crevasses; no green or black spots; no old potatoes, which are greyish in colour with low moisture content.
White radish	Long and thin; white in colour with no roots sprouting from the surface; the tip should break when twisted.
Snake gourd	Long and hollow inside with no holes; should break when bent.
Spring onions	Marble white with hard green shoots; skin of the onion should be soft and smooth and free of any black marks.

TABLE 9.7   General Specifications of Fruits to be Followed by Hoteliers

Item	Specifications
Cooking apple	Yellowish in colour; skin free from all spots.
Table apple	Golden red or bright brick colour with smooth skin; spotless and no packaging pressure marks.

(Contd)

TABLE 9.7 (Contd)

Item	Specifications
Banana	Greenish yellow colour; should not be pulpy or very hard to touch; no black patches or broken at the seams.
Tender coconut	Must have lots of water inside, which must be heard when shook; upon cutting, should have thick, marble white and juicy kernel; no rancid smell.
Grapes	Dark blue or light green colour; each grape attached to a bunch; thin skin with no spots or damage; sweet in taste.
Mangoes	Tight and smooth skin and small seed: firm pulp and not stringy; should not have a rotten or putrid smell.
Oranges	Bright orange in colour with smooth and wrinkle-free skin; firm if pressed; juicy and sweet segments with less seeds; should not have a rotten smell.
Papaya	Orange yellow colour with traces of green; sweet and firm pulp, which is bright yellow in colour.
Pears	Light greenish yellow in colour; juicy with firm pulp with no skin damage.
Plums	Reddish brown in colour, paper-thin skin with no skin damage; soft to touch but not pulpy; sweet in taste.
Peach	Dark brown in colour; thick smooth skin with no skin damage; soft and juicy with dark brown pulp; sweet in taste.
Pineapple	Tough outer skin; greenish yellow in colour; soft, juicy, and sweet inside but not pulpy which is yellow in colour.
Sweet lime	Bright green or yellow colour; smooth thin skin with no patches, firm to touch, juicy and sweet.
Water melon	Olive green or dark green in colour; heavy in size and hard to touch; white skin and red pulp.

Receiving

Receiving department is responsible for receiving all the goods that come into the hotel as indented by the various departments as per their specifications.

(i) No material should be accepted if it is off colour, has foul odours, and has extraneous substances or contaminants in it.

(ii) All fresh fruits and vegetables should be checked and cleaned physically in running water.

(iii) All fresh fruit and vegetables should be checked against the quality parameters indicated by the chef.

(iv) Proper records should be maintained of all items that are received.

(v) Once the items have been received they should be promptly sent to the stores or the kitchen as required. The general rule is to send all perishable items to the kitchen and non-perishable items to the stores.

(vi) All grocery items should be checked for the date of manufacture and the expiry or use by date.

(vii) The packaging should be intact and not open or damaged for all packaged products when being received by the hotel.

(viii) Receiving temperature of frozen food should be –18°C or below.

(ix) Vegetables and fruits should be segregated from meat, poultry, and seafood before being sent for storage.

Stores

The store is responsible for the proper storage of all materials received by the hotel. Stores have to be well planned so as to ensure that the area is easy to clean and maintain and is well ventilated.

Pest control should be done periodically to prevent contamination and breeding of pests. Stores in all hotels have walk-in refrigerators, which maintain a temperature between 5°C and 10°C and deep freezers where temperatures are maintained to –18°C.

(i) Fresh fruits and vegetables shall be stored in walk-in refrigerators at temperatures between 5°C and 10°C.

(ii) Meat, poultry, and seafood items that are frozen shall be stored in the deep freezers.

(iii) Vegetables and fruits will be segregated from meat, poultry, and seafood before storage.

(iv) Raw materials and food shall be stored in separate areas away from printed packaging materials, stationery, hardware, cleaning materials, and chemicals.

(v) Pre-packaged, processed food materials or products shall be stored as per the instructions given on the label.

(vi) Dried foods (such as grains and pulses) should be stored off the floor, ideally in sealable containers, to allow proper cleaning and protection from pests.

(vii) All items will be tagged with the date of receiving prior to storage.

(viii) Perishable food or foods with short shelf life should be sent to the kitchens to be used first.

(ix) The food materials shall be stored on racks that they are reasonably well above the floor level and away from the wall so as to facilitate effective cleaning and prevent harbouring of any pests, insects, or rodents.

(x) Containers made of non-toxic materials or food-grade material shall be used for storage of raw materials.

(xi) All products should be routinely checked for spoilage/contamination and shelf life.

(xii) Any spoiled/contaminated product should be promptly removed and discarded.

(xiii) Stores shall follow the policy of first in first out for effective and better management of the stores.

Kitchen

The kitchen is responsible for ensuring that food is prepared and cooked hygienically as per the recipe of the dish and served at the correct temperature to the guests—hot foods served hot and cold foods cold.

   (i) Whole fruits and vegetables should be washed in water before being peeled or cut before mixing them with other ingredients.

  (ii) Previously prepared/freshly cut fruits or vegetables should be kept in clean, properly covered containers under refrigeration.

 (iii) Raw meat and processed meat should be separated from other foods items.

 (iv) Cutting boards, utensils, knives, and preparation area for raw meats and poultry and marine products should be separate.

  (v) Frozen products should be thawed in refrigerator, microwave, or convection oven or under running potable water well before cooking.

 (vi) Only required quantities of food should be thawed at a time and it should be used immediately.

(vii) Thawed meats and vegetables should not be refrozen or kept in the chiller.

(viii) Food items that need to be chilled should be put straight away into the refrigerator.

 (ix) Cooked food should be cooled as quickly as possible and then put it in the refrigerator.

  (x) Semi-cooked or cooked dishes and other ready-to-eat foods such as prepared salads and desserts having short shelf life should not be left standing around at room temperature.

 (xi) Prepared confectionery products should be kept in chilled display windows.

(xii) All products should be routinely checked for spoilage/contamination and shelf life and should be promptly removed and discarded.

(xiii) Water used in the chutneys should be safe and potable.

(xiv) Sauces and chutneys should be placed in containers and stored in refrigerator when not in use.

 (xv) Perishable/uncooked chutneys should be consumed immediately.

(xvi) Proper quality or branded oils/fats should be used for food preparation, frying, and so on.

(xvii) Food should be cooked at the right temperature and as per the recipe and standards laid down it should not be overcooked, burnt, or charred.

(xviii) Whenever cooking or reheating of food is done, it should be hot all the way through.

(xix) Used or rancid oil should not be reused for cooking.

 (xx) Milk and milk products should be used immediately or pasteurized and refrigerated.

(xxi) Garnishes should be prepared using freshly cut vegetables and used immediately.

(xxii) There will be no smoke nuisance in the food preparation area.

(xxiii) There should be separate sinks for washing utensils and raw food items.

(xxiv) All items, fittings, and equipment that touch or come in contact to food must be kept in good condition. Chipped containers should not be used. Stainless steel, aluminium, glass containers, mugs, jugs, trays suitable for cooking and storing should be used.

(xxv) Equipment and containers that are used for food handling, storage, and preparation, processing and serving should be made from materials, which do not impart any toxicity to the food material.

(xxvi) Utensil or container used for cooking should not be used for any other purpose.

(xxvii) Every utensil or container containing any food intended for sale should be provided with a proper fitting cover/lid to protect the food completely from dust, dirt, and flies and other insects.

(xxviii) Proper exhaust and ventilation systems including air filters, wherever required, should be located in the kitchens.

(xxix) Suitable air curtains and pest-o-cutors should be installed at appropriate locations in the kitchen.

(xxx) Lighting fixtures must be protected to ensure that food is not contaminated by the fixtures accidently breaking.

(xxxi) Only potable water with appropriate facilities for its storage and distribution should be used in washing, processing, and cooking.

(xxxii) Drains and other places should be fitted with mesh or grills as required to prevent pests from entering or breeding in the premises.

Kitchen Stewarding

Kitchen stewarding is responsible for maintaining the cleanliness and hygiene in the kitchen—preparation areas, wash-up areas, storage cupboards, walk-in freezers, deep freezers, all utensils and equipment used in the kitchen and the restaurants. The department is also responsible for ensuring that all mechanical and electrical equipment are always maintained in good working order in close coordination with the engineering department.

(i) Kitchen stewarding should strictly follow the laid-down cleaning schedule to make sure that work surfaces, chopping boards, and equipment are thoroughly cleaned before and after food preparation.

(ii) Separate chopping boards and knives for raw fruits/vegetables/meat/poultry and ready-to-eat food should be used.

(iii) Refrigerator and display units should be maintained in the required temperature.

(iv) Processing area should be cleaned and disinfected promptly.

(v) All refuse/waste should be promptly removed from preparation area.

(vi) Personal hygiene of food handlers need to be ensured.

(vii) All mechanical equipment should be routinely cleaned, checked, and maintained.

(viii) Food handlers should undergo periodic medical checks to ensure that they do not suffer from any communicable disease.

(ix) Cleaning instructions should indicate the type of cleaning products to be used and for various types of equipment.

(x) Proper storage of cleaning agents should be done so as not to contaminate raw, cooked, or packed food.

Food and Beverage Outlets

Food and beverage outlets of a hotel are guest areas such as restaurants and banquets where the service of food is carried out.

   (i) Clean utensils/crockery and cutlery/disposables should be used for serving.
  (ii) Personal hygiene of food handlers need to be ensured.
 (iii) All mechanical equipment should be routinely cleaned, checked, and maintained.
  (iv) Buffet dishes should be washed with antibacterial cleaning agents, rinsed properly with water, and sanitized after every service cycle.
   (v) Display units should be maintained in good working conditions to avoid food spoilage and contamination.
  (vi) All refuse/waste should be promptly removed from the restaurant.
 (vii) Clean and intact containers should be used for storing sauces and chutneys.
(viii) All areas of the restaurant should be well lit and well ventilated.
  (ix) Food or beverages should not be stored in the same container used to store the ice intended for consumption.

Personnel

The personnel department is responsible for the recruitment, training, and career development planning of employees in a hotel company. It is responsible for providing proper rest and recreation facilities for employees, for example, staff locker rooms, staff cafeteria, and other welfare activities.

   (i) At the time of recruitment, steps should be taken to ensure that the employees are educationally qualified to hold the job.
  (ii) Staff should be made aware of steps to avoid cross-contamination.
 (iii) Staff lockers and canteen should be separate from food production and service areas.
  (iv) A display board mentioning the dos and don'ts for the workers should be put up in a prominent place in the premises in English or in the local language for everyone's understanding.
   (v) Staff lockers should be separate for male and female employees and maintained in sanitary conditions.
  (vi) Arrangements should be made to get the food handlers medically examined once in a year to ensure that they are free from any infectious, contagious, and other communicable diseases. A record of these examinations signed by a registered medical practitioner should be maintained for inspection purpose.
 (vii) Food handlers should maintain a high degree of personal cleanliness. The FBO should provide all food handlers with adequate and suitable clean protective clothing, head covering, face mask, gloves, and footwear. The FBO should ensure that the food handlers at work wear only clean protective clothes, head covering, and footwear daily.

(viii) Food handlers should not wear any belonging such as rings, bangles, jewellery, watches, pins, and other items that pose a threat to the safety and suitability of food.

(ix) Service staff engaged in food handling activities should refrain from smoking, spitting, chewing, or eating; sneezing or coughing over any food whether protected or unprotected food; and eating in food preparation and service areas.

(x) In general, visitors should be discouraged to go inside the food handling areas. However, proper care has to be taken to ensure that food safety and hygiene is never compromised.

In the fight against food adulteration, the Food Safety and Standards Act, 2006 is a major step forward. A review of the Act has been done by the FHRAI and the National Restaurant Association of India, and their observations are that there are certain provisions that require to be reconsidered as they are impractical, cumbersome, and outdated. Some of these observations are as follows:

(i) Doormats are to be kept at the entrance.

(ii) Hand wash to be provided for every 20 employees. FBOs as part of their SOPs follow more stringent hygiene guidelines in the food production areas.

(iii) Food is to be transported in temperature controlled vehicles.

(iv) Water purifiers to be provided in all food and beverage outlets. Currently all hotels use municipal water which is safe and potable.

(v) Cooking oil once used should not be reused for cooking. There are well-established practices that FBOs do not reuse oil that is rancid or stale.

(vi) Cold storage of perishables, cooked vegetarian, and cooked non-vegetarian food should be done at less than 4°C. These standards are incompatible with existing operating practices.

(vii) Cooking temperature for hot food should be 60°C and reheating temperature should be 74°C. These are contrary to the standards that are currently followed, for example, cooking temperature for hot foods is 65°C and reheating temperature is dependent on the food article being reheated.

(viii) Although there are provisions for migrating from the old registration procedure to the new licensing regime, the Act still retains some of the cumbersome documentation procedures which were being followed earlier.

(ix) The Act insists that any changes that are done should be with the permission of the licensing authorities. This ruling will impact any changes required to be done to menus on a need basis, for example, food festival menus, special occasion menus, and state dinners during visits of heads of states. This licensing requirement is totally impractical and needs to be revised.

(x) As mentioned earlier in this chapter, the Act would like the FBO to play a proactive role in implementing GHP and maintaining high quality standards in the procurement of ingredients and in the production of various food items. It is suggested that the SOPs being followed by the FBO should be certified by the licensing authorities.

(xi) The greatest fear is that it will be implemented by food safety officers who are not suitably trained to handle its effective implementation.

Insofar that this Act applies to food manufacturing and processing units, stringent guidelines are essential to assure the availability of quality packaged foods in the domestic market as well as to ensure that the exported packaged foods are internationally acceptable.

SUMMARY

This chapter gave a brief introduction to the history of food legislation and its evolution to encompass modern legal requirements. It compared two landmark pieces of food legislation in India and highlighted the shift in attitude from a regressive piece of legislation to a proactive legislation towards food adulteration and food preservation. The Food Safety and Standards Act, 2006 is a major step forward as it makes it mandatory for all types of FBOs to secure a licence prior to commencement of business. It ensures that hoteliers and restaurateurs play a proactive role in implementing GHP; in maintaining high-quality standards in the procurement of ingredients; and in the production of various food items by adhering to GHP and

HACCP procedures. The chapter detailed how this Act created a unified administrative and judicial structure for its effective implementation and provides for a graded penalty structure where the punishment depends on the severity of the violation. It provides for the first time an opportunity for the aggrieved person to seek compensation in the event of injury or death. The chapter discussed how Codex Alimentarius Commission's recommendations when applied to foods being packaged and marketed by Indian companies internationally will make it mandatory for processed and packaged food manufacturers to follow exceptionally high standards of hygiene at the procurement, production, and packaging stages.

KEY TERMS

Acids Added to food in order to make flavours 'sharper'. They also act as preservatives and antioxidants. Common food acids include vinegar, citric acid, tartaric acid, malic acid, fumaric acid, and lactic acid.

Acidity regulators Used to modify the acidity and alkalinity of foods.

Anti-caking agents Keep powders such as milk powder from caking or sticking.

Antifoaming agents Reduce or prevent foaming in foods.

Antioxidants Antioxidants such as vitamin C act as preservatives by inhibiting the effects of oxygen on food. They are also beneficial for health.

Adulteration Mixing of substances of an inferior quality making the food or beverage article unsafe and injurious to health or affecting the quality of the original food by altering its natural composition.

Adulterant Any material or substance which is or can be used by substitution, addition, or abstraction to or from food, so that the natural composition and quality of the original food substance is affected thereby making the food article unsafe and injurious to health.

Adulterated food Any food that contains an adulterant.

Bulking agents Substances such as starch added to increase the bulk of a food without affecting its nutritional value.

Codex Alimentarius Commission   Created in 1963 by Food and Agriculture Organization and the World Health Organization of the United Nations, to develop food standards, guidelines, and related texts such as codes of practice under the Joint FAO/WHO Food Standards Programme.

Concurrent List: List III of the Seventh Schedule whereby both the centre and the states enjoyed concurrent legislative powers to enact laws.

Contaminant   Any substance, whether added or not, which is present in food as a result of the production, manufacture, processing, preparation, treatment, packing, packaging, transport, or storage, or as a result of environmental contamination that makes the food harmful and injurious to health, but does not contain any extraneous matter.

Colour retention agents   Used to preserve a food's existing colour.

Doctrine of *Mens Rea*   In Latin means 'guilty mind' or 'criminal intent'. It is important to establish that there was a criminal intent to commit the offence before the guilty person could be prosecuted in a court of law.

Food   A substance or article of human consumption, either food (including primary food) or drink—other than water or drugs—which is of plant or animal origin, may be grown organically, genetically modified, or engineered, may be processed, partially processed, or unprocessed containing ingredients, flavouring matter, or condiments used in the preparation, which provides nutrition to the body, stimulates growth, and maintain life.

Primary food   An article of food, being a produce of agriculture or horticulture or animal husbandry and dairying or aquaculture in its natural form, resulting from the growing, raising, cultivation, picking, harvesting, collection or catching in the hands of a person other than a farmer or a fisherman.

Genetically modified or engineered foods   To harness the knowledge gained in the field of biotechnology and its application to agriculture so as to enhance agricultural yield and productivity by genetically making the crop resistant to pests and other harmful insects.

Unsafe food   An article of food whose nature, substance, or quality is so affected as to render it injurious to health.

Misbranded food   If the label, brand, tag, or notice under which a food is sold is false or misleading in any particular as to the kind, grade, or quality or composition; or if it is sold as the product of one manufacturer when in reality it is the product of another manufacturer; or if on the label, brand, tag, or notice under which it is sold there is any false statement concerning the sanitary conditions under which it is manufactured.

Food additive   Any substance not normally consumed as food by itself or used as a typical ingredient of the food, whether or not it has nutritive value, the intentional addition of which to food for a technological purpose in the manufacture, processing, preparation, treatment, packing, packaging, transport or holding of such food results, or maybe reasonably expected to result (directly or indirectly), in it or its by-products becoming a component of or otherwise effecting the characteristics of such food but does not include 'contaminants' or substances added to food for maintaining or improving nutritional qualities.

Food preservative   A substance that when added to food, is capable of inhibiting, retarding, or arresting the process of fermentation, acidification, or other types of decomposition of food.

Food colouring agents   Added to food to replace colours lost during preparation, or to make food look more attractive.

Food business operator   A person or an organization involved in running a food business whether for profit or loss, and is responsibly carrying out the activities related to any stage of manufacture, processing, packaging, storage, transportation, distribution of food, import of food including food services, catering services, and sale of food or food ingredients. He or she is required to operate his business after registering his business and/or obtaining the required licence.

Food poisoning   An unpleasant illness caused by eating contaminated foods.

Flavour enhancers   Enhance a food's existing flavours or give food a particular taste or smell. They may be extracted from natural sources (through distillation, solvent extraction, maceration, among other methods) or created artificially.

Flour treatment agents   Added to flour to improve its colour or its use in baking.

Glazing agents   Provide a shiny appearance or protective coating to foods.

Good hygiene practice   Involves identifying the essential principles of food hygiene applicable throughout the food chain.

Hazard analysis and critical control points   A systematic approach to food safety by identifying areas of concern and then taking remedial steps to rectify the problems and subsequently setting up a monitoring procedure to ensure production of safe foods for human consumption.

Humectants   Prevent foods from drying out.

Misleading advertising   An advertisement which falsely describes any food article or gives an inaccurate statement on the nature, substance, quality, or false guarantees through audio or visual publicity, print, electronic media, Internet, or website and includes any notice, circular, label, wrapper, invoice, or other document.

Stabilizers   Stabilizers, thickeners, and gelling agents, like agar or pectin (used in jam, for example) give foods a firmer texture by stabilizing emulsions.

Sweeteners   Added to foods for flavouring. Sweeteners other than sugar are added to keep the food energy (calories) low.

Thickeners   Substances which, when added to any mixture, increase its viscosity without substantially modifying its other properties.

EXERCISES

Define the Following

1. Unintentional adulteration
2. Bulking agents
3. Toxic food poisoning
4. Extraneous matter
5. Genetically modified foods
6. Contaminants
7. Primary foods
8. Hazard Analysis and Critical Control Points
9. Concurrent list
10. Unsafe food

Concept Review Questions

1. What are the salient differences between the Prevention of Food Adulteration Act, 1954 and the Food Safety and Standards Act, 2006?
2. Outline the licensing procedure as per the Food Safety and Standards Act, 2006.
3. When a food safety officer visits the hotel premises, what is a hotelier expected to do?
4. What steps should be taken by a hotel kitchen to implement good hygiene practices?
5. Under what circumstances is an aggrieved person entitled to compensation?
6. What is the role of an adjudicating officer?

7. What are the various types of offences related to food hygiene that would attract both imprisonment and fine?

Critical Thinking Questions

1. FSSAI mandates that good hygiene practice (GHP) should be implemented; yet it is not being done by hoteliers and restaurateurs. Analyse the reasons.
2. Hoteliers are familiar with the effects of food poisoning. How can they prevent its occurrence?
3. Does the Food Safety and Standards Act, 2006 simplify the licensing procedure for food chains like KFC and McDonalds, which operate across India?

Research Question

1. Industry associations FHRAI and NRAI oppose the single window clearance licensing procedure, the implementation of which has been deferred till 2014. Does the Food Safety and Standards Act simplify the licensing procedure for food chains like KFC and McDonalds that operate across India?

Project

1. Analyse the impact of India's adoption of the Codex Alimertarius Commission's recommendation on safety and standards in foods called Codex India on the business of food manufacturing and processing in India.

REFERENCES

Friedrich Accum, *A Treatise on Adulterations of Food and Culinary Poisons*. Longmans, London, UK, 1820. http://www.abebooks.com/products/isbn/9781406847703

<http://www.rsc.org/Library/Collections/Historical/Accum/PioneeringWork.asp> accessed on 18 March 2012.

<http://www.rsc.org/education/eic/issues/2005mar/thefightagainstfoodadulteration.asp> accessed on 18 March 2012.

<http://hansard.millbanksystems.com/acts/adulteration-of-food-act> accessed on 18 March 2012.

<http://www.legislation.gov.uk/ukpga/1875/63/introduction/enacted> accessed on 18 March 2012.

<http://www.macfisheries.co.uk/page17.htm> (Food Quality in London 1870-1938) accessed on 18 March 2012.

<http://www.codexalimentarius.net/web/index_en.jsp> accessed on 18 March 2012.

Cynthia A. Roberts, *The Food Safety Information Handbook*, pp. 8–9 <http://blogs.unpad.ac.id/souvia/files/2009/12/the-food-safety-information-handbook1.pdf> accessed on 18 March 2012.

http://zeenews.india.com/news/nation/now-food-samples-found-adulterated-after-milk_751916.html accessed on 12 April 2013

http://web.uri.edu/foodsafety/hazard-analysis-of-critical-control-points-principles/ accessed on 12 April 2013

http://books.google.co.in/books?id=MqLazH_MEzUC&pg=PA279&lpg=PA279&dq=Burnett,+%E2%80%98Plenty%E2%80%99,+pp.+228%E2%80%9329&source=bl&ots=BPwowwUi7N&sig=QkszfNXsWiNn7FsFDsKUSVwuAhU&hl=en&sa=X&ei=IU9qUc6hI4WrrAeGx4GQAQ&sqi=2&ved=0CDcQ6AEwAg#v=onepage&q=Burnett%2C%20E2%80%98Plenty%E2%80%99%2C%20pp.%20228%E2%80%9329&f=false

Liquor Licensing

LEARNING OBJECTIVES

After going through this chapter, the reader will be familiar with the following:

- Social importance of beverages
- Various types of non-alcoholic and alcoholic beverages
- Steps taken by governments to control the sale of alcoholic beverages through innovative legislative measures
- Purchasing, receiving, and storage of alcohol
- Serving alcohol responsibly and handling guests under the influence of alcohol
- The Dram Shop Act (USA)
- Laws governing the sale of cigarettes and tobacco products

INTRODUCTION

In his *History of the World in 6 Glasses*, Tom Standage remarks, 'The important drinks are still drinks that we enjoy today', the six being beer, wine, spirits, tea, coffee, and coke.

The word beverage is derived from the French word *boivre*, which means 'to drink'. In common parlance, beverages include a wide variety of liquids such as tea, coffee, liquor, beer, wines, milk, juices, and soft drinks excluding plain water. There are a variety of reasons for the consumption of beverages—for quenching thirst, for medicinal and antiseptic properties, for social enjoyment and relaxation, for conducting religious rituals, to enhance the flavour of foods, and so on.

Welcoming guests by offering them beverages is ingrained in various cultures. In India, a guest is welcomed by serving a glass of water, tea, or coffee; in America with a glass of lemonade or iced tea; in Morocco with a glass of almond milk; in certain European countries with a glass of wine; in Middle eastern countries with saffron-flavoured milk; and so on.

Beverages are classified into alcoholic and non-alcoholic beverages. Non-alcoholic beverages are defined as liquids that contain less than 0.5 per cent of alcohol, the popular ones being tea, coffee, aerated water, spring or natural water, mineral water, syrups, squashes, juices, and milk as illustrated in Fig. 10.1.

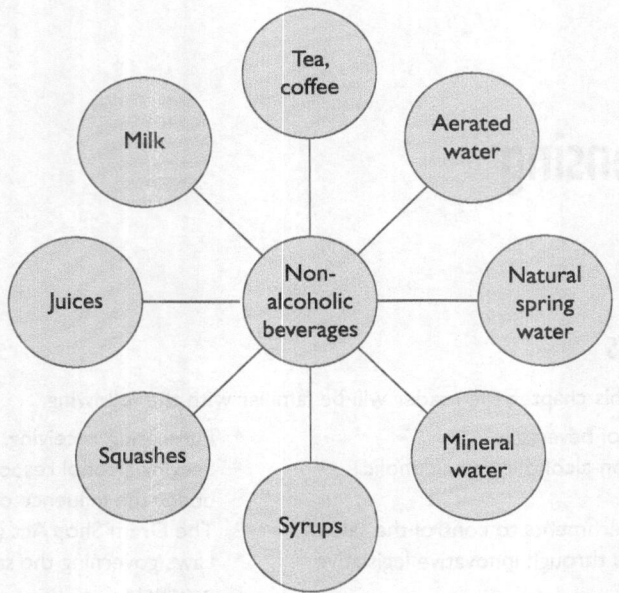

FIGURE 10.1   Types of Non-alcoholic Beverages

The *McGraw-Hill Dictionary of Scientific and Technical Terms* defines an alcoholic beverage as a 'potable preparation containing ethyl alcohol' and the *Encyclopaedia Britannica* defines it as 'any fermented liquor that contains ethyl alcohol as an intoxicating agent'. The *Pocket Oxford Dictionary and Thesaurus* defines alcohol as '(1) colourless volatile flammable liquid forming the intoxicating element in wine, beer, liquor, etc.: (2) spirits, liquor, (strong) drinks *colloq:* booze'.

In general terms, alcohol is a fermented potable clear colourless liquid that is an intoxicant, burns easily, blends well with water, and has a characteristic smell. The chemical formula for ethanol, which is an organic compound, is C_2H_5OH. It is composed of carbon, oxygen, and hydrogen.

Alcoholic beverages are classified into beers, wines, and spirits as illustrated in Fig. 10.2.

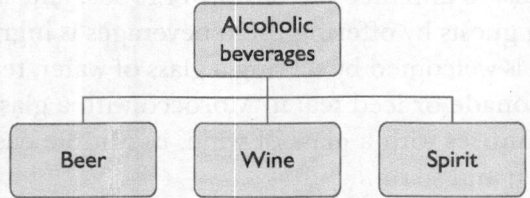

FIGURE 10.2   Types of Alcoholic Beverages

A brief history of non-alcoholic and alcoholic beverages is discussed in this chapter in order to familiarize the reader with the importance of beverages through the ages.

NON-ALCOHOLIC BEVERAGES

Non-alcoholic beverages such as tea, coffee, natural spring water, and mineral water besides being refreshing and stimulating have medicinal properties as they contain natural antioxidants that arrest the anti-ageing process.

Tea This is obtained from an East Asian evergreen shrub or small tree *Camellia sinensis* having fragrant, nodding, cup-shaped white flowers, and glossy leaves. The young, dried leaves of this plant, prepared by various processes, are used to make hot or cold beverages.

Tea as a drink is said to be discovered accidentally over 5000 years ago, when leaves from a tea bush fell into a pot of boiling water and the leaves delicately flavoured the liquid. Tea was originally drunk for its medicinal benefits, and it was not until the 1700s that it became to be consumed as a beverage. The flavour, quality, and character of tea are affected by the location, altitude, type of soil, and the climate of the region. The major tea-producing countries are China, East Africa (Kenya, Malawi, Tanzania, and Zimbabwe), India, Indonesia, and Sri Lanka.

Coffee This is obtained from various tropical African shrubs or trees of the genus *Coffea*, especially *Coffee arabica* widely cultivated in the tropics for their seeds that are dried, roasted, and ground to prepare a stimulating aromatic drink.

The story of modern coffee originates in the Arabian Peninsula, where roasted beans were first brewed around AD 1000. Sometime around the 15th century coffee spread throughout the Arab world. In the Arab world, coffee rose as an alternative to alcohol, and coffee houses as alternatives to taverns—both of which are banned by Islam (Standage 2005). The first commercial cultivation of coffee is thought to have been in Yemen. Although there are over 50 species of coffee, the best known are *Coffee arabica* and *Coffee camephora*. Coffee is grown in South and Central Americas, Africa, and Asia. The best coffee comes from Brazil and Colombia— the two largest producers of coffee.

Aerated water This is a beverage charged with carbonic gas, for example, soda water, brands such as Tonic Water, Dry Ginger, Bitter Lemon, Coke, and Pepsi. Standage (2005) remarks 'Coca-Cola encapsulates what happened in the 20th century; the rise of consumer capitalism and the emergence of America as a superpower. It's globalization in a bottle. It may be the second most widely understood phrase in the world after "OK"'.

Natural/spring water This refers to bottled water that can be still, naturally sparkling or carbonated water without mineral content, for example, Ashburn (England), Ballygoen (Ireland), Llanllyr (Wales), and Strathmore (Scotland).

Mineral water This refers to bottled water that can be still, naturally sparkling or carbonated water with mineral content, for example, Aix-la-Chapelle (France), Aix-la-Bains (France), Evian (France), Malvern (England), Perrier (France), Saint-Galmier (France), Selters (Germany), and Vichy (France).

Squashes   These are fruit flavoured concentrated syrups produced using artificial colours, flavours, and sweeteners. They have to be mixed with water or soda prior to drinking. Popular squashes are of orange, lemon, and grapefruit.

Juices   These are liquids that are naturally contained in fruits and vegetables and are obtained by extracting the same from them and are also commercially available in bottles or cans.

Syrups   These are thick viscous liquids consisting of sugar solution in water, artificially flavoured, and are used as a sweetener and as a base for cocktails and milkshakes. For example, Cassis (blackcurrant), Cerise (cherry), Citronelle (lemon), Framboise (raspberry), Gomme (white sugar syrup), Grenadine (pomegranate), and Orgeat (almond).

ALCOHOLIC BEVERAGES

Since time immemorial, alcoholic beverages have been used in religious ceremonies, for their curative medical properties and regarded as the 'elixir of life'. It is in recent time, that alcohol has come to be considered as a neccessary evil that requires to be controlled and regulated.

Beer   This is defined as a fermented alcoholic beverage made from grains such as barley, wheat, and rice flavoured with hops. The monks of northern Gaul called their concoction using the Celtic word 'Beor' which later became 'beer'.

Around 10,000 BC, the discovery of Stone Age beer mugs confirms the presence of fermented beverages. The first recipe for 'wine of grain' was inscribed on stone tablets in Mesopotamia about 7000 BC. The first batch of beer is thought to have been accidentally made by an individual who left a bowl of barley out in the rain. Mead, a fermented drink of water and honey mixed with malt, yeast, and herbs, was perhaps the first stimulating beverage the Persians, Phoenicians, and Egyptians were familiar with. By 1800 BC, the Babylonians were brewing beer and by 800 BC beer made from barley and rice was popular in India. The conquest of Gaul and Britain by Julius Caesar in 55 BC introduced beer to England. Saint Arnold was apparently the first person to introduce hops in the brewing of beer in the AD 6th century. In 1516, the German purity laws were passed making it mandatory for beer to be manufactured from barley, hops, and pure water. The purity laws forbade one to urinate in the river systems on Tuesdays to maintain the purity of water because water was diverted for brewing on Wednesdays.

Wine   According to the Wine & Spirit Association of Great Britain, wine is defined as an alcoholic beverage obtained from the juice of freshly gathered grapes, the fermentation of which has been carried out in the district of origin as per the local traditions and customs. Wines can be made from fruits other than grapes. Wines made from fruits are called country wines in Britain. Wines are usually classified into three main categories by place of origin or region; by type of wine—red, white, sparkling, rosé, or dessert wine; or by type of grapes—red or white.

Legend has it that the Persian King Jamshed was introduced to wine by his banished wife, who took a sip of wine that was labelled poison. She liked it so much that she made her husband taste it. Jamshed liked it as well and ordered the cultivation of grapes to produce wines throughout the kingdom. The Phoenicians and the Greeks learnt about wines from their travels to Iran and were instrumental in introducing wines and viniculture to Europe. The oldest known winery is located in Armenia and goes back to 4100 BC. The Egyptians used wine for religious ceremonies in 4000 BC, and by 2000 BC the Greeks discovered the art of wine making.

The *Appellation de'Origine Controlee* system introduced in the 15th century to establish and regulate the quality of wines according to the region that they were made gave a boost to the wine industry in France and is the benchmark for vintners to follow even today. The major wine producing countries are France, Italy, Australia, USA, South Africa, and Portugal.

Spirits   These are distilled alcoholic beverages containing ethanol produced by fermenting grains, fruits, or vegetables. The important ones commercially available are listed as follows:

Rum   It is produced from molasses obtained from sugarcane. It is the sweet, sticky residue that remains after sugarcane juice is boiled and the crystallized sugar is extracted.

Whiskey   Different grains are used for different varieties, including barley, malted barley, rye, malted rye, wheat, and maize.

Vodka   It is produced from grains such as sorghum, corn, rye, or wheat. Among grain vodka, rye and wheat vodka are generally considered superior; however, vodka can also be made from potatoes, molasses, soybeans, rice, and beetroot sugar.

Gin   It derives its predominant flavour from juniper berries.

Aquavit   It is from Scandinavia and made from potatoes or grain flavoured with caraway seeds. It is similar to *Schnapps*, which is from Germany and Holland.

Brandy   It is produced by fermenting grapes and distilling wine. The word brandy has its origins from the Dutch word *brandewijn*, which means 'burnt wine'.

Pomace—Grappa/Marc   Grappa is Italian whereas Marc is French style brandy made from the pressing of grapes after the required must has been removed for wine production.

Eau de Vie   This is also known as the water of life; it is the fermented and distilled juice of fruits.

Apple Brandy   Types of this are Calvados and Applejack.

Arrack   It is made from the sap of the palm trees.

Tequila   A Mexican spirit distilled from the fermented juice of the agave plant. It is traditionally drunk after a lick of salt and a squeeze of lemon.

Liqueurs   These are alcoholic beverages that are bottled with added sugar and have added flavours that are usually derived from fruits, herbs, or nuts.

EARLY INITIATIVES TO REGULATE ALCOHOL

In India, the earliest use of alcohol is mentioned in the Vedas (2000 BC) where it is called *Somras*. Subsequently, use of alcohol by small affluent groups of society was prevalent during the Indus Valley Civilization (1500 BC). In southern India, a local alcoholic brew called *masura* was popular with the working class. The first documented record of alcohol distillation is found in Italy in AD 1100 and the distilled liquids were called spirits. During the 17th and 18th centuries widespread use of alcohol was reported in England and its colonies besides other European countries.

The availability of inexpensive home-brewed beer and spirits encouraged alcoholism and drunkenness among the various strata of society. Widespread drunkenness came to be recognized as a crime and a social evil that needed to be curbed, compelling the English Parliament to pass 'The Act to Repress the Odious and Loathsome Sin of Drunkenness' in 1606. The Act imposed a fine of five shillings for drunken behaviour. In America, the colony of Massachusetts was the first to pass laws to control widespread drunkenness and to regulate the sale of alcoholic beverages in taverns.

In 1643, England introduced an excise tax on the distillation of alcohol in order to curb illicit brewing. Massachusetts on similar lines prohibited the brewing of home-made beer and introduced laws prohibiting the payment of wages in the form of alcohol. This led to the growth in the manufacture of illicit liquor popularly called 'moonshine'. In order to contain the growth of illegal distilleries a 'whiskey tax' was levied in 1791. Distillery owners and farmers resisted this tax as they made more money by converting the excess grains to whiskey. This culminated in the 'whiskey rebellion' in Pennsylvania, leading to the Act being repealed in 1802. These initial efforts of the government to tax the manufacture of alcohol met with resistance; it became clear that a modified form of taxation could be used in the future, which gave birth to the concept of licensing.

The sharp increase of alcoholism in America made the leaders of the country explore other avenues to curb this social evil. The idea of prohibition was born and it led to the passing of the 18th amendment to the US Constitution, commonly referred to as the Prohibition Act. With its ratification in 1920, the possession, manufacture, sale, transportation, import, and export of intoxicating liquors for beverage purposes were prohibited. Prohibition proved a failure in America and the Act was finally repealed in 1933 by the passing of the 21st amendment to the US Constitution. During the years in which prohibition was in force, the government exchequer suffered a sharp decline in revenues.

The experiment with prohibition in America, the measures to treat drunkenness as a crime, and taxing the manufacture of alcohol by England made the legislators realize that this perhaps was not the best way to control the widespread use of alcohol.

A policy has since evolved based upon the principles of possession, consumption, and transportation (PCT). The way to restrict possession was to define an age for the purchase of alcohol and to limit the units of alcohol a person could purchase; by imposing fines, and in extreme cases by awarding the punishment of imprisonment—the government attempted to control consumption as it was the main cause of drunkenness and unruly behaviour—and by the introduction of mandatory licensing on the manufacture, transportation, and sale of alcohol in public places.

LIQUOR LEGISLATION IN INDIA

In India, the British licensed the first brewery in 1862 and introduced taxes on the manufacture and sale of alcohol. This policy was similar to the one that they had implemented in England and their colonies based upon the PCT principle.

In legal terms, the Punjab Excise Act, 1914 defines 'liquor', 'country liquor', 'foreign liquor', and 'imported foreign liquor' under the Punjab Excise Liquor Definitions, 1954.

TEXT

(1) *The following shall be deemed to be 'liquor' for the purposes of Punjab Excise Act, (1 of 1914):*
  (a) *Methyl alcohol.*
  (b) *Spirituous preparation, namely:*
   (i) *Spirit Anisi* (ii) *Spirit Auranti Compo* (iii) *Spirit Cinnamon* (iv) *Spirit Rosae* (v) *Spirit Aetheris* (vi) *Tincture Aurenti* (vii) *Tincture Cinnamin* (viii) *Tincture Levandula Co.* (ix) *Tincture Limnois Conc* (x) *Tincture Zingiberis Mitis* (xi) *Tincture Card Co.* (xii) *Tincture Carminative* (xiii) *Tincture Capsici* (xiv) *Tincture Cinnamon Co.* (xv) *Tincture Zingiberis Fort* (xvi) *Tincture Calendules* (xvii) *Spirit Aethris Nitrosi* (xviii) *Tincture Krameria* (xix) *Tincture Gulancha* (xx) *Tincture Auristilla* (xxi) *Aqua Anisi Concentrate* (xxii) *Tincture Myrrh* (xxiii) *Tincture Curcuma* (xxiv) *Aqua Foeniculi Cone* (xxv) *Tincture Chinesis.*

(2) *The following shall, for the purpose of the Punjab Excise Act (Punjab Act 1 of 1914) be deemed to be 'Country Liquor' and 'Foreign Liquor', respectively:*
  (1) *'Country Liquor' means all liquor other than rectified spirit, denatured spirit and perfumed liquor not included in the definition of Foreign Liquor, normally manufactured from neutral spirit and de-mineralised water with added spices and essences, which do not imitate any imported liquors or cordials, and sold at prescribed strengths at country liquor ships, also including the substance commonly called. 'Laban' and also described as 'Punjab Medium Liquor'.*
  (2) *'Foreign Liquor' means:*
   (a) (i) *All liquor (other than country liquor, rectified spirit, denatured spirit and perfumed spirit) imported into India from other countries by sea or air, in original bottled form, and also termed as 'Imported Foreign Liquor';*
    (ii) *All beer, porter and stout including cider imported into India from other countries by sea or air, in bottled form; and*
    (iii) *All wines and sweets prepared from grapes or other fruits by a process of fermentation only with or without the addition of alcohol or any other ingredients imported into India from other countries by sea or air, in bottled form; and*
   (b) (i) *All liquor manufactured in India (other than country liquor, rectified spirit, denatured spirit and perfumed spirit) made in limitation of 'imported foreign. liquors' with or without any blend of such liquors, or direct import of such liquor in bulk from, and*

also on which excise duty at a rate higher than that levied on liquors falling under the definition of 'Country Liquor' is leviable;

(ii) All beer, porter and stout including cider manufactured in India; and

(iii) All wines and sweets prepared from grapes or other fruits by a process of fermentation only with or without the addition of alcohol or any other ingredient manufactured in India.

(3) 'Imported Foreign Liquor (bottled in origin)' means foreign liquor imported from abroad on which custom duty is leviable under any law for the time being enforce.

The Punjab Excise Act, 1914 and rules are attempts by the government to define alcoholic beverages and this definition has been adopted by most states; however, from a hotelier's and consumer's perspective, alcohol is any liquid that contains ethanol.

After Independence, the Indian government's desire was to implement prohibition in the country and this objective was stated under Article 47 of the Directive Principles of State Policy in the Indian Constitution: 'The State shall regard the raising of the level of nutrition and the standard of living of its people and the improvement of public health among its primary duties and, in particular they shall endeavour to bring about prohibition of the consumption, except for medical purposes, of intoxicating drinks and drugs, which are injurious to health.'

The states and union territories were given powers to legislate on the subject under List II of the Seventh Schedule of the Constitution—(State List):

Clause 8: Intoxicating liquors, that is to say, the production, manufacture, transport, purchase and sale of intoxicating liquors.

Clause 51: Duties of excise on the following goods manufactured or produced in the State and counter-vailing duties at the same or lower rates on similar goods manufactured or produced elsewhere in India-

Alcoholic liquors for human consumption

Opium, Indian hemp and other narcotic drugs and narcotics

But not including medicinal and toilet preparations containing alcohol or any substance included in sub-paragraph (b) of this entry.

The report 'Alcohol Related Harm: Implications for Public Health and Policy in India' (2011) prepared by Gururaj G. Pratima Murthy, N. Girish, and V. Benegal of the National Institute of Mental Health and Neurosciences, Bengaluru, confirms that alcoholism or addiction to alcohol and alcohol abuse have led to an increase in domestic violence, petty crimes, loss of jobs, lack of education, increase in car accidents, poor health, mental instability, and economic dependence culminating in debt. For these reasons state governments have been keen to curb alcoholism and alcohol abuse.

The states and union territories have attempted to implement the Directive Principles of State Policy by either enforcing prohibition or prohibiting the sale of alcohol on certain days called as 'dry days' in a calendar year and by determining the legal age for purchasing and consuming alcohol.

Besides these measures there is a pan-India ban on drinking in public places, on liquor advertising, promotions, and sponsorships by alcohol manufacturing and marketing companies. There is a direction that all packaging and labels shall carry statutory warnings that 'the consumption of alcohol is injurious to health'. The location of retail sale outlets is restricted by the density of population and zoning requirements; for example, a liquor sales outlet cannot be located within 75 metres of an educational institute, hospital, nursing home, religious places, and industrial estates.

Similarly, the sale and consumption of alcohol in a restaurant or hotel can only be done once it meets the zoning requirements, which are that it should not be located within 75 metres of an educational institute or religious place. Once the licence is granted, the hotel or a restaurant can sell alcoholic beverages to its patrons.

Prohibition

Prohibition is one of routes that certain state governments in India have adopted in order to regulate and curb the socio-economic impact of alcoholism.

(i) Total prohibition was implemented in Gujarat (with effect from 1 May 1960); however, foreigners and non-resident Indians can obtain a permit for 30 days upon arrival at Ahmedabad airport since 15 February 2010.

(ii) Total prohibition exists in the union territory of Lakshadweep, except in the island of Bangaram, where it is permitted for tourists alone.

(iii) Prohibition is in force in Nagaland by the Nagaland Total Prohibition Act, 1989, however, the policy is not enforced uniformly and liquor is easily available in hotels and restaurants.

(iv) Prohibition is implemented in Manipur by the Manipur Liquor Prohibition Act, 1991. Local brews are permitted but not Indian made foreign liquor (IMFL).

(v) Prohibition was introduced in Mizoram by the Mizoram Total Prohibition Act, 1997, which was subsequently amended in 2007 to allow for the manufacture and sale of wine made from grapes and guavas.

(vi) Both the states of Andhra Pradesh and Haryana experimented with prohibition for a brief period before relaxing it or completely doing away with it.

    (a) Prohibition in Andhra Pradesh came into effect by the Andhra Pradesh (Andhra Region) Prohibition Act, 1937. The Andhra Pradesh Prohibition Act, 1995 uniformly enforced prohibition in both the Andhra and Telengana regions; the law was finally amended in 1997 to permit the sale of IMFL and beer; however, the sale of arrack is still banned.

    (b) Haryana briefly flirted with prohibition for a period of 19 months from 1 July 1996 to 1 April 1998. Haryana's experiment with prohibition was a disaster; besides loss of revenue for the exchequer it encouraged smuggling of alcohol from the neighbouring states of Rajasthan, Uttar Pradesh, and Delhi.

In the rest of the country, alcohol is regulated through a prudent use of licensing procedures for the manufacture, transportation, import, and export of alcohol. By imposing taxes at the point of sale, governments have attempted to curb the consumption of alcohol by making it expensive for individuals to purchase it.

In Maharashtra, the Bombay Prohibition Act, 1949 regulates the sale, consumption, and transportation of alcohol and makes it mandatory for a person to acquire a drinking permit. Under the Delhi Liquor Licence Rules, 1976 the maximum alcohol possession limit for an individual is:

Foreign liquor whether imported or made in India	*18 litres*
Beer/wine (mild drinks) whether imported or made in India	*36 litres*
Cider	*9 litres*
Country liquor	*3 litres*

Note: An individual is allowed to carry one unsealed bottle of 750 ml while entering into the National Capital.

By implementing these measures Maharashtra and Delhi have attempted to restrict the quantity of alcohol that a person can possess at any given point of time.

Dry Days

On dry days mandated by the central government the sale of alcohol is prohibited. These days are 26 January (Republic Day), 15 August (Independence Day), and 2 October (Mahatma Gandhi's birthday) and are observed throughout the country. The states can declare additional dry days in keeping with the various religious festivals applicable to their respective states. Under the Representation of the Peoples Act, 1951, the Chief Election Commissioner is empowered to declare the date of polling, the dates of vote counting, and a day earlier as well as a day after as dry days. Hotel operators have to observe the designated dry days applicable to the state in which they are located. Failure to observe dry days results in a fine of ₹50,000 under the Punjab Excise Act, 1914.

Legal Age for Drinking

The legal drinking age in India varies from 18 years to 25 years depending upon the state of residency. In the states of Goa, Himachal Pradesh, Rajasthan, Sikkim, and Uttar Pradesh, the legal age is 18 years. Punjab, Haryana, Chandigarh, Delhi, Maharashtra, and Meghalaya observe 25 years as the legal drinking age, whereas for the rest of the country it is 21 years. It is suggested that there should be a single uniform legal age for drinking all over the country in the same way as 18 years is the age for voting uniformly throughout the country.

LIQUOR LICENSING PROCEDURES

Currently, there is no national policy on alcohol, as liquor licensing is a state subject and each state is free to enact its own liquor policy. For the purpose of our study we shall study the liquor policy that is currently being followed by the Delhi Government under the Delhi Liquor Licence Rules, 1976 and the Punjab Excise Act, 1914 as applicable to the state.

Liquor licences are issued under two categories: off premises or off-site and on premises or on-site.

Off Premises or Off-site Licence

Off premises or off-site licence permits the licensee to sell alcoholic beverages to individuals for consumption outside the licensee's premises, for example, wholesalers, liquor stores, and duty-free shops. The licences required are L-1, L-2, and L-6.

L-1 licence It has to be obtained by the manufacturer or owner of the distillery, and is a wholesaler's licence so that he or she can sell his or her product in the state.

L-2 licence It has to be obtained by the retailer to sell IMFL/beer in the state and is granted only to select Delhi Government undertakings, such as DSIDC and DTTDC.

L-6 licence It has to be obtained by the retailer to sell IMFL/beer in a duty-free shop.

On Premises or On-site Licence

On premises or on-site licence permits the licensee to sell alcoholic beverages to individuals for consumption within the licensee's premises; for example, restaurants and bars within hotels, room service, standalone restaurants and bars, beer bars, or sports bars. The licences required are L-3, L-4, L-5, L-5A, L-19, L-19A, L-53, L-20, L-49A, and L-18.

L-3 licence It permits a star-category hotel to sell IMFL/beer to resident guests through room service or by placing alcohol miniatures in the rooms in the mini-bars.

L-5 licence It permits the sale of Indian and foreign liquor in exclusive bars located inside star-category hotels.

L-4 licence It permits an independent restaurateur to sell IMFL/beer and foreign liquor to patrons in the specified bars and restaurants.

L-5A licence It permits sale of foreign liquor/beer to resident guests on luxury trains.

L-19 licence It permits a club to sell IMFL/beer to its members, for example, Gymkhana Club, Delhi Golf Club, and so on.

L-19A licence It permits a mess that is exclusively for government servants to sell IMFL/beer to its members, for example DSOI Club, Dhaula Kuan (New Delhi), and all clubs and mess of the armed forces.

L-53 licence It permits the sale of beer/mixed alcoholic beverages through a retail vend in departmental stores or malls.

L-20 licence It permits a hotel/restaurant/or club on a temporary basis for a specified guest function to sell IMFL/beer to guests. The licence has to be obtained in the name of the host who is hosting the function by paying a fee of ₹5000. The premises should be already licenced to sell alcohol—L-3, L-4, L-5, L-19, or L-19A.

L-49A licence It permits the service of alcohol for special occasions like marriages and engagements on any location that is properly screened, and the service of alcohol is restricted to people over 25 years of age. This licence has to be obtained by the host.

L-18 licence It permits the extension of hours of operation for an L-3, L-5, or L-4 licence holder.

PROCEDURE FOR ACQUIRING A LIQUOR LICENCE

The Delhi Liquor Licence Rules, 1976 do not draw any distinction between a hotelier applying for a bar licence and an independent restaurateur. The application form and the process followed by the government in both cases is similar and equally time consuming. The standard application form is shown in the box Exhibit A.

EXHIBIT A
APPLICATION FORM FOR L-3/L-4/L-5 LICENCE

1. Name and Address of Applicant/ Hotel
2. Its Constitution (whether Proprietorship/ Partnership of Society of Pvt. Ltd or Public Ltd Co.)
   Note: Please attach a copy of the Partnership Deed or Memorandum of Articles of Association in support of the constitution, wherever is relevant.
3. Letter No. and date of approval of Department of Tourism, Govt. of India with regard to Star Classification
4. Whether the premises are owned or leased or rented by the applicant
   Note: Please attach attested photocopy of the proof in support thereof.
5. Whether adequate space has been set out for Storage/Bar area in the Hotel
   Note: Please enclose a site and layout plan of the Hotel clearly demarking the Store Room, bar area (if any) and service area.

6. Whether the area where the Hotel is situated is an approved commercial area by the MCD/NDMC/DDA (please answer Yes/No)
7. Whether the applicant holds an Excise Licence in any form for any other premises (If so, details thereof)
8. Sales Tax Registration Certificate No. and date
   Note: Please enclose an attested photocopy of the Sales Tax Registration Certificate.
9. If assessed under the Income Tax indicate the Permanent Account No.
10. Have you been registered for an Eating House Licence with DCP (Licensing) and also Health Department of NDMC/MCD? If yes, please attach photocopy of the certificate.
11. Please attach a copy of the site plan and outline Map of the Hotel indicating sitting area segment wise & other facilities like toilets separately meant for Gents & Ladies.

12. Does the Hotel have parking space of its own? How many vehicles can be parked outside Hotel? Please indicate number of (a) Cars and (b) Scooters.
13. Whether the Hotel is centrally air-conditioned or provided with A.C.s. If with A.C.s number of air-conditioners provided
14. Whether the Pantry area is equipped with suitable gadgets and is hygienic (please answer Yes/No)
15. Details of fire-fighting equipment installed in the Hotel with dates/inspection by Fire Services Department and also NOC from Fire Services Department
16. Whether separate area has been earmarked for the smokers. Show the demarcation between smoking and no smoking areas of the restaurant, bar which has a seating capacity of 30 covers or more which is mandatory under the Cigarettes and other Tobacco Products (Prohibition of Advertisement and Regulation of Trade and Commerce, Production, Supply and Distribution) Act, 2003 (34 of 2003) as Section 4 of the act had made all enclosed spaces non smoking.
17. Whether Lodging House Licence from DCP (Licensing) and from NDMC/MCD issued (Please attach a copy thereof.)
18. Please indicate the distance from the premises of the Restaurant to the nearest:
    (i) Religious places
    (ii) Major educational institutions

We have gone through the Punjab Excise Act, 1914 as extended to the Union Territory of Delhi. Delhi Liquor Licence Rules, 1976 as amended from time to time, Delhi Intoxicant (Sales and Licence) Rules, 1976 and other relevant, excise rules and understood the same.

We have also understood that the application for the grant of L-3/5 licence shall be considered by the competent authority under the Delhi Liquor Licence Rules, 1976 as amended from time to time and the Delhi Intoxicant (Sales and Licence) Rules, 1976 and the other relevant Excise Rules for the grant of L-3/5 Licence.

Note: We further clearly understand the application/licence is liable to be rejected/cancelled for furnishing incomplete/incorrect particular and for any reasons whatsoever by the appropriate/competent authority. We understood that no compensation whatsoever on this account or on any other account shall be payable by the Delhi Administration in the event of non-grant/cancellation of L-4 Licence by the appropriate Competent Authority.

(Signature of Applicant)

Certified that the information given above is true and correct on the basis of the facts on record and to the best of my knowledge and belief.

(Signature of Applicant)

In the box Exhibit B, a detailed list of documents that are required to be furnished along with the application form is given:

EXHIBIT B
LIST OF DOCUMENTS REQUIRED FOR L-15/L-15F/L-16/L-16F/L17/18 LICENCE

1. Documentary proof regarding legal status of the Hotel i.e. whether Limited Liability Partnership / Company/Partnership Firm etc.
2. Trade Licence from the local authority i.e. MCD/NDMC as the case may be
3. Lodging House Licence from the local authority
4. Certificate of Registration of Eating House Licence issued by the DCP (Licensing)
5. Completion certificate in respect of the Building issued by the local authority
6. Documentary proof regarding applicant being an Income Tax Assesses

7. Documentary proof regarding Registration with Sales Tax Department
8. Site Plan of L-3 and L-5 stores
9. Key plans indicating the location of the Hotel
10. Proof of Department of Tourism indicating the project approval and also recommendation for the grant of L-3/L-5 Licence
11. NOC from Fire Department

12. Lodging House from DCP (Licensing)/NOC from the concerned DCP of the Area
The hotel or the restaurant have to confirm that under rule 11 of the Delhi Intoxicants Licence and Sales Rules, 1976 'No liquor shop for consumption "on" the premises shall be located within a distance of 75 metres from the following, namely:- (a) Schools, Colleges and other teaching institutions, (b) Religious Places'.

The structure of licence fees payable by hotels to the excise department for acquiring an L-3 licence to serve alcohol through room service and L-5 licence to serve alcoholic beverages in restaurants is illustrated in Tables 10.1 and 10.2.

TABLE 10.1 L-3 Licence Fee (for Service of Foreign Liquor to the Occupants in Their Rooms)

Description of Hotel	Fee (₹)
10 to 25 rooms	40,000
26 to 50 rooms	60,000
51 to 100 rooms	1,20,000
101 to 200 rooms	1,80,000
201 to 300 rooms	2,50,000
301 to 400 rooms	4,00,000
401 and more rooms	4,50,000

TABLE 10.2 L-5 Licence Fee (for Service of Foreign Liquor in a Bar or Restaurant Attached to a Hotel)

Description of Hotel	Annual Fee per Endorsement (₹)
Five star and above	8,50,000
Four star	7,00,000
Three star	6,50,000
Two star	6,00,000
One star	5,00,000
Budget	4,50,000

Once the inspection is done and the Commissioner of Excise is satisfied that all the requirements have been met, the licence is granted to a hotel/restaurant/standalone restaurant for a period of one year which is renewable annually.

MANDATORY COMPLIANCES OF A LIQUOR LICENCE

It is the responsibility of the food and beverage controller to ensure that the requirements of the licence are complied with by all the concerned departments of a hotel; for example, purchasing, receiving, stores departments, and the food and beverage outlet.

The mandatory requirements are listed as follows:

(i) Display the licence in a prominent place in the restaurant or bar premises.
(ii) Stock the bar with alcoholic beverages that have been purchased from the local vendors or imported under the Export Promotion Capital Goods (EPCG) scheme or under an Open General Licence (OGL).

(iii) Record the inventory in the excise register that is stamped and signed by the inspector. Inventories have to be maintained for each category of licence both at the bar and the stores separately:

(a) According to class of beverage, for example, rum, whiskey, or wine.

(b) Within the class of beverage by type of beverage, for example, whiskey— single malt whiskey, scotch, and so on.

(c) Within each class and type of beverage by brand, for example, whiskey— single malt—Glen Fiddich, Glenmorangie; Scotch—Johnny Walker Black, Whyte and McKay; and so on.

(iv) The inventory of the alcoholic beverages is maintained in 'units'. In India, for practical purposes of inventory a unit is regarded as 30 ml, which is the standard serving size for alcoholic beverages.

Example
- A 750-ml bottle of whiskey contains 25 units of standard serving size alcoholic beverage. When recording the inventory details all entries are made in millilitres (ml).
- A 750-ml bottle of wine contains 6 units of standard serving size alcoholic beverage. When recording the inventory details all entries are made in ml.
- Beer is bottled in various quantities right from a 650-ml bottle to 330-ml can; hence, the inventory is maintained in numbers of bottles or cans in store and not in ml.

(v) The liquor store has to be located in the hotel premises as per the floor plan submitted to the authorities at the time of application. The liquor store must have the correct signage, for example, Ricks Bar L-5 store or room service L-3 store.

(vi) All purchases are made as per the individual licence issued to the restaurants and bars.

Example The Ricks Bar, which operates under an L-5 licence, has raised a purchase requisition to the purchase department as follows:
- 12 bottles of Whyte and McKay whiskey (local purchase)
- 12 bottles of Glen Fiddich single malt (import under EPCG)

When placing the order the purchase department is required to raise two separate purchase orders mentioning the licence number of Ricks bar—one purchase order will be for Whyte and McKay whiskey being purchased locally, and the second one for Glen Fiddich single malt which is being imported under EPCG and is an import.

Under the EPCG scheme, hotels should be classified by the Department of Tourism and be members of the accredited trade bodies. This enables them to get the Import/Export Code (IEC), which is a must for an EPCG Licence. The EPCG scheme has been discussed earlier in Chapter 5.

Furthermore, under OGL, all types of alcoholic beverages such as spirits and wines can be imported. Customs duty is not payable immediately if the imported wine is kept in the customs bonded warehouse (CBW) for a period of three months. To secure the facilities of a CBW, the importer—in this case, the hotelier—will have to furnish a bank guarantee for double the value of the customs duty.

However, once it has to be removed, customs duty becomes payable along with excise that is levied by the state. From an economic perspective, hotels find it more beneficial to import wines and other alcohol beverages under the EPCG scheme.

Similarly, when receiving the alcohol the receiving department will generate two receiving documents mentioning the licence details so that there is no confusion when the items are transferred to the liquor stores.

All spoilages have to be recorded in the excise registers so that credits can be obtained once the spoilage is certified by the excise inspector. Until such time that the spoilage has been accounted for and certified, the material cannot be disposed. In the event of shortages that occur due to the negligence of the bartender, the monetary value of the shortage is recovered from the bartender. In case of overages the excess is recorded and added back to the opening stock at the time of inventory by the controller and subsequently certified by the inspector.

SERVICE OF ALCOHOL BEVERAGES

A variety of alcoholic beverages are served in restaurants and bars either as an aperitif before the meal, as an accompaniment during the meal, or as a digestive at the end of the meal. Whether they serve a fermented wine or a distilled spirit, all bartenders have to adhere to the standard serving size of a measure of alcohol, which is regulated by the Standard Weights and Measures Act, 1976 and the Standard Weights and Measures (Enforcement) Act, 1985.

From a hotelier's standpoint, it is important to understand the effect of alcohol on the human body. He or she should be able to identify the behaviour of a person who is intoxicated. Service staff is required to be familiar with the medical and legal aspects of alcohol consumption such as the rate of absorption and blood alcohol concentration (BAC).

An alcoholic beverage contains ethyl alcohol, which is an intoxicant. Even when taken in small quantities it impacts the central nervous system impairing the judgement of an individual. After consumption, alcohol passes from the stomach into the small intestine, where it is rapidly absorbed into the blood stream and distributed quickly throughout the body. Muscle cramps, nausea, loss of appetite, nerve disorders, and depression are related to excessive alcohol consumption.

Alcohol leaves the body after it is metabolized by the liver (90 per cent); kidneys, lungs, and skin account for approximately 5–8 per cent. The capacity of the liver to metabolize alcohol is one drink of 30 ml in one hour; if drinks are taken in quick succession the liver cannot metabolize it and alcohol enters the blood stream. The traces of alcohol take time to eliminate from the body.

An important factor that affects the level of intoxication is called the *rate of absorption*, which is the rate at which alcohol is absorbed by different parts of the body (Table 10.3).

TABLE 10.3 Absorption Rate of Alcohol

Area	Alcohol absorbed
Mouth	2% to 4%
Stomach	20%
Small intestines	80%
Bloodstream	80% of the alcohol travels to all the parts of the body
Brain	Within three minutes alcohol has an impact on the central nervous system

The other parameter to judge the level of intoxication is called BAC, which is defined as a way to measure the amount of alcohol still present in a person's blood stream and is expressed as a percentage of alcohol absorbed into the blood stream.

TEXT

The Motor Vehicles Act 1988 Section 185. Driving by a drunken person or by a person under the influence of drugs. Whoever, while driving, or attempting to drive, a motor vehicle,–

(a) Has, in his blood, alcohol in any quantity, howsoever small the quantity may be, or

(b) Is under the influence of a drug to such an extent as to be incapable of exercising proper control over the vehicle. shall be punishable for the first offence with imprisonment for a term which may extend to six months, or with fine which may extend to two thousand rupees, or with both; and for a second or subsequent offence, if committed within three years of the commission of the previous similar offence, with imprisonment for a term which may extend to two years, or with fine which may extend to three thousand rupees, or with both.

Explanation *For the purposes of this section, the drug or drugs specified by the Central Government in this behalf, by notification in the Official Gazette, shall be deemed to render a person incapable of exercising proper control over a motor vehicle.*

In India, the Motor Vehicles Act, 1988 under Section 185 specifies the permissible legal level as 30 mg per 100 ml of blood or 0.03 per cent BAC, which is stringent compared to USA, UK, and Canada that have specified the legal limit of 0.08 per cent BAC and China of 0.02 per cent BAC. If the BAC of a person crosses 0.15 per cent the possibility of an accident occurring goes up 25 times. On crossing BAC of 0.30 per cent a person can go into coma, and a BAC of 0.40 per cent can result in death. With cases of reckless and drunken driving on the increase in India, the government is proposing that stricter BAC standards be implemented. Some of the suggestions it has received are as follows: For 0.06 per cent to 0.15 per cent BAC a fine of ₹5000 and six months' imprisonment and for 0.15 per cent BAC and above ₹10,000 fine and one year's imprisonment.

In Washington, DC, drunken driving is classified as driving under the influence of alcohol (DUI) and driving while intoxicated (DWI); under DUI the BAC ranges from 0.20 per cent to 0.24 per cent BAC and in DWI it is above 0.25 per cent BAC.

Besides the punishment being meted out under the Motor Vehicles Act, 1988, a case can also be initiated under the Indian Penal Code Section 304(a) (causing death by rash and negligent act).

The two most significant cases of drunken driving are as follows:

(i) *Sanjeev Nanda vs the State Crl. Appeal No. 807/2008HC*   BMW case where Sanjeev Nanda along with his friends Siddharth Gupta and Manik Kapoor on 10 January 1999 killed six people including three policemen while driving under the influence of alcohol. He was awarded a punishment of two years' rigorous imprisonment under Section 304(a) of the IPC, which states, 'Causing death by negligence – Whoever causes the death of any person by doing any rash or negligent act not amounting to culpable homicide shall be punished with imprisonment of either description for a term which may extend to two years, or with fine, or with both.'

(ii) *Alistair Anthony Pereira vs State of Maharashtra Crl. Appeal Nos 1318–1320 of 2007 SC on 12 January 2012*   Seven persons were killed and seven others injured on Carter Road, Mumbai, when Alistair Pereira ran his car over them on 12 November 2006. The Mumbai High Court awarded him a jail term of three years and imposed a fine of ₹4.5 lakh to be distributed among the victims and relatives of the deceased. The high court's judgement was challenged by Alistair Pereira in the Supreme Court, which upheld the high court's decision under Section 304 Part II of the IPC, which states, 'Punishment for culpable homicide not amounting to murder. Whoever commits culpable homicide not amounting to murder shall be punished with imprisonment for life, or imprisonment of either description for a term which may extend to ten years, and shall also be liable to fine, if the act by which the death is caused is done with the intention of causing death or of causing such bodily injury as is likely to cause death; or with imprisonment of either description for a term which may extend to ten years, or with fine, or with both, if the act is done with the knowledge that it is likely to cause death, but without any intention to cause death, or to cause such bodily injury as is likely to cause death.'

The objective of the courts by meting out strict punishments was to ensure that society at large should not encourage drunken driving as an act of bravado but should treat it as a crime. Hoteliers have the responsibility to ensure that their guests are not inebriated to the point that will result in hazardous driving after leaving the premises.

Factors That Affect the Rate of Absorption and BAC

The following are some of the factors that affect the rate of absorption:

Body weight and size   A larger person can absorb more alcohol because alcohol passes through a larger cell mass and there is more blood to dilute its effects. Fat or obese people feel the effects of alcohol more as fatty tissues cannot dissolve their share of alcohol.

Gender   Females are generally of smaller built and have higher proportion of body fat, which impairs the dissolution of alcohol.

Fat-to-muscle ratio This is a measurement of the relative percentages of fat and muscle mass in the human body, in which mass in kilograms is divided by height in metres squared and the result used as an index of obesity. Body mass index (BMI) categories are shown in Table 10.4. Higher the BMI of a person, more is the fat-to-muscle ratio; therefore, it takes longer for a person with a high BMI to metabolize alcohol than a person who has lesser BMI.

Tolerance Regular and experienced drinkers have a high tolerance limit and it takes them longer to get intoxicated.

TABLE 10.4 BMI Categories

Category	BMI
Underweight	<18.5
Normal	18.5–24.9
Overweight	25–29.9
Obese	>30

Emotional state The state of being depressed or anxious as well as happy or emotionally relaxed can increase the absorption rate of alcohol

Food Eating food while drinking slows down absorption by delaying the opening of the pyloric valve of the stomach. However, eating a meal before drinking may reduce the peak alcohol level absorption by 50 per cent. Foods high in protein and fat should be consumed, for example, milk, cream, eggs, cheese, meats, and fried foods.

Amount and time taken to consume alcohol As a person consumes alcoholic beverages the amount absorbed into the blood stream increases. Normally, in the first hour a small person can absorb one to two drinks, a medium person two to three drinks, and a large person three to four drinks. Subsequently, the rate of absorption slows down to one drink of 30 ml per hour.

Although the government has a licensing procedure in place for hotels, restaurants, and bars, it has left to the individual establishments the definition of their own service standards.

For example, under the Food Safety and Standards Act, 2006, the owners or the company is required to file a nomination under Section 17(2) and Rule 12-B of the Prevention of Food Adulteration Rules, 1955 with the local health authorities nominating the manager or supervisor responsible for the day-to-day operations of the facility. Moreover, the Act makes it mandatory for the operations to be supervised by a manager who is a catering college diploma holder as per Rule 50 Clause 16(b).

The purpose of nomination and setting educational qualifications is to hold accountable an individual who is qualified to deal effectively and efficiently with unusual events that may happen during the operations of the facility.

However, in so far as the service of alcoholic beverages is concerned, surprisingly the government has not thought it prudent to give guidelines except that alcohol cannot be served by any person below the age of 25 years and no woman can work in a bar (Punjab Excise Act, 1914 Section 30).

CASE 10.1

APPELLANT: Anuj Garg and Others
              vs
RESPONDENT: Hotel Association of India CIVIL APPEAL NO. 5657 OF 2007 [Arising out of SLP
              (Civil) No. 12781 of 2006] WITH CIVIL APPEAL NO. 5658 OF 2007 [Arising out
              of SLP (Civil) No. 16127 of 2006]

DATE: 7/10/1936

The constitutional validity of Section 30 of the Punjab Excise Act, 1914 prohibiting employment of 'any man under the age of 25 years' or 'any woman' in any part of such premises in which liquor or intoxicating drug is consumed by the public is the question involved in this appeal, which arises out of a judgement and order dated 12 January 2006 passed by the High Court of Delhi in CWP No. 4692 of 1999.

In its judgement the Delhi High Court ruled—Section 30 of the Act has been declared to be ultra vires the Articles 19(1)(g), 14, and 15 of the Constitution of India to the extent it prohibits employment of any woman in any part of such premises, in which liquor or intoxicating drugs are consumed by the public.

In a special leave petition, the matter was referred to the Supreme Court on the grounds that if Section 30 of the Punjab Excise Act, 1914 was ultra vires, then it would lead to a dangerous situation that would encourage another Jessica Lal or BMW case.

The Supreme Court ruled that young men who take a degree or diploma in hotel management enter into service at the age of 22 years or 23 years. It, thus, cannot prohibit employment of men below 25 years. Such a restriction keeping in view a citizen's right to be considered for employment, which is a facet of the right to livelihood, does not stand judicial scrutiny.

The Supreme Court judgement was a boost for the Hotel Association of India and the Federation of Hotel and Restaurant Association of India (FHRAI) as all hoteliers can now employ women and men below the age of 25 years to serve alcoholic beverages in restaurants and bars.

All bartenders have to adhere to the standard serving size of a measure of alcohol, which is regulated by the Standard Weights and Measures Act, 1976 and the Standard Weights and Measures (Enforcement) Act, 1985.

TEXT

Section 39 (1) Whoever keeps any weight or measure other than the standard weight or measure in any premises in such circumstances as to indicate that such weight or measure is being or is likely to be, used for any:

(a) *weighment or measurement, or*

(b) *transaction or for industrial production or for protection, shall be punished with fine which may extend to two thousand rupees, and, for the second or subsequent offence, with imprisonment for a term which may extend to one year and also with fine.*

(2) *Whoever—*

(i) *in selling any article or thing by weight, measure or number, delivers or causes to be delivered to the purchaser any quantity or number of that article or thing less than the quantity or number contracted for and paid for, or*

(ii) *in rendering any service by weight, measure or number, renders that service less than the service contracted for and paid for, or*

(iii) *in buying any article or thing by weight, measure or number fraudulently receives, or causes to be received any quantity or number of that article or thing in excess of the quantity or number contracted for and paid for, or*

(iv) *in obtaining any service by weight, measure or number, obtains that service in excess of the service contracted for and paid for; shall be punished with fine which may extend to five thousand rupees, and for the second or subsequent offence, with imprisonment for a term which may extend to one year and also with fine.*

Section 39 stipulates the punishment that will be meted out in case a hotel or a restaurant does not implement the law by keeping a stamped peg measure or weighing scale certified by the Controller of Weights and Measures on the premises. Standard peg measure for spirits (gin, whisky, rum, and vodka) is 30 ml quantities or multiples thereof. Beer is served in bottles ranging from 650 ml to cans of 330 ml.

Bartenders and service personnel should be able to read and understand the Proof of the beverage, which is printed on the label. Proof is the concentration of alcohol in a beverage and is usually stated as the percentage of alcohol by volume (ABV). Depending on the source of alcoholic beverage, the proof is indicated on the label as British Proof (BP), United States (US), European Proof (GL), or OIML (International Organization of Legal Metrology)—the four standards of proof that are printed on bottle labels.

Traditionally, the spirit used to be mixed with gunpowder and ignited. In case of a mild explosion it was concluded that the alcoholic content was too strong for drinking, that is, *over proof*, and if it burnt gently with a blue flame or failed to ignite it was suitable for drinking, that is, *under proof*. Proof was regarded as 100 per cent.

British proof

The modern method of determining proof was devised by Bartholomew Sykes in 1816. Sykes observed that at a temperature of 10°C to 16°C, 57.1 per cent of ABV weighed the same as 42.9 per cent of water by volume. When they are combined in this proportion it is called proof spirit, the proof being 100 per cent. Based upon this scale, pure alcohol is 175 degrees proof or 75 degrees overproof, which means that it is 100 per cent alcohol.

Example	Calculation of alcoholic strength:
	30% (BP) underproof is $100 - 30 = 70\%$ proof
	50% (BP) overproof is $100 + 50 = 150\%$ proof
	Calculation of alcoholic content:
	If the label reads 70% degree proof
	$70 \times 100/175$ or $70 \times 4/7 = 40\%$ ABV
	$150 \times 100/175$ or $150 \times 4/7 = 85\%$ ABV

US proof

US proof spirits contain 50 per cent ABV as against the British proof spirits which contain 57.1 per cent ABV. Hence a 100 degree proof spirit contains 50 per cent ABV.

> **Example** If a bottle is marked 80 degree US Proof it contains 40% ABV. Calculation of proof: 80/2 = 40% ABV.

European proof

Named after the French chemist Guy Lussac and known as GL, in European proof standard, the spirit proof mentioned on the bottle is the same as the alcoholic strength expressed as percentage.

> **Example** If a spirit bottle is marked 40 degree proof then it contains 40% ABV.

International organization of legal metrology

Today, OIML is the widely accepted standard in the European Economic Community for expression of alcoholic strength.

> **Example** If a spirit bottle is marked 40 degree OIML then it contains 40% ABV.
> Volume per cent (V/v %) = [(volume of solute)/(volume of solution)] × 100%
> Here solute is the substance that dissolves in solution and solution is a homogeneous mixture of two or more substances, for example, sugar dissolved in water.

Note that volume per cent is relative to volume of the solution, not volume of the solvent. For example, wine is about 12 per cent v/v ethanol. This means there is 12 ml ethanol for every 100 ml of wine. If you mix 12 ml of ethanol and 100 ml of wine, you will get less than 112 ml of solution.

Table 10.5 illustrates the alcohol content in various beverages that are commercially available in the market.

TABLE 10.5   Alcohol Content in Various Beverages

Beverage	Alcoholic content (%)
Beer	3 to 6
Wine	12 to 14
Dessert wines	18 to 20
Spirits	40 to 90

BEHAVIOURAL TRAITS OF AN INTOXICATED PERSON

As guests consume more alcohol they undergo a variety of behavioural changes which should be observed by the hoteliers to determine whether alcohol should continue to be served or refused. When a guest walks into the hotel premises, his or her appearance, behaviour, and condition should be noted as this will give clues about his well-being. Using the LIST method helps identify behavioural changes in a guest. It is discussed as follows:

L—Lowered or relaxed inhibitions
- Becomes overly talkative and friendly to other guests
- Leaves a group of friends, broods, or drinks alone
- Uncontrolled outburst of emotional display
- Noisy or rowdy, speaks too loudly, or uses foul language or makes offensive comments

I—Impaired judgement
- Becomes tearful, argumentative, and emotional or starts a fight
- Complains that the drinks are too weak
- Becomes careless with money, for example, buys more drinks for the house
- Drinks faster and orders shots or doubles

S—Slowed response
- Motions become difficult, for example, difficulty in lighting a cigarette or picking up his or her glass
- Glossy eyes and slurred speech
- Drowsiness
- Becomes forgetful and is unable to think clearly, for example, ordering a second drink without finishing the earlier one

T—The loss of coordination
- Loses muscle control
- Spills drinks
- Stumbles, staggers, and has difficulty in walking or standing
- Handles money and wallet with great difficulty
- Unable to read or understand the menu, bill, and so on

Serving Drinks Responsibly
Serving drinks responsibly involves the following steps:
- Checking IDs before serving drink, and not selling to patrons who are under age
- Standardizing drink sizes and alcohol content
- Not allowing free-pour and using a peg measure to pour drinks
- Limiting guests to purchasing one drink per person at a time
- Not allowing guests to bring their own alcoholic beverages
- Selling food items as a practice when serving alcohol
- Allowing consumption on premises only
- Not allowing guest to take glasses filled with alcohol outside the premises
- Not taking orders at least 15–20 minutes before the closing of the bar

- Attending training programmes conducted by the bar/restaurant management to learn about the best practices in service
- Familiarizing oneself with any legal requirements that have to be met while doing service
- Ensuring the safety of patrons who are under influence of alcohol from any injuries while on premises

As mentioned earlier there is no law or directive at present in India to standardize the service of alcohol or to fix responsibility on individuals or establishments that serve alcoholic beverages. It is recommended that certain provisions similar to the Dram Shop Act of the USA should be implemented in the country.

'Dram shop' laws are named after establishments prevalent in 18th-century England, which sold gin by a spoonful or a dram. The Dram Shop Act was first passed in1872 by the state of Illinois and has been subsequently amended from time to time. Today, 43 states in USA and the District of Colombia have adopted this Act.

These laws are enforced through a civil suit in the court against the seller of the alcoholic beverage by the person who has sustained injuries at the hands of an intoxicated person. These laws are based upon the principle that those who profit from the distribution of alcohol should be held responsible for the resulting damages. For a seller to be held liable, it is unnecessary to show that he or she is negligent, provided it is proved that the seller sold liquor to a habitual drunkard or a person who was already drunk, which is illegal in itself.

However for a law suit to succeed it must be able to meet the following criteria:

(i) Proof of sale of alcohol to the patron
(ii) Injuries sustained by the patron
(iii) Proximate cause between the alcohol sale and the intoxication
(iv) Intoxication was at least one of the causes of the third-party damage

The salient features of the Act are culled from the various statutes of the states:

(i) All service personnel in bars require being certified or licenced by the government to serve and sell alcohol. The Act gives a new employee 45 days to obtain certification; in case it is not done, the hotel or restaurant has no choice but to relieve the employee. This certification is valid for a period of four years and has to be endorsed by the establishment where the employee works (Louisiana and California).

(ii) All service personnel are required to stop the service of alcohol to an intoxicated person and to record the details of such a person (all states).

(iii) All service personnel can be held personally liable for selling alcohol or tobacco to underage patrons; in case of any doubts the service personnel should ask the person to show his or her identification (all states).

(iv) Service personnel shall be held personally liable if they do not implement the smoking and non-smoking zoning laws in the restaurant and bar (all states).

(v) Service personnel and a liquor vend shopkeeper along with his staff would be held liable if an intoxicated customer caused an accident or injury upon leaving the server's restaurant, bar, or seller's establishment (all states).

(vi) Drunk, loud, and vulgar behaviour by an intoxicated patron in the bar can lead to the bar being fined, and for second or repeated incidents cancellation of the bar's licence (all states).

(vii) Carrying alcohol inside a car is prohibited but it can be carried in the boot of the car (Louisiana and California).

(viii) All bar owners are liable for the action of their customers (all states).

(ix) All bar owners are required to take additional insurance coverage called liquor liability insurance (all states).

(x) Sale of alcohol in an area other than the licenced area is not permitted (all states).

(xi) In some of the states the Dram Shops Act by extension makes corporate and individuals serving alcohol to large gatherings responsible for the safety of their guests. In case the guest has had excess alcohol and meets with an accident injuring a third party, the host can be sued for damages by the injured party.

In order to guard against costly litigations, hotels, restaurants, and liquor vendors have taken a variety of preventive measures such as eliminating 'happy hours', reducing late-night operations, offering free breathalyzer tests, instituting designated driver programmes, and training servers on how to deal with intoxicated patrons.

SALE OF CIGARETTES AND TOBACCO

Besides being knowledgeable about the laws governing the service of alcohol, servers in bars and restaurants have to be familiar with the laws governing the sale of cigarettes and tobacco as it is observed that the maximum sale of tobacco products—cigars and cigarettes—occurs in bars and restaurants. Sale of tobacco products is regulated by the following laws: Cigarettes and Other Tobacco Products (Prohibition of Advertisement and Regulation of Trade and Commerce, Production, Supply and Distribution) Act, 2003 (34 of 2003) and the Cigarettes and Other Tobacco Products (Prohibition of Advertisement and Regulation of Trade and Commerce, Production, Supply and Distribution) Rules, 2004, which came into force on 1 May 2004.

TEXT

Section 3 Prohibition of smoking in a public place.

(1) The owner or the manager or in charge of the affairs of a public place shall cause to be displayed prominently a board, of a minimum size of sixty centimetre by thirty centimetre in the Indian languages(s) as applicable, at least one at the entrance of the public place and one at conspicuous place(s) inside, containing the warning 'No Smoking Arec-Smoking here is an offence'.

(2) *The owner or the manager or in charge of the affair of a hotel having thirty rooms or restaurants having seating capacity of thirty persons or more and the manager of the airport shall ensure that,*
  (i) *the smoking and non-smoking areas are physically segregated;*
  (ii) *the smoking area shall be located in such manner that the public is not required to pass through it in order to reach the non-smoking area; and*
  (iii) *each area shall contain boards indicating thereon 'Smoking Area/Non-Smoking area'.*

Section 5 Prohibition of sale to minors.

(1) *The owner or the manager or the in charge of the affairs of a place where cigarettes and other tobacco products are sold shall display a board of minimum size of sixty centimetre by thirty centimetre at conspicuous place(s) containing the warning 'Sales of tobacco products to a person under the age of eighteen years is a punishable offence', in Indian language(s) as applicable.*
(2) *The onus of proof that the buyer of the tobacco products is not a minor lies with the seller of the tobacco products. The seller, in case of doubt, may request tobacco purchaser to provide appropriate evidence of having reached eighteen years of age.*

The Act forbids the sale of tobacco products to a minor or an individual below the age of 18 years, and it will be the hotel's responsibility to do the verification before selling the cigarettes. Restaurants that have more than 30 covers and hotels that have more than 30 rooms can permit smoking in designated areas, which are segregated and prominently display the signage 'Smoking Area'. It is recommended that the hotel can designate floors as 'Non-smoking Floors' for the convenience of resident guests.

In case the restaurant has 30 covers or less and the hotel 30 rooms or less, then smoking is strictly prohibited. It is suggested that for such properties an area outside the premises can be designated for the convenience of smokers.

Under the Courtesy of Choice programme, the FHRAI has been informing the members of the benefits of the anti-smoking legislation and how it will make a difference to the quality of service that is rendered by a hotel to its resident guests and patrons of its restaurants and bars.

SUMMARY

This chapter gave an introduction to alcoholic and non-alcoholic beverages and a definition of alcohol and various types of alcoholic beverages. It described the impact of alcohol on an individual's health and the social and economic problems caused by alcoholism. The chapter highlighted various attempts that have been made to regulate the possession and consumption of alcohol by governments. It further discussed various types of liquor licences issued by the government and the procedure for securing a restaurant/bar licence.

The chapter also explained the harmful effects of drunken driving and the resulting punishments under the laws and the methods of handling intoxicated persons and those under the influence of alcohol in a restaurant. The food and beverage controller has to ensure that all departments of a hotel, restaurant, or bar—especially purchasing, receiving, and stores—fulfil the requirements of a liquor licence. The chapter also highlighted the importance of establishing procedures to ensure responsible service of alcoholic beverages to guests.

KEY TERMS

Beverage Derived from the French word 'boivre', which means 'to drink'. Beverages include a wide variety of liquids, such as tea, coffee, liquor, beer, wines, milk, juices, and soft drinks, excluding plain water.

Non-alcoholic beverages Liquids that contain less than 0.5 per cent of alcohol, the popular ones being tea, coffee, aerated water, spring or natural water, mineral water, syrups, squashes, juices, and milk.

Tea Leaves of an evergreen shrub or small tree *Camellia sinensis* having fragrant, nodding, cup-shaped white flowers and glossy leaves. The young, dried leaves of this plant, prepared by various processes are used to make hot or cold beverages.

Coffee Include various tropical African shrubs or trees of the genus *Coffea* especially *Coffee arabica* widely cultivated in the tropics for their seeds that are dried, roasted, and ground to prepare a stimulating aromatic drink.

Aerated water A beverage charged with carbonic gas, for example, soda water, and brands such as Tonic Water, Dry Ginger, Bitter Lemon, Coke, and Pepsi.

Natural/spring water Bottled water that is naturally sparkling or carbonated water without any mineral content.

Mineral water Bottled water that is naturally sparkling or carbonated water with mineral content.

Squashes Fruit-flavoured concentrated syrups produced using artificial colour, flavouring, and sweeteners. They have to be mixed with water or soda prior to drinking.

Juices Liquids naturally contained in fruits and vegetables and obtained by extracting the same. Juices are commercially available in bottles or cans.

Syrups Thick viscous liquids consisting of sugar solution in water, artificially flavoured, and used as sweeteners and base for cocktails and milkshakes.

Alcohol Fermented potable clear colourless liquid that is an intoxicant, burns easily, blends well with water, and has a characteristic smell. The chemical formula for ethanol which is an organic compound is C_2H_5OH, which is composed of carbon, oxygen, and hydrogen.

Alcoholic beverages Classified as beers, wines, and spirits which contain ethanol.

Foreign liquor/imported foreign liquor (bottled in origin) Imported from abroad on which custom duty is leviable under any law for the time being enforced. It means all liquor, beer, porter and stout including cider, wines and sweets prepared from grapes or other fruits by the process of fermentation only with or without the addition of alcohol or any other ingredients.

Indian-made foreign liquor All liquor, beer, porter, and stout including cider, wines, and sweets prepared from grapes or other fruits by the process of fermentation only with or without the addition of alcohol or any other ingredient manufactured in India.

Country liquor All liquor other than rectified spirit, denatured spirit and perfumed liquor, not included in the definition of foreign liquor, normally manufactured from neutral spirit and de-mineralized water with added spices and essences, which do not imitate any imported liquors or cordials.

Beer Fermented alcoholic beverage made from grains such as barley, wheat, rice flavoured with hops. The monks of northern Gaul called their concoction using the Celtic word 'Beor' which later became 'beer'.

Wine Alcoholic beverage obtained from the juice of freshly gathered grapes, the fermentation of which has been carried out in the district of origin as per the local traditions and customs.

Spirits Distilled alcoholic beverages containing ethanol produced by fermenting grains, fruits, or vegetables, the important ones commercially available being Rum, Whiskey, Vodka, Gin, Aquavit, Brandy, Pomace—Grappa/Marc, Eau de Vie, Apple Brandy, Arrack, Tequila, and Liqueurs.

Rate of absorption Rate at which alcohol is absorbed by different parts of the body.

Blood alcohol concentration Amount of alcohol present in a person's blood stream and is expressed as the percentage of alcohol absorbed into the blood stream.

Prohibition To forbid the sale of alcohol by authority of the law.

Dry days Days designated by the government on which the sale of alcohol is prohibited.

Off premises or off-site licence Permits the licensee to sell alcoholic beverages to individuals for consumption outside the licensee's premises, for example, liquor stores.

On premises or on-site licence Permits the licensee to sell alcoholic beverages to individuals for consumption within the licensee's premises, for example, restaurants and bars within hotels, room service, standalone restaurants and bars, beer bars, and sports bars.

British proof The modern method of determining proof devised by Bartholomew Sykes in 1816. Sykes observed that at a temperature of 10°C to 16°C, 57.1 per cent of ABV weighs the same as 42.9 per cent of water by volume. When alcohol and water are combined in this proportion it is called proof spirit.

European proof Named after the French chemist Guy Lussac and known as (GL), under which the spirit proof mentioned on the bottle is the same as the alcoholic strength expressed as percentage.

OIML (International Organization of Legal Metrology) The widely accepted standard in the European Economic Community for expression of alcoholic strength. If a spirit bottle is marked 40 degree OIML then it implies that it contains 40 per cent ABV.

Legal drinking age in India Varies from 18 to 25 years depending upon the state of residence. It is 18 years in Goa, Himachal Pradesh, Rajasthan, Sikkim, and Uttar Pradesh; 25 years in Punjab, Haryana, Chandigarh, Delhi, Maharashtra, and Meghalaya; and 21 years in rest of India.

EXERCISES

Define the Following

1. Alcohol
2. Beverages
3. Off-premises licence
4. Tequila
5. OIML
6. Rate of absorption
7. Beer
8. BAC
9. Dry days
10. Wines

Concept Review Questions

1. What is the role of a food and beverage controller in the operations of a bar?
2. Explain the procedure for obtaining a liquor licence for a standalone restaurant.
3. Describe the cycle for the purchasing, receiving, and storage of alcohol.
4. What are the behavioural traits of an intoxicated person?
5. What are the laws that govern smoking and the sale of cigarettes in bars?

6. Briefly describe PCT alcohol policy that is followed by the government when framing the laws.

Critical Thinking Questions

1. Do you agree that liquor laws should have stipulations/guidelines for licensing of bartenders and service staff related to responsible service of alcoholic beverages to guests?
2. Drunken driving cases are on the increase in India. What steps can hoteliers and restaurateurs take to prevent this phenomenon?

Research Question

1. Liquor licensing is a state subject. Is it possible to develop a liquor licensing law that is centrally administered?

Project

1. Prepare a write-up on the Dram Shop law highlighting its important aspects. Concern for an individual's life and safety are paramount and these have been embodied in certain provisions of the Dram Shop Act USA. Do you agree?

REFERENCES

Tom Standage, *History of the World in 6 Glasses*, Walker and Company, USA, 2005.

<http://quotesnphrases.blogspot.com/2006/10/alcohol-sayings.html> accessed on 14 July 2012.

<http://news.nationalgeographic.com/news/2005/10/1003_051003_six_drinks.html> accessed on 14 July 2012.

<http://www.searo.who.int/LinkFiles/Facts_and_Figures_ch1.pdf> accessed on 14 July 2012.

<http://encyclopedia2.thefreedictionary.com/alcoholic+beverage> accessed on 14 July 2012.

<http://articles.timesofindia.indiatimes.com/2011-09-22/mumbai/30189043_1_superintendent-of-state-excise-bombay-prohibition-act-prohibition-law> accessed on 14 July 2012.

<http://www.xtimeline.com/timeline/History-of-Alcohol> accessed on 14 July 2012.

<http://www.duhaime.org/LawMuseum/LawArticle-360/Crazy-English-Laws-The-Sequel.aspx> accessed on 14 July 2012.

<http://en.wikipedia.org/wiki/Whiskey_Rebellion> accessed on 14 July 2012.

<http://www.drug-rehabs.org/cat/Properties_of_Alcohol> accessed on 14 July 2012.

<http://www.lmu.edu/Page25071.aspx> accessed on 14 July 2012.

<http://en.wikipedia.org/wiki/Non-alcoholic_beverage> accessed on 14 July 2012.

<http://www.nhlbisupport.com/bmi/> accessed on 14 July 2012.

<http://indiankanoon.org/doc/354941/> accessed on 17 July 2012.

<http://www.indiankanoon.org/doc/79026890/> accessed on 17 July 2012.

<http://www.answeringlaw.com/php/displayContent.php?linkId=638> accessed on 17 July 2012.

<http://en.wikipedia.org/wiki/Alcohol_proof> accessed on 17 July 2012.

<http://legal-dictionary.thefreedictionary.com/Dramshop+Acts> accessed on 17 July 2012.

<http://www.delhi.gov.in/wps/wcm/connect/DOIT_EXCISE/excise/licences/application+form+for+the+grant+of+l-3+or+l-5+licence> accessed on 17 July 2012.

<http://www.thefreedictionary.com/coffee> accessed on 16 July 2012.

<http://www.thefreedictionary.com/tea> accessed on 16 July 2012.

<http://www.thefreedictionary.com/Body+Mass+Index+(BMI)> accessed on 17 July 2012.

<http://excise.delhigovt.nic.in/ex6.asp> accessed on 18 July 2012.

<http://dictionary.reference.com/browse/solute> accessed on 18 July 2012.

<http://dictionary.reference.com/browse/solution> accessed on 18 July 2012.

<http://books.google.co.in/books?id=fUE0bazkcxAC&pg=PA20&dq=alcoholic++oxford+dictionary&hl=en&sa=X&ei=BD39UPLIBsH- rAes8YCADQ&sqi=2&ved=0CDoQ6AEwAQ#v=onepage&q=alcoholic%20%20oxford%20dictionary&f=false> accessed on 20 January 2013.

G Gururaj, Pratima Murthy, N. Girish, and V. Benegal (2011) *Alcohol Related Harm: Implications for Public Health and Policy in India* <http://www.nimhans.kar.nic.in/cam/CAM/Alcohol_report_NIMHANS.pdf> accessed on 12 April 2013.

Part V

Laws Related to Public Health and Safety

Chapter 11   Battle for a Healthy Environment

Battle for a Healthy Environment

LEARNING OBJECTIVES

After going through this chapter, the reader will be familiar with the following:

- Environment and its impact on our lives
- Legislative measures initiated to preserve the environment
- Key elements of a successful waste management programme
- Definition and implementation of good environment practices in eco-friendly hotels

INTRODUCTION

The earth will not continue to offer its harvest, except with faithful stewardship. We cannot say we love the land and then take steps to destroy it for use by future generations.

—Pope John Paul II

Concern for the environment is not a recent phenomenon, and we can trace back the origins of these concerns to the period of the Vedas. All the four Vedas, *Rig, Sama, Yajur,* and *Atharva,* mention that man should maintain a harmonious relationship with the five elements *Vayu* (Air), *Agni* (Fire), *Apah* (Water), *Prithvi* (Earth), and *Akash* (Firmament). It was understood that the well-being of humanity depended on the preservation and sustenance of the environment. The sages recognized that if the delicate balance was upset by human intervention, it could lead to the air, water, and earth becoming polluted, leading to changes in the climate and seasons. These ancient scriptures have recommended conservation of natural resources.

The *Oxford Dictionaries Online* define the environment as '(1) the surroundings or conditions in which a person, animal, or plant lives or operates (2) the natural world, as a whole or in a particular geographical area, especially as affected by human activity'. In India, the Environment Protection Act, 1986 defines the environment as 'including water, air and land and the interrelationship which exists among and between water, air and land, and human beings, other living creatures, plants, micro-organism and property'. Pollution is nothing but the introduction of extraneous matters or contaminants into the environment, which bring about a change in the quality of the air, water, or soil. The Environment Protection Act, 1986 describes an environmental pollutant as 'any solid, liquid or gaseous substance present in such concentration, as may be, or tend to be injurious to the environment'.

Since the Industrial Revolution of the 18th century, there have been rapid technological advancements that have increased environmental pollution worldwide. The reason for this is that man in his quest for advancement and economic growth paid scant heed to the impact his actions were having on the delicate balance that nature had maintained. In India, during the Mughal period and under British rule, exploitation of natural resources was the norm and post-Independence, this practice continued. Economic prosperity has improved lifestyles, but this has been achieved at the cost of upsetting the harmonious relationship between man and nature, resulting in a polluted environment. We keep reading in the newspapers about how the air and water quality is affecting our health in large cities and how use of pesticides by the farmers has affected the quality of the soil in which our grains, fruits, and vegetables are grown.

The environmental issue can be defined as the excessive exploitation of the Earth's natural resources, resulting in degradation and depletion of natural resources, which has impacted nature's capacity to sustain life. Depletion of natural resources is the result of the extraction of non-renewable resources such as metals and minerals and the extraction of renewable resources from the environment at a faster rate than they can be renewed, for example, excessive killing of wildlife. Degradation, on the other hand, is the destruction or damage to the natural resources, for example, deforestation, desertification, and pollution.

The first serious attempt to combat pollution and its impact on the environment was initiated when the UN Conference on the Human Environment held in Stockholm in 1972 laid down the 'common principles to inspire and guide the peoples of the world in the preservation and enhancement of the human environment'. In 1972, India set up the National Council for Environmental Policy and Planning within the Department of Science and Technology. This later, in 1985, became the Ministry of Environment and Forests, which together with the Central Pollution Control Board and State Pollution Control Boards, administers and regulates the various laws pertaining to environment protection.

With the passing of the 42nd Amendment to the Indian Constitution in 1976, an addition was made to the Directive Principle of State Policy Article 48-A, in which it became mandatory for the states to take steps to protect and preserve the environment, and under Article 51-A(g) of Part IV A of Fundamental Duties, it became the duty of 'every citizen of India to protect and improve the natural environment including forests, lakes, rivers, and wildlife and to have compassion for living creatures'.

However, it was the Bhopal gas tragedy, which occurred in 1984 at the Union Carbide pesticide plant that spurred the Indian government into taking affirmative steps. The Environment (Protection) Act and Rules were passed in 1986. Under this Act, the central government is empowered to take necessary measures to protect and improve the quality of the environment by setting standards for emissions and discharges; regulating the location of industries; management of hazardous wastes; and protection of public health and welfare. This legislation provides the framework for the coordination of central and state authorities.

Subsequently, a series of legislative measures has been taken to conserve and regulate the environment under various categories:

(i) Water
(ii) Air
(iii) Forest and wildlife
(iv) General
(v) Others
(vi) International agreements

Some of the important pieces of legislation that have been passed under various categories since 1882 are given in Table 11.1.

TABLE 11.1 Legislative Enactments Since 1882

1882: The Easement Act states that all surface water belongs to the state; however, it allows private use of groundwater, by viewing it as an attachment to the land.

1897: The Indian Fisheries Act has made the use of dynamite or other explosive with intent to catch, destroy, or poison any fish in order to kill fishes a crime.

1927: The Indian Forest Act and Amendment, 1984 consolidated the laws related to forests, the transit of forest produce, and the ground rules for the levy of duty on timber and other forest produce.

1956: The River Boards Act enables the states to request the central government in setting up River Advisory Boards to resolve interstate disputes and to encourage inter-state cooperation.

1970: The Merchant Shipping Act restricts the disposal of waste from ships along a specified radius along the coast.

1972: The Wildlife Protection Act, Rules 1973 and Amendment 1991 provide for protection to listed species of flora and fauna and establish a network of ecologically important protected areas. There is a blanket ban on carrying out any industrial activity inside these protected areas.

1974: The Water (Prevention and Control of Pollution) Act prohibits the discharge of pollutants into water bodies beyond a given standard and lays down penalties for non-compliance. The Act was amended in 1988 to conform closely to the provisions of the Environment Protection Act, 1986.

1977: The Water (Prevention and Control of Pollution) Cess Act provides for the levying and collection of fees from water-consuming industries and local authorities.

1980: The Forest (Conservation) Act and Rules, 1981 was adopted to protect and conserve forests. The Act restricts the powers of the state to de-reserve forests and use of forestland for non-forest purposes.

1981: The Air (Prevention and Control of Pollution) Act was adopted to counter the problems associated with air pollution. It establishes ambient air quality standards and seeks to combat air pollution by prohibiting the use of polluting fuels and substances as well as by regulating appliances that give rise to air pollution. Establishing or operating any industrial plant in the designated pollution control area requires consent from state boards.

1982: The Atomic Energy Act was introduced to deal with radioactive waste.

(Contd)

TABLE 11.1 (Contd)

1988: The Motor Vehicles Act was enacted to regulate vehicular traffic. It lays down the rules for the proper packaging, labelling, and transportation of hazardous wastes. Furthermore, stringent Euro I and II emission norms were notified for vehicle owners and manufacturers to control vehicular pollution.

1989: The Hazardous Waste (Management and Handling) Rules brought out a guide for the manufacture, collection, treatment, import, storage, and import of hazardous chemicals and for management of hazardous wastes.

1991: GSR 85E Scheme on Labelling of Environment Friendly Products certifies and labels household and other consumer products that meet certain environment criteria set by the Bureau of Indian Standards' quality requirements. Packaged food and beverage items should conform to the quality standards of the Food Safety and Standards Act, 2006 before they can be awarded the 'ECOMARK' label. This covers laundry detergents, packaging, and labelling materials that can be recycled, reused, and made from biodegradable materials

1991: The Coastal Regulation Zone Notification declares that coastal land up to 500 metres from the high tide line (HTL) and a stretch of 100 metres along the banks of creeks, estuaries, backwaters, and rivers that are subject to tidal fluctuations is declared as the Costal Regulation Zone (CRZ). CRZ is divided into four categories within 500 metres from the HTL for the regulation of various activities such as discharge of wastewater, including construction activities in the coastal lands, backwaters, and estuaries.

1991: The Public Liability Insurance Act and Rules and Amendment, 1992 makes it mandatory for companies to take out public liability insurance policy for the purpose of providing immediate relief to the persons affected by accident while handling any hazardous substance. Where death or injury results from an accident, this Act makes the owner liable to provide relief as is specified in the Schedule of the Act.

1994: National Ambient Air Quality Standards (NAAQS) ambient quality standards similar to those prevailing in many developed and developing countries were notified by the Central Pollution Control Board in April 1994 for major pollutants to protect public health, vegetation, and property.

1994: The Environmental Impact Assessment of Development Projects Notification includes all projects listed under Schedule I of the Act requiring environmental clearance from the Ministry of Environment and Forests if located in a fragile region. Moreover, any project with an investment of ₹500 crore requires to be approved by the Ministry of Environment and Forests.

1995: The National Environmental Tribunal Act was created for the speedy disposal of cases involving hazardous substances, resulting in an accident or damage to persons, property, and the environment and to award compensation for damages arising from any activity.

2000: The Municipal Solid Wastes (Management and Handling) Rules applies to every municipal authority responsible for the collection, segregation, storage, transportation, processing, and disposal of municipal solid wastes consisting of household, commercial, and industrial waste.

2002: The Noise Pollution (Regulation and Control) (Amendment) Rules lay down the terms and conditions that are necessary to reduce noise pollution, such as permissions and regulated use of loudspeakers or public address systems during night hours (between 10:00 p.m. and 12:00 midnight) on or during any cultural or religious festival.

These laws would have been toothless if the judiciary coupled with public interest litigations (PILs) had not espoused environmental causes through their various judgements, upholding the basic tenets of environmental legislation, which are as follows:

(i) Doctrine of public trust
(ii) Polluter pays principle

(iii) Principle of sustainable development

(iv) Precautionary principle

In one of the first legal cases *Municipal Council, Ratlam vs Vardhichand AIR 1980 SC 1622,* the Supreme Court interpreted Article 21 of the Indian Constitution, which guarantees fundamental right to life and personal liberty, to include the right to a wholesome environment and held that a litigant may assert his or her right to a healthy environment against the state by a writ petition to the Supreme Court or high court.

The facts of this case were that some residents of the Ratlam municipality filed a complaint before the Sub-Divisional Magistrate, Ratlam, alleging that the municipality was not constructing proper drains and there was stench and stink caused by the excretion by nearby slum dwellers and that this was a nuisance to the petitioners. The Sub-Divisional Magistrate directed the municipality to draw a plan within six months to remove the nuisance and passed an order, which was approved by the High Court, directing the municipality to construct the drains. The municipality filed an appeal in the Supreme Court of India and contended that it did not have sufficient funds to carry out the works as directed by the Sub-Divisional Magistrate. The Supreme Court held that paucity of funds could not be made an excuse by the municipality to shirk its basic duties and gave the judgement that it should comply with the Sub-Divisional Magistrate orders.

In a PIL by *Vijay Singh Punia vs Rajasthan State Board for the Prevention and Control of Pollution AIR 2003 Raj 286, RLW 2003 (2) Raj 1012, 2003 (2) WLC 465,* the Rajasthan High Court observed that when any person disturbs the ecological balance or degrades, pollutes, and tinkers with the gifts of nature such as air, water, river, sea, and other elements of nature, he or she not only violates the fundamental right guaranteed under Article 21 of the Constitution but also breaches the fundamental duty to protect the environment under Article 51A(g). Subsequently, in two other cases, namely *Subash Kumar vs State of Bihar and Others 1991 AIR 420, 1991 SCR (1) 5* and *Virender Gaur and Others vs State of Haryana and Others Appeal (Civil) 9151 of 1994,* the Supreme Court gave a wide-ranging interpretation of Article 21 of the Constitution stating that the right to life includes the right to clean air and water and made it mandatory for the state to protect this human right. These cases gave constitutional protection to the individuals against the actions of the state that may impact the individuals' right to a safe, healthy environment, ensuring clean air and water against the hazards of polluting industries.

In *Indian Council for Enviro-Legal vs Union of India & Others on 18 July, 2011 Civil Original Jurisdiction IA No. 36 and IA No. 44 in Writ Petition (C) No. 967 of 1989,* a case concerning serious damage by certain industries producing toxic chemicals to the environment of Bichhri District in Rajasthan, the Supreme Court applied '*the polluter pays principle*', which states that absolute liability rests with the polluter to pay for the damages done to the natural environment as a result of his or her actions.

In *M. C. Mehta vs Kamal Nath and Others AIR 2000 SC 1997*, the Supreme Court applied the '*doctrine of public trust*' and '*the polluter pays principle*' while awarding the judgement against the respondent Span Motels Private Limited. The Supreme Court applied the 'doctrine of public trust', which states that certain common properties such as rivers, forests, seashores, and air were held by the government in Trusteeship for the free and unimpeded use of the general public. Granting lease to a motel located at the bank of River Beas would interfere with the natural flow of the water and that the state government had breached the public trust doctrine. It further applied 'the polluter pays principle' while imposing penalties on Span Motels Private Limited.

Span Motels Private Limited was originally granted a lease to construct a motel on the banks of River Beas on 29 September 1981. Subsequently, Span Motels Private Limited was granted approval by the Ministry of Environment and Forests, Government of India, by a letter dated 24 November 1993 giving lease of forest land of 27 *bighas* and 12 *biswas* of area on the banks of the River Beas in Himachal Pradesh, which was regularized by the lease deed dated 11 April 1994. This encroachment of land led to the swelling of the river in 1995, leading it to change its course washing away the Span Hotel lawns, causing landslides, and an estimated property worth ₹105 crore was damaged.

In *Vellore Citizens Welfare Forum vs Union of India*, a PIL under Article 32 of the Constitution of India was filed against the pollution that was being caused by discharge of untreated effluent by the tanneries and other industries into the agricultural fields, road sides, water ways, open lands, and finally in the River Palar in Tamil Nadu, which was the main source of potable water to the residents of the area.

In this case, the Supreme Court applied the '*doctrine of public trust*', '*polluter pays principle*', and '*principle of sustainable development*', which is based on the '*precautionary principle*' when awarding its judgement.

The Supreme Court relied on the international interpretations of '*sustainable development*' and '*the precautionary principle*' that has been referred to by Sands (2003), which mentions the four recurring elements in the concept of sustainable development as stated in international agreements:

(i) The need to preserve national resources for the benefit of future generations (the principle of intergenerational equity)

(ii) The aim of exploiting natural resources in a manner which is 'sustainable', 'prudent', rational', 'wise', or 'appropriate' (the principle of sustainable use)

(iii) The 'equitable' use of natural resources, which implies that use by one state must take account of the needs of other states (the principle of equitable use, or intergenerational equity)

(iv) The need to ensure that environmental considerations are integrated into economic and other development plans, programmes, and projects and that development needs are taken into account in applying environmental objectives (the principle of integration)

The *precautionary principle* states any development activity that can cause serious and irreversible environmental damage must be prevented and is one of the tenets of sustainable development. Sustainable development balances environmental concerns with development, which improves the quality of human life without causing irreversible damage to the carrying capacity of the life-supporting ecosystem.

Through its various judgements, the Supreme Court has ensured that in any conflict between the concerns of development and the environment, the case will be decided based upon the touchstone of the '*doctrine of public trust*', '*polluter pays principle*', '*principle of sustainable development*', and '*precautionary principle*'.

Broadly speaking, these laws have attempted to uphold the well-established environmental principles for the control and disposal of pollutants or waste: prevention, reduce, reuse, and recycle (the three 'Rs'), and finally disposal. However, in Europe, the principle of recovery (also referred to as the fourth 'R') is followed after recycling and before the final disposal of pollutants or waste. This practice states that prevention is better than cure, similar to the precautionary principle failing which every attempt should be made to reduce consumption and to reuse items; in so far as it is practical, the item should be recycled after its useful life is over. The fourth 'R' recovery aims at recovering energy from the usable part of waste with the balance being disposed.

During the 1980s and 1990s, legislative measures and judicial activism awakened the conscious of industrialists, businesses, and hoteliers to the harmful effects of pollution. To encourage businesses to reduce harmful pollutants being discharged, governments decided to give incentives, for example, polluting industries could earn carbon credits by reducing the emissions and also by adopting technologies that support reduction of pollutants such as solar energy, biogas, and better waste disposal management techniques. The waste management hierarchy is illustrated in Fig. 11.1. In this hierarchy, the best option, prevention, is listed first and the least desirable option, disposal, is listed last.

Waste is commonly referred to as garbage or rubbish, and is created when any material becomes unusable or unwanted or has been discarded. Waste can be classified as solid, liquid, and gaseous waste, which can either be biodegradable or hazardous, as illustrated in Fig. 11.2.

Biodegradable waste is any substance that is capable of being decomposed by the action of micro-organisms such as bacteria, algae, fungi, for example, human and animal waste, cotton, and wool.

Hazardous waste is defined as a solid, liquid, or gaseous by-product of industrial processes that possesses at least one of the following characteristics: (i) corrosive, that is, has the potential of gnawing through the material; corrosive waste includes waste from rust remover, acid, or alkaline cleaning fluid, and battery acid; (ii) ignitable, that is, has the potential to catch fire; ignitable waste includes waste from paint, gasoline, diesel fuel, some degreasers, and some other solvents; (iii) reactive, that is,

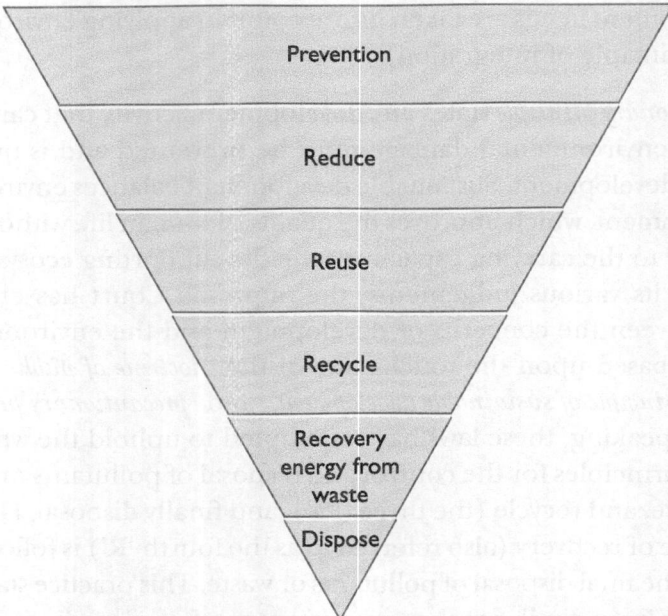

FIGURE 11.1 Waste Management Hierarchy

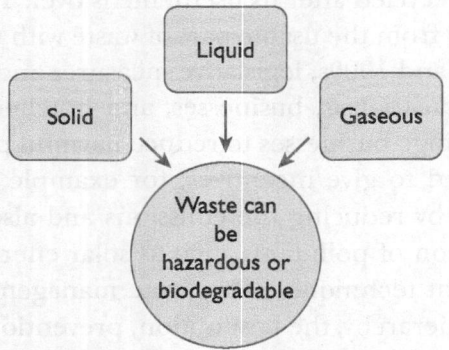

FIGURE 11.2 Classification of Waste

has the quality of bringing about a chemical or a physical change to any material or substance; reactive waste includes waste from cyanide plating, bleach, and other oxidizers; (iv) toxic, which is generated by poisonous substances (toxic substances) and which may have to be handled, stored, transported, and disposed in a controlled manner; toxic constituents include heavy metals, chlorinated solvents, or certain aromatic compounds. *Solid waste* consists of municipal waste (household, commercial, and industrial waste), construction waste, demolition waste, chemical waste, and special waste such as medical, abattoir, animal, and livestock waste and sludge as shown in Fig. 11.3. Solid waste is mostly sent to landfills for final disposal.

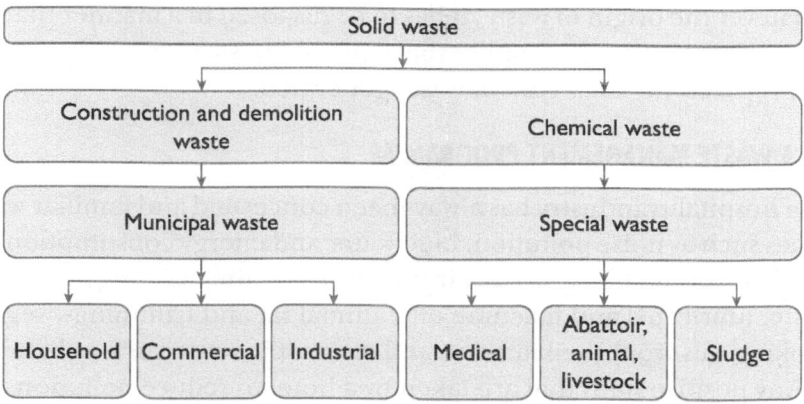

FIGURE 11.3 Sources of Solid Waste

Liquid waste or grey and black water is wastewater generated from domestic activities such as laundry, dishwashing, and bathing, which can be recycled onsite for use in drip irrigation of the landscaped gardens (Fig. 11.4). Black water is sewage and contains human waste and is therefore not usable for gardening until and unless it is treated. Treatment of grey and black water is done onsite by installing sewage treatment plants (STPs) in hotels. This is discharged as sewage.

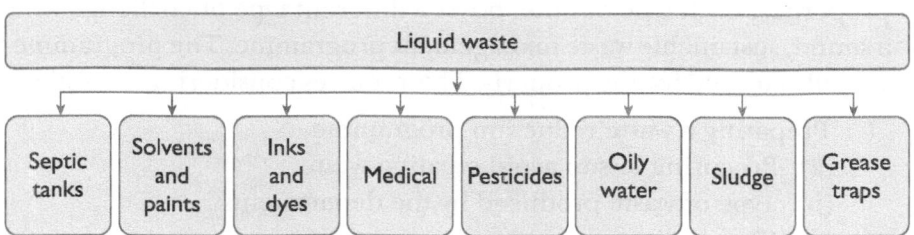

FIGURE 11.4 Sources of Liquid Waste

Gaseous waste consists of smoke, smog, fumes, and particles in the air such as soot, dust, carbon dioxide, nitrogen, and sulphur dioxide gas emissions, as shown in Fig. 11.5. Gaseous waste can only be controlled by preventing the polluting elements from being discharged into the air, as it is difficult to recycle or reuse.

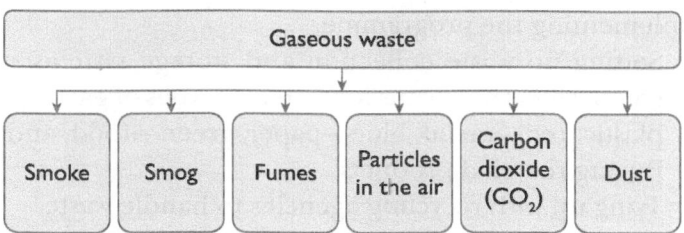

FIGURE 11.5 Sources of Gaseous Waste

Whatever the origin of waste, it has to be disposed in a manner that is least harmful to the environment. This implies that a proper waste management programme should be prepared for each type of waste generated.

DESIGNING A WASTE MANAGEMENT PROGRAMME

The hospitality industry has always been concerned and familiar with environmental issues such as noise pollution, high water and energy consumption from guest rooms and back-of-the-house areas, air quality inside the building, disposal of sewage, solid waste, lubricants and machine oils, animal fat and trimmings, vegetable waste, used cooking oils from the kitchens, and electronic waste such as batteries and bulbs.

Any positive steps that are taken by a hotel to reduce pollution and manage waste efficiently gets immediately recognized by the local community, as hotels are located in highly visible locations such as downtown, beaches or mountains, close to airports, wildlife parks, and game sanctuaries. This visibility gets further enhanced as hotels in any location are frequented by international and domestic guests having diverse profiles who become the hotels' ambassadors in spreading the message of good environmental practices being implemented by the hotel.

Hotels are flagged by different brands and operated by different management companies, and these could be heritage hotels, new-build properties, or existing properties. Each type of hotel poses a different type of challenge when formulating a sound, sustainable waste management programme. The programme has to be individually tailored for the property. This requires considering the following key points:

(i) Preparing a waste reduction programme
    (a) Procuring less to avoid creating waste
    (b) Type of waste produced by the departments
    (c) Cost of disposing waste
(ii) Reuse or recycling of waste making a commitment to manage waste
    (a) Creating employee awareness
    (b) Training the employees and getting them committed to participate in the programme
    (c) Preparing waste reduction targets
    (d) Organizing a waste reduction team to monitor the programme
(iii) Implementing the programme
    (a) Setting up waste collection and storage systems such as using different coloured garbage cans for different types of garbage, for example, yellow—plastic, red—metal, blue—paper, green—food, and black—glass
    (b) Buying recycled products
    (c) Tying up with recycling agencies to handle waste
    (d) Involving employees, guests, vendors, and the community to participate in the programme

   (iv) Getting feedback on the implementation
     (a) Establishing monitoring and evaluation procedures
   (v) Initiating improvements based upon feedback

PREPARING A WASTE REDUCTION PROGRAMME

The first step for preparing a waste reduction programme is to analyse the waste being generated by the departments and to classify it into broad categories such as paper, plastic, glass, aluminium, metal, cloth, chemicals, pesticides, cooking oils, lubricants, wood, vegetable, and animal waste, as illustrated in Table 11.2.

TABLE 11.2 Waste Analysis by Department

Department	Type of waste	Category
Front office	Office stationery, magazines, newspaper, plastic pens, computer toner and ink, and computer stationery	Paper and plastic
Food production and kitchen stewarding	Paper, metals, aluminium and stainless steel utensils, vegetable and animal trimmings (food wastage), wastewater, cooking oil, plastic containers, cling wrap, grease paper, aluminium foil, wooden utensils, cleaning agents—phenyl and dishwasher soap, packaging material, and broken plates	Paper, plastic, metal, wood, oils, food waste, wastewater, chemicals and detergents, ceramics, and aluminium
Food service	Paper, plastic bottles, leftover food and beverages, glass, matchsticks, cigarette butts, cloth, and packaging material	Paper, plastic, glass, food and beverage waste, and cloth
Housekeeping	Coat hangers, plastic bags, cloth, bottles, cans, newspaper, telephone books, guest stationery, and paper bags	Paper, plastic, glass, aluminium, and cloth
Laundry	Coat hangers, plastic drums, chemicals, detergents, waste cloth, laundry, and valet paper or plastic bags	Paper, plastic, lubricants, chemicals and detergents, and cloth
Engineering	Lubricants, chemicals, plastic switches, waste cloths, cleaning agents, diesel, scrap metals, discarded construction and demolition materials, paints, varnish, and solvents	Paper, plastic, diesel lubricants, chemicals, waste cloth, metal, batteries, and construction and demolition scrap
Sales and marketing	Office stationery, plastic pens, computer toner and ink, and computer stationery	Paper, plastic, and ink
Accounts, receiving, purchase, and stores	Office stationery, plastic bins, computer toner and ink, computer stationery, cardboard packaging material, and wooden crates	Paper, plastic, and ink
Horticulture	Grass, tree clippings, fertilizer, wood waste	Organic waste

Once the waste has been categorized, it has to be further segregated into hazardous or non-hazardous, biodegradable or non-biodegradable, and reusable or recyclable. This has been highlighted in Table 11.3.

TABLE 11.3 Category and Type of Waste That can be Reduced, Reused, or Recycled

Category	Type	Reduce	Reuse	Recycle
Glass	Non-hazardous waste	Purchase in limited quantities based upon the consumption pattern so as to minimize inventories	• Glass bottles to store condiments in the kitchen • Beverage bottles can be given back to the vendor for rebottling of beverages	• Keep separate bins for different types of recyclable materials on the service landings of guest floors, banquet function areas, and kitchens • Identify recycler who recycles glass
Paper	Non-hazardous waste	• Newspaper, serviettes, cardboard packing material, office stationery maintain minimum inventory • Newspaper magazines order as per occupancy • Print stationery when required	• Office stationery should be used on both sides • All brochures, in-house promotional material should be sorted and kept for recycling • Donate magazines to charities • Use partially used toilet rolls in staff lockers	• Keep separate bins for different types of recyclable materials on the service landings of guest floors, banquet function areas • Identify recycler who recycles paper
Plastic	Non-hazardous waste	Reduce the purchase of different types of plastic bottles, containers made from No. 1 PET; No. 2 HDPE; No. 3 PVC; No. 4 LDPE; No. 5 PP; No. 6 PS; No. 7 OTHERS	• Negotiate with vendors to supply goods in reusable crates and containers • Sell the plastic waste from Nos 1 to 6 to recyclers	• Keep separate bins for different types of recyclable materials on the service landings of guest floors, banquet function areas, kitchens • Identify recycler who recycles plastic
Aluminium/ Steel	Non-hazardous waste	Soft beverage cans, aerosol disinfectant spray cans, foil, tin cans	Aluminium and steel containers can be used for storage	• Keep separate bins for different types of recyclable materials on the service landings of guest floors, banquet function areas • Identify recycler who recycles aluminium

(Contd)

TABLE 11.3 (Contd)

Category	Type	Reduce	Reuse	Recycle
Cloth	Non-hazardous waste	Reduce the purchase of tablecloths, bed linen, napkins, waste cloths, by maintaining proper inventories and ordering items as and when required	Old tablecloths and bed linen can be converted into dusters, small cocktail napkins, and waste cloths for cleaning machines in the engineering and laundry departments	All discarded cloths should be stored separately and can be sold to recycle companies that convert it to other reusable materials
Wood	Non-hazardous waste	Reduce unnecessary trimming of trees and shrubs to generate waste	Use shaved wood trimmings to line the trees in the hotel campus	Collect in the compost pits allowing it to decompose into manure
Vegetable and animal waste (organic waste)	Non-hazardous waste	• Reduce trimmings by using potato peeling machines • Use pulverizing machines to make purees and fruit or vegetable pulp for cooking • Use various secondary cuts of meats fish and poultry to make stocks for soups	• Donate left-over foods to charities • Donate or sell vegetable and animal waste to food recyclers to prepare pet food • Use vegetable trimmings and odd cuts as garnish for dishes • Give choice to guests to order half or full portions of dishes and serve pre-plated meals to reduce waste	Recycle all disposable food into compost pits where it can decompose into manure
Lubricants	Hazardous waste	Machine oils, diesel grease, paints and oils should be reduced	Difficult to reuse	Can be used to create lube stock which can then be used
Cooking oils	Hazardous waste	Use less cooking oil in the preparation of foods; fat-free and low-fat meals are in keeping with the trend to remain healthy	Difficult to reuse	Can be used to create biodiesel fuel
Cleaning chemicals and pesticides	Hazardous waste	• Use minimum pesticides in the gardens reducing the level of chemicals in the area • Reduce the use of chemicals and sanitizers in the guest bathrooms • Reduce the use of chemicals and solvents in the laundry and engineering departments	Difficult to reuse	

Once waste has been identified, the amount of savings a hotel can achieve by these steps has to be quantified. This can be computed by systematically calculating category wise, for example, plastic, glass, paper, metal, and aluminium, as shown in Table 11.4. Similar tables should be developed for all other categories of waste, and once this has been done, the total income by disposing the waste to recyclers can be determined.

TABLE 11.4   Calculating the Weight and Income from Waste (Aluminium)

Item	Product weight (g)	Empty container weight (g)	Number of containers per case	Weight per container (kg)	Consumption per month in cases	Total weight per month (kg)	Income from disposal cost per kg	Income from disposal per month
Beverage cans	340	32	24	768	25	19.2	15	288
Juice cans	1304	160	12	1920	15	28.8	12	345.6
Coffee	1105	310	12	3720	6	22.32	12	267.84
Aerosol cans	36	8	24	192	15	2.88	8	23.04
Total						73.2		924.48
Annual savings								11,093.76

MAKING A COMMITMENT TO MANAGE WASTE

The foremost task for the management is creating employee awareness. It is achieved by initiating training programmes, handouts, and posters that create awareness among the employees; selecting team leaders who are responsible for the implementation of the programme; and finally recognizing and rewarding the team and its individual members.

A—*Awareness* of environmental laws and issues should be included in employee orientation programmes for new employees and part of the model standing orders. Training of employees should be done periodically to inform the employees why the hotel recycles waste, its benefits, and the resultant savings that accrue. Training plans should be developed which are specific to each department.

S—*Select team leaders* who shall, in consultation with the management, set up specific goals for their departments and will be responsible and accountable for evaluating their performance against the measurable goals that they have set for their departments. These team leaders will also give suggestions to the management on how to improve the programme, and steps that are considered necessary shall be initiated in consultation with the management.

R—Recognize individual employees that achieve their goals by giving them letters of appreciation and incentives. In order to encourage departments, a running trophy can be instituted, which can be awarded to the department that meets its targets. This will foster healthy inter-departmental competition and encourage them to perform.

A successful waste management policy results in 'Green hotels' that strive to be more environmentally friendly through efficient use of energy, water, and materials while providing quality services. Green hotels conserve and preserve by saving water, reducing energy use, and reducing solid waste.

IMPLEMENTING THE PROGRAMME

Besides employee participation, it is equally essential to encourage guest and vendor participation in the programme. Hotels can facilitate guest participation by placing recycling instructions in guest rooms, for example, as tent cards, inserts in the room directories, and flyers as guests are more than willing to participate in such initiatives.

Typically, in guest rooms, tent cards are placed for educating the guests of the hotel's eco-friendly policies covering the following points:

(i) In an effort to conserve water, the taps are to be closed when lathering and brushing teeth.

(ii) In an effort to conserve water, towels will not be replaced if hung and will be exchanged only when left on the floor.

(iii) In an effort to conserve water, tent cards should be left on beds in case change of bed sheets is not required.

(iv) In an effort to conserve energy, air conditioning temperature is to be controlled, and lights and TV are to be switched off when not in use.

(v) Guests should be recommended to open the drapes to allow natural light to come in.

(vi) Notices such as 'Rooms are ventilated by opening the windows by housekeeping on a daily basis in an effort to maintain the freshness of the rooms' are to be displayed.

(vii) Notices such as 'The management periodically cleans the dust and grime from the AC ducts and filters to maintain ambient air quality in the rooms' are to be displayed.

In public areas such as banquet halls and conference rooms, placing trash receptacles along with colour-coded recycling containers will facilitate collection and segregation of waste at the point of origin. Employees working in banquets should encourage guests to use these recycling containers by putting small tent cards at strategic places such as next to the plate warmers or plate pickup points, discreetly near the entry and exit points of the banquet venue, and near the dessert counters. Recycling containers can be placed in the gardens and swimming pool areas as unobtrusively as possible without causing disturbance to the ambience.

Vendors and suppliers of goods and services to the hotel have to be educated on the savings that will result if they follow good environmental practices. For example, if the vendor supplies fruits and vegetable in reusable crates or beverages in refillable bottles, the supplier effects a saving of having to purchase packaging material every time he has to affect deliveries to the hotel. These containers can be given on loan to the hotel against a deposit and returned back to the suppliers when empty.

Purchases should be made from suppliers who manufacture eco-friendly products that can be recycled, for example, stationery items made from recycled paper, handmade paper products such as guest pens, scribbling pads, wallpaper made from recycled materials, products that can be reused such as hotel guest slippers, loofah pads, hangers, crates for storage of meats, vegetables, glass bottles for storing condiments, refillable soap dispensers in guest rooms and public toilets, or products that are biodegradable such as combs, toothbrushes, corn starch, and shopping bags.

Collective efforts by the management, employees, guests, and vendors results in 'zero waste hotels', which are not necessarily hotels that produce no waste but are hotels that strive to minimize waste by using resources efficiently. As far as possible, they use products that are environment friendly and biodegradable, and when such products are not available, they use products that can be easily recycled, resulting in conversion of such waste into useful materials.

To keep the environment clean and healthy the hospitality industry has implemented suggestions under various categories such as the following.

Suggestions to Improve the Hotel Environment

Building and design   The best place to start the process is at the planning stage when the design of the building and its facilities are being prepared.

Some of the suggestions are listed as follows:

- Design and construct new hotels with facilities that account for the terrain, alignment of the sun, natural flow of water and wind.
- Renovate existing hotels taking advantage of newer materials and technologies to upgrade the hotel into a green hotel.
- Use materials that are non-toxic and natural materials in construction such as granite, stone, chalk and lime stone dust with clay and straws, bricks made from recycled fly ash, and so on.
- Use porous paving blocks in parking lots and on roads instead of concrete pavements, which will allow the water that would otherwise normally get wasted to flow through to the ground, thus increasing the groundwater supply.
- Build provisions for rainwater harvesting in the planning stage and for using the harvested water to water the gardens using drip irrigation rather than sprinklers.
- Fertilize the hotel grounds with composted kitchen and other organic waste rather than chemical fertilizers.
- Plant sturdy plants in the premises that require less water, fertilizers, herbicides, and pesticides.

Water conservation   The time-tested approach to water conversation is to reduce the consumption and to recycle grey and black wastewater that is generated by the hotel. Educate employees on the main aspect of The Water (Prevention and Control of Pollution) Act, 1974, which prohibits the discharge of polluted grey or black water into water bodies beyond a given standard and lays down penalties for non-compliance.

Some of the suggestions are listed as follows:

- Recycle grey water, generated from domestic activities onsite, for use in drip irrigation of the landscaped gardens and for washing driveways.
- Install STPs in hotels to treat black water for use in gardening.
- Monitor water consumption in the kitchens, guest rooms, and other areas of the hotel.
- Prepare action plan to reduce consumption for areas that consume more water.
- Train employees to report to maintenance department any water leakages in guest rooms, back of the house, kitchens, gardens, and laundry, promptly and regularly.
- Ensure maintenance department repairs leakages as soon as they are detected.
- Replace bathroom fittings such as shower heads, taps, and cisterns with high-pressure low-flow jets.
- Place tent cards in guest rooms to give guests an opportunity to decide when they want their towels and linen washed.
- Educate employees to turn off the water taps in their lockers and facilities when not in use.
- Request guests to help in conserving water by turning off the tap when brushing or lathering while bathing.
- Conduct regular water audits to monitor the success of the programme.

Energy conservation   The common-sense approach to save energy is to reduce energy consumption and purchase equipment that has a high energy star rating awarded by the Bureau of Energy Efficiency (BEE). Under Energy Conservation Act, 2001. The Ministry of Power in India has implemented the BEE Energy Star rating system for electrical appliances. It is mandatory since 2010 for manufacturers of electrical equipment to secure star ratings for their products. Typically, a five-star-rated product or equipment would consume less energy as compared to a three-star-rated appliance Higher the star rating, more the electrical efficiency.

Some of the suggestions are listed as follows:

- Monitor energy consumption in the kitchens, guest rooms, and other areas of the hotel.
- Alternative sources of energy such as solar and wind power should also be explored.
- Prepare action plan to reduce consumption for areas that consume more energy.

- Train employees to report to maintenance department any electrical equipment that is faulty in guest rooms, back of the house, kitchens, and laundry, promptly and regularly.
- Ensure maintenance department repairs the same as soon as they are informed.
- Sign annual maintenance contracts for plant and machinery such as lifts, boilers, AC plant, STP plant, pumps, and DG sets, and kitchen equipment such as ovens, grinders, and boilers.
- Service all equipment regularly and religiously following a 'Ken Fix It' programme, which is a programme instituted by hotels to keep all equipment in working condition at all times by following a proactive approach towards equipment maintenance.
- Install timers or sensors to turn off lights and equipment when they are not being used.
- Reduce the AC or heating in guest rooms and public areas as per the weather so as to save energy.
- Shut down floors to reduce energy consumption during low occupancy.
- Install lifts with floor access systems as a security measure and to control energy costs.
- Explore options of installing solar power panels to generate electricity.
- Encourage guests to turn off TVs, room lights, and other in-room electronic equipment when not in use.
- Replace electrical bulbs with energy-saving CFL bulbs.
- Use level controllers for sump pumps.
- Phase out inefficient high-energy consuming equipment and replacing it with newer efficient equipment.
- Operate all laundry dryers and washers on full-load basis
- Shut down pool filtration pumps when the pools are not in use
- Conduct regular energy audits to determine the success of the programme
- Track energy consumption to ensure that all equipment work as per the energy ratings indicated for them.

Noise reduction The objective of any noise reduction programme is to contain the level of noise being generated to permitted levels inside the building as well as to contain noise outside the building from travelling inside. The Noise Pollution (Regulation and Control) (Amendment) Rules, 2002 lay down the terms and conditions that are necessary to reduce noise pollution.

Some of the suggestions are listed as follows:

- Educate employees of the harmful effects of noise, such as permitted and regulated use of loud speakers or public address systems during night hours (between 10:00 p.m. and 12:00 midnight) on or during any cultural or religious festival. This is done by limiting loud outdoor music by restricting the hours as recommended in the Act and by reducing the decibel levels of the music.

- Plan during the design stage; for example, discotheques can be built with insulated walls so as to reduce the level of music going out of the area.
- Insulate the guest rooms to ensure that noise from one room does not travel to the others, as some guest are very susceptible to loud noises, for example, watching TV at higher volumes.
- Provide guest rooms with double-glazed glass windows to filter noise from outside.
- Create a suitable buffer by landscaped gardens to shield the hotel from outside noise.
- Use carpets to reduce noise in the guest corridors and in other public areas such as meeting rooms.
- Use noise dampers in engineering facilities in the plant room to keep the loud noise of the DG sets, AC plant, and boilers from travelling to the floors.
- Provide protective noise mufflers for the ears to employees who are exposed to loud noise while working around generators and large air-conditioning units.

Air quality   The Air (Prevention and Control of Pollution) Act, 1981 ambient quality standards similar to those prevailing in many developed and developing countries were notified by the Central Pollution Control Board in April 1994 and were known as National Ambient Air Quality Standards (NAAQS) for major pollutants to protect public health, vegetation, and property.

Air quality can be controlled by mixing fresh outside air with the air being circulated inside the building after it has been scrubbed to remove impurities. This involves isolating air that is in the back-of-the-house area of the hotel such as kitchens, stores, and laundry from air that is being circulated in the guest and public areas.
Some of the suggestions are listed as follows:
- There are various factors that affect indoor air quality in hotels, for example, smoke, soot, dust, fuel emission, bacteria in the air, smell from paints, air fresheners, food, and steam As a result of these factors, guests staying in the hotels may develop respiratory problems. It seeks to combat air pollution by prohibiting the use of polluting fuels and substances, as well as by regulating appliances that give rise to air pollution.
- Emissions from boilers and other equipment installed in the engineering plant room should be eliminated.
- The use of toxic chemicals to clean floors, blinds, upholstery, and other interior furnishing that give off smells and odours in the guest rooms should be eliminated.
- The Cigarettes and Other Tobacco Products (Prohibition of Advertisement and Regulation of Trade and Commerce, Production, Supply and Distribution) Act, 2003 (34 of 2003) and the Cigarettes and Other Tobacco Products (Prohibition of Advertisement and Regulation of Trade and Commerce, Production, Supply and Distribution) Rules, 2004 forbids the sale of tobacco products to a minor or an individual below the age of 18 years and prohibits smoking in hotels having less than 30 rooms and restaurants that have less than 30 covers.

- In case the restaurant has only 30 covers and the hotel 30 rooms, then smoking is strictly prohibited. It is recommended that an area outside the premises be designated for the convenience of smokers.
- Restaurants that have more than 30 covers can permit smoking in designated areas that are well ventilated and away from the other guests it needs to be ensured that the smoke from the smoking rooms is kept out of non-smoking areas by installing effective exhaust systems and prominently display the signage 'Smoking Area' or 'Non-smoking Area'.
- Hotels that have more than 30 rooms it is recommended that the hotel designate floors as 'Non- smoking Floors' for the convenience of resident guests.

Purchasing   The basic idea of purchasing is to buy only what is needed and, when it is needed, and to use products in a rational way to avoid unnecessary stocking of supplies. Some of the suggestions are listed as follows:

- Identify suppliers who manufacture products that can be recycled, reused, and/ or eco-labelled.
- Purchase from suppliers who agree to supply goods in reusable crates and containers made from recyclable materials.
- As far as possible, items should be purchased with the minimum packaging material on it as this helps in reducing waste.
- When purchasing new equipment, purchase energy-efficient appliances for kitchens, guest rooms, offices, and so on. For example, laundry machines should be energy star rated with low water consumption.
- Purchase items with little or no preservatives and food colouring.
- Use fresh products such as seasonal fruits and vegetables that are organically grown locally in bulk.
- Purchase stationery, other paper products, and toilet rolls made from recycled paper.
- Avoid purchasing disposal plates, forks, spoons, and napkins, which add to the waste.
- Purchase reusable and refillable inks and toner cartridges for use in the offices.
- Use refillable soap dispensers in guest rooms and public area toilets.
- Install hand dryers to save on the use of towels in public toilets.
- Choose least-polluting detergents and chemicals sold in refill packs for use in the laundry, kitchens, and guest rooms.
- Install rechargeable batteries to power equipment in offices and guest rooms where required.
- Use the '*energy saving*' functions that switch an appliance into sleep mode if it is not used for a certain length of time.
- Purchase beverages in glass bottles that can be refilled or in cans that can be recycled.

- Use organic fertilizers for the gardens and plants.
- Use table linen made with environmentally friendly materials that do not use hazardous dyes.
- Rent equipment that is seldom used by the hotel, instead of buying it.

Hotel chains have initiated environment-friendly programmes based upon the well-tested waste management hierarchy of prevention, reduce, reuse and recycle, recover energy from waste, and finally disposal by implementing some or all of the suggestions that have been listed earlier. These programmes are directed at achieving sustainable development, which has been defined 'as development that meets the needs of the present without compromising the ability of future generations to meet their own needs'.

Some of the programmes initiated by the hospitality industry are listed as follows:

The Orchid Hotel, Mumbai In the words of the Chairman, Vithal Kamat, at the EarthCare Awards 2012, 'The proof of success lies in reducing garbage. We have only one mantra—reduce, reuse, recycle. We took small steps like doing away with cut flowers.'

ITC Hotels—WelcomEnviron Programme 'The guiding principle is "Reduce, Reuse and Recycle". Each hotel has its own programme, encompassing local participation, creating awareness among employees and internal conservation through energy-saving gadgets and environment-friendly material. Our guests are also encouraged to be a part of our campaign, "Give back as much as you take from the environment."'

Taj Hotels, Resorts and Palaces (Environment Awareness and Renewal at Taj Hotels)—the EARTH Programme 'A project which reiterates the conscious effort of one of Asia's largest and finest group of hotels to commit to energy conservation and environmental management'.

Accor Hotels—Planet 21 Based on the Agenda 21 principles for Sustainable Development endorsed by 182 Heads of State at the United Nations Rio Earth Summit in 1992. This programme aims at 'making sustainable hospitality the focus of its strategic vision, as well as its development and innovation processes'.

IHG Hotels—Green Engage An innovative programme which allows IHG to design, build, and run even more sustainable hotels. The innovative and advanced online system allows individual hotels to measure the impact to the environment from the day-to-day running of their hotel. It is a system-wide approach to environmental management.

FEEDBACK ON THE IMPLEMENTATION

Although every hotel has its own waste management policy and has a built-in mechanism for feedback that is available from employees, guests, and vendors, it is recommended that the success of the programme be evaluated by an external agency. The advantage of independent evaluating agencies is that the feedback and comments shall be unbiased, fair, and not open to criticism by the team members.

EarthCheck: Green Globe Certification

There are various bodies that assess and certify hotel projects and the prominent among them is EarthCheck, which conducts the Green Globe certification programme. Assessment and certification of the environment programmes are carried out by various agencies of which EarthCheck is the only worldwide environmental certification programme for the travel and tourism industry with participants in more than 50 countries. EarthCheck is managed by EC3 Global, a subsidiary of the Sustainable Tourism Co-operative Research Centre. EarthCheck is the international benchmarking and certification programme for the travel and tourism industry based on the Agenda 21 principles for Sustainable Development endorsed by 182 Heads of State at the United Nations Rio Earth Summit in 1992. Taj Group, Accor, InterContinental Hotels Group, Langham hotels, Banyan Tree Hotels, and Orchid Hotels endeavour to meet the benchmarks set by EarthCheck.

- EARTH Programme of Taj Hotels, Resorts and Palaces' (Environment Awareness and Renewal at Taj Hotels) has been certified by Green Globe.
- IHG Hotels Green Engage has also been certified by Green Globe.
- Novotel Hyderabad International Convention Centre (HICC) is the first Green Globe certified convention centre in India.

The advantages of certification by EarthCheck are as follows:

(i) Competitive advantage
(ii) Return on investment
(iii) Reduction in operating costs
(iv) Easy recognition by travellers
(v) Contribution to sustainability

Leeds Building Certification: Leeds Platinum, Gold, Silver Certification

The other body that is well known is the US Green Building Council (USGBC), which awards the LEEDS certification to buildings. LEED stands for Leadership in Energy and Environmental Design and is an independent non-profit third-party rating system established by the USGBC. The LEED rating system is completely voluntary and consensus-based, incorporating both established industry principles and innovative environmental technology. LEED is the most widely recognized form of green building certification in the country.'

The advantages for LEEDS certification are as follows:

Lower operating costs
(i) Lower utility bills from increased energy and water efficiency

(ii) Lower maintenance cost as a result of detailed preventative maintenance plans

Increased property value
 (i) Higher market value for new and existing constructions
 (ii) Higher lease-up rate than conventional buildings

Healthier and safer for occupants
 (i) Improved indoor environmental quality
 (ii) Improved lighting and views

Certified recognition of green practices
 (i) Approval from a non-biased, accepted authority
 (ii) Physical proof of the values of the organization that owns and occupies the building

In India, the Indian Green Building Council (IGBC) is responsible for certifying hotels and other projects in India under the Platinum, Gold, and Silver categories. ITC Hotels have taken a lead in getting their hotels LEEDS certified and some of their important properties are as follows:

(i)	ITC Maurya, New Delhi	LEEDS Platinum Certified
(ii)	ITC Gardenia, Bangalore	LEEDS Platinum Certified
(iii)	ITC Grand Chola, Chennai	LEEDS Platinum Certified

International Organization for Standardization (ISO)—ISO 14001 Environmental Standard Certification

This standard specifies the requirements for an environmental management system and enables organizations to identify and control the environmental impact of its activities, products, or services. A systematic approach ensures that all activities that have an impact on the environment are critically reviewed, leading to benefits such as:

 (i) Reduced costs of waste management
 (ii) Savings in consumption of energy, water, and other resources
(iii) Sets up a framework for continued improvement of environmental performance

Some of the Indian hotels that have achieved ISO 14001 Environmental Standard Certification are as follows:

 (i) The Leela Palace Kempenski, Bengaluru
 (ii) The Taj Gateway, Madurai

These examples clearly show that concern for the environment is one of the most significant challenges that the hoteliers have to face in the 21st century.

EXHIBIT A

ENVIRONMENT-FRIENDLY WASTE MANAGEMENT MEASURES IN TAJ RESIDENCY, BENGALURU

Reproduced below is an extract of the report made by EarthCheck on the Taj Residency Hotel in Bengaluru highlighting the initiatives taken by the Taj group in facing the environmental challenge (EarthCheck website).

The Taj Residency is a five-star business hotel with 167 rooms and 6 function rooms capable of holding up to 1000 guests. Facilities include a swimming pool, fitness centre, a beauty parlour and hair salon, spa, and bookshop.

Reducing the Use of Freshwater and Wastewater Generation

Taj Residency, Bengaluru has implemented a number of initiatives to reduce water consumption, including treating and reusing wastewater onsite and installing water efficient fixtures.

Water-efficient Fixtures and Practice

Some of the practices for efficient use of water include the following:

(i) Electronic sensors are installed on all taps and urinals in the public and back areas to reduce water wastage.

(ii) Low-flow taps and shower roses have been installed in 99 per cent of the hotel.

(iii) All the hotel's toilets have low-flush volumes.

(iv) Laundry requirements are reduced by giving guests the option to have their linen changed on alternate days. Guest preferences are retained in the hotels records and implemented automatically on their next visit.

Water Recycling

Some of the measures for water recycling include the following:

(i) The hotel's effluent and pool backwash water is sent to an onsite single-phase treatment plant where it is treated to a quality suitable for reuse on the hotel's gardens and in the site's cooling tower. This ambitious wastewater recycling project saves the hotel 15–20 kL of water daily. Around three-quarters of the water savings are reinvested back into the system for maintenance.

(ii) The hotel's dishwasher collects final rinse water for reuse for the next load's initial wash, saving 15 L each cycle or 9 kL annually.

Reducing Operational Hours

Reducing the hours of operation of equipment and fixtures is often a quick and low-cost measure that can lead to considerable energy savings. The Taj Residency has implemented a number of initiatives including the following:

(i) Reducing the time delay on room key cards that turn off lighting when guests exit the room. Time delays were reduced from 30 seconds to 20–25 seconds.

(ii) Installing automatic timers on public and building lights

(iii) Switching off one of the site's three transformers at night to reduce energy loss and increase the transformer life

(iv) Implementing power-saver modes on all desktop monitors across the hotel

(v) Switching off air conditioning in function halls half an hour before guests leave

Heat Recovery

The hotel has installed a heat exchanger to recover heat from the site's air-conditioning refrigerant. This heat is used to preheat water used to feed its boiler. By mixing this water with water warmed using energy captured by 100 solar panels, the hotel is able to increase the boiler's feed water from 250°C to 400°C. This is equivalent to an energy saving of around 2.22 MJ (Mega Joules) per day or 52 litres of fuel per day.

Replacing and Retrofitting Old Inefficient Equipment

While the cost of replacing and retrofitting old inefficient equipment can be high, the initial financial outlay is often quickly recovered in reduced operational and maintenance costs.

The efficiency of the Taj Residency's air-conditioning compressor has been increased by 20 per cent by replacing an old reciprocating plant, which was continually cycling on and off, with a new screw compressor that operates more efficiently at part loads.

Other Initiatives
Some of the other initiatives include the following:
  (i) Replacing old DC elevators with energy efficient elevators with variable speed drives that can match the motor speed with the load
 (ii) Installing variable frequency drive starters to reduce unnecessary energy consumption on the air handling unit motors and chiller secondary pumps so they can operate over different speeds as opposed to a single- or two-speed motor starter
(iii) Reducing the environmental impact of fuel use and increasing boiler efficiency by using ultra diesel in the hotel's boilers, which has a lower sulphur content that reduces carbon monoxide emissions
 (iv) Replacing pumps used for air conditioning and building plumbing with high-efficiency pumps that save approximately 250–300 kWh per day

Installing Energy-efficient Lighting
By simply replacing old and inefficient lighting with energy-efficient alternatives, significant energy and financial savings can be made. Some of the measures are as follows:
  (i) The Taj Residency has installed compact fluorescence lights in guest rooms and corridors saving 100–150 kWh per day.
 (ii) Small power supply spikes can reduce the lifespan of these bulbs so the hotel has installed voltage regulators to maintain a constant operating voltage.
(iii) Energy efficient 30-watt LED lights have also been installed on the hotel's facade and spa, and lighting in the restaurants and lobby area have been connected to solid-state dimmer panels which automatically adjust ambience lighting levels to save energy.

Equipment Monitoring and Maintenance
The Taj Residency uses a Building Monitoring System (BMS) to quickly identify abnormalities and inefficiencies in its air-conditioning plant:
  (i) The BMS measures the temperature of chilled water in and out of the condenser to assess the load on the air-conditioning plant. This information, in conjunction with the ambient (outside) temperature,

is used to optimize the flow of the chilled water. For example, when the air is cooler outside the cooling tower will be more effective at cooling water so the water flow rate is reduced, lowering pumping requirements and reducing the load on the compressor.
 (ii) The boilers are regularly monitored, including adjusting fuel-to-air ratios, to ensure efficiency and boiler fuel consumption is checked against the manufacturer's recommendations. The water tube boiler is de-scaled when fuel consumption starts increasing. The air-conditioner condenser coils are also regularly de-scaled and the levels of dissolved solids in the chilled water closely monitored to minimize fouling of the coils.
(iii) The Taj Residency has established Total Preventative Maintenance schedules for all their equipment including preventative maintenance such as regular inspections, cleaning, and the replacement of worn parts and breakdown maintenance, which involves establishing a policy on dealing with problems as they occur and ways to reduce their impact on the hotel.

Solid Waste Management
The Taj Residency has a comprehensive solid waste management programme with 98 per cent of its waste either reused or recycled.
  (i) Waste is segregated into dry waste, such as paper, cardboard, plastics, and glass, and collected by recycling companies authorized by the Pollution Control Board (a non-government organization) at no cost.
 (ii) Wet waste such as food and floriculture waste is collected by a local piggery also at no cost.
(iii) All staff members are given regular on-the-job training on waste segregation and management and the hotel organizes seminars on waste management and other sustainability issues to foster greater environmental awareness among its staff and suppliers.
 (iv) Old cloths and bed sheets are sent to the Friend in Need Society, a home for the aged and destitute.

Sustainable Purchasing to Reduce Waste
  (i) The Taj Residency seeks to reduce the volume of solid waste it generates by purchasing supplies in bulk, which are then stored in reusable steel containers.

(ii) Daily supplies of vegetables are also procured in reusable boxes and water/mineral water supplied and stored in reusable crates.

(iii) The hotel gives preference to products and packaging that can be recycled or are made from recycled products. For example, all the hotel's serviettes, tissues, toilet tissues, and paper towels are made from 100 per cent recycled paper.

Purchasing to Reduce the Use of Harmful Substances

(i) The Taj Residency uses Johnson Diversey cleaning products because the company is committed to environmental stewardship not only in its products but also in the design, production, and use. More than 100 of its products have been certified by independent third-party groups such as Green Seal, Ecologo, EU Flower, and Nordic Swan. The supplier also trains staff in the correct use of its products.

(ii) All weedicides and fungal, rodent, and insect killers used by the hotel are eco-labelled Bayer's products, which have been identified as the world's sustainability leader using the Dow Jones Sustainability World Index for over a decade. The company has aligned itself with the voluntary 'Responsible Care' initiative of the chemical and pharmaceutical industries and signed the revised Global Charter of that initiative.

(iii) All spa beauty products provided to guests are natural and free of preservatives.

IMPACT OF COASTAL REGULATION ZONE ON THE DEVELOPMENT OF HOTELS IN INDIA

Resort hotels all over the world are located in coastal areas near beaches, in and around rivers, and in areas that have fragile ecosystems. In such locations, hotel projects require prior approval from the Ministry of Environment and Forests before any construction activity is undertaken as per the CRZ Notification. Currently, CRZ is divided into four categories within 500 metres from the HTL for the regulation of development activities.

Depending on the location of the land parcel falling in the CRZ, a hotel developer will have to get an environmental impact study done, which has to be submitted to the Ministry of Environment and Forests for approval. Once this has been obtained, the developer can seek other relevant permissions to build hotel from the local municipal authorities. If the land parcel falls under CRZ-I, then no construction will be permitted, if it is in CRZ-III then it will be allowed subject to the environmental impact study. The broad guidelines defining CRZ norms and the type of construction that is permitted in each category are discussed as follows.

CRZ-I (2011 Notification)

Ecologically sensitive areas and the geomorphologic features that play a primary role in maintaining the integrity of the coast fall under this category, which are discussed as follows:

(i) Mangroves. In case, mangrove area is more than 1000 square metres, a buffer area of 50 metres shall be provided.

(ii) Corals and coral reefs and associated biodiversity

(iii) Sand dunes

(iv) Mudflats that are biologically active

(v) National parks, marine parks, sanctuaries, reserve forests, wildlife habitats, and other protected areas under the provisions of Wildlife (Protection) Act, 1972 (53 of 1972), the Forest (Conservation) Act, 1980 (69 of 1980), or Environment (Protection) Act, 1986 (29 of 1986); including Biosphere Reserves

(vi) Salt marshes

(vii) Turtle nesting grounds

(viii) Horse shoe crabs' habitats

(ix) Sea grass beds

(x) Nesting grounds of birds

(xi) Areas or structures of archaeological importance and heritage sites

In this zone construction activity of hotels, beach resorts, and so on is not permitted.

CRZ-II (1991 & 2011 Notification)

The areas that have already been developed up to the shoreline fall under this category. For this purpose, 'developed area' is referred to as that area within the municipal limits or in other legally designated urban areas, which is already substantially built up and which has been provided with drainage and approach roads and other infrastructural facilities, such as water supply and sewerage mains.

Construction activities are restricted to the following:

(i) Buildings shall be permitted neither on the seaward side of the existing road (or roads proposed in the approved Coastal Zone Management Plan of the area) nor on seaward side of existing authorized structures. Buildings permitted on the landward side of the existing and proposed road or existing authorized structures shall be subject to the existing local town and country planning regulations including the existing norms of FSI/FAR.

(ii) Reconstruction of the authorized buildings to be permitted subject to the existing FSI/FAR norms and without change in the existing use. The FSI and FAR for construction projects shall be as on 19 February 1991 except for those specified in the CRZ Notification, 2011 which is mainly for slum redevelopment and redevelopment of dilapidated structures.

(iii) Other activities such as desalination plants and storage of non-hazardous cargo are also permissible.

(iv) The design and construction of buildings shall be consistent with the surrounding landscape and local architectural style.

CRZ-III (1991 & 2011 Notification)

The areas that are relatively undisturbed and those that do not belong to either category I or category II fall under this category. These include coastal zone (developed and undeveloped) and also areas within municipal limits or in other legally designated urban areas which are not substantially built up.

Construction activities permitted in this zone are as follows:

(i) The area up to 200 metres from the HTL is to be earmarked as 'No Development Zone'. No construction shall be permitted within this zone except for repairs of existing authorized structures not exceeding existing FSI, existing plinth area, and existing density. However, the activities that are permissible in this zone are agriculture, horticulture, garden pastures, parks, play fields, forestry, and salt manufacture from sea water.

(ii) Development of vacant plots between 200 metres and 500 metres of HTL in designated areas of CRZ-III with prior approval of Ministry of Environment and Forests is permitted for construction of hotels/beach resorts for temporary occupation of tourists or visitors subject to the conditions as stipulated in the guidelines at Annexure II.

(iii) Construction or reconstruction of dwelling units between 200 metres and 500 metres of the HTL is permitted so long it is within the ambit of traditional rights and customary uses such as existing fishing villages (*koliwadas*) and traditional ancient villages of farmers, traders, and craftsmen (*gaothans*) in Maharashtra. Building permission for such construction or reconstruction will be subject to the conditions that the total number of dwelling units shall not be more than twice the number of existing units, the total covered area on all floors shall not exceed 33 per cent of the plot size; the overall height of construction shall not exceed 9 metres and construction shall not be more than two floors (ground floor plus one floor).

(iv) Reconstruction or alterations of an existing authorized building is permitted subject to conditions (i) to (iii) mentioned above.

Practical suggestions that have been listed will assist hoteliers in implementing effective environmental practices in their hotels to effectively reduce pollution and creating a cleaner and healthy environment for guests.

It is true that hospitality management is all about giving exemplary services to guests, but it is equally true that protecting the business from all kinds of accidents and incidents that could potentially result in lawsuits is also important. This book gives the readers the opportunity to profit from the experience of others. It has been written not for lawyers but to make hoteliers aware of their legal responsibilities in a rapidly changing business environment. I trust that this book will serve students in understanding the nuances of hotel laws and practising hoteliers in applying this knowledge in diligently managing their hotels.

SUMMARY

Since the dawn of civilization, concern for the environment is in essence an attempt to balance the relationship between man and nature. With rapid economic prosperity the delicate balance between man and nature has been altered, resulting in the depletion and pollution of natural resources, which in turn began to impact the health and lifestyles of people. The chapter discussed the steps taken by the UN in 1972 to create awareness among the nations about the impact of pollution on the environment. It also discussed the legislation introduced in India to improve the environment and with the help of the judiciary to address and manage the environmental concerns. The chapter highlighted how the various pieces of legislation have resulted in hotels formulating waste management programmes to reduce waste and air and noise pollution and to save water and energy. Such programmes are independently evaluated by external agencies and based on their assessment hotels are certified as eco-friendly. The chapter also briefly discussed the impact of CRZ norms on the development of hotels in eco-sensitive areas.

KEY TERMS

Solid waste Municipal, household, commercial, industrial waste, construction waste, demolition waste, chemical waste, and special waste, for example, medical, abattoir, and animal and livestock waste and sludge.

Liquid waste or sewage Any water that has been used in manufacturing, cleaning, washing, and flushing containing impurities, and is discharged as sewage.

Gaseous waste Smoke, smog, fumes, and particles in the air, for example, soot, nitrogen and sulphur dioxide gases, carbon-di-oxide emissions, and dust.

Green hotels Hotels that strive to be more environment-friendly through efficient use of energy, water, and materials while providing quality services. Green hotels conserve and preserve by saving water, reducing energy use, and reducing solid waste.

Zero-waste hotels These are not necessarily hotels that produce no waste but are hotels that strive to minimize waste by using resources efficiently. As far as possible they use products that are environment-friendly, biodegradable, and when such products are not available they use products that can be easily recycled resulting in conversion of such waste into useful materials.

Ecotourism Tourism that is environmentally focussed and nature-oriented.

Energy star Rating awarded by the Bureau of Energy Efficiency. Higher the star rating more the electrical efficiency.

Biodegradable waste Any substance that can be decomposed by the action of micro-organisms, for example, human and animal waste, cotton, wool, and so on.

Hazardous waste A solid, liquid, or gaseous by-product of industrial processes that possesses at least one of the following characteristics: (i) corrosive, that is, has the potential of gnawing through the material, (ii) ignitable, that is, has the potential to catch fire, (iii) reactive, that is, has the quality of bringing about a chemical or physical change to any material or substance, and (iv) toxic, which is caused by poisonous substances (toxic substances) and which may have to be handled stored, transported, and disposed of in a controlled manner.

No. 1 PET—polyethylene terephthalate Containers made from this plastic sometimes absorb odours and flavours from foods and drinks that are stored in them. Items made from this plastic are recycled.

No. 2 HDPE—high-density polyethylene These products are very safe and they are not known to transmit any chemicals into foods or drinks. HDPE products are recycled.

No. 3 PVC—polyvinyl chloride Harmful if ingested and is often not recycled.

No. 4 LDPE—low-density polyethylene A very healthy plastic that tends to be both durable and flexible, and is not commonly recycled.

No. 5 PP—polypropylene Strong and can usually withstand higher temperatures and is not commonly recycled.

No. 6 PS—polystyrene Most commonly known as Styrofoam which is commonly recycled.

No. 7 Others Used to designate miscellaneous types of plastic such as polycarbonates and polylactide that are not defined by the other six codes. These types of plastics are difficult to recycle.

Building Monitoring Systems (BMS) Primary goal of building monitoring is to ensure that all building systems operate at peak efficiency and for ensuring that the systems operate as designed. Improperly operating systems waste energy and water, lead to unacceptable indoor environmental quality, and can cause premature equipment failures.

International Organization for Standardization (ISO)—ISO 14001 Environmental Standard Specifies the requirements for an environmental management system and enables organizations to identify and control the environmental impact of its activities, products, or services. A systematic approach ensures that all activities that have an impact on the environment are critically reviewed.

LEEDS Stands for Leadership in Energy and Environmental Design and is an independent, non-profit, third-party rating system established by the USGBC to certify green buildings. In India, the IGBC awards the LEEDS certification.

EarthCheck International benchmarking and certification programme for the travel and tourism industry based on the Agenda 21 principles for Sustainable Development endorsed by 182 Heads of State at the United Nations Rio Earth Summit in 1992.

Doctrine of public trust Certain common properties, such as rivers, forests, seashores, and air are held by the government in Trusteeship for the free and unimpeded use of the general public.

Polluter pays principle Absolute liability rests with the polluter to pay for the damages done to the natural environment as a result of his actions.

The precautionary principle Any development activity that can cause serious and irreversible environmental damage must be prevented and forms the basis of the principle of sustainable development.

Sustainable development Any development that balances environmental concerns with development which improves the quality of human life without causing irreversible damage to the carrying capacity of the life-supporting ecosystem.

Public interest litigation A litigation concerning any matter that is of public importance that requires a speedy redressal, which is achieved by filing a case in the court. The case can be filed by any member of the public, the aggrieved party, or by the court itself.

Depletion Of natural resources is the result of the extraction of non-renewable resources such as metals and minerals and the extraction of renewable resources from the environment faster than they can be renewed.

Degradation The destruction or damage to the natural resources by deforestation, desertification, pollution, and so on.

EXERCISES

Define the Following

1. Solid waste
2. Recycling
3. Waste hierarchy
4. Green hotels
5. Biodegradable waste
6. Non-hazardous waste
7. LEEDS
8. HDPE
9. Ecotourism
10. Construction and demolition waste

Concept Review Questions

1. What is the purpose of a waste management hierarchy?
2. Enumerate the common aspects of the various eco-friendly programmes launched by the hotels.
3. What are the sources, effects, and control measures to ease noise pollution?
4. Enumerate the measures followed by the purchase department to curb wasteful practices.
5. What is the role played by the various certifying agencies in controlling and encouraging eco-friendly practices?

Critical Thinking Questions

1. Building and operating Green Hotels is the mantra that hoteliers are following. Do you agree that these measures will translate into higher revenues?
2. In your opinion, how successful have the public interest litigations been instrumental in furthering the cause for the environment? Elucidate.
3. 'Zero waste hotels' produce no waste. Clarify.

Research Question

1. Are hotels blindly implementing eco-friendly policies without evaluating the relevance of the policy to a hotel environment?

Projects

1. Analyse ITC hotels' WelcomEnviron programme and suggest measures that will further improve the existing programme.
2. Based upon the environment-friendly suggestions, design a policy for an existing old-build hotel.

REFERENCES

P. Sands, *Principles of International Environmental Law*, 2nd edn, Cambridge University Press, Cambridge, UK, 2003, p. 253.

<http://www.goodreads.com/quotes/tag/environment> accessed on 07 September 2012

<http://articles.timesofindia.indiatimes.com/2009-06-30/vintage-wisdom/28197870_1_earth-environment-vedas> accessed on 07September 2012

<http://oxforddictionaries.com/definition/english/environment?view=uk> accessed on 07 September 2012

<http://indiatoday.intoday.in/story/world-environment-day-is-a-call-to-arms-albeit-a-green-one/1/199120.html> accessed on 07 September 2012

<http://www.unep.org/Documents.Multilingual/Default.asp?documentid=97&articleid=1503> accessed on 07 September 2012

<http://twocircles.net/legal_circle/constitutional_provision_and_environmental_protection_kamaluddin_khan.html> accessed on 07 September 2012

<http://en.wikipedia.org/wiki/Bhopal_disaster> accessed on 07 September 2012

<http://en.wikipedia.org/wiki/Waste_hierarchy> accessed on 09 September 2012

<http://www.greenworks.co.za/watchyourwastepage.html> accessed on 09 September 2012

<http://moef.nic.in/downloads/rules-and-regulations/eprotect_act_1986.pdf> accessed on 09 September 2012

<http://www.businessdictionary.com/definition/biodegradable.html> accessed on 09 September 2012

<http://www.businessdictionary.com/definition/hazardous-waste.html#ixzz27CcxgXF8> accessed on 09 September 2012

<http://www.sita.com.au/commercial-solutions/speciality-services/liquid-hazardous-waste/> accessed on 09 September 2012

1987 Brundtland report prepared by the UN's World Commission on Environment and Development <http://www.accor.com/fileadmin/user_upload/Contenus_Accor/Developpement_Durable/img/earth_guest_research/dossier_de_presse_eng_bd.pdf> accessed on 09 September 2012.

<http://www.ihgplc.com/index.asp?pageid=740> accessed on 10 September 2012.

<http://www.accorhotels.com/gb/sustainable-development/index.shtml> accessed on 10 September 2012.

<http://www.tajhotels.com/About-Taj/Company-Information/Earth.html> accessed on 10 September 2012.

<www.earthcheck.org> accessed on 11 September 2012.

<http://www.itchotels.in/Others/OthersWE.aspx> accessed on 10 September 2012.

<http://www.earthcheck.org/clients/case-studies1.aspx> accessed on 10 September 2012.

<http://www.earthcheck.org/media/7861/CS12%20Taj%20Residency%20Bangalore%20Case%20Study.pdf> accessed on 12 April 2013.

<http://www.ichotelsgroup.com/ihg/hotels/us/en/global/support/greenengagehotels> accessed on 10 September 2012.

<http://en.wikipedia.org/wiki/Units_of_energy> accessed on 11 September 2012.

Leeds Certification <http://www.usgbc.org/ShowFile.aspx?DocumentID=7760> accessed on 18 September 2012.

Georgia University Paper <http://www.greenbiz.com/sites/default/files/document/O16F6378.pdf> accessed on 18 September 2012.

<www.projectgaia.org/documents/.../Green%20Hotels%20Manual.pdf> Malta hotels accessed on 18 September 2012.

<http://en.wikipedia.org/wiki/Greywater> accessed on 21 September 2012.

<http://en.wikipedia.org/wiki/Blackwater_(waste)> accessed on 21 September 2012.

<http://earth911.com/> accessed on 21 September 2012.

<http://vijay028.hubpages.com/hub/SEMINAR-REPORT-OF-NATURAL-BUILDING-MATERIALS> accessed on 21 September 2012.

<http://www.getnaturalusa.com/BuildingMaterials.aspx> accessed on 21 September 2012.

<http://lhonline.com/green/leed/understanding_leed_1010/> accessed on 21 September 2012.

<http://www.hicc.com/press_releases/10/green_globe.pdf> accessed on 21 September 2012.

<http://www.hotelierindia.com/article-4844-profitable_green_trends/1/print/> accessed on 21 September 2012.

<http://www.iso.org/iso/home/about.htm> accessed on 21 September 2012.

<http://www.hinduwisdom.info/Nature_Worship.htm> accessed on 19 September 2012.

<http://www.brainyquote.com/quotes/keywords/environ-ment.html#Z7phZzq0XxcLhvXA.99> accessed on 17 September 2012.

Kamal Nath Case <http://www.indiankanoon.org/doc/1889473/> accessed on 23 September 2012.

<http://www.qualitylogoproducts.com/lib/different-types-of-plastic.htm> accessed on 23 September 2012.

Vellore Citizen's Welfare Forum <http://www.indiankanoon.org/doc/1934103/> accessed on 23 September 2012.

Legal Cases <http://legalservicesindia.com/article/article/fundamental-principles-of-environmental-protec-tion-755-1.html> accessed on 23 September 2012.

Indian Council For Enviro-Legal Action vs Union of India and Others Writ Petition (C) No. 664 of 1993 <https://www.elaw.org/node/2749> accessed on 23 September 2012.

Vijay Punia vs State of Rajasthan <http://www.indiankanoon.org/doc/1968630/> accessed on 23 September 2012.

Subash Kumar vs State of Bihar and Others 1991 AIR 420, 1991 SCR (1) 5 <http://www.indiankanoon.org/doc/1646284/> accessed on 23 September 2012.

Virender Gaur and Others vs State of Haryana <http://www.indi-ankanoon.org/doc/114802/> accessed on 23 September 2012.

<http://www.google.co.in/url?sa=t&rct=j&q=define+princi ple+of+sustainable+development+in+environmental+l aw+india&source=web&cd=8&ved=0CFAQFjAH&url= http%3A%2F%2Fwww.edo.org.au%2Fedosa%2Fresearch %2Fdavid%2520cole%2520on%2520precautionary%252 0principle.doc&ei=EXGGUMGNGcLPrQewy4CQAQ& usg=AFQjCNFfLVOAbXRtC0HXOpKKMAq-xZeYew> accessed on 23 September 2012.

<http://www.lec.lawlink.nsw.gov.au/agdbasev7wr/_assets/ lec/m4203011721754/speech_10jan06_preston.pdf> accessed on 23 September 2012.

<http://www.legalserviceindia.com/article/l54-Interpreta-tion-of-Polluter-Pays-Principle.html> accessed on 25 September 2012.

<http://www-group.slac.stanford.edu/esh/environment/ hazardous_waste/p_definitions.htm> accessed on 11 September 2012.

Glossary

Ab initio   From the very beginning.

Ad hoc   A solution that has been custom designed for a specific problem and cannot be adapted to other purposes.

Ad idem   In agreement.

Ad valorem   According to value.

Adjudication   A legal process of resolving a dispute and implies a hearing by a court, after notice, of legal evidence on the factual issue(s) involved prior to pronouncing of a judgement or decree in a court proceeding. It indicates that the claims of all the parties thereto have been considered and set at rest.

Administrative law   The procedure that is required to be followed in order to implement the law as intended by the statute and it derives its sanctity from it.

Affidavit   A formal sworn statement of fact.

Appellate jurisdiction   The privilege of the Supreme or High Courts to hear appeals that are filed against judgements given by the lower courts or tribunals.

Arbitration   The submission of a dispute to an unbiased third person designated by the parties to the controversy, who agree in advance to comply with the award—a decision to be issued after a hearing at which both parties have an opportunity to be heard.

Assentio mentium   Meeting of the minds.

Audi alteram partem   The concept that one cannot be fairly judged unless the cases for and against have been heard.

Bona fide   In good faith implies good intentions regardless of outcome.

Bona vacantia   Ownerless goods that generally go to the finder.

Casus fortuitous   A chance occurrence or unavoidable accident.

Causa proxima, non remota spectator   The immediate and not the remote cause has to be considered, also known as the doctrine of proximate cause, it literally means the nearest cause or direct cause and relates to the immediate cause of the mishap which has resulted in the loss establishing a relationship between the action and the result.

Caveat   May the person beware.

Caveat emptor   Let the buyer beware.

Certiorari   A writ passed by a higher court directing a lower court to send the record in a given case for review.

Civil law   Provides legal solutions to disputes involving ownership of personal property, interpretation of contracts, marriage disputes, divorce, damages for personal injury and to personal property, and so on.

Consensus ad idem   Free consent; this implies that the parties must agree about the subject matter of the agreement in the same sense as it is proposed without any ambiguity at the same time.

Constitutional law   Defines the relationship between the three arms of the government, and in a federal structure, the relationship between the centre and the states. It spells out the fundamental rights and duties of citizens and ensures that all statutory and administrative laws do not violate these rights.

Corpus juris   The complete collection of laws of a particular jurisdiction or court.

Criminal law   Crimes under various categories such as crimes against the state, persons and property, crimes relating to public order, health and safety, to religious affairs, marriage, decency and morals.

De facto   Something that is true in practice, but has not been officially instituted or endorsed.

De jure   Something that is established in law.

Dictum   A statement is given weightage or consideration due to the respect given to the person making it.

Doctrine of mitigation of loss   Based upon the principle that the insured as a prudent or sensible person will take all the steps necessary to save the property in the event that there is a mishap.

Doctrine of Public Trust Based upon the principle that certain common properties such as rivers, forests, seashores, and air are held by the government in trusteeship for the free and unimpeded use of the general public.

Endorsement When cheque, bill of exchange, or other negotiable instrument is indorsed so as to make it payable to another or encashable by any person.

Erratum Having been made in error.

Et al. Among others.

Etc. And so forth.

Ex ante Before the event.

Ex officio Something done or realized by the fact of holding an office or position.

Ex parte A decision reached, or case brought, by or for one party without the other party being present.

Ex post facto A thing done afterwards.

Ex post facto law A retroactive law, for example, a law that makes a past act illegal that was not illegal when it was done.

Ex-gratia In Latin means 'out of kindness'. Cash benefit or something given as a favour when no legal obligation exists.

Fait accompli A thing already done.

Fiat Let it be done.

Force majeure or act of God A flood, an earthquake, or other accident or event, which is without any human intervention and could not have been prevented by reasonable care or foresight, but is the result of natural causes (a snowstorm is an Act of God; driving in one is an act of man).

Fortuity doctrine States that the basic concept of insurance is to covers risks, rather than losses that were planned, intended, or anticipated by the insured.

Habeas corpus A writ issued by the supreme or high court to an authority or person to produce in court a person who is either missing or kept in illegal custody.

Hospitality law Covers a wide range of legal issues ranging from hotel business contracts, front-office operations, labour laws, duty of a hotel towards guests, hotel liability, food and beverage operations, public health, safety,

and security. It applies to the service sector that consists of the food service, travel, and hotel industries.

i.e. That is.

Ignorantia juris non excusat Ignorance of the law is no excuse.

In absentia A legal proceeding conducted without the presence of one party is said to be conducted in the absence of the party.

In camera Conducted in private, or in the chamber of a judge.

In flagrant delicto Being caught in the act of committing a crime.

In lieu In place of.

In pari delicto When both the parties are equally in fault.

In toto In total.

Indemnitas, indemnis In Latin means 'free from loss' is the basis of the principle of indemnity, which is to provide for compensation to the insured so as to place him in the same position that he was in prior to the loss and he should not enjoy a benefit from the occurrence of the loss.

Indorsement The act of the owner or payee signing his or her name at the back of a cheque, bill of exchange, or other negotiable instrument so as to make it payable to another or encashable by any person. Once this process has been completed the negotiable instrument is said to be endorsed.

Inter alia Among other things.

Intra vires An act being done within the powers or legal authority as opposed to ultra vires.

Ipso facto By the fact itself.

Jus commune Common law, refers to common facets of civil law. It is a body of unwritten customs and usages that are validated by the courts through judgements in civil or criminal cases thereby setting legal precedents for the courts to follow in the future when deciding cases.

Jus naturale Natural or customary law are laws common to all people that the average person would find reasonable, regardless of their nationality and is defined as unwritten norms, rules, moral strictures, religious beliefs that are followed voluntarily and universally accepted by society.

Lacunae A void or a situation that is not covered by any law.

Lex loci Law of the land as applicable to contract law.

Locus standi In Latin means 'place of standing' and is the right of a party to appear and be heard before a court.

Malafide In bad faith.

Mandamus Means 'we command', and is a writ issue by a higher court to a lower one, ordering that court or related officials to perform some administrative duty.

Mens rea In Latin means 'guilty mind' or 'criminal intent'. It was important to establish that there was a criminal intent to commit the offence before the guilty person could be prosecuted in a court.

Modus operandi The manner of doing things.

Nexus Connection.

Non sequitur An inconsistent statement.

Original jurisdiction Implies that the court is competent to hear the case filed before it and to take the case to trial before giving its verdict.

Pacta sunt servanda A fundamental principle of law that states that agreements are meant to be kept.

Par delictum Where both parties are at equal fault.

Pari passu On an equal footing.

Per capita Dividing money up strictly and equally according to the number of beneficiaries by the head.

Per se By itself or as a matter of law.

Praecautus In Latin means to 'take precaution or guard against' is instrumental in defining the precautionary principle, which states any development activity that can cause serious and irreversible environmental damage must be prevented which in turn forms the basis of the principle of sustainable development.

Prima facie On the face of it or at first sight.

Pro forma Things done as a formality.

Pro rata An proportional amount being charged based upon the time the space is occupied.

Pro tem Abbreviation of *pro tempore* means for the time being or being held for a temporary period.

Procedural laws or administrative law A body of law that governs the process prescribing the formal steps to be taken in enforcing legal rights. The implementation of civil and criminal law requires separate set of administrative procedures.

Proclamations Written documents announcing a King's intention to the public to act in a certain manner or to restrain from doing an action if it was not followed it resulted in suitable punishment (in historical context).

Prohibito or the writ of prohibition is issued by a superior court to a subordinate lower court or tribunal from exercising jurisdiction over a matter pending before it.

Quantum 'How much?'; for example, what is the quantum of punishment being meted out to the accused?

Quantum meruit As much as is deserved is earned or paid. In contract law, if no fixed price is agreed upon for the service, then one party would request a reasonable price for the said services at the end of the job.

Quid pro quo An equal exchange of goods or services, or of money.

Quo warranto A writ issued by a Supreme or High Court questioning the legal basis and authority of a person appointed to public office. A request made to someone exercising some power, to show by what legal right they are exercising that power.

Res ipsa loquitur The 'thing speaks for itself' used in tort law when there is no proof of what caused the harm, but it is most likely only the thing that could have caused the harm

Res judicata A legal principle that prevents a party to a case which has been finally decided from bringing an action on the same issue. For example, a case is barred by res judicata if an earlier case between the same parties has decided upon the same points. This is embodied in Section 11 of the Code of Civil Procedure, 1908.

Respondeat superior 'Let the master answer'. A concept that the master (e.g. employer) is responsible for the actions of his subordinates (e.g. employees). Also known as vicarious liability even though the person is being held responsible may not have done anything wrong.

Rule Nisi When admitting a writ petition for being heard, a court orders rule nisi which means that the respondents are asked to show cause why the petition should not be allowed, that is, why the rule issued may not be made absolute. If the petition is allowed, the court orders that the rule is made absolute. If the petition is dismissed, the court states that the rule has been discharged.

Sine qua non   Means without which there is nothing, for example, an essential event or action without which there can be no specified consequence.

Stare decisis   The principle that decisions of courts in previous cases must be followed in subsequent cases of similar nature.

Status quo   The current or existing state of affairs.

Statute law   A law that is enacted by parliament, which either forbids the doing of an action or makes it mandatory to do an action, failure to follow the law results in the imposition of penalties.

Sua sponte   In Latin means 'of one's own accord' or voluntarily. It normally refers to a situation when the court decides to addresses an issue that has not been presented for consideration by the litigants. For example the court can dismisses an action by determining that the jurisdiction is not proper even though both parties have agreed to appear in the court.

Sub judice   A matter pending decision by a court. Parties to such a matter are required not to do anything that would affect the outcome of the case.

Subpoena   An order compelling an entity to produce physical evidence in a legal matter.

Subrogation   The restitution of the rights of an assured in favour of the insurer against the third party for any damages caused by him in place of the assured after the insurer has indemnified him for the loss.

Substantive law   Creates, defines, and regulates rights, including, for example, the law of contracts, torts, wills, property; the essential substance of rights under law.

Sui generis   Means 'of his/her own kind'. It means that a person, place, or thing is of a distinctive nature.

Suo motu   The court may take action on its own when facts requiring legal intervention reach its notice. The court is then said to be acting *suo moto*.

Tort   French word for a wrong, a civil wrong, or wrongful act, whether intentional or unintentional (accidental), from which injury occurs to another. Torts include all negligence cases as well as intentional wrongs which result in harm. Negligence is unintentional tort whereas assault and battery; trespass, false imprisonment, defamation (libel or slander), invasion of privacy, private nuisance are examples of intentional tort.

Trial de novo   To commence a new trial on a matter previously decided and refers to a replacement trial for the previous one.

Uberrima fides   The principle of utmost good faith. Concept in contract law specifying that all parties must act in utmost good faith.

Ultra vires   Means 'beyond its power' or outside its scope of jurisdiction. An action that requires legal sanction to perform, but which is done without obtaining that sanction

Verbatim   Word by word exactly as said.
Veto   Means 'I forbid'.
Vice versa   The other way around.

Writ   A direction that a court issues, which is to be obeyed by the authority or the person to whom it is issued.
Writ of declaration   Issued to declare an executive, legislative, or quasi-judicial act to be invalid in law.

Index

A.K. Dave   8
Abandoned property   260, 274
Acceptance   30, 32, 59, 61, 87, 88, 90, 91, 95, 112
Accident and sickness insurance or health insurance   168
Accor Hotels—'Planet 21'   381
Acidity regulators   294, 325
Acids   294, 325
Act of God   99, 103, 160, 177
Actual cash value   157, 177, 178
Adjudicating officer   313, 327
Administrative law   31
Adulterated food   280, 281, 283, 286, 288, 325
Adventure tourism   12, 24
Advisory jurisdiction   32
Aerated water   284, 329–31, 355
Agency   6, 63, 86, 94, 104, 109, 110, 112, 128, 191
Agreement   6, 9, 17, 24, 25, 28, 35, 39, 50–2, 55
Agreement on Code of Practice between FHRAI & IATO (2005)   35, 39, 123, 128, 246
Agricultural Produce (Grading & Marking) Act, 1937 (AGMARK)   298
Aix-la-Bains   331
Aix-la-Chapelle   331
Alcoholic beverage   121, 145, 271, 329–34, 336, 337, 339, 340, 342–4, 347–9
Alcohol Related Harm: Implications for Public Health and Policy in India (2011)   336
Aleatory agreements   156
Alistair Anthony Pereira vs State of Maharashtra Crl. Appeal

Nos 1318–1320 of 2007 SC on 12 January 2012   346
Alteration of the contract   101
Amalgamation of unions   205
Amiable compositeur   197
Analytical Sanitary Commission   280, 282
Andhra Pradesh Grain and Seed Merchants Association vs Union of India A.I.R. 1971 S.C. 2346   284
Anil Madhok and Ajay Bakaya of Sarovar Hotels   10
Annual activity certificate (AAC)   62
Ante-dated cheque   115, 127
Anti-caking agents   294, 325
Antifoaming agents   294, 325
Appellate jurisdiction   37, 38
Appellation de'Origine Controlee   333
Apple brandy   333, 355
Appointment letters   209, 210, 212, 237
Aquavit   333, 355
Arbitration   86, 120–2, 125, 128, 190, 196, 197, 199, 201, 235
Area   136
Arms Length Pricing (ALP)   76
Arrack   333, 337, 355
Arthashastra by Kautilya   43
Arthur Hill Hassall   280
Article 32–35 Right to Constitutional Remedies   185
Articles 14–16 Right to Equality   185
Articles 19–22 Right to Freedom   185
Articles 23 and 24 Right against Exploitation   185

Articles 25–28 Right to Freedom of Religion   185
Articles 29 and 30 Cultural and Educational Rights   185
Ashburn   331
Assault   229, 243, 249, 250, 274
Associated Enterprise (AE)   76
Associated Hotels of India   4
Australian Carriers and Innkeepers Act, 1958   242
Automatic route   61–3, 65, 66, 69–70, 78, 79, 81–3
Babylon   34, 39, 151
Babulal Hargovindass vs State of Gujarat 1980 F.A.J. 40   310
Bacterial food poisoning   293
Bailee   98, 108, 109, 126, 127, 258–60, 272, 274
Bailment   86, 107–9, 125–8, 245, 257–9, 272, 274
Bailment and pledge   86, 107, 109, 125, 274
Bailor   107, 108, 126, 259, 272, 274
Ballygoen   331
Battery   243, 250, 274, 275, 367
Bearer cheque   115
Beer   329, 330, 332, 334–40, 343, 349, 350, 355, 356
Beor   332, 355
Best Western Hotels   9, 18
Bhagwat Purana   239
Bharatia Electric Steel Co. Ltd. vs State of Haryana 1998 LLR 322 (P&H HCDB)   201
Bhopal gas tragedy   362
Bilateral contract   96
Bill of exchange   113
Biodegradable waste   367, 389, 390

Blood alcohol concentration (BAC)   344
Blueprint of the hotel   137
Board and lodging licence   140
Boiler and pressure plant policy   169
Boivre   329, 355
Bombay Mutual (1871)   153
Bombay Prohibition Act, 1949   338
Bonus Commission in1961   215
Brandewijn   333
Brandy   333, 355
British proof   349, 350, 356
Building and design   376
Built-up area   136, 148, 149
Bulking agents   294, 325, 327
Bureau of Energy Efficiency (BEE)   377, 389
Bureau of Indian Standards (BIS)   137, 298, 364
Business law   86, 128
By release   117

Camellia sinensis   331, 355
Capital account transactions   66, 67, 82
Carpet area   136
Cash in counter   170, 171
Cash in safe   169, 171
Cash in transit   170, 171
Cassis   332
Casual leave   210, 222, 223, 236
Cecil Hotels   4
Census of India 2011   26, 130
Central Advisory Board of Health in 1937   282
Central Advisory Committee   308
Central Food Laboratories   284, 311, 312
Central Licensing Authority   307
Central Pollution Control Board in April 1994   362, 364, 379
Central Value Added Tax or Central Sales Tax   146
Cerise   332
Certificate of incorporation   60, 82, 83
Certificate of registration   49, 205, 341
Change of name of the union   205

Chender of Baljee Royal Orchid Hotels   10
Cheque bearing 'not negotiable'   116
Cheque crossed generally   115, 116
Cheque crossed specially   115
Chit funds   69, 82
Choice Hotels India Private Ltd.   8
Cigarettes and Other Tobacco Products (Prohibition of Advertisement and Regulation of Trade and Commerce, Production, Supply and Distribution) Act, 2003 (34 of 2003)   353
Cigarettes and Other Tobacco Products (Prohibition of Advertisement and Regulation of Trade and Commerce, Production, Supply and Distribution) Rules, 2004   353, 379
Citronelle   332
Civil complaint   37
Civil law   33, 38, 39
Class-I towns and also known as Tier-III cities   131
Class II preservatives   296
Class I preservatives   296
Closure   53, 66, 156, 176, 200, 202, 235, 238
Code of Conduct for Safe and Honourable Tourism   35, 270, 271
Code of Criminal Procedure, 1973   310
Code of Hammurabi   30, 34, 39, 151
Code of Manu   152
Codex Alimentarius Commission's   301, 325
Codex India   301, 327
Coercion   92, 93, 98, 126
Coffee   65, 171, 263, 296, 305, 317, 329–31, 355, 357, 374
Coffee arabica and Coffee camephora   331
Colour retention agents   294, 326
Commencement Certificate (CC)   135, 149

Commencement of Business (COB)   49
Commission agents   109, 110
Common law   30, 31, 37–9, 160, 239, 243, 245, 269, 273
Companies (Memorandum of Association) Act, 1890   45
Companies Act, 1850   46
Companies Bill, 2011   80
Companis   43
Comparative negligence   244, 245, 250
Conciliation officer   195, 237
Concurrent list   184, 186, 187, 234, 282, 326, 327
Consensus ad idem   92, 126
Consideration   48, 70, 72, 87, 91, 92, 94–6, 100, 101, 105
Constitutional law   33, 38, 39
Construction drawings   137, 149
Consumer dispute   174, 178, 255, 257, 275
Consumer Protection Act, 1986   155, 174, 175, 256, 285, 303
Contaminant   289
Contamination   288, 289, 293, 320, 321, 323, 326
Contingent contracts   98, 99, 178
Continuing guarantee   105, 106, 126, 127
Continuous service   200, 217–9, 236
Contour plans   137, 148
Contract   7, 9, 10, 15, 17, 24, 25, 27–9, 33, 35
Contract of guarantee   105, 106, 126
Contract of indemnity   103, 155, 157
Contractor   191, 214, 223–25
Contracts of adhesion   156
Contributory negligence   244, 245, 250, 252, 254, 258
Controller of weights and measures   349
Convertible term life insurance policy   165
Corporate tax   73, 74, 77, 79, 81

Counteroffer 90

Country liquor 335, 336, 338, 355

Courtesy of choice programme 354

Court of the adjudicating officer 313

Covered area 136, 148, 388

Cover note 162, 163

Creditor 51, 55, 91, 102, 104–7, 114, 126

Criminal 30, 33, 36–8, 68, 111, 112, 217, 228, 229, 250

Criminal intent or *Mens Rea* 280

Criminal law 33, 38

Crossed cheques 115

Cross offer 89

Cross section 138, 148

CRZ-I (2011 Notification) 386

CRZ-II (1991 & 2011 Notification) 387

CRZ-III (1991 & 2011 Notification) 387

Cultural tourism 12, 14, 24

Current account transactions 66, 67

Dean's hotel 4

Death of a guest 261, 262, 274

Debenture 53, 54, 57–9, 61, 71–3, 75, 85

Deductions from salary other than statutory deductions 220

Defendant 36–8, 104, 160, 161, 249, 251, 252, 275

Deficiency 120, 174, 256, 274, 275

Degradation 362, 390

Delhi Liquor Licence Rules, 1976 338–341

Delhi Municipal Corporation Bye-Law Order, 1964 (Regulation of Hotels, Loading Houses, and Similar Places) 240

Delhi Rent Control Act, 1958 240

Delhi Shops and Establishments Act, 1954 188, 189

Depletion of natural resources 362, 390

Derivative 71, 72, 85, 305

Designated officer 302, 309, 312

Development 4–9, 15, 17, 18, 23, 62, 66, 70, 72, 125

Dharamshastras 30

DIPP 25, 62, 69, 70, 82, 149

Directive Principles of State Policy 184, 186, 187, 324, 237, 282, 336

Directorate of Marketing and Inspection (DMI) 298

Director's Liability Act, 1890 45

Direct recruitment 209

Direct Tax Code (DTC) 2009 79

Disability 230

Disablement 168, 186, 217, 221, 222, 231, 232, 236

Discharge of a negotiable instrument 117
    By cancellation 117
    By endorsement 112, 117, 127
    By payment 117, 173

Discharge or performance of contracts 99
    By breach of contract 99, 103
    By Force Majeure or Act of God 103
    By mutual consent or agreement 99, 100
    By lapse of time 102
    By impossibility of performance 102
    By performance (Section 37) 99
    By release 117
    By operation of law 118
    By delay in presenting the cheque 119
    By tender 99

Dissolution of unions 205

District collector 129, 130, 218

Dividend distribution tax 73, 74, 79, 81–83

Doctrine of contribution 159

Doctrine of frustration 102

Doctrine of mitigation of loss 176

Doctrine of public trust 366, 367

Doing Business Report 2013 47, 48

Double Taxation Avoidance Agreements (DTAAs) 75

Dr Ambedkar 186

Dram Shop Act 329, 352, 356

Driving under the influence of alcohol (DUI) 345

Driving while intoxicated (DWI) 345

Dry days 337, 338, 355, 356

Due care 108, 244, 245, 251, 252, 262, 272

Due diligence 133, 134, 148, 149, 260

EarthCheck: Green Globe Certification 382

Eastern international hotels 6, 78

Eating house or restaurant licence 144

Eau de Vie 333, 355

Effect of mistake as to law 93

Eicher Goodearth Ltd. vs R K Soni (1993) XXIV LLR 524, 1993 LLR 524 (Raj HC) 211

Electronic equipment policy 169

Elevation 138, 148

Empire of India (1897) 153

Employee provident fund registration 145

Employee retention 22, 23

Employees provident fund scheme 1952 (EPF) 219

Employee state insurance scheme 145

Employees' deposit linked insurance scheme, 1976 207, 219

Employees' pension scheme, 1995 207, 219

Employment advertisement 208, 209

Employment Exchanges (Compulsory Notification of Vacancies) Act, 1959 188, 207

Emulsifiers 295

Encyclopaedia Britannica 330

Endowment assurance policy 167

Energy conservation 143, 377, 381

Engineered foods 288, 326

Engineering insurance 167, 169

Environmental Pollutant 362

Environment impact assessment or study (EIS) 135

Environment Protection Act, 1986 286, 361, 363

Eodem modo quo quid constituitur, eodem modo destruitur 100

EPCG licence 135, 142, 343

Equal Remuneration Act, 1976 187, 207, 213, 224

Essential Commodities Act, 1955 285

European proof 349, 350, 356

Evian 331

Ex-gratia and bonus 215

Excise duty 76, 83, 336

Excise tax 334

Exclusive agents 161, 177

Executive 27, 31, 32, 37, 39, 80, 186, 193, 204, 208, 209, 232, 234, 300

Expenditure tax 146

Export (Quality Control and Inspection) Act, 1963 285, 286

Export Promotion Capital Goods (EPCG) scheme 132, 342

Express contract 96

Extraneous matter 288, 289

Extraordinary leave 222, 236, 237

Factories Act, 1947, Shops and Establishments Act 222

Factories Act, 1948 187, 189, 190, 206, 210, 222, 236

Factory 121, 189, 206

Fair market value 157

Faletti Family 4

Faletti's hotel 4

False imprisonment 243, 244

FDI 9, 14, 25, 62, 63, 65, 66, 68–72, 78, 79

Federation of Hotels and Restaurant Association of India (FHRAI) 5, 24, 208

Festival holidays 145, 188, 215, 223, 236

Fidelity guarantee policy 170

FII 71, 79, 83

Fire insurance 160, 165, 167

Fire policy 168

Fire, natural disasters, terrorist attacks, war, pestilence, and other acts of God 261

First-cause test 160

Fixtures and equipment (FF&E) 132

Flashman's Hotel 4

Flavour enhancers 295, 326

Floor plans 138, 148

Flour treatment agents 295, 326

Flower vs Mayfair Joint Venture, 2000 WL 272187 (S.N.D.Y. 2000) 228

Food additives 280, 286, 294, 295, 299, 301

Food Adulteration Act, 1860 280, 282

Food Adulteration Committee in 1943 282

Food analyst 279, 302, 308–12

Food and Agriculture Organization (FAO) 301

Food and beverage controller 305, 342, 354, 356

Food and beverage outlets 28, 268, 316, 323, 324

Food colouring 294, 326, 380

Food inspector 280, 281, 286, 301, 304, 309

Food poisoning 286, 292, 293, 310, 326, 327

Food preservative 295, 296, 326

Food products order, 1955 284, 299

Food Safety and Standards Act, 2006 28, 144, 279, 285, 287–289, 294, 298, 299, 302–304, 306

Food Safety and Standards Authority of India (FSSAI) 144, 300

Food Safety Appellate Tribunal 315

Food Safety Management System 303, 307

Food safety officer 279, 302, 308, 309, 312, 314, 315, 327

Foreign direct investment (FDI) in 1991 9

Foreigner's Regional Registration Office 140

Foreign Exchange Management (Establishment in India of Branch Office or Other Place of Business) Regulations, 2000 58, 61, 63

Foreign Exchange Management (Transfer or Issue of Security by a Person Resident Outside India) Regulations, 2000 68

Foreign Exchange Management Act, 1999 43, 58, 61

Foreign Exchange Regulation Act, 1973 (FERA) 47

Foreign liquor 335–9, 342, 355

Foreign Technology Agreements 9, 24, 25

Foreigner's Regional Registration Office 140

Fourth 'R' 367

Framboise 332

Franchisee agreements 9, 24, 25, 81, 122, 124, 127, 270

Fraud 28, 34, 52, 53, 80, 83, 92, 93, 96, 113

Free consent 92, 94, 95, 126

Friedrich Accum 280, 282, 327

Function prospectus— Banquets 122, 123

Fundamental Rights 33, 38, 184, 185, 187, 226, 234, 283

FVCI 71, 83

Gaseous waste 369, 389

Generally Accepted Accounting Principles (GAAP) 77

General Anti-Avoidance Rules (GAAR) 80

General insurance 152–4, 156, 161, 164, 165, 167, 176

General insurance policies 154, 167

General offer 89

Genetically modified 287, 326, 327

Genoa, Italy 152

Gin 3–6, 8, 10, 12, 15, 18, 20–5, 27, 29–39, 43

Glazing agents 295, 326

Globalization and diversity 22

Gomme 332

Good hygiene practices (GHP) 303

Goods & services tax 80, 81

Gopal Dutt vs State of Haryana 1983 Cr L.J pp 303 at 304 (P&H) 311

Government route 61–3, 69–71, 82

Government servants 130, 189, 339

Gratuitous bailment 108, 126, 259, 274

Gratuity 187, 188, 198, 200, 207, 213, 215, 217–9, 221, 235

Green hotels 375

Grenadine 332

Grievance Cell of the Insurance Regulatory and Development Authority 175

Grievance redressal committee 190–4

Grievance redressal officer 175

Gross negligence 244

Group information sheet 122, 123

Guarantee 10, 44, 59, 65, 86, 95, 99, 103, 105, 106

Guest 3, 4, 9, 15, 20–5, 27–30, 34, 35, 38, 88

Guest arrival and departure register listing 241

Guild of merchants 44

Guy Lussac 350, 356

Hazard Analysis and Critical Control Points (HACCP) 303, 326, 327

Hazardous waste 364, 367, 372, 373, 389, 390

Headhunters 209

Health, sanitation, and hygiene 22

Health trade licence 143, 144

Henry de Bracton 30

History of the World in 6 Glasses, Tom Standage 329

Hospes 33, 239, 273

Hospitalite 239, 273

Hospitality Development and Promotion Board 139

Hostis 34, 239, 273

Hotel and Restaurant Approval and Classification Committee (HRACC) 8, 24, 324

Hotel Association of India (HAI) in 1996 10, 24

Hotel Classification 140, 141

Hotel India, New Delhi 5

Hotel Marina, New Delhi 5

Hotel Proprietors Act, 1956 (UK) 240, 242, 245, 254

House of Commons (Lok Sabha) 32

House of Lords (Rajya Sabha) 32

Humectants 295, 327

Hunar Se Rozgaar Scheme 208

IHG Hotels—Green Engage 381

Import Export Code (IEC) 135, 343

Imported foreign liquor 335, 336, 355

Income Tax Act, 1961 28, 68, 74, 76, 77, 79, 216, 220

Income tax rebates 220

Indecent Representation of Women (Prohibition) Act, 1986 229

Indemnity and guarantees 86, 103

Indentured labour or bonded labour 183

Independent agents or brokers 161, 177

India Tourism Development Corporation (ITDC) 6

India's labour policy 183, 187

Indian Arbitration Act, 1940 196

Indian Arbitration and Conciliation Act, 1996 120, 121, 196, 237

Indian Association of Tour Operators (IATO) 35, 123, 208

Indian Constitution 154, 184, 186, 189, 198, 226, 234, 302, 336, 362

Indian Contract Act 1872 28, 81, 86, 87, 90, 95, 97–9, 102, 104, 156

Indian Council for Enviro-Legal vs Union of India & Others on 18 July, 2011 Civil Original Jurisdiction IA No. 36 and IA No. 44 in Writ Petition (C) No. 967 of 1989 365

Indian Green Building Council (IGBC) 383

Indian Hotels Company Ltd 6

Indian Mercantile Insurance Company Limited 153

Indian Partnership Act, 1932 46, 49–52, 55, 105

Indian Penal Code, 1860 206, 229

Indian Performing Rights Society/Phonographic Performance Limited 142

Indian Standards Institute (ISI) 298

Induction 194, 209, 212, 213, 237

Industrial all-risk policy 169

Industrial dispute 184, 187, 189–96, 198, 201–3, 213, 235, 237

Between employers and employers 192, 204, 235

Between employers and workmen 192, 193, 235

Between workmen and workmen 192, 193, 204, 235

Industrial Revolution 152, 183, 362

Industrial tribunal 191, 198–201

Industry 1, 3–15, 17–21, 23–7, 35, 38, 39, 47, 69, 78

Information Technology (Amendment) Act 2008 270

Institute of Hotel Management at Aurangabad in 1989 19

Institution of Insurance Ombudsman 154, 175

Insurable interest 158, 159, 164, 177

Insurance 12, 28, 41, 44, 49, 54, 69, 96, 99, 124

Insurance Act, 1938 154, 173, 175
Insurance claim 151, 155, 156, 159, 160, 171–3, 175–8
Insurance policy 155–7, 159–61, 163–5, 167–71, 173, 174, 177, 178, 364
Insurance proposal 162
Insurance Regulatory & Development Authority Act, 1999 154
Insurance Regulatory and Development Authority (IRDA) 154
Intentional adulteration 291, 292, 327
InterContinental Hotel Group (IHG) 9
International Financial Reporting Standards (IFRS) 80
International Organization for Standardization (ISO)—ISO 14001 Environmental Standard Certification 383, 390
International Organization of Legal Metrology 349, 350, 356
International Union of Food, Agricultural, Hotel, Restaurant, Catering, Tobacco and Allied Workers' Associations (IUF) 229
Interstate Hotels Private Ltd 17
Intimation of Disapproval (IOD) 135
Invaluable items 98, 259, 260
Invasion of privacy 243, 248, 274
Involuntary bailment 108, 274
Irish Hotel Proprietors Act, 1963 245, 254
ITC Hotels—WelcomeEnviron Programme 381

J. W. Salmond 86, 243
Jamshetji Nusserwanji Tata 4
Jewellery 75, 259, 274, 324
Joint Stock Companies Act, 1844 44
Joint venture (JV) 46, 64
Judgement 30, 31, 36–9, 104, 118, 161, 174, 198, 226, 227

Judicial tribunals or commissions 35
Judiciary 27, 31, 32, 37, 39, 364, 389
Juices 329, 330, 332, 355

Kansas State Law Chapter 36 Article 602 268
Karma Hotels and Hospitality Consultants 16
Khakras and *Theplas* 279
King Henry II (1154–1189) 30
Kitchen 23, 28, 65, 144, 171, 193, 233, 262, 305, 316
Kitchen stewarding 233, 316, 322, 371

Labour courts 191, 193, 198
Last-cause test 160
Lawful object 93, 94, 126
Lay-off 199, 202, 218, 235, 236
Leadership in energy and environmental design 382, 390
Leave not due 222, 236
Leeds Building Certification: Leeds Platinum, Gold, Silver Certification 382
Legal age for drinking 338
Legal issues 22, 23, 27, 35, 38
Legal Metrological (Packaged Commodities) Rules, 2011 317
Legal Metrological Act, 2009 317
Legislative 31, 32, 43, 45, 81, 153, 154, 184, 186, 234
Lemon Tree Chain in 2012 10
Lex non cogit ad impossibilia. Impossibilium nulla obligatio est 102
Liability 28, 34, 35, 39, 44–6, 49–56, 61, 65, 80, 83
Liaison Office or Representative Office 61
Licence fees 342
Licensing 23, 28, 69, 70, 140, 299, 300, 304–7, 324, 325
Licensing authority 307
Life insurance 152–4, 157–9, 164–7, 175, 177, 218, 220
Lift operating licence 142
Limitation Act, 1963 86, 102, 118

Limited Liability Act in 1855 44
Limited Liability Partnership Act, 2008 46, 49, 51, 52
Liqueurs 333, 355
Liquid waste or grey and black water 369
Liquor 28, 121, 144, 287, 330, 334, 336, 338, 340, 342
Liquor licence 121
Litigants 36, 274
Livestock Importation Act, 1898 284, 300
Llanllyr 331
Lockout 190, 195, 200–3, 235, 236
Lord Curzon 281
Lord Justice Lindley 46
Loss of profit insurance 167
Loss Prevention Association of India 151, 176, 178
Lost property 157, 177, 260, 274
Lower courts or district courts 35
Luxury tax registration 146

M. C. Mehta vs Kamal Nath and Others AIR 2000 SC 1997 366
Machinery breakdown policy 169, 171
Mahatma Gandhi 183
Ma Huang 292
Malvern 331
Management contract 9
Management contracts 7, 9, 24, 78, 86, 122–5, 127
Manu 151
Manu Smriti 30
Marine cargo insurance 168
Marine freight insurance 168
Marine hull insurance 168
Marine insurance 152, 154, 164, 165, 167, 168
Marine liability insurance 168
Marriott Hotels, Accor Hotels 9
Massachusetts 334
Master plan 130, 131, 133, 147, 149
Masura 334
Maternity leave 210, 225, 236
McGraw-Hill Dictionary of Scientific and Technical Terms 330
Meat Foods Products Order, 1973 284

Mechanical drawings or technical drawings 138, 148

Mediation 120, 122, 125, 128, 190, 203

Medical or sick leave 222, 236

Medical tourism 12, 24, 25

Mega cities 130, 147, 149

Mesopotamia 332

Milk and Milk Products Order, 1992 (MPO) 284

Mineral water 257, 298, 329–31, 355, 386

Minimum alternate tax 73, 74

Minimum Wages (Central) Rules, 1950 213

Ministry of Environment and Forests 362, 364, 366, 386, 388

Misbranded food 289

Misbranding 279, 282, 286, 290

Misconduct 211

Misleading advertising 303

Misplaced property 260, 274

Misrepresentation 92, 93, 126

Mistake as of fact 92, 93

Moneyback policy 166

Money insurance 167, 169

Moonshine 334

Motor or car insurance 168

Motor Vehicles Act, 1988 161, 168, 345, 346

Municipal Corporation of Delhi vs Surja Ram 284

Municipal Council, Ratlam vs Vardhichand AIR 1980 SC 1622 365

Mutilated cheque 115, 127

N Radhabai vs D. Ramchandran 229

Napoleonic code (1804) 31

National Ambient Air Quality Standards (NAAQS) 364, 379

National Council for Environmental Policy and Planning 362

National Council for Hotel Management and Catering Technology (NCHMCT) 19

National holidays 223

National Institute of Mental Health and Neurosciences, Bengaluru 336

National Restaurant Association of India 324

National Tourism Policy of 2002 12

National tribunal 191, 193, 195, 198, 199, 201

Natural adulteration 291, 292

Natural food adulteration 293

Natural toxin 292, 293

Natural/spring water 331, 355

Navroze 152

Negligence 175, 178, 218, 234, 243–5, 250, 252, 254, 255, 257

Negotiable instrument 81, 86, 105, 112, 113, 115–18, 125, 127

Negotiable Instruments (Amendment and Miscellaneous Provisions) Act, 2002 112

Neon sign insurance policy 169

Nidhi company 70, 82

NOC from Chief Fire Officer 139

Noise pollution (Regulation and Control) (Amendment) Rules, 2002 364, 378

Noise reduction 378

Nomination 144, 305, 307, 347

Non-alcoholic beverages 329–31, 354, 355

Non-cash benefits 225

Non-gratuitous bailment 108, 126, 259, 274

Non-resident visitors (also called Patrons) 242, 243

Novation 22, 23, 100, 126, 127, 264, 381

NRI 71, 79, 85, 97

Oberoi Centre of Learning and Development 19

Oberoi Group 4, 78

Occupational disease 231, 233

Off premises or off-site licence 339, 355

Offer 34, 57, 82, 88–90, 95, 99, 100, 102, 155, 167

On premises or on-site licence permits 339, 355

Online Tax Accounting System 146

Open General Licence (OGL) 135, 342

Orgeat 332

Oriental Insurance (1874) 153

Oriental Life Insurance Company 152

Original jurisdiction 33, 36, 38, 39, 365

Overbooking 246, 273, 274

Oxford Dictionaries Online 29, 78, 134, 148, 361

Pacifica Group of Companies 17

Pacta sunt Servanda (agreements are to be kept) 91

Papnasan Labour Union *vs* Madura Coats AIR 1995 SC 2200 200

Parasites 292, 293

Park Hotel 10, 11, 18, 261

Parry's Employees Union vs Third Industrial Tribunal 2001 LLR 462 (Cal HC) 200

Partial completion certificate (PCC) 139

Partnership firm 50, 55, 341

Patu Keswani of Lemon Tree Hotels 10

Pawnee 108, 109, 272

Pawnor 108, 272

Payment of Gratuity Act, 1972 187, 207, 217

Payment of Gratuity Rules 217

Payment of Wages (Amendment) Act, 2005 187, 207, 213, 214

Payment of Wages Act, 1936, Payment of Wages Rules, 1937 214

Permanent Account Number 49, 54, 82, 140, 146

Permanent partial disablement 231, 232

Permanent total disablement 231

Perrier 331

Persian King Jamshed 333

Personnel 19, 21, 140, 144, 165, 193, 194, 210, 212, 213

Persons with Disabilities (Equal Opportunities, Protection of Rights and Full Participation) Act, 1995 266

Pesticide residue 292, 293

Physically challenged guests 266, 275

Plaintiff 36–8, 120, 158, 249–55, 258, 275

Plaint or complaint 36

Plate glass insurance policy 169

Pledge 72, 73, 86, 107–9, 125, 127, 128, 134, 148, 274

Pledging of goods 108, 271

Plot and survey 137, 148

Pocket Oxford Dictionary and Thesaurus 330

Pomace-Grappa/Marc 333, 355

Possession, consumption, and transportation (PCT) 334

Post-dated cheque 115, 127

Precautionary principle 366, 367

Predominant-cause test 160

Preference shares 59, 73

Preservatives 280, 284, 289, 292, 294–6, 301, 325, 380, 386

Presidency College of Hotel Management 19

Prevention of Food Adulteration Act, 1954 279, 283, 284, 286–8, 290, 299, 301, 302, 304, 305

Prevention of Food Adulteration Rules, 1995 144, 285, 294, 296, 299, 347

Pride Hotel 10, 11, 17, 18, 56

Primary food 288

Principal debtor 104–7, 126

Principle of *ex aequo et bono* 197

Principle of sustainable development 365, 366, 367, 390

Principle of utmost good faith or *uberrimae fides* 176

Private limited companies 45, 53, 55, 59, 65

Private nuisance 243, 248

Private sector employees 189, 190

Privilege leave or earned leave or annual leave 222, 236

Priya Paul of Park Hotels 10

Procedural law or administrative law 33

Proclamations 31, 38, 39

Profession Tax Enrolment Certificate 145

Prohibition 154, 185, 226, 227, 229, 271, 299, 334, 336–8, 341

Prohibition Act 334, 337, 338

Project office 63, 66, 82

Promise 11, 23, 86–8, 91, 92, 94, 96, 99, 101–3, 105

Promisee 87, 99, 101, 102, 103, 126

Promisor 87, 91, 92, 99–103, 126

Promissory note 113

Proof 104, 134, 149, 158, 226, 249, 307, 340–2, 349, 350

Property tax certificate 147

Proposal 87, 88, 90–2, 94, 121, 126, 162, 163, 177

Proposer 90, 91, 162–4, 177

Prospectus 57

Provident fund 54, 58, 144, 145, 186, 187, 198, 207, 213, 214

Province of Jurisprudence Determined (1832) 31

Provincial Insolvency Act, 1920 119

Proximate cause 159

Public analyst 280–3, 286, 301, 304, 311

Public duty 245

Public duty of a hotelier 245

Public liability insurance (third-party liability insurance) 170

Public limited companies 56, 59

Public Prosecutor vs Satyanarayana A.I.R. 1958 A.P.681; 1958 Cr L.J. pp 1375 301

Public provident fund account (PPF) 220

Public sector employees 189, 190

Punjab Excise Act, 1914 335, 336, 338, 339, 341, 347, 348

Purchase contract 90, 120, 122, 123, 317

Purchasing 65, 137, 148, 160, 161, 316, 329, 337, 342, 351

Qualified foreign investor (QFI) 71

Quality of service and pricing 23

Quasi contract 96, 97, 127

Ram Lal vs State of Rajasthan A.I.R. 2001 S.C.47 pp 48–49 310

Ranulf de Granville 30

Rate of absorption 344, 346, 347, 355, 356

Ready reckoner 134, 137, 148

Registration Act, 1902 86, 94, 127

Registration Act, 1908 28, 133

Registration and licensing of the food business 304

Registration of a union 204

Registration Office (FRRO) 28, 140

Registration of Foreigners Rules, 1991 270

Religious or spiritual tourism 13

Remission 100, 101, 126

Renewal notice 164, 177

Representation of the Peoples Act, 1951 338

Rescission 100, 101, 126, 128

Resident guest 243, 273

Resignation 209, 211, 217, 221, 235, 236, 238

Restricted Money Changers Licence 141

Retail food chains 306

Retirement 51, 64, 152, 165–67, 170, 200, 211, 215, 217, 219

Retirement plan, annuity, or pension policy 166

Retrenchment 192, 198–200, 235, 237

Rig, Sama, Yajur, and Atharva Vedas 361

Royal Charter 44

Royal Orchid Hotel chain 10

Rum 333, 343, 349, 355

Rupan Deol Bajaj vs KPS Gill 1998 SC 229

Rural tourism 12, 24

S.P. Jain 10, 11

Saint Arnold 332

Saint-Galmier 331

Sale of Cigarettes and Tobacco 329, 353

Sales Promotion Employees (Conditions of Service) Act, 1976 222

Sales tax registration 145, 340

Salmonella bacteria 293

Sanctioned area or buildable area 136, 148

Sanjeev Nanda vs the State Crl. Appeal No. 807/2008HC 346

Sarais Act, 1867 27, 28, 240, 241

Sarjoo Prasad vs State of Uttar Pradesh A.I.R. 1961 S.C. 631 284

Schnapps 333

Secretary, Thirumurugan Co-operative Agricultural Credit Society vs M. Lalitha, [(2004) 1 SCC 305] 174

Seljuk Empire 152

Service 3, 4, 6, 9–11, 15, 21–25, 27, 28, 38

Service tax registration 49, 145

Service tax 28, 49, 54, 58, 76, 77, 80, 81, 83, 145

Service Tax Statutory Provision Act, 1994 28

Set-off 216, 217

Set-on 217

Settlement stage 172, 173, 176

Share capital 45, 53, 54, 56–8, 65, 66, 73, 82, 83

Sheraton Group 6

Shops and commercial establishments and factories 188

Shops and Establishments Act, 1954 188, 189

Short-term capital gains and long-term capital gains 75

Signage 28, 142, 144, 169, 264, 267, 305, 307, 343, 354

Sir John Lawrence, Viceroy of India 35

Sir William Anson 86

Skippers 271, 272

Sohan Singh vs State of UP, 2000 Cr L.J. 3929 pp 3936 301

Solanine 292

Sole proprietorship 43, 46, 49, 51, 81

Sole selling agent and subagents 110

Solid waste 368, 369, 385, 389, 390

Somras 334

Span Motels Private Limited 366

Spanish Armada in 1588 34

Special offer 89

Spirit of hospitality 3, 24

Spirits 329, 330, 333, 334, 343, 349, 350, 355

Squashes 329, 330, 332, 355

Stabilizers 295, 327

Stale cheque or expired cheque 115, 127

Standard operating procedures (SOPs) 307

Standard Weights and Measures (Enforcement) Act, 1985 344, 348

Standard Weights and Measures Act, 1976 344, 348

Standards of Weights and Measures (Packaged Commodities) Rules, 1977 285

Standing orders 145, 184, 198, 210, 211, 213, 222, 227, 230

Standing, open, or continuing offer 90

Staphylococcus bacterium 293

Stare decisis 30, 39

State food safety commissioners 301

State of Tamil Nadu vs R. Krishnamurthy A.I.R. 1980 S.C. 538 287

State of Uttar Pradesh vs Kartar Singh A.I.R. 1964 S.C. 1135 284

State Pollution Control Boards 362

State vs T.R.M Subramanium, 1976 Cr L.J. 1982 pp 1983 301

Statute law 31, 38, 39, 270

Stores 316, 319, 320, 339, 340, 342–4, 354, 355, 371, 379

Strathmore 331

Strike 160, 168, 190, 195, 198, 200–3, 211, 218, 235, 236

Study leave 222, 236

Subash Kumar vs State of Bihar and Other. 1991 AIR 420, 1991 SCR (1) 5 365, 392

Subrogation 158, 177, 178

Substantive law 33, 38

Sukhdeo Krishna Kadam vs State of Maharashtra 1979 F.A.J pp 110–114 310

Super built-up area or sellable area 136, 148

Superannuation 200, 217, 219, 221, 222, 236, 237

Supreme Court 32, 35, 37, 38, 56, 116

Surety 104–7, 125–27

Surveyor or loss assessor 173

Sweeteners 295, 327, 332, 355

Syrups 284, 329, 330, 332, 355

Taittiriya Upanishad 34

Taj group 4, 19, 56, 78, 382, 384

Taj Hotel Resorts and Palaces 4, 6, 381, 382

Taj Hotels, Resorts and Palaces (Environment Awareness and Renewal at Taj Hotels)—the EARTH Programme 381, 382

Taj Mahal Hotel in Mumbai 4

Tax deduction and collection account number 146

Tax information network 147

TDR 70, 136, 137, 148, 149

Tea 8, 11, 14, 15, 25, 29–31, 34, 39, 101, 110

Technical services agreement 78, 81, 122, 125, 127

Technology innovations 23

Temporary partial or total disablement 232

Tequila 333, 355, 356

Termination 102, 103, 123–5, 193, 196, 197, 199, 200, 210, 211

The Act to Repress the Odious and Loathsome Sin of Drunkenness in 1606 334

The Air (Prevention and Control of Pollution) Act, 1981 139, 363, 379

The Apprentices Act, 1961 208

The Articles of Associations 44

The Australian Carriers & Innkeepers Act, 1958 (incorporating amendments as on 1 August 2010) 245, 255

The British Insurance Act 152

The Bureau of Indian Standards Act, 1986 298

The Carlton Hotel, Shimla (today known as the Oberoi Clarkes) in 1934 4

The Cigarettes and Other Tobacco Products (Prohibition of Advertisement and Regulation of Trade and Commerce, Production, supply and Distribution) Act, 2003 (COTPA) 271

The Companies (Acceptance of Deposit) Rules, 1975 61

The Companies Act, 1908, 1948, 1900, 1913, 1956 6, 27, 28, 45, 46, 49, 53–59, 62, 64, 65, 70

The Indian Partnership Act, 1932 46

The Constitution of India, List—III 282

The Dram Shop Act, 1872 329, 352, 356

The Environment (Protection) Act and Rules 1986 362

The Equal Remuneration Act, 1976 187, 213, 224

The Fatal Accidents Act, 1885 233, 234

The Food Adulteration Act, 1872 (UK) 280

The Foreigners Registration Act,1946 28

The Fortuity Doctrine 155

Theft 28, 169, 170, 177, 215, 243, 244, 254–8, 271, 272

The Grand, Calcutta (rechristened The Oberoi Clarkes) in 1938 4

The Gutenberg Galaxy 22, 26

The Hotel Rate and Structure Committee 240

The Imperial, New Delhi 5

the Indian Partnership Act, 1932 46

The Indian Stamp Act, 1899 28, 113, 114, 116, 134, 155

The Indian Trade Unions Act, 1926 203

The Industrial Disputes Act, 1947 184, 187, 190, 201, 202

The Industrial Disputes Act, 1948 213

The Infant Milk Substitutes, Feeding Bottles and Infant Foods (Regulation of Production, Supply and Distribution) Act, 1992 and Rules, 1993 286

The Innkeepers' Liability Act of 1863 34, 35

The Insecticide Act, 1968 286

The Lancet 280

The Maidens Metropolitan Hotel 5

The Margarine Act, 1887 (UK) 281

The Maternity Benefit Act of 1961 225

The Memorandum of Association 44, 45, 57, 82

The Minimum Wages Act, 1948 187, 207, 213, 214

The Monopolies and Restrictive Trade Practices Act, 1969 47

The National Building Code (NBC) 2005 137

The National Tourism Policy of 1982 7

The Negotiable Instruments Act, 1881 81, 105, 112, 117

The Oberoi, Taj, ITC, Welcomgroup 6

The Orchid Hotel, Mumbai 381

The Palace Hotel, Chail 5

The Patents Act, 1970, The Designs Act, 2000, and The Trademarks Act,1999 27

The Payment of Bonus Act, 1965, the Payment of Bonus Rules, 1965 and the Payment of Bonus Rules, 1975 215

The Polluter Pays Principle 364, 365, 390

The Protection of Women against Sexual Harassment at Workplace Bill, 2010 227

The Rugby, Matheran 5

The Sale of Food and Drugs Act, 1875 (UK) 281

The Savoy, Mussoorie 5

The Social Contract 29, 39

The Specific Relief Act, 1963 86, 120

The Supreme Court of India 32, 365

The Ten Commandments 30

The Three 'Rs' 367

The Trade Unions Act, 1926 and the Trade Unions (Amendments) Act, 2001 203

The Water (Prevention and Control of Pollution) Act, 1974 139, 363, 377

The Workmen's Compensation Act, 1923 and The Workmen's Compensation (Amendments) Act, 2000 231

Thickeners 295, 327

Thomas Wakley 280

Tier-I cities 130, 147

Tier-II cities 130, 147

Tort 33, 38, 239, 243, 244, 248, 250, 252, 254, 263

Total loss 157, 158, 173, 177

Toxin 293

Tracer gas 295

Trade union 183, 184, 186–8, 190, 194, 201–6, 215, 229, 234, 235

Trade Unions (Amendment) Act, 2001 190, 203

Trade Unions Act, 1926 184, 187, 190, 194, 203

Trading in transferable development rights (TDR) 70

Transfer pricing 43, 76, 77, 81, 83

Travel insurance 156, 168

Treatise on Adulterations of Food and Culinary Poisons 280, 282, 327

Trespass 243, 244, 250, 267, 268

Trial procedure 36
Triton Insurance Company 152
Types of cheques 115

Ubicunque est injuria, ibi damnum
  sequitur 233
Undue influence 92, 126
Unfair labour practices 201, 202
Uniform system of accounts for
  hotels 28
Unilateral contract 96
Unintentional adulteration
  292, 327
Unique identification number
  (UID) 62
Units 53, 67, 71, 267, 322, 323,
  325, 335, 343, 379
Unsafe food 288, 289
US Constitution 334
US Green Building Council
  (USGBC) 382
US proof 350
Uttar Pradesh Pure Food Act,
  1950 287

Valid contract 28, 86, 91, 95,
  125, 127, 155
Valuables 28, 257–9
Value Added Tax 49, 76, 83,
  145, 146
Vasudeva Kutumbhkam 22
Vayu (Air), *Agni* (Fire), *Apah*
  (Water), *Prithvi* (Earth) 361
VCF 71
Vellore Citizens Welfare Forum vs
  Union of India 366
Vendors or suppliers of
  goods 243

Verbal contracts 88
Vicarious liability 244, 263, 274
Vichy 331
Vijay Singh Punia vs Rajasthan
  State Board for the Prevention
  and Control of Pollution
  AIR 2003 Raj 286, RLW 2003
  (2) Raj 1012, 2003(2) WLC
  465 365
Viral food 293
Virender Gaur and Others vs
  State of Haryana and Others
  Appeal (Civil) 9151 of
  1994 365
Vishakha vs State of
  Rajasthan AIR 1997 (7)
  SCC323 226
Vodka 333, 349, 355
Voidable agreements 93, 126
Voidable contract 87, 88, 96,
  125
Void contracts 95, 96
Voluntary bailment 108, 274

Wages/salary 213
Warrants 71, 72
Waste management
  hierarchy 367, 368, 381, 390
Waste reduction programme
  370, 371
Water conservation 377
Wealth of Nations, Adam Smith
  (1776) 183
Wealth tax 73, 75, 259
Wealth Tax Act, 1957 75, 259
Weekly Holidays Act, 1942
  207, 222
Weekly offs 189, 222, 236

Weights and Measures Act 144
Welcomgroup Graduate School
  of Hotel Administration,
  Manipal 19
Whiskey 273, 333, 334, 343,
  355, 357
Whiskey rebellion 334
Whiskey tax 334
Whole life assurance policy
  166
Wholly owned subsidiary
  company (WOS) 58
Wildflower Hall, Shimla 5
Wine & Spirit Association of
  Great Britain 332
Wine 11, 89, 142, 271,
  287, 329, 330, 332, 333,
  335–8
Wine of grain 332
Withholding tax 73, 75, 82
Workman 138, 190, 191,
  198–200, 202, 213, 231,
  232, 235
Workmen compensation
  insurance 167, 169, 171
Workmen vs Management of
  American Express AIR
  1986 SC 548 = 1985(4)
  SCC 71 200
Workmen vs Meenakshi
  Mills Ltd. AIR 1994 SC 2696
  (5-member bench) 200
World Health Organization
  (WHO) 301

Yagnavalkya (Dharmasastra) 151

Zero waste hotels 376

Related Titles

INTERNATIONAL CUISINE AND FOOD PRODUCTION MANAGEMENT | 9780198073895

Parvinder S. Bali, Programme Manager, Culinary Services, Oberoi Centre of Learning and Development, Delhi

International Cuisine and Food Production Management is a comprehensive textbook specially designed for the final year degree/diploma students of hotel management. The book explores key concepts and illustrates them through numerous figures, photographs, and tables.

Key Features
- Elaborates on the culinary history, regions, specialties, and popular dishes of various international cuisines
- Devotes a complete part to advance confectionery
- Includes key managerial issues such as production planning and scheduling, production quality and quantity control, forecasting and budgeting, menu costing, yield management, and new product development

9780198066309 | TOURISM MARKETING

Manjula Chaudhary, Director, Indian Institute of Tourism and Travel Management, Ministry of Tourism, Government of India, Gwalior

Tourism Marketing explains the role of marketing in the tourism and hospitality industry through examples, illustrations, and cases.

Key Features
- Deals with an Indian context and provides case studies to understand the concepts better
- Discusses marketing management information system (MMIS) and the various methods of demand forecasting

HUMAN RESOURCE MANAGEMENT IN HOSPITALITY | 9780198069850

Malay Biswas, Assistant Professor, Indian Institute of Management, Rohtak

Human Resource Management in Hospitality is a comprehensive textbook, designed especially for students of hotel management programmes. It explores the core concepts of human resource management (HRM) and uses numerous industry-related examples and case studies to explain them.

Key Features
- Provides guidelines on the practical aspects of HRM in hospitality industry
- Provides a holistic view by also taking into account aspects of organizational behaviour

Other Related Titles

9780198061090 Raghubalan & Raghubalan: *Hotel Housekeeping* 2/e
9780198065272 Singaravelavan: *Food and Beverage Service*
9780195699197 Tewari: *Hotel Front Office*
9780198061816 Bali: *Food Production Operations*
9780198068495 Bali: *Quantity Food Production Operations and Indian Cuisine*
9780198084006 Seal: *Computers in Hotels: Concepts and Applications*
9780198064633 Bansal: *Hotel Facility Planning*
9780198062912 Ghosal: *Hotel Engineering*
9780195694468 Iyengar: *Hotel Finance*
9780198072362 Swain & Mishra: *Tourism: Principles and Practices*
9780198060017 Roday, Biwal & Joshi: *Tourism Operations and Management*
9780198078869 Roday: *Food Science and Nutrition* 2/e